Handbook of Gerontological Services

❖

SECOND EDITION

HANDBOOK OF GERONTOLOGICAL SERVICES

SECOND EDITION

Edited by Abraham Monk

COLUMBIA UNIVERSITY PRESS
New York

Columbia University Press
New York Oxford

Library of Congress Cataloging-in-Publication Data

Handbook of gerontological services / edited by Abraham Monk.
—2d ed.
p. cm.
Includes bibliographical references.
ISBN 0-231-06902-2
1. Aged—services for—United States—Handbooks, manuals, etc.
2. Social work with the aged—United States—Handbooks, manuals, etc.
I. Monk, Abraham.
HV1461.H34 1990
362.6′0973—dc20
89-28684
CIP

Casebound editions of Columbia University Press books are Smyth-sewn
and printed on permanent and durable acid-free paper

∞

Book design by Jennifer Dossin

Printed in the United States of America
c 10 9 8 7 6 5 4 3 2 1

Contents

PART III: *Basic Services*

PART IV: *Community-Based Services*

PART V: *Home-Based Services*

PART VI: *Long-Term Care and Institution-Based Services*

PART VII: *Special Issues*

Preface to the Second Edition

The first edition of *The Handbook of Gerontological Services* was published in 1985 and it apparently filled a substantial gap in the professional community, as evidenced by the fact that it had soon run out of print. This encouraged us to launch a new and revised edition. It is similar to the preceding one in its objectives, conceptual framework, and topical areas but it also registers the service developments of the intervening years.

As stated in the first edition, this *Handbook* aims to meet the need for a comprehensive review of the types of social intervention methods and the range of services available to the elderly. Written from a practice perspective, the *Handbook's* primary concerns are the issues that service providers confront on a day-to-day basis, from the time a particular program is planned and developed until it comes into contact with its intended beneficiaries.

Handbooks usually have a pretension to universality, but no such claim will be made here. To delve into all existing services for the aged would have required extending the book beyond all reasonable limits. Selectivity thus became the inevitable imperative, but priority criteria were not easily agreed upon. It is safe to admit that services that are in high demand and are repeatedly used by increasing numbers of consumers do merit inclusion. Yet there are specialized services used by small minorities that constitute critical components in the continuum of care. These services cannot be overlooked because they fill a sensitive need and reinforce the effectiveness of the more general services. A third order of services may not be as widespread or of immediate strategical importance, but may be tapping needs not yet fully recognized. This book seeks to do justice to all three types, but only time will tell whether it strikes a good balance among these services.

The *Handbook* is intended for several audiences: professional service practitioners, informal caregivers, community action groups, policymakers and administrators, researchers, academicians, students in the field of aging, and, last but not least, the elderly who wish to learn about the myriad of service systems impinging upon their lives. For some readers, this book will offer practical information, the nuts and bolts of the "how-to" variety. Others may extrapolate basic leads for research and concepts for teaching. In all instances, the *Handbook* offers an inventory of the state of the art and of the creative ferment permeating the gerontological services field. It is addressed to the wide audience of human service practitioners that staff the multidisciplinary teams in hospitals, long-term care facilities, multipurpose senior centers, mental health clinics, family service agencies, unions, Area Agencies on Aging, personnel departments, and the world of industry and business at large. It should be borne in mind that services for the aging constitute a complex and challenging endeavor that requires the collaboration of many professions.

The *Handbook* is made up of seven parts.

Part 1, "Concepts and Frameworks," serves as an introduction to professional interventions in the field of aging. It also examines the attitudes toward old age among service workers and in society at large. It concludes with a systematization of the continuum of formal services that has evolved to meet the needs of older persons.

Part 2, "Treatment and Intervention Modalities," begins with a review of the major approaches to psychosocial, medical, and functional assessment of elderly persons. It proceeds with the facilitation of access to services and the case management procedures required to coordinate an individual treatment plan. Contributors then review individual casework methods, specialized clinical approaches to individual services, group work, and resocialization methods and the macrosocietal strategies of social planning and social action.

Part 3, "Basic services," provides an overview of income maintenance resources for the aging population and continues with contributions on health and mental health services.

Part 4, "Community-Based Services," initiates the review of formally sponsored services. These services are focused on the family domain, work and retirement, older women, bereavement, assistance to crime and abuse victims, legal advice, and the multifaceted context of senior services.

Part 5, "Home-Based Services," includes the different types of residential and living arrangements available to older persons of varying degrees of functional ability, and the range of home-delivered services for the frail and homebound.

Part 6, "Long-Term Care and Institution-Based Services," includes the range of services for the chronically ill and the functional incapacitated. Attention is given to long-term care facilities, services for the dying, respite and adult day care programs, and protective legal and social services for those unable to fully assume responsibility over their lives.

Part 7, "Special Issues," wraps up the preceding exposition of services by highlighting two major generic issues that interest all practitioners. One is the ethnicity of the older person and how it affects both the delivery and the utilization of services. The other reflects on the moral and philosophical dilemmas practitioners face intermittently.

The contributors to parts 3, 4, 5, and 6 present the services in a continuum from wellness to chronicity. While the authors treat their subjects according to their individual perspectives and the idiosyncrasy of the topic, for the most part they follow a certain structural uniformity. All contributors thus tend to address the following five topical areas:

Need—the epidemiological scope and characteristics of the problem addressed by the service in reference

Assessment—ways of diagnosing and measuring the problem and need under scrutiny, both at the community and individual level

Interventions—the range of services devised to cope with the problem or need and determination of how clients learn about the service and come in contact with it; the role performed by social workers in conjunction with other professionals and paraprofessionals; the skills required for the provision of services and the effectiveness of the most commonly practiced forms of intervention; the specific needs of ethnic and minority elderly and differential approaches of attending to their needs; finally, ways in which this service is coordinated with other services

Theory—an interpretation of the problem and needs addressed by each service in terms of social-science theory; extent to which practice and intervention skills reflect different conceptual interpretations

Policy—a critical examination of public policies mandating or regulating each service; funding mechanisms, appropriations, and participation of different levels of government in the planning and provision of each service

By utilizing this model, service-related factors such as assessment, policy, service provision, etc., are integrated in the presentation of each service. Policy issues, for instance, are examined in conjunction with, say, protective services or nursing home care. A separate systematic presentation of all policies for the aged is therefore no longer needed.

The experts who contributed to the writing of this handbook bring to bear the vantage point of their day-to-day responsibilities. Some are front liners, the direct providers of the services they write about. Others are planners and administrators but still linked in a direct capacity with their assigned topics. Others are academic researchers with substantial familiarity with and deeply invested in their specialities. Some have written with almost exclusive reference to the settings where they carry out their practice. Others have adopted instead a comparative perspective that includes several settings.

In developing the content for this volume we were fortunate to count on the research assistance of Judith Whang and Ann McCann Oakley. Ms Linda Nye helped with preparation of the manuscript. This book would not have been possible without the earnest commitment made by the authors. They undertook their assignments with a sense of mission and accepted our suggestions for repeated modifications with patience and collegial understanding.

Abraham Monk

Contributors

Toby Berman-Rossi, D.S.W.
Columbia University School of Social Work
New York, New York

Elias S. Cohen, J.D., M.P.A.
Community Services Institute, Inc.
Narbeth, Pennsylvania

Carole Cox, D.S.W.
National Catholic School of Social Service
The Catholic University of America
Washington, D.C.

Barbara Oberhofer Dane, D.S.W.
Columbia University School of Social Work
New York, New York

Joseph Doolin, Ph.D., M.P.A.
Catholic Charities
Archdiocese of Boston

Ruth E. Dunkle, Ph.D.
University of Michigan
School of Social Work
Ann Arbor, Michigan

Irene A. Gutheil, D.S.W.
Fordham University
Graduate School of Social Service
New York, New York

Nancy H. Kuehn, M.S.W., J.D., L.L.M.
Prudential Insurance
Newark, New Jersey

Rosalie A. Kane, D.S.W.
School of Social Work and
School of Public Health
University of Minnesota
Minneapolis, Minnesota

Cary S. Kart, Ph.D.
University of Toledo
Sociology Department
Toledo, Ohio

Eric R. Kingson, Ph.D.
Boston College Graduate School of Social Work
Chestnut Hill, Massachusetts

Theodore H. Koff, Ph.D.
Long Term Care Gerontology Center
College of Medicine
University of Arizona
Tucson, Arizona

Jordan I. Kosberg, Ph.D.
Department of Gerontology
University of South Florida
Tampa, Florida

Regina Kulys, D.S.W.
Jane Addams College of Social Work
University of Illinois at Chicago
Chicago, Illinois

Louis Lowy, Ph.D.
Boston University School of Social Work
Boston, Masachusetts

Abraham Monk, Ph.D.
Columbia University School of Social Work
New York, New York

Harry R. Moody, Ph.D.
Brookdale Center on Aging
Hunter College of the City University of New York
New York, New York

Eloise Rathbone-McCuan, Ph.D.
School of Social Welfare
University of Kansas
Lawrence, Kansas

Edmund Sherman, Ph.D.
School of Social Welfare and Ringel Institute of Gerontology
The University at Albany
State University of New York
Albany, New York

Susan R. Sherman, Ph.D.
School of Social Welfare and Ringel Institute of Gerontology
The University at Albany
State University of New York
Albany, New York

Barbara Levy Simon, Ph.D.
Columbia University School of Social Work
New York, New York

Kenneth Solomon, M.D.
Saint Louis University Medical Center
Saint Louis, Missouri

Julia C. Spring, M.S.W., J.D.
Columbia University School of Law
New York, New York

Raymond M. Steinberg, D.S.W.
Andrus Gerontology Center
University of Southern California
Los Angeles, California

Cynthia Stuen, D.S.W.
National Center for Vision and Aging
The Lighthouse
New York, New York

Sheldon S. Tobin, Ph.D.
School of Social Welfare and Ringel Institute of Gerontology
The University at Albany
State University of New York
Albany, New York

Ronald W. Toseland, Ph.D.
School of Social Welfare and Ringel Institute of Gerontology
The University at Albany
State University of New York
Albany, New York

Monika White, Ph.D.
Senior Care Network
Huntington Memorial Hospital
Pasadena, California

Judith Wineman, M.S.W., C.S.W.
Retiree Service Department
International Ladies' Garment Workers' Union
New York, New York

Handbook of Gerontological Services

❖

SECOND EDITION

I

CONCEPTS AND FRAMEWORKS

1

Gerontological Social Services: Theory and Practice

ABRAHAM MONK, PH.D.
Columbia University School of Social Work

Gerontological and geriatric specializations are emerging in practically all human service professions, which is not surprising when we consider that American society is undergoing what Cowgill (1977) termed a "revolution of age," an unprecedented decline of mortality and fertility rates. The net effects are obvious: as few children are born and more adults survive into advanced senescence, the elderly are becoming a proportionally larger segment of society. Moreover, the average life expectancy is inching up relentlessly toward the ninth decade of life, and it is no longer uncommon to find two generations in retirement within the same family lineage. Retirement itself is a novel institution. It has created a life-style based upon economically nonproducing leisure roles that may eventually encompass a good third of a person's life span.

Initial professional responses to this demographic challenge were couched in a language of therapeutic pessimism and denials. Some practitioners felt that the aged were impervious to change, that their decline was irreversible, and that rehabilitative efforts on their behalf were altruistic but futile gestures. They similarly contended that there was no need for a separate geriatric specialization because the problems of the aged could be subsumed under more generic nosological entities or syndromes. One therefore dealt with arthritis, depression, or blindness in functional rather than in age-categorical terms.

No service discipline, however, could withstand for long the clamor of the elderly and their natural support networks seeking remediation for their multiple concerns. The public policies that ensued and the substantial apportionment of resources earmarked for those over age 65 became compelling inducements. Some professionals may have joined the new gerontological "bandwagon" for opportunistic reasons, while others have genuinely internalized an old-age consciousness, but their commitment to penetrate a barren and uncharted scientific domain was equally risky and praiseworthy.

The knowledge base at hand was initially too tenuous for guiding effective practice, and professions borrowed avidly from each other. No sooner did a breakthrough occur in one field than it was tested, metabolized, and incorporated into other disciplines. Because of this borrowing phenomenon, gerontologists soon developed a sense of kinship that on occasion transcended their primary occupational allegiances. Social workers working with the aged often sensed a greater affinity, and certainly interacted more frequently, with psychiatrists and nurses in the same field than with social workers specializing in a more remote area like criminal justice and probation. The resulting role-blurring was not always harmonious. Nor did it preclude feuds about claims to territorial exclusivity. Professions are still far from a consensus on their respective domains, but they are more aware that the knowledge explosion in gerontology is not owned by any one discipline, that the state of the art is in constant flux, and that new information is relentlessly generated to replace what was upheld as valid only yesterday. Moreover, professions are realizing that they cannot singly contend with the multiple ramifications of age-related problems. Multidisciplinary collaboration is a pragmatic necessity, but practitioners in each service profession are simultaneously expected to be "multiskilled," competent in a wide range of diagnostic and treatment modalities as well as thoroughly informed about the service options offered by sister disciplines.

It should not be surprising, therefore, that this handbook incorporates skills shared by many human service professions. It recognizes that all professionals wish to enable older persons to lead normal lives in their natural environments, and that they similarly want to assist in untangling situational problems as well as making irreversible chronic conditions more bearable. The successful provision of service, like the test of an effective therapist, ultimately depends on a keen understanding of the client for whom the service is intended. Because the elderly are so heterogeneous and because psychosocial theories underlying gerontological practice are so diverse, professional judgments must be, of necessity, eclectic and tentative. Gerontological practitioners find it a formidable enterprise to determine what all potential clients share in common, what may be specific to each group—racial, ethnic, religious, urban, rural, or socioeconomic—and ultimately what may be unique to each individual. To assist in this discerning function, I will explore first, how service providers initially approach their elderly clients; second, how theoretical frameworks guide the helping function; third, what critical issues and recurrent patterns are found in that function; and fourth, in what ways policy guides the provision of service.

PROFESSIONAL ATTITUDES TOWARD THE AGED

The first issue is an attitudinal one. First encounters in interpersonal relations are seldom neutral or devoid of emotional connotations. Providers of human services are no exception and, when entering the field of aging without proper training, they will act as unconscious carriers of the negative images perpetuated by their culture. They may therefore begin by exhibiting a fear of aging itself, followed by a phobic reaction of disgust and rejection, and end with a rationalization that conceives all dysfunctions and pathologies as inevitable correlates of old age for which, obviously, nothing can be done. Adverse reactions toward aging may be systematized in four categories: disvaluation, marginalization, internalization, and normativity.

Disvaluation

Disvaluation is the result of derogatory biases that deny the social and personal significance of the older person. The old, according to Butler (1974), are perceived as unproductive, rigid, uninteresting, withdrawn, and senile. It is further implied that they are a parasitical population voraciously demanding more than they contributed to society. When combined, all these myths seem to lend respectability to "agism," an active proces of discrimination against older persons that Butler likens to the prejudices of race, gender, religion, and color. Agism leads to a view of the elderly as less worthy, in cost-benefit terms, of receiving services. Schechter (1988) cites Butler's reference to a "new agism," the discrimination against the elderly in an era of fiscal and trade deficits and stagflation. These factors produce a "crisis" in which Social Security's legitimacy is questioned, as is the viability of public support to health care benefits for the aged. It is not surprising that this posture leads to the consideration of aged-based rationing of those benefits.

Marginalization

Older persons may be spared the traumatic effects of deliberate exclusion or discrimination, but they may still be ignored or forgotten. In a study of the images of old age in literature for adolescents, Peterson and Karnes (1976) found that, even when mentioned positively, the aged were not central characters. They were cast instead as peripheral shadows, unrelated to the mainstream of events. For the most part they were neither loved nor hated, simply unnoticed. Robertson (1976) examined the role of grandparents and similarly found that, although generally accepted by their grandchildren, they were not necessarily selected as role models.

There is more to marginalization, however, then sheer indifference or unawareness. The elderly who live alone are increasing in numbers. They are for the most part women. Some find it progressively more difficult to negotiate open spaces, stairs, distances, and public transportation. Others fear being assaulted and mugged. They become virtual recluses who sever their ties with the outside world unless assisted by the remnants of their natural support systems. They join, for the most part, the ranks of an invisible population seldom heard from again by social agencies and forgo services and benefits to which they may be rightfully entitled.

Internalization

One of the most devastating effects of prejudice occurs when victims end up accepting the prejudiced images of themselves and conforming their behavior to those images. Older persons may, for instance, introject the myths of rigidity and unproductivity and not trust themselves as capable of learning or doing new things. Their self-confidence is shattered, and the stereotypes become self-fulfilling prophecies. A study conducted by Louis Harris and Associates (1981) on behalf of the National Council on Aging found a rising discontent among the aged, compared to a similar survey seven years earlier. Cohen (1988), states that low goal formulation, and underestimated potentials for self-realization place constraints on the autonomy of elderly people with disabilities. He added that these older persons abandon all hopes of continuing growth and social participation, in order to focus all their energies in trying to avoid institutionalization, the ultimate defeat.

Service providers often find in their clinical experience certain behaviors that may suggest the internalization of dependence. The apparent helplessness exhibited by an elderly client may not be congruent, however, with his/her relatively good functional status. Brody et al. (1971) termed this behavior an expression of the "excess disability syndrome," often consisting of a manipulative strategy of feigning dependence in order to receive attention and ensure an uninterrupted flow of care.

Normativity

Logical derivatives from attitudes toward older persons are the culturally established norms that sanction what they should and should not do.

Norms prescribing age-appropriate behaviors are arbitrary and constantly changing, and they are made for all age groups. They tend, however, to be far more confining and restrictive for the older person. Neugarten, Moore, and Lowe (1965) suggest that this may be due to the fact that the elderly themselves ascribe greater importance to age norms. The young in turn tend to reject age as a valid yardstick by which to judge behavior.

Older persons may be ridiculed and dismissed as aberrant or senile for wearing youthful clothing, dating, or expressing sexual intimacy. Criticisms and sanctions leveled by their own peer group tend to be far more effective in inducing conformity to restrictive age norms than those imposed by professional outsiders. Negative attitudes are more visible in long-term care facilities simply because of the numerically larger concentration of older persons in a single location and their intensive interaction with staff. Kayser-Jones systematized the most frequently reported complaints of staff abuse in four categories:

1. *Infantilization*—treating the patient as an irresponsible, undependable child.
2. *Depersonalization*—providing services in an assembly line fashion, disregarding the patients' individual needs.
3. *Dehumanization*—not only ignoring elderly persons but stripping them of privacy and of their capacity to assume responsibility for their own lives.
4. *Victimization*—attacking the older person's physical and moral integrity through verbal abuse, threats, intimidation, theft, blackmail, or corporal punishments. (1981: 38–55)

Gubrium (1980) found that even in the absence of such harsh forms of treatment, nursing home residents may be affected by other subtle but equally demeaning exclusionary procedures. Staff, for example, will "plan ahead" without making the patient part of the decision-making process. They may also engage in "distancing," that is, treating the issues summarily and minimizing their importance in from the client. "Subplotting" consists, in turn, of a series of codes and subterfuges aimed at limiting the range of issues to be shared with the patient.

Most of these patterns or forms of staff-patient relations are typical, however, of all total or long-term care institutions and are not limited to the elderly alone. They reflect for the most part administrative expediency by an overburdened and often ill-trained staff rather than a malicious intent to debase the patient. The institutionalized elderly, however, constitute an easy target: they are too feeble and decompensated to assert their rights or retaliate, and they are truly powerless after having lost their networks of friends and relatives outside the institution. The fact remains too that, in advanced cases of frailty or organic brain syndrome, staff must take over and make decisions for the patient. Adult children often find themselves in the same predicament, and Blenkner (1965) advised them to treat their ailing parents with "filial maturity," which consists of communicating to their elders that they can truly rely on the care of their offspring without having to feel dependent. There is no role reversal whereby the older person becomes the child of his/her own children. Filial maturity simply means offering support without exacting the price of submission.

Filial maturity ought not be confined exclusively to the family domain. It has a comparable place in the professional helping relationship as a form of "therapeutic maturity" that begins by precluding all condescension, pseudofamiliarity, and attacks on the older person's sense of privacy. Have professional helpers ever thought what it does to senior persons who were always addressed with deference by their last name to suddenly be called by their first names by a worker half their age or even the age of their grandchildren? Therapeutic maturity is therefore launched with the empathetic endeavor of reaching out to the clients' feelings of self-esteem and playing them out as one's own. It continues with the helpers reflecting on their own feelings and attitudes toward aging as a life process and toward the aged as people. The actual intervention that ensues requires and immersion in the knowledge base, the plethora of facts that constitute the discipline of gerontology and their underlying meanings. The latter is the function of theory because, unless guided by sound conceptual interpretations, practice is reduced to an aimless application of techniques.

THEORETICAL FOUNDATIONS OF PRACTICE

The last quarter of a century has been a period of relentless theoretical productivity as far as the field of aging is concerned. While a sign of serious investigative commitment, it could also be very disconcerting to new practitioners seeking to anchor their interventions in a less shifting interpretative ground. Unable to contend with so much change, some practitioners tend to set their minds and lock themselves in a chosen theory, holding its propositions as unshakable truths. This has been true for both academic schools and social agencies. Seasoned practitioners, for the most part, have extricated themselves from canonized dogmas and opted instead for a greater intellectual openness and pragmatic eclecticism.

Professional helpers were initially attracted to Cumming and Henry's (1961) theory of intrinsic disengagement because of its functionalist appeal. It gave the process of aging a "purpose" consisting of the realization and acceptance of the terminality of life in the way that is least disruptive to society. It defined the older person's withdrawal or separation as natural, irreversible, universal, and gradual, irrespective of individual or cultural idiosyncrasies. It added a libertarian connotation by asserting that disengagement freed the person from the yoke of day-to-day obligations. Disengagement, finally, was consistent with a clinical predilection for contracting in the therapeutic relation, because it entailed a tacit understanding between person and society to reduce their reciprocal expectations.

The "activity"-oriented theoreticians (Carp 1968; Maddox 1963; Rose 1964) questioned whether disengagement is a natural process or whether it is culturally induced to make room for succeeding generations. The latter possibility, if true, is tantamount systematic discrimination and therefore regarded as morally reprehensible. If disengagement leads to stripping the aged of the instrumental roles that enabled them to remain independent agents, clinical intervention should be primarily addressed to neutralizing any further victimization. It must also assist in generating compensatory new roles, as proposed by Rosow (1973), to replace those that have been lost.

Contracting also plays a central, implicit role in exchange theory (Blau 1964; Dowd 1975; Emerson 1962). It hinges upon the older persons' capacity to perform their assumed obligations once power resources such as status, money, and skills have been substantially reduced or lost forever. Unable to offer such desirable attributes in return for social recognition, influence, or independence, the elderly become a powerless bunch. They have only one asset left to trade:

submission and the recognition of dependence on those who master and control resources. This is the very last contract they can enter into to secure protection and guarantee survival. Social workers have found exchange theory a helpful tool for better understanding phenomena such as alienation, dependence, and depression among the aged. It also gives them a ready-made framework to legitimize self-help and coalition program initiatives in community development.

The three theories under brief scrutiny—disengagement, activity, and exchange—implicitly state normative prescriptions of what life satisfaction or "good" aging is all about. From the disengagement perspective this consists of relinquishing social participation prior even to the onset of an inner sense of psychological detachment. For "activity" theory this involves harnessing new interactive skills, making oneself count, and shaping new roles. The exchange theory suggests in turn tapping one's hidden potentials and personal assets, joining forces with peers for mutual support, and entering into alliances with other disadvantaged groups. The three theories also give similar recognition, despite their conceptual disparities, to an omnipresent reality of loss. Rosenmayr (1982) criticized this concept of loss as a rather elementary form of reductionism and suggested paying attention instead to economic poverty as the underlying determinant of all forms of deprivation. Poverty in old age produces lack of stimulation, dependence on handouts and public assistance, illness, inadequate health care, and an overall shrinkage of opportunities. It also precipitates a "self-induced social deprivation," phenomenologically akin to disengagement, consisting of a passive and fatalistic resignation to one's fate, loss of all hope of ever being able to break the vicious circle of destitution and despondence.

The concept of life satisfaction has become for social workers and other service providers a powerful construct in its own right. It enables them to view a person's existence as striving for closure, in accordance with a script woven with values, expectations, and dreams—the ideals that confer meaning and purpose when a person approaching the end of life ponders whether it was all worth it. Even earlier, during middle age, crises often stem from a sense of discrepancy between a person's aspirations and what he or she has actually accomplished. The pursuit of unrealistic expectations that cannot come to fruition—like upward mobility or the highest rung of a career ladder—may lead to depression and alienation. Stock-taking, in these circumstances, causes a sense of defeat, not satisfaction. The mission of clinical intervention in such an instance is, according to Parkes (1971), to facilitate change of the individual's values and expectations, what he terms the person's "assumptive world." Old expectations must be questioned and discarded and new ones formulated and tested. The perceived discrepancy between the "assumptive world" in question and life realities ought not to bring an irrevocable crisis but lead to new insights, an accommodation to new alternatives, and perhaps even the discovery of hidden potential.

While the preceding psychosocial theories gained popularity among gerontological practitioners, Erickson's (1959) model of the life cycle has for years dominated the teaching of human behavior and life-transition counseling. Similar interests in other stage-structured theories also increased. Group counseling at a time of life transitions is termed by Freud-Loewenstein (1978) a "strikingly effective" and a "preferred" method for dealing with people in crisis and populations at risk. Some developmental or stage theories conceive of life as a fixed and universal sequence of maturational processes, evolving in a hierarchy of more complex life tasks (Duvall 1971; Loevinger 1976; Piaget 1976). For others like Erickson (1959) and Levinson (1978), there is no such ascending hierarchy: each period of life has its distinct characteristics and a series of tasks or challenges that must be mastered for optimal growth, but each stage is not necessarily better than the preceding stage. Brennan and Weick identified five assumptions shared by most theories of adult human development.

1. Human development continues throughout life.
2. The life cycle consists of a series of discrete stages.
3. Transitions from stage to stage are often marked by crises.
4. Growth may occur as the possible outcome of such crises.
5. Adulthood must be understood in terms of a person's capacity to cope with new challenges and crises. (1981:16)

Although not explicitly admitting it, most psychological theories of human development have imitated biological epigenetic models. They assume that human beings unfold all their potentialities in early adulthood and begin thereafter an invariant process of decline. Lerner and Ryff (1978) found however that cognitive development may continue throughout life and does not necessarily slow down at any fixed point of the life cycle. The rigidity and resistance to new learning that is often associated with aging is not an intrinsic developmental process, according to Botwinick (1978), but a defensive posture, possibly a maladaptive form of coping behavior when having to contend with threatening circumstances. Furthermore, differences in learning capacity between young and old may be accounted for by initial training, not age, according to Labouvie-Vief (1982). The young can better handle new informational inputs because of their more updated levels of scientific, mathematical, and computer-related training. Even when acknowledging that basic intellectual capacities show decline, especially in very advanced age, Plemons, Willis, and Baltes (1978) point out that intellectual functions can be practiced and have a reserve capacity that can be "activated." Besides, slower mental processing among the aged does not mean that less information is being stored and retrieved. Erickson describes the last stage of life, "integrity," as the acceptance of one's life the way it has been, not the way one would like it to have been, and taking full responsibility for it without blaming others. Being satisfied with one's life confers upon a person his/her ultimate authenticity, the realization of having become one's true self. This is an aspiration, however, that not all will reach. Some will fall prey instead to Erickson's dialectic opposite of integrity, "despair," so often manifested in depression and negative life review assessments.

Life cycle theories in general, and Erickson's in particular, offer a naturalistic, nonpathological foundation for social intervention. Transitions from stage to stage, according to Levinson (1978), entail a rather complex set of tasks: accepting the losses that result from the ending of the preceding state; reassessing the past; selecting those aspects one wants to continue; and formulating what course one wishes for the future.

Some of these tasks are unconscious, while other enter into the realm of awareness. They then produce emotional repercussions that oscillate form elation to panic or anxiety. In the latter case, as in all crises, the individual's coping skills may be strained beyond their limits. Rapoport (1967) advised in such instances to focus on the precipitating stresses. Her method of intervention consisted of fostering an adaptation to the new reality, reducing the anxiety by offering reassurance, relief from loneliness, a boost to the person's self-esteem, concrete information and advice as a sort of anticipatory guidance, and direct teaching of interpersonal skills. Yet the notion that the life cycle is organized in a sequence of stages and the hypothesis that both middle age and aging are characterized by pervasive crises and traumatic losses are far from receiving universal acceptance. Neugarten and Brown-Rezanka state that dominant themes and life concerns stay for life and reappear without a fixed order. The alleged predictability of life cycle transitions is disregarded as unreliable and capricious. "Some of the old regularities in timing have disappeared and some of the social clocks that tell people whether they are on time or off time are no longer operating" (1978–79:25–26).

Pearlin (1982) argues in turn that, instead of a dominant theme, as proposed by Erickson, there may be multiple patterns of aging and that not all members of a cohort are exposed to the same conditions of life: "While moving an equal distance across the life span from the same temporal starting point may provide a basis for some common experiences, such commonalities are not sufficiently powerful to erase the profound differences that result from people having different origins and from the variations in their current social and economic experiences" (1982:63). Individual variability within a cohort may then be greater than the differences that separate cohort from cohort. Pearlin also disputes the view that the negative effects of life accumulate with age. For some, the gratifications and compensations found throughout the years, and especially in maturity, may well cancel out negative residues. In the balance sheet of life not all the aged come out losers. Some may even find themselves ahead of the game. Defining what constitutes a detrimental experience in contrast to a positive one depends on each person's psychological makeup and cumulative life history. The "empty nest" syndrome, for instance, that allegedly begins when the last child leaves the parental home is experienced by some as a source of desolation and grief, but others may exult and rejoice in their newly gained freedom. People of the same cohort may react differently to the same situations, and Pearlin adds that aging itself does not produce more distress than the challenges faced by the young, although he circumscribes this statement to the healthy elderly. A life course approach, instead of a life cycle one, views life transitions as a continuous, uninterrupted process rather than as discrete segments of human experience. Even when conceptually isolating aging, youth, or middle age, each must be viewed in light of the entire life continuum, the pathways of a person's entire life, and how they were shaped in each instance by social and historical circumstances.

Rosenmayr (1985) points to the "cumulative deprivation" resulting from the interacton of adverse factors such as income, education, housing, consumption patterns, etc. Low-income elderly are particularly vulnerable and at risk of becoming trapped in such a cycle. Those who were poorly educated when young will go through life enjoying less opportunities, and will reap less benefits once reaching old age.

In sum, life cycle theories succeed in better explaining intrapersonal life sequences. They may be less effective in explaining differences across historical periods and cultural circumstances. Those who challenge the assumption that the life cycle is organized in fixed stages, as if these stages were ontological absolutes, do not mean to imply that defined life transitions do not exist. They contend instead that such transitions may be experienced differently by different people in different times and circumstances. The bottom line consists in relating to elderly clients, as with clients of any age, in terms of their personal uniqueness, without forcing them into preconceived conceptual schema. Theories and derived classifications will always remain tentative and partial explanations of reality. While offering a convenient framework for making a puzzling and confusing world more intelligible, they should not be accepted as immovable belief systems.

THE HELPING FUNCTION

The philosophical affirmation that all human beings have a right to complete their expected life cycle and that no stage of life is more valuable or more deserving of service inputs than others are the central premises of gerontological practice. This belief proceeds with the clinical recognition of each person's unique personality and coping patterns. Consequently, older persons should not be "homogenized" as if they were all alike.

Even when committed to the principle of individualization, however, service providers find it necessary to anchor their practice in some regularities or constancies characteristic of large populations. Practice-related taxonomies center, for the most part, on the functional capacities of older persons. While such taxonomies are too numerous to be reviewed here, the one outlined by the Gerontological Society (1978) for the Health Care Finance Administration can be cited as an example. It identified four target groups: the "unimpaired," the "minimally impaired," the "moderately impaired," and the "severely impaired" elderly. These classifications constitute a linear continuum from minimal to maximal impairment, taking into account some chronological parameters as well as the auspice of preventive, supportive, and protective services.

The category of "severely impaired" comprises people usually in their late 70's and older who exhibit advanced and multiple conditions such as osteo-arthritis, Parkinson's disease, paralysis, and cerebral vascular disease. A high incidence of confusion, disorientation, depression, and behavioral disorders is also present. The severely impaired have, for the most part, lost the capacity for self-care, and family supports, even when available, are not adequate to the need. Continuous and comprehensive long-term care is therefore required in either nursing homes or chronic care hospitals, but home care is not excluded if round the clock and properly monitored.

The "moderately impaired" are typically in their mid 70's or older. They are no longer self-sufficient; although not bedridden, they may be afflicted by the same conditions as the preceding group. Some may also have suffered mild strokes, heart failure, and amputations as well as visual and hearing impairments. They also exhibit memory loss and confusion, especially when subject to stress. While most individuals in this group can take care of some of their needs, they must be placed under medical, nursing, and social work supervision at home or in a protected environment. It is in this group that social workers find the greatest resistance to any interposited support that may suggest surrendering one's independence.

The "minimally impaired' tend to be in their late 60's and early 70's. Their illnesses may be acute and may cause temporary activity restrictions. Chronic impairments are, however, mild and do not impede continuity of life-style. There are signs of progressively advancing disability due to heart and circulatory disorders, arthritis, and visual defects. Occasional forgetfulness, while not serious in itself, may provoke anxiety and self-consciousness. Although these individuals can take care of themselves, they can also profit from community-based preventive services.

The "unimpaired elderly" are found in the youngest group, ranging from early to late 60's. They have minimal sporadic functional limitations and are fully capable of meeting all their needs. Major problems relate to the retirement transition and possible reduction in standard of living. Services are needed to assure continuity of interests, prevention of postponement of the onset of disabilities, and life enrichment.

Classifications based on functional ability and health status are commonly used because they offer a rationale for either institutional placement or community-based care decisions. Other classifications take into account the personality style in adjustment to retirement. Reichard, Livson, and Peterson found three well-adjusted and two poorly adjusted types among men. The positive types were:

1. *Mature.* They enter into old age without neurotic conflicts, exhibiting genuine satisfaction with whatever comes and without regretting the past.
2. *Rocking chair.* These individuals are the good disengagers, opting for a nonobligatory life and welcoming the freedom from responsibility. They find pleasure in "doing nothing."
3. *Armored.* Anxiously concerned about their waning resources, they ward off anxiety with compulsive activity. They make good adjustments as long as they can sustain intense activity levels.

The negative types were:

1. *Angry.* They despair over their failure to achieve life goals and blame others for it.

2. *Self-hating.* They experience a similar sense of failure but blame themselves for how their life turned out. Both these types exhibit high rates of depression, low self-regard, alienation, and feelings of worthlessness. (1962)

Reichard, Livson, and Peterson's typology is only one example of a number of psychosocial classifications evolved through analysis of empirical data. It has served to alert practitioners against simple dichotomic notions that all "disengagement-prone" behavior is bad and that an infusion of multifaceted program activities is a suitable prescription for all.

Classifications are auxiliary tools and should be used only as part of an overall evaluation procedure. Too literal an adherence to a typology based on functional ability, for instance, may lead, according to Illich (1975), to "structural iatrogenesis," namely, the possibility that health professionals, by appending a sick or disabled label on people, may destroy their resources for handling their deficits in an autonomous way. Determinations of who is capable and who is impaired are not easy to make. As Larson pointed out:

> One can seldom say, for example, that on this day or in this week, an adult who had previously been able to meet and resolve the problems of everyday living with reasonable prudence became incapable of doing so. Moreover loss of capability may be uneven. . . . An older person may be "childish" in his conversation but regular in meeting his financial obligations. (1964:248)

A comprehensive evaluation therefore goes beyond the fixed parameters of established classifications and taps for strengths and decrements into areas such as: self-care, physical and mental health, functional capacity, coping skills, present and past roles, occupational status, work and life satisfaction, family status, interpersonal relations, primary support systems, housing and environmental context; and economic conditions, including benefits that may accrue to a person for reasons of vesting, maturity of insurance plans, age, and proven need.

When an individual service plan is needed, social workers should keep in mind that, contrary to commonly held assumptions, many older persons can be helped with insight therapy. Prolonged forms of treatment may not be practical or feasible in all circumstances, and Oberleder (1966) suggests that interventions with the elderly should not be directed to changing their personality makeup but to alleviating their anxiety and maintaining adequate functioning. Verwoerdt (1981) similarly views psychotherapy as being supportive because regression and transference are not dealt with or interpreted. The basic goal then is to strengthen existing coping skills. A client's defenses should be understood as mechanisms to ward off an adverse reality and the anxiety it produces. Because older persons experience multiple and almost simultaneous stresses, defense mechanisms are not necessarily maladaptive in all instances. Some may be positive because they enable the person to contend with those blows. Ford (1965) observed, for instance, that denial gives the person a chance to reorganize, delay, or postpone dealing with a crisis until he or she can marshal inner or external resources more effectively. The same may be said about "withdrawal," when the person avoids taking risks and abandons the field. It may not be too high a price to pay in order to retain one's selfhood. Manipulation and aggression may also be interpreted on occasion as signs of vitality. They are proactive behaviors revealing a capacity to assess the environment and to increase personal gains.

The plan of treatment capitalizes on the older person's remaining strengths and coping resources, but it may also offer sincere reassurance, particularly when progressive disabilities have set in. It is much easier to accept one's dependencies when realizing that one is not alone and that others care. In any event, treatment objectives should be scaled down to a realistic expectation level, commensurate with the person's remaining strengths. Any improvement, regardless of how imperceptible, is an auspicious indicator of therapeutic effectiveness. It may produce the added benefits of enhancing the person's sense of control over his/her life and improving his/her battered self-esteem.

Rowlings (1981) observed that treatments for the elderly consist, for the most part, of the management of their dependence and the management of risk. The former is commonly handled through case management systems. The latter requires sheltered environments, community-based services, and preventive therapies. In addition, a "quality of life" orientation should be geared to enriching the overall circumstances of a person's life and adding more opportunities and alternatives. This is primarily attained through policy analysis, policy development, social planning, and community organization. It begins at the individual level with helping people obtain better and more suitable resources, a subject to be reviewed in the next section.

APPLYING SOCIAL POLICY

Social Security constitutes the leading source of income for older persons. Medicare covers nearly half of their acute health care costs, and Medicaid foots almost 60 percent of the nursing home bill. No other age group is so dependent on public entitlements, yet older persons are intimidated by complex eligibility requirements and the voluminous paperwork required to apply for a given benefit. There is the agony of waiting for decisions and not knowing how to seek redress when an application is disallowed on obscure statutory grounds. Overcome by sheer physical exhaustion, discouraged by transportation costs, long lines, and hurried expedience of clerical personnel, many seniors simply give up and do not press for their rights.

Social workers stepping in to facilitate access to services and to restore the provision of entitlements are similarly bewildered by the sheer number of programs addressed to the aged. According to the Senate Special Committee on Aging (1987), there are 80 federal programs to assist those with long-term care needs through cash assistance, in-kind transfers, and provisions of goods and services. Must an effective social worker become proficient in all of them? Kutza (1981) notes, to everybody's relief, that there are only eight programs that constitute the core of the aging-focused policies: Social Security (Old Age and Survivors Insurance), tax allowances and benefits, Medicare, Older Americans Act services, Medicaid, Supplementary Security Income, food stamps, and housing subsidies. Ultimately, a geriatric practitioner ought to have a good working knowledge of at least four: Social Security (OASI); Supplemental Security Income (SSI); Medicare (Title XVIII); and Medicaid (Title XIX). Only one piece of legislation is exclusively aimed at the elderly: the Older Americans Act, which focuses for the most part on the coordination of existing resources and the planning of new ones.

Social workers approach the myriad of programs for the aged wondering whether their clients qualify for services and how those who are entitled can obtain those benefits. A generic prescription for policy application therefore includes the following considerations:

1. *Eligibility* To whom is the program addressed? Who is entitled to apply for benefits and who does not qualify? Are there any retroactive eligibility provisions that compensate for services rendered prior to the application?
2. *Proof of eligibility*. What evidence must clients submit in order to establish whether they qualify for the benefits?
3. *Adequacy*. Are the benefits obtained commensurate with the client's needs? Assuming they meet those needs only partially, are there any other programs that can be used as backup or supplement? What is the best possible "package" of benefits that can be set up on behalf of a client?

4. *Costs.* Are there any known or hidden costs, deductibles, premiums, or "spend down" requirements that client must bear before becoming eligible for a specific benefit?
5. *Application.* What steps must the client follow in order to apply for a specific benefit? What is the waiting time, how quickly are applications acted upon, and how long does it take to obtain benefits?
6. *Confidentiality.* Are the client's rights to privacy assured during the application and service delivery process? Do clients have access to their files?
7. *Quality assurance.* Are the program personnel properly trained and equipped to deliver the benefits? Have quality standards and evaluative procedures been instituted to monitor the service delivery process?
8. *Plan of service.* Are clients involved in determining an eventual plan of service? What are the possible limitations or changes in duration, type, and level of service that may be subsequently introduced? Who has the authority to effect such changes?
9. *Due process.* How can the client request a review of a denial or termination of benefits? What are the mechanisms of appeal and grievance bearing? What information must the client submit when initiating an appeal?
10. *Advocacy.* If the program does not properly address a problem or does not reach its intended target population, how can clients and social workers bring this fact to the attention of policymakers? What are the best strategies for creating awareness and bringing about community pressure to effect change?
11. *Policy formulation* What are the best possible alternatives to a deficient or obsolete policy? What are their estimated benefits and what is their economic, political, and administrative feasibility?

Concerning the last two items—advocacy and policy formulation—it is to the social worker's advantage to know how existing policies evolved, whether they share a common pattern, and what future awaits them.

Policies for the aged, as for any other problem area, resulted from breakdowns in the provision of critical services by the voluntary or private sectors, thus forcing a reluctant government to intervene. As more needs were identified, additional remedial actions had to be sanctioned and instituted. This is the proverbial incrementalism of all policymaking in America, a step-by-step course guided by the pressures of interest groups and the circumstantial convenience of political agendas. There is no underlying commitment to a comprehensive and long-range strategy, and Estes (1979) suggests that many of the resulting policies are deliberately ambiguous precisely to avoid making definite value decisions. Incrementalism, however, has its advantages too: it permits trial-and-error adjustments, and it does not freeze providers in an ideological corner.

Value preferences, of course, enter into consideration when policymakers must contend with basic dilemmas: Are social policies for the aged meant to provide a floor of protection only, or should they seek to upgrade the quality of older persons' lives? Should they emphasize an income or a service strategy? Should services be universally responsive to all older persons or residually limited to those in greater need?

Should programs be based on a social insurance model, thus providing benefits in direct relation to a person's previous contributions? or should they seek to reduce income disparities by redistributing both money and resources? Is there a reason for separate programs for the elderly? or should they be integrated in a comprehensive service strategy for all needy members of society? Each of these questions merits an extensive discussion that would exceed the intent here. The issues, however, are more than academic since they touch upon the future scope and even the survival of the programs for the aged. The question whether there should be special separate services for the aged, for instance, received widespread attention at a time of the 1981 White House Conference on Aging, when those in favor of dismantling the network of gerontological services argued that services should exist to handle problems in general, regardless of the ages of those affected. Attacking problems separately for each age group results in a debilitated and fragmented strategy. Insisting on separate policies may lead to negative labeling, stigmatization, or token symbolic measures that fall short of the mark.

Advocates of an age-categorical approach claim, in turn, that doing away with the present system will not produce the alleged age "integration." It will lead instead to a functional specialization along disease or organ criteria. As in the traditional medical model, it will treat symptoms of dysfunctions but seldom the whole person, and may overlook the fact that illnesses in younger age groups are for the most part acute and episodic while chronicity is the dominant expression of pathology in old age. The very goals of treatment for the latter can no longer be restoration of health, as for the young, but compensation for loss of function. Moreover, older persons are often afflicted by a cluster of chronic conditions that might include arthritis, diabetes, deafness, recent widowhood, loss of income, absence of immediate relatives, and so on. These multiple conditions interact and combine in unpredictable ways, and they cannot be attacked piecemeal as separate functional entities.

The discussion may become superfluous when we take into account that the elderly tend to lose out when mixed with other age groups but are strengthened by peer interaction. Landmark initiatives concerning services for the aged in the United States were invariably spearheaded through age-categorical, not universalistic, programs. The four major public programs relevant to the aged—Social Security, Medicare, Supplemental Security Income, and nutrition (Older Americans Act)—began as "age specific" programs. Whenever generic programs were launched without making special provisions for older persons, the latter ended up discouraged at having to compete with the young for access to these services. In other instances they could not obtain the universal service because of deliberately discriminatory service practices. Disabled elderly are underrepresented in rehabilitative programs: although 40 percent of the disabled population are elderly, less than 10 percent of services rendered by state departments of rehabilitation are received by disabled elderly. Also, only 10 to 20 percent of services to the blind are provided to the elderly, while they represent 50% of the blind population (Kemp 1985).

There are recommendations to resolve the impasse by keeping services age-integrated until age 75 and then offering age-categorical services to the older cohort. The reasoning behind such an arrangement is expedient but not very rational. Some services, like preretirement counseling or occupational retraining, do not make sense at age 75. They are not needed at age 25, either, but may be useful only for those in the age 50–60 cohort.

Ideally, services should be organized in a two-tiered system: both universalistic and particularistic. A hospital may provide general outpatient services, but certain ailments may require the input of a pediatrician and other ailments the input of a geriatric specialist. A school system offers high school education for all, but a middle-aged adult who wishes to complete the requirements for a high-school diploma may need a didactic approach different from that targeted for adolescents. Besides, it is unlikely that an older person would feel comfortable in a class with teenagers. Age-categorical services have that advantage of being more individualizing. They employ differential assessment methods and a more profound understanding of the issues, crises, and developmental potentialities of each stage of the life cycle. Social policies will have to make special allowance for these specialized services, whether free-standing or as parts of universal programs, even when advocating greater closeness of generations and more effective utilization of primary support networks.

In essence, the application of social policy to practice goes beyond the knowledge and negotiations of entitlements. It requires as well an understanding of 1) the underlying philosophy of such policies; 2) the political climates that foster the adoption of new ideas or force the retraction of a too progressive advance; 3) the emerging issues that require societal intervention; and 4) the process that leads to the adoption of new policies, from grass-roots organization to lobbying, legislative drafting, and mobilization of political support.

Social workers are not passive implementers of programs even when seeking to maximize their potential benefits on behalf of elderly clients. They also assist in formulating the policies that authorize those programs. They take the lead in protecting good ongoing programs, when jeopardized, and in recommending changes when other programs are no longer adequate.

A MANPOWER AGENDA

Working with the aged, as it has unfolded here, is no light matter. It starts with an attitudinal self-appraisal and emotional preparation followed by the systematic learning of a vast knowledge base that encompasses theory, normal and pathological human development, and social policy issues. It finally requires the acquisition of a complex battery of practice skills, some of which give greater emphasis to institutional and sheltered care while others are addressed to the well or minimally impaired aged.

Where does such preparation take place? Although gerontological services are not in the forefront of the educational agenda of schools of health and social services, and most specialists have to improvise on their jobs, the number of undergraduate and graduate programs giving attention to or offering a concentration in aging have increased in recent years. According to a study of the National Institute on Aging (1987), 75 percent of the social work programs included gerontological content in their basic curricula; about 35 percent of faculty members expressed interest in the field. However, less than 10 percent of the 4,000 full-time faculty have any formal training in aging issues. The number of full-time equivalent professionally trained social workers needed to serve older persons and their families has been estimated to be in the range of 40,000–50,000 by the year 2000 and 60,000–

70,000 in 2020. These estimations exceed by many times the current levels of adequately trained personnel and the capacities of training programs.

Future estimates of manpower needs take into account not only the growing number of older persons, from about 24 million in 1980 to 35 million in 2000, but also the internal changes in the composition of the 65-plus cohort. Demographic projections estimate that the 75-and-older group, which represented 38 percent of the total aged in 1980 or about 9 million people, will rise to 44 percent or 15.4 million people by the turn of the century. Estimates of the proportion of the frailest and most dependent among the age group 75 and older range from 9 to 20 percent, depending on the definition of functional impairment (U.S. Census 1977). In any case, frail older persons, those who find it difficult to cope with the vicissitudes of life for reasons of health, economics, housing, and family supports, are the fastest growing segment of the elderly population. Services connected with the provision of long-term care for that group, whether community- or institution-based, will obviously follow suit.

There will also be an emerging demand at the other end of the age spectrum. During the late 1960s and early 1970s retirement before age 65 became a desirable option for nearly half of all prospective retirees. In recent years, a reverse trend emerged, aimed at abolishing mandatory retirement altogether or at least at gradually postponing it, as means of restoring fiscal viability of the Social Security system. However, with inflation rates dropping, early retirement is retaining its position as a favored alternative for older workers. Gerontological practitioners may then be confronted with vast numbers of leisured, younger retirees whose value primacy is no longer work but active exploration and search for self-renewal. Social workers will then have to come to terms with a new culture of leisure, centered around a sense of self-directedness, lifelong learning pursuits, and quality-of-life concerns.

Working with the aged holds many promises, but it will take time until these latent career opportunities will be fully realized. In the meantime, practitioners must attend to their clients' service needs without a ready-made and comprehensive service system. It is often up to them to design or even improvise new services. It is also their ultimate challenge to propose new legislation and advocate service reforms. Idealistic practitioners may find this a highly creative and pioneering task, but it is also a very demanding one in which the signs of "combat fatigue" show at an early stage. Excitement and frustration go hand-in-hand with building a new field of service.

REFERENCES

Blau P. M. 1964. *Exchange and Power in Social Life.* New York: Wiley.
Blenkner, M. 1965. Social work and family relationships in old age. In E. Shanas and G. F. Streib, eds., *Social Structure and the Family: Generational Relations.* Englewood Cliffs, N.J.: Prentice-Hall.
Botwinick, J. 1978. *Aging and Behavior* 2d ed. New York: Springer, 1978.
Brennan, E. M. and A. Weick. 1981. Theories of adult development: Creating a context for practice. *Social Casework* 62(1):13–19.
Brody, E. M., M. H. Kleban, M. P. Lawton, and H. A. Silverman. 1971. Excess disabilities of mentally impaired aged: Impact of individualized treatment. *The Gerontologist* 11(2):124–133.
Butler, R. N. 1974. Successful aging and the role of the life review. *Journal of the American Geriatrics Society* 22(12):529–535.
Carp, F. M. 1968. Some components of disengagement. *Journal of Gerontology* 23(3):382–386.
Cohen, S. 1988. The elderly mystique: Constraints on the autonomy of the elderly with disabilities. *The Gerontologist* (June), Supplement Issue, pp. 24–31.
Cowgill, D. O. 1977. The revolution of age. *Humanist* 37(5):10–13.
Cumming, E. and W. E. Henry 1961. *Growing Old: The Process of Disengagement.* New York: Basic Books.
Dowd, J. J. 1975. Aging as exchange: A Preface to theory. *Journal of Gerontology* 30(5):584–594.
Duvall, E. M. 1977. *Marriage and Family Development* 5th ed. New York: Harper and Row.
Emerson, R. M. 1962. Power-dependence relations. *American Sociological Review* 27(1):31–41.
Erickson, E. H. 1959. Identity and the life cycle. *Psychological Issues* 1(1):18–171.
Estes, C. L. 1979. *The Aging Enterprise: A Critical Examination of Social Policies and Services for the Aged.* San Francisco: Jossey-Bass.
Ford, C. S. 1965. Ego-adaptive mechanisms of older persons. *Social Casework* 46(1):16–21.
Freud-Loewenstein, S. 1978. Preparing social work students for life-transition counseling within the human behavior sequence. *Journal of Education for Social Work* 14(2):66–73.
Gerontological Society. 1978. *Working with Older People: A Guide to Practice.* Rockville, Md.: U.S. Department of Health, Education and Welfare.
Gubrium, J. F. 1980. Patient exclusion in geriatric settings. *Sociological Quarterly* 21(3):335–347.
Harris, L. and Associates 1981. "Aging in the Eighties: America in Transition" Washington, D.C.: National Council on the Aging.
Illich, I. 1975. *Medical Nemesis: The Expropriation of Health.* London: Calder and Boyars.
Kayser-Jones, J. S. 1981. *Old, Alone, and Neglected: Care of the Aged in Scotland and in the United States.* Berkely: University of California Press.
Kemp, B. 1985. Rehabilitation and older adults. In E. Birren and K. Schaie, eds., *Handbook of the Psychology of Aging.* New York: Van Nostrand Reinhold.
Kutza, E. A. 1981. *The Benefits of Old Age: Social Welfare Policy for the Elderly.* Chicago: University of Chicago Press.
Labouvie-Vief, G. 1982. Individual time, social time, and intellectual aging. In

T. K. Hareven and K. J. Adams eds., *Aging and Life Course Transitions: An Interdisciplinary Perspective.* New York: Guilford Press.

Larson, N. 1964. Protective services for older adults. *Public Welfare,* 22(4): 247–251, 276.

Lerner, R. M. and C. D. Ryff. 1978. Implementing the life-span view: Attachment. *Life-Span Development and Behavior,* 1:1–44.

Levinson, D. J. et al. 1978. *The Seasons of a Man's Life.* New York: Knopf.

Loevinger, J. 1976. *Ego Development: Conceptions and Theories.* San Francisco: Jossey-Bass.

Maddox, G. L. 1963. Activity and morale: A longitudinal study of selected elderly subjects. *Social Forces,* 42(2):195–204.

Neugarten, B. L. and L. Brown-Rezanka. 1978–79. *Midlife women in the 1980s.* Paper submitted to the House Select Committee on Aging. *Women in Midlife: Security and fulfillment.* 2 vols. Washington, D.C.: GPO.

Neugarten, B. L., J. W. Moore, and J. C. Lowe. 1965. Age norms, age constraints, and adult socialization. *American Journal of Sociology* 70(6):710–717.

Oberleder, M. 1966. Psychotherapy with the aging: An art of the possible? *Psychotherapy: Theory, Research and Practice* 3(3):139–142.

Parkes, C. M. 1971. Psycho-social transitions: A field for study. *Journal of Social Science and Medicine* 5(5):101–115.

Pearlin, L. I. 1982. Discontinuities in the study of aging. In T. K. Hareven and K. J. Adams, eds., *Aging and Life Course Transitions: An Interdisciplinary Perspective.* New York: Guilford Press.

Peterson, D. A. and E. L. Karnes. 1976. Older people in adolescent literature. *The Gerontologist* 16(3):225–231.

Piaget, J. 1976. *The Child and Reality: Problems of Genetic Psychology.* New York: Penguin.

Plemons, J. K., S. L. Willis, and P. B. Baltes. 1978. Modifiability of fluid intelligence in aging: A short-term longitudinal training approach. *Journal of Gerontology* 33(2):224–231.

Rapoport, L. 1967. Crisis-oriented short-term casework. *Social Service Review* 41(1):31–43.

Reichard, S., F. Livson, and P. G. Peterson. 1962. *Aging and Personality.* New York: Wiley.

Robertson, J. F. 1976. Significance of grandparents: Perceptions of young adult grandchildren. *The Gerontologist,* 16(2):137–140.

Rose, A. M. 1964. A current theoretical issue in social gerontology. *The Gerontologist* 4(1):46–50.

Rosenmayr, L. 1982. Biography and identity. In T. K. Hareven and K. J. Adams, eds., *Aging and Life Course Transitions: An Interdisciplinary Perspective.* New York: Guilford Press.

Rosenmayr, L. 1985. Changing values and positions of aging in Western culture. In J. Birren and K. W. Schaie, eds., *Handbook of the Psychology of Aging.* New York: Van Nostrand Reinhold.

Rosow, I. 1973. The social context of the aging self. *Gerontologist* 13(1):82–87.

Rowlings, C. 1981. *Social Work with Elderly People.* London: Allen and Unwin.

Schechter, M. 1988. The new ageism and social rationing: Why help old people? *Productive Aging News* (April), 22:2.

U.S. Bureau of the Census. 1977. Projections of the population of the United States: 1977 to 2050. *Current Population Reports,* series P-25, no. 704. Washington, D.C.: GPO.

U.S. Congress, Senate. 1987. Special Committee on Aging, "Developments in Aging: 1986." Washington, D.C.: GPO.

U.S. Department of Health and Human Services. 1987. National Institute on Aging. Personnel for health needs of the elderly: Through the year 2020. Washington, D.C.: GPO.
Verwoerdt, A. 1981. *Clinical Geropsychiatry.* 2d. ed. Baltimore: Williams and Wilkins.

2

Models of Services for the Elderly

❖

SHELDON S. TOBIN, PH.D.
RONALD W. TOSELAND, PH.D.
The University at Albany
State University of New York

Two kinds of models will be delineated. The first kind of model focuses on the classification of services, in this instance by relating the location, or geography, of services to levels of impairment. The second kind, in turn, reflects an attempt to develop configurations for the provision of services encompassing service delivery and organizational components. Service delivery components include the target group to be served, the services that will be provided to them, and how the services will be provided. In turn, organizational components include coordination and the planning and allocation of resources. Both kinds of models incorporate content in the preceding chapter, as well as content in the many chapters that follow, as will become readily apparent.

After an initial discussion of the first model for classifying services, a distinction will be made between discrete and integrating services. Then, to provide a basis in practice for the models, vignettes will be used to illustrate the matching of services with needs. Next is a discussion of some principles for developing service provision models by addressing three questions: For whom shall services be provided? What services shall be provided to them? And how shall these services be provided? Lastly, a preferred configuration and two effective alternatives will be offered for the provision of services to the elderly.

CLASSIFYING SERVICES

The organization of this book reflects a congruence between the geography of services and levels of impairment; that is, community-based services for the minimally impaired; home-based services for the moderately impaired; and long-term care and institutional-based services for the severly impaired. In this sequential presentation, the movement is from wellness to chronicity. Yet, another perspective can be offered on the relationship between the geography of services and levels of impairment. As shown in table 2.1, services within each of three geographical categories can be identified that can meet the needs of individuals who are at each level of impairment. Not shown, however, is the content in the papers in the next two sections of this book. Assessments and modalities of treatment and intervention transcend both geography and degrees of impairment because both are warranted, if not mandatory, across the spectrum of services and impairments.

For the three general levels of impairment, services can be indeed identified within each of the three kinds of geographical distinctions. A previous effort to show how services can be organized in various ways for individuals with the same general levels of impairment led to a trichotomy of home-based services, congregate-organized services, and congregate-residence services (Tobin 1975; Tobin, Davidson, and Sack 1976; Tobin and Lieberman 1976). The differences between the earlier trichotomy and the present one makes it apparent that there is no absolute way to classify the geography of services. Yet it is sensible to consider how elderly with the same general level of impairment can benefit from the use of differing organizing principles to make rational the current array of uncoordinated services. For the severely impaired, for example, care outside of institutions can be organized, primarily around services delivered into the home or around medically oriented as well as psychiatrically oriented, community or congregate day care treatment programs. The boundaries between classes of services, as well as between service components within each class, are obviously quite permeable. Additionally, sets of services can be clustered, as when services are delivered by a multipurpose senior center or through a case management system or when elderly live in a retirement village. Still, the trichotomy is useful.

A geography of services provides one way for planners and practitioners to understand the terrain of service delivery. Currently, a variety of services exists in all communities that needs to be coordinated if individual elderly are to benefit from their presence. Beyond

TABLE 2.1. A Classification of Services for Older Persons (Focus of Service Delivery)

Degree of Impairment	*Community-Based*	*Home-Based*	*Congregate Residential and Institutional-Based*
Minimal	Adult education Senior centers Voluntary organizations Congregate dining programs Individual and family information and referral, advice, and counseling	Home repair services Home equity conversion Share-a-home Transportation Telephone reassurance	Retirement communities Senior housing Congregate residential Housing with meals
Moderate	Multipurpose senior centers Community mental health centers Outpatient health services Case management systems (social/health maintenance organizations, etc.)	Foster family care Homemaker Meals-on-wheels Case management for family caregivers and elderly impaired members	Group homes Sheltered residential facilities Board and care (domiciliary care) facilities Respite care
Severe	Medical day care Psychiatric day care Alzeheimer family groups	Home health care Protective services Hospital care at home	Acute hospitals Mental hospitals Intermediate (health related) nursing facilities Skilled nursing facilities Hospice care in a facility

a way of identifying available, but not necessarily accessible, services, a geography of service reaffirms the importance of having diverse services for individuals with similar levels of impairments. Two elderly persons with similar levels of impairment may need very different kinds of services because of, for example, the presence or absence of family able and willing to provide assistance in caregiving. For the elderly person with such family members, home-based services may suffice but for another elderly person who does not have these supports, an enriched congregate environment may be necessary. In turn, the family that is overburdened from caregiving may need respite care (a vacation or holiday from caregiving), which can be organized by providing a bed in a congregate facility for the elderly person. A twenty-four-hour homemaker, in turn, may provide sufficient assurance to the anxious family when a case-management system offers around-the-clock backup to the homemaker. Yet, as noted by Kane and Kane (1987), it is indeed unfortunate that the usefulness of the diverse services have not been evaluated for their effectiveness for meeting targeted needs.

DISCRETE AND INTEGRATING SERVICES

Discrete services for older persons have existed since antiquity (Beattie 1976). In modern industrial society, particularly since the inception of social security, there has been an enormous increase in programs and services for both the young-old and the old-old. These programs and services, however, have not arisen as part of a carefully thought-out plan for meeting the needs of older persons (Kahn 1976). Rather, these programs and services have been developed, in large part, in a "band-aid," patchwork fashion, as needs were identified and political pressures were sufficient to bring about the development of specific programs and services. The Older Americans Act of 1965 reflects how political pressures result in statements of intent but not with organizing principles for service delivery (Estes 1979). Some subgroups among the elderly were targeted as particularly needy and discrete services identified for development, but integrating mechanisms were not identified. Funding nutrition programs and multipurpose senior centers can be interpreted as only a modest attempt develop ways of organizing or integrating services. Several of the services discussed earlier in this volume, and some that appear in table 2.1, however, are programs that do attempt to integrate services such as one-step intake services, multiservice centers, and case management. Yet the Older Americans Act when amended in 1973 (P.L. 93-29) did not mandate any forms of service integration but rather focused upon a clearer specification of programs that needed to be coordinated for specific subgroups among the elderly. At the same time, however, the Allied Service Bill of 1974 (92d Cong., 2d Sess; S.3643, H.R. 15856), did go beyond the listing of services to encompass the need for integration of services. To integrate services, Frank Carlucci, who was then under secretary of the Department of Health, Education, and Welfare, emphasized in 1974 the need for common intake and case management: "a comprehensive assessment of a person's multiple need for services at a single entry point, then [taking] responsibility for seeing to it that appropriate services are provided" U.S. House (1974:9).

It is now almost one decade later and little has been done to attain the lofty goal of integrating services. Case management exists more in word than deed, and whereas coordination has replaced service integration as the *ingua franca* it also is more of a cliche that refers to a desired outcome rather than to the reality of the achievement of service integration through adequate funding. All but a few direct practitioners must still function in a fragmented nonsystem of services. Yet service integration for those who can benefit from alternatives to institutional care has been shown to be effective (Applebaum, Seidl, and Austin 1980; Eggert, Bowlyow, and Nichols 1980; Hodgson and Quinn 1980). In these times of austerity, however, the favorable experiences of the three cited programs—the Wisconsin Community Care Organization, Access in Monroe County, New York, and Triage in Connecticut—have not led to a national program but rather to the newest set of demonstration projects, the channeling grants of the Health Care Finance Administration.

The National Long-Term Care Demonstration project, the "channeling demonstrations," was to have been the definitive study on long-term case management cost effectiveness. This social experiment was motivated to show the efficacy of substituting community care for nursing home care (Carcagno and Kemper 1986). Although more treatment than control group members developed greater confidence about receiving household and personal care, other benefits for caregivers were not found, except for a transient increase in feelings of well-being, and none for their care receivers. An important finding, however, was that the services did not substitute for informal case. Still, according to Weissert (1988), because of deficiencies in targeting those who would otherwise be institutionalized, it cannot be stated with any certainty that case management does not have the potential to reduce rates of institutionalization. The only evidence for this potential was obtained by the South Carolina site where applicants for

Medicaid Nursing Home placements were selected for the study (Nocks et al. 1986). In turn, Kane criticized the outcome measure of decreased institutionalization because "Some persons can be best served in a residential setting. . . . Indeed, some people can achieve greater independence and well-being in a facility than isolated in their homes" (1988:196). As will become apparent in the paper on case management, this integrating service can provide for appropriate services being provided simultaneously and sequentially as needed.

Until coherent and rational service systems are developed, when knowledgeable persons describe services for the elderly, the narrative is more likely to be a catalogue of services rather than a description of a coherent system of services (Beattie 1976; Gelfand and Olsen 1980; Gold 1974; Holmes and Holmes 1979; Lowy 1979). Cataloguing and detailing the effectiveness of services, as well as how they can function for individual elderly, however, is useful because it familiarizes practioners and planners with the diversity of services currently available to older people, suggests gaps in services, and raises issues about organizing services.

MATCHING SERVICES WITH NEEDS

Basic to all models of service delivery is the assumption that an array of services is available for the direct service worker to provide to individual clients as needed. The geography of services presented initially in this chapter reflects this assumption. Comprehensive taxonomies for organizing services for the elderly, however, as noted earlier, are relatively rare. A quite ambitious and laudatory attempt was undertaken by Golant and McCaslin (1979), who built on Lawton's (1972) formulations for assessing the functional status of individual elderly. They based their taxonomy on Lawton's dimensions of competence and independence to generate levels of functioning. In their schemata, competence is measured on seven levels of increasingly complex tasks: 1) life maintenance; 2) functional health; 3) perception and cognition; 4) physical self-maintenance; 5) instrumental self-maintenance; 6) effectance; and 7) social-role preformance. Independence, in turn, similar to one dimension of our typology, is measured on three levels: 1) services for those whose impairments necessitate institutional care or its equivalents; 2) services that provide alternatives for preventing premature institutionalization; and 3) services for the comparatively well elderly. Using these two dimension, Golant and McCaslin categorized a variety of services that are available to meet the needs of older persons. Because Golant and McCaslin have been so ambitious, and thus so comprehensive, their classification system is rather complex. Indeed, our simpler system becomes rather complex when focusing on individual cases.

The following case vignettes illustrate the diversity of services that can be developed to meet the needs of the heterogeneous population of the elderly. They also illustrate ways that service integration can occur, including through individual initiative in the marketplace, within a retirement community, by medically oriented sheltered housing, and by case management. Additionally, gaps in service are evident, particularly in the last illustration, that of Mrs. Jansen, who remained in a costly hospital bed for five weeks while awaiting nursing-home placement.

The first two vignettes illustrate the different ways that services are organized for those whose degree of impairment is minimal. In the first case, Mrs. Larandi relies on a number of community and home-based services to keep her functioning at an optimal level while living in her own home. In the second case, Mr. and Mrs. Texter rely on severly community-based and home-based services while residing in a retirement community.

> Mrs. Larandi is a 69-year-old widow who lives in her own home in an ethnic community in a large city. Except for her chronic arthritis, which affects her knees and makes walking somewhat painful, Mrs. Larandi is in good health. She does, however, utilize several community services in addition to the outpatient services she receives at the local hospital for her arthritis. To utilize her leisure time productively, she is involved with RSVP. Through this program, she works for a local hospital's patient-services department four hours a day, three days a week. Two other days during the week she has her lunch at the senior citizens center, where she remains to play Bingo with her friends during the afternoon. She also used the home repair service that is available through the senior center and is considering becoming involved in the home equity conversion program. This program allows her to use the equity she has accumulated in her home to pay her taxes and her heating bill so she can continue to live in her own home.

> Mr. Texter is 73 and Mrs. Texter 72. When Mr. Texter retired twelve years ago, they moved to Leisure World, a retirement community in a southwestern state. Although they miss having more contact with their children and grandchildren, who continue to live in the community from which they migrated, both Mr. and Mrs. Texter are very pleased that they moved away

from the frigid weather of north central states. Not only have they made many new friends, but they enjoy the self-contained nature of leisure world, which has a wide variety of services to meet their needs. For example, when Mr. Texter had difficulty with retirement benefits he was receiving, he received help in straightening out the problem from a worker at the residents service office (information and referral), which is centrally located in the community center of Leisure World.

For Mr. Texter's hearing problem and for Mrs. Texter's glaucoma, they rely on private physicians who have offices in the community. They are both involved with a variety of leisure time activities through the men's club and the women's club, which are housed in the fitness center at Leisure World. Because they have no transportation, they rely on the senior van service, which takes them on shopping trips to two medium-sized cities some distance from Leisure World.

The next two case examples illustrate the different ways that services may be arranged for those who are moderately impaired. With the help of a variety of support services, both Mrs. Bishop and Mr. Fendel are able to function at optimal levels and avoid being institutionalized.

Mrs. Bishop is a 77-year-old widow who lives in a one-bedroom apartment in a rent-controlled building in a large urban area, almost seven years ago. Mrs. Bishop was hospitalized for a short time for agitation and sleeplessness. Her condition, diagnosed as a severe depression, was stabilized with Lithium. Since that time, she is seen monthly by a worker at an after-care community mental health clinic, where her Lithium blood level is monitored and her prescription is renewed. Because of her chronic arthritis and hearing difficulties, she found it increasingly difficult to keep her clinic appointments. Her Department of Social Services (DSS) adult services worker arranged for a light to be attached to her bell so she could be aware when someone was at her door even if she did not hear the doorbell ring. The DSS worker also arranged for escort services to take her to and from her clinic appointments. Since she qualifies for Meals-on-Wheels, and had difficulty preparing meals for herself, this service was begun two years ago. Through Title XX of the Social Security Act, she was also eligible for homemaker services. The homemaker helps her with her household chores three hours a day, three days a week. On days the homemaker does not come, two neighbors in her apartment building look in on her. She gave both these neighbors keys to her apartment just in case "something should happen and I can't answer the door."

Mr. Fendel, who was a migrant farm worker, fell on icy pavement last year just before his seventy-sixth birthday. He received treatment for his broken hip at the community hospital. Because he had no family in the area to care for him, Mr. Fendel could not return to his apartment. However, since he was able to get around with the help of a walker, his medical social worker at the hospital decided that Mr. Fendel might be a good candidate for a supportive living program sponsored by the Visiting Nurse Association (VNA). This program provides sheltered housing in which Mr. Fendel could have his own room while sharing kitchen facilities with three other persons. Although he had a little difficulty getting adjusted, Mr. Fendel has done quite well in the new setting. The building, which was recently rehabilitated, was designed with the needs of the physically handicapped in mind. A homemaker and the Meals-on-Wheels service, which he obtained with the help of his medical social worker and a VNA nurse, who acted cooperatively in planning for Mr. Fendel's discharge from the hospital, are perfect for Mr. Fendel's needs. In case of an emergency such as falling down, the VNA has a nurse's aid stationed in the building twenty-four hours a day. In addition, there is a registered nurse available during the day. Other services, such as physical and occupational therapy, are available from the central office of the VNA if they are needed in the future.

The last two case examples illustrate the ways services may be organized for the severely impaired older person. In the first case, the availability of a caregiver makes it possible for Mrs. Hunter to remain at home. In the second case, despite a variety of community-based and home-based services, it was not possible for Mrs. Jansen to remain at home.

After some "periods of forgetfulness" and a serious incident in which the gas range was left on, Mr. Hunter decided to seek help for his wife. He was referred by his family physician to a geriatric unit in a state hospital fifteen minutes by car from his home. After a home visit, psychological testing, and a medical evaluation, the geriatric screening team decided that Mrs. Hunter, age 63, was suffering from Alzheimer's disease. Because of her proximity to the hospital, it was decided that she should attend the day treatment program, which operates six hours each week.

This program, designed especially for those with Organic Brain Syndrome, was especially useful because it gave Mr. Hunter some relief from the burdens of caring for his wife. It also provided supportive counseling, including involvement in a group for family members of patients with Alzheimer's disease, for Mr. Hunter, who was psychologically devasted by the rapid deterioration of wife's condition. After several months, further diagnostic testing was ordered by the geriatric team's physician and a CAT Scan revealed two small lesions, one in the frontal lobe and one at the base of Mrs. Hunter's brain. The latter was inoperable. The diagnosis was changed, and after some deliberation it was decided to change Mrs. Hunter's plan of care and involve her with a home-based hospice program. A worker from the geriatric team, acting as case coordinator, stayed involved with Mr. and Mrs. Hunter. In addition to coordinating a variety of services, including medical care, SSI, and legal counseling to prepare a will, the worker helped Mr. Hunter to cope with his wife's illness.

Eight months after Mr. Hunter had contacted his family physician, Mrs. Hunter died at home. The worker from the geriatric unit had several contacts with Mr. Hunter following his wife's death. These were designed to ensure that he was successfully coping with the loss of his wife. Through these contacts he was helped to become involved in a men's club at a local senior citizens center.

Mrs. Jansen is an 81-year-old black female who resided with her brother in subsidized senior housing in a poor, high-crime, urban area. For eight years, Mrs. Jansen has suffered from Alzheimer's disease. At first, only her short-term memory was impaired, but in recent years the disease has progressed and she is no longer oriented to person, place, or time. In the last six months she has also become incontinent. She received homemaker services as well as Meals-on-Wheels. These services would have been insufficient, however, to maintain Mrs. Jansen at home due to the severity of her confusion, if it were not for the devoted attention of her husband, who provided 24-hour care for Mrs. Jansen.

Unfortunately, while the homemaker was attending to Mrs. Jansen, Mr. Jansen went out shopping for groceries and was mugged by two teenagers, who robbed him and knocked him to the ground. Because of the injuries he sustained, he had to be hospitalized, creating an emergency situation for Mrs. Jansen, who could not be left unsupervised in her apartment. An adult protective service worker at the county social service office became involved immediately after the problem was reported by the homemaker. Placement in a nursing home was the only alternative, but because a nursing home bed was not immediately available the protective service worker advised the Jansens' physician to hospitalize her, which he did. Although Mrs. Jansen was needlessly occupying a costly hospital bed, nursing homes were reluctant to accept her because of her mental impairment and intermittent incontinence and, also, because she was a Medicaid patient. Mr. Jansen was recovering nicely and wished to care for his wife at home, but the Jansens' physician advised against it because of Mr. Jansen's immobility and the burden of caregiving and told Mr. Jansen that "it is time for her to go to a home." After three weeks in the hospital she was accepted into a voluntary sectarian home.

The case examples illustrate that many different kinds of service arrangements are necessary to meet the diverse needs of older persons. In addition to the general rule of developing a flexible and diverse service delivery system to meet the unique and disparate needs of different older persons, a variety of questions should be resolved when considering models for organizing services for older persons.

FROM CLASSIFICATION TO MODELS

To translate classifications of services for the heterogeneous elderly to models first necessitates a statement of purposes. The case vignettes suggest that goals vary by functional status. For the relatively unimpaired, services should enhance well-being and prevent deteriorations; for the moderately impaired, they should facilitate activities of daily living, enhance the caregiving of informal supports, prevent further deterioration and, whenever possible, restore lost functioning; and for the severely impaired, in addition to the goals for the impaired, services should limit unnecessary and premature institutional care and, when necessary, offer appropriate institutional care. To be effective, a service system must be accessible to the target population, receptive to the idiosyncratic needs of clients, and able to provide options and multiple services for each client, both simultaneously and in appropriate sequence, as needed. Thus goals, in turn, can be achieved only by a system of services that is coordinated so that diverse parts function in concert to assure that service delivery goals are attained and planned so that resources may be allocated and distributed rationally, giving major attention to client needs.

This set of goals can be applied to all human services, not only social services. Social services, according to Kahn, pertain to "programs that protect or restore family life, help individuals cope with external and internal problems, enhance development and facilitate access through information, guidance, advocacy, and concrete help of several kinds" (1973:19). Focusing on social services *per se,* however, does not resolve issues of who should be provided with social services, what social services should be provided, and how social services should be delivered. Stated another way, a social-service model for the elderly could focus on people of all ages, including the elderly, or specifically on the elderly, and if on the elderly, on all the elderly or on elderly identified as more in need; could encompass all possible social health services or be concentrated in specific services to meet the most unmet of needs; and could be fully coordinated and planned or partially so, through, for example, informal arrangements. (For a fuller discussion of these issues, see Tobin, Davidson, and Sack 1976).

PRINCIPLES FOR A COMPREHENSIVE MODEL

Any comprehensive model must answer three questions: For whom? What? And how? These three questions will be discussed in order.

For Whom?

The elderly could be served as part of the larger society. Indeed, Neugarten (1983) has argued for an age-irrelevant society in which chronological age becomes extraneous. With adjustments of Social Security by the cost of living index, the percentage of elderly below the poverty level now approximates the percentage for other age groups (about 15 percent). Moreover, because the elderly receive a diversity of in-kind benefits, the elderly may now be considered to be relatively advantaged. For example, whereas the amount of chronic impairment among the elderly is similar to the amount among other age groups, the elderly receive Medicare. The graying of the federal budget (Hudson 1978) reflects the increased expenditures for the elderly. Thus, in years past, providing services to all the elderly, through age-based entitlement, was sensible because attributed need could be demonstrated by population statistics. This particularistic approach, however, is no longer valid, and increasingly advocated are universalistic approaches using demonstrated need-that is, need-based programs (Etzioni 1976). Illustrations of the argument for basing programs on need rather than age occur in our vignettes. Mrs. Hunter, for example, was only 63 when diagnosed as afflicted with Alzheimer's disease, whereas Mrs. Jansen was 81.

Kutza and Zweibel (1983) have contrasted the arguments for each approach. An age-based (or attributed-need) allocative policy is attractive because of political expediency, administrative efficiency, simplicity of measurement, and lack of stigmatization. A need-based policy, on the other hand, more efficiently targets the most needy. In turn, Ozawa (1976) has shown that SSI, a need-based program, does not stigmatize elderly recipients as does welfare programs for the chronically poor. Because of the political viability of programs for the elderly, Austin and Loeb (1983) argue that age is relevant and, for this reason, Kutza and Zweibel (1983) advocate programs that combine age and need, such as mandating group eligibility of the elderly for those receiving SSI or Medicaid. This kind of combination is certainly better than recent programs such as those of the Administration on Aging, that have disproportionately benefited the more affluent (U.S. General Accounting Office 1977b; Estes 1979; Estes and Newcomer 1973; Kutza 1981; Nelson 1983). Apparently funding through Title XX of the Social Security Act has not heretofore proved an effective remedy to maldistribution for the most needy among the elderly (Gilbert 1977; Gilbert and Specht 1979; Schram 1983; Schram and Hurley 1977).

A concrete example of how the age-based program has not reached those with the greatest need is the nutrition, or congretate dining program for the elderly (Title III-C of the Older Americans Act, formerly Title VII). This program was founded to redress nutritional and social interaction deficiencies. Although great numbers of the elderly have participated in this program, the evidence suggests that those who have participated have been the healthier and the more socially active. Tobin and Thompson (1981) have referred to one aspect of this phenomenon as the "countability paradox" because, in their study of programs in one community, those nutrition sites with greater numbers (and thus judged more successful by the local office on aging) had fewer impaired participants than programs with fewer participants (that were judged as less successful by the group that allocated funds for dining sites). Where accounting is based on numbers rather than need, it is easy, and perversely sensible, to exclude those with impairments because they make the well elderly feel uncomfortable, create additional management problems, and necessitate consideration of programs beyond recreational activities.

Determining eligibility by need rather than by age, however, does not resolve two other kinds of questions. Should personal assets also be used, such as a means test, in determining eligibility? And, independent of eligibility considerations, do the special needs of the elderly dictate special kinds of service systems?

Regarding the first of these two questions, there are at least two reasons why means tests may not be appropriate in determining eligibility for the chronically impaired. First, means tests generally stigmatize individuals. Second, few families have the resources necessary to provide home care for their impaired elderly members. Currently, for example, the percentage of families providing care at home for their elderly members is at double the percentage of elderly with comparable functional statuses in nursing homes. The percentage of elderly in nursing homes may be approaching 6 percent, but about 8 percent of all the elderly are homebound (about 3 percent are bedridden) and certainly more than 4 percent are not homebound but need surveillance to remain in the community. Weissert (1985) has estimated the total at-home percentage to be 12.4. The value of family caring, in turn, is much greater than the cost of agency services. In this "shared function" (Litwak 1978) by family and agency, for example, the average monthly cost or value by both family (including friends) and agencies for those greatly impaired is $407, but the value of family and friends caregiving is $287 and agency cost is only $120; for the extremely impaired, the total cost is $845, with the value of family and friends caregiving placed at $673 and agency costs for their services at $172 (U.S. General Accounting Office 1977a). The task, therefore, is to facilitate family and friends caregiving to the greatly and extremely impaired elderly so that all costs are not covered through agency and public expenditures. Because very few can afford this kind of monthly outlay of dollars, the solution in Great Britain has been to provide a modest Constant Attendance Allowance to families, regardless of income or assets (Moroney 1976). Thus advocated is eligibility determined not by age or income through a means test but through assessment of need. The distinction between means and needs assessment, as well as the problems in needs assessment, has been cogently discussed by Austin and Loeb (1983).

Regarding the second question, whether the needs of the elderly dictate special services for them, it can be argued that the elderly are too often screened out of services, that family caregiving to the elderly may necessitate special kinds of programs and knowledge, and that the impairments and kinds of services needed for the elderly also demand special expertise that can be gained only in age-specific programs. Cook (1983) has detailed the following steps in deciding whether the organization and delivery of services should be age-based: the "specialness" of the problem, the importance of the special problem, the likelihood of successful targeting, the probability of ameliorating the problem, and the probability of minimizing unintended side affects. These steps, or criteria, in decision making do suggest the usefulness of an age-specific strategy in the organization and delivery of services, particularly for the more chronically impaired elderly. Because dependency from impairments rises precipitiously beyond age 75, priority should be given to the old-old—that is, the most vulnerable—using a criterion of attributed need or a combination of age as a reflection of attributed need and demonstrated need.

A service system designed specifically for the most vulnerable and impaired elderly, as noted earlier, must also attend to issues of prevention. Unless consideration is given to the needs of the less impaired, predominantly young-old, all resources will be allocated for the severely impaired elderly with no attention to prevention. There are three kinds of prevention; primary prevention refers to reducing the incidence of a disease, secondary prevention to reducing the effects of acute illness through early detection and vigorous intervention, and tertiary prevention to limiting the effects of chronic illness by stabilizing and enhancing functioning and, also, to reducing the likelihood of acute flare-ups. If resources are not specifically allocated for prevention, services will be concentrated for more desperate situations. Moroney (1976) found that, in Great Britain, personal care services were almost exclusively used for those elderly without viable family supports. From the social workers' perspective, families with elderly could continue to manage for a time even if severely overburdened by caregiving. Whereas prevention of deterioration in family caregiving was an explicit goal, it could not be achieved if resources allowed only for attention to crisis and emergency situations.

For the severely impaired, however, institutional care can absorb all resources, leaving little for community-based services. Alternatively, prevention of institutionalization can lead to a focus on community alternatives without allocations for those who need institutional care. Other modern societies, as now we are, have confronted the reality that shifting resources from institutional to community-based services can eventuate in the prevention of institutionalization but leave only benign neglect and custodial care for those who can no longer remain in the community. Given the reality of limited resources, this may be a deplorable necessity, but to have it occur without a rational debate on long-term care policies is to relinquish our responsibility to make the most critical of decisions.

What?

Services that can be provided in a comprehensive social-service system are too numerous to mention. Listed in table 2.1 were only some of the services that can be provided to the elderly. The vignettes incorporated, among others, the following services: volunteer activities, senior centers, home repair, home equity conversion, information and referral, retirement communities, case management, homemaker and home health services, sheltered housing, day treatment, hospice care, hospital care, and nursing home placement. Must, however, a comprehensive system provide all possible services? It may not be feasible to do so. A classic example is that of homemaker. No society can provide all the homemaker services that every citizen desires. Even a comprehensive system would, therefore, have to confront the issue of rationing services. In addition, it is certainly necessary to echelon services so that more intense and more expensive services with less usage are developed for larger population bases than more everyday services. The corollary is in medical services, where primary care physicians must be available in every community; secondary medical services, such as general hospitals, distributed among larger groups of people; and specialized tertiary care facilities developed for even larger population bases. Rationing and echeloning of services, therefore, must be incorporated into any comprehensive system. This consideration of rationing and echeloning of services is particularly relevant to the case of Mrs. Jansen, who lingered in a costly bed in an acute general hospital while awaiting placement in a skilled nursing home.

Most clear is that income maintenance must be provided to meet basic daily survival needs; and where there is heightened vulnerability and impairment, medical and social service needs must then additionally be met. Any attempt to meet social service needs must go beyond a proliferation of discrete services and include one or more strategies for assuring the availability of an appropriate mix of discrete services and those services that provide for their integration. A distinction between discrete services and integrating services has been noted earlier and is reflected also elsewhere in this handbook. How to accomplish integration is our next question.

How?

The "how" in this context of models of social services for the elderly refers to service integration at the delivery level and to coordination and planning, as well as allocation, at the organizational level. Some solutions to service integration, as just noted, are covered in this volume and were also reflected in the vignettes. The Texters, who were minimally impaired, lived in a retirement village in which the senior center functioned as a one-step multipurpose center but without decentralized common intake and case management. Mrs. Bishop, who was moderately impaired, had a Department of Social Service worker who functioned for her as case manager. Mrs. Fendel, also with moderate impairment, benefited from the service integration provided within medical oriented sheltered housing that Sherwood et al. (1981) found to limit nursing home usage. Mrs. Hunter's case manager was a worker on the geropsychiatric team.

An alternative to a coherent professional system is, of course, to use the marketplace. Even if cash were provided for the purchase of service, when the purpose is to enhance the shared function of formal supports and the family for the impaired elderly member, would it best be given to the primary family caregiver or to the older person? Frankfather, Smith, and Caro (1981) argue that too much attention to the caregiving family diminishes the autonomy of the older person. They also apply this argument to professional case managers who they perceive as intrusive and likely to impose their own bias, which can result in supporting family members at the expense of the elderly person—as was apparently the case in the Blenkner, Bloom, and Nielsen (1971) social experiment but not in Goldberg's (1970) study. If a case management system is advocated for the integration of services for individuals and their families, then professional judgment obviously must include a sensitivity to the wishes of clients, and professional judgment of need must be tempered by a principle of minimal intervention (Kahn and Tobin 1981).

Organizing a case management system in which services are assured obviously necessitates reimbursement for the services. Three forms of insurance are emerging: LTCI (Long-Term Care insurance), CCRCs (Continuing Care Retirement Communities) and SHMOs (Social Health Maintenance Organizations) (Branch, Sager and Meyers 1987; Tobin, in press; Wiener et al. 1987). LTCs may provide reimbursement for discrete services but are unlikely to eventuate in provider organizations using case managers to provide services and to prevent unnecessary and premature institutionalization (see for example, Rivlin and Wiener 1988). CCRCs which are available to the more affluent (Ruchlin 1988), and SHMOs, are likely, however, to use case management because of capitation funding. That is, the pool of money from clients to the organization must be cautiously spent to avoid heavy hospital and institutional costs. SHMOs, now in the experimental stage, when under the auspices of established HMOs not only rely heavily on case management but also on innovative GEUs, geriatric evaluation units, and rehabilitative services to maintain and restore ADL functioning. Even efficient use of personnel and facilities, however, cannot eliminate hospital stays, which may be covered by Medicare and catastrophic health insurance, and extended stays in nursing homes which can quickly overtax revenues. Thus, most SHMOs limit the number of nursing home days reimbursed necessitating their members to spend down to Medicaid.

Case management focuses on integration of services at the client level, whereas SHMOs and CCRCs also do so at the systems level. LTC, in turn, resolves the issue by letting consumers purchase their services for which they are then reimbursed. In either instance, the agency providing services must decide on the comprehensiveness of its service provision. To what extent can any service provider own all the specialized services necessary for long-term community care? Some, such as Kaiser-Permanente's SHMO (Leutz et al 1988) can be quite comprehensive owning hospitals and rehabilitation centers. Most, however, must develop purchase agreements with specialized agencies.

However, can any kind of case management system be comprehensive? No primary care system can control the specialized services provided in a tertiary care agency or facility. Thus the interaction between primary care and tertiary care providers can never be simple. Kane and Kane (1980), in their excellent study of long-term care in diverse modern societies, quickly discovered the many dynamic tensions among providers at different levels of service and among providers at the same service level. In Great Britain, for example, a major mechanism for assuring coordination among community-based care, hospitals, and long-term care facilities was the lodging of authority to place the elderly person in a long-term facility in the hands of the community-based social worker. Only when the community-based worker judges that community care no longer assures independent living is institutional care provided.

Ownership of all services by an integrating provision mechanism, such as by a case-management system is indeed not feasible. For coordination at the organizational level there must be formal agreement among service providers, particularly between providers who integrate services and discrete service providers. To be sure, decentralized local care services can increase accessibility for clients, capitalize on informal supports, respond to clients and family needs, and increase local autonomy but at the same time must assure the delivery of more centralized services—the more costly secondary and tertiary services. Only, however, through centralized planning and allocation of resources can there be the capacity to assess the total needs of large segments of the population; a balancing of priorities among conflicting organizational demands; a setting of uniform standards and common objectives; increasing efficiencies; increasing coordination; and an assuring of formal commitments among agencies.

Coordination among agencies can take many forms, including hierarchical, egalitarian, and reciprocal relationships. It can also extend from informal agreements to collaborating through formal agreements to confederations to federations. Such complexities often suggest how simple it is to favor marketplace coordination. Yet through formal as well as informal agreements that include mechanisms for reimbursement for services, a great amount of coordination can be developed (Davidson 1976; Tobin, Davidson, and Sack 1976).

DESIGN OPTIONS FOR MODELS

The optimum model for service provision emerges from the previous discussion of some basic principles. Still, as noted in the discussion, optimum solutions to the questions for whom, what, and how do not permit an ideal model. There are none; there are, at best, trade-offs. Our task, however, is to ignore reality for a moment and to advocate a more idealized model, but one that can accommodate rules of eligibility based on need and personal resources.

Tobin, Davidson, and Sack (1976) contrasted a preferred option for the design of services with two effective alternative designs. As shown in Table 2.2, reproduced from that monograph, the preferred model focuses on the most vulnerable among the elderly. Services for these elderly would not be restricted to the elderly with the lowest incomes because elderly above the poverty level need costly services even with moderate degrees of impairments if independent community living is to be assured. A full set of services would be provided through service integration, decentralized coordination would be extensive, and planning and allocation would be centralized.

The two effective alternatives vary on the five dimension, but both contain mechanisms necessary for service integration. In turn, from

TABLE 2.2. Options for Configurations: The Preferred and Two Other

Central Questions	*Preferred Design Options*	*Effective Alternatives*	
I. Service delivery components			
Who	Elderly-vulnerable services as a right of all elderly, with priority given to the vulnerable	Universal-vulnerable services as a right to all in need, with the vulnerable elderly given priority	Low-income elderly services provided only to low-income elderly
What	Full service comprehensive social service strategy providing social services, including income maintenance	Centralized I & R broad social service strategy relying on disparate providers to meet service and income needs	Limited service A limited range of services available at the neighborhood level with decentralized I & R
How	Social integration A system which features decentralized intake, multipurpose centers, and professional integrators	Confederation A loose association of agencies which together provide a relatively full range of services through centralized intake without professional integrators	Neighborhood nonprofessional A system which features decentralized intake and multipurpose centers through nonprofessional integrators

II. Organizational components			
Coordination	Full coordination A system with formal inter- and intra-level agreements, with shared staff, intake, and information	Partial coordination A system with formal intra-level agreements and informal inter-level agreements, with shared intake and information, but with separate staff	Informal coordination A network with informal intra- and inter-level agreements, with agency-specific intake and staff and shared information
Planning and allocation	Centralized A system with centralized point planning, common objectives, and pooled resources	Cooperative A system with separate planning and decentralized decision making, with a combination of agency-specific and stated objectives, with some pooling of resources	Autonomous community A system with decentralized planning at the neighborhood level, with agency-specific objectives and little pooling of resources

the discrete options within each of the three general models, further models can be proliferated that combine solutions for the five dimensions. Given the realities of human services, for example, partial coordination may be preferred because of the need for dynamic tensions among providers with different missions and different expertise. This is most apparent, as noted earlier, in relationships among community care providers, hospitals, and long-term care facilities. A "fully" coordinated system could too easily lead to domination by hospitals.

The design options detailed in table 2.2 do not provide a fine-grained set of models. Returning to table 2.1, it is possible, however, to build models from a variety of integrating services. Among community-based services, the multiple service center is a natural setting for service integration; among home-based services, diverse housing options and case management also offer rare opportunities for service integration; and all the kinds of institution-based services can likewise provide these opportunities. To single out only two kinds of special facilities, enriched group living for a dozen or so elderly has been found to be an excellent alternative to institutional care in other countries, and Sherwood et al. (1981) have similarly shown that medically enriched housing is effective for those with chronic impairments regardless of age.

A FINAL COMMENT

Models for the provision of services for the elderly are probably as varied as the elderly themselves. It is possible, however, to develop logical classification systems for the varied and uncoordinated services that currently are available for the elderly, as was discussed in the initial section of this chapter. Case vignettes were useful for illustrating how services with differing geographical organizing principles can meet the needs of elderly individuals with similar levels of impairment and also a variety of ways services can be integrated. Principles can, and were, indentified that must guide the development of service-integration models. These principles must answer three kinds of questions. For whom among the elderly are services to be provided? What services must be provided to meet the needs of these elderly? And how can these services be integrated in their delivery and, at the organizational level, how can they be coordinated and planned? A modest attempt was made to develop an optimum model, as well as two alternative models that contained many design options. Albeit the accumulated knowledge permits the construction of optimum and also sensible alternative models, trade-offs would be necessary even in an ideal world. In a less-than-ideal world, obviously characteristic of the current state of affairs, alternatives that at least provide for some beneficial integration are to be preferred over simplistic solutions that maintain the current fragmented nonsystem of services for the elderly.

REFERENCES

Adams, J. P., Jr. 1980. Service arrangements preferred by minority elderly: A cross cultural survey. *Journal of Gerontological Social Work* 3(2):39–57.

Applebaum, R., F. W. Seidl, and C. D. Austin. 1980. The Wisconsin community care organization: Preliminary findings from the Milwaukee experiment. *The Gerontologist* 20(3):350–355.

Austin, C. D. and M. B. Loeb. 1983. Why age is relevant in social policy and practice. In B. L. Neugarten, ed., *Age or Need: Public Policies for Older People.* Beverly Hills, Calif: Sage.

Beattie, W. M., Jr. 1976. Aging and the social services. In R. Binstock and E. Shanas, eds., *Handbook of Aging and the Social Sciences.* New York: Van Nostrand Reinhold.

Blenkner, M., M. Bloom, and M. Neilsen. 1971. A research and demonstration project of protective services. *Social Casework* 52(10):483–499.

Branch, L. G., A. Sager, and A. R. Meyers. 1987. Long-term care in the United States: A study in trench warfare. In R. A. Ward and S. S. Tobin, eds., *Health in Aging: Sociological Issues and Policy Directions.* New York: Springer.

Carcagno, G. J. and P. Kemper. 1988. The evaluation of the National Long-Term Care demonstration. I: An overview of the channeling demonstration and its evaluation. *Health Services Research* 23(1):1–22.

Cook, F. L. 1983. Assessing age as an eligibility criterion. In B. L. Neugarten, ed., *Age or Need: Public Policies for Older People.* Beverly Hills, Calif.: Sage.

Davidson, S. M. 1976. Planning and coordination of social services in multiorganizational context. *Social Service Review* 50(3):117–137.

Eggert, G. M., J. E. Bowlyow, and C. W. Nichols. 1980. Gaining control of the long term care system. First returns from the ACCESS experiment. *The Gerontologist* 20(3):356–363.

Estes, C. 1979. *The Aging Experience: A Critical Examination of Social Policies and Services for the Aged.* San Francisco: Jossey-Bass.

Estes, C. and R. Newcomer. 1973. State units on aging: Discretionary policy and action in eight states. San Francisco: University of California.

Etzioini, A. 1976. Old people and public policy. *Social Policy* (November/December), pp. 21–29.

Frankfather D. D., M. J. Smith, and F. G. Caro. 1981. *Family Care of the Elderly: Public Initiatives and Private Obligations,* Lexington, Mass.: Lexington Books.

Gelfand, D. E. and J. K. Olsen. 1980. *The Aging Network.* New York: Springer.

Gilbert, N. 1977. The transformation of social services. *Social Service Review* 51(12):624–641.

Gilbert, N. and H. Specht. 1979. Title XX planning by area agencies on aging; Efforts, outcomes and policy implications. *The Gerontologist* 19(6):264–274.

Golant, S. M. and R. McCaslin. 1979. A functional classification of services for older people. *Journal of Gerontological Social Work.* 1(3):187–209.

Gold, B. D. 1974. The role of the federal government in the provision of social services to older persons. *Annals of the American Academy of Political and Social Sciences* 415:55–69.

Goldberg, E. M. 1970. *Helping the Aged: A Field Experiment in Social Work.* London: Allen and Unwin.

Hodgson, J. H. Jr. and J. L. Quinn, 1980. The impact of the Triage health care delivery system upon client morale, independent living and the cost of care. *The Gerontologist* 20(3):364–371.

Homes, M. and D. Holmes. 1979. *Handbook of Human Services for Older Persons.* New York: Human Sciences Press.

Hudson, R. 1978. The graying of the federal budget and its consequences for old age policy, *The Gerontologist* 18(10):428–440.

Kahn, A. J. 1973. *Social Policy and Social Services.* New York: Random House.

Kahn, A. J. 1976. Service delivery at the neighborhood level: Experience, theory, and fads. *Social Service Review* 501(1):23–56.

Kahn, R. L. and S. S. Tobin. 1981. Community treatment for aged persons with altered brain function. In N. E. Miller and G. D. Cohen, eds., *Clinical Aspects of Alzheimer's Disease and Senile Dementia,* New York: Raven Press.

Kane, R. A. 1988. The noblest experiment of them all: Learning from the National Channeling evaluation. *Health Services Research* 23(1):189–198.

Kane, R. A. and R. L. Kane. 1987. *Long-Term Care: Principles, Programs, and Policy.* New York: Springer.

Kane, R. L. and R. A. Kane. 1980. Alternatives to institutional care of the elderly beyond the dichotomy. *The Gerontologist* 20(3):249–259.

Kutza, E. A. 1981. *The Benefits of Old Age: Social Welfare Policy for the Elderly.* Chicago: University of Chicago Press.

Kutza, E. A. and N. R. Zweibel. 1983. Age as a criterion for focusing public programs. In B. L. Neugarten, ed., *Age or Need: Public Policies for Older People.* Beverly Hills, Calif.: Sage.

Lawton, M. P. (1972). Assessing the competence of older persons. In D. P. Kent, R. Kestenbaum, and S. Sherwood, eds., *Research Planning and Action for the Elderly.* New York: Behavioral Publications.

Leutz, W., R. Abrahams, M. Greenlick, R. Kane, and J. Protas. 1988. Targeting expended care to the aged: Early shared experience. *The Gerontologist* 28(1):4–17.

Litwak, E. 1977. Theoretical base for practice. In R. Dobrof and E. Litwak, eds. *Maintenance of Family Ties of Long-Term Care Patients.* Washington, D.C.: Department of Health, Education and Welfare.

Lowy, L. 1979. *Social Work with the Aging: The Challenge and Promise of the Later Years.* New York: Harper and Row.

Moroney, R. M. 1976. *The Family and the State: Considerations for Social Policy.* London: Longman.

Nelson, D. W. 1983. Alternative images of old age as the basis for policy. In B. L. Neugarten, ed., *Age or Need: Public Policies for Older People.* Beverly Hills, Calif.: Sage.

Neugarten, B. L. 1983. *Age or Need: Public Policies for Older People.* Beverly Hills, Calif.: Sage

Nocks, B. C., M. Learner, D. Blackman, and T. C. Brown. 1986. The effects of a community-based long-term care project on nursing home utilization. *The Gerontologist* 26(2):150–157.

Ozawa, M. N. 1976. Impact of SSI on the aged and disabled poor. *Social Work Research and Abstracts* 14:3–10.

Schram, S. F. 1983. Social Services for older people. In B. L. Neugarten, ed., *Age or Need: Public Policies for Older People.* Beverly Hills, Calif.: Sage.

Schram, S. F. and R. Hurley. 1977. Title XX and the elderly. *Social Work* 22(3): 95–102.

Sherwood, S., D. S. Greer, J. N. Morris, and V. Mor. 1981. *An Alternative to Institutionalization: The Highlands Heights Experiment.* Cambridge, Mass.: Ballinger.

Tobin, S. S. 1975. Social and health services for the future age, Part II. *The Gerontologist* 15(1):32–37.

Tobin, S. S. (in press). The "ideal" long-term care system. In Z. Harel, P. Ehrlich, and R. Hubbard, eds., *Understanding and Serving Vulnerable Older Adults and Aged.* New York: Springer.

Tobin, S. S., S. M. Davidson, and A. Sack. 1976. *Effective Social Services for Older Americans.* Ann Arbor: Institute of Gerontology, University of Michigan–Wayne State University.

Tobin, S. S. and M. A. Lieberman. 1976. *A Last Home for the Aged: Critical Implications of Institutionalization.* San Francisco: Jossey Bass.

Tobin, S. S. and D. Thompson. 1981. The countability paradox. In H. Wershaw, ed., *Controversial Issues in Gerontology.* New York: Springer.

U.S. Congress. Senate Special Committee on Aging. 1971a. Alternatives to nursing home care: A proposal. Washington, D.C.: GPO.

U.S. Congress. Senate. Special Committee on Aging. 1971b. Making services for the elderly work: Some lessons from the British experience. Washington, D.C.: GPO.

U.S. General Accounting Office. 1977a. Home health: The need for a national policy to better provide for the elderly. Washington, D.C.: GAO.

U.S. General Accounting Office. 1977b. Local area agencies help the aging but problems need correcting. Washington, D.C.: GAO.

U.S. House of Representatives 1974. Committee on Education and Labor, Statement of Frank Carlucci on the Allied Services Bill. July 10, 1974. Washington, D.C.: USGPO, 9.

Weissert, W. G. 1985. Estimating the long-term care population: Prevalence rates and needs. *Health Care Finance* 6(4):1373–1379.

Weissert, W. G. 1988. The National channeling demonstration: What we knew, now know, and still need to know. *Health Service Review* 23(1):175–187.

Wiener, J. M., R. Hanley, D. Spence, and D. Coppard. 1987. Money, money, who's got the money?: Financing options for long-term care. In R. A. Ward and S. S. Tobin, eds., *Health in Aging: Sociological Issues and Policy Directions.* New York: Springer.

II
TREATMENT AND INTERVENTION MODALITIES

3

Assessing the Elderly Client

❖

ROSALIE A. KANE, D.S.W.
University of Minnesota, Minneapolis

Multidimensional assessment is a crucial component of service to the elderly. Regardless of where they work, human service professionals must develop strategies to collect, weigh, and interpret relevant information about the client. Properly used, assessment becomes a decision-making tool. The major clinical purpose of assessment is to facilitate decisions about the type and amount of services that should be offered to a particular client. Periodic reassessments then determine whether the services or treatments should be continued, discontinued, or changed.

Human service professionals, and social workers in particular, are no strangers to the concept of assessment. Social workers have been taught to assess the client thoroughly, sensitively, and almost continuously. They are conditioned to consider both social history and current functioning. They are urged to take a family-centered approach. And, above all, a social worker's assessment deals with both the *person* and the *environment* in which the person functions. All these familiar principles pertain to geriatric assessment. What then is so special about assessment of the aged?

First, the assessment of an older client is likely to be complex. The history-taking is complicated because seniors have accumulated many life experiences to take into account. Assessment of current functioning is complicated because such functioning is not usually a product of interacting physical, mental, and social factors, making interpretation of observed or reported behavior difficult. The process of assessment can also be complicated by compromised communication abilities of older clients or even by the generation gap that sometimes yawns between the assessor and the assessed. Despite these complexities, assessment takes on a powerful imperative with elderly clientele. As the general population becomes proportionately older and the numbers of persons in the late 1970s and '80s increases, the pressure on social programs will also increase. Service providers must allocate types of resources and services according to an equitable and justifiable formula, and assessment is the key to that allocation.

A second characteristic of assessment of the elderly is its emphasis on measurement. The reliance on uniform instruments is perhaps the most troublesome feature to human service workers, who may be more comfortable drawing conclusions from unfettered clinical judgment. The aging field has spawned hundreds of assessment instruments, including many that yield one or more summary scores (Kane and Kane 1981; Israel, Kozerevic, and Sartorius 1984). Some instruments measure a single attribute (e.g., social involvement, ability for self-care), whereas other multidimensional assessment tools covers several aspects of physical, mental, and social functioning. Some instruments are essentially questionnaires that elicit the client's self-report, whereas others use ratings and observations made by professionals. Some screening tools can be completed in a matter of minutes, but assessments take several hours and involve the participation of a multidisciplinary team. The professional is challenged to choose an instrument wisely and to use it well, which may require consideration of issues of reliability and validity that were formerly the exclusive province of the researcher or program evaluator.

This article presents some specific purposes of assessment, discusses appropriate content for assessment of an older person, offers criteria for selecting an assessment tool, reviews some commonly used instruments, and concludes with practical issues relevant to making assessments of older persons and their families. It emphasizes assessments typically required in social work practice within the context of the current proliferation of specialized geriatric assessment centers (Kane, Kane, and Rubenstein, in press) and case management programs.

PURPOSE OF FORMAL ASSESSMENTS

Formal assessments take a toll in time and energy for both workers and clients. If performed, analyzed, and used consistently, they represent a distinct budget item. Nevertheless, uniform, systematic assessment approaches are critical to serving the elderly. They are used for screening and case finding, for care planning, and for monitoring and quality assurance. Furthermore, clinically derived assessment often forms the basis for program evaluation and research. At each clinical step, the assessment organizes the worker, provides a checklist for items that might be forgotten, and offers a comparison point against which to observe improvement or deterioration.

Screening And Case Finding

Screening is a brief assessment procedure that triggers a fuller assessment in specified circumstances. It is often appropriate to screen large populations of older persons to identify those needing a particular service. For example, an Area Agency on Aging might want to know who in its catchment area would benefit by an activities program or by respite services for caregivers of the frail elderly. Or, to take another common example, a hospital social work department that realistically could offer counseling to only some of the many older hospital patients might wish to choose those clients systematically rather than let caseloads fill up haphazardly. In each instance, a screening tool is needed. Obviously such a screening process should be brief, inexpensive, and yet capable of pinpointing the target group of interest.

Screening requires consideration of two epidemiological terms: sensitivity and specificity. As sensitive screen tends to pick up most persons with the targeted condition but may at the same time pick up "false positive," who are dropped after later assessment. In contrast, a specific screen will tend to eliminate persons without the targeted condition, thus minimizing false positive; however, the specific test may have a high rate of false negatives, meaning that persons with the condition of interest will *not* be identified in the screening. The desirable sensitivity of the test will depend on the frequency, severity, and remediability of the condition sought. For instance, when screening for elder abuse, a life-threatening condition with relatively low frequency and with the possibility of effective action, one prefers a sensitive tool. It is important to pick up all the true cases, and sorting out the false positive is unlikely to become onerous. But when screening for depression among the bereaved, a common phenomenon, a specific test will be more useful since the second-stage assessment and the elimination of false positive could be prohibitively expensive. Those individuals planning screening tests must take these issues into account in setting the thresholds for action.

Determining eligibility for a service or benefit requires a special type of screening. Especially in the case of long-term care services for the frail elderly, clients often need to meet a measurable threshold of income, disability, or both before receiving service. For example, to be eligible for nursing home care under Medicare, the beneficiary must be deemed to require "skilled" care as defined by the legislation. Equity demands a uniform approach to eligibility testing. But the service provider must distinguish *eligibility* for a service from *need* for that service. For example, an elderly man may be eligible for Title XX homemaking services on the basis of his income and his restricted ability to ambulate and care for the household. But he may not need the service because his spouse provides it, just as she has for the last forty years. Eligibility categories are usually defined rather broadly, but the subsequent full assessment of those eligible should determine the mix of services (if any) is appropriate for the particular case. Rarely will the situation be as clearcut as in the example. More often, the program must struggle for forge rules for determining the desirability of offering a particular service once formal eligibility has been established.

Care Planning and Service Delivery

A comprehensive assessment forms the basis for decisions about intervention. From such an assessment, the professional decides whether a problem exists, whether needs are unmet, and what type and quantity of assistance should be recommended. The advantages of collecting information according to a routine format are compelling:

1. In the case of a team of providers (multidisciplinary or otherwise) everyone can gain the same view of the client and communication is enhanced.
2. In the case of complex problems, a consistent assessment format can enhance the likelihood that the assessor will review most relevant information.
3. Those serving older people need to identify *change* on dimensions of interest. For the elderly, a change in functioning (e.g., a drop in the amount of social contact) may be more important than the actual description of functioning (e.g., the absolute amount of social contact). Even if no services are deemed necessary, the initial assessment offers a baseline against which subsequent change can be observed.
4. If resources are scarce, caregivers will be able to compare the

functional abilities, social needs, and social resources of clients and offer services where they would seem to have the most benefit.

5. A comprehensive assessment touching on a variety of important dimensions allows the worker or the team to make a judgment about the reasons for a problem and therefore to decide how to intervene. For example, on self-care dimensions, two clients may show identical failure to cook and eat their meals, but further assessment on cognitive and affective dimensions might show memory loss in one and depression in the other. The treatment plan would differ markedly for those two individuals.

A common complaint is that the sophistication of assessment outstrips the variety in service prescriptions. Sometimes this results from the entrenched habits or lack of imagination in the human service professionals and agencies. Sometimes the problem is a genuine paucity of service in the community. To guard against the former, professional personnel should spend time consciously developing decision rules (sometimes called algorithms) that outline the type of services to be used, given specific assessment results. Time should be set aside for creative "brainstorming" about the kinds of innovative service packages that could be priced together in specific circumstances.

Monitoring and Quality Assurance

Another purpose of assessment is ongoing monitoring of the service. Such monitoring can be done by the individual provider to establish whether a particular intervention (e.g., day care or group therapy) is having its desired effect. Often monitoring is also done by an umbrella organization that has responsibility to authorize payment for a particular service. The latter agency needs to keep sufficient track of the client to know whether the need for the service continues and whether changes on significant dimensions would suggest a different service package.

Too often, assessment (like diagnosis) is reserved for the front end of an association with a client. Thus social service or rehabilitation records may show extensive multidisciplinary workups and team interpretation of the data, but the subsequent record is often comparatively unimportant because changes can be precipitous and unpredictable.

In some circumstances, client assessments are used as a form of quality assurance. This is particularly true in residential settings where the condition of the older person is construed as a positive outcome of care. Monitoring for quality assurance requires careful consideration of the outcomes that the program should reasonably be expected to influence. Quality assurance may also require that functioning be assessed in terms of actual performance (i.e., what the client does) rather than the capacity to perform (i.e., what the client is capable of doing). For example, if a client is capable of ambulating and bathing by herself or himself but is permitted neither to go outside nor to take a bath without supervision, one could hardly applaud the nursing home for fostering a higher quality of life as reflected by increased independence. Assessors need to be clear about whether they should measure capacity, actual performance, or both.

Assessment as an End in Itself

Later articles discuss one-stop intake programs and case management services. In such programs, skilled assessment and subsequent case planning is the major part of the service offered. Legislation is periodically introduced at the federal or state level to allow Medicaid funding for comprehensive assessments before nursing home placements are permitted. Inherent in such policy is the idea the review entailed in the comprehensive assessment is a worthwhile benefit to the client, resulting in plans that are more humane and less costly than placement in a nursing home.

It is, of course, possible to oversell assessment, nobody is cured by diagnosis, nor are anyone's problems solved by assessment. However, caregivers conducting an assessment and clients participating in an assessment can generate more imaginative solutions to problems. For example, a client typically reviews his/her resources and considers sources of assistance as part of the assessment; this process serves as a review and an organizer for the client as well as for the worker.

CONTENT OF ASSESSMENT

Function versus Diagnosis

In assessing the elderly, an accurate medical and/or psychiatric diagnosis is essential. Medical diagnosis for elderly patients is often inadequate. Treatable medical conditions can easily be missed, and many physicians currently in practice have not been trained to distinguish aspects of normal aging from pathological processes, which could lead to both undertreatment and overtreatment (Kane, Ouslander, and Abrass 1984). Geriatric assessment units, where a specially trained team thoroughly assesses physical functioning, identify an average of 3.5 treatable conditions, undiagnosed in previous medical care (Rubenstein, Abrass, and Kane 1981; Kane, Kane and Rubenstein, in press). Senile dementia is an overused diagnosis (Garcia, Redding, and Blass 1981) and is sometimes bestowed without a careful examination of physical (e.g., infections, high drug dosages), emotional (e.g., depression), or environmental causes of confusion. For all these reasons, a social worker or other multipurpose assessor should establish whether a creditable geriatric workup has been done and arrange for one if necessary (particularly in the context of "old-old" clients—those over 75—seeking long-term care).

Indeed, the importance of comprehensive geriatric assessment has been stressed since the early 1980s with the increase in specialized inpatient and outpatient assessment centers where complex interacting medical, psychological and social problems can be sorted out. Such centers typically are staffed by multidisciplinary teams and use standardized functional inventories as well as laboratory tests. Short-range treatment (especially medication reductions and/or changes) are often tried and the patient's reactions to these interventions becomes part of the data base of the assessment. In 1987, a consensus panel convened by the National Institute on Aging agreed that functional assessment—i.e., assessment of the patient's "ability to function in the arena of everyday living,"—is integral to medical decision making (Solomon 1988; Consensus Development Panel 1988). Therefore, although at present, one cannot assume all elderly patients have received adequate medical diagnosis, perhaps in time geriatrically sensitive medical workups will become more the norm.

Similarly, psychiatric diagnosis should not be short-circuited. Although DSM-III describes many of its diagnostic entities as having a typical onset in adolescence or early adulthood (e.g., schizophrenia, most affective disorders, substance abuse), the document acknowledges that new cases can develop in later years (American Psychiatric Association 1980). Reactive disorders (including both post-traumatic stress and adjustment disorder) can appear at any age and can harken back to much earlier stimuli. Personality disorders, although appearing early, are lifelong phenomena and may become more troublesome to others with the dependencies of old age. In addition, DSM-II gives considerable direct attention to organic mental disorders and the differential diagnosis between delirium and chronic dementias further explicated by Sloane (1980).

Unfortunately, older persons tend not to receive mental health services, especially diagnostic and treatment services, on an outpatient basis (Task Panel on Elderly 1978). True age-specific prevalence figures for psychiatric disorders are therefore hard to determine. Dohrenwend and his colleagues (1980) estimated that 18 to 25 percent of persons over 65 suffer from functional (i.e., nonorganic) mental disease, particularly affective disorders. The assessor will be less likely to omit a psychiatric diagnosis if the older person has a history of mental illness, however, the possibility of new incidence or existence of a previously unrecognized psychiatric condition that must be considered. Many of these conditions are eminently treatable.

The complexity of psychiatric diagnoses among older people is highlighted by a series of chapters in the research book *Handbook of Mental Health and Aging* (Birren and Sloane 1980). Miller (1980) describes the differential diagnosis between dementia and functional disorders and discusses "terminal drop" and the phenomenon of declining cognitive ability in the months before death. Lawton, Whelihan, and Belsky (1980) review the problems of personality tests for older people and raise many cautions about validity. (Dye's discussion of the same topic in another volume [1982a] abstracts and critiques the most common personality tests used with the elderly, including tests of personality rigidity, and is a good resource for further information on available tests.) Post (1980) offers a lucid discussion of paranoid, schizophrenic, and schizophrenic-like states in the elderly, describing little-studied phenomena such as the "senile recluse" as well as the range of paranoid-type disorders, with and without hallucinations, with and without affective components. Post's discussion is recommended for a cogent account of clinical pictures.

Although careful medical and, if appropriate, psychiatric diagnosis is a crucial part of the assessment of older clients, diagnosis is insufficient for care planning. Older persons tend to accumulate chronic diseases, and a simple list of active diagnosis does not explain the *functional* abilities of the individual. Nor does it accurately predict the need for services. Two people with diabetes, osteoarthritis, or even schizophrenia may manifest very different functional abilities.

Functioning is a product of an individual's abilities, motivation, and environment (with environment construed broadly to include the physical environment, the task expectations, and the availability of social support). Any individual can experience large increases or decreases in functional performance with environmental changes. For example, a previously competent person might be rendered incompetent in a foreign country where an unfamiliar language is spoken. Conversely, a somewhat inept person may be rendered competent by a secretary or household staff. Those assessing the elderly must examine both actual abilities and environmental issues. In moving from assessment data to a plan, the assessor must consider ways to increase capacity and motivation (e.g., educational approaches, physical therapy, occupational therapy, psychological therapy, medical treatments, prosthetic devices) and ways to render the environment less complicated and demanding. Because the older person is vulnerable to environmental insult and sudden, far-reaching changes in social support, the environmental component of the functional assessment should not be neglected.

Multidimensional Assessment

Figure 3.1 summarizes components of a thorough, multidimensional assessment of the functioning of an older person. Each box represents a domain worthy of separate assessment, but the various domains for inclusion, though different authorities subdivide or title them differently. Figure 3.1 suggests nine content areas for assessment; environmental, service use, value preferences, and finally, burden on the support system.

PHYSICAL FACTORS

Even those without medical training can gather useful information about a client's health. Determining the diagnoses the client has accumulated, the drugs the client uses, and his/her hospital and physician-utilization patterns will present a composite picture of health status. Pain and discomfort is also important to gauge, although instruments to do so are rudimentary. Kane et al. (1983a,b) have developed an approach to measuring pain and discomfort among nursing home residents, using headache, joint pain, itching, dizziness, and chest pain as indicators. Physical conditions highly relevant to functional ability and not usually the province of an internist or general practitioner include vision, hearing, dentition, and podiatric status. The assessor might determine whether impairment exists in any of these areas, whether full evaluation and treatment has been sought, and when applicable, whether the client has appropriate prostheses and devices. Finally, self-report of physical health has been shown to be a good predictor of mortality (Mossey and Shapiro 1982). Assessors should be warned, however, that although the measures discussed in this section afford a capsule view of cumulative morbidity, they will not account for etiology of problems and do not substitute for a

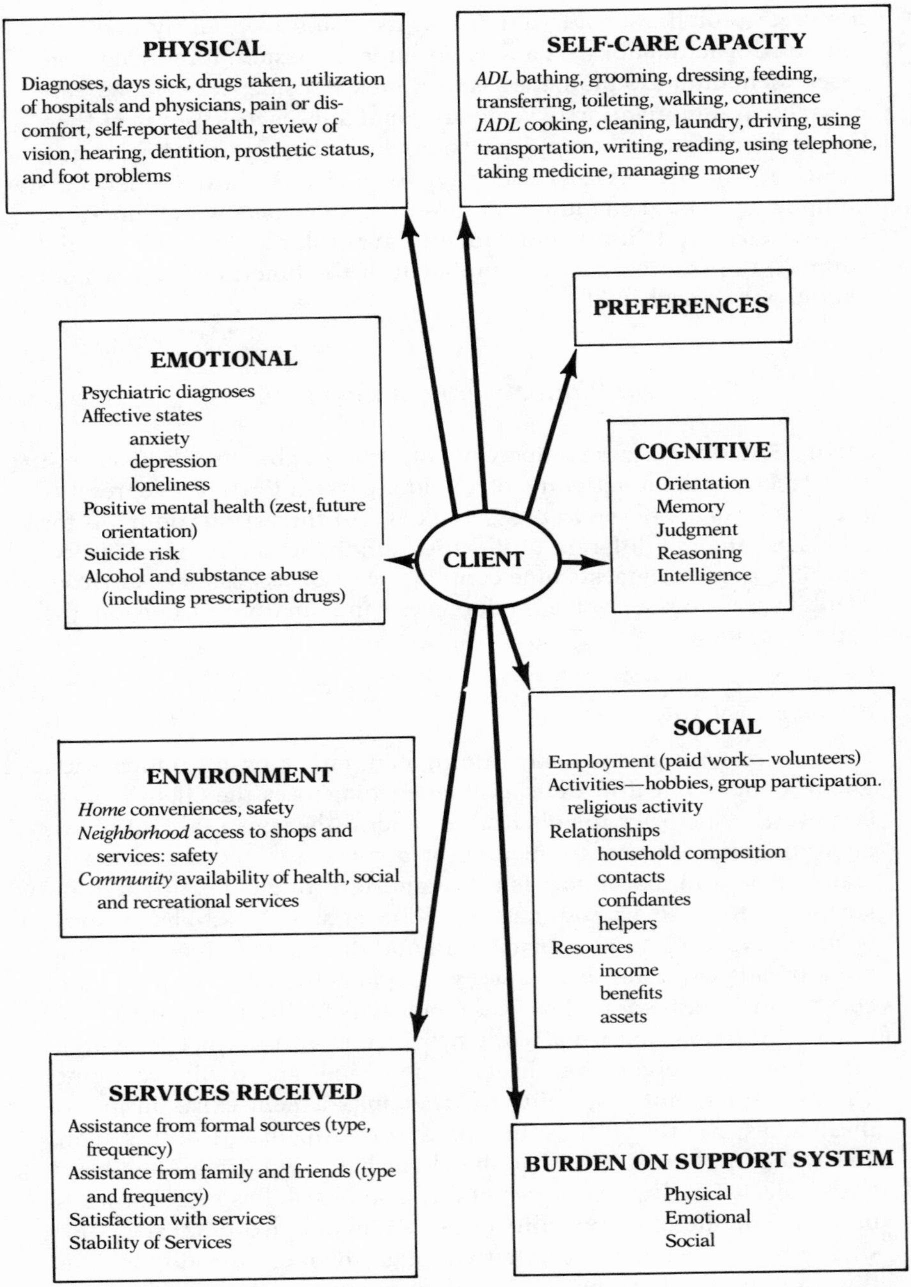
PHYSICAL
Diagnoses, days sick, drugs taken, utilization of hospitals and physicians, pain or discomfort, self-reported health, review of vision, hearing, dentition, prosthetic status, and foot problems
SELF-CARE CAPACITY
ADL bathing, grooming, dressing, feeding, transferring, toileting, walking, continence
IADL cooking, cleaning, laundry, driving, using transportation, writing, reading, using telephone, taking medicine, managing money
PREFERENCES
EMOTIONAL
Psychiatric diagnoses
Affective states
anxiety
depression
loneliness
Positive mental health (zest, future orientation)
Suicide risk
Alcohol and substance abuse (including prescription drugs)
CLIENT
COGNITIVE
Orientation
Memory
Judgment
Reasoning
Intelligence
SOCIAL
Employment (paid work—volunteers)
Activities—hobbies, group participation. religious activity
Relationships
household composition
contacts
confidantes
helpers
Resources
income
benefits
assets
ENVIRONMENT
Home conveniences, safety
Neighborhood access to shops and services: safety
Community availability of health, social and recreational services
SERVICES RECEIVED
Assistance from formal sources (type, frequency)
Assistance from family and friends (type and frequency)
Satisfaction with services
Stability of Services
BURDEN ON SUPPORT SYSTEM
Physical
Emotional
Social

geriatric workup. In fact, if the assessors determine that the individual is taking ten or more prescription or non-prescription drugs and has accumulated numerous diagnoses, referral to a geriatric assessment unit might be indicated. (This is especially true if the evaluation of self-care capacity shows substantial impairment as well.)

EMOTIONAL FACTORS

The emotional category includes a review for functional psychology, particularly affective disorders. Several short batteries of questions have been developed to screen for depression. Most often used with the elderly are the Zung Self-Rated Depression scale (Zung 1965) and the Beck Inventory of Depression (Beck et al. 1961). Both are shown in table 3.1. Common indicators of depression such as appetite loss, fatigue, insomnia, palpitations, and sexual disinterest may be masked by the physical and social circumstances of the elderly. Some recommend that the assessment emphasize indicators of dysphoric mood rather than psychophysiological signs of depression (Gallagher, Thompson, and Levy 1980). Positive well-being is sometimes measured through scales such as Life Satisfaction Index (LSI) (Havighurst, Neugarten, and Toblin 1961), or the Philadelphia Geriatric Morale Scale (Lawton 1972), although there is some overlap between the common measures of depression and the common measures of morale. (See table 3.2 for these two morale scales.)

Suicidal ideation should be assessed directly whenever evidence of depression or despair is found. (The incidence of completed suicides in persons over age 65, particularly among men, is high and probably underreported.) Although assessors may be uncomfortable asking, older persons will respond willingly and reliably to the question "How often have you thought of killing yourself?" with response categories such as "never," "occasionally," "often," and "almost all the time" (Kane et al. 1983b).

COGNITIVE FACTORS

A cognitive appraisal is important whenever the assessor suspects that memory and intellectual functioning are impaired. Several tests have been developed to assess memory and intellectual functioning are impaired. Several tests have been developed to assess memory and cognitive function. The best-known brief tests ascertain orienta-

FIGURE 3.1. Components of a Multidimensional Assessment.

tion for place, time, and person; recent and remote memory; and calculation. Table 3.3 presents the Short Portable Mental Status Questionnaire, which is part of a larger instrument developed at Duke University (1978). Other instruments tap higher levels of functioning by presenting simple problems and checking abstract thinking through proverb interpretation; the Folstein Mini-Mental Status Questionnaire (Folstein and McHugh 1975) is an example. Dye (1982b) abstracts and critiques seventeen measures of intellectual functioning that have been applied to the elderly, including elaborate batteries. On the other end of the spectrum, simpler tests of cognitive ability have been developed for nursing homes, using indicators like knowledge of the season of the year, the next meal, and the location of one's

TABLE 3.1. Examples of Scales to Measure Affective Status

Zung Self-Rated Depression Scale[a]

1. I feel downhearted and blue.
2. Morning is when I feel the best.
3. I have crying spells or feel like it.
4. I have trouble sleeping at night.
5. I can eat as much as I used to.
6. I still enjoy sex.
7. I notice that I am losing weight.
8. I have trouble with constipation.
9. My heart beats faster than usual.
10. I get tired for no reason.
11. My mind is as clear as it used to be.
12. I find it easy to do the things I used to.
13. I am restless and can't keep still.
14. I feel hopeful about the future.
15. I am more irritable than usual.
16. I find it easy to make decisions.
17. I feel that I am useful and needed.
18. My life is pretty full.
19. I feel that others would be better off if I were dead.
20. I still enjoy the things I used to do.

SOURCE: Zung scale adapted from W. W. K. Zung. (1965). Beck inventory from A. T. Beck et al. 1961.

[a]For each item, the respondent rates the statement as "a little of the time," "some of the time," "good deal of the time," or "most of the time."

room (Lawton 1972). These have the advantage of not relying on information about the date and current events that may seem somewhat irrelevant nursing home residents.

Two cautions about brief mental status assessments. First, such assessments are sometimes used to determine whether a client is capable of answering the rest of the questions on an assessment instrument. Decision rules often state that if a client gets a specified number of questions incorrect, a significant other will provide the remaining information. However, cognitive abilities are spotty, and persons making errors on the Short Portable Mental Status Questionnaire are capable of reliably answering other questions, particularly those pertaining to their activities, relationships, moods, and prefer-

TABLE 3.1. (*Continued*)

Modified Beck Depression Inventory[b]

1. I do not feel sad.
   I feel sad.
   I am sad all the time and can't snap out of it.
   I am so sad or unhappy that I can't stand it.
2. I am not particularly discouraged about the future.
3. I do feel like a failure.
4. I get as much satisfaction out of things as I used to.
5. I don't feel particularly guilty.
6. I don't feel I am being punished.
7. I don't feel disappointed in myself.
8. I don't feel I am any worse than anyone else.
9. I don't have thoughts of killing myself.
10. I don't cry any more than usual.
11. I am no more irritated now than I ever am.
12. I have not lost interest in other people.
13. I make decisions about as well as I ever could.
14. I don't worry that I look worse than I used to.
15. I can work about as well as I used to.
16. I can sleep as well as usual.
17. I don't get any more tired than usual.
18. My appetite is no worse than usual.
19. I haven't lost much weight, if any, lately.
20. I am no more worried about my health than usual.
21. I have not noticed any recent change in my interest in sex.

[b]Each item has 4.5 responses, representing a range of mood; the respondent picks the one most appropriate. We included all four responses only for item no. 1.

ences. And certainly nobody else is likely to give an accurate answer to this type of question. It is dangerous to eliminate the client as a source of further information on the basis of marginal cognitive score.

The second caution is that the assessor should supplement information from short tests with other kinds of information. The histori-

---

TABLE 3.2. Examples of Scales Measuring Subjective Well-Being in the Elderly

---

Philadelphia Geriatric Center Morale Scale

1. Things keep getting worse as I get older. (No)[a]
2. I have as much pep as I did last year. (Yes)
3. How much do you feel lonely? (Not much)

ttle things bother me more this year. (No)

5. I see enough of my friends and relatives. (Yes)
6. As you get older, you are less useful. (No)
7. If you could live where you wanted, where would you live? (Here)
8. I sometimes worry so much that I can't sleep. (No)
9. As I get older, things are (better, worse, the same) than/as I thought they'd be. (Better)
10. I sometimes feel that life isn't worth living. (No)
11. I am happy now as I was when I was younger. (Yes)
12. Most days I have plenty to do. (Yes)
13. I have a lot to be sad about. (No)
14. People had it better in the old days. (No)
15. I am afraid of a lot of things. (No)
16. My health is (good, not so good). (Good)
17. I get mad more than I used to. (No)
18. Life is hard for me most of the time. (No)
19. How satisfied are you with your life today? (Satisfied)
20. I take things hard. (No)
21. A person has to live for today and not worry about tomorrow. (Yes)
22. I get upset easily. (No)

Life Satisfaction Index (LSI-A)

Here are some statements about life in general that people feel differently about. Would you read each statement in the list and, if you agree with it, put

---

[a] The correct answer, shown in parentheses, is scored one point.

SOURCE: Moral scale adapted from M. P. Lawton, 1972. The dimensions of morale. In D. Kent, R. Kastenbaum, and S. Sherwood, eds., *Research Planning and Action for the Elderly* (New

cal onset of the cognitive impairment is important, as is the presence of absence of personality change or antisocial behavior. The differential diagnosis between pseudodementia (i.e., depression present with dementia symptoms) and true cognitive loss is assisted by information about suddenness of onset and accompanying behavior (see Salzman and Shader 1979, for tabular comparisons of pseudodementia

TABLE 3.2. (*Continued*)

a check mark in the space "agree." If you do not agree, put a check mark in the space under "disagree." If you are not sure one way or the other, put a check mark in the space "?."

1. As I grow older, things seem better than I thought they would be. (Agree)
2. I have gotten more of the breaks in life than most of the people I know. (Agree)
3. This is the dreariest time of my life. (Disagree)
4. I am just as happy as when I was younger. (Agree)
5. My life could be happier than it is now. (Disagree)
6. These are the best years of my life. (Agree)
7. Most of the things I do are boring or monotonous. (Disagree)
8. I expect some interesting and pleasant things to happen to me in the future. (Agree)
9. The things I do are as interesting to me as they ever were. (Agree)
10. I feel old and tired. (Disagree)
11. I feel my age, but it doesn't bother me. (Agree)
12. As I look back on my life, I am fairly well satisfied. (Agree)
13. I would not change my past life, even if I could. (Agree)
14. Compared to other people my age, I've made a lot of foolish decisions in my life. (Disagree)
15. Compared to other people my age, I make a good appearance. (Agree)
16. I have made plans for things I'll be doing a month or a year from now. (Agree)
17. When I think back over my life, I didn't get most of the important things I wanted. (Disagree)
18. Compared to other people, I get down in the dumps too often. (Disagree)
19. I've gotten pretty much what I expected out of life. (Agree)
20. In spite of what people say, the lot of the average man is getting worse, not better. (Disagree)

York: Behavioral Publications). Life satisfaction index adapted from R. J. Havinghurst, B. L. Neugarten and S. S. Tobin, 1961. The measurement of life satisfaction, *Journal of Gerontology*, 16:134–143.

and true dementia). Furthermore, the planning for and with the client with memory loss is influenced by other factors such as social intactness and appropriateness. It is also useful to look for strengths in the behavior of the person with cognitive impairment. If that individual takes care of someone else, for example, he is exhibiting positive signs of cognition that should counterbalance any test score (Gurland et al. 1982).

SOCIAL FACTORS

As figure 3.1 shows, the social assessment should take into account social activities, social relationships, and social resources. Activities include interests and hobbies that can be pursued in solitude and those that involve participation in social or membership groups. Relationships include the frequency of human contact and interaction, the availability of necessary assistance from others, and access to a

TABLE 3.3 Short Portable Mental Status Questionnaire (SPMSQ)

Short Portable Mental Status Questionnaire (SPMSQ)

1. What is the date today (month/day/year)?
2. What day of the week is it?
3. What is the name of this place?
4. What is your telephone number? (If no telephone, what is your street address?)
5. How old are you?
6. When were you born (month/day/year)?
7. Who is the current president of the United States?
8. Who was the president just before him?
9. What was your mother's maiden name?
10. Subtract 3 from 20 and keep subtracting from each new number you get, all the way down.

0–2 errors	= intact
3–4 errors	= mild intellectual impairment
5–7 errors	= moderate intellectual impairment
8–10 errors	= severe intellectual impairment

Allow one more error if subject had only grade school education.
Allow one fewer error if subject has had education beyond high school.
Allow one more error for blacks, regardless of education criteria.

SOURCE: Duke University, 1978.

trusted confidante. Although a minimum threshold of social activity and contact is probably intrinsically good (e.g., associated with feelings of well-being, good sleeping patterns, lessened depression), the major goal is for the individual to have *meaningful* activities and social contacts. Simple counts do not tell the story—the person with four friends is not twice as well off as the person with two friends. The person with balanced activities is not better off than the bridge or tennis fanatic. Certainly the person who participates in a range of activities that he/she perceives as tedious and unfulfilling has not achieved social well-being. Therefore, social well-being has a subjective as well as an objective component; the assessor should determine whether the activities and contacts are satisfying to the individual. The importance of a pet in promoting social well-being should not be discounted nor should the seriousness of the loss of a pet be underestimated. Many instruments have been developed for quick screening of social functioning. Table 3.4 presents one of these (Lubben 1988).

Work should not be forgotten, even if the person is retired. Because our identities are so enmeshed with our work, the assessor should know what kind of work the individual did and where his/her skills lie. This is particularly true for men in the elderly cohorts, and women increasingly identify with their work. A knowledge of work history and general abilities may suggest volunteer involvement compatible with the individual's physical capabilities and interests. Certainly the assessment of a person bound for or already in a nursing home should not neglect the occupational component. Demonstration projects in nursing homes (see, for example, Jorgenson and Kane 1976) have shown that individuals with utilizable skills, such as a concert pianist or an expert gardener, often have no opportunity to use them in the nursing home environment because no one is aware of the person at that human level. On a positive note, Laufer and Laufer (1982) describe how nursing home residents with foreign language skills become adjunct instructors to local college students and formed mutually important relationships through that exchange. This type of model program shows the payoff from assessments that try to encapsulate the abilities, interests, and skills older people have developed in a lifetime of work and community involvement.

In a social assessment, baseline values become increasingly important. Typically, for example, social isolation is measured by the absolute amount of face-to-face, telephone, and even mail contact between the older person and others in a particular (or typical) week. But some people are more gregarious than others. Social contact amounting to a daily telephone call and two or three outings or visits during a week might be a comfortable pattern for some people and represent an

TABLE 3.4. Lubben Social Network Scale

Family networks

Q1. How many relatives do you see or hear from at least once a month? (NOTE: Include in-laws with relatives.) Q1 ____

0 = zero	3 = three or four
1 = one	4 = five to eight
2 = two	5 = nine or more

Q2. Tell me about the relative with whom you have the most contact. How often do you see or hear from that person? Q2 ____

0 = <monthly	3 = weekly
1 = monthly	4 = a few times a week
2 = a few times a month	5 = daily

Q3. How many relatives do you feel close to? That is, how many of them do you feel at ease with, can talk to about private matters, or can call on for help? Q3 ____

0 = zero	3 = three or four
1 = one	4 = five to eight
2 = two	5 = nine or more

Friends networks

Q4. Do you have any close friends? That is, do you have any friends with whom you feel at ease, can talk to about private matters, or can call on for help? If so, how many? Q4 ____

0 = zero	3 = three or four
1 = one	4 = five to eight
2 = two	5 = nine or more

Q5. How many of these friends do you see or hear from at least once a month? Q5 ____

0 = zero	3 = three or four
1 = one	4 = five to eight
2 = two	5 = nine or more

Q6. Tell me about the friend with whom you have the most contact. How often do you see or hear from that person? Q6 ____

0 = <monthly	3 = weekly
1 = monthly	4 = a few times a week
2 = a few times a month	5 = daily

TABLE 3.4. (*Continued*)

Confident relationships

Q7. When you have an important decision to make, do you have someone you can talk to about it? Q7 ____

Always	Very Often	Often	Sometimes	Seldom	Never
5	4	3	2	1	0

Q8. When other people you know have an important decision to make, do they talk to you about it? Q8 ____

Always	Very Often	Often	Sometimes	Seldom	Never
5	4	3	2	1	0

Helping others

Q9a. Does anybody rely on you to do something for them each day? For example: shopping, cooking dinner, doing repairs, cleaning house, providing child care, etc.
NO—if no, go on to Q9b. YES—if yes, Q9 is scored "5" and skip to Q10.

Q9b. Do you help anybody with things like shopping, filling out forms, doing repairs, providing child care, etc.? Q9 ____

Very Often	Often	Sometimes	Seldom	Never
4	3	2	1	0

Living arrangements

Q10. Do you live alone or with other people? (NOTE: Include in-laws with relatives.) Q10 ____

5 Live with spouse
4 Live with other relatives or friends
1 Live with other unrelated individuals (e.g., paid help)
0 Live alone

TOTAL LSNS SCORE: ____

SCORING:

The total LSNS score is obtained by adding up scores from each of the ten individual items. Thus, total LSNS scores can range from 0 to 50. Scores on each item were anchored between 0 and 5 in order to permit equal weighting of the ten items.

alarming narrowing of social contact for others. With repeated assessment, it might be important to inquire whether the information given represents a change.

ENVIRONMENTAL FACTORS

The environmental assessment has not been well developed or standardized. There is increasing awareness of the importance of assessing the adequacy of the immediate environment, both home and neighborhood, in terms of safety factors, convenience, and manageability for a person with other impairments. Often household equipment or renovation can make a person more functional in a particular setting. In the neighborhood, the proximity to shops, buses, beauty parlors, libraries, parks, and pharmacies may be important. Delivery policies of nearby businesses may also be important. So far, instrumentation on environment tends to concentrate on the perceived adequacy of residential or institutional environments (Windley 1982). Research by Carp and Carp (1982) on perceptions of the elderly about ideal features of a residential neighborhood might ultimately lead to yearly checklists for that neighborhood.

SELF-CARE CAPACITY

Self-care capacity is based on functional performance, which, as already indicated, is a product of the person's physical and mental capabilities, his/her psychological motivation, and the environmental pressures. Therefore, the entire physical, emotional, cognitive, and environmental assessment will yield information about the ability of the individual to sustain an independent life-style. But a more direct way of tapping into this content is to assess self-care performance directly. Two acronyms come into prominence in this functional assessment; ADL (activities of daily living) and IADL (instrumental activities of daily living).

ADL activities refer to basic self-care skills such as bathing, feeding, dressing, transferring into and out of bed or onto and off of the toilet, walking or using a wheelchair, and grooming oneself. Continence is often included in an inventory of ADL activities, although it is a psychological function. One of the most parsimonious and frequently used ADL measures is the Katz ADL scale (Katz et al. 1963) a six-item scale that divides each function only two ways (independent or dependent; see table 3.5). In contrast, other approaches gather more information. For instance, ability to eat can be broken down further to distinguish complete independence from need for some assistance with cutting meat, from need for special equipment, and from complete dependence. Similarly the function itself can be broken down into component parts: for example, drinking from a cup, eating from a plate. The level of detail required will depend on the type of organization sponsoring the assessment and its purpose. Usually it is useful to distinguish between independence with the help of equipment and independence with the help of another person. If one can move with a walker, one has gained a degree of independence over the person who requires another individual to help with the walking. Value judgments are involved in assessing ADL capacity—for example, if the speed and competence with which dressing is performed does not meet the abstract standards of a particular assessor, the persons might be deemed dependent. An ADL assessment also varies as to whether the information comes from the report of the client, the report of a relative, the rating of a caregiver, or actual observation of the client. Some assessment tools use simulated equipment, allowing the client to demonstrate the capacity to perform certain skills (e.g., butter a slice of bread, use the telephone) (Kuriansky et al. 1976).

IADL functions are more complex activities that support independence. Typically cooking, cleaning, doing laundry, using transportation or driving, telephone use, self-medicating abilities, and money management are included. Some assessors also examine the capacity for heavy work such as major cleaning or gardening. IADL performance is rendered more or less difficult by the kind of equipment that the client has at his/her disposal (compare a washtub to automatic washing machine to a coin laundry down three flights of stairs). IADL performance also depends somewhat on learned abilities—homemaking skills for men and money management skills for women may be lacking in the cohorts now elderly. Such skills can be developed, however, as part of a plan. A plan can also be directed at simplifying the activities so that they can be performed within an individual's reduced capacities (e.g., presorted medication doses, telephone modifications, step-reducing devices).

SERVICES RECEIVED

The assessor must contrast the client's needs uncovered by the assessment with the services the client is currently receiving. Knowledge of the extent to which the client needs and receives assistance not only gives guidance for care planning but permits estimation of the cost of service. This part of the assessment should separate several aspects of assistance.

1. It should distinguish assistance from agencies or paid personnel and assistance dependent on volunteer labor of family or friends.
2. It should distinguish between services purchased by the individual and services reimbursed under a benefit or insurance program.
3. It should identify both the *actual services* needed and the *source* of the assistance. In our pluralistic form of social organization similar services can be received from a variety of agencies and programs (both residential and community-based). A true picture of the service pattern requires "disaggregating" discrete services (e.g., homemaking assistance, financial planning assistance, shelter, recreation) from the source of that assistance. As part of Duke University's OARS methodology (Duke University

TABLE 3.5. Katz Index of ADL

Index of Independence in Activities of Daily Living

The Index of Independence in Activities of Daily Living is based on an evaluation of the functional independence or dependence of patients in bathing, dressing, going to the toilet, transferring, continence, and feeding. Specific definitions of functional independence and dependence appear below the index.

A	Independent in feeding, continence, transferring, going to toilet, dressing, and bathing.
B	Independent in all but one of these functions.
C	Independent in all but bathing and one additional function.
D	Independent in all but bathing, dressing, and one additional function.
E	Independent in all but bathing, dressing, going to toilet, and one additional function.
F	Independent in all but bathing, dressing, going to toilet, transferring, and one additional function.
G	Dependent in all six functions.
Other	Dependent in at least two functions, but not classifiable as C, D, E, or F.

Independence means without supervision, direction, or active personal assistance, except as specifically noted below. This is based on actual status and not on ability. A patient who refuses to perform a function is considered as not performing the function, even though he is deemed able.

Bathing (sponge, shower or tub)
Independent: assistance only in bathing a single part (as back or disabled extremity) or bathes self completely

Transfer
Independent: moves in and out of bed independently and moves in and out of chair independently; (may or may not be using

1978) services were disaggregated into twenty-four discrete functions. (See table 3.6 for the service list and the applicable unit of measurement.) The Cleveland GAO study (U.S. Comptroller General 1977) used this method to study the relationship between functional impairment and use of services.

4. It should distinguish services purchased on a discretionary basis from services needed to maintain functioning.

If the client receives considerable long-term service from family and friends, the assessment should examine components of that "informal support". It is useful to know how much time is actually being given by family and neighborhood helpers and how much of that time is needed to maintain functioning. "Personal time dependency" is a phrase coined by Gurland and his colleagues (1978) to express the

TABLE 3.5 (*Continued*)

Dependent: assistance in bathing more than one part of body, assistance in getting in or out of tub or does not bathe self

Dressing

Independent: get clothes from closets and drawers; puts on clothes, outer garments, braces; manages fasteners; act of tying shoes is excluded

Dependent: does not dress self or remains partly undressed

Going to toilet

Independent: gets to toilet; gets on and off toilet; arranges clothes, cleans organs of excretion (may manage own bedpan used at night only and may or may not be using mechanical supports)

Dependent: uses bedpan or commode or receives assistance in getting to and using toilet

mechanical supports)

Dependent: assistance in moving in or out of bed and/or chair; does not perform one or more transfers

Continence

Independent: urination and defecation entirely self-controlled

Dependent: partial or total incontinence in urination or defecation; partial or total control by enemas, catheters, or regulated use of urinals and/or bedpans

Feeding

Independent: gets food from plate or its equivalent into mouth (precutting of meat and preparation of food, as buttering bread, are excluded from evaluation)

Dependent: assistance in act of feeding (see above); does not eat at all or parenteral feeding

SOURCE: S. Katz et al, 1963, "Studies of Illness in the Aged. The Index of ADL: A Standardized Measure of Biological and Psychosocial Function," *Journal of the American Medical Association* 185: 94 ff.

essence of the long-term care dilemma. One goal of the plan is to decrease "personal time dependency," which, in the long run, is likely to create a burden on the support system.

The assessor should also examine the stability of the assistance that the individual is receiving. Some persons may be at the end of their financial benefits. Others may enjoy excellent help from the family, but the family support may rest with one individual alone. The services received by such people lack depth. For example, some-

TABLE 3.6. Disaggregated Long-Term-Care Services

Category of Service	*Unit of Measurement*
Basic maintenance	
Transportation	Passenger round trips
Food, groceries	Dollars
Living quarters (housing)	Dollars
Supportive	
Personal care	Contact hours
Continuous supervision	
Checking services	
Meal preparation	Meals
Homemaker-household	Hours
Administrative, legal and protective	Hours
Remedial	
Social/recreational	Sessions
Employment	Number of times provided
Sheltered employment	Hours of employment
Education—employment related	Training session hours
Remedial training	Number of sessions
Mental health	Sessions
Psychotropic drugs	
Nursing care	Contact hours
Medical	Number of visits/dollars
Supportive devices and prostheses	Dollars
Physical therapy	Sessions
Relocation and placement	Moves
Systematic multidimensional evaluation	Hours
Financial assistance	Dollars or dollar equivalent
Coordination, information and referral services	Hours

SOURCE: Adapted from Duke University, 1978.

one may be depending on one son alone, and if he were transferred to another community no backup assistance would be available (Kulys and Tobin 1980). The assessor should know which proportion of the caseload has support systems that are one deep.

FAMILY BURDEN

Closely related to the previous category is the assessment of the burden on the social support system—most notably the family. Presently there are no widely used instruments to tap this dimension, although some investigators are doing work that should isolate features of burden. Often the caregiver is also over 65 (a postretirement "child," a sibling or, most frequently, a spouse). In such instances, each older person in the constellation is assessed individually. It may be that the amount of care needed by a husband is beyond the physical and emotional capacity of the wife. The service plan may be directed then to providing some respite or assistance for the primary caregiver.

Families in the so-called "middle generation" who struggle with responsibilities related to minor children as well as aging parents may be experiencing enormous cumulative pressures. Intuitively one would expect that pressure to be a function of the extent of multiple physical and financial demands and the duration of these demands. Research does report certain phenomena related to an elderly relative in the household that strain the family's endurance; incontinence and night wandering are most notable and should be flagged as signs that the family needs help even before such help is demanded. Another elusive factor is the relationship of spouses as affected by care given to one or another spouse's parents, and such reactions are probably conditioned by the affective tides between parents and their adult children, the formative experience of middle-generation husband and wife with grandparents in their own original households, and personal concepts of duty and religious responsibility. In the 1980s, several measures of burden have been developed (Zarit, Reever, and Bach-Peterson 1980; Robinson 1983; Montgomery, Stull, and Borgatta 1985).

PREFERENCES

Assessment of the preference of the older person is of paramount importance and may be the most neglected aspect of a multidimensional assessment. Long-term care arrangements (be they in institutions or in the community) involve compromise with the ideal. Even if funds were not constrained, a program that sets out to achieve a maximum goal in one area (say, ADL and ADL capacities) may need to compromise on pain relief and even social well-being. If such trade-offs must be made, surely the opinion of the older person should be sought about what should be maximized and what should be traded off (Kane and Kane 1982). Some older persons may wish to emphasize physical safety and freedom from risk of accidents more than goals of independence, but others may prefer to accept the risks of falling or the knowledge that services will be incomplete at home rather than to accept the dependence and "quality of life" loss inherent in nursing-home placement. Unfortunately, these issues are seldom put squarely to the persons most concerned. The value preferences and risk-aversion of professionals and family members often dictate the ultimate plan.

Of course the professional cannot be irresponsible and allow the older person to take the risks that are dangerous to the entire community. Even here, however, it is important that a double standard not develop. For example, if a teenager or a middle-aged adult leaves on a faucet or forgets his or her keys, there is no particular cause for alarm. Few housewives have *never* burned the bottom out of a kettle. However, if such an event occurs once or twice for a person over age 75, the question about ability for self-care is often raised.

MULTIDIMENSIONAL TOOL

A multidimensional assessment tool or battery gathers together information about many aspects of an older person's functioning and well-being to present a composite picture. Such procedures are now well-integrated into a variety of programs, both to establish eligibility for various levels of service and to plan care. For example, most states have developed multidimensional assessment tools to gauge the need for nursing home care. Some of these measures are merely descriptive, but others, such as New York's DSM-III, yield a score upon which action is taken. For the most part, the measures used to determine nursing home placement are easily manipulated to generate the desired result. Various monitoring groups such as state nursing home inspection agencies and professional standards review organizations have developed patient-specific assessment tools designed to provide baseline information about the nursing home residents and form the foundation for a nursing care plan (Kane et al. 1979). By now, many states have developed multidimensional assessment tools for preadmission screening programs prior to admission to nursing homes, and for assessing clients to receive community care under their Medicaid waiver programs (Kane and Kane 1987).

Many multidimensional assessments are modeled after early efforts of the Department of Health and Human Services to develop a minimum standard for recordkeeping in nursing homes (U.S. HEW 1978; Jones, McNitt, and McKnight 1974). Typically, they contain sections to be completed by each member of the multidisciplinary team. Although they fail to produce any scores through which clients can be compared, such tools are useful formats for uniform recording and, as such, have potential to improve care. In late 1987, by Congressional mandate, the Secretary of Health and Human Services appointed a commission to recommend a minimal data set to assess the needs of older people at discharge from hospitals. This work may incorporate some brief scales, but is expected to be largely an organized recording format (U.S. Congress 1986). Similarly, in 1988, the Health Care Financing Administration commissioned a study to develop a standardized assessment tool for nursing home care (Health Care Financing Administration 1988). Both these efforts are designed to improve care through systematic assessment, and to encourage comparable information that can be used by regulators, and perhaps even payors.

Some multidimensional assessment tools do produce a single score that takes into account physical, mental, and social dimensions of functioning. The Sickness Impact Profile (SIP) is such a device (Bergner et al. 1976). The tool was designed from a health perspective and was not particularly designed for the elderly. In all probability, the information is too condensed to be useful for care planning.

Gerontologists have produced multidimensional instruments that yield several scores in different domains. The CARE battery (Gurland et al 1977–78) is one such example. The best-known multidisciplinary assessment technique in gerontology is the OARS methodology, developed by the Older Americans Resource and Service Center at Duke University (1978, 1988). OARS collects information in five areas (physical health, ADL capacity, mental health, social well-being, economic well-being); information is gathered through an interview with the client or (if the client fails a brief cognitive test) a significant other. The instrument takes an average of ninety minutes to administer and, with training, interviewers achieve reliability of judgment when present with the same interview stimulus.

The scores in the OARS instrument are derived from clinical judgment as refined by reviewing responses to the questions on the instrument. After the administration, the assessor rates each of the five areas on a six-point scale ranging from excellent functioning to totally impaired. The assessor is reminded which responses to read over for each rating and is given anchoring statements. The scores can then be added up for an overall scores (i.e., two score of six would be the most independent, and thirty the most dependent) or the person can be rated according to the number of domains impaired. The domain scores can also be examined separately.

The OARS instrument represents one of the best-studied and most widely accepted approaches to gerontological assessment. Initially it presented some problems: 1) it is inadequate to assess functioning at the lower end of the spectrum; 2) the score still relies on judgment rather than on a numerical treatment of the individual questions in each domain; and 3) in summary treatments, all domains are considered equal and independent. More recently, however, researchers have worked to develop scales from the actual answers to questions on the instrument (Duke University 1988; George and Fillenbaum 1985; Fillenbaum 1988).

INTERVIEWING CONSIDERATIONS

Some practical considerations are important for eliciting reliable and valid information from older persons, particularly those with physical impairments. Some are common sense, but others may be overlooked because they are embodied in the instrument and its language or procedures.

Older persons may have visual, hearing, or communication difficulties. The pace should be geared to the client's abilities. If visual prompts are used, they should be oversize. The room should be quiet and the interviewer should speak slowly (though not necessarily loudly) and sit so that his/her lips can be observed. Privacy should be arranged; many older persons do not speak as comfortably about matters of bodily function as does the current generation. If the assessment is long, it may need to be broken into component parts so as not to tire the client. Many of these guidelines pertain to clinical encounters with the elderly as well as with initial assessment. Besdine (1982) provides an excellent review of the physical conditions that promote a good diagnostic enccunter with an older person.

Sometimes the very language of the instrument is inappropriate to the age group or the cultural cohort. Psychological jargon has crept into the general language, but it is not familiar to older persons. Even concepts like "service" may be unfamiliar to a large number of elderly middle-class respondents, whereas they could readily describe help that they needed or received. Some words are unsuited to many older ears. In our own work in nursing home assessments, we needed to change the word "anxious" to "tense" because the former was heard as "ancient." Similarly, we had to reword a question about satisfaction with the word "residence" because it sounded as though we were inquiring about satisfaction with the other "residents."

CRITERIA FOR AN ASSESSMENT TOOL

The nine areas of multidimensional assessment pose an enormous challenge. Somehow the assessment, with the help of standardized tools, needs to be streamlined and organized so that it generates accurate, useful information with relative speed. Several criteria should be considered in choosing and using an assessment tool.

RELIABILITY

Reliability simply means that, in the absence of real change, repeated assessments will yield the same results. Factors that may make assessment of the elderly unreliable include changes in the way an assessment is done from one assessor to the next (interrater reliability) or from one time to the next (interrater or intertemporal reliability). In programs serving the elderly, the whole staff must speak the same language, and it is imperative that they use uniform definitions and approaches for their assessment. Merely using a standard instrument does not assure reliability, especially if each worker rates abstract factors like depression, social support, or self-concept according to personally developed criteria. Few assessment tools for the elderly have undergone rigorous tests of reliability (Kane and Kane 1981; Mangen and Peterson 1982).

VALIDITY

Validity is the ability of the instrument to measure what it sets out to measure. Reliability is necessary but not sufficient for validity. A false bathroom scale, for example, can yield 100 percent reliability but 100 percent inaccurate results. Similarly, all nurses aides might in good faith agree that a client was incapable of self-care, but their rating could be invalid. Some factors that affect the validity of a measure are the opportunity for raters to make observations, the anxiety of the person being assessed, or the familiarity of the testing environment. A client may be incapable of self-care in a hospital, but that test may not validly reflect his abilities when at home with familiar surroundings and equipment. Because physical, mental, and social factors are so intertwined in the elderly, an effort to measure one component may be rendered invalid by one or more of the others. For example, a tool to measure cognitive impairment may produce a poor score, but actually the individual's physical status (e.g., deafness) may have produced the result. Finally, many scale are used to measure abstract aspects of well-being in the elderly, and those scales may not be valid reflections of the dimension being measured. The social worker should always go back to the actual questions used to measure an abstraction (say, social isolation, loneliness, or family burden) and see if, at least on the face of it, the measure seems to tap all aspects of the phenomenon.

SUITED TO POPULATION

Assessment procedures must be appropriate for measuring change in the particular population being assessed. Some tools will fail to pick up changes that have great meaning for better or worse for clients already substantially impaired because the instrument is not calibrated finely enough. For example, a community planner might find it sufficient to divide people into those who are not bedbound, but the person who is bedbound experiences great differences in quality of life, depending on his/her ability to sit up and move in bed. Similarly, on social dimensions, instruments used in nursing homes should be able to pick up finer nuances of differences at the lower end of the functional spectrum than those used, for example, in a multipurpose senior center.

Because the elderly population is so diverse, many agencies will need the capacity to assess persons with wide-ranging functional abilities. (This is particularly true of one-stop assessment centers.) "Branching techniques" should be developed so that, on the basis of a particular response or observation, the assessor eliminates some procedures and turns to others. It is frustrating and embarrassing for people if they are asked to perform procedures that are obviously difficult or too simple. It is also time consuming to go through elaborate processes to prove the obvious.

PRACTICAL

Assessment procedures should be comfortable for the assessor to use and the client to undergo. Questions should be ordered to fit clinical criteria about interview flow. As much as possible, expensive equipment should be eliminated and instruments developed that can be used by persons without extensive professional training.

In developing practical approaches, the assessor should not underestimate the ability of the older person himself to make systematic observations. For screening and monitoring, the older person is an important aide. Generally speaking, no one has better opportunity or more motivation to make the observation. (The latter point is tempered somewhat by the human tendency to prevaricate to protect a status or benefit or to prevent a feared outcome such as being sent to a nursing home.) The ability of paraprofessional aides (e.g., homemaker/home health aides or nursing home attendants) to make important observations should also not be discounted. Such personnel need to know what to look for, when, how often, and why. They also need to be provided with convenient formats for recording that recognize the minimal literacy in the English language for many such personnel.

FUTURE PROSPECTS

Comprehensive multidimensional assessments of the elderly, complete with standardized questions, subscales, and scoring systems, clearly are becoming a fixture in health and social service delivery for the frail elderly. As we have seen, a plethora of individual scales are available to measure specific aspects of functioning and well-being. There are also a large number of assessment batteries that combine individual scales in various ways. Some of the latter form the basis for data systems that permit monitoring the effectiveness and costs of service systems for the frail elderly.

Practitioners and program developers have become quite familiar with comprehensive assessments and, if not enthusiastic, at least reconciled to their use. Many leaders still engage in a wistful search for the single "best instrument," but there is a growing recognition that no single tool will serve for all purposes and, conversely, many tools can work for the same purpose. Moreover the magical thinking of the early 1980s, that is, the expectation that assessments alone would help the elderly, is giving way to a salutory recognition that assessments are useful only if they help organize actions.

Thus the 1990s can be expected to usher in a new era in comprehensive assessments, an era that gives greater attention to developing information systems to guide service delivery and monitor its quality in a proactive way. Computer technology will be an important element in this capacity, but no hardware or software can replace sound choice of data elements worth collecting and feedback mechanisms to ensure that the information gets back to the right people at the right time in usable forms.

Some formidable but possible challenges lie ahead. One is a relatively narrow matter of measurement development, and the other two relate to information systems.

On the measurement front, more attention must be given to development and consistent use of measures of psychological and social well-being. There has been consistent attention over a twenty-year period to the challenges of measuring activities of daily living (ADL). By now, ADL is routinely incorporated into medical and social service records and has been used as an outcome for scores of demonstration projects. There is wide consensus about the tasks that are part of an ADL scale and, despite differences in nuances, most authorities go about measuring ADL in about the same way. Social well-being and psychological well-being, in contrast, have been measured sporadically and inconsistently, and many authorities tend to dismiss these elements as important but essentially unmeasurable. Those who believe that genuine differences in social and emotional well-being can be attributed to the programs we develop will need to invest in the development and the consistent use of these measures in studies and operational programs.

The challenges of information systems are twofold. First, as already indicated, information systems need to be developed that are actually *used* to inform service plans. Sometimes fewer data elements are better, if the tradeoff is between a large information system where output is irregular and late and a lean system that produces regular information to those who actually give care. Second, and of critical importance, is the development of assessments that generate data permitting case managers and others to track a client who uses multiple kinds of services over time, as well as compare characteristics and results of users of different services. We must strive to identify and use measures that are appropriate regardless of whether the client is receiving home care, day care, nursing home care, or some other type of service. If each service sector has its own incompatible information system, it becomes impossible to really describe the effects of services overall. Moreover, we have begun to understand that individual clients use different service packages over time, and even a nursing home stay does not represent "the end of the line" for many clients, but rather a phase of care. A major challenge for the future is to make sure that the comprehensive multidimensional assessment moves with the client and does not become a parochial feature of individual service programs.

REFERENCES

American Psychiatric Associations. 1980. *Diagnostic and Statistical Manual of Mental Disorders.* 3d ed. Washington, D.C.: APA.

Beck, A. T., C. H. Ward, M. Mendelson, J. Mock, and J. Erbaugh. 1961. An inventory for measuring depression. *Archives of General Psychiatry* 4:53–63.

Bergner, M., R. A. Bobbitt, S. Kressel, W. E. Pollard, B. S. Gilson, and J. R. Morris. 1976. The Sickness Impact Profile: Conceptual formulation and methodology for the development of a health status measure. *International Journal of Health Services* 6:393–415.

Besdine, R. 1982. The data base of geriatric medicine. In J. W. Rowe and R. Besdine, eds. *Health and Disease in Old Age,* Boston: Little, Brown.

Birren, J. E. and R. B. Sloane, eds. 1980. *Handbook of Mental Health and Aging.* Englewood Cliffs, N.J.: Prentice-Hall.

Carp, F. M. and A. Carp. 1982. The ideal residential area. *Research on Aging* 4:411–439.

Consensus Development Panel, D. Solomon, Chairman. 1988. National Institutes of Health Consensus Development Conference Statement: Geriatric Assessment Methods for Clinical Decision-Making. *Journal of the American Geriatric Society,* 36:342–347.

Dohrenwend, B. P., B. S. Dohrenwend, M. S. Gould, B. Link, R. Neugehauer, and R. Wunsch-Hitzig. 1980. *Mental Illness in the United States: Epidemiological Estimates.* New York: Praeger.

Duke University. 1978. Center for the Study of Aging and Human Development. *Multidimensional Functional Assessment: The OARS Methodology.* Durham, N.C. Duke University.

Duke University 1988. Center for the Study of Aging and Human Development. Gerda G. Fillenbaum, ed., *Multidimensional functional assessment of older adults.* Hilldale, N.J.: Lawrence Erlbaum Associates.

Dye, C. J. 1982a. Personality. In D. J. Mangen and W. A. Peterson, eds., *Research Instruments in Social Gerontology.* vol. 1: *Clinical and Social Psychology.* Minneapolis; University of Minnesota Press.

Fillenbaum, G. G. 1988. *Multidimensional Functional Assessment of Older Adults: The Duke Older American Resources & Services Procedures,* Hillsdale, N.J.: Lawrence Erlbaum Associates.

Folstein, M. F. and P. R. McHugh. 1975. Mini-mental state: A practical method for grading the cognitive state of patients for the clinician. *Journal of Psychiatric Research* 12:189–198.

Gallagher, D., L. W. Thompson, and S. M. Levy. 1980. Clinical psychological assessment for older adults. In L. Poor, ed., *Aging in the 1980s: Selected Contemporary Issues in the Psychology of Aging.* Washington, D.C.: American Psychological Association.

Garcia, C. A., M. J. Redding, and F. P. Blass. 1981. Overdiagnosis of dementia. *Journal of the American Geriatric Society* 29:407–410.

George, L. K. and G. G. Fillenbaum. 1985. OARS methodology: a decade of experience in geriatric assessment. *Journal of the American Geriatric Society* 33:607–615.

Gurland, B. J., L. L. Dean, J. Copeland, R. Gurland, and R. Golden. 1982. Criteria for the diagnosis of dementia in the community elderly. *The Gerontologist* 22:180–186.

Gurland, B. J., L. Dean, R. Gurland, and D. Cook. 1978. Personal time dependency in the elderly of New York City: Findings from the U.S.–U.K. cross-national geriatric community study. In Community Council of Greater New York, *Dependency in the Elderly of New York City: Policy and Service Implications of the US-UK Cross-National Geriatric Community Study.* New York: Community Council of Greater New York.

Gurland, B., J. Kuriansky, L. Sharpe, R. Simon, P. Stiller, and P. Birkett. 1977–78. The Comprehensive Assessment and Referral Evaluation (CARE): Rationale, development, and reliability. *International Journal of Aging and Development* 8:9–42.

Havighurst, R. J., B. L. Neugarten, and S. S. Tobin. 1961. The measurement of life satisfaction. *Journal of Gerontology* 16:134–143.

Health Care Financing Administration. 1988. Development of a Resident Assessment System and Data Base for Nursing Home Care. RFP-HCFA-88-039/EE.

Israel, L., D. Kozerevic, and N. Sartorius. 1984. *Source Book of Geriatric Assessment.* (English edition ed. A. Gilmore). Basel and New York: Karger AG.

Jones, E., B. McNitt, and E. McKnight. 1974. *Patient classification for long-term care: User's manual.* (HRA 75-3107) Washington, D.C.: GPO.

L. A. Jorgenson, and R. L. Kane. 1976. Social work in the nursing home: A need and an opportunity. *Social Work in Health Care* 1:471–482.

Kane, R. A. and R. L. Kane. 1981. *Assessing the Elderly: A Practical Guide to Measurement.* Lexington, Mass.: D.C. Heath.

Kane, R. A. and R. L. Kane. 1987. *Long-term Care: Principles, Programs, and Policies.* New York: Springer.

Kane, R. A., R. L. Kane, D. Kleffel, R. H. Brook, C. Eby, G. A. Goldenburg, L. Z. Rubenstein, and J. Van Ryzin. 1979. *The PSRO and the Nursing Home.* Vol. 1: *An Assessment of PSRO Long-Term Care Review.* Santa Monica, Calif.: Rand Corporation.

Kane, R. L. and R. A. Kane. 1982. *Values and Long-Term Care.* Lexington, Mass.: D.C. Health.

Kane, R. A., R. L. Kane, and L. Z. Rubenstein. (in press). Comprehensive assessment of the elderly patient. In M. D. Petersen and D. L. White, eds., *Health Care for the Elderly: An Information Sourcebook.* Newbury Park, Calif.: Sage., Inc.

Kane, R. L., R. Bell, S. Z. Reigler, A. Wilson, and R. A. Kane. 1983a. Assessing the outcomes of nursing home patients. *Journal of Gerontology* 38:385–393.

Kane, R. L., R. Bell, S. Z. Reigler, A. Wilson, and E. Keeler. 1983b. Predicting the outcomes of nursing-home patients. *The Gerontologist* 23:200–206.

Kane, R. L., J. G. Ouslander, and I. Abrass. 1984. *A Manual of Geriatric Medicine.* New York: McGraw-Hill.

Kulys, R. and S. S. Tobin. 1980. Older people and their "responsible others". *Social Work* 25:139–145.

Kuriansky, J. B., B. J. Gurland, J. L. Fleiss, and D. W. Cowan. 1976. The assessment of self-care capacity in geriatric psychiatric patients. *Journal of Clinical Psychology* 32:95–102.

Laufer, E. A. and W. S. Laufer. 1982. From geriatric resident to language professor: A new program using the talents of the elderly in a skilled nursing facility. *The Gerontologist* 22:551–554.

Lawton, M. P. 1972. The dimensions of morale. In D. Kent, R. Kastenbaum, and S. Sherwood, eds., *Research, Planning and Action for the Elderly.* New York: Behavioral Publications.

Lawton, M. P., W. M. Whelihan, and J. K. Belsky. 1980. Personality tests and their uses with older adults. In J. E. Birren and R. B. Sloane, eds., *Handbook of Mental Health and Aging.* Englewood Cliffs, N. J.: Prentice-Hall.

Lawton, M. P. 1972. The dimensions of morale. In D. Kent, R. Kastenbaum, and S. Sherwood, eds., *Research, Planning, and Action for the Elderly.* New York: Behavioral Publications.

Lubben, J. E. 1988. Assessing social networks among elderly populations. *Family and Community Health* 11:42–52.

Mangen, D. J. and W. A. Peterson, eds. 1982. *Research instruments in social gerontology*, Vol. 1: *Clinical and Social Psychology*. Minneapolis: University of Minnesota Press.

Miller, E. 1980. Cognitive assessment of the older adult. In J. E. Birren and R. B. Sloan, eds., *Handbook on Mental Health and Aging*. Englewood Cliffs, N.J.: Prentice-Hall.

Montgomery, R. J., D. E. Stull, and E. F. Borgatta. 1985. Measurement and the analysis of burden. *Research on Aging* 7:137–152.

Mossey, J. M. and E. Shapiro. 1982. Self-rated health: a predictor of mortality among the elderly. *American Journal of Public Health* 72(8):800–808.

Post, F. 1980. Paranoid, schizophrenia-like, and schizophrenic states in the aged. In J. E. Birren and R. B. Sloane, eds., *Handbook of Mental Health and Aging*. Englewood Cliffs, N. J.: Prentice-Hall.

Robinson, B. 1983. Validation of a caregiver strain index. *Journal of Gerontology* 38:344–348.

Rubenstein, L. Z., I. B. Abrass, and R. L. Kane. 1981. Improved patient care on a new geriatric evaluation unit. *Journal of the American Geriatric Society* 29:531–536.

Salzman, C. and R. I. Shader. 1979. Clinical evaluation of depression in the elderly. In A. Raskin and L. F. Jarvik, eds., *Psychiatric Symptoms and Cognitive loss in the elderly: Evaluation and assessment techniques*. Washington, D.C.: Hemisphere Publishing Corporation.

Sloane, R. B. 1980. Organic brain syndrome. In J. E. Birren and R. B. Sloane, eds., *Handbook of Mental Health and Aging*. Englewood Cliffs, N.J.: Prentice Hall.

Solomon, D. 1988. Geriatric assessment: methods for clinical decision making. *Journal of the American Medical Association* 259:2450–2452.

Task Panel Reports Submitted to the Presidents Commission on Mental Health, 1978. Washington, D. C.: GPO.

U.S. Comptroller General. 1977. *The Well-Being of Older People in Cleveland, Ohio*. Washington, D.C.: GPO.

U.S. Congress. (1986). Omnibus Budget Reconciliation Act, Section 9305.

U.S. Department of Health, Education and Welfare. 1978. *Working Document on Patient Care Management: Theory to Practice*. Washington, D.C.: GPO.

Windley, P. G. 1982. Environments. In D. J. Mangen and W. A. Peterson, eds., *Research Instruments in Social Gerontology*. Vol. 1: *Clinical and Social Psychology*. Minneapolis: University of Minnesota Press.

Zung, W. W. K. 1965. A self-rating depression scale. *Archives of General Psychiatry* 12:63–70.

Zarit, S. H., K. E. Reever, and J. M. Bach-Peterson. 1980. Relatives of the impaired elderly: correlates of feelings of burden. *The Gerontologist* 20:649–55.

4

Case Management: Connecting Older Persons with Services

MONIKA WHITE, PH.D.
Huntington Memorial Hospital, Pasadena

RAYMOND M. STEINBERG, D.S.W.
University of Southern California, Los Angeles

How do older people and their families find their way to the vast array of programs and services such as those described elsewhere in this handbook? How does the complex and often overloaded service system reach out and facilitate the search for help with problems, in maintaining independence and in enriching the quality of life? This paper addresses access points and interventions aimed at making connections between those who need services and the services and entitlements that are most appropriate to their needs. The focus is on case management, which has emerged in the 1980s as a primary means of assisting older persons and their families to obtain resources.

NEED

Since the 1960s, special programs for chronically ill or impaired older persons have been implemented. Most states and localities have established formal and informal services and linkages to respond to their older populations. The array of services can be staggering: nursing home, acute care, medical, health, mental health, emergency response systems, social, rehabilitation, residential, legal, financial, employment, home health care, meals, day care, transportation, respite care, homemaker, escort and shopping, personal care, friendly visiting and telephone reassurance. Services such as these comprise the long-term care "system."

In spite of large numbers of programs in each locality that purport to link clients to services and to coordinate service delivery, the need for assistance in accessing the long-term care system remains largely unmet (Koff 1988; Steinberg and Carter 1983; Palmer 1985; Oriol 1985; Kapp, Pies, and Doudera 1986; Austin 1987). Many older persons are not connecting at all with services they need. Some find partial or incoherent combinations of services, and others receive services that, at best, fail to address their most important problems or, at worst, have harmful effects on their well-being. While some deficiencies result from gaps in the availability and ineffectiveness of services, many of the problems can be traced to mismatches between persons and services. Case management, i.e., working at the client, program, and system levels, seeks to achieve appropriateness in fit between needs and services.

Case management has become a major intervention that not only connects those who seek service but, through coordination and advocacy activities, also serves to broaden public awareness about problems and remedies, monitors effective service delivery, assists agencies in reaching or working with hard-to-serve clients, and documents needs for improving the community's service delivery system. Clearly, the need for case management would become unnecessary if a rational, coordinated and easily accessible system of services was in place. But, with the trend to care for the elderly needing long-term care through community-based, rather than institutional services, it has become increasingly difficult to locate needed services without a knowledgeable person to function as an expert guide.

There are a number of reasons why older people do not find nor receive appropriate services:

- few people are aware of noninstitutional service options;
- services are usually sought out at a point of crisis when neither the client nor the family is in a condition to engage in consumer research;
- many problems and needs are a first-time experience—there is no basis for comparison of services or providers;
- few of the elderly or their families know where to find competent help or reliable information;

- many people turn to their physicians, ministers, neighbors, or others who are also uninformed about service options;
- most of the elderly have little understanding of their entitlements or knowledge of eligibility regulations for programs and services;
- many elderly resist or refuse help when it is offered and/or deny problems even in the face of great hardship;
- many elderly fear that a call for help will result in institutionalization;
- many needy elderly or caregivers are unaware that they may be able to receive help in their own homes;
- most elderly and their families are unprepared for the care needs that may arise with advancing age;
- many elderly and/or their families "over-solve" problems, using expensive and often inappropriate services without ever seeking alternatives;

While case management is just one type of linking mechanism, it is seen by some to be a "panacea to improve health and human services by making them more accessible" (Kane 1988: 5). The fact that case management is now offered in virtually every kind of human services setting speaks for its success as a problem-solving and coordinating function (see Grisham, White, and Miller 1983).

INTERVENTIONS

In addition to case management, there is a wide spectrum of ways by which agencies attempt to connect the people who need services with appropriate programs. Table 4.1 summarizes the types and purposes of some of these linkage programs and activities briefly described below.

Information Campaigns/Special Events

There are several strategies used by agencies to build public awareness of their functions. Human-interest stories in newspapers and TV interviews or documentaries usually result in new requests for information and services. Other strategies include utilization of existing resources in the community such as utility company newsletters and speakers bureaus (Cardwell 1988). Some agencies produce a resource directory for distribution to consumers and professionals as a way of providing information about services. Often, special events, such as a health fair, are held to attract older persons. While such activities may not identify new clients, they do provide an opportunity for face-to-face interactions.

Outreach/Personal and Telephone Friendly Visiting

The term "outreach" may refer to a number of different activities, but it most commonly means that someone goes into the community to introduce potential clients to services, usually at gatherings of seniors. Agencies also use outreach to indicate any ongoing or follow-up contact with clients that is made at locations outside of the agency site. A popular activity of this type is friendly visiting, which provides a personal interaction for homebound seniors. Another form of this is

TABLE 4.1. Linking Interventions: Types and Purposes

Type	*Purpose*
Information campaigns/special events	Educate; publicize; inform market
Outreach/personal and telephone friendly visiting	Promote participation; offer services; establish personal contacts; follow up on services, provide social interaction
Information and referral	Inform; explain services; answer questions; help identify problems; direct to resources
Special case advocacy	Obtain fair share of resources; lobby; mediate in grievances
Client tracking systems	Inventory of clients; service utilization; share information with other agencies
Assessment centers	Complete physiological, psychological, neurological work-up; clarify level of care needs, refer
Case management	Identify problems; plan care; provide options; coordinate/arrange service delivery; monitor utilization/client status

telephone reassurance, where the older person receives a phone call on a regular basis.

Information and Referral

Information and Referral (I & R) services are available in most communities, often at senior centers. They specialize in maintaining up-to-date inventories of available services in their areas to facilitate speedy responses to telephone requests. Responses to I & R requests may range from giving a name, location, and telephone number of an agency to conducting a brief assessment prior to directing the caller to appropriate resources. Sometimes there are formal referral agreements between agencies to facilitate access to each other's services.

Special Case Advocacy

Some programs have been established to serve populations with special needs to assure that clients receive their share of resources. Often, such programs handle grievances about quality of care or denial of service. Included in these client groups would be elderly persons who are deaf, blind, minority, isolated, mentally ill, retired members of a union or residents in care facilities. For example, ombudsmen who troubleshoot grievances of nursing home residents are now established in every state (U.S. AoA 1982). The role of the advocate is to help the client get what is wanted, not necessarily to assess other needs or alternatives.

Client Tracking Systems

In most programs using a client tracking system, the purpose is to record, monitor, and report about the clients being served and their utilization of the services. To the extent that such systems permit the identification of unmet service needs, they do enhance access by highlighting gaps in services, excessive delays in response times and high-cost care (Steinberg and Carter 1983). Most programs now utilize some form of computerized tracking of clients and services which enhances information exchange between agencies where appropriate. Such information is also critical to research projects which help to shape future programs.

Assessment Centers

A relatively new modality in the care of the elderly is comprehensive geriatric assessment centers, especially as a free-standing service. Such centers are viewed as having no vested interest in the diagnosis, hence are trusted to bring extra skills and objectivity to the process. By performing complete physical, neurological and psychological evaluations, they assist in planning the most suitable care and prevent inappropriate service utilization because of misdiagnosis. Some centers do assume responsibility for linking patients to case management programs or service providers for follow up (Hageboeck 1981). With the exception of the Veteran's Administration which has developed comprehensive assessment units, assessment centers have not yet become major entry points to the long-term care system (Koff 1982: 52).

CASE MANAGEMENT

Case management is a valuable and versatile approach to meeting the service needs of the homebound elderly and other persons with complex situations that place them at risk of institutionalization. Case management can be defined in many ways because it is practiced with so much variation. While the setting, staffing, funding, targeting and duration of service vary considerably, the core activities of case management remain constant: they are case-finding, assessment, care planning, service coordination, monitoring and reassessment (White 1987). Although there is no consistant data to substantiate exactly what the impact of case management has been on long-term care costs, it has been—and continues to be—used in both public and private programs and practice.

Case Management in Public Programs

Throughout the 1970s and 1980s, the public sector has taken an active role in testing and developing programs for the elderly. While the major impetus has been cost savings, a large number of individuals has been able to remain in less restrictive environments because of them. The focus of these programs is on reaching the appropriate target groups. An additional benefit has been the outreach and access efforts that have accompanied the program development. Almost all of them utilize case management. Table 4.2 summarizes the types and purposes of some of the major public programs discussed below:

MEDICARE/MEDICAID WAIVERS

Since the early 1970s, waivers to Medicare and Medicaid have been given to states by the Health Care Finance Administration (HCFA). Rules are waived to permit greater flexibility in eligibility criteria, allowable reimbursements, and expanded services in the interest of demonstrating cost effectiveness of nursing home alternatives. The most significant of these waivers is the Medicaid waiver enacted in the 1981 Omnibus Budget Reconciliation Act. Known as the Section 2176 waiver, states used it to develop statewide programs for poor, frail elderly that substituted community services for nursing home care (see Kane 1984; Hamm, Kickham, and Cutler 1985; Oriol 1985). To date, almost every state has applied for the waiver and all but a small percentage of them include case management to locate, coordinate, and monitor services.

These programs operate within many settings including hospitals,

TABLE 4.2. Public Programs Using Case Management: Type and Purpose

Type	*Purpose*
Medicare/Medicaid waivers	Cost effective community-based care as alternative to institutionalization for targeted groups
Pre-admission screening	Determine appropriate target for placement; divert, find service alternatives
State LTC programs	Special programs designed to respond to statewide needs and populations
Area Agencies on Aging	Planning/coordination within specific localities; information & referral
Channeling demonstrations	Testing of referral and purchase models of coordinated service delivery
S/HMO (social/health maintenance organizations)	Pre-paid, capitated insurance for health and supportive services; cost containment

area agencies on aging, county or state human services departments, family services and other health and social service agencies. In order to achieve the goal of cost effective alternatives by serving the appropriate target groups, the programs developed outreach and referral systems and a variety of contractual agreements. Such targeting efforts have greatly enhanced access to services for this population.

PRE-ADMISSION SCREENING PROGRAMS

Screening of nursing home applicants is another way of assuring that only those who are appropriate for this level of care are placed. Others are diverted to community care. Most states have some form of pre-admission screening program with varying success. Issues have emerged in some states regarding who makes the placement determination; hospital discharge planners, medicaid field office, or special agencies. Another issue is that pre-admission screening has not been applicable to private pay applicants. Cost savings in these programs is closely associated with targeting. As Kane notes, savings may be realized not by identifying those who are inappropriate for nursing home placement, but by diverting those who are (1984:14). This represents another setting that can serve to connect frail elderly to community care systems.

STATE LONG-TERM CARE PROGRAMS

In addition to the waiver programs noted above, states are establishing special programs to address the needs of their local elderly. Many of these programs include case management as a method of addressing the need to access long term care services. California, for example, has established a Department of Aging which administers statewide programs providing coordinated care for younger disabled and elderly at risk of institutionalization, adult day care, and Alzheimer's resource centers. Austin (1987) compared case management programs in four Northwestern states (Washington, Oregon, Idaho and Alaska), and found that they varied greatly in their targeting, financing, and organizational auspice, but all were aimed at dealing with services fragmentation. Massachusetts has one of the oldest long-term care programs and has committed sizable state funds to community care programs including housing, respite care and home care (Oriol 1985:157). These are only a few examples of the types of state programs currently in operation.

AREA AGENCIES ON AGING

Area Agencies on Aging (AAA) were mandated through the Older Americans Act. The AAAs, along with the State Units on Aging, form the "only national system of community-based agencies focused solely on the needs of elders" (Austin 1988:9). Through these planning and coordinating entities, a nationwide network of nutrition, information and referral, legal services and nursing home ombudsmen were established. Some offer case management, but most encourage or provide financial support for senior centers or other agencies to provide it. All of the approximate 800 AAAs in the United States direct considerable attention to connecting older persons with resources, including many of the types of linkages programs described earlier.

CHANNELING PROGRAMS

The National Long-Term Care Channeling Demonstration was designed to test community care through case management to contain costs for long-term care services. Two different models were implemented: one "basic" model which provided case managers whose primary function was to fully utilize individual and family resources before linking the client to the formal service system; the other, a "complex" model which operated with a full range of waivers, expanded service coverage; financial control, case management authority, and a cap on service expenditures (Kane 1984:16). The outcomes from the ten-site demonstrations were that cost savings were not realized but unmet needs were met, life satisfaction was improved for both the clients and their families; and home care services were increased (see Kemper et al. 1986). It remains to be seen whether the benefits will be considered to outweigh the costs of achieving them, but the models did strengthen access to a range of long-term care services.

SHMO (SOCIAL/HEALTH MAINTENANCE ORGANIZATION

The Social Health Maintenance Organization (SHMO), which integrates acute and chronic care on a prepaid, capitated basis, was implemented in 1985 as a demonstration. The project expands coverage of community, nursing home and hospital care for Medicare beneficiaries through monthly premiums paid by a combination of Medicare, Medicaid and the enrollees, themselves. Case management is an integral part of the SHMO design. While referrals are made by medical staff and other health care professionals, it is the case managers who determine eligibility and authorize services. Among the many questions being studied is exactly how to determine eligibility and then identify individuals who meet those criteria (Leutz et al. 1988). The experience and outcomes at the four SHMO sites (Elderplan, Brooklyn, N.Y.; Kaiser Permanente, Portland, Oreg.; SCAN Health Plan, Long Beach, Calif.; and Seniors Plus, Minneapolis), are likely to influence the formulation and development of future long-term care programs.

While on-going public funding is always questionable, efforts to address long-term care problems continue. And, although there is as yet no conclusive evidence of cost reductions as originally hoped, case management dominates the methods for linking clients and services in new program planning and implementation. Both the public and private sectors are expanding the use of case management in a widening circle of settings, thus improving the chances of access to and appropriate utilization of, the long-term care system.

Case Management in the Private Sector

Table 4.3 summarizes the types and purposes of case management programs in private sectors. The adoption of case management across such a wide range of settings has helped many individuals and families access services not available to them through public sources. In order to facilitate access, many of these programs are designed to be available where potential clients or their families will normally spend some of their time. This enhances the prospect of exposure to, and utilization of, the service.

HOSPITAL-BASED PROGRAMS

The acute care system is most likely to see more elderly than any other, and is a natural access point to the long-term care system. Nationally, the average hospital census is 40 percent Medicare. While managed care programs that coordinate care and monitor costs within the hospital are quite common, DRGs (diagnostically related groups which pre-set reimbursement for specific procedures) have led to increased concerns over length of stay and safe discharges. Many hospitals are now developing programs to follow patients beyond the discharge plan, to assure continuity of care and to avoid inappropriate readmissions. In these programs, medical social workers, discharge planners and case managers coordinate their distinct functions to assist patients and their families in leaving the hospital on a safe, timely and cost effective basis and accessing the most appropriate post-hospital care (see Simmons and White 1988). Physicians and other health care professionals are ideal referral sources to case management programs.

LEGAL-BASED PROGRAMS

Because of the legal complexities involved in protecting both the person and the person's estate, the legal community is closely tied to issues of aging. In addition to relationships with private attorneys in establishing trusts and wills, individuals and families often interact with legal entities through probate courts in conservatorships. Case management programs as well as private practitioners are forging new partnerships in this arena. Judges, attorneys, and conservators find the assistance of a case manager invaluable in a number of ways: objective assessments can help in planning suitable care options; linkages to trusted care providers can be made by the case manager who knows the local resources; the older person's health and mental status can be monitored and reported to the appropriate legal authorities. Sometimes, attorneys or conservators themselves can benefit from consultation about the client's condition or in thinking through

TABLE 4.3. Private Programs Using Case Management: Type and Purpose

Type	*Purpose*
Hospital-based programs	Continuity of care; shorter stays; decrease readmits; control quality, costs
Legal-based programs	Adjunct to legal services; protective supervision; conservatorships
Finance-based programs	Adjunct to banking services; estate/financial planning; money management
Insurance-based programs	Control utilization & costs
Corporate/business programs	Assist employed caregivers
Private practice	Individual/group, for-profit practice providing care consultation and coordination for elderly & families on fee basis

placement decisions. In rare cases, a private case management program or individual case manager serves as a conservator as well. Legal (as well as financial) areas related to the elderly are fraught with ethical issues such as consent and voluntary participation (see Kapp, Pies, and Doudera 1986). The relationships between the legal system and the long-term care system represent new access points for the elderly and their families.

FINANCE-BASED PROGRAMS

As with the legal community, financial planners, bank trust officers, and those persons legally responsible for the finances of an older person finds case management helpful. Because they are primarily involved with older persons of considerable means, financial professionals often lack knowledge of public benefits or of the long-term consequences of expensive placements. Again, close working relationships between the financial professional and the case manager can mean expanded options for economically viable care plans.

Many case management programs provide or refer to daily money management services for the poor or near-poor elderly. This is an emerging arena in long-term care that assists older persons who can remain at home but need help with such tasks as bill paying. These, in coordination with other in-home services, can make a great difference in someone's ability to remain independent.

INSURANCE-BASED PROGRAMS

Most insurances that offer a long-term care policy for the elderly provide benefits for nursing home care and limited home care. The current available policies are also very expensive. Rivlin and Weiner (1988) discuss four ways of lowering long-term care insurance prices: 1) reduce benefits; 2) sell to younger individuals; 3) incorporate in employee benefit policies; and 4) combine with health care insurance. A number of insurance companies are now working on expanded benefits, including considerable in-home care, and affordable rates. Many of these companies are hiring "case managers" whose function is to determine eligibility and coordinate benefits for enrollees. Others contract with established case management programs for these services and to facilitate access to community-wide services. The case management component related to long-term care insurance policies and programs will become increasingly critical as more older persons are enrolled and begin to utilize their benefits.

CORPORATE/BUSINESS PROGRAMS

The private corporate and business sectors are concerned about the growing numbers of caregivers in their companies. Several studies have shown that approximately 25 to 30 percent of employees over 40 years old carry significant caregiving responsibilities for an older relative (see Traveler's 1985). Because of their knowledge of resources and the services system, case managers are being invited to participate in employee assistance or personnel department programs to help the caregivers plan and access services for their relatives. Education and informational seminars, caregiver support groups, individual consultation and special caregiver hotlines are being offered to these employed caregivers. The employees during lunch hours. Other models, such as national I & R networks designed especially for employed caregivers are being developed (see Piktialis 1988). Such programs have long-range benefits, since they provide respite for the caregiver as well as assisting the older person. In addition, caregivers are better educated about service access and options for their own futures.

PRIVATE PRACTICE

Private case management on a fee-for-services basis is growing rapidly. Many nonprofit agencies, including family services, senior centers, and hospitals, have developed programs aimed at more affluent elderly or families willing and able to pay for care coordination and access to services. Given the culture of the nonprofit agencies, a number of issues must be addressed in developing fee-based services including marketing, targeting, pricing, billing and staffing (see, for example, Goldis and Chambers 1988). There are now many individuals who are establishing private practice businesses providing case management.

The majority of these private practitioners are master's level social workers, often utilizing a nurse consultant. Some case managers are nurses, gerontologists, or other related professionals. Because case management is such a new service, private practitioners have a more difficult task in reaching clients than agencies which usually have other services or relationships within a community. Thus private case managers must "market" their services much like attorneys, accountants, or therapists. Nonagency practitioners are more flexible in their ability to respond quickly (even after hours and weekends) and to operate without the constraints of regulations and agency procedures. Both agency and nonagency private case managers are proving useful in assisting groups of elderly and their families who have been unable to access service through public sources.

POLICY

Several kinds of trends in the United States are reinforcing the need for case management or other linkage programs. There are broad policy trends reflected in specific pieces of governmental legislation and in comparable changes in approaches of the private sector. The major emphasis in this decade has been, and will continue to be, cost containment of health and social services. The move toward community, rather than institutional, care and the recognition of non-acute, long-term care needs, has led to the development of alternative services that were to be less costly. Though not proven, there is evidence that proper targeting, resource allocation and service management may impact costs. However, if savings are realized (as in some of the Medicaid Waiver programs), they must be shared appropriately, otherwise economic responsibilities will simply be shifted from one entity to another (Lubben 1987:20). At the same time, policymakers are concerned that noninstitutional programs will not decrease the demand for institutional care but will be used in addition, thus significantly increasing long-term care costs (Jette and Branch 1983:54–55).

Cost containment is not only a concern of government but has also commanded the attention of private health insurance companies, employer coalitions, and employee groups that must pay for the insurance. This part of the private sector is watching, and beginning to experiment with, case management approaches that may reduce the length of hospital stays and the overuse of skilled nursing facilities by substituting home care. While these functions are primarily carried by nonprofit agencies supported with public and United Way funds, there is a trend toward proprietary, private practice agencies, and firms in which assessment and service brokerage assistance is provided for a fee.

Cutting across general trends is the rapid ascendency of policies and legislation that directly and indirectly promote the use of case management in behalf of the frail elderly. Among the important benchmarks of this trend have been the Medicare and Medicaid waiver programs, which promoted case-managed alternative services. Since the early 1980s, new bills have been considered for expanding or amending home care so that case management and alternative services can become reimbursable and more widely available.

The same time period has seen policies reflecting a national administration that has reduced programs and services and expects increased individual responsibility (Torres-Gil 1988:5–6). This situation has exacerbated the need and desire for ways to insure care. As we head into the 1990s, the need to insure long-term care continues to be the focus of legislative attention. New public private partnerships, such as the states now testing the development of long-term care insurance with grants from the Robert Wood Johnson Foundation, may represent the future means of partially addressing this area.

Finally, other trends, not necessarily reflected in public policy, deserve mention because they either adversely or favorably affect the development of access assistance and case management programs. One is the general inability to arrive at minimum program standards or practitioner qualifications. In the specific instance of case management, there has been a preeminence of social workers as practitioners and administrators. Two kinds of trends may change the configuration of staffs and relative career opportunities among the professions. First is the emergence of nurses and others in comprehensive assessment and care-planning with the elderly. A new wave of professionals with degrees in gerontology is moving into case management, bridging particular knowledge and skills for working with the elderly. In addition, paraprofessional aides have demonstrated their competence to establish rapport and to deal with instrumental and environmental needs of elders.

A parallel trend in schools of social work was to view case management as a less than professional area of practice (because it minimizes therapeutic counseling and emphasizes functional needs). This was discouraging new recruits; however, there is now great interest on the part of NASW in social work involvement in case management and setting standards for quality, professional coordination. The National Association of Social Workers (NASW) has now developed standards for case management practice. Many social work curricula now incorporate aging content and case management as a service approach.

Meanwhile, the experience of community care organizations has demonstrated that social work skills are highly desirable because of the complexities of working with multiply impaired elderly and their families. Work with these populations has highlighted the importance of dealing with mental health needs and sensitive value preferences as well as service system development. All programs that provide access to information and services call for capabilities in technical assistance to and maintaining interorganizational linkages with a wide range of human service agencies on behalf of individual clients and groups of clients. Thus, competence in community organization and group work, as well as casework, are required. In summary, and in spite of trends to the contrary, quality access assistance and case management demand professional generalists with strong clinical grounding.

THEORY

The spectrum of levels of intervention described here, the diversity of personnel who perform the functions, and the lack of uniformity in the organizational contexts in which they are conducted, all suggest a lack of common theoretical bases. Instead, it is necessary to adapt a wide range of systems, organizational and clinical theories from other fields. Although there is some recent case management literature that discusses these theories and their application, most of it refers to earlier works that still apply (see White 1980; Norman 1985).

There is a body of theory that supports the coexistence in a given community of multiple approaches to access assistance, variability in the structure of programs from community to community, and a variety of responses for different sets of help-seekers. Much of contingency theory has been developed in the analysis of organizations and systems of organizations. Weiner summarized contingency theory as based on two assumptions: there is no one best way to organize and any way of organizing is not equally effective (for all purposes or all environments). He further noted research on administrator or worker style and concluded that "there is no one best way or style far surpassing others in effectiveness" (1978:53).

Relevant theories comparable to organizational contingency theory may be found in social service and clinically oriented literature (Aiken et al. 1975: Kahn 1976). For example, differentiation of worker roles (and program roles within the system) was outlined by Demone (1978) in terms of the change agent, the lobbyist, the ombudsman, the coordinator, and the advocate. Similarly, Demone differentiated approaches to change as consensus, process, collaboration.

There are commonly accepted principles of practice that apply to the many different kinds of programs discussed here: the client's right of self-determination; partializing problems in complex cases; beginning where the client is; and involving all persons who will be affected by any proposed change. Lippett, Watson and Westley (1958) developed a set of generic guidelines based upon numerous helping disciplines at various levels of practice (individual, group, and community). The authors described the phases that lead to "choosing an appropriate helping role" as 1) a diagnostic clarification of the problem; 2) assessment of the client motivation and capacity to change; 3) assessment of the change agent's motivations and resources; and 4) selecting appropriate change objectives. The particular community problems for which a program was established, as well as the particular needs and preferences of individual clients, will influence program design and clinical approaches.

Rothman (1974) summarized the findings from social science research into "generalizations" and formulated "action guidelines" for practitioners. These generalizations have relevance for the programs and statements made earlier:

> Organizations employing indigenous workers are successful in reaching clients who not previously receiving services. (p. 186)
>
> The rate of adoption of an innovation is directly elated to the extent to which it is diffused in a manner compatible with the target system's norms, values, and customs. Innovations with a compatible diffusion process will have a higher adoption rate than innovations with an incompatible diffusion process. (p. 446)
>
> Different client populations prefer different styles of participation. These preferences may change over time. (p. 382)
>
> Different modes of communication are used by different adopters. Relatively early adopters of innovations tend to use mass media information sources whereas later adopters tend to use face-to-face information sources. The rate of adoption of an innovation is related to the degree to which information is passed through the appropriate communication mode. (p. 448)

In the above quotations, the term "adopters of innovation" may be compared with concerns here about assisting older persons to utilize services with which they are unfamiliar. There must not only be a good match between the problem and the solution but also flexibility and sensitivity to adjust to the norm, values, and customs of each client. The above generalizations may also be viewed in the context of introducing a new kind of program (such as a community-care organization) into a community. Not only must the new program take into account preexisting programs, it must also be initiated with the appropriate communication mode (local advocates vs. outside consultants or research reports) and awareness of the norms and customs that prevail in the community.

REFERENCES

Aiken, M. et al. 1975. *Coordinating Human Services.* San Francisco: Jossey-Bass.

Austin, C. 1987. *Improving Access for Elders: The Role of Case Management. Final Report.* Seattle: Institute on Aging, University of Washington.

Austin, C. 1988. History and politics of case management. *Generations* 12(5):7–10.

Cardwell, S. 1988. Marketing: making it work. *Discharge Planning Update* 8(1):12–17.

Demone, H. W. Jr. 1978. *Stimulating Human Services Reform.* Washington: Project Share.

Employee Caregiver Survey. 1985. Hartford, Conn.: The Travelers Companies.

Goldis, L. and R. Chambers. 1988. Development and operation of a private hospital-based case management program. Presented at the American Hospital Association Conference: Revenue Generating Program for Hospital Social Work, San Diego, Calif., September 30, 1988.

Grisham, M., M. White, and L. Miller. 1983. Case Management as a problem-solving strategy. *PRIDE Institute Journal of Long-Term Home Health Care* 2(4):21–28.

Hageboeck, H. 1981. Training the trainers manual: Iowa gerontology model project. Iowa City: University of Iowa.

Hamm, L., T. Kickham, and D. Cutler. 1985. Research demonstrations, and evaluations. In R. Vogel and H. Palmer, eds., *Long-Term Care: Perspectives from Research and Demonstrations.* Rockville, Md.: Aspen.

Jette, A. and L. Branch. 1983. Targeting community services to high-risk elders: Toward preventing long-term care institutionalization. *Prevention in Human Services,* 3(1):53–69.

Kahn, A. J. 1976. Service delivery at the neighborhood level: Experience, theory, and fads. *Social Service Review* 50(1):23–56.

Kane, R. 1984. Case management in long-term care: Background analysis for hospital social work. Chicago, Ill.: American Hospital Association.

Kane, R. 1988. Introduction. *Generations* 12(5):5.

Kapp, M., H. Pies, and A. Doudera, eds. 1985. *Legal and Ethical Aspects of Health Care for the Elderly.* Ann Arbor, Mich.: Health Administration Press.

Kemper, P. et al. 1986. *The Evaluation of the National Long-Term Care Demonstrations: Final Report.* Princeton, N.J.: Mathematica Policy Research.

Koff, T. 1982. *Long-Term Care: An Approach to Serving the Frail Elderly.* Boston: Little, Brown.

Koff, T. 1988. *New Approaches to Health care for an Aging Population: Developing a Continuum of Chronic Care Services.* San Francisco: Jossey-Bass.

Leutz, W. et al. 1988. Targeting expanded care to the aged: Early SHMO experience. *The Gerontologist* 28(1):4–17.

Lippett, R., J. Watson, and B. Westley. 1958. *The Dynamics of Planned Change.* New York: Harcourt, Brace and World.

Lubben, J. 1987. Models for delivering long term care. *Home Health Care Services Quarterly* 8(2):5–22.

Norman, A. 1985. Applying theory to practice: The impact of organizational structure on programs and providers. In M. Weil, J. Karls, et al., eds., *Case Management in Human Service Practice.* San Francisco: Jossey-Bass.

Oriol, W. 1985. *The Complex Cube of Long-Term Care: The Case for Next-Step Solutions—Now.* Washington, D.C.: American Health Planning Association.

Palmer, H. 1985. The system of provision. In R. Vogel and H. Palmer, eds., *Long-Term Care: Perspectives from Research and Demonstrations.* Rockville, Md.: Aspen.

Piktialis, D. 1988. The elder care referral service. *Generations* 12(5):71–72.

Rivlin, A. and J. Weiner. 1988. Caring for the disabled elderly: Why will pay? Washington, D.C.: The Brookings Institution.

Rothman, J. 1974. Planning and organizing for social change: Action principles from social science research. New York: Columbia University Press.

Simmons, W. and M. White. 1988. Case management and discharge planning: Two different worlds. In P. Volland, ed., *Discharge Planning: An Interdisciplinary Approach to Continuity of Care.* Owings Mills, Md.: National Health Publishing.

Steinberg, R. and G. Carter. 1983. *Case Management and the Elderly.* Lexington, Mass.: Lexington Books.

Torres-Gill, F. 1988. Aging for the twenty-first century: Process, politics and policy. *Generations* 12(3):5–9.

U.S. AoA (Administration on Aging). 1982. The long-term care ombudsman program: National summary of state ombudsman reports for FY 1981: Executive summary. Washington, D.C.: U.S. Administration on Aging.

Weiner, M. E. 1978. Application of organization and systems theory to human services reform. Washington, D.C.: Project Share.

White, M. 1980. Toward a conceptual framework for case coordination program design: Lessons from the past, guidelines for the future. PhD dissertation, University of Southern California.

White, M. 1987. Case management. In Maddox et al., eds., *The Encyclopedia of Aging.* New York: Springer.

5

Casework Services

EDMUND SHERMAN, PH.D.
The University at Albany
State University of New York

Today's casework service is characterized by a number of different theoretical orientations and models. This chapter will describe these models and how they have been adapted to work with the elderly. Hopefully, this will serve the purpose of making the content both prescriptive and descriptive for the gerontological practitioner.

OVERVIEW

There are several ways of defining, and in so doing distinguishing, casework from other interventions within the broad arena of service provisions that comprise gerontological practice. Fischer's (1978) identification of casework as the branch of social work "whose defining characteristic is the provision of individualized services" has the virtue of brevity. It also identifies casework as a social work method, which serves to differentiate it from individualized services provided by other professional disciplines. However, in order to serve the purposes of this paper, there is need of a definition or characterization that delineates certain crucial elements in casework practice. Helen Harris Perlman's (1957) characterization of casework seems to do this very well. Essentially, she sees casework as a process of helping people deal with their problems through: 1) the provision of resources; 2) the problem-solving work; and 3) the therapeutic relationship.

It is largely in terms of elements (2) and (3) that one is apt to see differences among the several casework treatments models to be outlined here. There is general agreement in the casework literature on the need for the provision of "hard" and "soft" services. The importance of the linkage, brokerage, and advocacy roles of caseworkers cannot be overestimated when it comes to the reality of practice with older persons, a population with particularly great economic and medical needs. Also it must be distinguished from case management which may include casework but also encompasses the ongoing provision of concrete assistance to the elderly and often, as well, to family caregivers.

Although there have been changes in the relative emphasis on the provision of resources over the years, the major development in casework with the aged have been in the areas of "problem-solving work" and the "therapeutic relationship." These represent, in short, the counseling aspects of casework service. These changes or developments are to a large degree related to changing social work conceptions of aging and work with the aged, as well as to a growing diversification of direct practice orientation and methods in social work generally. Whatever the reasons, these changes have been rather dramatic over the past twenty years.

It should be added quickly that these changes have been largely in terms of approach rather than volume of casework service. Lowy (1985), who has described casework mostly in terms of its counseling function in settings such as family service agencies, public welfare departments, and mental health clinics, noted that only in a minority of cases are such services available to the community aged living in their own homes. The situation is certainly no better in residential settings and institutions such as nursing homes and other long-term care facilities as far as employment of professionally trained caseworkers is concerned (Garner and Mercer 1980). Much of this, of course, is due to attitudes on the part of many social workers about working with the elderly in such settings, a fact which was dramatically highlighted by Kosberg (1973) fifteen years ago and which still holds true to a large extent.

Nevertheless, there have been some important events and changes that have taken place with respect to casework with the elderly and these need to be placed into some kind of historical perspective. They have to do with new theoretical and research perspectives on aging, the call for accountability and evaluation of the effectiveness of services, and above all a changing attitude among social workers. Evidence for this was found by Cormican (1980), who reviewed three traditional social work journals *(Social Casework, Social Service Review,* and *Social Work)* for the five year period from the start of 1970 through 1974. He found a marked change even within that brief span of five years. The findings indicated that social workers began that period with an essentially negative view of aging. They tended to view aging as a process of losses and to emphasize protective services. In the middle of this period a more positive view of aging emerged, with an emphasis on counseling services. By the end of the period there was a recognition of the diversity in the aging process and the need for differential treatment and services. This change in general social work thinking was also reflected in casework in particular.

Casework, especially casework within the context of protective services, had to undergo a wrenching reappraisal in that period as a result of the findings reported by Blenkner, Bloom, and Nielsen (1971) from the research and demonstration project of protective services under the auspices of the Benjamin Rose Institute of Cleveland. The predominant service provided within the project (treatment) group was more intensive casework counseling (provided in 82 percent of those cases), and yet the treatment group demonstrated a higher mortality rate and a higher rate of institutionalization than did the control group. This was one of the eleven controlled studies reviewed by Fischer (1973) in which he came to the conclusion that casework was no more effective than no intervention at all. In fact, the higher mortality and institutionalization in the Cleveland study suggested to him that casework might even be more harmful than no intervention.

Later, using more sophisticated statistical techniques, Berger and Piliavin (1976) reanalyzed the data from the Cleveland study and found that the experimentals were significantly more debilitated and at risk than the controls on the basis of combined age, mental status, and physical functioning *before* treatment. Thus, the difference in survival or mortality rates could not be attributed to the experimental (casework) condition. Although the reanalysis did not account for the higher rate of institutionalization, there was some retrospective reasoning among the professionals involved in the project that institutionalization had been viewed as a legitimate and often appropriate protective service among trained practitioners who preferred not to take the great risks involved in leaving alone many elderly people who wished to continue in their marginal and self-endangering way of life (Wasser 1971). In addition, a similar study which was somewhat more advanced in terms of research methodology was conducted in England, and it showed markedly different findings (Goldberg 1970). The special project groups, which also had casework as the core of service delivery, showed significantly more positive measures of morale, activity level, and social need, with no higher rates of mortality or institutionalization.

Nevertheless, the findings of the Cleveland study brought about a great deal of soul searching and reappraisal through the 1970s concerning the role of casework in protective services, the status and use of institutional care within the spectrum of service, and the need for more accountability and demonstration of the effectiveness of casework services.

These developments combined with the changing views of aging and the emergence of different theoretical orientations toward casework practice have made for a much more diversified range of services and approaches in the casework repertoire of the 1980s.

The casework treatment models to be presented here represent the dominant ones in social work with the elderly at the present time. Some are much more indigenous to social work than others, some are more recent than others, and some are more prevalent and appropriate in particular kinds of practice settings and with particular problems of aging. One major factor in differential use is the community/institution dimension. Casework approaches, even within the same theoretical orientations, can vary in important respects in work with aged clients in institutional settings as opposed to work with clients in their own homes.

As noted earlier the major differences in the models to be presented are with respect to the problem-solving work and the therapeutic relationship, particularly with respect to the nature and the objectives of these two elements of casework. In a sense, then, each model can be viewed as prescriptive for the application of particular treatment procedures and techniques within its own frame of reference so practitioner-readers with a strong single theoretical preference can use it that way. At the same time it should be apparent to the reader that there is a great deal of commonality among the models in terms of actual skills, techniques, and methods used in practice with respect to certain kinds of problems. In fact, there appears to be much convergence occurring in actual practice. Where these convergences and commonalities occur it will be noted in the course of presenting each model.

However, it is also evident that the different treatment models can represent *alternative* ways of approaching the same problem and that certain of these alternatives have been found to be more appropriate and/or effective in dealing with the problem. Furthermore, it is also evident that approaches and techniques from different models can *complement* one another and can be used very effectively in conjunction with one another. The implications of these points will be considered later under "Future Directions."

TREATMENT MODELS

The Psychodynamic Model

This has been perhaps the most influential model for the longest period of time with respect to casework with the aging. It is largely Freudian and psychoanalytic in its theoretical origins, and it is represented to a large extent in the psychosocial casework theory of Florence Hollis (1972) and more recently Francis Turner (1986). The first and most complete explication of this model for work with older persons was done by Edna Wasser in *Creative Approaches to Casework with the Aging* (1966).

Essentially, this model incorporates concepts from ego psychology with respect to adaptation (Hartmann 1958), as well as Erikson's (1963) developmental tasks and psychosocial crises. When applied to the elderly, this ego psychological framework provides a particular perspective which has been concisely summed up as follows: "The aged person is constantly making an adaptation to his environment in minor as well as major ways. Indeed, it is in the later years that losses and changes are most likely to occur, when the individual has less psychic and physical energy to deal with crises and maintain equilibrium. A breakdown may be manifested in regressive behavior; there may be a breakdown of instincutal drives and disturbances in the executive functions of the ego" (Wasser 1966:17).

This brief quote incorporates a number of key ideas which very much influence both assessment and intervention. Foremost is the concept of loss, and the specific ego problem is one of coping with progressive losses: physical, financial, and social status, and above all loss of significant object relations, which leads to loss of cathexis and its resultant impoverishment of ego. This has been referred to as "depletion," which can have profound emotional effects from lowered self-esteem and guilt to depression and despair. There are therefore attempts at "restitution," which might include rather regressive adaptations on the part of the ego. Stanley Cath's (1963) psychological construct of depletion-restitution balance is central to this model. Essentially, the construct holds that efforts to strike a balance between external and internal depleting and restorative forces go on throughout life, especially in old age. Efforts at restitution that appear to be regressive have to be seen as defenses against depletion anxiety, which probably has its roots in dread of abandonment.

What is particularly important about this is that in practice the caseworker might have to shore up defenses that would be considered maladaptive for younger persons. In fact, mechanisms such as regression and denial can be adaptive rather than pathological in old age. This means dependency faced on a realistic appraisal of limitations. Thus an elderly woman with heart trouble who lives alone will accept outside help with heavy housekeeping tasks, despite her prior sense of accomplishment and independence in carrying out such tasks.

Consequently, the caseworker will eschew some of the uncovering, insight-oriented techniques such as confrontation and deeper interpretation. The emphasis is definitely *not* on getting behind the defenses but rather to support many of them. Wasser put it rather succinctly: "Treatment of the older persons gives priority to supportive techniques. In helping the client build on his remaining strengths, supporting his useful defenses, and relieving his inner and outer stress, the caseworker encourages his capacity for self-mobilization" (Wasser 1966:25).

Warmth (including physical expression of it), encouragement, promoting realistic feelings of hope, positive reinforcement of coping efforts, and acceptance of regressive and dependent behavior are all to be heavily drawn upon in casework with the elderly. Furthermore, these techniques are apt to be appropriate throughout the course of long-term treatment with many elderly, unlike work with younger persons in which supportive techniques are more heavily used in the early stages of treatment. With the elderly, these supportive procedures are frequently intended to help the client to feel better, more comfortable, stronger, and better able to cope over the long haul as well as immediately.

Nelson (1980) proposed four types of supportive procedures which she sees as necessary conditions for change: protection, acceptance, validation, and education. Each of these has particular relevance for casework with the older client.

Protection involves the worker literally *taking over* for the client in some area of functioning. For example, in the case of confused elderly persons living alone whose utilities have been shut off for nonpayment due to mental confusion, the worker would have to step in and take over the contacts and payments necessary to obtain the utilities. Other such actions would probably have to be undertaken by the worker *with* the client in this protective service situation. It might even be necessary, depending on the physical and mental status of the client, for the worker to take over completely by arranging for institutional placement. This was reflected in the Cleveland study in which this particular model was used in the treatment condition. However, it should be emphasized that the primary emphasis in this model was and is still very much on maintaining the older person in her/his home situation of choice. Thus, the model calls for use of the entire range of concrete services that can maintain the older person at home: financial, medical, homemaker, transportation, and so on. Not only do these meet material, social and health needs, but "they can help make restitution for the losses (the client) has suffered and they can sustain him until he can mobilize his own forces" (Wasser 1971:45).

Acceptance, in Nelsen's scheme, means providing confirmation that the client is worthwhile and valued despite occasional wrong behavior. In an elderly client this is apt to mean such confirmation in the face of regressive or possible aberrant behavior.

The supportive technique of *validation* is feedback to clients indicating *in what ways* they are good, strong, or likely to be effective. Because of depletion and lowered self-esteem older people need to know and be reminded of positive attributes and aptitudes, past and present.

Education is a supportive procedure which involves teaching clients how to cope by providing information and/or modeling of different ways to behave, communicate, control emotions, etc. An example might be the situation of an older person whose increased dependency and anger is being expressed inappropriately and is alienating family members who are needed for support and nurturance. The worker might teach the client how to express dependency needs appropriately, assertively, rather than aggressively by angry demands. Further, the worker might indicate how the client can suppress angry feelings in the context of the family but ventilate them in sessions with the worker. The family, too, can be taught how to understand and cope with these restitutional behaviors. It should be noted at this point that the family is seen as the primary restitutional resource for the older person, just as it is apt to be a source of some depletion through insensitivity, nonresponsiveness, and dysfunctional interactions.

The therapeutic relations, Perlman's third element of casework, is markedly different in this model than in the others to be presented. Issues of transference and countertransference are immediately taken into account and transference is seen as an inevitable factor in the relationship. Whether to encourage or discourage it and to what extent are key questions for treatment planning. It has already been noted that a certain amount of dependency needs will be met by the worker directly or indirectly and frequently in conjunction with the client's family. In general there will be an evolution in the treatment process from the development of trust in an initially dependent sort of relationship to the degree of independence of which the client is capable in terms of ego functioning. This frequently involves a certain amount of identification by the client with the worker as a model for problem-solving, which should then develop into a self-identification based upon new or recovered ways of coping effectively (Wasserman 1974).

The goals and course of relationship with the institutionalized elderly are apt to be different (Brody 1977). Goldfarb (1981) has indicated that independence cannot be a realistic goal in such cases and instead the aim should be simply to make the person less dependent. Therefore, the worker should accept the role of surrogate parent and allow the person to grow more independent in a secure relationship.

The therapeutic use of reminiscence has become an integral part of psychodynamic work with the elderly ever since Butler's (1963) explication of the role of reminiscence in the life review process. Much of the social work treatment literature on reminiscence has been on its use with individuals and groups in institutional settings (Ingersol and Goodman 1980; Ingersol and Silverman 1978; Lewis and Butler 1974; Liton and Olstein 1969), but it can just as appropriately be used in casework with aged individuals living in the community (Kaminsky, 1978; Lowy, 1985; Sherman, 1985).

Lewis (1971) found that the self-concepts of elderly men living in the community were enhanced by reminiscence through positive memories of past pleasures and accomplishments. Pinkus (1970) noted that reminiscence not only can enhance self-esteem but enables the elderly to identify with the past. This can help reinforce a sense of identity for the purposes of sustaining self *continuity* (Grunes 1981). The sense of a continuity of self has been found to be extremely important in helping the "old-old" to withstand the trauma and narcissistic assaults involved in institutionalization and further organic deterioration (Tobin, in press).

More specifically, reminiscence can be used as a casework technique to deal with depression by evoking memories of positive self-images which have been decathected in the course of the depression (Liton and Olstein 1969). It can also be useful in grief work, for it is similar to mourning in that the lost person can be brought to mind which then allows for further release of emotion (McMahon and Rhudick 1967). Of course, one has to be aware of possible dangers in the use of reminiscence, for as Butler (1963) noted, panic, guilt, and depression can sometimes occur in the process. Consequently, it is important to assess the content and quality of the client's expressed memories before engaging in systematic use of reminiscence. Such an assessment also has broader uses for both diagnosis and focusing of treatment in that it provides information about the client's self-image, how much stress is being experienced, and the types of relationships being sought (Pinkus 1970).

There has been a strong emphasis on exploration of the meaning of grief and mourning in this model as a means for developing techniques for dealing with the aged person's reaction to loss. Wasser (1966) called attention to the implications for casework practice of the work of Bowlby (1961), Lindemann (1944), and Bibring (1953). There is insufficient space to go into the actual techniques at this point. The work of Kubler-Ross (1969) and others, which was soon incorporated into this model (Wasser 1971), is well known and readily accessible to readers.

It can be surmised from the foregoing that much of the casework using this model deals with depression, particularly reactive depressions resulting from loss and depletion. This takes on added significance when it is recognized that depression is the most common psychiatric problem of the aged (Zarit 1980).

Another common emotional problem among the elderly is anxiety. Because it is so general a term and emotion, it would be difficult to document that it is more common among the elderly than other age groups. However, the kinds of concerns and fears related to possible further physical, financial, and object losses, together with a concomitant lessening of a sense (internal locus) of control in their lives, has to increase the incidence of dysfunctional anxiety. This can be particularly true for the more vulnerable elderly who might require casework and other services in order to maintain themselves in the community in crisis situations. Crisis intervention will be described as a separate brief treatment model later in this chapter, but it should be noted that it is very closely related to if not a part of this psychodynamic (ego-psychological) model (Parad 1965; Wasser 1966). Consequently, dynamic casework handling of anxiety that hampers or prevents effective coping will be covered under "Crisis Intervention."

The second most common psychological disorder after depression among the institutionalized elderly is paranoia (Pfeiffer 1977). Late life paranoia is not as apt to manifest itself in delusions involving grandiose persons or plots as in earlier paranoia, and the delusions are apt to involve people who have been close to the older persons: family, friends, neighbors, and so on. Of course, paranoid beliefs are more apt to occur in older persons with some significant sensory deficit, particularly in hearing and sight. Consequently, how a caseworker handles paranoid ideation and behavior is a most pertinent question in work with the elderly.

There are several ways within this model of handling this problem, but each of them requires development of trust and strong supportive casework activity within the treatment relationship. Two examples of this were selected from the treatment literature. One case illustrates the results of two years of intensive casework services with a man in his late eighties who was functioning at a psychotic, paranoid level in a large geriatric center (Ross 1981). The worker had weekly half-hour sessions with the client, who was a major source of irritation to other residents and staff with his constant angry accusations and outbursts. The worker allowed herself to be seen by him as an "omnipotent protectress" who would act as advocate for him and manipulate his environment to assure his safety and security. On the basis of this relationship "the patient incorporated into his fragile ego enough discipline so that he could function in a manner acceptable to continued living in the institution" (Ross 1981; 108).

Another case example within this model involved some creative use of reminiscence (Liton and Olstein 1969). Again, the client's paranoid ideas and behaviors created problems with other residents, whom she suspected of trying to harm her, poison her food, and attack her from behind. Since talking about these ideas distressed her greatly the worker deflected discussion in their casework sessions to recollections of the client's happier past. Her paranoid symptoms were greatly alleviated and she regained some former social abilities in telling numerous and colorful stories. This enhanced her relationship with the other residents and provided positive feedback from them, thereby reducing any environmental reasons for paranoid ideation.

This psychodynamic model has incorporated important new developments over the years, and it continues to do so (see later notations on cognitive methods under "Crisis Intervention"). Therefore, we can expect that this model will continue to be influential and contribute heavily to casework practice with the elderly in the future.

The Behavioral Model

The behavioral model has not been used as extensively or as long as a specifically social work intervention approach with the elderly as has the psychodynamic model. However, references in the social work literature on its use with the elderly has increased markedly since 1975. It is essentially a behavior modification approach which was originally called the "socio-behavioral" approach when it was introduced into social work by Edwin J. Thomas (1967). Its origins are in learning theory, and most of the behavior modification techniques were developed by leading clinical theorists from psychology, such as Albert Bandura (1975) and Frederick Kanfer and Jeanne Phillips (1970).

Since Thomas' 1967 monograph, there has been an increasing number of behavioral offerings by social work educators including, among others: Fischer and Gochros (1975), Shinke (1981), Schwartz and Goldiamond (1975), Thomas (1970), and Thomlinson (1986).

Basically, in this model the caseworker makes planned and systematic use of the principles and techniques of behavior modification so as to decrease undesirable behaviors and increase desired behaviors in the individual. Furthermore, it is seen as a parsimonious approach: "Most of its procedures are derived from three basic perspectives on human learning—the fields of operant learning, respondent learning, and imitative learning" (Fischer 1978:157).

The initial use of behavioral methods in work with the elderly tended to be almost exclusively in institutional settings (Tobin 1977). It is in such settings, of course, that stimulus control procedures, contingency management, token economies, and other forms of reward and reinforcement can be put into operation most readily and efficiently. The kinds of target problems identified and worked on initially concerned self-care and activities of daily living involving locomotion, dressing, eating and continence. The contribution of behavioral methods to dealing with these problems cannot be underestimated, and they have become highly valued additions in institutional settings for the elderly.

One of the first documented social work efforts to move beyond these problems to more psychosocial concerns was a report on research-based behavioral group work in a home for the aged (Linsk, Howe, and Pinkston 1975). Using applied behavior analysis the team devised data-based treatment approaches to encourage more active participation of group members in the home as a way of dealing with the frequent problem of elderly people becoming isolated and uncommunicative in such settings. Observation methods that include reliability measures were developed for the purposes of planning and evaluating the treatment. Results showed a strong relationship between the social worker's use of task-related questions to group members and increased levels of appropriate verbalization by residents in activity groups. Although this study involved a group work approach, the authors indicated that this type of behavior analysis could appropriately be applied to individualized treatment and evaluation.

This has in fact happened, and the remainder of this section will deal with individualized behavioral casework services. One example of this is a case in which behavioral contracting was used to reduce the problem behaviors of an 85-year-old male resident of a nursing home (Adams 1979). The behaviors that were identified target problems included temper tantrums, combativeness, and long episodes of crying. A functional analysis was done in which antecedents, dysfunctional behavior, and consequences were charted and interventions planned. The behaviors to be increased and those to be decreased were written into a contract. A token system was devised which included goods and privileges such as candy, soda, extra television viewing time, game-room privileges, special field trips to sights and sports events. Verbal reinforcement of positive behaviors was systematically used by staff as well as the worker with positive results.

This case illustrates some well-established behavioral procedures (token systems and verbal reinforcement) to deal with some fairly common behavioral problems in nursing home settings. What about dealing with problems of a clinically pathological nature, particularly those classified as paranoid? One example of behavioral work with such a problem was described by Cartensen and Fremouw (1981).

This was a case of a 68-year-old woman in a nursing home displaying paranoid behaviors that included hysterical crying because of the belief she was going to be murdered, probably by poisoning. This was potentially life-threatening because it led her to refuse necessary cardiac medication. The individualized treatment program that was designed for her consisted of fourteen weekly counseling sessions in which her verbalizations of positive experiences were rewarded and in which she was asked to keep a daily record of behavior that focused on positive rather than negative events. A training session was also provided to staff members in which concepts of reinforcement and extinction were explained and they were shown how to respond to the patient in terms of these principles. They were asked to initiate conversations with the client at times when she was not expressing paranoid concerns. On the basis of a consistent program for staff-client interactions there was an extinction of frequent paranoid verbalization which in turn served to lessen staff tension and avoidance behavior so that staff could provide a supportive environment.

These examples of individualized service relate to casework with the elderly in institutional settings, but what represents a more recent development of note is home-based behavioral casework with the elderly (Linsk, Pinkston, and Green 1982). This approach utilizes family or other involved caretakers who are willing to help, and the focus is on changing the home environment of the elderly person in ways that increase the amount of positive support received. The worker directly teaches these support persons applied behavior analysis. The treatment procedures include prompts, praise, contracting, and instruction geared toward increasing the elderly person's rate of reinforcement and opportunity to receive reinforcement.

A practice illustration of this model from the Elderly Support

Project in Chicago, which was designed to demonstrate means of keeping elderly clients in their own homes, was provided by Linsk et al. (1982). It was a case of a 69-year-old retired man who was depressed and had a number of health problems, including emphysema, tardive dykenisia, and possible Parkinson's disease. This case therefore represents one behavioral form of work with depression as well as an example of home-based behavioral casework. Most behavioral therapists have linked depression with the amount of social reinforcement available, and in one conceptualization of intervention the assumed weak schedule of reinforcement requires an increase in the amount of positive reinforcement (Lazarus 1968).

In this case a more reinforcing environment was constructed from simple daily activities which had been identified, specified, and measured according to behavior analysis procedures for the purposes of treatment and evaluation. This involved specific written contacts, behavioral frequency counts, and review of trends and patterns in graphic form with the client and his wife. Levels of daily activities by the client were targeted as dependent variables, and activities were added serially to his daily functioning while his wife was taught to reinforce him for desired responses such as getting out of bed, cutting down on his smoking, taking daily walks, and so on. The results in this case prompted the authors to conclude that they provided "preliminary support" for the use of home-based procedures for treating the impaired elderly" (Linsk et al. 1982; 231).

It should be noted here that some behavior therapists emphasize the absence of demonstrated social skills as an antecedent condition for the occurrence of depressed behaviors (Lewinsohn 1976). A major ingredient in treatment therefore is the teaching of social skills so that the client can more effectively evoke the social reinforcements that are necessary to allay the depression. There is, of course, no reason why the two approaches cannot be combined in practice, with the social skills training complementing the planned social reinforcements.

Having presented behavioral approaches to problems of depression and paranoid behaviors there is need to consider the other ubiquitous emotional and behavioral problem facing older persons—anxiety. As noted earlier, anxiety can become dysfunctional and incapacitating when it is overwhelming or chronic, and the elderly are apt to be more at risk for the stress or events and circumstances that can lead to chronic and/or overwhelming anxiety. The classic behavioral approach to treatment of anxiety has been systematic desensitization, usually in the form proposed by Wolpe (1973). Basically, this technique involves the use of a subjective scale of anxiety of SUDS "subjective units of disturbance," with a value of 0 for absolute calm and 100 SUDS for the most extreme anxiety the person can imagine. Then a hierarchy of anxiety-provoking stimuli or situations is constructed on the basis of the client's assessment of SUDS level associated with the situations, which are of the most focal concern to the client. While this is going on the client is trained in deep-muscle relaxation on the basis of the empirical fact that one cannot be anxious (which includes muscle tension) while at the same time being relaxed. The client then simultaneously maintains the relaxed state and imagines the anxiety-associated stimuli from the hierarchy. When the highest (100 SUDS) stimulus on the scale has been reduced to near 0 by this process, the dysfunctional anxiety associated with the focal problem-stimulus should be extinguished.

While demonstrably effective in dealing with conditioned anxiety of various sorts, it does not fit into the characteristic format of casework practice in its typical settings of family agencies, public welfare agencies and social service departments. The element of rather lengthy and repetitive physical (muscle relaxation) training and practice seems somewhat incompatible with the usual "talking therapy" or client-worker dialogue in agency office or client home.

Vattano (1978) proposed some stress-management procedures in addition to systematic desensitization which can be readily adapted to the usual casework settings. These include relaxation training involving a rather brief muscle relaxing procedure and some empirically tested forms of meditation and the "relaxation response" technique (Benson 1975). It is interesting to note in this regard that there has been a proliferation of yoga and meditation classes in many current senior service center programs, and one wonders about the effect of these programs on the lives of the participants.

The virtues of these techniques lie not only in their adaptability to conventional casework practice with the elderly, but more important that they are autogenic and they provide the older person with the tools and techniques for self-management or control. The advantage of *self*-control in contrast to the *external* control of the more conventional environmental, social reinforcement techniques in behavioral practice is that it can be used with the isolated as well as other elderly persons living in the community. It can also be used by older persons in institutional settings, and by those going through the stressful transition of relocation from community to institution. Self-management or autogenic techniques also answer, in part, one of the criticisms of behavioral approaches in work with the elderly-the-problem of too little generalization of therapeutic gains to new situations (Rebok and Hayer 1977: Tobin 1977). The fact that a client learns an adaptive response within a specific behaviorally controlled situation unfortunately does not lend itself to new problematic situations.

Another new development that has vastly enhanced the range and effectiveness of applied behavioral techniques has been the addition of cognitive techniques. Use of the cognitive capacities of memory, imagination or imagery, logical reasoning, and problem-solving in clients allows them to learn how to develop adaptive responses on their own, so that they can cope with situations that are new or different from those in which situation-specific learning takes place in conventional behavior modification. Thus, cognition has been found to be a powerful "mediating variable" in the basic S–R paradigm of behaviorists. These newer cognitive behavioral techniques could just as legitimately be put in this behavioral section of the chapter, for many of the leading contributors to the combined approach are basically behaviorists.

The Cognitive Model

Mahoney and Arnkoff (1978) in a review of the cognitive therapies identified three major types: rational psychotherapies, coping skills therapies, and problem-solving therapies. The rational type is most closely identified with Ellis (1962 and 1974) and Beck (1976) and it usually forms the cognitive core of the other two types of cognitive therapies. It is also the one that is central to most of the social work literature on the use of cognitive methods in casework (Combs 1981; Lantz 1978; Sherman 1987; Werner 1965, 1982, and 1984), including casework with the aged in particular (Sherman 1979, 1981 and 1984).

The central idea in the cognitive approach is that human emotion is much more a result of what people think, believe, or tell themselves about a situation or event than the event itself. Ellis built this into a cognitive "ABC theory of emotion in which A is the *activating event* or situation, B is the *belief* or thoughts about that event, and C is the emotional *consequence* of the thoughts or belief." Thus, B is an intervening factor in the experiential process, and if it is an irrational belief (iB) it can lead to irrational and dysfunctional emotional consequences (iC), and the person will experience A as extremely stressful or catastrophic. In fact, Ellis frequently talks about "catastrophic thinking" and notes that irrational beliefs usually contain a "must," an "ought," or a "should"—an implicit absolutistic demand that the person *must* obtain what she or he wants. In other words, what any person might reasonably want—love, acceptance, respect—is irrationally transformed into an absolute *need* or demand and not receiving it is experienced as traumatic and catastrophic.

In the cognitive approach, the client is taught how to explore the implicit thoughts or self-talk that are associated with the explicit disproportionate and dysfunctional emotions. Then the client identifies the unsubstantiated or irrational elements within the implicit thoughts, and with the guidance of the therapist learns how to dispute them and replace them with rational beliefs (B). This *disputation* (D) represents the core activity of the treatment process and it should lead to a new *evaluation* (E) of the problem situation and the activating event (A). Thus, there is an A–B–C–D–E sequence involved in the total process.

Beck (1976) uses essentially the same approach and he asks the client to monitor the whole process by identifying "automatic thoughts" or beliefs and the associated emotions on a form called a "Daily Record of Dysfunctional Thoughts," which calls for the following:

1. Describe actual events or thoughts and daydreams of the day leading to unpleasant emotions.
2. Describe the type of emotion (sad, angry) and rate the degree of emotion involved on a scale of 1 to 100.
3. Write down the automatic thought(s) associated with the emotion and rate the degree of belief in the thought on a scale of 1 to 100.
4. Then write a rational response to the irrational automatic thoughts and rate the degree of belief in the rational response (1–100).
5. Re-rate the belief in the automatic thought (1–100) and specify and rate the subsequent emotions (1–100).

By the process of identifying and disputing the negative cognitions leading to the negative emotions, the client should be able to gradually decrease the incidence and intensity of those emotions. Clients are given the regular "homework" assignment of monitoring their thoughts and emotions on a continuous basis throughout treatment.

Homework assignments are very much a part of cognitive practice, and clients are encouraged to test out and challenge their irrational ideas, beliefs, and fears in real life. The term "cognitive" might belie the rather active type of treatment it often is. It is also one that provides for a great deal of client self-management and control. The basic A–B–C or dysfunctional thoughts approach is very easily and quickly taught and learned, and elderly persons are able to incorporate it into their repertoires quite readily (Sherman 1981).

The cognitive model, particularly Beck's version, has been most noted for its use in the depressions where it has some empirical evidence of effectiveness (Rush et al. 1977; Rush, Khatami, and Beck 1975; Shaw 1977). His model posits three specific concepts to explain depression: 1) the cognitive triad; 2) schemas; and 3) cognitive errors or faulty information processing (Beck et al. 1979). The cognitive triad consists first of the client's negative view of self; second, a negative interpretation or construction of her/his experiences; and third, a negative view of the future. These depressive views emerge from a personally unique but relatively stable cognitive pattern called a schema. It is the way the schema processes incoming information that leads to the cognitive errors that are characteristic of depressogenic thinking and feelings.

Therefore, the core of the treatment processes is to have the client "restructure" (re-pattern) cognitions by continuous uses of procedures like the daily analysis of dysfunctional thoughts, together with other techniques. In fact, the term "cognitive restructuring" is a generic term for a number of specific cognitive-behavioral techniques used in different combinations. However, the cognitive review or disputation process is always at the center of these techniques as the mediating treatment variable.

In addition to the disputation or reanalysis of depressogenic thoughts and cognitive errors, certain other techniques are used in treating depression. One of these is called "mastery and pleasure therapy," and it is particularly helpful for dealing with the characteristic belief of depressed persons that they never enjoy anything and they never will, as well as the belief that there is nothing they can do with any degree of competence or mastery (Beck et al. 1979). This technique requires that the client keep a daily record of activities and mark down an "M" for every activity during the day that provides a sense of mastery and a "P" for every activity that provides some pleasure. For each M or P the client has to rate how much mastery or pleasure is experienced, on a scale from 0 (none) to 5 (a great deal). Almost invariably it will be found that there are some activities that provide a modicum of pleasure or mastery, whether a 1 or 2 rating, which provides evidence to dispute the belief that there is absolutely no sense of mastery or pleasure in life.

Another related technique for depression is "graded task assignment," which is called "success therapy" by Beck (1976) because the client is first assigned a simple task that the therapist is sure can be accomplished and is then assigned increasingly difficult tasks. Of course, care has to be exercised so that the tasks are not too difficult, for failure will produce even more feelings of incompetence and worthlessness.

"Bibliotherapy" is a commonly used technique in cognitive treatment. It involves homework assignments of readings specific to the client's problems and about how the client's dysfunctional cognitions are related to the problems. Obviously, the caseworker has to be sensitive to the client's degree of literacy and potential resistence to a technique as didactic as this. The literature has to be simply, clearly, and directly written for it to be effective, but it can be quite effective with elderly clients when used in conjunction with other techniques. Beck and Greenberg (1974) prepared a clearly written booklet of this sort, which is routinely provided to their depressed patients at the start of treatment.

An example of the rational form of cognitive therapy associated with Beck and Ellis is provided in the case of Mrs. L., a 69-year-old woman who was referred to Jewish Family Service because of the emotional distress she was experiencing in apparent reaction to her 44-year-old daughter's separation and imminent divorce. The daughter, her only child, lived with her own two daughters, aged 17 and 20, in a city 300 miles away. Mrs. L. was very worried and actually doubtful about her daughter's ability to cope with the separation and the responsibilities of single parenthood. Mrs. L. felt that her worries were well-founded, but she could not understand the extreme sadness she was feeling along with bouts of increased insomnia, lethargy, and feelings of worthlessness.

In the course of six sessions with the agency caseworker, Mrs. L. was asked to monitor the cognitions associated with her negative emotions by using Beck's Daily Record of Dysfunctional Thoughts (Beck et al. 1979:403). In addition, she was asked to read a section of a book (Ellis and Harper 1975) that provided a list of prevalent irrational beliefs that could possibly help her identify any depressogenic thoughts she might be having that would explain her depressed state. The monitoring of her dysfunctional thoughts revealed a series of automatic thoughts going from immediate situation-specific issues to deeper levels of belief. At the more immediate level she doubted that her daughter could cope with her life after divorce. Mrs. L. also recognized that she was disappointed in her daughter but that she was much more disappointed in herself. In fact, she believed she was a bad mother and therefore a failure as a person. So much of her life and identity was wrapped up in being a "good" mother that she was feeling utterly incompetent and worthless in all respects. Thus, it was her irrational belief (iB) of total worthlessness because of perceived failure as a parent that was leading to the irrational consequences (iC) or state of depression after the activating event (A) of her daughter's marital separation.

She was given homework assignments involving disputation and continued monitoring of these dysfunctional thoughts and beliefs. In addition, the worker suggested Mrs. L. visit her daughter to check out if there was a sound empirical base for her concerns and beliefs, as well as to offer whatever support she could to her daughter. Mrs. L. did make the visit and in the course of it learned that her daughter felt (and actually was) able and competent to cope with the impending divorce. In fact, she was looking forward to it. Therefore, she did not perceive Mrs. L. to be a failure as a mother, but rather as a mother who provided her with an emotional foundation and a role model to enable her to cope with this stressful time in her life.

Mrs. L.'s depressed state was lessening after several sessions with the caseworker, and her symptoms lifted almost completely after her visit to her daughter.

A cognitive technique which can be used to deal with problems of anxiety as well as depression is "cognitive rehearsal" (Beck and Emery 1985). The client is asked to imagine going through some selected activity or situation and identify the anticipated obstacles and conflicts. This allows for advance preparation for coping and problem-solving strategies, and it enables the client to pinpoint ahead of time the automatic thought(s) that represent obstacle(s) in the situation. This all serves to allay anticipatory anxiety and depressed cognitions of incompetence and failure.

Other similar cognitive preparatory techniques are "vicariation" or cognitive modeling (Raimy 1975) and "rational imagery" (Lazarus 1971). These are often combined with behavioral techniques in a form of cognitive-behavior modification of the coping skills or problem-solving variety (Meichenbaum 1977). These cognitive behavioral therapies and techniques are proliferating rapidly, and a strong case has been made for their incorporation into mainstream social work practice (Berlin 1982; Fischer 1978).

One of the better known and more influential coping skills techniques is "systematic rational restructuring" (Goldfried, Decenteco, and Weinberg 1974). It is similar in almost every respect to the behavioral technique of systematic desensitization in that it includes construction of a hierarchy of anxiety-probing situations, with successful coping at one level a prerequisite for progression to the next. However, it substitutes rational reevaluation in place of muscle relaxation by having the client identify what dysfunctional thoughts are occurring when anxious or depressed and then reevaluating the situation in more rational terms while noting any changes in subjective units of disturbance (SUDS) This is a good alternative for older persons who cannot do the muscle relaxation part of desensitization because of their physical condition. The author has elsewhere described a case of a 74-year-old woman who was in an anxiety state over her physical condition and recent surgery (Sherman 1981;122–126). This included the use of systematic rational restructuring in conjunction with the techniques of rational imagery and "changing attributions" (Mahoney 1974).

Problem solving therapy includes a diverse collection of procedures that include such behavioral ones as assertiveness training, modeling, and positive reinforcement, along with cognitive review and rehearsal (D'Zurilla and Goldfried 1971). Basically, it trains clients how to solve problems in a six-step process: 1) general orientation; 2) defining the situation; 3) identifying positive and negative thoughts about the situation; 4) brainstorming alternative solutions; 5) deciding on the best solution, and 6) practice and implementation of the solution. It has been used by social workers with community-based older persons with generally positive results (Toseland 1977; Waskel 1981).

Generally, it is with problems of depression and anxiety related to stress and coping that the cognitive model seems to have the greatest applicability. When it comes to actual organic brain syndromes, loss of cognitive capacities rule out many of the rational therapy options. Also, in true paranoid thought the delusional systems and distortions rule out a number of cognitive techniques (Werner, 1974). Finally, Emery (1981) has found it necessary to adapt certain procedures, such as the type of diagnostic tests and behavioral task assignments, because of the physical limitations of elderly clients.

BRIEF TREATMENT MODELS

The Crisis Intervention Model

The crisis intervention model has certain focal concepts that make it particularly applicable for casework with the community-based elderly in both preventive and protective situations.

"Crisis intervention means entering into the life situation of an individual, family, or group to alleviate the impact of a crisis inducing stress in order to help mobilize the resources of those directly affected, as well as those who are in the significant 'social orbit'," according to Parad (1965:p. 2). Its origins go back to the work of Eric Lindemann (1944) in his study of the mourning reactions of the bereaved relatives of victims of the Coconut Grove disaster of 1942 in Boston and to the further development and extension of his concept by Gerald Caplan (1961). Thus, from its very beginnings crisis theory dealt with the trauma of object loss and sharp dislocations in the lives of the bereaved, which of course are problems very pertinent to old age. Again, Erikson's (1963) epignetic theory contributed with its explication of maturational stages and the potential for crisis at each stage. As noted earlier, ego psychology is very central to it, and a number of social science concepts dealing with role theory and role transition are also pertinent.

In its simplest terms "crisis" can be defined as an upset in a steady state, but it must be added that the habitual problem-solving activities are not adequate to the new situation and do not lead rapidly to the previously achieved balanced state (Rapoport 1965). What usually happens is that a hazardous event creates a problem in the person's life situation, and this event can be conceived of as a loss, a threat, or a challenge. If it represents a threat to basic need and/or sense of identity, it is met with *anxiety;* if it represents loss or deprivation it is met with *depression;* but if it represents a challenge it is apt to be met with energetic and purposive problem-solving activities. Thus, crisis theory addresses the two most commonly experienced emotional problems of the elderly—anxiety and depression.

One other central concept of crisis theory is the time-limited nature of the crisis state. Caplan (1961) claims that the actual period lasts from one to six weeks, in which an adequate solution has to be found to restore equilibrium. If it is not found a lower level of functioning and mental health will ensue. This makes it essential that intervention take place quickly and actively, and this accounts for the brief treatment nature of the crisis model (Rapoport 1970).

There are certain patterns of response that provide for healthy crisis resolution, and these provide the guidelines for our interventions with the elderly. First, there is a need for cognitive grasp and restructuring as a first step in problem solving, so the role of the caseworker is to help the client identify and isolate the factors (often preconscious and unintegrated) that have led to disruption of functioning. Then, together, worker and client arrive at a formulation of the problem that facilitates cognitive restructuring (Rapoport 1965). This in itself might provide the kind of problem-solving activity sufficient to reestablish the previously achieved balanced state.

Perlman (1975) has provided an excellent analysis of cognitive functioning in the process of ego adaptation to stress and crisis states which adds significant focal power to the crisis model. In fact, Golan (1978) has identified Perlman's problem-solving model as having contributed directly to the crisis intervention approach.

The second practice guide is that there needs to be an explicit acceptance by the caseworker of the disordered affect, the irrational and negative attitudes, and the need for the expression and management of feelings on the part of elderly clients. Not only do these behaviors have to be met with empathy and acceptance, but they have to be placed in the rational context of their natural history. This is extremely important for casework with the elderly, in order to assure that the affect and responses of the client are not immediately labelled as evidence of senility or organicity. These behaviors should first be viewed as efforts at coping and possible restitution.

The third major guide is the availability and use of interpersonal and institutional resources. The use of formal institutions, agencies, and caretakers has been incorporated in crisis intervention from its inception. So has the recognition and use of significant others, particularly family, for comfort, support, and need-satisfaction. The potential for use of a broader network of human relationships was recognized in the past but not systematically pursued. As far as work with the aged is concerned, the development and availability of mutual support groups has been of major importance (Caplan and Killilea 1976) as have the self-help groups with more of a social-action orientation (Gartner and Riesmann 1977; Hess 1976). In some instances case workers have helped to develop informal helping networks in order to initiate helping interaction or to provide for continuity in the informal helping process (Smith 1975).

All of these happenings bode well for the continued use and further development of the crisis intervention model for casework service to the elderly. It is also clear that this model can enhance and be enhanced by some of the other models that have already been discussed.

The Task-Centered Model

The task-centered model is probably the only one of those covered here that is truly indigenous to social work, for it was developed and empirically tested in social agency settings where social work was the host discipline (Reid and Shyne 1969; Reid and Epstein 1972; Reid 1977; Reid and Epstein 1977; Epstein 1980). If it has any theoretical origins, they come out of Helen Harris Perlman's (1957) problem-solving theory of casework, which is also an indigenous social work practice theory. At any rate, the task-centered approach has been found to be particularly promising for short-term casework with the aging (Cormican 1977). Its special strengths as well as certain possible limitations for work with the aged will be noted after a brief recapitulation of the essential features of the model.

Task-centered work normally consists of six to twelve client-worker sessions once or twice a week over a period of time to four months. Assessment is concentrated in the first one or two sessions, with an emphasis on exploration and specification of problems, culminating in a problem-reduction program which focuses on certain target problems. The target problem(s) will usually be only one or two, but no more than three in number, so that client's and worker's task activities can be focused and concentrated enough for problem resolution within the brief allotted time.

Next, the client and worker mutually agree upon target problem priorities, set goals, and specify their respective tasks to be carried out in or to achieve the specified goals. A "task" states a general direction for action, and general tasks can be broken down into operational tasks and subtasks. For example, the target problem for a socially isolated, ambulatory older person in the community might be stated as "lack of sufficient social contact for emotional well-being," in which case the general task will be to substantially increase the number of social contacts within the specified period of service. Specific subtasks of the client might include, sequentially, to inquire about, visit, enroll, and finally attend a local senior service center. To initiate a certain number of contacts per week with friends and neighbors might also be an operational task for the client. The worker's task in this instance might be to provide information about available senior centers or possible social programs, about transportation service, if distance is a problem, as well as providing specific instruction, guidance, or modeling of how the isolated person can initiate these contacts.

There is contracting with the client about the duration, scheduling, and conditions of the intervention. The contract does not have to be written, but it can be if the client wishes. At any rate, the conditions, specification of tasks, and third party involvements (family members, referring or collaborative agencies, and so on) all have to be mutually and explicitly agreed upon between client and worker. The whole emphasis is to quickly identify and work on the problems that the *client* sees as most pressing.

The actual implementation or problem-solving part of treatment consists of the client carrying out the specified tasks and subtasks while the worker obtains the necessary resources and ancillary services and, if necessary, instructs the client in the skills and actions necessary to accomplish the stipulated tasks. The client's task performance is reviewed and any necessary adjustments made in each session, and at the end there is a review of the overall progress made in alleviating the target problems. If the progress has been sufficient, service is terminated at the contracted time. Certain exceptions of from one to four additional sessions can be made, and there might also be some follow-up at a later date with some monitoring of client task functioning.

In general, the task-centered model is eclectic in nature, drawing upon behavioral, cognitive and ego-psychological methods and techniques. For example, Epstein (1980) used a five-step variation of the problem-solving therapy noted earlier (D'Zurilla and Goldfried 1971). Graded-task assignment is used just as in behavioral and cognitive approaches. And, in fact, task-centered and cognitive-behavioral methods can be combined almost in their entirety in work with certain kinds of problems. A case example of this kind of combined use of these two methods was provided by this author in the treatment of a 66-year-old woman with a reactive depression (Sherman 1981:127–136).

Golan (1981) has noted that the task-centered approach is also well-suited for crisis intervention in that its emphasis on quick formulation and systematic work on the most pressing problems of clients fits well into the time trajectory of crisis states. She further noted that it is very appropriate for use during transitional periods, because within its eight-problem typology the model addresses three problems—difficulty in role performance, decision problems, and reactive emotional distress—that can be crucial in transitional situations. For example, a too-frequent problem among elderly couples occurs when one spouse is endangering her/his own health and well-being in maintaining a deteriorating partner at home. This involves a difficulty in role performance for which the care taking spouse could use help in the form of home care and other concrete supportive services which the task model was well equipped to provide. The example could also be viewed as a decision problem in that there might be a need to come to a decision about institutional placement of the deteriorating spouse. Finally, it could be a problem of reactive emotional distress in helping the caretaking spouse deal with the fact of loss and institutionalization of the partner.

On the other hand, Golan (1981) sees some problem with the time-limited aspects of the model for some transitional work "where the entire linking interval may cover several months or even years." Of course, this precludes setting in advance a specific number of sessions within a definite span of time. However, this would be true of most short-term models, so the task-centered model is not alone in this. On the other hand, the model does function best as a voluntary service in which the client recognizes a problem and is prepared to work on it. The model could be problematic in protective situations with clients who are negative toward and refuse to see the need for any such service.

With these few limitations, the task-centered model has a great deal to contribute to casework with the elderly. It has not only been found useful in work with the community-based elderly but also for dealing with the psychological problems of the elderly in a long-term residential facility (Dierking, Brown, and Fortune 1980). This has led some social work educators in an MSW program to attempt to develop the task-centered model as an effective base for social work with the elderly by integrating it with gerontological and clinical knowledge and experience (Fortune and Rathbone-McCuan 1981).

In concluding, it should be noted that crisis intervention and task-centered are by far the most influential of the brief casework models. There are no other, competing short-term *social work* approaches that are cohesive enough to be considered a model for casework practice with the aged.

FUTURE DIRECTIONS

It must be evident to the reader by now that there is a trend toward convergence and a degree of commonality among the above models of casework. Therefore, one very promising direction for the future lies in the synergistic development and use of these different models in a more integrative manner with the elderly.

If we begin with the fact that in many instances of community casework with the elderly there has been a depletion of tangible, material resources as well as psychosocial resources, a combined task-centered and crisis intervention approach immediately suggests itself. The task-centered model is particularly well suited for quick provision of concrete services without "taking over" for the client and thus incurring unnecessary dependency. The crisis model is well equipped for handling the emotional aspects of the situation, of the need for appropriate support based on an assessment of ego functioning, which in turn will indicate the range and limitations of the client's coping capacities. The task-centered model can also provide the kind of structure for rational, sequential coping and problem-solving work required at this stage.

Additionally, some of the stress-management techniques from the behavioral repertoire might be applied if anxiety impinges too much on the client's problem-solving capacities. Also, coping skills techniques from the cognitive-behavioral repertoire might be taught to the client, according to the demands of the situation (Meichenbaum 1977). Furthermore, if the brief supportive and problem-solving work of the combined task centered/crisis intervention approach is not sufficient to resolve the problem, it might be necessary to provide the elderly client with the more specifically focused problem-solving therapy (D'Zurilla and Goldfried 1971). This would be particularly appropriate if the client had a functional deficit in systematic problem-solving skills (Goldfried and Goldfried 1975). When it comes to more extended casework such as the transitional work mentioned by Golan (1981), where issues of role transition, identity, and intrapersonal and interpersonal functioning are prominent, the psychodynamic model appears most appropriate. However, even here the work under that model could be enhanced by some of the cognitive restructuring techniques to bring about necessary changes in self-concept, which is essentially based on a cognitive schema.

The growing application of cognitive, behavioral, and task-centered approaches in casework with the aged may lead in the direction of greater specification of service input and outcome. There might also be a growing use of quantified methods in assessment and evaluation, since these approaches lend themselves to these methods. This certainly has implications for accountability and for empirical testing of the differential effectiveness of treatment approaches. (Tolson 1988).

There will undoubtedly be a greater need for couples and family casework in the future with the elderly using one or a combination of the models covered here. Getzel (1982), for example, has described the use of a crisis model in helping elderly couples. Wolinsky (1986) has described a somewhat more eclectic approach to work with older couples, while Herr and Weakland (1979) have described work with elderly families which takes into account the structural and intergenerational characteristics of such families.

Not only is there an increasing practice literature on this, the actual demand for couples and family casework with older persons is increasing. Kosberg and Garcia (1987) carried out a survey of elderly clients served in a multiservice family agency in Florida and found that marital counseling was the second most frequent form of treatment method, with family counseling less frequent but still requested in a number of cases. Individual counseling was the most common form of casework service, but this was a function of the fact that at least half of the elderly clients were living alone. Thus, there will be a continuing need for the individual casework models outlined here together with increasing application of them in treatment involving elderly couples and families.

A number of training and educational implications are inherent in the influx of cognitive, behavioral, and task-centered methods into casework practice with aged individuals, couples, and families. The sheer numbers and varieties of tested and untested but promising techniques are such that only a fraction of them can be taught and learned in a two-year MSW curriculum, even in curricula with practice theoretical orientations that are compatible with them. This suggests the need for additional training opportunities outside the regular curriculum in the form of continuing education workshops and classes and in-service training programs in gerontological practice settings.

Certainly, these techniques should not be offered cafeteria-style in either training programs or in practice. None of them should be used in the absence of a guiding treatment framework and a sound assessment. Some of them, especially those using muscle relaxation, should only be used in the light of medical advice because of the greater possibility of physical complications with elderly clients.

There is another important concern about the proliferation and increased use of techniques. It has to do with the kind of professional stance the worker assumes with such a repertoire, which can all too easily become that of technical expert and virtuoso with a bag of "scientific" techniques and procedures. This can lead to inadequate attention to the pervasive social, medical, and economic needs of many elderly individuals. Furthermore, work with the elderly requires a broader view, a life-span perspective, one that "argues that only in gerontological practice are social workers confronted with a person's final destiny and with the true meaning of a person's life" (Monk 1981:62). The idea of a social technician or therapist providing casework services to our aged clients is not compatible with the more profound humanistic perspective on aging and work with the aged which is required of us.

REFERENCES

Adams, J. M. 1979. Behavioral contracting: An effective method of intervention with the elderly nursing home patient. *Journal of Gerontological Social Work* 1(3):235–250.

Bandura, A. 1975. *Principles of Behavior Modification.* New York. Columbia University Press.

Beck, A. T. 1976. *Cognitive Therapy and the Emotional Disorders.* New York: International Universities Press.
Beck, A. T. and G. Emery. 1985. *Anxiety Disorders and Phobias: A Cognitive Perspective.* New York: Basic Books.
Beck, A. T. and R. L. Greenberg. 1974. *Coping with Depression.* New York: Institute for Rational Living.
Beck, A. T., A. J. Rush, and G. Emery. 1979. *Cognitive Therapy of Depression.* New York: Guilford Press.
Benson, H. 1975. *The Relaxation Response.* New York: William Morrow.
Berger, R., and Piliavin, I. 1976. The effect of casework: A research note. *Social Work* 21(3):205–208.
Berlin, S. B. 1982. Cognitive behavioral interventions for social work practice. *Social Work* 27(3):218–226.
Bibring, E. 1953. The mechanism of depression. In P. Greenacre, ed., *Affective Disorders.* New York: International Universities Press.
Blenkner, M., M. Bloom, and M. A. Nielsen. 1971. A research and demonstration project of protective services. *Social Casework* 52(8):483–499.
Bowlby, J., 1961. Process of mourning. *The International Journal of Psychoanalysis* 42:317–340.
Brody, E. M. 1977. *Long-Term Care of Older People: A Practical Guide.* New York: Human Sciences Press.
Butler, R. 1963. The life review: An interpretation of reminiscence in the aged. *Psychiatry* 26(1):65–76.
Caplan, G. 1961. *An Approach to Community Mental Health.* New York: Grune and Stratton.
Caplan, G. and M. Killilea. 1976. *Support Systems and Mutual Help: Multidisciplinary Explorations,* New York: Grune and Stratton.
Cartensen, L. L. and W. J. Fremouw. 1981. The demonstration of a behavioral intervention for late life paranoia. *The Gerontologist* 21(3):329–333.
Cath, S. H. 1963. Some dynamics of middle and later years. *Smith College Studies in Social Work* 33(2):97–126.
Combs, T. D. 1980. A cognitive therapy for depression: Theory, techniques, and issues. *Social Casework* 61(6):361–366.
Cormican, E. 1977. Task-centered model for work with the aged, *Social Casework,* 58(8):490–494.
Cormican, E. J. 1980. Social work and aging: A review of the literature and how it is changing. *Aging and Human Development* 11(4):251–267.
Dierking, B., M. Brown, and A. E. Fortune. 1980. Task-centered treatment in residential facility for the elderly: A clinical trial. *Journal of Gerontological Social Work* 2(3):225–240.
D'Zurilla, T. and M. Goldfried. 1971. Problem-solving and behavior modification. *Journal of Abnormal Psychology* 78:107–126.
Ellis, A. 1962. *Reason and Emotion in Psychotherapy.* Secaucus, N.J.: Citadel Press, McGraw-Hill.
Ellis, A. 1974. *Humanistic Psychotherapy: The Rational-Emotive Approach.* New York: McGraw-Hill.
Ellis, A. and R. A. Harper. 1977. *A New Guide to Rational Living.* New York: Prentice-Hall.
Emery, G. 1981. Cognitive therapy with the elderly. In G. Emery, S. D. Holon, and R. C. Bedrosian, eds., *New Directions in Cognitive Therapy.* New York: Guilford Press.
Epstein, L. 1980. *Helping People: The Task-Centered Approach.* St. Louis: C. V. Mosby.
Erikson, E. 1963. *Childhood and Society.* 2d ed. New York: Norton.

Fischer, J. 1973. Is casework effective? A review. *Social Work,* 18(1):5–20.

Fischer, J. 1978. *Effective Casework Practice: An Eclectic Approach.* New York: McGraw-Hill.

Fischer, J. and H. L. Gochros. 1975. *Planned Behavior Change: Behavior Modification in Social Work.* New York: Free Press.

Fortune, A. E. and E. Rathbone-McCuan. 1981. Education in gerontological social work: Application of the task-centered model. *Journal of Education for Social Work* 17(3):98–105.

Garner, J. D. and S. O. Mercer. 1980. Social work practice in long-term care facilities: Implications of the current model. *Journal of Gerontological Social Work* 3(2):71–77.

Gartner, A. and F. Riesmann. 1977. *Self-Help in the Human Services.* San Francisco: Jossey-Bass.

Getzel, G. 1982. Helping elderly couple in crisis. *Social Casework* 63(9):515–521.

Golan, N. 1978. *Treatment in Crisis Situations.* New York: Free Press.

Golan, N. 1981. *Passing Through Transitions: A Guide for Practitioners.* New York: Free Press.

Goldberg, E. M., A. Mortimer, and B. T. Williams. 1970. *Helping the Aged: A Field Experiment in Social Work.* London: Allen and Unwin.

Goldfarb, A. I. 1981. Psychiatry in geriatrics. In S. Steury and M. L. Blank, eds., *Readings in Psychotherapy with Older People.* Washington, D.C.: National Institute of Mental Health.

Goldfried, M. R., E. T. Decenteco, and L. Weinberg. 1974. Systematic rational restructuring as a self-control technique. *Behavior Therapy* 5:247–254.

Goldfried, M. and A. Goldfried. 1975. Cognitive change methods. In F. Kanfer and A. Goldstein, eds., *Helping People Change.* New York: Pergamon Press.

Grunes, J. M. 1981. Reminiscences, regression, and empathy—a psychotherapeutic approach to the impaired elderly. In S. I. Greenspan and G. H. Pollock, eds., *The Course of Life,* vol. 3. Washington, D.C.: GPO.

Hartmann, H. 1958. *Ego Psychology and the Problem of Adaptation.* New York: International Universities Press.

Herr, J. J. and J. H. Weakland. 1979. *Counseling Elders and Their Families.* New York: Springer.

Hess, B. B. 1976. Self-help among the aged. *Social Policy* 7:55–62.

Hollis, F. 1972. *Casework: A Psychosocial Therapy.* 2d ed. New York: Random House.

Ingersol, B. and L. Goodman. 1980. History comes alive: Facilitating reminiscence in a group of institutionalized elderly. *Journal of Gerontological Social Work* 2(4):305–319.

Ingersol, B. and A. Silverman. 1978. Comparative group psychotherapy for the aged. *The Gerontologist* 18(2):201–206.

Kaminsky, M. 1978. Pictures from the past: The use of reminiscence in casework with the elderly. *Journal of Gerontological Social Work* 1:19–32.

Kanfer, F. H. and J. S. Phillips. 1970. *Learning Foundations of Behavior Therapy.* New York: Wiley.

Kosberg, J. 1973. The nursing home: A social work paradox. *Social Work* 18(2):104–110.

Kosberg, J. J. and J. L. Garcia. 1987. The problems of older clients seen in a family service agency: Treatment and program implications. *Journal of Gerontological Social Work* 11:141–153.

Kubler-Ross, E. 1969. *On Death and Dying.* London: Macmillan.

Lantz, J. E. 1978. Cognitive theory and social casework. *Social Work* 23(5):361–366.

Lazarus, A. A. 1968. Learning theory and the treatment of depression. *Behavior Research and Therapy* 6:83–89.

Lazarus, A. A. 1971. *Behavior Therapy and Beyond.* New York: McGraw-Hill.
Lewis, C. N. 1971. Reminiscing and self-concept in old age. *Journal of Gerontology* 26(2):263–269.
Lewis, M. I. and R. N. Butler. 1974. Life review therapy: Putting memories to work in individual and group psychotherapy. *Geriatrics* 29:165–169, 172–173.
Lewinsohn, P. M. 1976. A behavioral approach to depressions. In R. J. Friedman and M. M. Katz, eds., *The Psychology of Depression: Contemporary Theory and Research.* New York: Brunner/Mazel.
Lindemann, E. 1944. Symptomatology and management of acute grief. *American Journal of Psychiatry* 101:141–148.
Linsk, N., M. W. Howe, and E. M. Pinkston. 1975. Behavioral group work in a home for the aged. *Social Work* 20(6):454–463.
Linsk, N. L., E. M. Pinkston, and G. R. Green, 1982. Home-based behavioral social work with the elderly. In E. M. Pinkston, J. L. Levitt, G. R. Green, N. L. Linsk, and T. F. Rzepnicki, eds., *Effective Social Work Practice: Advanced Techniques for Behavioral Intervention with Individuals, Families, and Institutional Staff.* San Francisco: Jossey-Bass.
Liton, L. and S. C. Olstein. 1969. Therapeutic aspects of reminiscence, *Social Casework* 50(5):263–266.
Lowy, L. 1985. *Social Work with the Aging: The Challenge and Promise of the Later Years.* 2d ed. New York: Harper and Row.
Mahoney, M. J. 1974. *Cognition and Behavior Modification.* Cambridge, Mass: Ballinger.
Mahoney, M. J. and D. Arnkoff. 1978. Cognitive and self-control therapies. In S. L. Garfield and A. E. Bergin, eds., *Handbook of Psychotherapy and Behavior Change* 2d. ed. New York: Wiley.
McMahon, A. S. and P. J. Rhudick. 1967. Reminiscing in the aged. In S. Levin and R. J. Kahana, eds., *Psychodynamic Studies on Aging: Creativity, Reminiscing, and Dying.* New York: International Universities Press.
Meichenbaum, D. 1977. *Cognitive-Behavior Modification: An Integrative Approach.* New York: Plenum Press.
Monk, A. 1981. Social work with the aged: Principles of practice. *Social Work* 26(1):61–68.
Nelsen, J. C. 1980. Support: A necessary condition for change. *Social Work* 25(5):388–393.
Parad, H. J., ed. 1965. *Crisis Intervention: Selected Readings.* New York: Family Service Association of America.
Perlman, H. H. 1957. *Social Casework: A Problem-Solving Process.* Chicago: University of Chicago Press.
Perlman, H. H. 1975. In quest of coping. *Social Casework* 56(4):213–225.
Pfeiffer, E. 1977. Psychopathology and social pathology. In J. E. Birren and W. K. Schaie, eds., *Handbook of the Psychology of Aging.* New York: Van Nostrand Reinhold.
Pinkus, A. 1970. Reminiscence in aging and its implications for social work practice. *Social Work* 15(3):47–53.
Raimy, V. 1975. *Misunderstandings of the Self.* San Francisco: Jossey-Bass.
Rapoport, L. 1965. The state of crisis: Some theoretical considerations. In H. J. Parad, ed., *Crisis Intervention: Selected Readings.* New York: Family Service Association of America.
Rapoport, L. 1970. Crisis intervention as a mode of brief treatment. In R. W. Roberts and R. H. Nee, eds., *Theories of Social Casework.* Chicago: University of Chicago Press.
Rebok, G. W. and W. J. Hayer. 1977. The functional context of elderly behavior. *The Gerontologist* 17:27–34.

Reid, W. J. 1978. *The Task-Centered System.* New York: Columbia University Press.
Reid, W. J. and L. Epstein. 1972. *Task-Centered Casework.* New York: Columbia University Press.
Reid, W. J., and L. Epstein, eds. 1977. *Task-Centered Practice.* New York: Columbia University Press.
Reid, W. J. and A. Shyne. 1969. *Brief and Extended Casework.* New York: Columbia University Press.
Ross, F. 1981. Social work treatment of a paranoid personality in a geriatric institution. In S. Steury and M. L. Blank eds., *Readings in Psychotherapy with Older People.* Washington, D.C.: National Institute of Mental Health, (DHHS No. ADM 81-409.)
Rush, A. J., A. T. Beck, M. Kovacs, and S. Hollon. 1977. Comparative efficacy of cognitive therapy and imipramine in the treatment of depressed outpatients. *Cognitive Therapy and Research* 1:17–37.
Rush, A. J., M. Khatami, and A. T. Beck. 1975. Cognitive and behavioral therapy in chronic depression. *Behavior Therapy* 6:398–404.
Schinke, S. P., ed. 1981. *Behavioral Methods in Social Welfare.* Hawthorn, N.Y.: Aldine.
Schwartz, A. and J. Goldiamond. 1975. *Social Casework: A Behavioral Approach.* New York: Columbia University Press.
Shaw, B. F. 1977. Comparison of cognitive therapy and behavior therapy in the treatment of depression. *Journal of Consulting and Clinical Psychology* 45:543:551.
Sherman, E. 1979. A cognitive approach to direct practice with the aging. *Journal of Gerontological Social Work* 2(1):43–53.
Sherman, E. 1985. A phenomenological approach to reminiscence and life review. *Clinical Gerontologist* 3:3–16.
Sherman, E. 1981. *Counseling the Aging: An Integrative Approach.* New York: Free Press.
Sherman, E. 1984. *Working with Older Persons: Cognitive and Phenomenological Methods.* Boston: Kluwer-Nijhoff.
Sherman, E. 1987. Cognitive therapy. In A. Minahan, ed., *Encyclopedia of Social Work,* 18th ed. New York: National Association of Social Workers.
Smith, S. A. 1975. Natural Systems and the Elderly: An Unrecognized Resource. Report of Title III model project grant, School of Social Work, Portland State University.
Thomas, E. J., ed. 1967. *Socio-Behavioral Approach and Application to Social Work.* New York: Council on Social Work Education.
Thomas, E. J. 1970. Behavioral modification and casework. In R. Roberts and R. Nee, eds., *Theories of Social Casework.* Chicago: University of Chicago Press.
Thomlinson, R. J. 1986. Behavior theory in social work practice. In F. J. Turner, ed., *Social Work Treatment.* 3d ed. New York: Free Press.
Tobin, S. S. 1977. Old people. In H. Maas, ed., *Social Service Research: Review of Studies.* New York: National Association of Social Workers.
Tobin, S. S. (in press). Psychodynamic treatment of the family and the institutionalized individual. In N. E. Miller and G. D. Cohen, eds., *Psychodynamic Research Perspectives on Development, Psychopathology, and Treatment in Later Life.*
Tolson, E. R. 1988. *The Metamodel and Clinical Social Work.* New York: Columbia University Press.
Toseland, R. 1977. A problem-solving group workshop for older persons. *Social Work* 22(4):323–324.
Turner, F.J. 1986. *Psychosocial Theory.* In F. J. Turner, ed., *Social Treatment,* 3d ed. New York: Free Press.
Vattano, A. J. 1978. Self-management procedures for coping with stress. *Social Work* 28(2):113–119.

Waskel, S. 1981. The elderly, change, and problem solving. *Journal of Gerontological Social Work* 3(4):77–81.

Wasser, E. 1966. *Creative Approaches in Casework with the Aging.* New York: Family Service Association of America.

Wasserman, S. L. 1974. Ego psychology. In F. J. Turner, ed., *Social Work Treatment.* New York: Free Press.

Werner, H. D. 1965. *A Rational Approach to Social Casework.* New York: Association Press.

Werner, H. D. 1982. *Cognitive Therapy: A Humanistic Approach.* New York: Free Press.

Werner, H. D. 1986. Cognitive theory. In F. J. Turner, ed., *Social Work Treatment.* 3d ed. New York: Free Press.

Wolinsky, M. A. 1986. Marital therapy with older couples. *Social Casework* 67(8):475–483.

Wolpe, J. 1973. *The Practice of Behavior Therapy.* New York: Pergamon Press.

Zarit, S. H. 1980. *Aging and Mental Disorders: Psychological Approaches to Assessment and Treatment.* New York: Free Press.

6

Group Work and Older Persons

TOBY BERMAN-ROSSI, D.S.W.
Columbia University School of Social Work

Groups are universal and ever present. They are central to our lives. From the first moment of our birth when we are ushered into the family, we live within groups. As we move beyond that initial group, new collective experiences must take up the tasks of nurturing and sustaining social living. Traveling through life, groups become the fabric of our daily lives, joining us to each other in common cause, through the affection of common bonds. Connections to kin, kith, work, school, recreation, political life and community all achieve form and are sustained through groups. Taken together, groups become the touchstone by which we develop and sustain our connections to each other. Our sense of ourselves as social beings is created in interaction with others and is sustained by collective experience. With aging the attenuation of group connections becomes a significant threat to the social self of older persons. Such a threat, intensified by increasing loss of attachments to the physical and social environment can ultimately place life itself at risk.

While groups are a normative part of our lives, once placed in a professional context they immediately assume another character. Articulation of purpose and function, method and skill, becomes a compelling task for the professional social worker. Clarity is required as we define how our helping activities are responsive to human need, how they enrich clients lives, and how social workers make a difference.

The author is appreciative of the helpful editorial suggestions of Professor Irving Miller.

NEEDS OVER THE LIFE COURSE

A consideration of the needs of this population across the life course is indispensable to planning group service for them. The aging process itself represents a significant and often severe challenge to older persons. Central to this challenge is the presence of a high degree of change, loss, and uncertainty. Assaults and insults to the older person's sense of self often result. Current demographics of aging suggest that older persons fall within two fairly distinct groups: 1) those relatively healthy and active; and 2) those more vulnerable and at risk (Mayer 1983). All older persons must, however, cope with change, loss, and unpredictability, as well as the normal dependencies of aging (Blenkner 1969), regardless of Mayer's categories. These inevitable dependencies of aging lie within four areas: economic, physical, mental, and social, and become the context for the events over which the elderly have increasingly little control (Seligman and Elder 1986). Older people know and fear the reality of decline in health status and intensification of functional impairment with increasing age (Mayer 1983). The fact that suicide occurs more frequently among aged peers than any other age group (Brody and Brody 1987) is often known among the elderly. Just when the need for social supports is greatest, their availability is steadily declining. The threat to loss of self image, is greatest when one is elderly. "At no other point in the life cycle of the normal individual is one's narcissism and the integrity of the self challenged so forcefully" (Sorensen 1986:534).

How older people cope with and adapt to continuous narcissistic injuries (Sorensen 1986) and survive physically, socially, and emotionally, within their environment, becomes a riveting question. Kaufman (1986) sought to elucidate this issue by looking at the meaning of aging to the elderly themselves. Her findings indicate that all of her subjects did not think of themselves as aging or aged per se; they thought of themselves as themselves. To them their selves were ageless. They acted based upon the sense of self they knew throughout their lives. Kaufman learned that it was exactly this ageless self which mediates the demands of change and provides the continuity and meaning older people need to cope with change. If the self is constant, the impact of change is lessened. When older people aged well they maintained their ageless selves. When problems arose in coping and adaptation, chinks in the self became evident. If older persons could no longer preserve their selves and were not whom they knew themselves to be, who were they? Loss of identity is clearly correlated with decline and unsuccessful aging. Tobin (1985), in the course of a lecture, told the story of a student's beginning experience in aging. Essentially the following occurred:

> When the student asked the old woman who the young woman was in the picture, she answered that it was she. The student thought, oh, that's the old woman when she was young. The woman thought, yes, that's me. She had no need to say "that's me when I was younger." Her sense of self provided the unity for her in a way which the student had yet to understand.

In their examination of the social and psychological conditions explaining differences in adapting to stress Lieberman and Tobin (1983) similarly note that maintenance of a sense of self, in the face of adversities of later life, is correlated with successful aging.

If a sense of self develops over time, through activity, and "is a product of interaction between the growing human organism and its environment" (Bronfenbrenner 1979:16), what occurs if interaction with the environment diminishes? Rose (1963) believes that a part of the self dies with each loss and that a segment of the self is consequently called upon to change. This change is not necessarily a positive one. If loss is associated with role change, as with retirement and widowhood, and is not matched by role replacement, a narrowing of the self-conception occurs (Rose 1963; George 1980). Self-identities are reflected in the numbers of social roles and social engagements the individual entertains. The depreciation of the self as a result of a process of depersonalization becomes a natural outcome of an increasingly restricted social world in which the numbers of social contacts are diminished for the older person (Coe 1965). An uninterrupted process of loss can result in an emotional state reflecting a sense of helplessness and hopelessness so profound that the development of disease itself can be hastened or induced (Engel 1968). Agism burrowed within can prompt the older person to withdraw (Seligman and Elder 1986) and deprive the older person available opportunities or those which can be created.

This state of psychological and environmental impotence is not a natural outgrowth of the aging process, but rather a profound distortion of the symbiotic tie between older people and their physical and social environments (Schwartz 1961; Germain and Gitterman 1980). Given the ubiquity of power inbalances between the elderly and society (Nahemow 1983) such a distortion is not surprising. Older persons are continuously asked to adapt to a world in which the power of others looms increasingly larger in their lives. In this society with an inequitable distribution of wealth, two-thirds of older black women live alone in hopeless poverty (Brody and Brody 1987), while those who make the strongest claim fare better in receiving their share of limited resources. As age and the likelihood of frailty increases, the expressions of the elderly become muted unless others help to swell their voices.

Much of the literature on assertion and control of one's environment has concerned itself with those institutionalized (Berman-Rossi 1986; Gubrium 1974; Kahana 1974; Pastalan 1983; Schutz and Brenner 1977; Tobin and Lieberman 1976). The conclusions of these works, particularly that passivity is a predictor of vulnerability, is applicable to all older persons. Assertion is required for psychological, social, and actual physical survival. Aging in role is an active, not a passive process. Activity mediates "the impact of role on the aging process" and shapes or reshapes the role itself (White Riley 1986:161). The greater the perceived control over ones' stressors the lesser are the actual aversive and harmful effects of the stressors themselves (Schutz and Brenner 1977). The greater the degree of control, the greater is the decrease in trauma associated with change (Pastalan 1983). The sense of oneself as competent rises dramatically as one experiences oneself as capable of influencing the environment. Competence, like the sense of self, is created through interaction with the environment (Germain 1987).

DEFINING PRACTICE STRATEGIES

Three central sets of life course needs of older persons influence our definition of practice strategies. Our previous discussion had highlighted: 1) the need to continue a meaningful life in the face of the inevitability of loss, change, the unpredictability of an uncertain future, and death; 2) the need to sustain, strengthen, and give expression to the "ageless self"; and 3) the need to exert influence in interaction with one's physical and social environment. These needs exist whether the older person is part of Mayer's (1983) first category of comparatively well and able elders, or whether she or he falls into the second group of frail elderly.

Our practice strategies are set within the value perspective that all older persons, irrespective of capabilities, have the human right to live their lives as fully as possible (Monk 1985). In addition, the worker must believe in the potential of all elderly persons to change and in their potential to sustain their own lives. Such beliefs are rooted in the corollary belief that only when the environment is responsive to the needs of older persons can their full potential be realized.

Our practice strategies therefore eschews establishing a dependent, paternalistic relationship in which the worker "does good to" the client "for the client's sake" (Gaylin et al. 1981). We seek a special partnership relationship through which the elderly can increasingly command more of their own lives, thereby mitigating some of the power inequities between them and the world around them. These ideas about helping are based on a wish to empower clients, and are designed to enhance opportunities by which the older person can reaffirm his or her sense of a competent self. A model focused on strengths, not deficits, is required (Miller and Solomon 1979). A competence oriented perspective (Libassi and Turner 1981; Maluccio 1981) assumes that self is reaffirmed in the course of experience. A high degree of congruence between older people and their environments supports the most competent self. The distance the older person travels from the sense of self she or he has known or desires, is the distance the social worker must travel with the older person to counteract the depersonalization of the self with aging. Increasing the predictability and controllability of the physical and social environment, become core means for preserving the ageless self.

There is a common belief that this practice approach has greater applicability to the well elderly than with those frail, or to the young-old than with the very-old. While the greater dependence of the frail clearly requires an active professional approach to structuring a responsive environment, it runs some risk of sliding into unnecessary paternalism. The risk of paternalism can be reduced by professional discipline, skill in implementing this strategy, and a differential assessment unequivocally justifying it. Putting these approaches into practice should not exclude the older person from the process irrespective of their functional capacity. Choice is critical to life for all people (Lee 1983). It is the professional who must find the way to involve the older person and be sensitive to their cues or wish for assertion. An example from my own practice will illustrate:

> It was the second meeting, in a long-term care facility, for a group of five women all of whom had severe Alzheimer's disease. The group was formed to lessen some of the social isolation they experienced. It was hoped that if social connections could be established among the women during the group, these connections might be transferred to everyday living. At the first session the women agreed to meet together to enjoy themselves. When they were not able to suggest anything they might want to do or talk about, I offered to bring music. They agreed. After spending several hours finding recordings representing their ethnic groups

> I excitedly arrived for the meeting. I arranged the members in a circle and began serving juice and cookies. The mood was pleasant and relaxed. As we finished, I mentioned that I had brought records I thought they would enjoy. A change in Mrs. C. became readily apparent. She began to grimace, talk to herself, and started rolling the skirt of her dress in knots. The other members seemed not to notice and were finishing their refreshments. I said Mrs. C., "you look a little unhappy right now." There was silence. Some of other members looked up. She leaned toward me and placing her face five inches from mine said, with great force, "I hate listening to music." I moved back a little and said "oh, I didn't know that" and asked her what she did like to do. She moved her face away, smiled, and said "I like to listen to stories." I smiled and said to the other members that Mrs. C. would rather listen to stories than listen to music and then asked what they would like to do. The two other women who seemed to understand the discussion said they liked stories too and asked me if I would tell them a story. I looked at Mrs. C. and she agreed. I rolled the phonograph away and began a story about myself. My tale lead to wonderful reminiscing on the part of the women. They asked for more stories next week. I agreed. As Mrs. C. wheeled herself away she grabbed my hand, put her head on it, smiled and said "I like you." I smiled, held her hand and said "I like you too."

The issue of control and predictability in the environment was strikingly clear for Mrs. C. Her words of the initial session were insufficient to assert herself. She needed to see the phonograph and be in the group. Through verbal and nonverbal action, in the community of her peers, Mrs. C. asserted her ageless self. As a result, she felt and actually became more competent in creating the kind of world in which she wanted to live. Her effort to establish a personal connection with the worker helped mediate differences in power (Nahemow 1983). For a moment, at least, she created a microcosm in which her world was again satisfying (Kastenbaum 1983).

GROUP EXPERIENCE FOR OLDER PERSONS: THE MUTUAL AID GROUP

Group services become an ideal form to actualize our practice strategies for empowering older persons. The very existence of groups becomes the affirmation and realization of a belief in the older person's ability to contribute meaningfully to the lives of others as well as his or her own.

Contributing in groups occurs naturally. Tropp put it this way: "And this is the way it is in life; people have from time immemorial helped each other, sans benefit of therapy. Just as people do not have to be taught to breathe, so they move to help each other" (Tropp 1968:270). The powerful heuristic conception of the group as a mutual aid system is built upon this familiar phenomenon: Even when the obstructions of a complex, competitive, industrial, society are present, the movement of people, faintly or strongly, will be towards each other. Though all who work with people in groups understand this centripetal movement, Schwartz (1961) brought the unifying concept of mutual aid into the professional arena and provided the base for the development of future writings on mutual aid (Gitterman 1979; Lee and Swenson 1986; Shulman 1984; 1985/86). Schwartz's definition of a group for social work purposes, allows us to see how powerful is this concept of mutual aid. He writes:

> The group is an enterprise in mutual aid, an alliance of individuals who need each other, in varying degrees, to work on certain common problems. The important fact is that this is a helping system in which the clients need each other as well as the worker. This need to use each other, to create not one but many helping relationships, is a vital ingredient of the group process and constitutes a common need over and above the specific tasks for which the group was formed. (1961:p. 15).

This definition enlivens elements which have special relevance to work with older people in groups and helps elucidate the nature of the helping process within groups. The value, to the elderly, of these mutual aid properties intrinsic to groups are affirmed by the extensive use of groups in practice with older people. Both Burnside (1978) and Hartford (1980, 1985) document these efforts.

Shulman (1984, 1985/86) elaborates nine aspects of the mutual aid group and provides an organizing frame to consider the meaning of mutual aid group experience for older persons. The nine components are interdependent and reciprocal.

1. *Sharing Data:* When group members help each other work on a variety of tasks, they simultaneously share ideas, beliefs, and solutions which are derived from their rich lives. Whether it is how to secure services within a long-term care facility, how to cope with the loss of a loved one, or how to knot a tie, the group provides the chance to share personal truths of help to others. The older person's sense of self is validated as others try out his or her suggestions.

2. *The Dialectical Process:* A dialectical process ensues as members consider different aspects of a point. As they listen, and clarify the opinions of others, their own thinking emerges and as it is shared back and forth the group to moves toward a synthesis. The group provides, for the older person, a safe environment in which to formulate his or her thinking and once again confirms a belief in their own ability to do so. Regardless of the simplicity or complexity of the discussion, group member have the experience of participating in a process where their ideas are valued by the worker and some in the group. A sense of self is further established and affirmed when one can distinguish oneself from others.

3. *Discussing a Taboo Area:* Stereotyping of the older person carries with it a definition of what is appropriate for older people to think, feel, and do. These restricting images, once internalized constitute powerful forces with which the elderly must struggle. The mutual aid group provides an opportunity for members to create a culture in which an alternate definition of acceptability can be spelled out. Personal and collective liberation occurs from discussing personally significant content, such as, sexuality, anger at loved ones or helpers, as well as acceptance after one has discussed such forbidden areas. This process of discussing "forbidden" material takes on special significance as one approaches the latter part of one's life. A consideration of the limits of future time provides a strong incentive to use the present to work on material which a life review may have highlighted (Butler 1963).

4. *The "All-in-the-Same-Boat" Phenomenon:* Evidence from practice and theoretical and empirical literature indicates that group association reduces isolation, alienation, and loneliness by providing a medium for strengthening connections between older people and their social world (Lowy 1962; Mayadas and Hink 1974). The social identity of the elderly is strengthened by social experiences and other links to the social environment. Mutual aid emphasizes the connections among group members and thus fortifies the social bond among them. The knowledge that one is not alone in one's thoughts, feelings or deeds provides invaluable support for older people who are among the most isolated and alienated in our society. Such universal and universalizing phenomena serve to mitigate some of the stigma of agism. Forman's (1971) notion of "shared jeopardy" becomes a centripetal force drawing older people towards each other.

5. *Mutual Support:* Offering help to another can have electrifying power. For many, particularly the frail elderly, negative self-images crowd out feelings of worth. Such feelings become obstacles to giving to others. The knowledge that one can give and be given to connects one to the core of humanity in a manner unrivaled by other experiences. Lee's (1981) experience with a group of mentally frail women is founded upon enormous faith in the ability of all human beings to connect meaningfully and give to each other in some way. A worker in a community center, with a more competent group, tells a similar story:

> A poetry group was discussing a poem about the loss of a loved one. Mrs. Ramen, a widow of four months, began to sob uncontrollably. The members were silenced. No one moved to comfort her. The worker said she could see how strongly she was feeling and wondered if she were thinking about her own recent loss. Mrs. Ramen lashed out shouting that no one there knew what she felt. No one had lost a mate. Miss Santiago, a quiet woman who rarely spoke said she thought she could understand. Mrs. Ramen continued shouting, that she of all people couldn't understand because she had never even been married. Miss Santiago's eyes filled with tears. In her quiet, shy, manner she said she thought she could understand. She lost her sister two years ago. They had lived together for eighty-one years. She said she knew she would never love anyone else again. As she spoke, she picked up her belongings and started to leave the room. Mrs. Ramen, stilled by Miss Santiago's words, walked over, said she was sorry, and hugged Miss Santiago. Both women, in tears, embraced for a long while. Miss Santiago remained in the room after everyone had left. I sat next to her. She said she had vowed to never tell anyone about her sister; it was too private, but something moved her. I asked how she felt now. She was silent for a while and as if from some place deep inside she said she felt good, really good. It was the first time since her sister died that she ever felt close to anyone.

Moments such as these have the power to alter the remaining life of the older person. Once connections between group members are established on a deep emotional level, the possibilities for engagement are virtually or almost limitless. A view of oneself as capable of giving radiates into the nooks and crannies of our lives.

6. *Mutual Demand and Mutual Expectations:* Bennett (1963) states that older persons are among the least regimented, least structured,

and least observed members of society. Given a life of quiet isolation, many elderly go largely unattended. A social worker writes:

> After a visit to a colleague, I encountered a woman of about 85 years in the elevator. Her wool coat, stockings, and shoes were urine soaked. She walked hesitatingly with her walker and offered not a single sign of acknowledgment as I carefully held three sets of doors for her. In conversation with my colleague, she shared that she knew Mrs. Schwartz for years and it simply hadn't occurred to her that she do anything to try to be of help. She noted that if it were a family/child neglect situation she automatically would have acted.

Negative stereotypes and reluctance to become involved prompts us to ask less and less of the elderly. Abilities atrophy and the deterioration of skills becomes progressive. Mutual aid groups can be a radical departure from the insults of agism. The underlying belief that older persons are capable of growth and giving, prompts mutual demand and mutual expectations. What is intrinsically striking about an interactive helping system is that members demand and expect from each other, as well as form the worker. The distinctive position of a peer means that one has known much of what is experienced by others. This personalized knowledge, and process of identification among peers, increases the determination not to allow others to languish with their problems. In saving others, one is saved.

7. *Helping with Specific Problems:* The mutual aid group provides an opportunity for members to be assisted with specific problems. It allows members to move from a sometimes formless sense of generalized worry, to naming the specific nature of the concern. This helps members to act and points the way for problem solving activity. Such assistance is specifically helpful for enabling older persons to develop an active, assertive stance, in matters of importance to them.

8. *Rehearsal:* Group members are encouraged to audition new skills and ideas in a safe environment. The experience of going over how one would handle difficult, particularly taboo themes increases notably a sense of competence. Such support is particularly strengthening to those who have come to mistrust their abilities. The unity of thinking, feeling, and doing is marvelous and exhilarating.

9. *Strength in Numbers Phenomenon:* Challenging the powerful in society is a complex, if not fearsome, experience for most of us. Obstacles to assertion are omnipresent and began to develop very early in

life. Agism, an increasingly unresponsive environment, and an increasing sense of personal vulnerability of the older person, makes self-declaration even more difficult. If assertion is required for survival, then such assertion becomes more possible when one is supported by others. Needs often have a greater chance of being met when voiced by a collective, rather than an individual. Individual potency increases with collective potency.

The following example illustrates the interrelation of our last three components of the mutual aid group. The other six components are readily apparent as well. The group is an open ended floor group made up of residents on a health-related service in a long-term care facility. The work of the group was to help residents work on problems, issues, and concerns emanating from their life together as older persons on a particular floor in the institution.

> *June 2d:* Midway into the meeting, after a brief pause, two of the members began speaking about how they no longer felt as safe as they used to on the floor. They continued on about how the home was not as good as it used to be. Others joined in and the general sense of discouragement was strong. I said I wondered what was contributing to their feeling less safe because I hadn't heard them express these feelings as strongly before. The members continued in general terms, stating that's just the way it feels. Nothing I tried facilitated their being more precise.

> *June 9th:* After we finished a piece of work on selecting members for a variety of committees, I said I was still thinking about last week's discussion of how unsafe they had come to feel and I wondered if we could return to that discussion. Without much energy they agreed. I said I had left feeling quite unsettled last week and I imagined that they might be feeling that way as well. I said I had known them for a while and because these were new feelings I couldn't help but think that something had changed for them, to contribute to their feeling so unprotected. The members looked at each other. I waited. The silence went on for almost a minute. Mr. Brown took a deep breath and said: "The reason we feel so unsafe is that the Home is admitting sicker people to our floor and since there is no staff on the floor after nine, we all feel responsible for the newcomers and we also feel unable to take care of them." Mr. Brown's courage in sharing what the members were struggling with paved the way for our discussion of the nature of the problem and how they would rectify the situation. We agreed to discuss next steps at the following meeting.

June 16th: At this meeting the members decided they wanted to speak to Administration. They felt that if "they" wanted to bring in sicker residents (which the floor didn't want) then "they" would have to provide for them. They rehearsed who would say what to whom and also role played a number of "what if" situations. When Mr. Kelly said he was worried that the Home could get back at them, most of the other members said that there were too many of them and that the Home couldn't punish them all. Besides, if any one of them sensed any of that going on, they would all go down to the administrators office.

The talks between residents, the floor social worker, and the administrator continued off and on over the next six weeks. The Home ultimately agreed to provide an aid for the night shift and agreed to provide a nurse if the numbers of frailer residents increased on the floor. After all, they said, they too were concerned about the residents.

OBSTACLES TO ENGAGEMENT IN GROUPS

The development and offering of group services for the elderly, must be considered carefully. Bringing older people together in groups does not, of itself, ensure that the group will be a satisfying experience in which members help themselves and each other. Obstacles to mutual aid and to the ability of people to use each other are inevitable. These are compounded by particular characteristics of the aging experience and the meaning of group experience for the aging.

First, the preponderant experience of loss, change, and unpredictability, militates against the establishment of stable relationships and a cohesive sense of self. An increase in the here and now aspects of life adds to ambivalence about involvement. Second, the nearness of death, especially for the frail older person, makes him or her thoughtful about how to use remaining time. The extending of the self into new territory may or may not be what is sought. Ambivalence about involvement becomes prevalent. Involvement in a life review process further heightens the importance of choice (Butler 1963). Time and continuity of services become particularly salient for those whose personal time is limited. Third, participation in groups reflects one's cohort group attachment and life experience. Many older persons have not had much formal experience in groups. For example, groups focused upon social action and groups working on life transitional issues may feel alien. The newness of the collective experience may reawaken self-doubt and performance anxiety. Withdrawal or refusal to be engaged can also be a response when the sense of self as competent is challenged. Fourth, as the physical and social environment retreats, as frailties increase, risk and the possibility of failure looms larger. For the frail elderly who have the fewest resources, failure is an experience to be particularly avoided. Remaining alone and within ones own world is at least a familiar experience with which one might make peace. Such aspects of group experience for the elderly will inform all components of practice with the aged in groups.

CONTINUUM OF GROUP SERVICES

A continuum of group services is based upon the assumption that all groups are capable of simultaneously making demands and providing opportunities. Demands and opportunities are interdependent concepts and when considered together give depth to practice. This continuum is structured along two lines: 1) the nature of the involvement required of the older person; and 2) what the group provides the older person. Gitterman (1979, 1986) proposes that many group related ideas commonly thought of as absolute are actually relative in nature. This notion is especially pertinent to work with older persons, because the aged are not a homogeneous group. At the least they are made up of four categories; 1) those physically and mentally able; 2) those physically able and mentally frail; 3) those physically frail and mentally able; and 4) those physically and mentally frail. The wide range of needs and abilities demonstrated by these groups of older persons requires specifying all conceptions of the value of group activities, group properties, and group structure. Gitterman highlights three for consideration: factors of time, size, and the physical environment.

Time: The limits of time are often thought to be an energizing force enabling group members to proceed with greater consciousness. Time-limited groups, for example, a new residents orientation group, help members engage quickly, do their work, and then move apart. However sensible, this idea of bounded time may well become a negative reality for members who have little conception of time beyond the immediate experience. Discrepancies between worker time and member time orientations introduces discordant notes into the working relationship. On the other hand, open-ended ongoing groups, in long term residential care facilities though lacking the spur of time limits provide the chance to have a secure, ongoing group experience in which members can come and go. Such groups reassure members that it will always be there for them and this provides the kind of support not available from a time-limited group.

Group size: It is commonly held that large group activities such as lectures and concerts are valuable precisely because they make few demands upon participants. Friedlander (1983) observers that in community centers, such groups allow for a minimum of exertion while enabling members to feel part of a group simply by virtue of their common presence. Demand is low and opportunity high. Miller and Solomon's (1980) experience echoes Friedlander's. But take the same exact group and consider involving those cognitively more limited. We can see that the size of the group and the largeness of the physical environment may prove too great for even passive involvement. The movement from small, intimate groups, with familiar faces, to large groups with unfamiliar faces in unknown spaces may raise anxiety and may not provide the essential support necessary for engagement. Small face to face groups are conducive to a high degree of intimacy as well as demands upon participants. Each member is more visible by virtue of size. The greater demands on individual members in the small group is more than offset by increased support to each member as well as by the higher staff to member ratio. These qualities of the small group makes them useful to the very capable as well as the least able.

Physical environment: The physical environment is a critical element of group experience. If structured positively, the physical setting can facilitate mutual aid and the experiencing of competence. Environmental distractions can be overwhelming even to those with only minor difficulty. Consequently particular care must be taken with those cognitively limited who can only concentrate on a few stimuli at a time. Room arrangements which inhibit premature intimacy, may militate against feelings of comfort for those who need to make physical contact to establish connections.

The following illustrates the interrelation of time, size, and the physical environment. It suggests that what may be true for older people in general, may not be true for a particular one. A senior center worker reports the following:

> Mrs. Diaz, a 73-year-old woman, widowed four years ago, recently decided to "try" the senior center. The worker's first choice of activity for Mrs. Diaz was an afternoon musical performance. She thought the music would be pleasant and little would be

asked of Mrs. Diaz. When Mrs. Diaz arrived at the auditorium she froze. She had never seen so many older people together and couldn't bring herself to go into such a large room where she knew no one. She chose instead a baking group.

This small face-to-face group allowed her to enter at a point of competence, to continue a familiar social role and to perpetuate her ageless less by recreating the past in the present.

In creating groups, the social worker seeks a correspondence between demands and opportunities and the abilities and needs of older persons. While some generalizations can be offered with confidence, all must be adapted to the individuals under consideration. An assessment of demands, opportunities, abilities, and needs becomes the basis for a strategy for practice. If the worker determines that there is close congruence between them little else is required. If on the other hand there is a tenuous fit the worker is than called upon to ask the following questions: 1) If the physical and social environmental were more responsive, would the older person be able to use the group in a satisfying manner? 2) Is the older person's sense of competence better served by choosing another group or by trying to master the group demands with additional support? 3) Is the group out of the person's grasp regardless of what supports are provided? Offering groups which strengthen abilities can only be achieved if the worker understands what she or he is asking when inviting an older person to enter a particular group. Moving from their own positions of competence, workers often underestimate the demands made on older people in group services. The worker must not unwittingly participate in creating an additional failure for the elderly. Too much is at stake. Establishing a continuum of services allows participants to enter groups where they feel comfortable. The availability of a wide range where needs and abilities and demands and opportunities are well balanced, ensures that all older persons, regardless of distinguishing characteristics, can participate in growth producing, satisfying group experiences. The professional's task is to create such opportunities.

GROUP PROPERTIES AND GROUP PURPOSE

While all group attributes have intrinsic properties they do not have intrinsic value. Value is ascribed or determined in keeping with group function, i.e., what the work of the group is, and group purpose, i.e., what it hopes to achieve. To the question is this group too large, we must ask, too large for what. When we wonder whether the group session is long enough, we must again ask, long enough for what. When we ask how a group should be composed we must ask for the relationship between members and purpose. Even the value of particular group structures can only be determined in concert with a definition of what one hopes to achieve and what the members have come together to do. A functional/operational approach allows us to think in action terms and to particularize our knowledge for each group proposed.

TYPES OF GROUPS

Groups services for older persons can be organized by a variety of conceptualizations found in the literature (Cohen and Hammerman 1974; Euster 1971; Friedlander 1983; Kubie and Landau, 1953; Lowy 1985; Miller and Solomon 1979). For example, in an early schema, Kubie and Landau (1953) suggest the following kinds of groups: self-government, programming, woodworking and painting, poetry, birthday parties, music, dramatics, and discussion groups. These groups evolved out of their nine year experience of working in a recreation center for the aged. Remarkably, these designations are very similar to more current ideas, be they groups within institutions, or groups within the community. Euster (1971) proposes that within institutions for the aged groups might include: resident councils, living unit groups, activity planning groups, special interest groups and enrichment groups. Miller and Solomon (1980) put forward four kinds of groups: formal and informal educational groups, life task or problem solving, self-government groups, and social action groups.

One unintended consequence of these designations has been the further separation of "activity and discussion, process and program, and task and growth" (Shulman 1971:222). The polarization between work with tasks and work with feelings becomes especially troublesome for both workers and group members. Dualisms distort the nature of reality. All tasks generate feelings and all feelings exist in a social context definable through a delineation of important tasks. All groups contain both instrumental and expressive functions though either may appear more apparent at any one point in time. In working with older persons in groups it becomes particularly important to eliminate such polarizations, lest the meaning of the experience be lost to the older person and only half of the experience become available to the worker. This issue is particularly troublesome to new workers with the elderly.

A first year, direct practice, social work, student, placed in a mental health clinic which served a high percentage of older persons, came to supervision all upset because she had been assigned to work with an entitlement group. She said she was afraid that she wouldn't have a chance to develop her "clinical" skills. She knew entitlements were important, but didn't know why a volunteer or case aid couldn't do that. Her supervisor asked how Mr. Farmer felt about applying for Medicaid. The student was eloquent in describing how powerfully negative that felt to him and she was excited about the chance to help him with those feelings. Her supervisor asked her to imagine where those feelings would go if Mr. Farmer were in an entitlement group. The student saw immediately that those same feelings would still be present. Then she said, but the entitlement group is a task group and has nothing to do with feelings. The rest of supervision was spent on helping the student understand how work with complex tasks involves work with the complex feelings generated by the tasks.

Gitterman (1979) and Germain and Gitterman (1980) put forth a way of thinking about groups which transcends these problematic dichotomies and provides a framework for developing, offering, and sustaining group services. These groups might be organized for and offered to members, or might be arranged so that members can choose their own focus for the group. Germain and Gitterman suggests that people's needs, or "problems-in-living" fall within three areas: life transitional, interpersonal troubles, and environmental obstacles. These labels are not intended to signify mutually exclusive categories but rather to highlight a way of organizing groups based upon the propensity for certain kinds of content to predominate. It is understood that within their lifetime, all groups may focus upon all three problems in living. In addition, groups within each arena may use both activity and discussion, and will work on tasks and feelings associated with the tasks for which the members have gathered. As we discuss these three problems-in-living, the reader will immediately be reminded of our previous discussion of the needs of older persons across the life course.

Life Transitions: Stress associated with life transitions arises from three sources: developmental changes, status and role demands including stigmatized life statuses, and crisis events. Each and every need defined within these boundaries can become the basis for a group service. They might be organized to help older people cope with the physical, biological, and cognitive changes associated with aging and may range from a lecture series open to a wide audience, to a smaller face to face group of selected older people to work on coping with change and loss in their lives. The nature and varieties of efforts to create group services to help the elderly cope with the vicissitudes of change and loss are very numerous. Only a few examples can be cited: Parry (1980) reports on helping members manage the ravages of chronic illness and disability; Rosengarten (1986) writes of establishing extended social networks of home care groups to help beyond the period of acute recovery form illness; Orr (1986) draws a poignant description of efforts to help group members to deal with the death of one of their own. Groups might also concern themselves with the shift from a work centered life, to a life of "retirement" activity. The need to sustain meaningful activity continues throughout ones lifetime and is strikingly exemplified in the Retired Senior Volunteer Program. In this program, seniors perpetuate their ageless, competent selves serving others. Leisure-time groups become prime examples of groups which simultaneously foster continuation of social roles and social competencies and development of new interests to replace or supplement former pastimes. Getzel (1980) believes that certain groups, e.g., poetry groups, by their very existence, convey a belief in the creative potential of older persons, which encourages the elderly to participate and create poetry in their lives. Recent appraisals of the use of reminiscence with the aged demonstrate the usefulness of this activity (Kaminsky 1984). Reminiscence groups (Pincus 1970; Greenhouse Gardella 1985) and groups utilizing a life-review process (Butler 1963) enable the older person to validate their past, recapture their lives in the present and forge links between both (Lowy 1962). Howell puts the experience of many older people into poignant words when she states "I am what I remember about myself" (1983:105). Reminiscence, as a psychological mechanism, is especially helpful to sustaining the sense of self in the very old (Tobin 1988). The mutual aid group, with its understanding mutual support and shared jeopardy provides an ideal vehicle for assisting with the crises of loss of spouses, loved ones, illness and infirmity.

Environmental Obstacles: Environmental needs, physical or social, can be approached in two ways: 1) through groups specifically organized for that purpose; and 2) as an accompaniment or outgrowth of work on life transitional stressors or interpersonal obstacles. Institutional settings often establish groups designed to help residents deal with the complexities of institutional life, a good example of which is the Resident Council. These groups have as their daunting task helping residents negotiate life in an institution. Focused upon such issues as service procedures, e.g., when medication is administered, and the quality of services, e.g., the temperature of food, they can also serve the interests of the institution as well. Similar groups can be found in community and senior centers, and everywhere the elderly are encouraged to take charge of their lives. As group members work on life transitional or interpersonal needs, distance from the environment may become apparent. Coping with disability may lead to the need for changes in the physical environment to facilitate connection with the world outside. The flow back and forth between life transitional and environmental needs is a natural one. It is facilitated by the worker's consciousness of the interconnections.

As with the physical environment, groups can be designed to enhance the social environment. Social network linkages and similar efforts flow from the work on life transitional and interpersonal issues. These groups become powerful forces connecting people to each other and to the world around them. For example, groups for relatives in institutions, welcoming committees in unions, community centers, and senior centers, are there to connect new members to each other, thereby lessening isolation. Birthday groups, holiday celebrations and a whole host of social occasion groups all re-create normative social occurrences not otherwise possible for isolated elderly. Work on life's transitions and interpersonal tensions also becomes associated with the need for social linkages. Loneliness after the loss of a spouse can lead to an increased need for companionship; coping with illness can prompt joining a survivors group; and being helped can prompt one to volunteer help to others.

Interpersonal Obstacles: The stresses of life can generate increased interpersonal tensions within all natural groups in which individuals live or are closely associated. Members of groups, roommates within institutions, families, and floor mates, all can develop problematic relationships and communication patterns. As with other problems-in-living, special groups such as roommate groups, or family groups can be created to help members understand and develop new ways of relating.

Role of the Worker

A conceptualization of a group as a mutual aid system inevitably has strong implications for defining the role of the social worker in the group. While there are a multiplicity of helping relationships the social worker's activity is directed toward helping others act (Schwartz 1961). It is in empowering members to attend to the needs which have drawn them together that the worker's highest aspirations are achieved.

The social worker becomes that force within the group directed towards helping members: move beyond the bounds of their individual isolation, believe in the possibility of change through group association, and find the connections between their definition of social need and the group's defined social purpose. This helping network of peers counter balances the power of the worker and provides members with an experience which helps them once again exert influence. This kind of success encourages efforts to influence their larger environment.

STAGES OF GROUP DEVELOPMENT AND SOCIAL WORK SKILL

Workers are more likely to act more consciously, skillfully, and relevantly if they understand the stages of group development. More fully developed groups are better able to attend to the needs which have brought them together (Berman-Rossi 1987). Most group development literature (Bennis and Shephard 1956; Garland, Jones, and Kolodney 1965) has been concerned with time limited, closed groups. Schopler and Galinsky (1984) have extended our understanding by identifying different developmental patterns in open-ended groups.

Our practice literature has paid scant attention to working with groups of older people over time. Lowy (1985) and Miller and Solomon (1979) are exceptions. Without such knowledge workers will have limited understanding about how to engage and sustain older persons in groups. Five interdependent component of worker and group life, across stages of group development will be briefly touched upon here (Berman-Rossi 1988). All are informed by our knowledge of the elderly within groups: 1) character of group system; 2) character of member behavior, 3) member and collective tasks; 4) tasks of the social worker; and 5) skills of the social worker. The classification of Garland, Jones, and Kolodney (1965) will be used.

Stage 1: Pre-Affiliation

At this initial stage, the group lacks a sense of group identity. Uncertainty predominates and exacerbates the older person's sense of insecurity. A climate of trust is undeveloped and stress rather than support is felt. An atmosphere of mistrust prevails. Previous life and cohort experiences militate against intimacy. Members fear failure. Vulnerability increases dependence and the need for support. The group must develop a collective understanding of its work in which all members interests are represented. Members fear that their needs are unique and cannot be satisfied. The social worker is called upon to understand the members' fear of failure, their hesitancy to assert themselves, and their need to develop an understanding of what they will do together. Skills include offering an understanding of how the group can serve the members, even the frailest members; helping members express their ideas about the group in whatever form they can, and to respond to covert messages by making their meaning clearer.

Stage 2: Power and Control

Issues of power and control dominate. Regardless of functional capacity members are most concerned about their power in relation to the worker. Issues of power and control are intimidating to members and the group is closest to possible dissolution. Many elderly are unused to challenging those in authority, particularly those trying to be helpful. Age differences make difficult work even harder. Those with fewer environmental resources feel even greater vulnerability. Members express themselves in oblique and indirect terms. Group energy is strong. Though members begin to look to each other for support, ambivalence predominates. The group does come to grips with the power of the worker and moves on with its work. The worker must help members use each other and tackle his or her power. The worker must accept the challenge to his or her authority and assist members to express their feelings and ideas about task performance. Unless group members are successful in this stage, their development as a mutual aid system will be hampered. An example from practice will illustrate. A social worker in a union sponsored Retirees Reach Out Program writes:

> It was the sixth meeting of our Welcoming Committee Group. In the previous meeting we had agreed that I would call each new retiree, welcome them to the program, and describe what it offered. Shortly after we began, Mr. Rivera stood up, looked at me and the seven men and women gathered around the table, and said: "Some of us were talking and we don't agree that you should be the one to call the new retirees first. We believe that

the members should make the first call. It really is our program and we would like to have this first chance at welcoming new members." I looked around the room and everyone nodded in agreement. There was a solemn tone in the air. I paused for a moment to take in the suggestion and said: "I think that's a great idea and it's really fine with me." I smiled and with a little laugh said, "Can I at least get to call them second." They all laughed and Mrs. Samson said, "Of course, we just want to be first."

Without missing a beat they quickly moved on to figuring out how they could get the names of new retirees in a timely manner. Their manner was energetic, focused, and relaxed. As they began to serve coffee I said; "There's something I've been thinking about, as I've been sitting here, and would like to hear your thinking on it." They nodded for me to continue. I said I was struck by how strongly they all seemed to feel about this suggestion. They nodded in agreement and commented on how it was important to them. I continued and said: "It makes me wonder what you felt or thought last week when you all agreed with my suggestion that I call each new member." The room was silent. There was a heaviness in the air. I waited. The members were obviously uncomfortable. Mr. Brown said: "I didn't agree with you but didn't want to hurt your feelings." Ms Niman said, "I didn't agree either, but no one else was saying anything, so I didn't." We continued to discuss their hesitancy to confront my suggestion. When all but Mr. Strocchia had spoken, Mr. Brown called upon him to give his thoughts. Mr. Strocchia said: "It is very hard for me to disagree with you. First you are a lady, and second you are in charge. I always felt this way with all my bosses." The weight of his expression sat heavy in the room. No one spoke. Members began to gather up their belongings to go to the next program. I said I was very taken with what they had all said. I knew it took a lot of strength from all of them. I said I knew we needed to end now but I wanted them to know that I was thankful that they shared their thoughts with me and had the courage to put forth their own ideas. I said that if it was o.k. with them I would like to continue our talk about my power in the group and our working relationship. They agreed and I said I thought they had helped me understand a lot about our working together and their working with each other.

The worker learned that the group had a life outside its formal meeting time which influenced what occurred during the group meeting. She also learned that in this partnership arrangement, her helping relationship with the group was one of many, i.e., "client and worker roles shift from those of subordinate recipient and superordinate expert, [is] often assumed to be characteristic of a 'professional' relationship" (Germain and Gitterman 1980:14). The group, in this practice example, had the power to strengthen its most fearful member and in challenging the worker's authority the group had become stronger as had each of the members (Berman-Rossi 1987).

Stage 3: Intimacy

Having managed the power and control stage, members can move on towards the development of more intimate peer relationships. They have proven to each other that they have the strength necessary to assist each other. Their sense of competence has increased significantly and becomes a potent force in the movement of the group as a whole. Members trust each other and see the group as a source of strength, capable of meeting their needs. Criticism of the group is not tolerated. The worker is called upon to support the growing intimacy and to challenge remaining obstacles to engagement. Problem solving activity becomes especially strong at this point.

Stage 4: Differentiation

The group is at its most mature stage and is most preoccupied with fulfilling member needs. Relationships among members are strongest. Members feel strong attachment to each other and differences are most accepted. As a result, members can differentiate themselves from each other and in so doing individual selves are strengthened. The worker is called upon to help members use the group for satisfaction of remaining needs before disbanding the group.

Stage 5: Separation

Successful handling of this final stage of group development is imperative, if the gains of the previous stages are to remain firm. As in all endings previous losses are reawakened and reenacted in the present experience and thus poses a considerable challenge for both worker and members. An approach-avoidance pattern often appears as a means of coping with loss. The members must realistically evaluate their work, and say good bye and do so without minimizing gains in coping with their loss. The worker is called upon to: assist members in a realistic appraisal of gains, translate coded messages into overt communication, credit gains, and participate with members in an authentic appraisal of the experience. Sensitivity to the members' need to leave the group "whole" is particularly important as a means of enabling participant to integrate a successful experience into their sense of a competent self.

CONCLUSION

> Deep within every man there lies the dread of being alone in the world, forgotten by God, overlooked among the tremendous household of millions and millions. That fear is kept away by looking upon all those about one who are bound to one as friends or family, but the dread is nevertheless there and one hardly dares think of what would happen to one of us if the rest were taken away.
>
> —Soren Kierkegaard

Well-developed and skillfully offered group service programs for all older persons ensures that others will never be taken away. Group association becomes a primary means to mitigate the isolation and alienation so often the experience of older persons. A sense of belonging engendered by group participation has a powerfully beneficial effect upon the terms of engagement between the elderly and their physical and social environment. Strengthened individuals and strengthened collectives can even better the power inbalance between them and society. The decisiveness necessary for endurance is increased through belonging and participating in groups. The mutual aid group offers the elderly opportunities which sustain a sense of self. Self-expression and self-acceptance enhance self-esteem. The development of caring relationships in the midst of a continuous process of loss ensures that affective, relational, and environmental involvement will remain possible for older persons.

REFERENCES

Bennett, R. 1963. The meaning of institutional life. *The Gerontologist.* 3(3):117–125.

Bennis, W. and H. Shephard. 1956. A theory of group development. *Human Relations.* 9:415–57.

Berman-Rossi, T. 1986. The fight against hopelessness and despair: Institutionalized aged. In A. Gitterman and L. Shulman, eds., *Mutual Aid Groups and the Life Cycle.* Itasca, Ill.: F. E. Peacock Press.

Berman-Rossi, T. 1987. Empowering Groups Through Understanding Stages of Group Development. Paper presented at the Ninth Annual Program Meeting, Association for the Advancement of Social Work with Groups. Forthcoming.

Berman-Rossi, T. 1988. Tasks and Skills of the Social Worker Across Stages of Group Development. Paper presented at the 10th Annual Program Meeting, Association for the Advancement of Social Work with Groups.

Blenkner M. 1969. The normal dependencies of aging. In R. A. Kalish, ed., *The Later Years: Social Applications of Gerontology*. Monterey, Calif.: Brooks/Cole.

Brandler, S. M. 1985. The senior center: Informality in the social work function. *Journal of Gerontological Social Work* 8(3/4):195–210.

Brody E. M. and S. J. Brody. 1987. Aged: Services. *Encyclopedia of Social Work*. 18th ed. Silver Spring, Md.: National Association of Social Workers.

Brofenbrenner, U. 1979. *The Ecology of Human Development*. Cambridge, Mass.: Harvard University Press.

Burnside, I. 1984. *Working with the Elderly: Group Process and Techniques*. North Scituate, Mass.: Duxbury Press.

Butler, R. N. 1963. The Life Review An Interpretation of Reminiscence in the Aged. *Psychiatry* 26(1):65–76.

Coe, R. M. 1965. Self-Conception and Institutionalization. In A. M. Rose and W. A. Peterson, eds., *Older People and Their Social World*. Philadelphia: F. A. Davis.

Cohen, S. Z. and J. Hammerman. 1974. Social work with groups. In E. M. Brody, ed., *A Social Work Guide for Long-Term Care Facilities*. Rockville, Md.: National Institute of Mental Health.

Engel, G. L. 1968. A life setting conducive to illness: The giving-up complex. *Annals of Internal Medicine* 69:293–300.

Euster, G. L. 1971. A system of groups in institutions for the aged. *Social Casework* 52(8):523–529.

Forman, M. 1971. The alienated resident and the alienating institution. *Social Work* 16(2):47–54.

Friedlander, H. 1983. Differential use of groups in mainstreaming the handicapped elderly. In S. Saul, ed. *Group Work with the Frail Elderly: Social Work with Groups* 5(2):33–42.

Garland, J., H. Jones, and R. Kolodney. 1965. A model for stages of development in Social work groups. In S. Bernstein, ed., *Explorations in Group Work: Essays in Theory and Practice*. Boston: Boston University School of Social Work.

Gaylin, W., I. Glasser, S. Marcus, and D. J. Rothman. 1981. *Doing Good: The Limits of Benevolence*. New York: Pantheon Books.

George, L. K. 1980. *Role Transitions in Later Life*. Monterey, Calif.: Brooks/Cole.

Germain, C. B. 1987. Human development in contemporary environments. *Social Service Review* 61(4):565–580.

Germain, C. B. and A. Gitterman. 1980. *The Life Model of Social Work Practice*. New York: Columbia University Press.

Getzel, G. G. Old people, poetry, and groups. 1981. *Journal of Gerontological Social Work* 3(1):77–85.

Gitterman, A. 1979. Development of group services. *Social Work with Groups in Maternal and Child Health*. Columbia University School of Social Work and Roosevelt Hospital Department of Social Work, Conference Proceedings, June 14–15.

Gitterman, A. 1986. Developing a new group service. In A. Gitterman and L. Shulman, eds., *Mutual Aid Groups and the Life Cycle*. Itasca, Ill.: F. E. Peacock.

Gitterman, A. 1989. Building mutual support in groups. *Social Work with Groups* 12(2):5–21.

Greenhouse Gardella, L. 1985.The neighborhood group: A reminiscence group for the disoriented old. *Social Work with Groups* 8(2):43–52.

Gubrium, J. F. 1974. On multiple realities in a nursing home. In J. F. Gubrium, ed., *Late Life: Communities and Environmental Policy.* Springfield Mass.: Charles C. Thomas.

Halpern J. and G. Dlugacz. 1982. Working with groups on an inpatient psychiatric setting. In A. Lurie, G. Rosenberg, and S. Pinsky, eds., *Social Work with Groups in Health Settings.* New York: Prodist.

Hartford, M. E. 1980. The use of group methods for work with the aged. In J. E. Birren and R. B. Sloan, eds., *Handbook of Mental Health and Aging.* Englewood Cliffs, N.J.: Prentice-Hall.

Hartford, M. E. 1985. Group Work with Older Adults. A Monk, ed., *Handbook of Gerontological Services.* New York: Van Nostrand Reinhold.

Howell, S. C. 1983. The meaning of place in old age. In G. D. Rowles and R. J. Ohta, eds., *Aging and Milieu.* New York: Academic Press.

Kahana E. 1974. Matching environments to needs of the aged: A conceptual scheme. In J. F. Gubrium, ed., *Late Life: Communities and Environmental Policy.* Springfield Mass.: Charles C. Thomas.

Kaminsky, Marc. 1984. The uses of reminiscence: A discussion of the formative literature. *Journal of Gerontological Social Work.* 7(½):137–156

Kastenbaum, R. 1983. Can the clinical milieu be therapeutic? In G. D. Rowles and R. J. Ohta, eds., *Aging and Milieu.* New York: Academic Press.

Kaufman, S. R. 1986. *The Ageless Self.* Madison: University of Wisconsin Press.

Kubie, S. H. and G. Landau. 1953. *Group Work with the Aged.* New York: International Universities Press.

Lee, J. A. B. 1981. Human relatedness and the mentally impaired older person. *Journal of Gerontological Social Work* 4(2):5–15.

Lee, J. A. B. 1983. The group: A chance at human connection for the mentally impaired older person. In Shura Saul, ed. *Group Work with the Frail Elderly. Social Work with Groups* 5(2):43–55.

Lee, J. A. B. and C. Swenson. 1986. The concept of mutual aid. In A. Gitterman and L. Shulman, eds., *Mutual Aid Groups and the Life Cycle.* Itasca Ill.: F. E. Peacock.

Lieberman, M. A. and S. S. Tobin. 1983. *The Experience of Old Age.* New York: Basic Books.

Libassi M. F. and N. S. Turner. 1981. The Aging Process: Old and New Coping Tricks. In A. N. Maluccio, ed., *Promoting Competence in Clients.* New York: Free Press.

Lowy, L. 1962. The group in social work with the aged. *Social Work.* 7(4):43–50.

Lowy, L. 1985. *Social Work with the Aging.* 2d ed. New York: Longman.

Maluccio, A. N. 1981. Competence-oriented social work practice: An ecological approach. In A. N. Maluccio, ed., *Promoting Competence in Clients.* New York: Free Press.

Mayer, M. J. 1983. Demographic change and the elderly population. In Shura Saul, ed. *Group Work with the Frail Elderly. Social Work with Groups* 5(2):7–12.

Miller, I. and R. Solomon. 1979. Group service for the elderly. C. B. Germain, ed., *Social Work Practice: People and Environments.* New York: Columbia University Press.

Monk, A. 1985. Gerontological social services. In A. Monk, ed., *Handbook of Gerontological Services.* New York: Van Nostrand Reinhold.

Nahemow, L. 1983. Working with older people: The patient–physician milieu. In G. D. Rowles and R. J. Ohta, eds., *Aging and Milieu.* New York: Academic Press.

Orr, A. 1986. Dealing with the death of a group member: Visually impaired elderly in the community. In A. Gitterman and L. Shulman, eds., *Mutual Aid Groups and the Life Cycle.* Itasca, Ill.: F. E. Peacock.

Parry, J. K. 1980. Group services for the chronically ill and disabled. *Social Work with Groups* 31:59–67.

Pastalan, L. A. 1983. Environmental displacement: A literature reflecting old person-environment transactions. In G. D. Rowles and R. J. Ohta, eds. *Aging and Milieu.* New York: Academic Press.

Rose, A. M. 1963. Social and cultural factors. *Social Group Work with Older People.* New York: National Association of Social Workers.

Rosengarten, L. 1986. Creating a health-promoting group for elderly couples on a home care program. *Social Work in Health Care.* 11(4):83–92.

Schopler, J. and M. Galinsky. 1984. Meeting practice needs: Conceptualizing the open-ended group. *Social Work with Groups* 7(2):3–19.

Schutz, R. and G. Brenner. 1977. Relocation of the aged: A review and theoretical analysis. *Journal of Gerontology* 32(3):323–333.

Schwartz, W. 1961. The social worker in the group. *New Perspectives on Services to Groups: Theory, Organization and Practice.* New York: National Association of Social Workers.

Schwartz, W. 1971. On the use of groups in social work practice. In W. Schwartz and S. Zalba, eds., *The Practice of Group Work.* New York: Columbia University Press.

Seligman M. E. P. and G. Elder, Jr. 1986. Learned helplessness and life-span development. In A. B. Sorensen, F. E. Weinert, and L. R. Sherrod, eds., *Human Development and the Life Course: Multidisciplinary Perspectives* Hillsdale, N.J.: Lawrence Erebaum Associates, Pubs.

Shulman, L. 1971. "Program" in group work: Another look. In W. Schwartz and S. Zalba, eds., *The Practice of Group Work.* New York: Columbia University Press.

Shulman, L. 1984. *The Skills of Helping Individuals and Groups.* 2d ed. Itasca, Ill.: F. E. Peacock.

Shulman, L. 1985/86. The dynamics of mutual aid. In A. Gitterman and L. Shulman, eds., *The Legacy of William Schwartz: Group Practice as Shared Interaction: Social Work with Groups* 8(4):51–60.

Sorensen, M. H. 1986. Narcissism and loss in the elderly: Strategies for an inpatient older adults group. *International Journal of Group Psychotherapy* 36(4):533–547.

Tobin, S. S. 1985. The Psychology of the Very Old. Paper presented at Lecture Series, Brookdale Institute on Aging and Adult Human Development, Columbia University.

Tobin, S. S. 1988. Preservation of the self in old age. *Social Casework* 69(9):550–555.

Tobin, S. S. and M. Lieberman. 1976. *Last Home for the Aged.* San Francisco: Jossey-Bass.

Tropp, E. 1968. The group: In life and in social work. *Social Casework* 49(5):267–74.

White Riley, M. 1986. Overview and highlights of a sociological perspective. In A. B. Sorensen, F. E. Weinert, and L. R. Sherrod, eds., *Human Development and the Life Course: Multidisciplinary Perspectives.* Hillsdale, N.J.: Lawrence Erebaum Associates, Pubs.

7

Community Organization, Social Planning, and Empowerment Strategies

❖

CYNTHIA STUEN, D.S.W.
The Lighthouse, New York

Community organization, social planning, and empowerment have a variety of interrelated meanings for different groups, disciplines, and professions. The terms relate to such concepts as community problem-solving, community work, community development, neighborhood organizing, mutual aid, self-help, community action, and social movement.

To address problems such as inadequate income, incapacitating illness, deteriorating housing, and lack of access to educational opportunities, which may disproportionately affect older adults, the people and institutions of a community must first recognize that they are the problems of a total community. Therefore, the change efforts required must be organized with a strategic plan of action.

Job forecasters predict social work with older adults to be a top growth area (Kahl 1988). Gerontological social workers are well suited for the tasks involved in community organization, social planning and empowerment. The professional value base and the skills employed in macro practice are most appropriate to these areas of concern. Unfortunately not all social workers bring adequate skills to the job. (Rothman 1979).

Community organization and social planning focus on a population needing redress and on the outside forces of the community at large that effect their problem. The practice areas are not ends, but processes in which a problem is addressed by helping a group of people focus on the issue, enabling, and empowering them to act on their own behalf.

This paper provides information on the macro areas of practice, specifically community organization and social planning. Its primary focus is the empowerment of older persons based on social work values. Social work has not been exempt from agist attitudes, hence practice knowledge with older adults is not as rich and certainly not as well documented as that with younger age groups. Fortunately the graying of the population and key legislation of the 1960s has brought forth an era of greater attention to older persons among all disciplines, social work included.

NEED

Individuals inevitably grow old but societies do not necessarily age commensurately. Populations can become older or younger, depending on shifts in the proportion of people within various age levels. Fertility rates, infant mortality rates, and changes in life expectancy are factors that affect a population's youth or age. What is startling about the aging of America today is the rapid rate at which it is proceeding. There are two separate and simultaneous events which account for a rapidly aging America: the speed with which the number of older and very old people is growing, and the dramatic decline in the proportion of young people—a decline expected to continue in the decades ahead (Pifer and Bronte 1986).

Stephen Golant (1988) predicted that the beginning decades of the twenty-first century will be known as the "Golden Era" for older people. While our attention as this century closes is on the population we now refer to as Yuppies, in the twenty-first century the spotlight will be on the *Yeepies* that is *Y*outhful, *E*nergetic, *E*lderly *P*eople *I*nvolved in *E*verything. This has important implications for empowerment activities. The old-old (age 85 plus) will have grown at an extraordinary rate of 87 percent between 1950 and 1990.

The decrease in younger cohorts raises concerns for who will financially support and physically provide the increasing services needed by an aging population? This has prompted debates on generational equity, pitting young against old in advocacy for services and goods.

Advances in robotic technology offer hope to older persons in coping with functional impairments. Voice-activated robots to assist with activities of daily living, such as lifting and transferring, housekeeping, medication reminding, security are just some of the uses being promoted (Lesnoff-Caravaglia 1987).

The increased segment of life spent in retirement creates a new leisure role for the elderly, for which there is no previous cultural experience. From an economist's point of view, there is a lengthened period of nonproductivity and an increased drain on resources; an unfavorable dependency ratio is occurring due to the increase in life expectancy and the decrease in the birth rate. Women continue to outlive men on the average by seven to ten years; there is, therefore, a sizable population of older women who are usually poorer than their male counterparts. Many of these elderly women are widows, and the role changes experienced with the loss of a spouse present an increasing need for social adjustment for the older adult. For older black women, the classic triple jeopardy—racism, sexism, and poverty—may often be operative.

Social work in general, and with the elderly in particular, has primarily been practiced in urban areas, but rural areas have been gaining the attention of gerontologists. A large percentage of the U.S. older population live and will continue to live in metropolitan or urbanized America, primarily in its suburban areas. The high incidence of home ownership among today's older population is likely to continue over the next twenty years (Cheven 1987). This trend reflects the strong desire by the majority of older people to experience the material, symbolic and emotional advantages of homeownership (Golant 1984).

Some of the major concerns of the rural elderly are focused on access issues such as transportation and the availability of multiple services in their localities. In place of the racial and ethnic differences of urban neighborhoods, rurality brings regional variations in cultures and life style; rural areas are generally felt to be more heterogeneous than urban environments.

The surge of legislative activity in the mid-1960s that affected the elderly was in response to the recognized needs of this growing population. Community organization emerged as an important social work method particularly applicable to the development of community-based programs for older adults.

IMPLICATIONS OF THEORIES ON AGING

Individuals react differently to the changes that occur in the latter decades of life. Reactions to these changes can affect general functioning and social relations as well as physical health (Birren and Schaie 1977).

A major social and psychological change that older adults experience is role loss and role change. Most of the aged are given very limited roles in our society. Leaving the occupational roles of many decades, due to mandatory retirement or by choice may create a loss of socialization, loss of gratification and perhaps loss of confidence in one's abilities (Kell and Patton 1978).

The elderly can become "roleless" as Burgess (1960) portrays in his activity theory. A restructuring of society to include significant roles for the aged, is required to catch up with demographic and technological changes. The activity theory holds that higher levels of social involvement of an older adult will result in higher morale and increased life satisfaction (Havinghurst and Albrecht 1953).

From a community organization point of view, this would lead to development of programs to provide social involvement of older adults. The Older Americans Act of 1965 seems to be based on an outlook similar to the activity theory. The developmental theory of Neugarten, Havighurst, and Tobin (1964) state there are life tasks that must be achieved in order to integrate the older-adult role just as there are in other life-cycle stages. This theory prompts a more evolutionary policy approach to program planning.

The theory of social exchange is built on the assumption that interactions between individuals or collectivities are attempts to maximize rewards while keeping costs at a minimum. A major proposition of the exchange theory is that the interaction between two or more people will probably be continued and positively evaluated if they each see a "profit"—a reward from the interaction (Dowd 1975). Having the potential to offer rewards confers power, a central concept of this theory. The power of the aged is diminished by losses in employment, health, social network, and finances. Emerson (1962) delineated four possible strategies to redress power imbalances:

1. Withdrawal—no involvement (which is commensurate with disengagement);
2. Extension of power—cultivating new roles in order to obtain new rewards;
3. Emergence of status—the dependent partner seeks more power through reemergence of status, by a revaluing of a skill possessed by the dependent (older adult) party;
4. Coalition formation—the less powerful partner seeks alliance with others of similar dependence in hopes of counteracting the more powerful.

The last balancing strategy, coalition formation, is perhaps the most popular with community organizers. In work with elderly, one occasionally observes the coalescing of elderly with younger cohorts.

The "Gray Panthers" organization is an advocate for equal rights, equal opportunity and dignity for the elderly. They are intergenerational in their base, recognizing the importance of intergenerational supports and not being isolated. "Generations United" is a national coalition of agencies concerned with intergenerational issues and programs.

It is helpful for community workers to the cognizant of the theoretical views of aging that undergird their assessment of need and hence their choice of strategy in working with older persons. One caution is in order. However, useful a theoretical perspective may be for explanatory purposes, no single theory can be used to make judgments about normativity in such a diverse population as older adults.

An understanding of the social, economic, health and current political issues affecting older adults in the community will guide the needs assessment process and will lead the professional and/or consumer to the selection of an appropriate intervention strategy. Community organization, social planning, and empowerment are well suited for many areas of problem solving relative to older adults, as will be illustrated here.

ETHNIC DIMENSIONS OF MACRO PRACTICE

Organizing, planning, and empowerment practice requires a knowledge of ethnic and cultural differences among older adults. The heterogeneity of older adults is accepted, however policies are made and programs designed which are still not sensitive to ethnic differences. Even when differences are acknowledged, they frequently compare white and nonwhite, or report only black and Hispanic differences. For example, the definition of Hispanic by the U.S. Census includes persons of Spanish, Mexican, Cuban, Puerto Rican, and Central and South American heritages. Manuel and Reid (1982) argue that individual differences in physical (racial) and cultural (ethnic) traits, even within a specific minority group, produce different degrees of identification and minority victimization. Perhaps the social work ethic of starting where the individual is promotes the best approach for community organizers and social planners. Social workers need to recognize and be sensitive to the historical and cultural diversity of older adults.

Social planning cannot begin until access to the community is achieved. In many instances obtaining access in ethnic communities can be very difficult.

In most ethnic groups, the least assimilated, those with the strongest sense of ethnic identity will be the elderly (Cox 1987). There may be cultural traditions which insulate the older person from the realities of their new culture as well as continuing expectations of their own family which are no longer realistic (Cox and Gelfand 1987).

Ethnic and minority elderly are further hindered by linguistic and citizenship barriers. Some persons come from countries where there is no history of active civic participation (Torres-Gil 1987). Cultural traditions and attitudes based on mistrust and suspiciousness of outsiders are factors which may impede the planning process also. A working relationship with an ethnic community is only possible if sensitivity to the culture is maintained.

Certain issues have similarity for minority populations, and income is certainly a major one. The feminization of poverty is a factor for women of all age groups, but most especially for women of ethnic minorities. Health is also a key issue. Minority populations have poorer subjective reporting and functional health status than their white counterparts (Manuel and Berk 1983).

The 1980 Census delivered more information about older adults than ever before (Longino 1982). There are two major improvements in the Census reports, the first, is that the age group 65 years and over is not treated as a homogeneous group but is reported in five-year age groups up to the category "75 years and over." The other is a better reporting of the race/ethnicity category. Special subject reports are available from U.S. Census data that provide detailed tabulations on a variety of socioeconomic variables by race and ethnic group.

Caution should be exercised, however, when utilizing census data on the older population. It is probable that the data suffer from a greater measure of error and biases than do data for the younger population (Siegel and Taeuber 1983).

Research documents that, knowledge about and access to benefits and services plays an important role in the prediction of service utilization (Krout 1983). Ralston (1984) found that senior center utilization by black elderly was predicted by a commitment to become involved, their perception of the center and contact with family and friends. Sociodemographic variables, health and transportation did not have significant effect.

In a study of counties with high proportions of minorities, Holmes found:

- As the minority population proportion in a county decreases, minorities are less likely to be served.
- A minority living in sparsely populated areas is most likely to be overlooked by service providers.

- The strongest predictors of the extent of older minority persons being served by an agency are the staffing pattern and location of program offices in the minority neighborhood. (1982:397)

There is limited knowledge however about the influence of one's racial/ethnic group as a determinant of service knowledge and utilization (Harel et al. 1987). There is also limited research to document that ethnic populations do not tend to take advantage of health and social services (Bell 1975; Biegel and Sherman 1979; Davis 1975; Fujii 1976; Guttman 1979). Some argue that age acts as a leveler on ethnic variation but others claim minorities may be favored for services (Dowd and Bengston 1978; McCaslin and Calvert 1975; Cull and Hardy 1973).

National organizations do exist which represent minority groups of older adults, e.g., National Caucus on Black Aged, National Hispanic Council on Aging, but mainstream national organizations, e.g., AARP and NCOA, have not been particularly successful in attracting minority participants. Political organizations of minority persons such as the Urban League, the Rainbow Coalition, National Council of La Raza are recognized as effective political forces, however, none of these organizations have defined aging issues as key priorities (Torres-Gill 1987).

The minority baby boom cohort will become the minority elderly after the year 2000. Perhaps this group of minority elderly will be more assimilated than their predecessors. An interesting question for planners to address is whether the minority elderly will take the side of the "aging" group or retain allegiance to the ethnic concerns of their community. Without doubt, knowledge of the implications of ethnic and racial background is critically important to any work with older adults.

MODELS OF INTERVENTION

Rothman (1979), has characterized community organization as consisting of locality development, social planning, and social action. Locality development (also called community development) is most concerned with capacity building and self-help. Social planning, which emphasizes program-development goals and the use of a problem-solving approach, seems to have arisen along with the growth of the welfare state. Laws and regulatory practice in the social welfare arena frequently mandate a social-planning process—for example, the Older Americans Act of 1965 and Title XX of the Social Security Act. Social action, which gained much attention in the 1960s, is concerned primarily with organizing disaffected groups of the community and looks to promote power shifts and institutional change.

Locality Development

Social participation, primarily voluntaristic, is heavily relied on for locality development. From the tactical point of view of the community organizer, participation is a conditional means to be utilized selectively, depending on selected goals and strategies (Rothman et al. 1981). Federal legislation such as the Older Americans Act promoted citizen involvement in the design of services. Whether this involvement has resulted in significant input or mere tokenism is a subject for further study.

The organizer needs to remember that the path to full participation of the elderly individual in community organizing begins with the awakening of the concept that "I count." Match (1970) provides numerous tasks the community organizer must complete in order to mobilize the entire community, not just individuals. To summarize, the community worker must

1. Foster a focused desire for change at the grass-roots level
2. Identify, involve, and train formal and informal leaders
3. Develop and time change strategies consonant with the capability and culture of the community

Self-help groups gained in popularity through the 1960s when anti-institutional attitudes prevailed, and in the 1970s as service resources began to diminish. There has been a dramatic growth of the self-help ethos in recent years that has the promise of helping older americans pursue broad goals of health care, social well-being and general welfare.

Katz and Bender (1976) define a self-help group as a small, voluntary group established to provide mutual aid in the achievement of a specific purpose. While an individual group may be small, there are increasing numbers of networks of self-help groups operating across the country.

Older adults and their concerned relatives and care supporters are represented in the growth phenomenon of self-help groups. Such self-help groups meet a variety of needs; the provision of information, social/emotional support, and coping strategies useful by others with similar problems.

There is a broad spectrum of self-help groups; some require ongoing professional intervention, some occasional professional support, and some no professional involvement at all. The level of professional support required for self-help groups at different stages of development and with different goals is on a continuum. An extensive review of the literature on the role of ideology for such groups is provided by Suler (1984).

A growing number of self-help groups have focused on the needs of widowed persons. The American Association of Retired Persons, through its Widowed Persons Service, assists communities in providing programs for widowed persons of all ages. Although women comprise the bulk of widowed—as high as 75 percent—it is men who appear to suffer more from being widowed (Gartner 1984:37). Two major studies have reported that widows receiving self-help intervention in widow-to-widow programs adjusted to their bereavement more rapidly than those who did not (Vachon 1980; Lieberman and Borman 1981).

Given the growing older-adult population and high likelihood that older women and an increasing number of men will experience widowhood or widowerhood, gerontological social workers need to be aware of the variety of effective self-help modes available that they can foster as well as the variety of roles they may perform as initiator, consultant, broker, and evaluator.

Older women in the labor market have been recognized by AARP in the development of Senior Gleaners, a self-help group in California, was organized to travel around California to glean fruits and vegetables after the harvest for distribution to themselves and thirty or more charities. The group was composed mainly of low-income retired persons. It is to be noted that this self-help group was organized and implemented by older adults themselves (Pilusk and Minkler 1980).

Support groups for specific health problems such as cancer and arthritis allow members to share their experiences and their strategies for coping with life. Others may help people follow treatment regimens like hypertensive groups or weight reduction groups.

A number of caregiver support groups have emerged. One of the first demonstration projects addressing caregiver needs was the Natural Support Project of the Community Service Society of New York. This project documented that caregiver groups operate along a continuum which required total to no professional support or maintenance. This project also documented that caregiver groups can also evolve into social action groups (Zimmer and Mellor 1981).

A very rapid proliferation of support groups has emerged for families of Alzheimer victims. The national organization for Alzheimer's disease promotes support groups across the country.

To some extent, self-help increased during the Reagan era. Self-help became a euphemism for cutbacks in professional and paid services and, unfortunately, some policymakers view self-help groups as a substitute for formal services. Self-help participation may however increase the demand for services. When individuals get involved in self-help, they often become more aware of services and resources available (Riessman et al. 1984).

Self-help groups can provide a valuable interface between the professional bureaucracy that delivers the health and human services so vital to older persons, and the informal support network of the elderly. Litwak and Meyer (1974) posit that both the formal and informal networks are better able to carry out their respective tasks if they are interdependent rather than operating separately, in complete autonomy. Self-help groups can aid the informal network in negotiating the maze of bureaucratic organizations offering services in the community. Hence the community worker needs to be cognizant of the self-help model and foster it appropriately.

A few criticisms have been however levelled at self-help groups. One is that self-help is less likely to attract low-income, less educated older adults. Another criticism is that self-help potentially blames the victim and does not promote structured changes in the health and human service systems. While this may be true it seems a poor excuse for inaction and doing nothing.

Self-help for home-bound persons has also emerged in our society and should be given consideration by community workers. Chain "correspondence," magazines, and telephone reassurance programs are a few examples. Institutional settings such as nursing homes are also possible sites for support groups to flourish—victims of stroke, widows, persons with diabetes.

Social Planning

The community action programs of the 1970s tried to develop indigenous leadership and enhanced participation at the neighborhood level. Social planning involving the elderly was slower to evolve. There are illustrations of effective community organization in the social planning model. The following case study demonstrates not only the social planning process but its relationship to community development and social action.

A massive housing project was planned for an urban community with only a token number of units for older persons. Popular opinion held that low priority was given to housing units for the elderly because neighborhood residents were black and their voting records poor. A community organizer worked with the residents for two months gathering facts to support a comprehensive plan to obtain more housing units for the elderly. A number of residents, mostly elderly, canvassed the neighborhood, explained the problem, and asked for a commitment "to come out if ever needed." Keeping the neighborhood network informed of events and progress was a key element of the project. Later, when a voter registration campaign was undertaken, the mayor offered to visit on only three-days notice. The community developed a statement explaining the demand for more housing units for the elderly and residents again canvassed the neighborhood, reminding residents of their previous commitment to "come out." When the mayor arrived, residents filled the auditorium; the mayor subsequently promised to allocate more housing for the elderly, a promise that was kept. The success of the effort was attributed to the meeting turn-out and to the increased number of registered voters (Corbett 1970).

Although the concept of "contracting" is more commonly used in casework, it is equally important to establish a contract with a community group. It is the responsibility of the community worker to negotiate the timetable, strategies, expected outcomes, and completion or "success" measures.

PROGRAM MODELS

There are three basic models of program implementation that can be put into effect; the decision-making unit model, the spontaneous contagion model, and the advocacy model. Practical illustrations of these models from the gerontological field follow.

The decision-making unit model progresses from participants to a partial target population to decision-making to a general target population. The concern that older adults were not being utilized in volunteer roles prompted a demonstration project known as Serve and Enrich Retirement through Volunteer Experience (SERVE). Participants were elderly persons; the target population was the elderly of Staten Island, New York; the time of the demonstration project was the late 1960s. Upon conclusion of the demonstration project, a decision was made to translate this volunteer program model to the older-adult population nationwide; it became the Retired Senior Volunteer Program (RSVP). This decision-making unit model is applicable in many program development arenas; it is a rational approach to planning service programs.

The spontaneous contagion model occurs when the practitioner sees a need among a target population, develops a program to meet the need, and recruits a pilot population, for example, homeless persons. The goal is a program that can be replicated elsewhere.

Both of the above models utilize a small group of "converts" to promote the targeted program. These models make broad goals more manageable to implement. They set short-term goals and force the practitioner to think through the entire process on a small scale, to build a support base, and to run on a trial basis with a small group.

Another approach for social workers in gerontological practice is the *advocacy model* that emerged in the 1960s. Community organizers of the Saul Alinsky school would "organize organizations" and then try to get the unaffiliated poor to join one of the organizations involved. One case study of Alinsky's work utilized senior centers as a key network.

The Citizens Action Program (CAP) in Chicago began in 1969, originally as the Campaign Against Pollution; when it became concerned with broader issues such as property taxes and consumer issues, the name was changed. By 1973 CAP represented thirty neighborhood associations and fifty senior-citizen centers throughout the city and had succeeded in getting reductions in proposed telephone rate increases and pharmaceutical prices and a tax rebate program for the elderly in Illinois (Lancourt 1979).

Alinsky (1972) considered it critical to utilize an active committee structure staffed by organizers. These were democratic committees with elected memberships. Although Alinsky used the term "radical," extreme measures were not used. Alinsky was a systems-oriented person, interested in making government, landlords, and business more responsive to citizens, which is also the current aim of the Gray Panther movement. In a "how-to" organizing manual for older adults prepared by a Gray Panther officer (Bagger n.d.), the basic recommended reading is Alinsky's *Rules for Radicals*. Advocacy planning, in summary, is that which demands that recipients or consumers of service should be partners in all decisions affecting the operation of such service.

Older adults can and need to be involved in all levels of social planning, implementing, and evaluating through direct responsibility and/or advisory committees, boards, coalitions, councils and planing teams. The diversity of older-adult participation should be represented; the customary upper middle class, "Muppies" (the mature urban professionals) and the disenfranchised—all needs must be balanced to reflect the priorities of the constituency.

LEGISLATIVE IMPACT ON SOCIAL PLANNING

Two major amendments in 1965 to the Social Security Act, specifically Title XVIII (Medicare) and XIX (Medicaid), were designed to have significant impact on older adults. They were written and passed without much involvement of the elderly (Pratt 1976). By 1970, a power swing away from the elderly and back to the "professionals" was underway, and revenue sharing is illustrative of the original good intentions to allow citizen participation in local planning and fund allocation. It has not however proved a successful participatory model, even though Title XX of the Social Security Act provided for training of the elderly to enable them to garner their fair share of funds.

The Older Americans Act of 1965 created an opportunity to turn the tide of "negligible" planning *for* the elderly to planning *with* the elderly. Social movements and planning of services relative to the older-adult population were initially instigated and engineered by interested professionals; the 1973 amendments created an area agency planning network and mandated opportunities for constituent input. Each state has established a state unit on aging to which local Area Agencies on Aging (AAA) channel their input. The AAAs are responsible for coordinating existing services and designing future programs for the elderly. Generally, three-year plans that coincide with federal-funding cycles and allocations are developed by each AAA and forwarded to the state unit on aging.

There are now over 700 AAAs across the country mandated to define service priorities and establish comprehensive service systems to improve services to the elderly. AAAs can use their allocation powers to fill gaps in services by contracting for such services, but an AAA has no authority over major system providers, for example, those in the health field that are not directly funded through Older American Act funds. This means that the director and staff of an AAA can operate only by persuasion; they cannot offer any economic incentive for cooperation, nor do they have the legal capacity to sanction.

Several services mandated by the Older Americans Act require a community organization perspective, for example, services intended to encourage and assist older persons to use the facilities and services available to them or to assist older persons to obtain adequate housing. Advocacy is a primary skill necessary to identify and gain access to a service or to lobby for its availability. It has been common for advisory bodies of AAAs to be involved in legislative advocacy for the "class of elderly." Amendments to the Older Americans Act of the 1970s and 1980s have incrementally introduced targeting of services to older adults who are most in need.

Social Action

Social action is the third category of Rothman's typology of community organization models. Understanding the history of social movements relative to older adults can be enlightening to the contemporary gerontological social worker who is planning social activities and can provide insights to today's social action agenda. The impetus for social movements addressing the needs of the elderly at the turn of the century was provided by the desire for a social insurance program similar to models already in place in Germany and England. Leaders of various movements advocating pensions for older persons had large followings but were resented by policymakers.

A number of plans were initiated to address the depression economy. Francis Townsend's plan in the 1930s was to pay a pension of $200 per month to each person over age 60. The Ham-and-Eggs Plan of the 1920s proposed by Robert Noble recommended issuance of special scrip that could be spent only by older adults. The Wisconsin Plan, while emphasizing the need for organizations to set aside funds against risk of unemployment, was also concerned with old-age security. The philosophy of dealing with unemployment and the needs of the elderly was promoted by the American Association for Labor Legislation (AALL). Isaac Rubinow, later joined by Abraham Epstein, founded the leading pension-reform organization, the American Association of Old Age Security. This group modeled its recommendations on the European plans and arbitrarily set 65 as the retirement age. All of the movements faded with the passage of the Social Security Act in 1935.

One overriding similarity characterized these early movements. They were all developed and promoted by nonaged charismatic leaders rather than by the elderly themselves. Pratt (1976) concludes that the total lack of elderly constituents in the pension efforts was a critical error and short-sighted in their effects. He also speculates that if a more aggressive aging organization had existed, it would have advocated a more comprehensive act and it would not have taken five years to pass the subsequent amendments to Social Security. What these movements did accomplish was to raise the nation's consciousness of the existence and special needs of its aging population.

The impetus for the founding of the American Association of Retired Persons came from Ethel Percy Andrus. She had been turned down by dozens of insurance companies as she sought health insurance for the several thousand members of the National Retired Teachers Association. An insurance broker, Leonard Davis, recognized the opportunity and obtained an insurance underwriter. In 1958, Andrus formed the American Association of Retired Persons (AARP). It has grown phenominally and currently boasts 28 million members, anyone over the age of 50 may join for $5. In a lengthy article on the AARP in the *New York Times Magazine* (October 23, 1988, p. 99), the organizations legislative division director stated: "This nation has a suspicion of bigness, and we're bending over backward so people aren't afraid of us. We play by the rules. We don't have a political action committee, we don't give money, we don't give endorsements. We do what the civics books say: get out the word on the issues."

The AARP has a reputation of being more moderate then other lobbies for the elderly. Its most important social action strategy is the flood of paper it is able to transmit which gets information on the issues out to its 28 million member constituency.

The National Council of Senior Citizens (NCSC) is a national advocacy group with its roots in the struggle for health legislation in the early 1960s. Its membership comes from organized labor and has a more liberal philosophy than AARP. A much smaller organization, based in Washington, D.C., is the National Association of Retired Federal Employees (NARFE). Another mass activist group of uncertain membership size deserves mention, the Gray Panthers, founded by Maggie Kuhn in 1970 and merged in 1973 with one of Ralph Nader's public citizen groups, the Retired Professional Action Group. The Gray Panthers is an activist, universal, citizen-initiated social movement that promotes a basic restructuring of society and in which retirement is seen as a new age of liberation and self-determination. The Gray Panthers promote a coalition of young and old to explore alternative life-styles, advocate the elimination of agism, and "radicalize" older persons to assume responsibility for their own lives.

The Older Women's league, founded by Tish Sommers, is a national organization with local chapters. They address concerns of old women and particularly the issue of the feminization of poverty among the old. They have conducted a national telephone organizing project to promote their concerns.

Long-Term Care '88 was a consortium of more than a hundred national organizations focused on educating the public about the critical family issue of long term care. Long-Term Care '88, a nonpartisan group which sought to encourage presidential and congressional candidates to speakout on the issue. The unique strategy to be noted by this social action group was that it focused on long-term care as an issue across the life span. Unfortunately the presidential candidates did not respond and raise long-term care as a major issue in the 1988 campaign.

A relative newcomer to the foundation world is the Villers Foundation, established in 1982 by Phillippe and Katherine Villers. The foundation places primary interest on activities that empower elders, affect public policy, change institutional behavior toward elders and low-income people, and raise public consciousness about the lives and contributions of older people (Villers Foundation 1986). It is involved directly in projects such as the production of a slide show titled, *Off Our Rockers: Senior Organizing in the 80's*. This educational project seeks to show people new to organizing what senior organizing is all about.

To counteract what it considers a dangerous divisionary by-product of the generational equity movement leaders, the Villers Foundation published a report about the economics of old age, *On the Other Side of Easy Street: Myths and Facts About the Economics of Old Age* (1987). Their concern is that everyone, regardless of age, has an opportunity to live in economic security.

Indirectly, the Viller's Foundation, has been a leader in funding grass-roots groups which seek to empower older adults in areas such as adequate low-income housing, adequate health care, and access to jobs.

Broad-based advocacy groups provide an opportunity for alliance when community organizers develop change strategies. Depending on the goal of the change effort, the involvement of another organization with a similar goal either at the national or local level, may enhance the prospects for success. Contact with organizations not specifically focused on issues of older adults can also enlarge the base of support, for example, the Americans with Disabilities Act, which is pending before Congress, would protect people with disabilities in employment, transportation, and public accommodations.

The Adults Only Movement in Arizona provides an unusual illustration of an older adult social movement. It is theoretically akin to Rose's (1965) subculture theory of aging, that older persons have common generational experiences, feel more comfortable with their own peers, and work to self-segregate. Rose felt this trend was supported by an increase in old-age dominated areas like housing complexes for the elderly and retirement communities.

The Adults Only Movement began in 1973 when a group of elderly were concerned about two minor children living in their adults-only mobile-home subdivision. A court battle resulted in a ruling that supported the concept of an adults-only community (Anderson and Anderson 1978). The movement comprised home and property owners concerned about this one problem. The common background and similar values of the participants provided the basis for effective advocacy. This example, while raising a dilemma for civil libertarians who claim that this type of movement is disciminatory, also presents the social worker with a significant social policy issue of age-segregated voting blocs.

The increased interest of the elderly in political activity has been widely observed and encouraged. The elderly and those acting on their behalf recognize the power base they represent in promoting legislation and funding in the constituencies' best interest.

The relationship of political activity and age has fortunately been studied in depth. When voting behavior is studied and socioeconomic status and length of residence in the community are controlled, one finds a gradual increase in political activity over the life span. For overall political participation, a minor decline is seen after the "standard" retirement age of 65. In general, the longer one is exposed to politics the more likely one is to participate (Verba and Nie 1981).

It is a stereotype that individuals become more conservative as they age. Empirical testing of the relationship of age and conservatism is fraught with methodological problems. Defining "conservatism," for example, has to take into account societal trends toward liberalism or conservatism as well as the aging process per se. Cohort analysis it is hoped will be a much-improved method of documenting how a cohort changes over time when exposed to the same societal influences. Analyzing cohorts over a thirty-year period, Glenn reached two conclusions:

1. According to almost any constant definition of conservatism, people have typically become less, rather than more, conservative as they have aged in conformity with general societal trends.
2. Cohorts who have aged into and beyond middle age during the past three decades have become more conservative in a relative sense, that is, relative to the total adult population and prevailing definitions of conservatism and liberalism. Paradoxically, people may become more likely to consider themselves conservative while, according to a constant definition, they become less conservative. (1974:26)

There has been concern in some sectors that the elderly will become an overwhelmingly powerful voting bloc and will receive an unfair proportion of diminishing resources at the expense of other age groups. Opinion differs, however, on actual voting behavior. Rose

(1965) argued that the elderly forsake old alliances and join new age-segregated groups. The NCSC and the AARP encourage age-segregated voting, but empirical data supports the claim that this occurs only in the area of health care (Weaver 1976). The only historically significant effort to organize the elderly into a political force, the Townsend Movement, began in 1933 and introduced a senior-power element into American politics, but died out with the passing of the Social Security Act. Binstock and others argue that historically there has not really been an elderly voting bloc and that one is not likely to emerge (Campbell 1971; Binstock 1972).

Community organizers need to be equipped with the knowledge of political participation behavior of older adults. Whether employing the models of social action, social planning, or locality development, organizers should not minimize the power of an organized interest group of older adults.

Two national advocacy groups have developed in the 1980's to address concerns of generational equity. A national bestseller entitled *Megatraumas: America at the Year 2000,* written by Colorado Governor Richard D. Lamm, states that our whole public policy bias is toward the elderly who are no longer disproportionately poor. He states that ten times more resources were allocated for elders in 1984 than for the young.

Americans for Generational Equity (AGE) was established to inform the public that while the aged population is better off than before, younger people are worse off because of the inequitable distribution of resources. AGE publicity has been criticized for promoting devisiveness and conflict (Zweck 1986).

Advocates for elderly persons state that the promotion of information that fosters intergenerational conflict, pitting older persons against young families and children, is a dangerous ploy. At this time of scarce federal resources and an increasing deficit, the inequalities of wealth and power have fostered a "zero sum game" that tends to grant benefits to only one constituency at equal cost to the other (Kingson et al. 1985).

Generations United was formed in 1986 as a coalition on intergenerational issues and programs to counteract the AGE advocates. Their intent is to enlist a broad base of organizations to join in advocating for public policies and programs that recognize the interdependence of children, youth, families, and the elderly. It is co-chaired by the executive directors of the Child Welfare League of America and the National Council on the Aging.

Blaming the elderly as a primary cause of the 1980s fiscal crisis has deflected attention from the more real causes of the economic woes of this time (Minkler 1987). A generational equity group like AGE has fostered resentment of the elderly and resembles the victim-blaming approaches of earlier decades.

MAJOR TYPES OF CHANGE STRATEGIES

Social work deals fundamentally with change. Warren's (1977) typology of change strategies, which acknowledges the relationship between change agents and the targeted system for change, its consonant with social work's definition of change.

The most benign strategy to effect change is *collaboration* where mutually agreed-upon goals of change are carried out through consensus and cooperation. There are three primary methods of collaboration: informal cooperation, coalition building, and the creation of coordinating organizations (Turock 1983).

The most sophisticated method of collaboration is the coordinating organization. It is formally established and is usually a legal entity with bylaws specifying governance and membership.

The *difference-campaign strategy* is appropriate when consensus has not been achieved but hoped for. A campaign strategy is inaugurated to win support for an objective or idea. Campaign strategies recognize that differences of opinions and values are present. The social worker implementing this type of strategy is in the role of persuader, trying to convert people to look at an issue differently.

The Social Security "crisis" of 1982 provided an example of campaign strategy. A national organization called Save Our Security (SOS) evolved to address the crisis. It mounted a major campaign urging solution of the fiscal problems of Social Security without benefit cuts. Newsletters, letter-writing, delegations to elected officials, and visits to Congress were tactics utilized in the campaign to win support for identified objectives.

The *contest strategy,* which has as its goal the defeat of the opposition, is appropriate when there is disagreement as to the desired outcome and the campaign strategy is deemed ineffective. Strikes, boycotts, sit-ins, and demonstrations are common tactics of this strategy.

The experiences of an elderly activist organization in Cape Cod, Massachusetts, in 1979 illustrates several of the strategies just described. In an attempt to gain access to nursing homes that were considered by the elderly to be poorly managed, various change strategies were incrementally applied. First, letter-writing, "befriending" residents and staff through visitation, and educational activities to raise the consciousness of the community about nursing homes were undertaken. Later, one of the contest strategies utilized by older adults was a sit-in, which resulted in the arrest and conviction of the older adults on charges of trespassing (Holmes 1982).

In selecting a strategy, the purpose of the change effort must be considered, as well as the support base and/or constituencies. For example, if locality (community) development is the goal, a campaign strategy is usually effective in bringing together all significant community groups. Organization of client groups, such as families of Alzheimer patients, to provide education, mutual support, and resource sharing for a group with similar concerns and stresses would equally, best be accomplished by a campaign strategy.

At times a practitioner may see his or her role as limited only to facilitation. Morris has suggested: "The exercise of professional leadership requires us to select our goals for action. . . . Our concern with helping others to make up their minds does not excuse us from the obligation of making up our own (minds)" (1962:168). In decision making, constituent goals, agency goals, and goals of the professional may be in conflict. It is the role of the social worker to identify the differences and creatively find the path to meet the constituent goals while being cognizant of agency self-interests. The organizational context sets many boundaries for allowable degrees of involvement for the employed worker.

ORGANIZATION CONTEXT

Community organization, social planning, and social activism are practiced in many types of settings in both the public and private sectors. Prior to 1935, they were primarily associated with coordinating voluntary agencies such as community chests or health and welfare councils. Since 1935, the federal government's increased role through financial support of programs has meant that most community organization workers in the field of aging have been in the public sector. The type of interorganization planning referred to by Perlman and Gurin (1972), in which the role of the social worker is to determine how to organize and allocate resources, is illustrated by the network of Area Agencies on Aging created by the Older Americans Act. Among the network of service agencies for older adults, the AAAs have contributed to a diminished role of local community health and welfare councils.

Institutionalized Elderly

Approximately 5 percent of those 65 and over are in a residential-care facility at any given time. However, between 20 and 40 percent of the elderly are estimated to spend time in their later years in a nursing home. This is a significant number of people who come in contact with long-term residential care. Three community organization strategies are suggested by Litwan and associates (1982) for organizing older persons at the residential care facility level. These strategies apply to health care settings of all types; however, macro-level social workers are more prominent in acute care settings.

Organizing the nursing home from within through residents' councils is one strategy. The pioneering work on establishing such councils was done by Silverstone (1974), who advocated that all residents be involved. As more severely disabled persons are now being admitted, however, questions are raised about the degree of participation and self-governance possible. One possibility is to involve others in the residents' council, particularly outside advocates who could represent the interests of the severely disabled.

The second strategy is the nursing home ombudsman mandated by the Older Americans Act Amendments of 1978. An ombudsperson is responsible for responding to resident complaints. Litwin notes that generally the ombudsperson is not empowered to change policies and therefore tactics oriented toward consensus rather than contest are appropriate given the lack of authority in the role. The ombudsperson is viewed most commonly as an advocate. Few would describe the ombudsperson as a militant advocate working to change the balance of power rather than as a spokesperson knowledgeable about the system (Berger 1976).

Advocacy for the residents from outside the nursing home is a third strategy applicable to residential facilities. Family and visitors council and consumer-rights group of the institutionalized elderly are examples. FRIA (Friends and Relatives of Institutionalized Aged) in New York City orients friends and relatives to the long-term care system and provides strategies and support for case-by-case interventions. Consumer-rights groups are also flourishing, for example, the Elderly Activist Project in Cape Cod, Citizens for Better Care in Michigan, and hotlines for abuse reporting. The National Citizens' Coalition for Nursing Home Reform lobbies for national reform in the long-term care industry. Their recent project was monitoring the effects of Diagnosis Related Groups on nursing home admissions.

A study of ethnic differences regarding patient advocacy services in long-term care facilities provides insight for gerontological social workers. Black residents were significantly more likely to have heard of the Patient's Bill of Rights than their white counterparts and were more convinced that outsiders were needed to intervene in response to patient grievances (Monk and Kaye 1984:9).

The rural elderly as a population group can be characterized as having a double burden—being old and inhabiting a rural environment (Cryns and Monk 1975). The rural environment poses special problems and hazards relative to elderly who need services and socialization due to geographical expanse and hence lack of proximity to service.

The Advocacy for Rural Elderly Committees recommended to the 1981 White House Conference on Aging that selected federal agencies be required to provide outreach and that the "traveling van" concept of outreach services be adopted for rural communities (Huttman 1985).

Rural service-delivery planners can be encouraged that the 1980 Census includes a one-in-two subsample of the population in rural counties, which increases the reliability of the data. In addition, the over-65 age group is documented in five-year segments in many of the reports. Information not available to planners from census data is the changing characteristics of older people resulting from in or out migration patterns (Deimling, 1982; Longino and Bigger 1982). It is of interest to note that in farming communities, many retired farmers and spouses retire to the nearest local town and hence many small towns are characteristically becoming retirement communities.

Lifelong Learning

"Most of the major problems in the lives of older people—economic security, physical and mental health, social well-being—can be addressed effectively by *education* that gives older people the capacity to cope. Education is the neglected necessity in dealing with the basic needs of older people. (White House Conference on Aging 1981).

Ongoing education is also critical in enabling older adults to remain viable in our high technology, knowledge-based society. The opportunity to fine-tune current skills, to develop or retool for a second or third career, or merely to acquire knowledge for its own sake is an important element for social planners and policy makers to bear in mind. The local library, senior centers, community colleges, and universities should address themselves to lifelong learning based on a life-cycle education approach (Turock 1983). The library, which has a tradition of independent, self-planned, self-directed education, can be tapped appropriately for older adults by community workers focused on preventing the isolation created by lack of knowledge. The National Council on the Aging's Self-Discovery Through the Humanities and most recently their Educational Goals Inventory project are illustrations of concrete activities that address information gaps for older adults (Jacobs 1984).

A Seniors Teaching Seniors model project developed at the Columbia University Brookdale Institute on Aging in New York City promoted a unique learning experience. The program trained seniors to become teachers, leaders, and organizers of educational programs utilizing their skills and expertise (Stuen et al. 1982). The university is an appropriate setting for older adult to be affiliated for learning and sharing purposes. Another innovative project at Columbia University involved the utilization of retired faculty to assist community agencies and public schools in various educational endeavors (Stuen and Kaye 1984).

Elderhostels have become popular not only in the United States but around the world. Older adults sign up for single or multiple classes at colleges and universities. Oftentimes courses are offered during non-peak times of the academic year, enabling the university to exercise better utilization of its facilities and the adult learners to benefit from the economics.

Professional Responsibility

In any organizing and planning effort, individuals are the building blocks. For older persons, the new unrehearsed role of retirement may be traumatic and the thought of community action may be threatening. Approaching community organization, planning and empowerment in an orderly, incremental way and pacing the activities will usually ensure, a project's durability. Negative reactions from the elderly should be viewed positively because they reflect discontent with the status quo and are essential ingredients for promotion of change. A first goal may be educational in the sense of empowering older adults. The audio/slide show titled *Off Our Rockers* produced by the Villers Foundation is an example of a resource to empower older adults through education.

Collective action is particularly difficult with a diverse population of older adults. The worker must communicate effectively the commonalities of the issue and the need to coalesce individuals to work together for mutually beneficial goals, sometimes in the face of skeptical reactions from the constituents who feel that the changes are too late for them. The problem to be worked on must be subdivided into realizable goals in order to retain an element of hope. To discuss a five year strategy with a group of 90-year-olds may not spur the desired commitment to participation.

In any community, the worker needs to recognize the psychosocial fabric and its variety. It is important to seek involvement of all classes and ethnic groups and to build bridges for "different" people to come together and work on a common goal. Working with, not for, will ensure that the worker is well grounded in community planning and organizing work.

Policy Considerations and Future Directions

Certain words have become commonplace in the '80s that reflect the macro practice area. Words such as "empowerment," "networking," "advocacy," "peer support," and "self-help" have replaced catch words of previous decades such as "consciousness-raising," "grass roots," or "maximum feasible participation" (Riessman 1988). In an era or rights of the disabled, gay rights, and patient rights, where do older adults fit? Should older adults coalesce around a specific problem/disability or age? Given the backlash against older persons promulgated by the Social Security solvency issues and the myth that older persons are living on easy street at the expense of children, it is probably wise to promote intergenerational strategies to address social problems. Aging is still perceived by many as a problem (while it beats the alternative), Americans have a long way to go to correct our basic agist attitudes.

Empowerment requires respect for what people already know and can do. Lay persons control of self-care education projects has proven to be effective strategy for the diffusion of self care knowledge and skills in the community (Savo 1983). Professionals need to radically change their modus operandi to include older adults *in all phases* of their work involving them.

We have moved beyond believing that organizing older adults to stuff envelopes, signing petitions or addressing form letters to politicians represents empowerment of older adults. While such activities are important, in and of themselves do not lead to empowerment. However, organizing interest groups to research and study the issues, organizing forums for citizens of all age groups to address issues relevant for older adults and personally visiting legislators are much more empowering (Aronstein 1986).

Calhoun (1978) provides documentation for two policy options that were open to lawmakers during the 1940s, when it was first recognized that the elderly constituted a growing segment of the population. These two options, material intervention and institutional reform, remain relevant today. The New Deal-type programs of which Social Security is the best example, illustrate material intervention. Institutional reform, which focuses on changing attitudes, was more favored, according to Calhoun, by pioneers in the field of gerontological social work. Grace Rubin-Rabson, a geriatric social worker writing in 1948, rejected massive material intervention on behalf of the elderly, favoring instead long-range changes in the social climate designed to improve the position of older citizens. Reformers in the 1940s chose to change the image of older persons on the assumption that improvements in social and economic status would follow.

The objectives of the Older Americans Act support the institutional-reform option. Social Security is one instance of material reform favored over institutional reform. The Social Security crisis was fostered by partisan political forces and provides a good illustration of how a crisis can be engineered by the media and partisan forces. Derthick's (1979) prediction that when the system had reached maturity, improvements in benefits would become increasingly difficult came true in 1982 (Anderson 1983).

One recurring theme of social policy in macro social work with the aged is the difficulty in establishing a cohesive identity among older persons for social action. Binstock (1972) advocates that the aged need to develop nonelderly identity ties such as with nonaged minority groups. Since the elderly cannot stop consuming essential goods and services, nor have jobs to strike from they have no leverage, no power, and therefore must join forces with other groups.

Atchley (1972) agrees with Binstock that the elderly as a group are too diverse to provide a singular group identity and cannot therefore make effective pressure groups, but they can be effective in making their plight visible, especially to politicians and the media.

Examination of their Older Americans Act as a case study of how the legally mandated organizational caretaker of the "problems of the aged" promote and perpetuate the aging "enterprise" was carried out by Estes (1979). It is Estes' opinion that the continuation of age-segregated policies assists only the professionals who thrive on jobs in the aging enterprise and that this is a divisive, isolating tragedy for U.S. society. One overall allegation she makes of the Older Americans Act is that it promotes a problem focus in dealing with older persons and hence seeks to improve the individual's adjustment to society rather than promoting long-range structural changes. The basic assumption is that the system to which older adults should adjust is a basically good one (Kuhn 1978).

The policy decisions adopted in the 1960s to foster separate services for older adults reemerged in a critical debate in the 1980s. The blame for increasing federal budget deficit has been placed on the elderly in this backlash era. This debate echoes the social welfare controversy whether programs should be offered on a universalistic or particularistic basis. A universalistic service orientation advocates that all persons in need, regardless of age, should be served, however, experience with age discrimination in the workplace, Title XX, and community mental-health centers suggest that, unless the elderly are specifically targeted, they will not receive their fair share.

The advantage of utilizing the elderly as a focal point for social legislation in the remainder of this century is certainly in their numbers; they are a rapidly increasing segment of the population. Their general popularity in partisan politics and the ethos that supports them as "deserving" is a historical advantage not to be discarded lightly.

The main skill of social workers in community organization is the ability to enable constituents to act on their own behalf. Etzioni (1978) encouraged by mobilization of older people who with the help of professionals, could systematically refine and expand the senior movement by identifying forces that support reform at the system level. In our industrial society, where mandatory retirement and skill obsolescence have tipped the balance of power in favor of the younger working population, only a well-organized interest group espousing rights of older adults can hope to have an impact.

REFERENCES

Alinsky, S. D. 1972. *Rules for Radicals.* New York: Vintage Books.

Anderson, H. The social security crisis. *Newsweek,* January 24, 1983, pp. 18–28.

Anderson, W. A. and N. D. Anderson. 1978. The politics of age exclusion: The adults only movement in Arizona. *The Gerontologist* 18(1):6–12.

Aronstein, L. 1986. Empowerment by senior centers or trivial pursuit. *Social Policy* 15(4):11–13.

Atchley, R. C. 1972. *The Social Forces in Later Life.* Belmont, Calif: Wadsworth.

Bagger, H. S. n.d. *A study program for the elderly and friends of the elderly: An interdisciplinary approach.* New York: Whitney.

Bell, B. D. 1975. Mobile medical care to the elderly: An evaluation. *Gerontologist.* 15(2):100–103.

Berger, M. 1976. An orienting perspective on advocacy. In P. A. Kerschner, ed., *Advocacy and Age: Issues, Experiences, Strategies.* Los Angeles: Andrus Gerontology Center. University of Southern California.

Biegel, D. E. and W. R. Sherman. 1979. Neighborhood capacity building and the ethnic aged. In D. Gelfand and A. Kutzik, eds., *Ethnicity and Aging: Theory, Research, and Policy*. New York: Springer.

Binstock, R. H. 1972. Interest-group liberalism and the politics of aging. *The Gerontologist* 12(3):265–280.

Birren, J. E. and K. W. Schaie, eds. 1977. *Handbook of Psychology of Aging*. New York: Van Nostrand Reinhold.

Bragar, G. and H. Specht. 1973. *Community Organizing*. New York: Columbia University Press.

Burgess, E. W. 1960. *Aging in Western Societies*. Chicago: University of Chicago Press.

Calhoun, R. B. 1978. *In Search of the New Old: Redefining Old Age in America*, 1945–1970. New York: Elsevier.

Campbell, A. 1971. Politics through the life cycle. *The Gerontologist* 11(2):112–117

Chevan, A. 1987. Homeownership in the Older Population: 1940–1980. *Research in Aging* (June), 9:226–255.

Corbett, F. 1970. Community organization involving the elderly. In S. K. Match, ed., *Community Organization, Planning, and Resources for the Older Poor*. Washington, D.C.: National Council on the Aging.

Cox, 1987. Overcoming access problems in ethnic communities. In D. E. Gelfland and C. M. Barrisi, eds., *Ethnic Dimensions of Aging*. New York: Springer.

Cox, C. and D. Gelfand. 1987. Familial assistance, exchange, and satisfaction among the ethnic elderly. *Journal of Cross-Cultural Gerontology* 2:241–256.

Cryns, A. and A. Monk. 1975. *The Rural Aged: An Analysis of Key Providers of Services to the Elderly*. Albany: State University of New York at Buffalo.

Cull, J. C. and R. E. Hardy, eds. 1973. *The Neglected Older Americans*. Springfield, Ill.: Thomas.

Cumming, E. and W. E. Henry. 1961. *Growing Old: The Process of Disengagement*. New York: Basic Books.

Davis, K. 1975. Equal treatment and unequal benefits: The Medicare program. *Milbank Memorial Fund Quarterly* 53:449–488.

Deimling, G. T. 1982. Macro- and microlevel aging service planning and the 1980 census. *The Gerontologist* 22(2):151–152.

Derthick, M. 1979. No more easy votes for Social Security. *Brookings Bulletin* 16(4):1–16.

Dowd, J. J. 1975. Aging as exchange: A preface to theory. *Journal of Gerontology* 30(5):584–594.

Dowd, J. and F. Bengston. 1978. Aging in minority populations: An examination of the double jeopardy hypothesis. *Journal of Gerontology* 33(3):427–436.

Emerson, R. M. 1962. Power-dependence relations. *American Sociological Review* 27(1):31–41.

Estes, C. 1979. *The Aging Enterprise*. San Francisco: Jossey-Bass.

Etzioni, A. 1978. From Zion to diaspora. *Society* 15(4):92–101.

Faison, B. H. 1985. The development of community organization practice theory, 1956–1983. Monticello, Ill.: Vance Bibliographies #P 1463.

Fujii, S. M. 1976. Elderly Asian Americans and use of public services. *Social Casework* 57:202–207.

Garcia, A. 1981. Factors affecting the economic status of elderly chicanos. *Journal of Sociology and Social Welfare* 8:529–537.

Gartner, A. 1984. Widower self-help groups: A preventive approach. *Social Policy* 14(3):37–38.

Glenn, N. 1974. Age and conservatism: *Annals of the American Academy of Political and Social Science* 415:176–186.

Golant, S. M. 1984. *A Place to Grow Old: The Meaning of Environment in Old Age.* New York: Columbia University Press.

Golant, S. M. 1988. Housing in the year 2020: What does the future hold? In *The Aging Society: A Look Toward the Year 2020.* Issues in Aging No. 5. Chicago: Center for Applied Gerontology.

Guttmunn, D. 1979. Use of informal and formal supports by the ethnic aged. In D. Gelfand and A. Kutzik, eds., *Ethnicity and Aging: Theory, Research and Policy.* New York: Springer.

Harel, Z., E. McKinney, and M. Williams 1987. Aging, Ethnicity, and Services: Empirical and Theoretical Perspectives. In D. Gelfand and M. Barresi, eds., *Ethnic Dimensions of Aging.* New York: Springer.

Havighurst, R. J. and R. Albrecht. 1953. *Older People.* New York: Longmans, Green.

Holmes, J. 1982. *The Elderly Activist Handbook.* Hyannis, Mass.: Cape United Elderly.

Huttman, E. D. 1985. *Social Services for the Elderly.* New York: Free Press.

Jackson, J. J. 1978. Retirement patterns of aged blacks. In E. P. Stanford, ed., *Retirement Concepts and Realities.* San Diego: Center on Aging, San Diego State University.

Jacobs, B. 1984. Establishing goals for older adult educational programs. *Perspective on Aging* 13:17–19.

Kahl, A. 1988. Careers in the field of aging. *Occupational Outlook* (Fall), pp. 3–21.

Katz, A. H. and E. I. Bender. 1976. *The Strength in Us: Self-Help Groups in the Modern World.* New York: New Viewpoints.

Kell, D. and C. Patton. 1978. Reactions to induced early retirement. *The Gerontologist* 18(2):173–178.

Keller, J. B. 1978. Volunteer activities for ethnic minority elderly. In E. P. Stanford, ed., *Retirement Concepts and Realities.* San Diego: Center on Aging, San Diego State University.

Kingson, E., B. A. Hirschorn, and J. M. Cornman. 1986. *Ties that Bind.* John Cobin, Md.: Seven Locks Press.

Krout, J. 1983. Correlates of service utilization among the rural elderly. *The Gerontologist* 23:500–504.

Kuhn, M. 1978. Open letter. *The Gerontologist* 18(5):422–424.

Lamm, R. D. 1985. *Megatraumas: America at the Year 2000.* Boston: Houghton Mifflin.

Lancourt, J. E. 1979. *Confront or Concede: The Alinsky Citizen-Action Organizations.* Lexington, Mass: Lexington Books.

Lesnoff-Caravaglia, G. 1978. Trends to watch: Applications of technology in long-term care. *Retirement Housing Report* (June), 1:5–6.

Lieberman, M. and L. D. Borman. 1981. The impact of self-help intervention for widows' mental health. *National Reporter* 4:2–6.

Litwak, E. and H. J. Meyer. 1974. *School, Family and Neighborhood: The Theory and Practice of School-Community Relations.* New York: Columbia University Press.

Litwin, H., L. Kaye, and A. Monk. 1982. Holding the line for the institutionalized elderly: Strategic options for community organizers. *Social Development Issues* 6(3):15–24.

Longino, C. F. 1982. Symposium: Population research for planning and practice. *The Gerontologist* 22(2):142–143.

Longino, C. F. and J. C. Bigger. (1982). The impact of population redistribution on service delivery. *The Gerontologist* 22(2):153–159.

McCaslin, R. and W. R. Calvert. 1975. Social indicators in black and white: Some ethnic considerations in delivery of service to the elderly. *Journal of Gerontology* 30(1):60–66.

Manuel, R. C. and M. L. Berk. 1983. A look at similarities and differences in older minority populations. *Aging*, no. 330.

Manuel, R. C. and J. Reid. 1982. A comparative demographic profile of the minority and non-minority aged. In R. C. Manuel, Ed., *Minority Aging: Sociological and Social Psychological Issues*. Westport, Conn: Greenwood Press.

Match, S. K. ed. 1970. *Community Organization, Planning, and Resources and the Older Poor*. Washington, D.C.: National Council on the Aging.

Minkler, M. 1987. The politics of generational equity. *Social Policy* 17:48–52.

Monk, A. 1981. Social work with the aged: Principles of practice. *Social Work* 26(1):61–68.

Monk, A. and L. W. Kaye. 1984. Patient advocacy services in long term care facilities: Ethnic perspectives. *Journal of Long-Term Care Administration* 12(1):5–10.

Morris, R. 1962. Community planning for health: The social welfare experience. In *Public Health Concepts in Social Work Education*. New York: Council on Social Work Education.

Morris, R. 1977. Caring for vs. caring about people. *Social Work* 22(5):353–359.

National Association of Social Workers. 1987. *Encyclopedia of Social Work* 18th ed. Silver Spring, Md.: National Association of Social Workers.

National Council on Aging. 1988. *Case Management Standards*. Washington, D.C.: The Council.

Neugarten, B., R. J. Havighurst, and S. S. Tobin. 1964. Personality types in aged population. In B. L. Neugarten, ed., *Personality in Middle and Late Life*. New York: Atherton.

Perlman, R. and A. Gurin. 1972. *Community Organization and Social Planning*. New York: Wiley.

Pifer, A. and L. Bronte. 1986. *Our Aging Society: Paradox and Promise*. New York: Norton.

Pilusk, M. and M. Minkler. 1980. Supportive networks: Life ties for the elderly. *Journal of Social Issues* 36(2):95–116

Pratt, H. J. 1976. *The Gray Lobby*. Chicago: University of Chicago Press.

Ralson, P. A. 1984. Senior center utilization by black elderly adults: Social, attitudinal and knowledge correlates. *Journal of Gerontology* 4:224–229.

Riessman, F. 1988. The language of the 80s. *Social Policy* 16(4):2.

Riessman, F., H. R. Moody, and E. H. Worthy, Jr. 1984. Self-help and the elderly. *Social Policy* 14(4):19–26.

Rose, A. 1965. The subculture of aging: A framework for research. In A. M. Rose and W. Peterson, eds., *Older People in Their Social World*. Philadelphia: Davis.

Rothman, J. (1974). *Planning and Organizing for Social Change: Action Principles from Social Science Research*. New York: Columbia University Press.

Rothamn, J. 1979. Three models of community organization practice. In F. M. Cox et al., eds., *Strategies of Community Organization*. 3d ed. Itasca, Ill.: Peacock.

Rothman, J., J. L. Erlich, and J. G. Teresa, 1981. *Changing Organizations and Community Programs*. Beverly Hills, Calif.: Sage.

Savo, C. 1983. Self-care and empowerment: A case study. *Social Policy* 14(1):19–22.

Siegel, J. S. and C. M. Taeuber. 1982. The 1980 census and the elderly: New data available to planners and practitioners. *The Gerontologist* 22(2):144–150.

Silverstone, B. M. 1974. *Establishing Resident Councils*. New York: Federation of Protestant Welfare Agencies.

Stuen, C. and L. W. Kaye. 1984. Creating educational alliances between retired academics, community agencies and elderly neighborhood residents. *Community Services Catalyst* 14(4):21–24.

Stuen, C., B. B. Spencer, and M. A. Raines. 1982. *Seniors Teaching Seniors: A*

Manual for Training Older Adult Teachers. New York: Brookdale Institute on Aging, Columbia University.

Suler, J. 1984. The role of ideology in self-help groups. *Social Policy* 14(3):29–36.

Torres-Gil, F. 1987. Aging in an ethnic society: Policy issues for aging among minority groups. In D. Gelford and C. Barresi, eds., *Ethnic Dimensions of Aging.* New York: Springer.

Turock, B. J. 1983. *Serving the Older Adult.* New York: Bowker.

U.S. Congress. House Select Committee on Aging. 1980. *Future Directions for Aging Policy: A Human Service Model.* Washington, D.C.: GPO.

U.S. Congress. Senate Special Committee on Aging. 1983. *Aging Reports.* Washington, D.C.: GPO.

Vachon, M. L. S. 1980. A controlled study of self-help interventions for widows. *American Journal of Psychiatry* 37:1380–1384.

Verba, S. and N. Nie. 1981. Age and political participation. In R. B. Hudson, ed., *The Aging in politics: Process and policy.* Springfield, Ill.: Thomas.

Villers Foundation, The. 1987. *On the Other Side of Easy Street: Myths and Facts About the Economics of Old Age.* Washington, D.C.: Villers Foundation.

Villers Foundation, The. 1986. *Report 1983–1985.* Washington, D.C.: Villers Foundation.

Warren, R. L. 1977. *Social Change and Human Purpose: Toward Understanding and Action.* Chicago: Rand McNally.

Weaver, J. 1976. The elderly as a political community: The case of national health policy. *Western Political Quarterly* 29(4):610–619.

White House Conference on Aging. 1981. Mini-Conference Report, vol. 1.

Zimmer, A. H. and J. M. Mellor. 1981. *Caregivers Make the Difference: Group Services for Those Caring for Older Persons in the Community.* New York: Community Service Society.

Zweck, B. 1985. 'AGE' Supports Legislation That Urges Benefit Shift From Old to Young. *Older American Reports,* November. Business Publishers, Inc., Silver Spring, Md.

Zweck, B. 1986. Generational equity associates file lawsuit against federal government. *Older American Reports,* January. Business Publishers, Inc., Silver Springs, Md.

III

BASIC SERVICES

8

Health Services

RUTH E. DUNKLE, PH.D.
University of Michigan, Ann Arbor

CARY S. KART, PH.D.
University of Toledo

Defining the need for health services is a complex task influenced by many factors. The most obvious of these include the severity of illness symptoms and level of physical disability. In general, individuals with the most disability tend to make the most intensive use of health services (Lubitz and Prihoda 1984). Factors unrelated to illness symptoms or level of physical disability are also important predictors of health service use. Gender (Verbrugge and Madams 1985), health knowledge and beliefs (Andersen and Newman 1973), the availability of social support (Brody 1981; Litwak 1985; Homan et al. 1986), the presence of health insurance (Wan and Soifer 1974; Kronenfeld 1978; Wan 1982), transportation (Garitz and Peth 1974; Ward 1977), and the organization of the health care delivery system itself (Harris 1975; Hammerman 1975) are just a few of the variables that affect utilization of health services by older adults.

In an effort to establish parameters for evaluating health service utilization, we begin with an assessment of the health status of the United States aged population. Explanations of health service use among the elderly are reviewed and strategies for enhancing service use among the needy are identified. Finally, the organization of public policies and their impact on the types of services consumed by the elderly is discussed.

HEALTH STATUS

Understanding the reasons that underlie the health problems of older persons is a complex task. Genetics, environmental issues, personality and social context all play a part. Health may be defined in terms of social roles and performance tasks, rather than in biological terms (Parsons 1958, 1965). Age itself can impact the recognition of physical changes such as the presence of pain or an elevated temperature (Pathy 1967). Illnesses of older people may be further developed than in younger people at the time symptoms are recognized. Over attribution of symptoms to the aging process directs the attention of the elderly person (and the health care professionals) away from real disease and/or environmental factors that may affect health. Such misattributions may have tragic consequences (Kart 1981).

Focusing on the environmental and social issues of aging and health has ramifications for the actual functioning of the older person. Kuypers and Bengtson's (1973) notion of the social breakdown syndrome highlights the interplay between the physical changes that come with aging and the social meaning they subsequently have for the older person (see figure 8.1). The social changes that occur in the Western world as one grows older include role loss, ambiguous norms, lack of reference group, and a view of aging as an irreversible decline. These social changes lead to a sense of vulnerability of competence for the older person, the initial phase of the breakdown cycle. The elder grows more dependent on the external definition of the situation and begins to doubt his/her competence with increasing health problems that lead to unprecedented dependencies. The person is labeled as incompetent and then gradually grows more dependent with the resultant deterioration of previous skills.

An individual's social functioning cannot be understood apart from the environment in which the individual interacts. As the older person's functional capacities decrease, the constraints of the environment increase. Assessing transportation and meeting basic health needs becomes difficult, and the community can in effect become less hospitable and even dangerous for the elderly person. An individual's ability to adapt to or change the environment is central to their capacity to maintain autonomy. As Kane and Kane note: "The elderly have less and less opportunity to change an environment to meet their particular needs. Adaptation then seems to be the major option" (1981:140).

Assessment of the person-environment fit plays an important role in the understanding of the older person's health and service needs. It

FIGURE 8.1. SOURCE: J. A. Kuypers and V. L. Bengtson, 1973: 181–201.

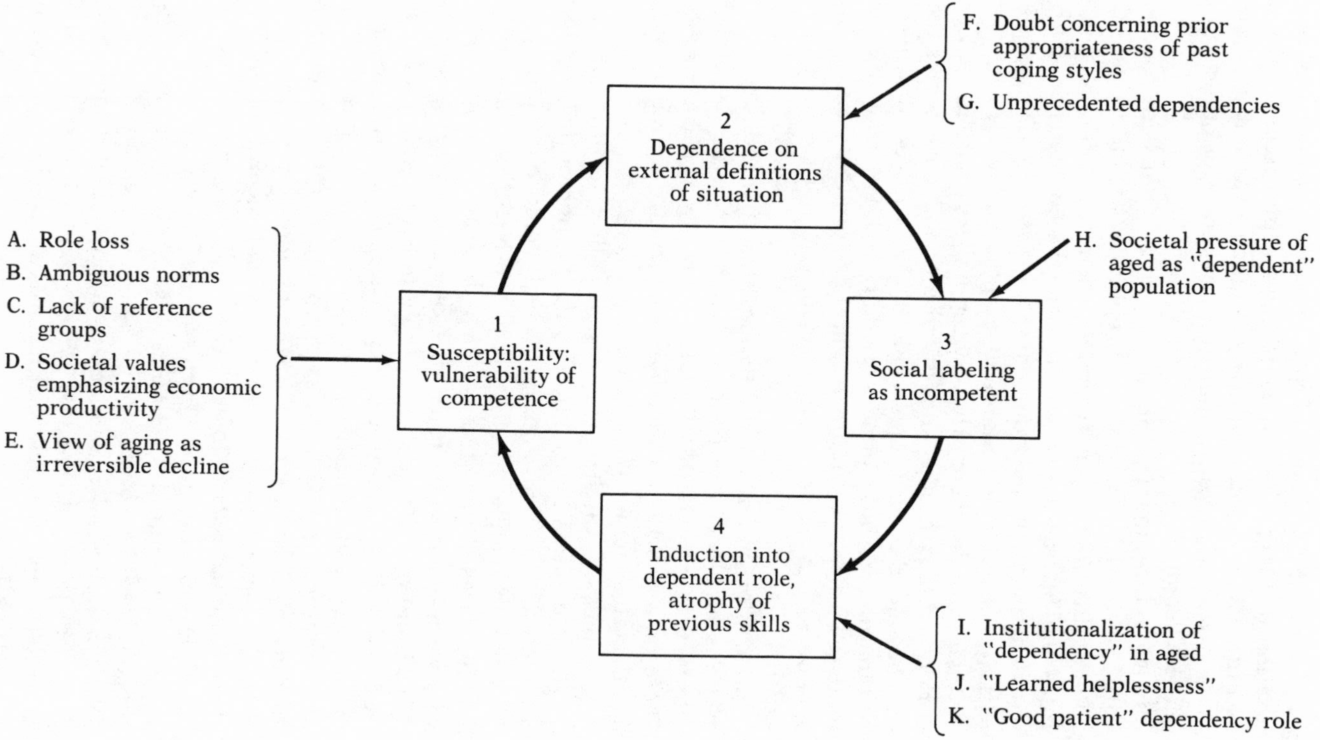
A. Role loss
B. Ambiguous norms
C. Lack of reference groups
D. Societal values emphasizing economic productivity
E. View of aging as irreversible decline
1
Susceptibility: vulnerability of competence
2
Dependence on external definitions of situation
F. Doubt concerning prior appropriateness of past coping styles
G. Unprecedented dependencies
3
Social labeling as incompetent
H. Societal pressure of aged as "dependent" population
4
Induction into dependent role, atrophy of previous skills
I. Institutionalization of "dependency" in aged
J. "Learned helplessness"
K. "Good patient" dependency role

may be that the provision of specific services to compensate for deterioration of functioning in some areas could preclude the need for institutional care. Interventions should strive to ensure that a situation exists where the environment meets the needs of the older person and vice versa.

Lawton and Simon (1968) have suggested the "environmental docility hypothesis" as a way to conceptualize the individual's degree of vulnerability to the environment. Their transactional model illustrates the interaction of the individual's competence, and the demands made by the environment as well as the individual's adaptive behavior, affective responses and adaptational level.

Organizational theory that conceptualizes relations between a network of primary groups and formal organizations carries the discussion beyond the need for specific health services into the realm of explanations for how services are delivered. Provision of service from acute to chronic health arenas via the community and/or institution is more or less facilitated by certain types of relationships (Litwak 1985).

In an effort to understand the health status and service utilization patterns of older Americans, data from the 1984 National Health Interview Survey (NHIS), Supplement on Aging (SOA) was examined. These data provide an excellent opportunity to understand current health status among older Americans.

The purpose of the SOA was to collect health and community service utilization information on the portion of the 1984 NHIS sample that was aged 55 and over which could be related back to the information regularly collected in the NHIS on these respondents. The SOA was administered to half the persons in the NHIS sample who were age 55 to 64 at the time of the interview and all those then age 65 and over. Over sixteen thousand persons are included in the SOA. As is the case for the NHIS, SOA data is derived from individuals' reports of their health status, not from medical records. Individuals' awareness and willingness to report accurate information is taken as a given. There are no estimates of under- or overreporting. Thus, SOA data should be viewed as a social record of health, different though not necessarily inferior to a medical or clinical record.

While some doubt has been cast on the accuracy of self reported health, a substantial correlation exists between subjective health status and measures of functional status in aged adults (Ferraro 1980, 1985) and physical examinations or physician ratings (LaRue et al. 1979; Maddox and Douglass 1973). About 70 percent of the SOA respondents reported their health status as excellent, very good, or good (see table 8.1).

Most health survey data show a pattern in which vigorous old age predominates (Gilford 1988). The great majority of older Americans live in the community and are cognitive intact and fully independent in their activities of daily living. While almost three out of four (74.9 percent) persons 55 to 64 years assess their health in positive terms, less than two out of three (63.6 percent) of those 85 years and older do similarly. Even among the very-old living in the community, however, only about one-third (36.4 percent) assess their health status as fair or poor. Gender differences in self-assessment of health status among the aged are quite modest. This is particularly interesting in light of the significant female advantage over males in mortality rates and life expectancy (Marcus and Siegel 1982; Zopf 1986).

Examining demographic characteristics further qualifies these self-reports of health status. Almost one-half (46.9 percent) of the aged

TABLE 8.1. Self-Assessed Health Status by Selected Characteristics (1984 Supplement on Aging, NHIS)

	SELF-ASSESSED HEALTH STATUS			
	Excellent or Very Good	*Good*	*Fair*	*Poor*
Age				
55–64 years	44.1%	30.8%	16.6%	8.4%
65–74	36.5	32.0	21.1	10.3
75–84	36.0	31.1	20.7	12.2
85+	35.0	28.6	23.2	13.2
Gender				
Male	39.4	30.3	19.1	11.2
Female	37.9	32.0	20.4	9.7
Family income				
Under $15,000	30.2	30.5	24.7	14.6
$15,000 or more	46.9	31.8	15.2	6.1
Race				
White	39.5	31.8	19.1	9.6
Nonwhite	28.7	25.6	27.1	18.5
Residence				
Central city	38.0	31.1	20.6	10.3
Suburban	42.0	32.3	17.5	8.2
Rural	35.3	30.3	21.7	12.7

with family incomes of $15,000 or more reported their health status as excellent or very good; 30.2 percent of those with family income under $15,000 reported similarly. Less affluent elderly were almost twice as likely as were more affluent elderly (39.3 percent vs. 21.3 percent) to assess their health status as fair or poor.

Racial differences in self-assessment of health status show a similar pattern. Whites are more likely than nonwhites to assess their health positively; 45.6 percent of nonwhites assess their health as fair or poor. This differential is consistent with prior research (Schlesinger 1987). Almost 86 percent of nonwhites in the SOA are black. Black/white differences in self-assessment of health status may reflect real differences in health status and health service utilization (Gonnella, Louis, and McCord 1976; U.S. Office of Health Resources 1979; Gibson and Jackson 1987). Geographic locale is also an important consideration. Elderly suburbanites have more positive assessment of their health status than do elderly residents of central city and rural areas.

Examination of self-reporting of health status does not differentiate between concerns relating to acute health and chronic health problems. Today, chronic conditions represent the key health problems affecting middle-aged and older adults.There has been a reduction in the incidence of infectious diseases in the United States and an increase in the importance of chronic conditions (Kart, Metress, and Metress 1988). There are now many more persons suffering from conditions that are managed or controlled rather than cured. These conditions are long-lasting, and their progress generally causes irreversible pathology. However, many of these chronic disease conditions do not cause death. Chapman, LaPlante, and Wilensky (1986) calculate that only 36 to 41 percent of all disability is related to "fatal" disease.

Table 8.2 shows the proportion of SOA respondents having selected chronic conditions by age, gender, family income, race, and residence. In the case of each chronic condition listed, a higher proportion of the old-old (85 years and older) reports that condition than is the case for the young-old (those 55–64 years). Compared to the young-old, the old-old are about twice as likely to report having cancer, four times as likely to have trouble with their hearing, about four times as likely to have had a stroke, and almost five times as likely to have trouble seeing in one or both eyes. Arthritis/rheumatism, cancer, heart disease, and hypertension seem to peak among those 75 to 84 years in the SOA.

Among the elderly, women appear to be more likely to be troubled by arthritis or rheumatism, hypertension, and vision impairments. Men are more troubled by heart disease, stroke and hearing impair-

TABLE 8.2. Percent Reporting Selected Chronic Conditions by Age, Gender, Family Income, Race, and Residence (1984 Supplements on Aging, NHIS)

	Arthritis or Rheumatism	*Cancer*	*Hearing Trouble*[a]	*Heart Disease*[b]	*Hyper-tension*	*Stroke*	*Vision Trouble*[c]
Age							
55–64 years	41.1%	6.9%	6.2%	9.9%	35.6%	2.5%	4.6%
65–74	50.9	11.0	8.9	14.4	42.7	5.1	7.4
75–84	55.5	13.0	13.8	16.3	46.4	8.1	11.2
85+	54.0	13.0	25.5	14.8	44.4	10.6	21.2
Gender							
Male	40.4	10.3	12.1	16.1	35.5	5.9	7.3
Female	55.7	10.4	8.6	11.7	45.9	4.9	8.6
Family Income							
Under $15,000	55.6	10.4	11.2	15.1	46.7	6.8	10.5
$15,000 or more	43.8	10.7	9.5	12.6	37.4	4.0	5.8
Race							
White	48.7	11.0	10.5	13.9	40.2	5.1	7.8
Non-White	55.3	4.0	5.6	10.0	55.8	7.1	10.9
Residence							
Central City	47.7	9.0	9.0	13.3	42.6	5.4	7.6
Suburban	46.4	10.4	9.4	13.8	38.7	5.2	7.1
Rural	53.4	11.4	11.4	13.5	43.8	5.4	9.5

[a] Deafness in one or both ears.
[b] Includes rheumatism, heart disease, coronary heart disease, myocardial infarction, angina pectoris, any other heart attack.
[c] Trouble seeing in one or both eyes.

ments. SOA respondents show almost no gender differentiation in cancer. Women live longer than men, on the average, so they are more likely to suffer from a variety of chronic conditions. They also may be more willing to report chronic illness during the household interviews used to collect the SOA data.

The relationship between family income and the percentage of SOA respondents reporting the selected chronic conditions in table 8.2 is fairly clear-cut. For each chronic condition, except cancer, those elderly who have family income of less than $15,000 are more likely than those with family income of $15,000 or more to report the presence of the condition. Most older people with low incomes had lower incomes before old age. Thus their access to medical care and their capacity to generate a favorable living environment have likely been reduced for an extended period of time (Kart, Metress, and Metress 1988). This may result in higher rates of disease as well as earlier death. For some number of individuals, reduced income is the consequence of illness or disability.

Racial differences in chronic conditions are evident in table 8.2, although there is generally thought to be more undetected disease among blacks than whites (Anderson et al. 1987). Elderly whites are advantaged relative to nonwhites in the proportion reporting having arthritis, hypertension, stroke, and vision trouble. A smaller proportion of elderly nonwhites than whites report having cancer, hearing trouble, or heart disease. Only modest differences in the reporting of chronic conditions seems related to place of residence.

As we have already seen, one way to define health status is in terms of the presence or absence of disease or disability. An alternative way is based on level of functioning (Katz 1983; Branch 1980; Kane and Kane 1981; Katz 1983). From this view, individuals may be said to be ill if they believe they are ill and behave as though they are ill (Shanas and Maddox 1985). Table 8.3 reports the percentage of SOA respondents needing assistance with usual instrumental activities of daily living (IADL) and more basic activities of daily living (ADL). IADL items include preparing meals, shopping, managing money, using the telephone, and doing light and heavy housework (Katz 1983). Items adapted from the Katz ADL Index (Katz 1983) include eating, dressing, bathing, going to the bathroom, walking, getting in or out of bed or a chair, and getting outside.

IADL items are more complicated multifaceted tasks than the individual ADL items. For example, shopping requires being able to get out of bed, dress, walk, *and* leave the home. Thus we expect functional decrements to show up first in IADL items and more older people to require assistance in carrying out these instrumental activities than

TABLE 8.3. Percent Needing Assistance with Instrumental Activities of Daily Living (IADL) and ADL by Selected Characteristics (1984 Supplement on Aging, NHIS)

	IADL[a] NUMBER OF ACTIVITIES				*ADL*[b] NUMBER OF ACTIVITIES			
	One	*Two/ Three*	*Four/ More*	*Total*	*One*	*Two/ Three*	*Four/ More*	*Total*
Age								
55–64 years	9.8%	2.5%	1.6%	13.9%	5.4%	3.9%	2.5%	11.8%
65–74	13.0	4.2	3.3	20.5	7.9	5.6	3.7	17.2
75–84	15.9	9.0	7.6	32.5	11.1	9.1	7.3	27.5
85+	14.9	14.2	30.6	59.7	12.7	17.2	19.6	49.5
Gender								
Male	7.5	2.5	3.5	13.5	7.6	4.8	3.8	16.2
Female	16.0	6.8	5.7	28.5	8.5	7.6	5.7	21.8
Family Income								
Under $15,000	16.5	7.6	5.6	29.7	10.7	8.7	6.1	25.5
$15,000 or more	9.3	2.7	3.6	15.6	5.6	4.0	3.5	13.1
Race								
White	12.5	4.9	4.6	22.0	8.0	6.3	4.7	19.0
Non-White	15.5	7.7	7.1	30.3	9.6	7.8	7.1	24.5
Residence								
Central City	12.7	6.6	4.6	23.9	8.5	7.1	5.1	20.7
Suburban	11.3	3.8	4.9	20.0	7.1	5.1	4.7	16.9
Rural	14.3	5.4	4.9	24.6	9.0	7.4	5.1	21.5

[a] IADL includes preparing meals, shopping, managing money, using telephone, doing light housework, and doing heavy housework.
[b] ADL includes eating, bathing, dressing, walking, getting in/out of a bed or chair, going to the bathroom, and getting outside the house or apt.

is the case for basic activities of daily living. This expectation is supported by the data in table 8.3. In every case, except that of males, a greater proportion of SOA respondents report needing assistance with instrumental activities than is the case for basic ADLs. The oldest-old, women, those with family incomes under $15,000, non-whites and those residing in rural areas report needing the greatest assistance with both instrumental and basic activities of daily living.

HEALTH SERVICES UTILIZATION

There are inherent problems in gathering accurate data in order to identify and design appropriate service interventions to maximize the health and functioning of the older person. Beyond this, in many instances, the elderly are reluctant to admit need or accept help and may even deny using services (Moen 1978). Not all older people are likely to find information regarding services that they need (Dunkle et al. 1982; Branch 1978). In asking community residents what they would do if they became ill and needed constant care, Stoller (1982) found that about thirty percent did not name any strategy for obtaining care. Silverstone (1984) argues that lack of knowledge about resources and services reduces the effort made to locate services or even information about them. She found that even for people who have some knowledge about available services, they may not be able to relate them to their own needs. Matching need to service may be difficult for an older person because they simply may not be inclined to use services. Further, they may not know how to negotiate services from agencies even if they wanted to use them (Bild and Havighurst 1976; Cantor 1975; Comptroller General 1972).

When elders do use services, it is most likely those services perceived as earned, not ones that are based on a means test where income is the root of eligibility (Moen 1978). It has been argued that the elderly as a group do not give accurate information during the initial self report interview. The procedure of assessing functioning during initial contacts is thus questioned and the need for adequate reassessment and follow-up highlighted (Steinberg and Carter 1983).

Over the last two decades, several researchers in different parts of the Western world have noted the effects of social class and income on the use of health services. Andersen et al. (1968) in Sweden and Snider (1981) in Canada have described the inverse relationship between social class or income and utilization; older individuals from lower socioeconomic backgrounds used more health services. In general, higher levels of annual physician visits are related to advanced age, higher educational attainment, being female, and being married (Andersen and Aday 1978; Marcus and Siegel 1982). Wan (1982), in a study of 2,000 elderly living in low-income urban areas, found that regular users of neighborhood health care centers were more likely to be older, black, have little education, low family income, and acute illness or chronic disabilities.

Racial factors play a part in utilization of health services as well. Neighbors (1986) found that blacks using hospital emergency rooms for basic health services were more likely to have lower incomes and be older and unemployed. A recent study examining ambulatory health care utilization among a national sample of 2,000 blacks revealed that users were in poorer health and had higher psychological distress (i.e., lower personal efficacy and self esteem) than nonusers (Luckey and Tran 1988). Even after controlling for need factors, Mutran and Ferraro (1988) report that minority elderly are less likely than elderly whites to be hospitalized. Black elderly, in particular, are more likely to be poor than white elderly and remain significantly disadvantaged on a broad range of health measures (Manton et al. 1987). Racial differences in physician visits may reflect real differences in need. We have already seen nonwhites less likely than whites to assess their own health status in positive terms. In addition, nonwhites are more likely than whites to require assistance with IADLs and ADLs and, as table 8.4 indicates, they spend considerably more days in bed on average. The effects on service utilization of race, family income, and even place of residence may be difficult to disentangle.

We examined two areas of health service utilization available in the SOA, physician visits and short stay hospitalizations. About 80 percent of SOA respondents had at least one contact with a physician during the previous twelve months (see table 8.4). The average number of physician visits during the past year was highest among those aged 75 to 84 years. As table 8.4 shows, when those with no physician contacts during the past twelve months are excluded, the average number of physician contacts more than doubles. Women, those with family income under $15,000, nonwhites, and central city residents average the most physician contacts.

Haug (1981) has raised the question of whether health service utilization among the elderly is appropriate to the symptoms they experience. She finds that the elderly report overutilization of physicians for less serious complaints. Haug argues that utilization of physicians for these complaints may be physician-initiated, a result of physicians advising their patients to come in for "check-ups" or other treatments. Others have identified the importance of physician diagnosis and/or recommendation in health service use (Aday and Andersen 1975; Shuval 1970; Wilensky and Rossiter 1983).

Gender differences in utilization of physician services is not peculiar to the aged. It exists in all age groups except among children. The largest differential occurs during those ages when women are most likely to be making use of obstetrical and gynecological services. Explanations for these gender differences in utilization of health services have focused primarily on the social situation of women. Nathanson (1975) offers three categories of explanation for why women use more medical services than do men: 1) it is culturally more ac-

TABLE 8.4. Average Number of Physician Days, Bed Days, and Hospital Days per Year by Selected Characteristics (1984 Supplement on Aging, NHIS)

	Physician Visits		*Bed Days*		*Hospital Days*	
	(1)	*(2)*	*(1)*	*(2)*	*(1)*	*(2)*
Age						
55–64 years	4.5%	9.9%	9.4%	32.4%	1.5%	11.9%
65–74	5.2	10.6	10.7	40.2	2.2	12.9
75–84	6.4	13.5	14.9	52.2	3.0	13.4
85+	5.5	12.4	20.9	67.8	3.4	13.7
Gender						
Male	4.8	10.6	10.9	40.5	2.5	14.3
Female	5.5	11.5	12.4	43.4	2.1	11.8
Family Income						
Under $15,000	5.8	11.6	15.1	50.8	2.7	13.5
$15,000 or more	4.8	7.5	8.4	29.3	1.8	11.6
Race						
White	5.1	10.2	11.4	39.9	2.3	12.7
Non-White	6.8	20.5	16.2	63.7	2.3	14.5
Residence						
Central City	6.0	13.2	13.1	45.2	2.2	13.0
Suburban	5.1	10.3	10.6	38.1	2.3	13.3
Rural	4.8	10.6	12.0	44.3	2.3	12.4

(1) Average visits or days per last twelve months, all cases.
(2) Average visits or days per last twelve months, *excluding* all cases with zero visits or days.

ceptable for women to be ill; 2) women's roles are relatively undemanding, thus reporting illness and visiting the doctor is more compatible with their role responsibilities than is the case for men; 3) women's social roles are, in fact, more stressful than those of men—consequently, they have more real illness and need more care. The merits of these explanations continue to be debated (e.g. Verbrugge and Madans 1985).

Less than two out of ten (17.8 percent) SOA respondents had occasion to experience a short-stay hospitalization during the twelve months prior to being interviewed. The oldest-old tend to remain in the hospital longer than the young-old. The average number of days spent in the hospital during the past twelve months by those 85 years and older was 13.7 days; the comparable figure for those 55 to 64 years was 11.9 days.

Currently, very little is known about the actual decision making that leads to service utilization. This is the case for use of community or institutional long-term health care services. Although several researchers have identified sets of predictors of institutional versus home based long-term care (Branch and Jette 1982; Greenberg and Ginn 1979), few have investigated how older adults select among various types of care and, further, what impact these services have on their adjustment to the care.

Many individuals enter care arrangements in the community or an institution following an acute care hospitalization. In exploring the reason 288 persons moved to 27 nursing homes, Smallegan (1985) found that about two-thirds were admitted directly from the hospital, and more than 80 percent had been hospitalized recently. Often, decisions to return to the community and receive services are not based on the person's level of need, but rather on the availability of resources to cope with these needs (Smallegan 1985). In fact, Smallegan regards any decision to enter a nursing home a consequence of inadequate resources in finances, health, or social and emotional supports.

Older patients come to the hospital setting with various physical, psychological and social resources that bear on the type of long-term care setting chosen as well as their adjustment to the setting. These predisposing factors also play a part in whether the patient becomes involved in the care decision.

The sense of urgency that often accompanies discharge from the hospital may interfere with the older person's usual patterns of problem solving. The result is that patients may be in a less than ideal situation for making decisions regarding their post-hospital care. These constraints on usual decisions making practices may have a negative effect on post-hospital adaptation. Failure to consider alternatives, and the ability or lack of freedom to make a choice have been linked to negative consequences in some circumstances (Kemph 1969).

A recent study by Dunkle et al. (1986) presents a model of the predisposing factors that affect the older patient participating in the discharge planning process, the resultant choice of care arrangement, and the subsequent adjustment in terms of level of satisfaction and depression. Patients who were in better health were more likely to be involved in the decision-making process. But involvement had no significant relationship to the type of setting chosen. Institutional placement was directly affected by the individual's ability to perform activities of daily living as well as their socioeconomic status. Less healthy and poorer patients were more likely to be institutionalized following hospitalization. Those patients who were discharged from the hospital back into the community were more likely to be satisfied with the setting than patients who were institutionalized. While there was reason to believe that being institutionalized following hospitalization could result in the patient being depressed (Borup 1981), the results indicated that the effect of placement on depression is indirect and mediated by satisfaction with the long-term care setting. If the patient was satisfied with the long-term care arrangement, then he or she was less likely to be depressed. The satisfaction of the patient, though, was more likely if they had been involved in the decision making process, returned to a community setting, had a higher socioeconomic status, were in better health, and were less depressed before being hospitalized.

INTERVENTIONS

By and large, health services for the elderly may be listed under the heading of long-term care, a concept that is complex as well as confusing. "Long-term care" describes diverse services offered in a variety of settings ranging from nursing homes to noninstitutional settings such as adult day care centers and a person's own home (U.S. Senate 1988). Long-term care involves two client groups: those requiring temporary support and those in need of permanent or extended support (Brody and Magel 1986). Temporary services are regarded as short term, long-term care while the extended care is described as long term, long-term care. Short-term care lasts less than ninety days and currently affects 1.5 million elderly. The types of services included are inpatient and outpatient rehabilitation services, hospital, day care, hospice care, home health care and community outreach services. Hospitals service more elderly than any other community agency, figure 8.2 displays the range of services available to elders in the community as well as in institutions. Many communities in which older people reside offer a substantial number of these services, however, only a limited number of communities are able to provide a complete set of services. The range of needed services is in all likelihood going to increase.

Litwak (1985) predicts that the delivery of appropriate services to older people may ultimately require that three moves be made. First, when the older person's health is good, he or she is likely to benefit from living in an age homogeneous community. Second, when disability occurs, the ideal living arrangement is an age-heterogeneous community near the older person's children. Finally, if disability progresses to the point where the person needs 24-hour care, the best environment is a nursing home.

Each of these moves involves an attempt to match the caregiving task with the most appropriate group structure. According to Litwak (1985), making the match requires completing five main tasks: 1) tasks requiring continual proximity or distance; 2) tasks requiring long- or short-term commitment; 3) tasks requiring large or small groups; 4) tasks requiring common or different life-styles; and 5) tasks requiring internalized forms of motivation versus those requiring instrumental ones. Older people can optimize their goal achievement if they have a network consisting of friends, neighbors, spouses, kin, and acquaintances. Litwak (1985) believes that all groups are necessary. One group cannot easily substitute for another in providing appropriate care.

In 1985, an estimated 1.5 million people, or more than 5 percent of the aged population, were confined to nursing homes (U.S. Senate 1988). Women who are 85 years of age and over show much higher nursing home utilization than their younger counterparts.

Community-based services include the use of home health aides, homemaker services, meals-on-wheels, visiting nurse service, adult day care, and telephone checking services, among others. Only about 20 percent of SOA respondents report using one or more of these community-based services. Generally, those 75 years and over, women, the poor, and those needing most assistance with IADLs and ADLs are most likely to use the types of community-based services described above.

To this point, the service utilization contexts we have described include a service provider and a service recipient. One important area that should not be overlooked is self-care. This form of treatment has been a common practice in all parts of the world (Williamson and

FIGURE 8.2. Inventory of recommended available services appropriate to a long-term care/support system. (From Brody and Masciocchi 1980. *America Journal of Public Health 70)*

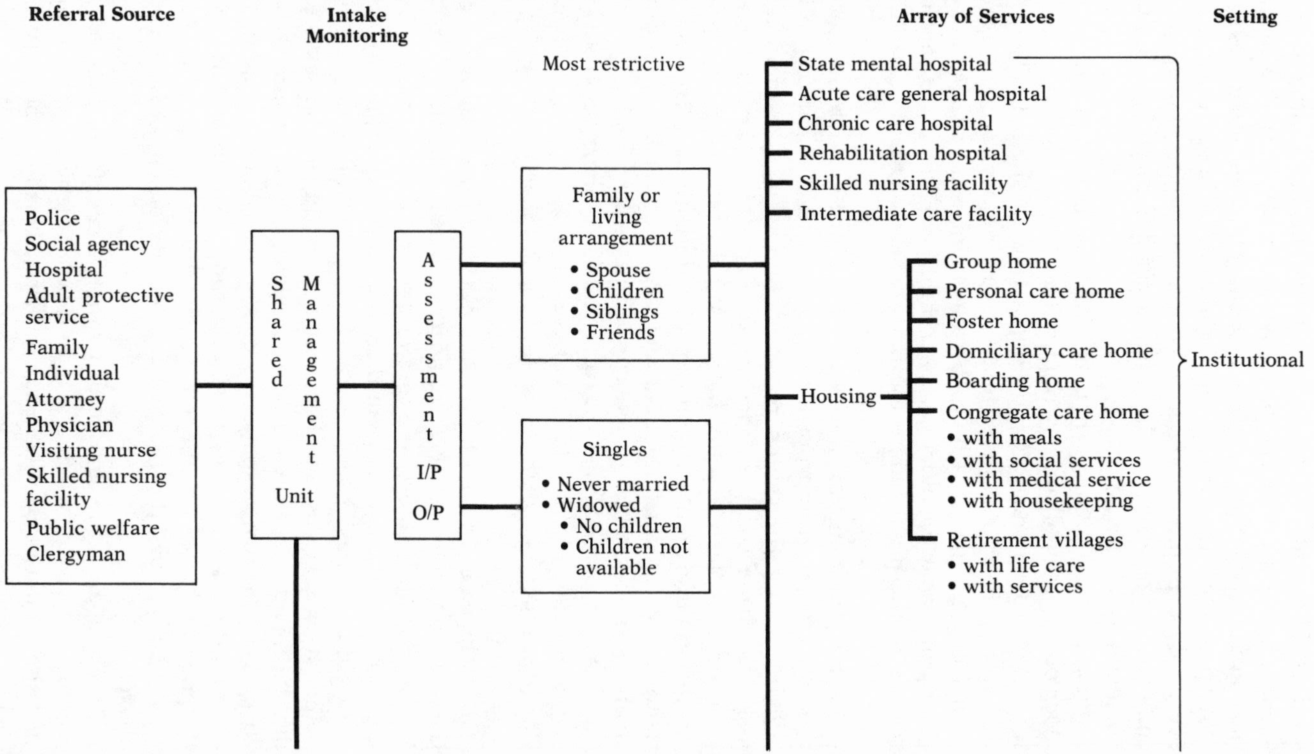

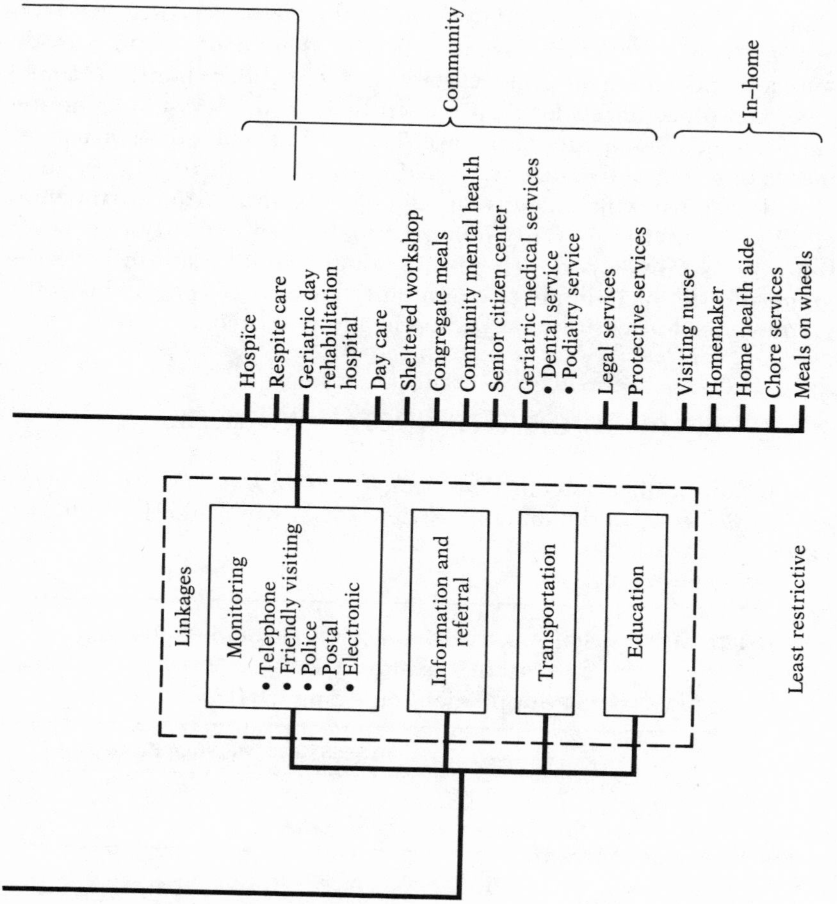

Community
In–home
Hospice
Respite care
Geriatric day rehabilitation hospital
Day care
Sheltered workshop
Congregate meals
Community mental health
Senior citizen center
Geriatric medical services
• Dental service
• Podiatry service
Legal services
Protective services
Visiting nurse
Homemaker
Home health aide
Chore services
Meals on wheels
Linkages
Monitoring
• Telephone
• Friendly visiting
• Police
• Postal
• Electronic
Information and referral
Transportation
Education
Least restrictive

Danaher 1978; Levin and Idler 1981) as a response to doctors' neglect, lack of services, or unacceptably harsh treatment of symptoms (Risse, Numbers, and Leavitt 1977; Schott 1984; Lock 1980; Ohnuki-Tierney 1984; Levin, Katz, and Horst 1979). Unfortunately, little is known about the content, range and determinants of self-care (Dean 1981).

SOA respondents were asked to assess their capacity to provide self-care. Sociodemographic variables, age, gender, family income, race, and place of residence, provided little in the way of explaining variation in assessment of self-care. Table 8.5 provides data on assessments of self-care by IADLs and ADLs. About one-third of those individuals requiring the greatest amount of assistance with instrumental and basic activities of daily living evaluate their capacity to provide self-care as fair or poor. These individuals would seem to have the greatest need for in-home or community-based services and be in the greatest risk for institutionalization in a long-term care setting.

ROLE OF THE SOCIAL WORKER

In a recent publication entitled, *Social Work in Health Care: A Review of the Literature,* Berkman et al. review social work practice in health care:

TABLE 8.5. Self-Assessed Capacity to Provide Self-Care by IADLs and ADLs (1984 Supplement on Aging, NHIS)

	ASSESSMENT OF SELF-CARE			
	Excellent/ Very Good	*Good*	*Fair*	*Poor*
IADL[a]				
Needs assistance with				
one activity	48.1%	37.1%	13.0%	1.8%
two or three	42.8	37.1	16.9	3.2
four or more	35.0	32.1	21.8	11.2
ADL[a]				
Needs assistance with				
one activity	44.9%	38.9%	14.0%	2.3%
two or three	41.2	38.5	15.0	5.3
four or more	36.0	34.9	22.1	7.0

NOTE: See table 8.3 for listing of activities included in IADL and ADL indices.

> The emphasis of social work practice in health care has shifted from the intrapsychic dynamics of the individual patient to the mutual interaction of the patient and the patient's context (Falck 1987). Depending on one's theoretical perspective, that context may be the family (Hartman and Laird 1983), social membership (Carlton 1984), the larger ecological system (Germain 1984), social membership (Carlton 1984), or a specific disease entity (Kerson 1982). This shift in emphasis has been important in helping the profession to develop clearer concepts and thus to intervene more effectively. (1988:15)

The social worker frequently finds him- or herself functioning in an interdisciplinary health setting to provide social work services as a part of the broader health service package. This medical context promotes patient confusion about the exact nature of social work service. For many social workers, the medical setting may create a less than predictable service delivery context. Sometimes the social workers may work in a context of medical specialization. At other times, the worker may find him/herself among patients with diverse medical histories. Even with this variability, many argue that social workers do the same things with health clients regardless of program diversity (Kane 1981).

The services of hospital social workers encompass a vast array of services to elderly hospital patients, ranging from individual counseling with the older patient to working with the older person in the larger context of their family. But counseling is only part of the services provided. Frequently, discharge planning involves providing information regarding community resources as well and linking the patient to these services. At times, the worker draws upon community organization skills to educate patients, their families, the hospital staff and the broader community on various issues such as AIDS, Alzheimer's, etc.

HEALTH ASSESSMENT AND EVALUATION

The interdependence of the physical, psychological and social factors of the health status of the older person makes assessment a complicated issue (Kane and Kane 1981). Further complicating matters is the relationship between diagnosis and assessment, and the functional capacities of the older person. From our perspective, health care to the elderly should focus on maintaining functioning capability, identifying deficits that may be reversible, and increasing active life expectancy (Gilford 1988).

There are numerous assessment instruments that separately test physical, cognitive, mental health and social function. These are described in a number of existing compilations (Kane and Kane 1981; Mangen and Petersen 1982; Fillenbaum 1984). Fillenbaum has argued for the merits of employing a multidimensional approach to assessing functional status. She argues that "the tendency of care givers and research workers alike has been to measure single dimensions of well-being . . . However, elderly people are subject to multiple disadvantages, and their physical, mental, social and economic well-being are closely interrelated . . . so that combined assessment of the various dimensions of well-being is necessary" (1984:5).

Fillenbaum identifies three multidimensional functional assessment instruments that meet standards of validity and reliability: the Comprehensive Assessment and Referral Evaluation (CARE), the Philadelphia Geriatric Center Multilevel Assessment Instrument (MAI), and the Older Americans Resources and Services Multidimensional Functional Assessment Questionnaire (OARS).

PUBLIC POLICIES AND HEALTH SERVICES UTILIZATION

Increased access to health services was provided to the elderly through the enactment of Medicare and Medicaid in 1965. Rates of health and nursing home use by the elderly, for example, increased dramatically between the late 1960s and the late 1970s (Rice and Feldman 1983; Gornick et al. 1985). And, according to Rabin (1985), much of this increase in service use reflected previously unmet needs. Medicare (Title XVIII of the Social Security Act) provides health insurance protection to most individuals 65 years of age and older, to persons who have been entitled to Social Security or railroad retirement benefits because they are disabled, and to certain workers and their dependents who need kidney transplantation or dialysis. Medicare is a Federal program with a uniform eligibility and benefit structure throughout the United States. Protection is available to insured persons without regard to their income or assets.

Medicaid (Title XIX of the Social Security Act) was intended as a catchall program to handle the health care needs of the nation's poor. Estimates are that the program covers approximately 36 percent of the aged poor (U.S. Senate 1988). Medicaid is jointly funded by federal and state governments with the federal government contributing in excess of 50 percent in "poorer" states. There are two ways to qualify for Medicaid: Categorical eligibility is linked to eligibility for

Supplemental Security Income (SSI), while "medically needy" eligibility is determined by spending down through medical costs to 133 percent of the Aid to Families of Dependent Children (AFDC) level. Unfortunately, in both cases, the individual's income must be well below the poverty level.

In 1987, Medicare insured 29 million aged and 3 million disabled individuals at a cost of approximately $80 billion. Changes in hospital reimbursement under Medicare have been phased in since 1983 from an "after-the-fact" cost-based reimbursement method of payment to a prospective payments system (PPS) based on diagnosis related groups (DRGs). Under PPS, hospitals are paid a set price for each case that fits into one of 473 DRG's (U.S. Senate 1988). Some argue that this PPS provides incentives to hospitals to admit patients at a later stage in the progression of illness and discharge them at an earlier stage of illness recovery (for an analysis of the potential impact of hospital DRGs, see Office of Technology Assessment 1985).

Medicare does not cover the hospital costs of truly extended acute illnesses, and does not protect beneficiaries against potentially large co-payments or charges above the Medicare payment rate for physician services. As a result, about two-thirds of older Americans purchase supplemental private insurance coverage sometimes referred to as "medigap" coverage. In addition, Medicare long-term care benefits are minimal.

As we have already established, chronic conditions represent the major health problems affecting middle-aged and older adults. Nevertheless, Medicare's emphasis is on shorter-term acute illnesses, while Medicaid provides nursing home care only to the poor. The maintenance of chronic health conditions and quality of life issues do not receive adequate attention. Services that are delivered across the continuum of long-term care are fragmented, and the range of services used and the pattern of use are more complex than is revealed by most data bases (Densen 1987). Community-based long-term care programs comprise a heterogeneous collection of agencies, institutions and programs of both a private and public nature (Somers 1985). The extent to which any of these services will be used depends on their availability within a community, ease of access, and the financing mechanisms (Gilford 1988).

Recent amendments to Medicare have shown increased sensitivity to connecting acute care services to long-term care services. The Omnibus Reconciliation Act of 1980 liberalized Medicare home health care benefits and made provision for greater participation by proprietary home health agencies (Rabin and Stockton 1987). The 100-home health visit limit was removed as was the requirement of a prior hospitalization for Part A skilled nursing home coverage (Somers 1983).

Congress has enacted the Medicare Catastrophic Coverage Act of 1988, the largest single expansion of Medicare in the history of the program, but then repealed the amendments in 1989. Even if those amendments to Medicare remained, major shortcomings of the program would have continued. These include a failure to provide coverage for long-term nursing home care, absence of protection from non-Medicare-covered physician charges including charges above the Medicare assigned rate, and lack of coverage for expenses incurred from optical, dental, and hearing services and products.

Medicaid benefits have also been adjusted in an attempt to meet the acute and long-term care needs of the elderly poor (Davis and Rowland 1986). Chore services, homemaker aid, and other types of social services are now covered by Medicaid under a waiver provision if a state can demonstrate that total expenditures are not increased by the use of this type of service. A recent study by the General Accounting Office (1982) found that expanded home health services do not necessarily reduce nursing home or hospital use or total services costs. Even with these changes in Medicare and Medicaid, public spending has reinforced the use of institutions for providing long-term care (Davis and Rowland 1986).

Suggestions for policy changes have been taken from the results of federally supported demonstration projects that have emphasized new approaches to the provision of community care (Benjamin 1985). Such suggestions include 1) coordinating and managing a mix of social services to meet clients' needs and reduce the rate of institutionalization; 2) providing Medicare and Medicaid coverage to pay for travel to medical services or changing the location of services to reduce costs; and 3) innovating with reimbursement methods that test whether costs are reduced without adversely affecting patient outcomes (Hamm, Kickham, and Cutler 1983). It should be noted, however, that not all students of long-term care view federal demonstration projects in positive terms (Trager 1981). Some argue that the money could better be put to use by funding additional services.

In some ways, fear has blocked legislation to expand noninstitutional long-term care benefits. These fears are related to predictions about the increasing numbers of older people, the difficulty in assessing need for long-term care, and the fear that with added services, families will abandon their elders. In general, though, it is recognized that service delivery has been hampered due to policy constraints. As Brody and Magel state:

As an outcome of the separate financial and professional lineages of medicine, social work and other health disciplines, long-term care systems have evolved into a collection of poorly related, multiple, parallel, overlapping and noncontinuous services. Continuity of care, which is a sine qua non to effective health service delivery, is rarely achieved. Services are funded inadequately by public auspices at the federal, state and local levels, and are multiply administered at these different levels in a bewildering arrangement of eligibilities and benefits" (1986:2).

REFERENCES

Aday, L. A. and R. Andersen. 1975. *Development of Indices of Access to Medical Care.* Ann Arbor, Mich.: Health Administration Press.

Andersen, R., and L. Aday. 1978. Access to medical care in the U.S.: Realized and potential. *Medical Care* 17:533–546.

Andersen, R. and J. Newman. 1973. Societal and individual determinants of medical care utilization in the U.S. *Milbank Memorial Fund Quarterly* 51:95–124.

Andersen, R., O. Anderson, and B. Smedby. 1968. Perceptions of and response to symptoms of illness in Sweden and the U.S. *Medical Care* 6:18–30.

Andersen, R., M. Chen, L. Aday, and L. Cornelius. 1987. Health status and medical community utilization. *Health Affairs* 6(1):135–156.

Benjamin, A. 1985. Community based long-term care. In C. Harrington, R. Newcomer, C. Estes, and Associates, eds., *Long-Term Care of the Elderly: Public Policy Issues.* Beverly Hills, Calif.: Sage.

Berkman, B., E. Bonander, B. Kemler, L. Marcus, I. M. Rubinger, I. Rutchick, and P. Silverman. 1988. *Social Work in Health Care: A Review of the literature.* Chicago: American Hospital Association.

Bild, B. and R. Havighurst. 1976. Senior citizens in great cities: The care of Chicago. *The Gerontologist* 16:4–88.

Borup, J. 1981. Relocation: Attitudes, information network, and problems encountered. *The Gerontologist* 21(5):501–511.

Branch, L. G. and A. M. Jette. 1982. A prospective study of long-term care institutionalization among the aged. *American Journal of Public Health,* 72:1373–13798.

Branch, L. 1978. *Boston Elders.* Program Report: University of Mass. Center for Survey Research.

Brody, E. 1981. "Women in the Middle" and family help to older people. *The Gerontologist* 21(5):471–480.

Brody, S. and J. Magel. 1986. Long-term care: The long and short of it. In C. Eisdorfer, ed., *Reforming Health Care for the Elderly: Recommendations for National Policy.* Baltimore, Md.: Johns Hopkins University Press.

Brody, S. J. and C. Masciocchi. 1980. Data for long-term care planning by Health Systems agencies. *American Journal of Public Health* 70(11):1194–1198.

Cantor, M. 1975. Life space and the social support system of the inner city elderly of New York City. *The Gerontologist* 15:23–27.

Carlton, T. 1984. *Clinical Social Work in Health Settings: A Guide to Professional Practice with Exemplars.* New York: Springer.

Chapman, S. H., M. P. LaPlante, and G. Wilensky. 1986. Life expectancy and health status of the aged. *Social Security bulletin* 49(10):24–48.

Comptroller General of the United States. 1972. *Study of Health Facilities Construction Costs.* Washington, D.C.: General Accounting Office.

Davis, K. and D. Rowland. 1986. *Medicare Policy: New Directions for Health and Long-Term Care.* Baltimore: Johns Hopkins University Press.

Dean, K. 1981. Self-care responses to illness: Selected review. *Social Science and Medicare* 15:673–687.

Densen, P. M. 1987. The elderly and the health care system: Another perspective. *Milbank Memorial Fund Quarterly* 65(4):614–638.

Doty, P. 1986. Family care of the elderly: The role of public policy. *Milbank Memorial Fund Quarterly* 64(1):34–75.

Dunkle, R., C. Coulton, J. MacKintosh, and R. Goode. 1982 .1 The decision-making process among the hospitalized elderly. *Journal of Gerontological Social Work* 4(3):95–106.

Dunkle, R. and C. Coulton. 1986. Decision making for long term care. Research project funded by the National Institute of Mental Health.

Falck, H. S. 1987. Social and psychological care before and during hospitalization. *Social Science and Medicine.* 25(6):711–720.

Ferraro, K. F. 1985. The effect of widowhood on the health status of older persons. *International Journal of Aging and Human Development* 21:9–25.

Fillenbaum, G. G. 1984. *The Wellbeing of the Elderly: Approaches to Multidimensional Assessment.* Geneva: World Health Organization.

Garitz, F. and P. Peth. 1974. An outreach program of medical care for aged highrise residents. *The Gerontologist* 14:404–407.

General Accounting Office. 1982. *The Elderly Should Benefit from Expanded Home Health Care but Increasing These Services Will Not Insure Cost Reductions.* (Public No. GAO/IDE-83-1). Washington, D.C.: GPO.

Germain, C. 1984. *Social Work Practice in Health Care: An Ecological Perspective.* New York City: Free Press.

Gibson, M. 1984. Family support patterns, policies and programs. In C. Nusberg, ed., *Innovative Aging Programs Abroad.* Westport, Conn: Greenwood Press.

Gibson, R. C. and J. S. Jackson. 1987. The health, physical functioning, and informal supports of the black elderly. *Milbank Memorial Fund Quarterly* 65(Suppl. 2):421–454.

Gibson, D. M., 1988. *The Aging Population in the Twenty-First Century: Statistics for Health Policy.* Washington, D.C.: National Academy Press.

Gonnella, J. S., D. Z. Louis, and J. J. McCord. 1976. The stage concept: An approach to the assessment of outcome of ambulatory care. *Medical Care* 14:13–21.

Gornick, M., J. N. Greenberg, P. W. Eggers, and A. Dobson. 1985. Twenty years of Medicare and Medicaid: Covered populations, use of benefits, and program expenditures. *Health Care Financing Review,* Annual Supplement.

Greenberg, J. N. and A. Ginn. 1979. A multivariate analysis of the predictors of long-term care placement. *Home Health Care Services Quarterly* 1:75–99.

Hamm, L. V., T. Kickham, and D. Cutler. 1983. Research, demonstrations and evaluations. In R. Vogel and H. Palmer, eds., *Long-Term Care: Perspectives from Research and Demonstrations.* Washington, D.C.: Health Care Financing Administration.

Hammerman, J. 1975. Health services: Their success and failure in reaching older adults. *American Journal of Public Health* 64:253–256.

Harris, R. 1975. Breaking the barriers to better health-care delivery for the aged. *The Gerontologist* 15:52–56.

Hartmen, A. and J. Laird. *Family-Centered Social Work Practice.* New York: Free Press.

Haug, M. 1981. Age and medical care utilization patterns. *Journal of Gerontology* 33:103–111.

Homan, S. M., C. C. Haddock, C. A. Winner, R. M. Coe, F. D. Wolinsky. 1986.

Widowhood, sex, labor force participation, and the use of physician services by elderly adults. *Journal of Gerontology* 41(6):793–796.

Kane, R. and R. Kane. 1981. *Assessing the Elderly.* Lexington, Mass.: Lexington Books.

Kane, R. 1981. Social workers in health: Commonalities and differences. *Health and Social Work* (November), 6(4):25–85.

Kane, R. A. and R. L. Kane. 1981. *Assessing the Elderly: A Practical Guide to Measurement.* Lexington, Mass.: Lexington Books.

Kart, C. 1981. Experiencing symptoms: Attribution and misattribution of illness among the aged. In M. Haug, ed., *Elderly Patients and Their Doctors,* New York: Springer.

Kart, C. S., E. Metress, and S. Metress. 1988. *Aging, Health and Society.* Boston: Jones and Bartlett.

Katz, S. 1983. Assessing self-maintenance: Activities of daily living, mobility, and instrumental activities of daily living. *Journal of the American Geriatrics Society* 31:721–727.

Katz, S., L. G. Branch, M. H. Branson, J. A. Papsidero, J. C. Beck, and D. S. Greer. 1983. Active life expectancy. *New England Journal of Medicine* 309:1218–1224.

Kemp, B. 1981. The case management model of human service delivery. In E. Pan, T. Barker, and C. Vash, eds., *Annual Review of Rehabilitation,* vol. 2. New York: Springer Publ.

Kemph, J. 1969. Kidney transplants and shifts in family dynamics. *American Journal of Psychiatry* 125:1485–1490.

Kerson, T. *Social Work in Health Settings: Policy and Practice.* New York: Longman.

Kobrin, F. 1981. Family extension and the elderly: Economic, demographic and family cycle factors. *Journal of Health and Social Behavior* 19:68–76.

Kronenfeld, J. 1978. Provider variables and the utilization of ambulatory care services. *Journal of Health and Social Behavior* 19:68–76.

Kuypers, J. A. and V. L. Bengtson. 1973. Social breakdown and competence. *Human Development* 16:181–201.

LaRue, A., L. Bank, L. Jarvik, and M. Hetland. 1979. Health in old age: How do physicians' ratings and self-ratings compare? *Journal of Gerontology* 34:687–691.

Lawton, M. P. and B. B. Simon. 1968. Ecology of social relationships: housing for the elderly. *The Gerontologist* 8:108–115.

Levin, L. S. and E. L. Idler. 1981. *The Hidden Health Care System: Medicating Structures and Medicine.* Cambridge, Mass.: Ballinger.

Levin, L. S., A. H. Katz, and E. Holst. 1979. *Self-Care: Lay Initiatives in Health.* 2d ed. New York: Prodist.

Litwak, E. 1985. *Helping the Elderly: The Complementary Roles of informal Networks and Formal Systems.* New York: Guilford Press.

Lock, M. M. 1980. *East Asian Medicine in Urban Japan.* Berkeley: University of California Press.

Lubitz, J. and R. Prihoda. 1984. Use and costs of Medicare services in the last 2 years of life. *Health Care Financing Review* 5:117–131.

Luckey, I. and T. Tran. 1988. Classification of users and nonusers of public health clinic among older blacks. Paper presented at the Gerontological Society meetings, San Francisco, November 1988.

Maddox, G. L. and E. B. Douglass. 1973. Self-assessment of health: A longitudinal study of elderly subjects. *Journal of Health and Social Behavior* 14:87–93.

Mangen, D. L. and W. A. Peterson, eds. 1982. *Research Instruments in Social Gerontology.* Vol. 1: *Clinical.* Minneapolis: University of Minnesota Press.

Manton, K. G., C. H. Patrick, and K. W. Johnson, 1987. Health differential between blacks and whites: Recent trends in mortality and morbidity. *Milbank Quarterly* 65(1):129–199.

Marcus, A. C. and J. M. Siegel. 1982. Sex differences in the use of physician services: A preliminary test of the fixed role hypothesis. *Journal of Health and Social Behavior* 23:186–196.

Moen, E. 1978. The reluctance of the elderly to access help. *Social Relations* 23(3):293–303.

Mutran, E., and K. Ferraro. 1988. Medical need and use of services among older men and women. *Journal of Health and Social Behavior* 43:171.

Nathanson, C. 1975. Illness and the feminine role: A theoretic review. *Social Science and Medicine* 9:57–62.

Neighbors, H. W. 1986. Ambulatory Medical Care Among Adult Black Americans: The Hospital Emergency Room. *Journal of National Medical Association* 78(4):275–282.

Office of Technology Assessment. 1985. *Medicare's Prospective Payment System: Strategies for Evaluating Cost, Quality, and Medical Technology.* Washington, D.C.: GPO.

Ohnuki-Tierney, E. 1984. *Illness and Culture in Contemporary Japan.* Cambridge: Cambridge University Press.

Parsons, T. 1958. Definitions of health and illness in the light of American values and social structure. In E. Jaco, ed., *Patients, Physicians, and Illness.* Glenco, Ill: Free Press.

Parsons, T. 1965. *Social Structure and Personality.* New York: Free Press.

Pathy, M. 1967. Clinical presentation of myocardial infarction in the elderly. *British Heart Journal* 29:190–199.

Rabin, D. L. 1985. Waxing of the gray, waning of the green. In *America's Aging: Health in an Older Society.* Committee on an Aging Society, Institute of Medicine and National Research Council. Washington, D.C.: National Academy Press.

Rabin, D. L. and P. Stockton. 1987. *Long-Term Care for the Elderly: A Factbook.* New York: Oxford University Press.

Rice, D. P. and J. J. Feldman. 1983. Living longer in the United States: Demographic changes and health needs of the elderly. *Milbank Memorial Fund Quarterly* 61(3):362–396.

Risse, G. B., R. L. Numbers, and J. W. Leavitt. 1977. *Medicine Without Doctors: Home Health Care in American History.* New York: Science History Publication.

Roos, N. P., P. Montgomery, and L. l. Roos. 1987. Health care utilization in the years prior to death. *Milbank Memorial Fund Quarterly* 65(Suppl. 2):270–296.

Schlesinger, M. 1987. Paying the price: Medical care, minorities, and the newly competitive health care system. *Milbank Memorial Fund Quarterly* 65(Suppl. 2):270–296.

Schott, L. J. 1984. The medicines of knaves and fools? Patent medicine in nineteenth-century America. *Journal of the Cleveland Medical Library Association* (Spring/Summer), pp. 26–28.

Shanas, E. and G. L. Maddox. 1985. Health, health resources, and the utilization of care. In R. H. Binstock, and E. Shanas, eds. *Handbook of Aging the Social Sciences.* 2d ed. New York: Van Nostrand Reinhold.

Shuval, J. 1970. *The Social Functions of Medical Practice.* San Francisco: Jossey-Bass.

Silverstone, B. 1984. Informal social support systems for the frail elderly. In Institute of Medicine/National Research Council, ed., *America's Aging: Health in an Older Society.* Washington, D.C.: National Academy Press.

Smallegan, m. 1985. There was nothing else to do: Needs for care before nursing home admission. *The Gerontologist* 25(4):364–369.

Snider, E. 1981. Young-old versus old-old and the use of health services. Does the difference make a difference? *Journal of the American Geriatrics Society* 29(8):354–358.

Soldo, B. J. and K. G. Manton. 1985. Changes in the health status and service needs of the oldest-old: Current Patterns and future trends. *Milbank Memorial Fund Quarterly/Health and Society* (Spring), 63:286–319.

Somers, A. R. 1983. Medicare and long-term care. *Perspectives on Aging* (March/April), pp. 5–8.

Somers, A. R. 1985. Financing long-term care for the elderly: Institutions, incentives, issues. In Committee on Aging Society, Institute of Medicine and the National Research Council, eds., *America's Aging: Health in an Older Society.* Washington, D.C.: National Academy in Press.

Steinberg, R. and G. Carter. 1983. *Case Management of the Elderly.* Lexington, Mass.: Lexington Books.

Stoller, E. P. 1982. Sources of support for the elderly during illness. *Health and Social Work* 7:111–122.

Trager, B. 1981. In place of policy: Public adventures in non-institutional long-term care. Paper presented at the annual meeting of the American Public Health Association, Los Angeles, November.

Troll, L., S. Miller, and R. Atchley. 1979. *Health Status of Minorities and Low-income Groups.* DHEW Pub. No. (HRA) 79-627. Health Resources Administration. Washington, D.C.: GPO.

U.S. Office of Health Resources. 1979. *Health Statuses of Minorities and Low Income Groups.* Department of Health, Education, and Welfare Resources Administration. Washington, D.C.: GPO.

U.S. Senate. Special Committee on Aging. 1988. *Developments in Aging: 1987*, vol. 1. Washington, D.C.: GPO.

Verbrugge, L. M. and J. H. Madans. 1985. Social roles and health trends of American women. *Milbank Memorial Fund Quarterly* 63(4):691–735.

Wan, T. 1982. Use of health service by the elderly in low income communities. *Milbank Memorial Fund Quarterly* 60:82–107.

Wan, T. and S. Soifer. 1974. Determinants of physician utilization: A causal analysis. *Journal of Health and Social Behavior* 18:61–70.

Ward, R. 1977. Services for older people: An integrated framework for research. *Journal of Health and Social Behavior* 18:61–70.

Wilensky, G. R. and L. F. Rossiter. 1983. The relative importance of physician-induced demand in the demand for medical care. *Milbank Memorial Fund Quarterly* 61(2):252–277.

Williamson, J. D. and K. Danaher. 1978. *Self-care in Health.* London: Croom Helm.

Zopf, P. E. 1986. *America's Older Population.* Houston: Cap and Gown Press.

9

Mental Health and the Elderly

❖

KENNETH SOLOMON, M.D.
Saint Louis University Medical Center
Saint Louis, Missouri

Older individuals are more likely to demonstrate evidence of acute or chronic psychopathology than are individuals in any other stage of life. Indeed, Post (1968) suggests that 20 to 30 percent of the elderly have psychiatric disorders. Older people make up a large percentage of new admissions and the majority of long-term-stay clients in state hospitals and other institutions. Approximately 5 percent of the elderly are institutionalized because of psychopathologic or behavioral difficulties (Redick, Kramer, and Taube 1973).

Psychiatric dysfunction in the elderly is not caused by the biologic changes that occur with aging, although some changes in the biochemistry and physiology of the brain may increase the vulnerability of the elderly to certain psychologic dysfunctions and organic neurologic disease. Rather, the development of psychopathologic dysfunction in the elderly arises from the interaction of the triggers of current psychosocial stressors and the older person's lifelong learned ability to cope adaptively with stress.

STRESS AND COPING IN THE ELDERLY

New psychiatric symptoms in the elderly are always triggered by current stress. The elderly have a characteristic set of psychodynamic responses to stress, regardless of its biologic, psychologic, or social nature (Goldfarb 1968, 1974; K. Solomon 1981a, 1981b, 1982a, 1982c, 1983a, b, c). As this stress is experienced by older people, it leads to a sense of diminished mastery over their environment and therefore to increased feelings of helplessness and ambivalence about dependency needs. It is at this stage that the older person may experience the development of learned helplessness (Maier and Seligman 1976; Seligman 1975; K. Solomon 1982e), a process often inadvertently enhanced and reinforced by members of the person's social support system and, especially, by the mental health, health, and human services delivery system. This concept is crucial, as the development of learned helplessness almost invariably leads to the development of psychopathology; whereas, the avoidance of learned helplessness is preventive of this process.

These feelings may produce three affects. One is fear, as the older person worries about what is to become of him/her as he/she works to resolve the stress. Another affect is anger at self or others, anger over what has happened to the older person as well as anger at experienced powerlessness and loss of mastery. These affects, also conceptualized as flight or fight, are mediated biologically by the general adaptation syndrome, which triggers the organism to either cope or to become biologically exhausted (with subsequent illness or death) (Selye 1950). Whether the person feels fear or anger or a mixture of the two depends on how that person has responded to stress throughout his/her life. The basic stress response does not change with increasing age. The third affect is loss and a sense of narcissistic injury. How much loss is experienced by the older person is inversely related to the manifest anxiety noted to the observer.

Acute and Unexpected Stress

The stress experienced by the older person may be acute and unexpected or chronic. The events that cause acute, unexpected stress may be grouped into three major categories, all characterized by loss.

The first set of losses is in the social support system. They include loss of spouse, siblings, friends, parents, children, other relatives, and neighbors. The most psychologically devastating of these is the loss of a spouse (Guttmann, Grunes, and Griffin 1979; Homes and Rahe 1967; Wolff 1977).

A second set of losses concerns social role and involves a shift from institutional to tenuous and informal roles and a shift as well in gender roles. By their very nature, tenuous and informal roles, which exist at the whim of the primary group or society, are sources of stress for the elderly (Rosow 1976). Particularly stressful for men is the loss of opportunities for the expression of gender-role expectations (K. Solomon 1982b 1982c; Solomon and Hurwitz 1982).

The third major set of losses falls into a miscellaneous group that includes loss of health, independence, adequate income, mobility, adequate housing, and leisure activities. These losses are the result of societally determined changes, such as retirement (Friedmann and Orbach 1974; Sheppard 1976), and chronic diseases that inhibit the functioning of the older person (Wilson 1970).

Chronic Stress

Besides these acute episodic stressors, chronic stressors arise from the "victimization" of the elderly (K. Solomon 1983a, b). This victimization has four dimensions: economic, attitudinal, role, and physical. Like all chronic situations in which the individual is "one down," the individual feels oppressed, angry, despondent, and helpless and may turn the anger onto himself/herself or explosively outward toward others or society at large (Brody 1974).

Economic victimization includes not only illegal "ripoffs" and fraudulent schemes but also legal and sanctioned policy, such as inadequate pensions, the effects of inflation, business practices that bilk the elderly consumer of needed funds, and inadequate Medicare coverage.

Physical victimization includes abuse of the older person by his/her children or spouse as well as the effects of crime against person and property. It also includes much of the poor treatment that the elderly frequently receive from health caregivers in the form of inadequate diagnostic evaluations, inappropriate medication or surgery, and inadequate care in custodial institutions.

Attitudinal victimization is the result of the stereotyping of the elderly (Ryan 1976; Tuckman and Lorge 1953a). As Butler (1975) and Solomon and Vickers (1979) note, stereotyping leads to misdiagnosis and the provision of inadequate and irrelevant services. Individual needs of the elderly are not identified, and their individuality is lost. This contributes to the learned helplessness of many older individuals, especially in the health care setting (Maier and Seligman 1976; Seligman 1975; K. Solomon 1979c, 1982e).

Role victimization comes with the shift from institutional to tenuous and informal social roles. The elderly may then lapse into a state of rolelessness with subsequent alienation, anomie, apathy, and psychopathologic symptomatology if they are unable to adopt even tenuous or informal roles (Akisal and McKinney 1975; Bibring 1961; K. Solomon 1981a).

THE PSYCHOGERIATRIC EVALUATION

Before an intervention can be planned for the older individual with significant psychologic dysfunctions, a complete psychogeriatric evaluation is necessary. The goal is to get as much information as possible for a comprehensive understanding of the person's psychosocial state. The evaluation requires examination of the person's current stresses, his/her psychodynamic response to these stresses, the responses of various social subsystems that interact with the individual, and the strengths and weaknesses of the individual's personality. The evaluation also includes the elimination of any treatable medical causes of symptoms that may be present.

The psychogeriatric evaluation has eleven components. While it is presented in its entirety here, it is not expected nor required that any individual member of the geriatric team be responsible for the entire evaluation. Many authors have examined the roles of various mental health professionals and have divided them into two major categories: generalist and specialist. Generalist roles are those clinical roles that are not limited by disciplinary boundaries or training. Rather, these roles are used by all professionals in the fulfillment of various professional tasks. They are discussed in more depth elsewhere (Cohen 1973; Smith 1972; K. Solomon 1979b, 1982d). Specialist roles allow for differentiation of professionals on the team and utilization of specific skills, knowledge, and personality traits of these professionals in the total care of the individual (Harris and Solomon 1977; Howard 1979; Pons 1979; Romaniuk 1979). Most work accomplished in the psychosocial aspects of caring for the elderly person in a mental-health/human-service setting utilizes generalist skills of all members of the team. The psychogeriatric evaluation is one task that can be largely completed using only generalist skills.

The components of the psychogeriatric evaluation are:

1. *History of the Present Episode.* One needs to know exactly what the client is feeling and experiencing, how long the problem has been going on, what seemed to trigger it, what makes it better (even temporarily), what seems to make it worse, and what interventions the client, family, and mental-health personnel have tried to improve this particular problem. It is in the history of the present episode that one asks specific questions regarding the various symptoms needed to

make a diagnosis as well as to assess blocks to need satisfaction, including presence or absence of vegetative, depressive, psychotic, phobic, and obsessive-compulsive symptoms.

2. *Past Psychiatric History.* One not only needs to ask if the client has had inpatient or outpatient psychiatric treatment in the past, but whether he/she has received intervention for emotional problems from other personnel such as psychologists, social workers, psychiatric nurses, and clergy. In addition, a history of receiving "nerve pills" or other psychotropic drugs from a family physician is important. This information will help clarify the client's ability to cope and his/her coping mechanisms. The presence of a history of a severe psychiatric disability would be an indication either for a prescription of specific interventions (especially psychopharmacologic) that have been successful in the past (Ayd 1975) and the avoidance of interventions that have been unsuccessful.

3. *Past and Present Medical Status.* The client's medical history is necessary to assess his/her overall functional capabilities and to know what problems to expect in the future. The presence or absence of certain medications may impair or enhance the overall treatment process. This history may also hint at certain somatic disorders or medications that may be causing the psychopathology noted in the client (e.g., depression secondary to hypothyroidism or toxic psychosis secondary to antidepressants).

4. *Drug History.* The client's use of drugs must be ascertained, which not only includes presecription medications, but also over-the-counter drugs and street drugs. Many older people have problems with alcohol or drugs, which may interfere with their overall functioning as well as with the treatment program or which may otherwise cause specific psychiatric disorders. Besides alcohol, the most commonly abused drugs in the elderly are over-the-counter "nerve pills," benzodiazepines, marijuana, barbiturates, amphetamines, and legal narcotic analgesics; the use of these drugs must be specifically ascertained.

5. *Psychosocial Evaluation.* The purpose of the psychosocial evaluation is to gather information about the client's past coping skills, factors that may enhance or inhibit psychiatric and physical rehabilitation, and to assess other stresses and resources in the patient's environment.

The psychosocial evaluation begins with a family history, which includes information about the client's parents, siblings, and children. The evaluation includes the medical and psychiatric histories of these individuals, and what kind of relationships these people had and have with each other and with the client. The family history also includes occupational and social class background of the client's parents, their immigration status, and the relationship between the parents.

In the developmental history, the client's meeting of developmental landmarks is assessed. The examiner also gathers information about the client's life as a child.

In the educational history, one asks questions about the client's level of education and use of this education. Why the client stopped or continued educational pursuits at different times in his/her life is ascertained. The client's interest in lifelong learning, vocational rehabilitation, and attitudes toward education are also assessed.

In the client's occupational history, the examiner looks at the jobs the client has held, his/her ability to hold a job, and the kind of work he/she is interested in. One also examines for exposure to occupational hazards that might have diagnostic or therapeutic implications.

In the marital and sexual history, one examines these relationships as a major resource and stress. These factors need to be examined regardless of marital status, sexual orientation, or sexual exclusivity or nonexclusivity. If the client has never married or cohabited, the reasons need to be assessed. The entire spectrum of the individual's interpersonal relationships is examined in this way. One also ascertains the client's interest in and level of sexual activity with its obvious implications for treatment.

One then looks at the client's current financial situation, which not only includes examination of his/her sources of income but which also includes other social services that substitute for income. These sources include food stamps, health insurance coverage, and Title III nutrition programs.

The examiner then investigates the client's current housing, which is examined for the presence or absence of barriers and to see how the house can be made barrier-free. Thus housing becomes both a stress and a resource to the individual.

How the client uses leisure time is also assessed. This factor is important not only to provide relaxation for the client but also to gather information about the client's ability to relax, experience positive affects, and develop meaningful rather than just time-consuming activities.

In planning intervention, knowledge of the client's premorbid personality is crucial. This information will tell the therapist what kind of defense and coping mechanisms the person uses. The examiner will also learn how the person has satisfied various needs in the past and whether or not the person has been capable of adapting to stress in the past. It will clarify other psychologic stresses and resources the individual brings into the rehabilitation situation and helps to assess the risk of the individual developing major psychopathology in the future. For example, those with labile personality disorders are at risk for developing depression and those with stable personality disorders are at risk for developing either depression or paraphrenia when stressed in old age (Solomon 1981b; Weiss 1973). Those without personality disorders are more likely to cope successfully with stress. At the same time that one assesses the premorbid personality of the client, one examines the entire environment to assess other stresses and resources that are present.

6. *Review of Systems.* While a review of systems has traditionally been part of the medical examination, it can be done by any professional. During the review of systems, the examiner asks about various symptoms of disease, including pain, visual problems, bowel habits, diet and appetite, sleep, and sexual functioning. Formal guides to a review of systems have been published elsewhere (Adams 1958; Delp 1968; Friedland 1967; Judge and Zuidema 1963).

7. *Physical Examination.* The physical examination should be complete, including a rectal and pelvic examination. Although this must be done by a physician, nurse practitioner, or physician's assistant, the mental health/human service worker must be apprised of this information in order to understand the problems of the older person and plan appropriate interventions.

8. *Neurologic Examination.* As may older individuals have or are suspected to have neurologic disease, a thorough neurologic examination must be done. This examination does not have to be done by a neurologic consultant since all physicians and other health professionals who do physical examinations are trained to do neurologic examinations. This information must be transmitted to the members of the team.

9. *Mental Status Examination.* The mental status examination has fifteen parts in addition to observation of the client during the conduct of the psychogeriatric examination. Delineation of psychopathologic symptoms is necessary for an accurate assessment of the psy-

chosocial status of the older client. Accurate, value-free descriptions of behavior, without labels, are the backbone of the mental status examination. In reviewing the mental status examination, one can easily see many forms of behavior that vary from the expected normative behavior of the client. These variations are not necessarily psychopathologic. For example, a sad affect would be very appropriate to someone who has recently had a cerebrovascular accident but would not be appropriate for someone who has just won a lottery.

There are several descriptions of the conduct of the mental-status examination (MacKinnon 1980; Menninger 1962; Stevenson and Sheppe 1974). The parameters of the mental status examination will be discussed in turn.

First one notes the client's appearance. How is the person dressed? Is the person in a bed or wheelchair or ambulatory? What is his/her posture? Are there any other signs that might indicate the possibility of physical disease? Appearance is either appropriate or inappropriate for the client's medical condition and social setting. For example, it would not be generally considered appropriate for a client to wear pajamas to an outpatient appointment but it would be appropriate to wear them in a hospital. The social context of a client's appearance must be taken into account. The same holds true for posture, which may be relaxed, tense, indicative of physical pathology, or bizarre and unusual as in some psychotic individuals.

One then notes the client's level of consciousness and alertness. The level of consciousness may be normal or the client may be hyperalert with wide eyes and furtive scanning of the environment or drowsy, sleeping, obtunded, semicomatose, or comatose.

The third part of the examination is evaluation of the client's attention span. The client may have marked difficulty paying attention because of distractability or hearing deficit. On the other hand, a client may be demonstrating denial or selective attention, and may, for unconscious reasons, not attend to the examiner. Selective inattention is usually under some conscious control, but denial is not. Distractability is usually noted in severe psychotic or cognitive disorders.

Mood is ascertained by asking the client how he/she feels and what is his/her underlying mood. For example, is he/she happy, sad, angry? Mood may be euthymic; it may be happy or sad within the realm of human experience. Or the client may experience extremes of mood including elation or euphoria on the one hand or severe depression on the other. The client may be angry or hostile or be experiencing anxiety or fear.

Associated with mood is the fifth parameter of the mental-status exam, affect. This is the behavioral manifestation of the underlying mood, and is usually ascertained through examination of the client's facial expression. Is the facial expression angry, sad, happy, dull, or blunted? Also, the examiner wants to know if the affect corresponds to the expressed thought content. The client's affect may be appropriate or inappropriate. Inappropriate affect is affect that does not fit the underlying mood or the content of the person's thoughts. If inappropriate, it may also be blunted or flattened, which is when the person does not facially express underlying feelings.

Sixth, one examines the level of activity. Is it normally active, hyperactive, or hypoactive? Are there tremors or other abnormal movements? The client may demonstrate psychomotor retardation, in which all physical functions are slowed up, or psychomotor agitation, in which he/she is restless or agitated. Mild agitation may be manifested by mild finger tapping and hand wringing. Severe agitation is manifested by difficulty staying still for more than a few moments, which must be differentiated from akathisia, which is a common Parkinsonian symptom.

One then examines the quality of the client's speech. One considers the quantity, volume, tone, inflection, speed, and understandability (coherence). Speech may be incoherent or indistinct because of aphasia or dysarthria. It may be rapid or slow, monotonous or inflected, too low or too loud. It may or may not be appropriate to the situation, content, or affect.

The examiner then considers the client's thought process. Is it rational, logical, and oriented toward a goal? Does the client attempt to answer questions in a reasonably concise manner? Is the client able to express himself/herself or is there evidence of receptive or expressive aphasia? Deficiencies of thought include paucity of thought, which is a relative lack of expressed thought. Preservation occurs when the same thought is repeated over and over again regardless of its relevance to the question asked. Other disorders of thought process include a loss of the normal logical pathways. When mild, this is called tangentiality, in which the client seems to constantly digress from topic, of circumstantiality, in which the client "beats around the bush" but eventually answers the question. More severe loss of logical aspects of thought is called loose associations or derailment. When severe, the client's speech may be almost impossible to understand. This situation is called a word salad. In addition, the client may use neologisms, newly invented words that may have idiosyncratic meanings known only to the client.

Next, one examines the content of the client's thought. What is it that the person is specifically thinking and is it relevant to the business at hand. Disturbances of thought content include vagueness, compulsive repetition, or obsessive intrusion of a thought alien to the client's ego. The client may demonstrate *idées fixes,* which are unshakeable, encapsulated ideas that may or may not be delusional. The client may also be preoccupied with phobic ideas or fantasies. He/she may demonstrate delusions, which may be reasonably logical beliefs but which are not based in reality. Delusions are frequently paranoid in the elderly. They may be encapsulated or limited to only a small part of the client's life and not affect the client's functioning in other ways, or they may be unencapsulated, global, and severely disruptive. They may be organized into a delusional system or they may be disorganized. The client may also demonstrate confabulation or the creation of "factual" information to cover up memory deficits, which must be differentiated from willful lying. Depressive thought content, including self-deprecation, statements of irrational guilt, and feelings of helplessness, hopelessness, worthlessness, and uselessness may also be demonstrated. Finally, certain specific Schneiderian first-rank symptoms of schizophrenia are included as disturbances of thought. These symptoms include thought insertion (the belief that an outside force or person is putting thoughts in the client's head), thought control (the belief that an outside force is controlling the client's thoughts), behavioral control (a similar belief associated with behavior), thought withdrawal (the belief that an outside force is taking thoughts out of the client's head), and thought broadcasting (the belief that people are able to hear the client's thoughts). Schneiderian first-rank symptoms are believed to be pathognominic of schizophrenia in younger people (Kendell, Brockington, and Leff 1979), but have no specific pathognomonic consequence in the elderly.

In examining perception, one examines the client's ability to understand the spoken and written word as well as looking for unusual perceptual experiences. Many major disorders of perception are pathophysiologic in nature and include receptive aphasias and the results of major sensory deficits.

Another common disorder of perception is the illusion, in which things are perceived in ways that do not match the reality. The optical illusion is an example with which everyone is familiar. Misperceptions are another form of perceptual disorder, in which something is misidentified as something it is not. The most severe perceptual disorders are hallucinations, in which the client creates sensory inputs not based in the external environment. These hallucinations may be auditory, visual, olfactory, gustatory, tactile, or kinesthetic. Specific

Schneiderian perceptual symptoms include the experience of hallucinating two voices communicating with each other or a single voice keeping up a running commentary on the client's behavior.

Memory is examined, in part, during the process of obtaining a history, a process that allows the examiner to ascertain the accuracy of the client's recent and remote memory. Questions about the client's activities over the few days prior to the examination test for recent memory. To test for immediate recall, one gives the client three items to remember and checks back with him/her several minutes later to see if they are recalled. Memory disturbances includes specific amnesias and hypomnesias as well as more global disturbances of immediate recall, recent memory, and remote memory, and the part processes of registration, retention, recognition, and recall.

One then tests for orientation. Does the client know the day of the week, date, month, year, and season? Does the person know the name of the place he/she is in, the address, the floor, the room number? Can the client give a reasonable account of himself/herself? Is the client aware of the present situation? In other words, does the client understand the environmental parameters surrounding him/her? Difficulty with orientation is called disorientation and is marked by the client's inability to identify the time, the place, or basic information about himself/herself.

One assesses the client's level of intelligence by examining his/her ability to perform higher cortical functions. Can the client serially subtract seven from a hundred? Can the client follow simple instructions? Can the client read and write a simple sentence? How well does the client interpret proverbs? Are these proverbs interpreted abstractly or concretely? The proverbs I usually use are: "You can lead a horse to water but you can't make it drink" and "People in glass houses shouldn't throw stones." Can the client identify similarities and differences between items such as an apple and an orange? Disorders of intelligence may include life long intellectual deficits, as in mentally retraded individuals, or acquired intellectual deficits. The latter may be specific, like dyslexia, or global as in dementia, and include difficulties following simple instructions, reading, calculating, and writing sentences. These disorders may also include loss of the ability to abstract proverbs, which is partially dependent upon the educational level and cultural background of the client.

One tests judgment by assessing what the client would do in hypothetical situations. The situations I use are: What would the client do if he/she found a letter lying on the ground in front of a mailbox, and what would the client do if he/she smelled smoke while at the movies.

These questions give the examiner information about client's ability to integrate environmental cues and choose between several alternative behaviors. Difficulties of judgment include impulsivity, the failure to take the consequences of one's behavior into account prior to action.

The final part of the mental status examination is the assessment of the client's level of insight, which is accomplished by asking the client why he/she feels he/she has developed the specific emotional, behavioral, or cognitive difficulty. Levels of insight range from a complete denial of all symptoms to the ability to identify symptoms but not their consequences or etiology, to the ability to identify symptoms and consequences but not their etiology, to insight as to the nature and cause of the psychosocial difficulties. The level of insight will often determine the type of intervention planned with the client.

10. *Laboratory Examination.* The specific laboratory examination is dependent upon the nature of the psychologic difficulty considered. For geriatric clients who develop psychopathology, the laboratory examination should include a complete blood count, renal, liver, and thyroid function studies, electrolytes, fasting blood sugar, electrocardiogram, chest x-ray, serology for syphilis, urine alcohol and drug screen, and serum concentrations of drugs that the client is taking. In addition, if a diagnosis of brain failure is being considered, the client should also have vitamin B_{12} and folate blood levels assessed, and a computerized axial tomography of the head, with and without contrast. An electroencephalogram or magnetic resonance imagery of the head, or other specific laboratory evaluations may also be necessary.

11. *Social Examination.* This examination is the final part of the psychogeriatric evaluation. It includes information gathered from review of the client's chart and from discussions with social-service staff, nursing staff, family members, neighbors, and other important individuals in the client's life. It will corroborate the history the client gives the examiner and will also give the examiner insight into other symptoms that the client may be unwilling or unable to discuss. It will also help assess and enlist the interpersonal resources available to the client. If feasible, the social examination should include a tour of the client's home to assess resources, stresses, and barriers in the environment.

THE MAJOR PSYCHIATRIC DYSFUNCTIONS

Depression

Depression is the most common psychiatric disturbance in the elderly. Estimates of the incidence of depressive episodes that significantly interfere with life functioning in persons 65 and over range from 15 percent to 68 percent, with most researchers noting an incidence of 30 to 40 percent (Ban 1978). This finding compares with a 10 percent incidence of depression in the general population (Sartorius 1975), making depression three to six times more frequent in the elderly than in the young. The prevalence of depression in the elderly in the community has been estimated by Blazer and Williams to be approximately 15 percent (Blazer and Williams 1980). The frequency of depression in the elderly is associated with the many stresses that they face. The elderly may also be biologically predisposed to the development of depression.

DESCRIPTION

Depression is manifested by sad mood (or its equivalent) and various vegetative disturbances (American Psychiatric Association 1987). There is a change in appetite (usually loss but occasionally increase) and change in the sleep cycle (usually difficulty falling asleep, difficulty remaining asleep, and early morning awakening, but occasionally hypersomnia). The client demonstrates either psychomotor agitation or retardation and may complain of anxiety, weakness, or feeling slowed up, but not sadness. The client feels fatigued, even after adequate sleep, and feels that he/she does not have the energy or the motivation for rehabilitation and other tasks. The client feels guilty and blames himself/herself for these problems. The client has difficulty concentrating and demonstrates a cognitive disturbance manifested by a disturbance of recent memory and immediate recall, concrete thinking, pervasive doubt, and what the author has described as "viewing the world through gray-colored glasses." In addition, the depressed individual manipulates himself/herself and others into situations that will guarantee failure (Bonime 1966; Kovacs and Beck 1978) and then internalizes the guilt and anger at others who do not respond to these manipulations. The severely depressed person may verbalize suicidal feelings, ideation, or plans. As suicide is one of the leading causes of death in the elderly (Weiss 1974), the examiner must always ask the client about suicidal ideation. Some severely depressed individuals will also demonstrate a variety of psychotic symptoms, including delusions and hallucinations.

The phenomenology of depressive disorders in the elderly varies with the premorbid history of the older person. Many elderly present the classic semiology of depression, including sad mood, psychomotor agitation, guilt, self-deprecation, hopelessness, worthlessness, helplessness, appetite and weight disturbance, sleep disturbance, and suicidal ideation. However, many elderly exhibit psychomotor retardation without guilt, anger, and self-deprecation. Those elderly with a premorbid history of an affective disorder or difficulty in handling conflicts about hostility and dependence are more likely to develop a depressive picture that fits the classic description. The elderly with good premorbid histories who suffer a multitude of losses are likely to experience predominantly affective loss leading to a clinical picture more consistant with a retarded depression. Loss and grieving are not as intimately associated with anger as they are in younger individuals; this lack of association contributes to the clinical picture just noted.

Depression is the major psychiatric disturbance that may be fatal; the major reason is suicide. One-fourth of all suicides in the United States occur in individuals over 65. The rate of suicide in white men over 65 is three times that of white men aged 25. White men over 75 have the highest incidence of successful suicide, followed by white men 65 to 74 and white women over 65 (Weiss 1974). The elderly are the only age group in which successful suicides outnumber suicide attempts; when the elderly are suicidal, they are likely to be successful.

Death of the depressed elderly person may also result from major physiologic consequences of the depression, even in the absence of suicidal intent. The appetite disturbance that accompanies depression may lead the older person to withdraw from food and drink. Severe fluid and electrolyte disturbances may rapidly develop, which may be fatal because of secondary pneumonia or seizures. The immobility caused by depression may lead to the development of decubitus ulcers, which may become secondarily infected, leading to sepsis. Thus depression in an older person is potentially more dangerous and the need for treatment more urgent than in a younger person.

DIAGNOSIS AND TREATMENT

The diagnosis of depression involves the differentiation of depression from physical diseases, particularly dementia, and drug abuse or withdrawal. Depression is a common cause of pseudodementia in the elderly (Libow 1973); since depression is treatable and many of the dementias are not, an accurate diagnosis is absolutely essential. One difficulty in differential diagnosis is that depressive symptoms may be noted in the demented individual early in the course of the brain disease (Solomon 1982f). The severely depressed individual, especially one with a retarded depression, may be so anergic as to make it impossible to differentiate between depression and dementia. Kahn (1978) has noted that many cognitive changes, primarily deficits of immediate recall and recent memory, occur in the depressed individual. In addition to the cognitive changes, there are severe difficulties of attention that may seem to be a memory deficit. The anergic, depressed individual may be so retarded that he/she may become incontinent and unable to care for basic bodily needs. Because of anergia, the depressed individual may think more concretely than in the premorbid state, which may also give the impression of a loss of cognitive functioning. Agitation and an inability to respond to the examiner may lead to a false impression of cognitive disturbance. Secondary physiologic changes may lead to delirium, with subsequent missed diagnosis of the underlying depression.

Drug and alcohol withdrawal syndromes are frequently characterized by symptoms that are identical to depression, especially in patients addicted to short-acting benzodiazepines. Depressive symptoms are also common after detoxification and remit spontaneously over time. Thus, an addicted patient must usually be "clean" for at least one month before a diagnosis of depression can be made and treatment instituted.

Endocrine disorders may present as an affective disturbance distinguishable from a major depressive disorder (Whybrow and Hurwitz 1976). Depression is commonly seen in clients with chronic renal disease, anemia, and brain tumors, and as a result of head trauma. Mood changes, lethargy, fatigability, weight loss, and sleep disturbances are seen in a myriad of systemic diseases and as side effects of many medications, especially hormones, psychotropic drugs, and antihypertensive medications.

The diagnosis of depression is made by a combination of inclusion and exclusion criteria (American Psychiatric Association 1987). These criteria include at least four of the following eight:

1. Appetite/weight disturbance
2. Sleep disturbance
3. Disturbance in activity level
4. Cognitive disturbance
5. Disturbance in energy level

6. Disturbance in usual interests
7. Disturbance of attention
8. Suicidal ideation/plans/behavior

Other features that should be noted include mood disturbance of at least two weeks duration. Exclusion criteria—that is, that the depression is not part of a physical disorder or other major psychiatric disorder or that it is not a normal grief reaction—should be noted. It is absolutely essential to differentiate between depression (a major disturbance) and sadness (a universal experience).

Once the diagnosis of depression is made, treatment should be rapidly and aggressively instituted because of the potentially fatal outcome of this disturbance. A combination of pharmacotherapy with antidepressant medication (or, if the client has delusions or hallucinations, with antipsychotic medication), psychotherapy (especially of a cognitive therapy orientation), and environmental manipulation is indicated.

Alcoholism and Chemical Dependency

Approximately 25 percent of people over the age of 65 are at risk for developing alcoholism or chemical dependency. A major problem at this time is the addiction to short-acting benzodiazepines (table 9.1), especially alprazolam, lorazepam, and triazolam. Indeed, there is a virtual epidemic occurring in the USA at this time. Many of these individuals have a long history of drug and alcohol abuse, with the short-acting benzodiazepines being the latest of a long line of abused medications. But many other patients were placed on these drugs

TABLE 9.1. Benzodiazepines

1. Chlordiazepoxide (Librium)
2. Diazepam (Valium)
3. Oxazepam (Serax)
4. Clorazepate (Tranxene, Azene)
5. Prazepam (Verstran, Centrax)
6. Lorazepam (Ativan)
7. Halazepam (Paxipam)
8. Alprazolam (Xanax)
9. Flurazepam (Dalmane)
10. Temazepam (Restoril)
11. Triazolam (Halcion)

after complaining to their physician about anxiety, depression, insomnia, or vague somatic complaints. Because of their short half-lives in the body, tolerance to these medications develops rapidly, with withdrawal the consequence. Anxiety, agitation, and sleeplessness (withdrawal) is followed by either an increased dose of medication or increased frequency of dosage. Tolerance and withdrawal are the inevitable result and a cycle of increased drug and increased withdrawal develops. While this pattern occurs with all addictive drugs, it may take months to years to develop with alcohol or longer-acting medications. With the short-acting medications, however, a full-blown withdrawal syndrome, characterized by severe agitation, anxiety, panic attacks, depression, delirium, poor attention span, and even seizures may occur in the patient who has been taking these drugs for only two or three weeks, at very low dosage, *while the patient is still taking the drug*. Even when detoxification is complete, these symptoms may recur as long as six months after the last dose of drug has been taken. These medications should never be abruptly discontinued, as a full-fledged withdrawal syndrome can be fatal. For example, 20 percent of untreated delirium tremens (alcohol withdrawal) is fatal.

Reactive alcoholics may or may not have been premorbid social drinkers but who, after experiencing a series of stresses in old age, begin to drink heavily for the first time. Some differences have been noted between male and female alcoholics who begin to drink for the first time in later life. Men tend to drink alone rather than with friends, and the major reason they give for their drinking is self-medication to cope with severe losses. Many of these men have been extremely dependent on someone whom they have lost, and they have become severely depressed. They are unable to cope with many of the stresses of daily life without the use of alcohol. Their alcohol use rapidly accelerates to an addiction, frequently in a matter of months.

Women tend to drink in the company of others. Many of these women have been somewhat compulsive and dependent individuals who have characterologically been unable to express anger. In the presence of stress, usually the loss of a significant other, they use alcohol to release the hostile feelings that they have repressed and suppressed for a lifetime.

The treatment of alcoholism and chemical dependency first involves confrontation of denial and rationalization, education about the effects of addictive drugs and alcohol for the patient and family, confrontation of the family's enabling behaviors, and attendance at Alcoholics Anonymous, as well as supportive psychotherapy and appropriate detoxification. Once the patient is "clean" for at least one month, and preferably longer, then treatment of the underlying depression, if present, by appropriate psychotherapy, sociotherapy, and psychopharmocology is indicated.

Brain Failure

The third most common psychiatric disorder in the elderly is brain failure, which denotes a functional neurologic loss. Brain failure has four mutually nonexclusive dimensions, and the clinical presentation of any individual may be conceptualized as a mixture of factors on these axes. These axes are continual and an individual may shift on any or all of them at any time during the course of the disease.

One axis is the symptomatologic. One terminus is delirium, which is a disorder of attention and which is associated with an altered state of consciousness. The other terminus is dementia, which is a disorder of memory and which is associated with a normal state of consciousness. Some people with dementia may also have symptoms of delirium and vice versa. The second axis is the time of onset of symptoms and ranges from acute and sudden, as seen in drug toxicity or a cerebrovascular accident, to very slow, chronic, and insidious, as seen in Alzheimer's or Creutzfeldt-Jakob disease. The third axis is that of etiology, from completely extrinsic, as in head trauma, to completely intrinsic, as in multi-infarct dementia. Finally, there is the prognostic axis, ranging from completely reversible to completely irreversible.

It has been estimated that approximately 6.2 percent of individuals over age 65 will develop brain failure. At age 65, the incidence is 2 to 3 percent, which gradually increases to approximately 20 percent at age 80 (Kay 1977). It then levels off and remains at 20 percent for the rest of the life cycle. Although only 5 percent of the elderly are institutionalized, the diagnosis of dementia is present in 50 percent of institutionalized elderly (Redick, Kramer, and Taube 1973). However, approximately one of every four individuals who present with evidence of brain failure has a completely treatable cause of the disorder.

CLINICAL FEATURES

The primary signs and symptoms of brain failure are those symptoms that are completely attributable to the neurological deficit *per se* and include memory loss, aphasias, agnosias, apraxias, and disorientation. There are also secondary symptoms. These symptoms are part of the individual's attempts to adapt to or cope with the loss of functioning, personality traits that become accentuated into symptoms when previously acquired coping mechanisms are lost, and the consequences in and response of the environment and support network to the individual with brain failure.

In early dementias, depression is frequently seen and may cloud the diagnostic picture (K. Solomon 1982f). The depressive symptoms develop from the individual's grief over loss of functioning and memory as a body part. This loss, like the loss of any other body part, is experienced as a narcissistic injury and requires that the individual work it through and find new modes of functioning (Kolb 1975).

Anxiety is also frequently seen, with a constant worry of what will happen to the self or family or with fears that children will inherit the disease. This anxiety has a strong existential component and is frequently relieved by honest sharing of prognostic information with the elderly client.

Psychotic symptoms may develop as the dementing individual attempts to reestablish psychologic homeostasis. The individual with brain failure has difficulty remembering and integrating parts of the environment, which may be further accentuated by the presence of a visual or hearing deficit. The person may then develop delusions to explain what is happening to him/her and to the world around him/her. The presence of a sensory deficit may further lead these individuals to create their own sensory input in the form of hallucinations, a form of sensory deprivation psychosis (P. Solomon 1961).

Confabulation may also be noted. As the individual attempts to reestablish psychic homeostasis, he/she "invents" a reality that is plausible and that allows for denial of the unpleasant blanks in memory.

As the individual loses cognitive capabilities, he/she may act in ways that cause the family, neighborhood, and community alarm (Mace and Rabins 1982). He/she becomes more dependent on others in the community to successfully manage activities of daily living, which may lead to anger, recriminations, guilt, overdependency, helplessness, inappropriate attempts at maintaining autonomy, or denial by the family, community, or the demented client. The secondary family problems not only cause anxiety and depression in themselves, which further complicate the clinical picture, but may lead to major family psychopathology, including the development of psychiatric symptoms in other members of the family. Behavioral difficulties, although derived from sources in the individual's premorbid personality, become a constant source of difficulty for the client and the caregivers.

DIAGNOSIS AND TREATMENT

Twenty-five percent of individuals with brain failure have a treatable cause of the symptomatology. If the symptoms are not treated within a reasonable time, permanent brain disease may occur secondarily. Therefore, it is incumbent upon the evaluating physician to do a thorough evaluation of all individuals with brain failure. This includes a complete psychogeriatric evaluation, as described above. If a full evaluation is otherwise negative, and if there is cortical and central atrophy on cranial tomography, one can make a presumptive diagnosis of Alzheimer's disease (which cannot be proved except at autopsy). The history, examination, and results of laboratory tests will lead to a specific diagnosis for almost all causes of reversible and irreversible brain failure. If the history and examinations reveal hints of another condition that may lead to pseudodementia, other tests (e.g., magnetic resonance imagery, angiography, lumbar puncture) must be performed.

Whenever possible, treatment is aimed at the specific cause of the brain failure. However, if that is not possible, treatment must be symptomatic with an emphasis on maintaining environmental homogeneity and helping the person continue to function at maximum levels. The use of cognitive-acting drugs, such as cerebral vasodilators or dihydrogenated ergot alkaloids, is not recommended, as the clinical efficacy of these drugs has never been demonstrated. Individual psychotherapy may be helpful and family counseling is mandatory.

Paraphrenia

Paraphrenia is a diagnosis rarely made in the United States, although there is no paucity of paranoid elderly encountered in clinical practice. This diagnosis is frequently subsumed under other labels. Paraphrenia is a paranoid psychosis that develops in an older person without a premorbid history of major psychiatric problems and in the absence of organic brain disease. Premorbidly, most individuals with paraphrenia have been schizoid, aloof, or suspicious (Isaacs 1973); however, they have never evidenced frank psychotic symptomatology. In some individuals, the paranoid ideation is limited to only certain sharply delineated areas of thought. In other individuals, it is a more global and systematized delusional process. Schneiderian symptoms may be present, which has frequently led to a misdiagnosis of late-onset schizophrenia. However, schizophrenia rarely begins after age 35 and has a poor prognosis. Paraphrenia rarely begins prior to age

55, and its prognosis is excellent. The paranoid delusions frequently have more than a kernel of truth in them and indeed may be so plausible that a thorough evaluation of the person's social history may be necessary for the examiner to be thoroughly convinced that the individual is dealing with delusion rather than reality. In about two-thirds of cases of paraphrenia, the paranoid symptomatology develops as a defense against a potentially overwhelming depression. In these cases, treatment of the psychotic symptomatology frequently leads to the elucidation of depressive symptomatology that had been masked by the paranoid ideation. Treatment of the subsequent depression is then necessary. Kay, Cooper, and Garside (1976) have noted that sensory deficits occur in approximately 70 percent of elderly individuals with paranoid ideation; investigation and correction of this problem are an important part of the diagnosis and intervention of clients with paraphrenia. Paraphrenia is treated with a combination of reality-testing, supportive psychotherapy, and antipsychotic medication.

Mania

Mania is much less common than depression in the elderly. In some ways, it is the extreme opposite of depression, as the manic individual's mood is elated or euphoric. He/she demonstrates extreme impulsivity, diminished need for sleep, increased energy, psychomotor agitation, and rapid speech. Many manic individuals are quite hostile and may be overtly paranoid. Some also demonstrate hallucinations or delusions. Older manic individuals are less likely to demonstrate the physical hyperactivity and rapid speech than younger people, so that the mood disturbance becomes the paramount sign of the disorder. The treatment of mania is also psychopharmacologic, psychotherapeutic, and sociotherapeutic.

Personality Disorders

Personality disorders affect approximately 5 percent of the elderly (K. Solomon 1981b) and are lifelong maladaptive interpersonal behavior patterns that may become evident for the first time or intensified in old age. Individuals with personality disorders may seek or be referred for therapy for the first time in old age because their social network has either broken down or is no longer willing or able to put up with the maladaptive behavior or because they have become uncomfortable with their behaviors. There is some "maturing out" of the more impulsive labile disorders, such as narcissistic and borderline disorders, as they become less affectively and behaviorally intense. These individuals, especially if dependent, are prone to the development of depression when under stress in late life. Individuals with a stable disorder, such as the obsessive-compulsive, paranoid, or schizoid disorders, tend to remain stable or become worse throughout life. These individuals are prone not only to the development of depression but also to paraphrenia and other psychotic syndromes of late life because they are no longer able to control their environment and have a cognitive style of doubt, guardedness, and suspiciousness.

Neuroses

Neuroses, phobias, and anxiety disorders are syndromes that are rare in the elderly. When they do occur, they are frequently indicative of an underlying depression or organic problem. However, an occasional individual may develop neurotic symptoms for the first time when his/her adaptational mechanisms break down because of psychosocial problems. Therapy for both personality disorders and neuroses is long-term individual or group psychotherapy or psychoanalysis.

Other Psychiatric Disturbances

All psychiatric disturbances that occur at a younger age may also occur in the elderly. Elderly schizophrenics with chronic symptoms have been noted to have a somewhat diminished affective intensity to their psychotic symptomatology (Verwoerdt 1976). They frequently have developed and maintained some kind of social stability that allows for fairly consistent daily functioning, even in the presence of psychotic symptomatology (Zusman 1966). The same is also true of those who are mentally retarded, although psychotic symptomatology is absent and their functioning frequently depends on an institutional environment. Sexual dysfunctions may also occur for the first time in old age. Besides demythologizing and education, treatment follows the techniques developed by Masters and Johnson (1970).

PSYCHOPATHOLOGIC SYMPTOMS OF MEDICAL DISEASES AND MEDICAL SYMPTOMS OF PSYCHOPATHOLOGY

Psychopathologic Symptoms

1. *Memory Loss.* As stated above, the causes of memory deficits are legion; indeed, almost any disease listed in standard medical textbooks can cause reversible or irreversible memory loss and loss of intellectual functioning in the elderly (Libow 1973). The major reversible causes are depression, drug abuse or withdrawal (alcohol, addictive psychotropic drugs, and over-the-counter drugs), or side effects of medication, malnutrition and hypovitaminoses, reversible neurologic diseases (especially the sequlae of head trauma), hypothyroidism or hyperthyroidism, other endocrine disorders, cardiovascular disease, severe and acute systemic infections, and any severe acute medical disease. As the usual symptoms of these various diseases often are not present in the elderly (Exton-Smith and Overstall 1979)—for example, an older person may not experience pain with a heart attack or symptoms of diminished metabolism with hypothyroidism—referral to a physician in all cases of memory loss is absolutely necessary for a complete evaluation.

2. *Depression.* While depression may seem to be a reasonable response to real life situations in the elderly, it may be a result of drug abuse or withdrawal, side effects of medication, neurologic disease, endocrine disorders (especially thyroid disease), infections (even minor ones), and chronic illness. Indeed, the majority of clients with Alzheimer's disease also experience concurrent depression, and the differentiation of these two disorders may be difficult if not impossible (K. Solomon 1982f).

3. *Psychotic Symptoms.* Hallucinations are commonly related to drug withdrawal, side effects of a variety of medications, head trauma, other neurologic disorders, endocrine disorders, and any severe acute illness. Paranoid symptoms may be seen in a variety of acute and chronic neurologic disease, as a manifestation of drug toxicity, and in a variety of endocrine diseases, infections, and post-traumatic states, as well as masking depression.

Medical Symptoms

1. *Fatigue.* Fatigue is a common symptom of any chronic illness, anemia, malignancies, infectious processes, and as a side effect of medications. It is also a common symptom of depression, Alzheimer's disease, and a variety of labile personality disorders and neuroses.

2. *Constipation.* Constipation is seen in a variety of gastrointestinal diseases, as side effects of medications, and as a common complaint of older people who are unaware that the older gastrointestinal tract normally slows down its functioning. Constipation is also frequently seen as a vegetative symptom of depression, obsessive-compulsive personality, and neurotic disorders.

3. *Difficult or Rapid Breathing.* Difficulty in breathing or shortness of breath is commonly seen in a variety of pulmonary and cardiovascular diseases. It is also a frequent symptom of anxiety (along with hyperventilation) and labile personality disorders, and in drug withdrawal.

4. *Weakness.* Weakness is part of a variety of chronic musculoskeletal and many neurologic diseases of an acute or chronic nature. It is also a common complaint in Alzheimer's disease, in depression, and in labile personality disorders.

5. *Pain.* Pain may be indicative of localized disease or may be referred from disease elsewhere in the body. When accompanied by other physical concomitants of pain (e.g., sweating, facial grimacing, pallor) and if acute in onset, it is almost always due to bodily disease. Chronic pain has both psychologic and physiologic components, and the etiology may be difficult to ascertain. Aside from a legion of chronic physical conditions causing pain, chronic pain is a common symptom of depression, personality disorders, schizophrenia, and drug abuse.

6. *Sleep Difficulties.* Although the most common cause of sleep difficulties is depression, this symptom is commonly seen as a result of any chronic illness, the use of hypnotics, the presence of pain or respiratory difficulties, as a response to any acute biologic or psychosocial stress, and the presenting symptom of the primary sleep disorders, especially sleep apnea. It is frequently seen in drug abuse and withdrawal. It is a frequent end result of boredom, as the individual

takes naps during the day, then goes to bed early, and having had a good night's sleep during the day, still expects to sleep until the usual waking hour. Dreams and nightmares may be side effects of a variety of medications, especially psychotropic drugs.

PRINCIPLES OF INTERVENTION

The goal of intervention is to change symptoms into adequate coping, adaptation, and growth by reversing the psychodynamic schema just cited. Most of this can be accomplished by members of the team, utilizing generalist skills. As Rogers (1959) has pointed out, the major qualities of a good psychotherapist are not technical skills but rather empathy (the ability to psychologically put oneself in the other person's place), unconditional positive regard (the ability to accept the client as he/she is; this is not the same as liking the client), and genuineness (accepting oneself as one is).

Based on the sequence of psychodynamic events outlined earlier in this chapter, intervention should follow a predictable sequence of events. There is some overlap in the sequence to allow for maximal therapeutic flexibility when working with the elderly person with a psychologic disturbance. These principles of intervention hold whether or not the disturbance is primarily organic or functional in nature.

Intervention is divided into two phases. The first is the phase of crisis intervention and may be easily accomplished by mental healthcare workers. This is the reversal of the psychodynamic sequence of events noted earlier. The second phase of therapy is relevant only for those individuals who have a lifelong history of inadequate coping skills or those who wish to pursue further personal growth; it consists of long-term psychotherapy and should be done by a psychotherapist.

Crisis Intervention

The first step in therapy is a direct attack on the symptoms. If the person has psychotic symptoms (mania, delusions, hallucinations), catastrophic reactions or organically based agitation that has been uncontrolled by nonpharmacologic measures, antipsychotic medication (table 9.2) is indicated. Antipsychotic medications should not be used as the treatment of symptoms of anxiety, as there is no evidence that these medications are efficacious for these problems (K. Solomon 1976; K. Solomon and Hart 1978). Nor should they be used in the treatment of organically based symptoms until the underlying causes of the symptoms are eluciated. If the client meets the criteria for a diagnosis of major depressive disorder, antidepressant medication (table 9.3) is indicated. Antidepressants should not be used in the treatment of anxiety or for adjustment disorders, sadness, or grief reactions. If the client is manic, lithium is the treatment of choice.

One must be careful with psychopharmocologic agents in the elderly. The reasons for this can be elucidated by pharmacokinetics of drugs in the elderly (Friedel 1977). Both therapeutic effects and side

TABLE 9.2. Antipsychotic Drugs

I. Phenothiazines

A. Aliphatic

1. Chlorpromazine (Thorazine)
2. Promazine (Sparine)
3. Triflupromazine (Vesprin)

B. Piperidine

1. Thioridazine (Mellaril)
2. Mesoridazine (Serentil)
3. Piperacetazine (Quide)

C. Piperazine

1. Prochlorperazine (Compazine)
2. Trifluoperazine (Stelazine)
3. Butaperazine (Repoise)
4. Perphenazine (Trilafon)
5. Fluphenazine (Prolixin, Permitil)
6. Acetophenazine (Tindal)

II. Thioxanthenes

1. Chlorprothixene (Taractan)
2. Thiothixene (Navane)

III. Butyrophenones

1. Haloperidol (Haldol)

IV. Dihydroindolones

1. Molindone (Moban, Lidone)

V. Dibenzoxazepines

1. Loxapine (Loxitane, Daxolin)

VI. Diphenylbutylpiperidine

1. Pimozide (Orap)

effects increase as the concentration of free drug in the blood increases. It takes less medication to provide higher blood levels in the elderly because of changes in the factors responsible for the maintenance of the concentration of drugs in the blood. The absorbed dose may be somewhat erratic, as gastrointestinal motility is diminished, leading to an increased opportunity for the drug to be absorbed. However, arterial blood flow and transport enzyme activity are diminished, leading to decreased absorption. Because of changes in liver enzyme activity and renal function, the time it takes to metabolize and eliminate the drug is extended, resulting in an increased concentration of the drug in the blood. Since there is proportionally more fat tissue than water in the older body, and psychopharmacologic agents (lithium excepted) are all fat-soluble, this too leads to

TABLE 9.3. Antidepressant Drugs

I. Tricyclics

A. *Iminobenzyls*
1. Imipramine (Tofranil)
2. Trimipramine (Surmontil)
3. Desipramine (Norpramin, Pertofrane)

B. *Dibenzoheptadienes*
1. Amitriptyline (Elavil, Endep)
2. Nortriptyline (Aventyl, Pamelor)
3. Protriptyline (Vivactil)

C. *Dibenzoxepins*
1. Doxepin (Sinequan, Adapin)

D. *Dibenzoxazepines*
1. Amoxapine (Asendin)

II. Tetracyclics
1. Maprotiline (Ludiomil)
2. Trazodone (Desyrel)

III. Monoamine Oxidase Inhibitors
1. Isocarboxazid (Marplan)
2. Tranylcypromine (Parnate)
3. Phenelzine (Nardil)

IV. Bicyclics
1. Fluoxitene (Prozac)

increased concentration of the drug in the blood. Furthermore, the amount of free drug in the blood also increases as the concentration of albumin diminishes with age (Greenblatt 1979), reducing plasma binding of the drug. In addition, the central nervous system is more sensitive to the effects of these drugs, and the barrier protecting the brain from drugs is weakened with age, increasing the effects of these drugs in the older person.

Psychotropic drugs have many side effects. Commonly occurring side effects include oversedation, constipation, dry mouth, dizziness, a "drunken" gait, falls, increased anxiety, cognitive disturbances, psychotic symptoms, depression, a metallic taste in the mouth, heartburn, and indigestion. Less common are disturbances of liver function, changes in heart rhythm, allergic reactions (especially skin rashes), increased sensitivity to sunlight, difficulty controlling body temperature in hot environments, increased vulnerability to seizures, anemia, difficulty urinating, high fever, disturbances of endocrine function, increased risk of infections, and sudden death. Specifically, antipsychotic drugs also commonly produce a variety of neurologic side effects resembling Parkinson's disease (tremor, increased muscle tones, difficulty with coordination, gait disturbances, a mask-like face) and a chronic neurologic disorder called tardive dyskinesia, manifested by involuntary wiggling of the facial and tongue muscles, fingers, arms, toes, and torso, and facial grimacing. Benzodiazepines are all potentially addictive, even when taken for a brief period of time in low dosage. Thus psychotropic drugs cannot be prescribed with impunity, since they are far from benign. On the other hand, they should always be prescribed when indicated, for therapy will not be of benefit unless the client is capable of responding to it, something precluded by the presence of severe psychopathology.

A variety of nonpharmacologic techniques may be used in the treatment of anxiety. For episodic anxiety, the breathing exercises used in Lamaze childbirth (Bing 1962) are of help. For more continuous anxiety or tension, relaxation exercises such as described by Jacobson (1938) and Wolpe (1969) may be of help. For some clients, cognitive therapy (Kovacs and Beck 1978), regular strenuous physical exercise (e.g., jogging or swimming), transcendental meditation, tantric or other forms of yoga, massage or other body work, sex (including masturbation), or biofeedback may also be of benefit in mastering anxiety. Acupressure to the junction of the mastoid process and base of the skull may be helpful in the treatment of tension headache. Because of the unproven efficacy of benzodiazepines (K. Solomon 1976; K. Solomon and Hart 1978) and other antianxiety agents such as hydroxyzine or meprobamate (Greenblatt and Shader 1971), and their high addictive potential, these drugs probably have little place in the treatment of the elderly.

If the older person demonstrated phobic, compulsive, or obsessive symptoms, the use of traditional behavior-modification techniques is indicated (Schaefer and Martin 1969; Wolpe 1969). Sexual dysfunctions may be treated by sexual therapies developed by Masters and Johnson (1970). Hypnosis may also be used for specific neurotic symptoms. Acting up, whether it be aggressive, dependent, or helpless, is managed with behavioral paradigms that emphasize environmental manipulation and limit-setting of the inappropriate behavior.

Following the direct attack on symptoms, the therapist next helps the client ventilate the underlying affect. This involves giving the client permission to feel fear, anger, or loss and to verbalize these feelings. Permission must be especially given to individuals who are afraid of antagonizing the therapist if they get angry at the therapist. It should be made clear that it is "OK" to be angry at members of the team and to direct this anger at them rather than toward oneself. Clients who are particularly labile in expressing affect must learn how to channel affect into verbal communication conducive to therapy. Those who do not express affect must be pushed to do so. Ventilation is sometimes enhanced through the use of movement, poetry, art, or music therapies.

The next step is the minimization of helplessness and dependency. The major modalities used in this part of therapy are environmental manipulation and behavioral techniques. The client is given graduated behavioral tasks that the therapist knows he/she can definitely manage. At first these tasks should be graded according to the individual's current level of functioning. For example, severely depressed individuals may be required just to get out of bed by a certain time. A better functioning individual may be required to attend a senior center or take care of certain tasks in his/her environment. It is frequently necessary to enlist the aid of family members or other resources in the community to aid in the accomplishment of these tasks. This is especially true if the individual suffers from brain failure. Remotivation and rehabilitative therapies are also quite useful at this juncture in therapy. The patient must internalize feelings that counter helplessness and dependency.

Regaining mastery requires that the client have control over his/her life. That requires choice and options. The client must be told that he/she is responsible for his/her behavior. This responsibility is more than just an existential statement, for without responsibility there can be no need to master and manipulate one's environment. Mastery requires that the older person have choice. The client should be allowed to make all decisions for himself/herself. In an institution, this includes decisions regarding clothing, menu, visitors, activities, and therapeutic goals. The client should not be cut off from his/her network, but must use this network to help maintain autonomy and mastery. The older person must be encouraged to take risks and to try out new options that may not be comfortable for the therapist yet may be comfortable for the older person. For the individual without brain failure, however, these choices require that the therapists give and even create options appropriate for the individual's problems, so that he/she may be able to choose from a wide range of options to resolve the problems that led to the development of the symptomatology.

The last step in this phase of therapy is to attempt to reverse the stress. Losses in the social-support system are frequently managed by helping the individual create a new support system. For example, the older person may attend a senior center, reestablish contact with other family members and friends, or find a new job. Loss of role requires that the individual seek out new meaningful roles, give positive valence to old roles, realign himself/herself with old interests, or attempt to create new roles. The memory deficits of brain failure may be partially reversed with reality orientation and other modalities (Ernst et al. 1978; Stephens 1969). Specific stresses that can be reversed through appropriate use of the human-service delivery system should be tackled early, as these stresses usually affect basic activities of daily living. A major goal, however, is not to use this system to *do for* the older person (and thus create further dependency and helplessness) but to teach the older person how to advocate for himself/herself and control the human-service delivery system (and thus further mastery, choice, and self-responsibility). For the older person who has previously functioned well, this is frequently all the therapy that is necessary.

Psychotherapy

For those older persons who wish to continue their self-examination and grow or for those individuals with a lifelong history of inadequate coping skills, one then enters the second stage of intervention, the stage of psychotherapy. Older individuals are quite motivated for help, and resistances are fewer. As such, they are quite amenable to various psychotherapeutic modalities.

THERAPEUTIC MODALITIES

If the problems are primarily intrapsychic, a form of individual psychotherapy is the treatment of choice. For those who are psychologically minded, an insight-oriented psychotherapy (psychoanalysis, psychoanalytically oriented psychotherapy, Gestalt therapy, transactional analysis, client-centered psychotherapy, or existential therapy) is the treatment of choice, occasionally augmented with a movement therapy, such as Feldenkrais or dance therapy, massage therapy, neurolinguistic programming, or art therapy. If the problems are primarily interpersonal, group psychotherapy, family therapy, or marital therapy is indicated. For those individuals who are not good candidates for an insight-oriented psychotherapy, such as those with an overlay of somatization, those who are not psychologically minded, or those who cannot tolerate a transference relationship, long-term supportive psychotherapy may also aid in coping with future stress.

Some technical modifications of psychotherapy may become necessary in working with this age group. Because some clients may fatigue easily, it may be wise to limit sessions to thirty minutes rather than the traditional fifty minutes for these clients. Sessions should be scheduled at such times as to maximize the older person's alertness and diurnal and other biologic rhythms, as well as special travel needs. Many elderly rely on public transportation, limit their driving to daylight hours because of limitations in night vision, or avoid nocturnal excursions into or out of high-crime areas. Taking the history requires a much longer time because there are more years of experience. History-taking should emphasize an assessment of the person's lifelong strengths and how he/she coped with stress (Butler 1974) so that these techniques may be utilized and reinforced during psychotherapy. As older persons have frequently had many years of self-examination, it may be possible to start psychotherapy at a level of insight that is deeper than with younger clients. In addition, older persons are aware of their limited life span and are more motivated for psychotherapy than are younger persons (LeShan and LeShan 1961). Because of this, resistances are diminished, which allows for a more rapid identification and working through of major dynamic issues, followed by willingness on the part of the older person to put these insights and affective changes into their behavioral repertoire. Interpretations thus may be given earlier in therapy and concentration on resistances may be minimized.

Techniques of Gestalt therapy and transactional analysis may be particularly helpful in working with an older person with a personality disorder. If there is a degree of somatization, identification of the emotional concomitants of the somatization may be translated into verbal affective statements. For example, somatic pain may first be concretized so that the older person is asked what his/her stomach is feeling. The person is then asked, using a Gestalt technique (Perls 1969), to translate that into a statement about what he/she is feeling and own the statement and feeling. That statement is then used as a bridge to the identification of the underlying affective state. Once that underlying affective state is identified, the person's maladaptive responses to it can be further identified in a way consistent with supportive or insight-oriented therapy. Because many older people with unresolved dependency issues behave in a childlike way, various transactional analytic techniques, as well as responses to the individual as an adult and pointing out the childlike ways in which he/she behaves, may be a particularly helpful form of interpersonal insight (Maxwell and Falzett 1974). It is particularly important for the therapist at this stage not to behave in a parental way.

Group psychotherapy with older persons can be quite successful in promoting therapeutic changes (Goldfarb 1971). It tends to work better when the groups are homogeneous and consist only of older people because many older persons have a reluctance to share in a mixed-age group in which they may be the only older person and in which younger clients dominate. However, in a geriatric therapy group, this is generally not so. In addition, because older psychiatric clients are more likely to be women, there are frequently not enough men in the group to dominate it, thus allowing for greater intimacy and sharing. The group may be utilized to be supportive, to confront, and to suggest specific behavioral modifications, as well as to give insight and feedback on the interpersonal aspects of the individual's personality disorder. Group psychotherapy is particularly helpful in individuals with dependent personality disorders or passive-aggressive personality disorders because the group is frequently unwilling to tolerate the pathologic behavior, thus forcing change in the maladaptive responses to stress with the support and advice of the group. In addition, as there is an element of social isolation in many elderly clients, the group brings to the client a consistent social network that can be expected to be helpful in times of crisis (K. Solomon and Zinke 1981).

Family or couple psychotherapy may consist of a behaviorally oriented approach in which the family is used as behavioral engineers to modify—with classical reinforcement, extinction, or punishment paradigms—the behaviors of the identified client. Or a communications, functional, or structural model may be utilized to help clarify the person's needs and to help the family members or spouse behave in a way that maximizes appropriate response-outcome. With the relatively nonverbal individual with interpersonal difficulties living at home, utilization of a family member or a substitute for a family member, such as a home health aide, as an intervenor may be an important element in family or behavioral therapy.

For clients with severe dependency needs or for those who are schizoid, day hospitalization or attendance at special social groups for the elderly may be helpful. These social groups may involve nonthreatening activities and may allow for the gradual desensitization of the older withdrawn individual to a social network that may be supportive. Day hospitalization may allow clients to structure their lives. In the context of nonthreatening recreational activities, plus therapeutically oriented groups and individual sessions, moderate success can result with a severely disturbed older person with a dependent, schizoid, or schizotypal personality disorder. In addition, ancillary social and rehabilitative services may be necessary and helpful within the context of any of the therapeutic modalities. There may be a need to teach budgeting, shopping, or advocacy skills, especially for the chronically dependent or schizoid individual. Assurance that the older person is receiving appropriate and complete social services such as food stamps, Medicare, etc., may become an important part of developing the therapeutic alliance as well as a way of minimizing some of the social and day-to-day stresses on the client that would interfere with ongoing therapy.

TRANSFERENCE ISSUES

Major transference issues develop during the course of any psychotherapy. A particularly important one in working with the elderly is the development of dependency upon the therapist. The therapist is frequently perceived as a consistently caring and nurturing individual (a perfect mother), who is always helping out and who frequently does so in concrete ways. The older person, especially one with conflicts around dependency needs, may transfer dependency from family or social network to the therapist and may expect the therapist to make all major and minor life decisions for the client. Some therapists, such as Goldfarb (1968, 1974), encourage the dependency in the hope that the client will identify with the therapist and incorporate the therapist's superego as his/her own, thus leading to changes in maladaptive interpersonal paradigms. Thus, even after termination of therapy, the dependency is encouraged so that therapeutic headway may continue. Other therapists, myself included, emphasize growth and autonomy on the part of the older client and tend to de-emphasize dependency. In therapy with older clients, I prefer to emphasize choice, responsibility, and risk-taking behaviors to try out new interpersonal skills that are necessary to maximize autonomy and independent functioning on the part of the older client.

Parentification of the therapist is an important form of transference in psychotherapy for the elderly with personality disorders. In many ways this parentification is no different from the parentification seen in the context of any transference relationship, in which the therapist is seen as if he/she were various significant others in the client's life. However, because the parents of older clients are frequently either deceased, ill, or dealing with many of the same stresses as the older client, parentification brings out many unresolved psychodynamic issues related to loss, separation, and parent/child relations that have been repressed for several generations. Thus parentification becomes an important part of the therapeutic involvement as it rapidly brings up important dynamic issues that are dealt with by the usual psychotherapeutic modalities of explanation, clarification, questioning, and interpretation (Bibring 1954; Olinick 1954). Goldfarb (1968, 1974) emphasized parentification without interpretation, so that the elderly client will identify with the therapist to facilitate the incorporation of the therapist's superego. I prefer to interpret it, so as to foster resolution of the conflicts noted immediately preceding.

On the other hand, however, the client is usually older and frequently quite significantly older than the therapist. The individual may infantilize the therapist and may relate to the therapist either as a child or a grandchild. This brings up important therapeutic issues, especially intergenerational issues and issues of control and dependency, for the therapist is seen as if he/she were the patient's own child or grandchild.

COUNTERTRANSFERENCE ISSUES

Countertransference issues are many in psychotherapy with older individuals. As just mentioned, adherence to stereotypes may lead to an inappropriate denial of the therapeutic growth potential of the older client as well as the inappropriate reinforcement of dependency and helplessness of the older client. In addition, working with the older client may bring up many anxieties and stresses about the therapist's own aging, which leads both to status inconsistency and to a state of cognitive dissonance (Festinger 1957). A frequent response to these states in dealing with the elderly is to reinforce the stereotypes of older people (K. Solomon 1979a), which then becomes a therapeutic blind spot in working with older clients. Stereotyping and the subsequent development of learned helplessness can be combatted through a variety of educational and experiential techniques that emphasize issues of the therapist's own aging, demythologizing, correction of cognitive dissonance, and the development of nonstereotyped attitudes toward the elderly. (K. Solomon 1983a, K. Solomon and Vickers 1980, 1981).

Because of the age differential between therapist and client, the therapist may parentify the client, which may have important consequences as the therapist may fear bringing up certain dynamic issues because they are unresolved between him/her and his/her parents. The therapist may not allow himself/herself to experience anger at the client and therefore may allow the client to act out or to continue various forms of maladaptive behavior rather than confronting the effects of the behaviors. The therapist may be overly gentle or may avoid dealing with issues related to sexuality in the older client because of countertransference problems.

On the other hand, the therapist may infantilize the older client. The infantilization may take the form of being overly helpful and reinforcing dependency on the part of the client. This may lead to a crisis in therapy as the therapist has to deal with his/her own relationship with his/her children. Infantilization also diminishes the growth potential of therapy as well as leading to a gentleness in therapy that may be inappropriate.

Other issues that the therapist must deal with when doing psychotherapy with older people are the issues of illness and death. Older persons miss sessions when they become acutely ill or suffer exacerbations of chronic medical illness that may or may not require hospitalization. The vulnerability of the client, the therapist, and the therapy then become important issues with which the therapist, too, must work and leads to many existential questions, such as limits, attitudes, *weltanschauungen,* and the meaning of life, which the therapist may not have worked through with himself/herself. Illness interrupts the flow of therapeutic sessions and, if accompanied by brain changes such as delirium, may actually lead to a major therapeutic reversal; it may take months of therapy to regain premorbid levels of psychologic functioning. Medical illness also leads to the prescription of drugs that may adversely interact with either the person's psyche or with psychotropic medications that may be prescribed.

Dying may be an acute or a chronic, protracted process. In any case, it may lead to the therapist being unable or unwilling to work with the client during his/her final hours, when the therapist may be most needed. The therapist may be angry at the client for leaving and may take out his/her anger by missing or canceling sessions, being late for sessions, or prematurely terminating therapy. The therapist has to experience and work with his/her own grief over the loss of the client. The loss is not only that of the individual client, but also loss and grief as a generic life issue. Because death is a frequent occurrence in the life of the therapist working with the elderly, the therapist must confront his/her own finitude and limits of his/her own life.

WHEN TO CALL THE PHYSICIAN

All clients with major psychopathology who have not had a thorough medical evaluation should be evaluated by a physician, who can complete the physical examination, neurologic examination, and laboratory examination portions of the psychogeriatric examination. If there is any question about the possibility of drug interactions, drug side effects, or medical diseases that may cause psychopathology, or if information about the client's medical condition and prognosis are germane to the therapeutic process, referral to a physician is also necessary. Referral is necessary whenever the client develops new medical symptoms, even if the therapist suspects that these symptoms are psychogenic in origin. A geropsychiatrist should see the client if the client has symptoms of major psychopathology for which psychopharmacologic intervention is necessary or if the mental-health worker simply feels the need for consultation and another opinion, even if things are going well therapeutically. In choosing medical/psychiatric consultants, it is important to choose a physician with skills working with the elderly and with positive attitudes toward this age group.

REFERENCES

Adams, F. D. 1958. *Physical diagnosis.* Baltimore: Williams and Wilkins.

Akisal, H. S. and W. T. McKinney, Jr. 1975. Overview of recent research in depression: Integration of ten conceptual models into a comprehensive clinical frame. *Archives of General Psychiatry* 32:285–305.

American Psychiatric Association. 1987. *Diagnostic and Statistical Manual of Mental Disorders.* 3d ed. rev. Washington D.C.: American Psychiatric Association.

Ayd. F. J. Jr. 1975. Treatment-resistant patients: A moral, legal and therapeutic challenge. In F. J. Ayd, Jr. ed., *Rational Psychopharmacotherapy and the Right to Treatment.* Baltimore: Ayd Medical Communications.

Ban. T. 1978. The treatment of depressed geriatric patients. *American Journal of Psychotherapy* 32:93–104.

Bibring, E. 1954. Psychoanalysis and the dynamic psychotherapies. *Journal of the American Psychoanalytic Association* 2:745–770.

Bibring, E. 1961. The mechanism of depression. In P. Greenacre, ed., *Affective Disorders.* New York: International Universities Press.

Bing, E. 1962. *Six Practical Lessons for an Easier Childbirth.* New York: Bantam.
Blazer, D., and C. D. Williams. 1980. Epidemiology of dysphoria and depression in an elderly population. *American Journal of Psychiatry* 137:439–444.
Bonime, W. 1966. The psychodynamics of neurotic depression. In S. Arieti, ed., *American Handbook of Psychiatry,* vol. 3. 1st ed. New York: Basic Books.
Brody, E. B. 1974. Psychosocial aspects of prejudice. In S. Arieti et al, eds., *American Handbook of Psychiatry,* vol. 2. 2d ed. New York: Basic Books.
Butler, R. N. 1974. Successful aging and the role of life review. *Journal of the American Geriatrics Society* 12:529–532.
Butler, R. N. 1975. *Why Survive? Being Old in America.* New York: Harper and Row.
Cohen, R. E. 1973. The collaborative co-professional: Developing a new mental health role. *Hospital and Community Psychiatry* 24:242–246.
Delp, M. H. 1968. Study of the patient. In M. H. Delp and R. T. Manning, eds., *Major's Physical Diagnosis.* Philadelphia: Saunders.
Ernst, P., B. Beran, F. Safford, and M. Kleinhauz. 1978. Isolation and the symptoms of chronic brain syndrome. *Gerontologist* 18:468–474.
Exton-Smith, A. N., and P. W. Overstall. 1979. *Geriatrics.* Baltimore: University Park Press.
Festinger, L. 1957. *A Theory of Cognitive Dissonance.* Stanford: Stanford University Press.
Friedel, R. O. 1977. Pharmacokinetics of psychotherapeutic agents in aged patients. In C. Eisdorfer and R. O. Friedel, eds., *Cognitive and Emotional Disturbance in the Elderly.* Chicago: Year Book Medical Publishers.
Friedland, E. 1967. Clinical clerk case study outline. Buffalo: State University of New York at Buffalo.
Friedmann, E. A. and H. L. Orbach. 1974. Adjustment to retirement. In S. Arieti et al., eds., *American Handbook of Psychiatry,* vol. 1. 2d ed. New York: Basic Books.
Goldfarb, A. I. 1968. Clinical perspectives. In A. Simon and L. F. Epstein, eds. *Aging in Modern Society.* Washington: American Psychiatric Association.
Goldfarb, A. I. 1971. Group therapy with the old and aged. In H. I. Kaplan and B. J. Sadock, eds., *Comprehensive Group Therapy.* Baltimore: Williams and Wilkins.
Goldfarb, A. I. 1974. Minor maladjustments of the aged. In S. Arieti et al., eds., *American Handbook of Psychiatry,* vol. 3. 2d ed. New York: Basic Books.
Greenblatt, D. J. 1979. Reduced serum albumin concentration in the elderly: A report from the Boston Collaborative Drug Surveillance Program. *Journal of the American Geriatrics Society* 27:20–22.
Greenblatt, D. J. and R. I. Shader. 1971. Meprobamate: A study of irrational drug use. *American Journal of Psychiatry* 127:1297–1303.
Gutmann, D., J. Grunes, and B. Griffin. 1979. The Clinical Psychology of Later Life: Developmental Paradigms. Paper presented at the 32d Annual Meeting of the Gerontological Society. November 29, Washington, D.C.
Harris, M. and K. Solomon. 1979. Roles of the community mental health nurse. *Journal of Psychiatric Nursing and Mental Health Services* 15:35–39.
Holmes, T. H., and R. H. Rahe. 1967. The social readjustment rating scale. *Journal of Psychosomatic Research* 11:213–218.
Howard, M. 1979. The community mental health nurse and geropsychiatry. Paper presented at the 32d Annual Meeting of the Gerontological Society, November 26, Washington, D.C.
Isaacs, A. D. 1973. Geriatric psychiatry. *Practitioner* 210:86–95.
Jacobson, E. 1938. *Progressive Relaxation.* Chicago: University of Chicago Press.
Judge, R. D., and G. D. Zuidema. 1963. *Physical Diagnosis: A Physiologic Approach.* Boston: Little, Brown.

Kahn, R. L. 1978. Learned helplessness and cognitive impairment in the elderly. Paper presented at the 31st Annual Meeting of the Gerontological Society. November 19, San Francisco.

Kay, D. W. K. 1977. The epidemiology and identification of brain deficit in the elderly. In C. Eisdorfer and R. O. Friedel, eds., *Cognitive and Emotional Disturbances in the Elderly.* Chicago: Year Book Medical Publishers.

Kay, D. W. K., A. F. Cooper, and R. R. Garside. 1976. The differentiation of paranoid from affective psychoses by patients' premorbid characteristics. *British Journal of Psychiatry* 129:207–215.

Kendell, R. E., I. F. Brockington, and J. P. Leff. 1979. Prognostic implications of six alternative definitions of schizophrenia. *Archives of General Psychiatry* 36:25–31.

Kolb, L. C. 1975. Disturbances of the body image. In S. Arieti et al. eds., *American Handbook of Psychiatry,* vol. 4. 2d ed. New York: Basic Books.

Kovacs, M. and A. T. Beck. 1978. Maladaptive cognitive structures in depression. *American Journal of Psychiatry* 135:525–533.

LeShan, L. and E. LeShan. 1961. Psychiatry and the patient with a limited life span. *Psychiatry* 24:318–322.

Libow, L. S. 1973. Pseudo-senility: Acute and reversible organic brain syndromes. *Journal of the American Geriatrics Society* 21:112–121.

Mace, N. L. and P. V. Rabins. 1982. *The 36-Hour Day: A Family Guide to Caring for Persons with Alzheimer's Disease. Related Dementing Illnesses, and Memory Loss in Later Life.* Baltimore: John Hopkins University Press.

MacKinnon, R. A. 1980. Psychiatric history and mental status examination. In H. I. Kaplan. A. M. Freedman and B. J. Sadock, eds., *Comprehensive Textbook of Psychiatry,* 3d ed. Baltimore: Williams & Wilkins.

Maier, S. F. and M. E. P. Seligman. 1976. Learned helplessness: Theory and evidence. *Journal of Experimental Psychology: General* 105:3–46.

Masters, W. H., and V. E. Johnson. 1966. *Human Sexual Response.* Boston: Little, Brown.

Masters, W. H., and V. E. Johnson. 1970. *Human Sexual Inadequacy.* Boston: Little, Brown.

Maxwell, J., and B. Falzett. 1974. OK childing and parenting. El Paso: Transactional Institute of El Paso.

Menninger, K. A. 1962. *A Manual for Psychiatric Case Study.* 2d ed. New York: Grune and Stratton.

Olinick, S. L. 1954. Some considerations of the use of questioning as a psychoanalytic technique. *Journal of the American Psychoanalytic Association* 2:57–66.

Perls, F. 1969. *Gestalt Therapy Verbatim.* Lafayette. Real People Press.

Pons. S. L. 1979. Roles of the community geropsychiatric social worker. Paper presented at the 32d Annual Meeting of the Gerontological Society. November 26, Washington, D.C.

Post, F. 1968. Psychological aspects of geriatrics. *Postgraduate Medical Journal* 44:307–318.

Redick, R. W., M. Kramer and C. A. Taube. 1973. Epidemiology of mental illness and utilization of psychiatric facilities among older persons. In E. W. Busse and E. Pfeiffer, eds., *Mental Illness in Later Life.* Washington: American Psychiatric Association.

Rogers, C. R. 1959. A theory of therapy, personality and interpersonal relationships as developed in client-centered framework. In S. Koch, ed., *Psychology: A Study of a Science.* New York: McGraw Hill.

Romaniuk, M. 1979. A look at the psychologist's role on a community geropsychiatry team. Paper presented at the 32d Annual Meeting of the Gerontological Society. November 26, Washington, D.C.

Rosow, I. 1976. Status and role change through the life span. In R. H. Binstock and E. Shanas, eds., *Handbook of Aging and the Social Sciences.* New York: Van Nostrand Reinhold.

Ryan, W. 1976. *Blaming the Victim.* New York: Vintage.

Sartorius, N. 1975. Epidemiology of depression. *WHO Chronicles* 29:423.

Schaefer, H. H., and P. L. Martin. 1969. *Behavioral Therapy.* New York: McGraw-Hill.

Seligman, M. E. P. 1975. *Helplessness.* San Francisco: W. H. Freeman.

Selye, H. 1950. *The Physiology and Pathology of Exposure to Stress.* Montreal: Acta.

Sheppard, H. L. 1976. Work and retirement. In R. M. Binstock and E. Shanas, eds., *Handbook of Aging and the Social Sciences.* New York: Van Nostrand Reinhold.

Smith, F. S. 1972. *Definition of a Generalist* (mimeo.). Albany: Capital District Psychiatric Center.

Solomon, K. 1976. Benzodiazepines and neurotic anxiety: Critique. *New York State Journal of Medicine* 76:2156–2164.

Solomon, K. 1979a. The development of stereotypes of the elderly. Toward a unified hypothesis. In E. P. Lewis, L. D. Nelson, D. H. Scully, and J. S. Williams, eds., *Sociological Research Symposium Proceedings (IX).* Richmond: Virginia Commonwealth University.

Solomon, K. 1979b. The geropsychiatrist and the delivery of mental services in the community. Paper presented at the 32d Annual Meeting of the Gerontological Society, Washington, D.C.

Solomon, K. 1979c. Social antecedents of learned helplessness of the elderly in the health care setting. In E. P. Lewis, L. D. Nelson, D. H. Scully, and J. S. Williams, eds., *Sociological Research Symposium Proceedings (IX).* Richmond: Virginia Commonwealth University.

Solomon, K. 1981a. The depressed patient: Social antecedents of psychopathologic changes in the elderly. *Journal of the American Geriatrics Society* 29:14–18.

Solomon, K. 1981b. Personality disorders in the elderly. In J. R. Lion, ed., *Personality Disorders: Diagnosis and Management,* 2d ed. Baltimore: Williams and Wilkins.

Solomon, K. 1982a. The elderly patient. In J. A. Spittell, Jr., ed., *Clinical medicine,* Vol. 12: *Psychiatry.* Hagerstown: Harper and Row.

Solomon, K. 1982b. The masculine gender role: Description. In K. Solomon and N. B. Levy, eds., *Men in Transition: Theory and Therapy* New York: Plenum.

Solomon, K. 1982c. The older man. In K. Solomon and N. B. Levy, eds., *Men in Transition, Theory and Therapy.* New York: Plenum.

Solomon, K. 1982d. The roles of the psychiatric resident on a community psychiatric team. *Psychiatric Quarterly* 54:67–76.

Solomon, K. 1982e. Social antecedents of learned helplessness in the health care setting. *Gerontologist* 22:282–287.

Solomon, K. 1982f. The subjective experience of the Alzheimer's patient. *Geriatric Consultant* 1:22–24.

Solomon, K. 1983a. Intervention for the victimized elderly and sensitization of health professionals: Therapeutic and educational efforts. In J. I. Kosberg, ed., *The Abuse and Maltreatment of the Elderly.* Boston: Wright-PSG.

Solomon, K. 1983b. Victimization by health professionals and the psychologic response of the elderly. In J. I. Kosberg, ed., *The Abuse and Maltreatment of the Elderly.* Boston: Wright-PSG.

Solomon, K. 1983c. Assessment of psychosocial status in the aged. In O. L. Jackson, ed., *Clinics in Physical Therapy.*Vol. 6: *Geriatrics.* New York: Churchill Livingstone.

Solomon, K. 1984. The geriatric patient with cognitive dysfunction. In L. Robinson, ed., *Psychological Aspects of Care of Hospitalized Patients*. Philadelphia: F. A. Davis.

Solomon, K., and R. Hart. 1978. Pitfalls and prospects in clinical research on antianxiety drugs: Benzodiazepines and placebo—A research review. *Journal of Clinical Psychiatry* 39:823–831.

Solomon, K., and R. Hurwitz. 1982. Stress, coping, and the older gay man. Paper presented at the 59th Annual Meeting of the American Orthopsychiatric Association. April 2. San Francisco.

Solomon, K., and R. Vickers. 1979. Attitudes of health workers toward old people. *Journal of the American Geriatrics Society* 27:186–191.

Solomon, K., and R. Vickers. 1980. Stereotyping the elderly: changing the attitudes of clinicians. Paper presented at the 33d Annual Meeting of the Gerontological Society of America. November 25, San Diego.

Solomon, K., and R. Vickers. 1981. Stereotyping the elderly. Further research on changing the attitudes of clinicians. Paper presented at the 34th Annual Meeting of the Gerontological Society of America and the 10th Annual Meeting of the Canadian Association on Gerontology. November 10, Toronto.

Solomon, K., and M. R. Zinke. 1981. Group psychotherapy with the depressed elderly. Paper presented at the 58th Annual Meeting of the American Orthopsychiatric Association. March 31, New York.

Solomon, P. 1961. *Sensory Deprivation*. Cambridge: Harvard University Press.

Stephens, L. 1969. *Reality Orientation: A Technique to Rehabilitate Elderly and Brain Damaged Patients with a Moderate to Severe Degree of Disorientation*. Washington, D.C.: American Psychiatric Association.

Stevenson, I., and W. M. Sheppe, Jr. 1974. The psychiatric examination. In S. Arieti et al., eds., *American Handbook of Psychiatry*, vol. 1. 2d ed. New York: Basic Books.

Tuckman, J., and I. Lorge. 1953. Attitudes toward old people. *Journal of Social Psychology* 37:249–260.

Verwoerdt, A. 1976. *Clinical Geropsychiatry*. Baltimore: Williams and Wilkins.

Weiss, J. A. M. 1973. The natural history of antisocial attitudes: What happens to psychopaths? *Journal of Geriatric Psychiatry* 6:236–242.

Weiss, J. A. M. 1974. Suicide. In S. Arieti et al., eds. *American Handbook of Psychiatry*, vol 3. 2d ed. New York: Basic Books.

Whybrow, P. C., and T. Hurwitz. 1976. Psychological disturbances associated with endocrine disease and hormone therapy. In E. J. Sachar, ed., *Hormones, Behavior, and Psychopathology*. New York: Raven Press.

Wilson, R. N. 1970. *The Sociology of Health: An Introduction*. New York: Random House.

Wolff, C. T. 1977. Loss, grief, and mourning in adults. In R. C. Simons and H. Pardes, eds. *Understanding Human Behavior in Health and Illness*. Baltimore: Williams and Wilkins.

Wolpe, J. 1969. *The Practice of Behavior Therapy*. New York: Pergamon Press.

Zusman, J. 1966. Some explanations of the changing appearance of psychotic patients: Antecedents of the social breakdown syndrome concept. *Milbank Memorial Fund Quarterly*, 44(Suppl.):366–396.

10

Public Income Security Programs for the Elderly

❖

ERIC R. KINGSON, PH.D.
Boston College Graduate School of Social Work, Chestnut Hill

Because income services are critical to the well-being of today's and tomorrow's elderly, social workers and other human services practitioners need to understand how these programs work. Equally important, their participation in the policy discussions that shape these programs is needed.

Writing for practitioners concerned both with assisting elderly persons and their families in accessing needed income services and with improving these services, I begin with a brief overview of the economic status of the elderly. Next the need for public and private means of assisting retirees and their families in maintaining living standards is discussed, followed by a review of the theories behind the major public income security programs. Then the old age income support system—the range of public and private income security interventions—is briefly described, followed by a more detailed discussion of the major public income maintenance programs affecting the elderly, including points of access, eligibility and the major benefits. The concluding section identifies several policy issues and sug-

I wish to acknowledge with appreciation that this paper has benefitted from the comments of Kirk Little, graduate assistant, Boston College, Graduate School of Social Work, Chestnut Hill, Massachusetts; Robert J. Myers, F.S.A., consultant, Silver Spring, Maryland; and Joseph Quinn, Ph.D., Boston College, Department of Economics, Chestnut Hill, Massachusetts. Needless to say, the opinions and any errors that may remain are mine.

gests ways in which service providers can work to improve income security policies.

OVERVIEW OF THE ECONOMIC SECURITY OF THE ELDERLY

A few summary points about the economic status of the elderly should be kept in mind. First, the overall improvement in the economic well-being of the elderly during the past thirty years should be recognized as an important societal achievement, attributable primarily to post-World War II economic growth and to the expansion of protections under Social Security, other public programs and private pensions. Economic growth has enabled society to afford more income security. Relative to the elderly of the past, new cohorts of the elderly have arrived at old age with higher levels of Social Security protection, greater receipt of other retirement income and greater asset holdings, very notably home ownership.

Second, there is no doubt that today's elderly, as a group, are considerably better off than previous cohorts of the elderly. This is true whether their economic status is measured in terms of poverty rates,[1] real (that is, inflation-adjusted) income, the real value of assets or in terms of how they are doing relative to the entire population. For instance, poverty rates for persons aged 65 and over have declined from 35.2 percent in 1959 to 12.2 percent in 1987.[2] Similarly, for families headed by persons age 65 and over, median incomes in constant (1986) dollars have, on average, increased from $12,024 in 1965 to $19,932 in 1986. That is, after adjusting for inflation, elderly households have experienced a 60 percent increase in income during this period. As Brandeis University economist James Schulz observes: "From a statistical point of view, *the elderly in this country are beginning to look a lot like the rest of the population;* some very rich, lots with adequate income, lots more with very modest incomes (often near poverty), and a significant minority still destitute. This is very different from the past when most were destitute" (1988: 18).

Third, the diversity of their economic circumstances must be recognized (Chen 1985; Quinn 1987; Schulz 1988). As Boston College economist Joseph Quinn warns, when discussing the economic status of the elderly we should "beware of the mean:" "never begin a sentence with "The elderly are . . ." or "The elderly do . . ." No matter what you are discussing, some are, and some are not; some do, and some do not. The most important characteristic about the elderly is their diversity. The least interesting summary statistic is the mean because it ignores the tremendous dispersion around it" (1987:64).

Fourth, and very importantly for social workers and other human service providers, the problems of income insecurity for the elderly, while reduced, certainly have not been resolved. The income position of a substantial portion of older Americans, composed disproportionately of widowed, very old, female and minority elders, is, at best, marginal. For example, while 12.4 percent of persons aged 65 and over were officially defined as poor in 1986, 21 percent of widowed women in this age group, 22.5 percent of elderly Hispanics and 31 percent of elderly blacks had incomes below the poverty threshold. Also, an astonishing 63.7 percent of women age 72 and over who were living alone fell below the poverty line (U.S. Senate 1988)!

Because Social Security represents such a large portion of the elderly's total incomes (38 percent in the aggregate), their well-being is very sensitive to alterations in the program and to the maintenance of a sound program. And, as Schulz (1988) points out, the elderly face some unique threats to their economic well-being. Quite notably, relatively few elderly households are free from a major risk to their economic well-being—the possibility that chronic and disabling illness will undermine their own and their family's financial security. And so, although the economic status of the elderly is greatly improved, much yet remains to be done, especially for vulnerable populations for whom social workers and other human service providers hold special commitment. But for now let us turn to examining the need for public and private means of protecting against loss of income in old age.

THE NEED FOR INCOME SECURITY FOR THE ELDERLY

The need for mechanisms to protect employees from old age dependency and to promote the orderly turnover of the labor force grew out of the industrialization and modernization of America. As America responded to this need, retirement emerged as a new period of leisure, reinforced by the establishment of pensions that both support and encourage retirement. Now, virtually all American workers and their families depend on pensions (e.g., Social Security) and other public and private means to assist in maintaining prior living standards during their retirement years.

Changes associated with modernization such as improved sanitation, public health and health care contributed to the increase in the numbers and proportion of the population that are elderly (Atchley 1971). Other related demographic trends (Achenbaum 1983), including increased life expectancies and changes in the structure of the family, contributed to the aging of America and the need for income support of the elderly.

With changes in the economy, including a shift from a largely agrarian to an industrial economy (Achenbaum 1983), the labor force became more wage-dependent (Axinn and Levin 1982; Schulz 1988), subject to the large uncertainties inherent in a market economy. Also the bureaucratization of the workplace and push for greater efficiency worked to the disadvantage of the aged (Latimer 1932; Lubove 1968), accentuating the need for mechanisms to protect the elderly against economic dependency.

Emerging concomitantly with these changes were the needs of employers and the economy as a whole for mechanisms to promote the orderly turnover of the labor force, encouraging older workers to retire in exchange for a pension and thereby creating job opportunities for younger ones (Graebner 1980; Schulz 1988). Thus, the emergence of public and private pensions responded to the need to "grease" the intergenerational transfer of employment opportunities.

Very importantly, modernization and the economic growth that followed meant that America could afford to support a large group of older persons who did not work (Schulz 1988). In fact, approximately one third of the economic growth during the twentieth century has been taken in the form of increased leisure (e.g., vacation, reductions in hours worked per week), much of it in the form of retirement (Kreps and Spengler 1966).

As retirement became institutionalized, workers and their families adjusted their expectations in anticipation of an extended period of leisure towards the latter part of the life cycle. The availability of Social Security and, though less widespread, other pensions, created new opportunities to choose to leave work. These pensions have also responded to the needs of many workers and their families who, because of disabling health conditions and/or limited employment opportunities, have little choice but to leave the labor force.

Today, the vast majority of workers (74 percent in 1987) first accept Social Security retirement benefits prior to their 65th birthday—often because they choose to but also in many cases because they have no other viable income alternative. And most leave paid employment by or before their 65th birthday. Largely reflecting the increased availability of pensions and the retirement incentives they are intended to provide, the labor force participation of men aged 65 and over has dropped from 45.8 percent in 1950 to 16.3 percent in 1987.

That of men aged 55 through 64 has declined from 86.9 percent to 67.6 percent during this period. Among women the trends are somewhat different. From 1950 through 1987 the labor force participation of women aged 65 and over has been fairly stable, varying between roughly 11 and 7 percent. However, the participation of women aged 55 through 64 has actually increased, from 27.0 percent in 1950 to 42.7 percent in 1987. Apparently the long-term trend of increased labor force participation among women has substantially offset the powerful early retirement trend.

Finally, it should be noted that the emergence of retirement pensions and other forms of protecting the incomes of the elderly (especially Social Security and Medicare) respond to the desire of individuals, families and the society for a dignified and stable means of support for the elderly (Kingson, Hirshorn, and Cornman 1986). Older family members highly value their financial independence, preferring to rely on a combination of public programs and private savings mechanisms rather than their children's resources. Pensions, especially Social Security, respond to the need for a rational approach that enables individuals to contribute at a relatively small rate over time in exchange for protection for themselves and their families against loss of income and costs resulting from illness in old age (Kingson, Hirshorn, and Cornman 1986). They also assist young and middle-aged adults to direct most of their financial resources towards their children because pensions enable the retirement income needs of their parents, in many cases, to be adequately met.

THEORIES BEHIND PUBLIC INCOME SECURITY PROGRAMS

Every society must decide on the combination (and types) of public and private efforts needed to protect individuals and their families from risks substantially beyond their control, for example, loss of income due to retirement and health care expenses (Kingson and Berkowitz, forthcoming). Ours expects individuals and families to shoulder a substantial portion of these risks through the family, private savings and other private mechanisms (e.g., private pensions, private insurance). Also in place is a system of public income security programs.

The major public income security programs, most notably Social Security and Medicare, affecting the well-being of the elderly are based on social insurance principles. Second, important public assistance programs are directed primarily at low-income persons, e.g.,

Supplemental Security income (SSI) and Medicaid. In addition, programs for veterans are justified in part on the grounds that the nation owes veterans, especially those serving during war periods, special consideration "as a result of their unique social and economic contribution through service in the armed forces" (Axinn and Levin 1982: 3–4)

Social insurance provides a practical way to protect against common risks and meet the needs of citizens. Former Social Security Commissioner Robert Ball notes: "The purpose of social insurance is to prevent economic insecurity by pooling the contributions paid by covered earners and their employers (and in some systems other sources of income as well) to provide protection against the loss of earned income" (1978:5).

By applying insurance principles, program costs can be estimated and premiums set, thereby enabling individual and familial risk to be spread across the entire insurance pool. To provide widespread protection and to maintain a fair balance between good (e.g., healthy persons) and bad risks (e.g., unhealthy persons) participation in social insurance programs must be universal and compulsory. (Unlike private insurance which generally requires screening out bad risks, participation in social insurance programs includes everyone. If it did not it would undermine one of its fundamental goals, to provide widespread protection to the citizenry.)

To finance social insurance programs, workers generally make direct contributions—usually through a highly visible payroll tax—and indirectly through employer contributions. This reinforces their earned right to a benefit and helps underwrite the dignity of beneficiaries and the stability of these programs. It also encourages responsibility in financing the program because workers have a strong stake in its soundness (Social Security Administration 1987). The authority and taxing power of government stand behind the financing of social insurance programs and these programs are often viewed as involving compacts between generations.

Concern for meeting the basic needs of persons covered by social insurance programs is a driving goal. As Robert J. Myers, Chief Actuary of the Social Security Administration for many years, points out, the main reason for having social insurance programs is "that social benefits on a social-adequacy basis can only in this way be provided to a large sector of the population" (1985:11). While social insurance programs often reflect this concern through such mechanisms as cost-of-living adjustments and benefit formulas that provide proportionately larger benefits to low- and moderate-income workers, persons who make (or whose employers make on their behalf) larger contributions into social insurance programs generally receive larger benefits. By preventing poverty, it is often argued that social insurance programs add an important measure of stability to families and the society as a whole. (Kingson, Hirshorn and Cornman 1986; Kingson, Berkowitz, and Pratt, 1989).

Public assistance programs (also called welfare programs) are based on the assumption that society should not let poor persons and families fall below a defined standard of living (Clark 1985) or fail to have access to a minimal level of needed services (e.g., health care, housing). Some consider the public assistance approach to be the most appropriate way of protecting the incomes of the poor because means-testing enables program costs to be contained and benefits to be targeted to low-income persons. Others suggest that programs for poor people undermine the dignity of beneficiaries and generally become poor programs because they lack political support necessary to sustain benefit level (Cohen 1972). However, those strongly favoring the universal social insurance approach, generally also see an important role for public assistance programs in assisting some persons who fall through the first layer of the safety net, social insurance.

PUBLIC AND PRIVATE INCOME SUPPORT INTERVENTIONS

This section provides an overview of the old age income support system which includes various types of cash income (e.g., Social Security, earnings), tax policies affecting the elderly, and in-kind transfers (e.g., Medicare and the care provided by family members). While the discussion here emphasizes the major sources of cash income, it is important to recognize that the economic well-being of the elderly is also affected by in-kind transfers (both private and governmental), and the use of consumer durables (especially homes) acquired over a lifetime as well as the levels of taxation to which the elderly are subject (Clark, et al. 1984).

Sources of Cash Income

The major sources of cash income for persons aged 65 and over are Social Security (38 percent of the reported income going to aged units in 1986), assets (26 percent), earnings (17 percent) and other public and private pensions (a combined 14 percent) (see table 10.1). Public assistance and cash transfers from family members represent a small portion of reported income.[3]

SOCIAL SECURITY

For most aged households Social Security, the Old-Age, Survivors, and Disability Insurance program, provides the foundation for economic security in old age. This is especially true for modest- and low-income elderly units. For example, aged units with incomes below $10,000 in 1986 reported that Social Security provided, on average, three-quarters of their total incomes. In fact, about 57 percent of persons aged 65 and over report that Social Security provided at least 50 percent of their total cash income in 1986 (Grad 1988).

PRIVATE AND PUBLIC-EMPLOYEE PENSIONS

The proportion of the elderly population receiving private and public-employee pension income has shown very substantial increases so that by 1982 an estimated 23 percent of aged units received some private pension income and 12 percent received income from government employee pensions. In spite of this growth in pension receipt, the relative contributions of these pensions to aged households is

TABLE 10.1. Importance of Various Sources of Income to Aged Units, 65 and Over in 1986

	PERCENTAGE SHARE OF TOTAL INCOME PROVIDED TO				
Source of Income	*All aged units*	*Units under $5000*	*$5000–$9999*	*$10,000–$19,999*	*$20,000 or more*
Social Security	38	77	75	51	21
Railroad retirement	1	0	1	1	0
Private pension	7	1	3	9	8
Public employee pension	7	1	3	7	9
Asset income	26	4	9	19	34
Earnings	17	0	3	9	24
Public assistance	1	14	3	0	0
Other	2	2	2	2	1

SOURCE: Grad 1988.

fairly small. Each provide about 7 percent of the total income flowing to aged units, much of it going to the more financially comfortable elderly. Not surprisingly, private pension income is rarely the major source of income for the elderly because such pensions are almost always designed as supplements to Social Security and because persons who receive private pensions generally receive other sources of income too (Upp 1983).

ASSET INCOME

Asset income has become an increasingly important source of income in old age, received by approximately two-thirds of aged units and accounting for 26 percent of their total income (probably more if these data were corrected for under-reporting error). Assets income is particularly important for the more financially comfortable elderly, reported as providing in 1986 34 percent of all the income going to aged units with $20,000 or more in income.

Individual Retirement Accounts (IRAs), Keough plans, and 401K plans are savings devices that can be properly classified as either private pensions or assets. They are treated in this discussion as assets since they are primarily a result of savings decisions made by individuals. Although IRA and Keough assets exceeded 105 billion dollars in 1983 (Employee Benefit Research Institute 1984), they represent a miniscule portion of the income going to the elderly since the development of these savings mechanisms is fairly recent.

EARNINGS

Earned income is reported in 1986 to provide, on average, 17 percent of the income going to aged units. Most, of course, accrues to higher-income units. In terms of the economic status of the elderly, the presence of earnings is one of the major distinguishing factors (Schulz 1988). For example in 1985, data from the Current Population Surveys suggest that the median incomes of all men aged 65 and over was $10,900, while among those who worked full-time throughout the year it was $26,146. The comparable figures for elderly women are $6,313 and $18,336 (U.S. Census 1986).

CASH PUBLIC ASSISTANCE

Public assistance payments, mainly Supplemental Security Income (SSI), provide a small portion of the incomes going to elderly households, about 1 percent. Such payments are, however, an important part of the incomes for persons that social workers and other human service providers have special responsibility to serve, for example, representing 14 percent of the income received by aged units reporting less than $5,000 in 1986. Therefore, special attention will be paid to describing these programs below.

OTHER SOURCES OF INCOME

Other sources of income—mainly veterans benefits, railroad retirement and transfers from family members—also represent a small portion of the incomes of household income for the elderly.

In-kind Income

The importance of in-kind government transfers, in-kind private transfers and the use of consumer durables to the economic well-being of the elderly is briefly discussed now.[4]

IN-KIND GOVERNMENT TRANSFERS

The in-kind program of greatest importance to the elderly is Medicare, the hospital and physicians insurance program for disabled persons and the elderly (65 and over). Of necessity, elderly persons consume a disproportionate amount of the health care dollar. In 1984 the per capita cost of health care for the elderly was $4,202, with Medicare picking up 49 percent of the cost, mostly for treatment in hospital settings. Medicaid, the means-tested program that provides access to health services (including nursing home care) for persons receiving SSI or Aid to Families with Dependent Children (AFDC) and for certain persons that states define as "medically needy," picked up 13 percent of the elderly's health care costs in 1984. About one-third was paid by the elderly "through direct payments to providers or indirectly through premiums for insurance" (U.S. Senate 1988). Of course, out-of-pocket expenditures were relatively small for many elderly, and extremely large for some, primarily those requiring nursing home and other expensive long term care services. Food Stamps and public elderly housing programs also provide important in-kind services for low-income elderly persons in the case of the Food Stamp program and for certain low- and moderate-income elderly persons in the case of elderly housing.

IN-KIND PRIVATE TRANSFERS

Most private transfers flowing toward the elderly are in-kind, primarily care and other personal services provided by spouses, children other family members and friends, and secondarily housing at reduced or no cost. While there are numerous measurement problems concerning how to estimate the value of these services, it is clear that they represent very substantial contributions to the economic as well as the personal well-being of many elderly persons. Of course, over time and at any given time, many transfers flow from the elderly toward younger family members.

VALUE OF CONSUMER DURABLES

Home ownership is usually the most important asset of the elderly. The elderly have a very high rate of homeownership, with about 80 percent of elderly couples and 40 percent of single elderly persons being homeowners. About four-fifths of these elderly homeowners are free of debt (Schulz 1988). And it is estimated that about half (51 percent) of the elderly in 1984 had at least $40,000 in equity in their homes.[5] Converting such non-liquid assets into a source of income without the sale of a home is difficult.[6] Newly available mechanisms like reverse annuity mortgages may provide a solution for some elderly wishing to stay in their homes but also wishing to take advantage of the equity they have accumulated to provide additional income. Such mechanisms, available through some federally chartered savings and loans associations, enable elderly homeowners to sell some equity in their homes, "receiving in return a fixed monthly sum based on a percentage of the current market value of the house" (Schulz 1988:40). Of course, an important factor that many elderly persons would want to consider is the reduction in the value of their estate for their heirs. Also, they may want to know that the income produced from a reverse annuity mortgage would be countable when determining eligibility for Medicaid. Homeownership, however, does not count toward Medicaid eligibility. However, in some states the equity in a house is attachable under very limited circumstances—primarily at the death of unmarried persons for whom Medicaid has paid nursing home costs.

Taxation

The income position of the elderly is also affected by tax policy. The elderly, particularly the higher income elderly, benefit from the generally favorable tax treatment of their incomes. For example, throughout life many elderly have benefited from tax policies that exclude interest on mortgage payments and state property tax payments for homeowners from taxable income and from the favorable tax treatment afforded to private pension savings and income and Social Security income.[7] Moreover, the tax reductions that have taken place during the 1980s have been particularly beneficial to the high-income elderly (Storey 1983).

The tax code has a number of special provisions affecting the elderly and their families. Even though recent changes brought about by the 1986 Tax Reform Act eliminated the extra personal exemption afforded the elderly, the new basic standard deduction has been increased and the elderly receive an "additional standard deduction," $1,200 for a couple ($600 each) where both persons are 65 or over and $750 for a single person aged 65 or over in 1988. Another important provision of the tax code for some older persons is the one-time exclusion from the capital gains tax of up to $125,000 in gains from the sale of the principal residence available to persons age 55 or over if they have owned and lived in their house for three of the last five years. Also, family members who, in order to work, have dependent care expenses (e.g., paying someone to provide care) for a physically or mentally disabled person of any age (or a child under age 15) may be eligible for a tax credit if they reside with the disabled person. States, too, have special provisions in their tax codes for the elderly. Notably, thirty-one states have property tax circuitbreakers providing substantial relief to elderly, disabled and sometimes other households from property taxes, often including renters as well as homeowners (Shapiro and Greenstein 1988).

MAJOR PUBLIC INCOME SECURITY PROGRAMS FOR THE ELDERLY

To assist social workers and human service providers with information and referral, the major public income security programs affecting the elderly are now described, including points of access, eligibility, and basic benefits. Certain programs affecting older disabled persons (e.g., disabled workers in their 50's) are also described because such persons are often functionally older than persons many years their age, and should therefore be of special concern to service providers.

This overview is quite general and does not present many important details. Excellent pamphlets made available to the public at no cost by the Social Security Administration, the Health Care Financing Administration, the Veterans' Administration and state public assistance agencies are useful sources of more detailed information. Because the laws governing these programs are complex and often change, be sure to check and doublecheck your information when assisting older persons. Additionally, keep in mind that persistence often pays off. You should assist and encourage older persons to appeal decisions if it appears that they have been wrongfully denied benefits (e.g., disability eligibility or Medicare reimbursement).

Social Security

Social Security—the Old-Age, Survivors, and Disability Insurance program (OASDI)—provides benefits to about 38.6 million persons each month, mostly retired workers and their spouses (about 27 million) and aged survivors (about 5 million) but also to disabled workers (about 2.8 million) and their spouses, to surviving spouses caring for children under age 16 and to over 3 million children of disabled and deceased workers (Kingson, Berkowitz, and Pratt 1989).

Access to benefits is provided through approximately 1,300 local Social Security Administration offices and over 3,000 small contact stations (e.g., in a designated senior center) for more isolated communities. Questions and application for benefits can be made in person, or often, via telephone or the mail. If someone is confined to home because of illness or disability and if their claim cannot be handled via telephone and mail, Social Security Administration regulations require that a SSA representative make a home visit. Unfortunately, this is not always done. SSA is also expected to provide special assistance to non-english speaking persons.

Through employment covered by the Social Security program, workers build protection for themselves and their families. Because of the widespread coverage of the program, nearly all elderly people are eligible to receive Social Security benefits. Very importantly, annual cost-of-living adjustments assure that benefits, once received, maintain their purchasing power.[8] The amount of benefits which insured workers and eligible family members receive is related to the prior earnings of the insured worker. Although workers with higher earnings generally receive larger benefits, the Social Security benefit formula provides special assistance to moderate- and low-income workers by replacing a higher proportion of previous earnings for such workers.

Benefit amounts will also vary according to the age at which they are first accepted and can be reduced as a result of earnings. For example, nondisabled beneficiaries under age 65 with earnings in excess of $6,480 in 1989 and persons age 65 through 69 with earnings in excess of $8,880 in 1989 lose one dollar in benefits for every two dollars of earnings above the earnings ceiling. Each year the ceiling is adjusted for changes in average wages (Kingson 1987; Kingson and Berkowitz, forthcoming). As of 1990, benefits will be reduced by only one dollar for every three above the earnings ceiling for persons reaching normal retirement age (65 in 1990).

Social Security provides retirement, survivors and disability benefits to covered workers and eligible family members (see table 10.2). Covered workers receive full retirement benefits if claimed at the normal retirement age (65 today, but scheduled to be gradually increased to 67 essentially over a 24 year period beginning in 2003). Benefits received from ages 62 through 64 are permanently reduced for each month of receipt prior to normal retirement age (to 80 percent of a full benefit for persons receiving benefits at age 62 and a little lower as the new normal retirement age is phased in). Persons in a position to choose whether to accept early benefits should carefully assess the long-term implications of this reduction on their retirement finances. Because of the delayed retirement credit, the benefits of persons claiming benefits after the normal retirement age can

TABLE 10.2. Average and Maximum Social Security Benefits in January 1989

Average Monthly Benefits	
All retired workers	$537
Aged couple, both receiving benefits	$921
Widowed mother and two children	$1,112
Aged widow alone	$492
Disabled worker, wife	$943
All disabled workers	$529
Maximum Benefits at age 65 for Worker Retiring in 1989	
Retired worker	$899
Total family maximum on retired worker's earning record	$1,575
Maximum Benefits at age 62 for Worker Retiring in 1989	
Retired worker	$668

SOURCE: Social Security Administration Press Office, *Fact Sheet: 1989 Social Security Changes*

be increased, although currently not by very much. There is also a special minimum benefit designed to assist workers who have worked for many years, but at low wages.

Workers under age 65 who are severely disabled and whose disability is expected to last at least twelve months and/or result in death, may, after a five-month waiting period be eligible to receive disability insurance benefits under Social Security. After twenty-four months of entitlement to disability benefits, they become eligible for Medicare benefits. Assistance by service providers in completing and following the progress of disability applications and appeals is often helpful.

Family members of retired (and disabled) workers may be eligible to receive some benefits as well. Importantly, spouses, aged 62 and over, of retired workers (including divorced spouses married for at least ten years to a worker) may be eligible to receive a spouse benefit. The benefit amount will vary depending on the age the spouse first receives it. In some cases spouses of a disabled or retired worker caring for a child under 16 or an adult disabled child may be eligible for auxiliary benefits as may be unmarried dependent children under 18 of such workers, dependent grandchildren under 18 and children over 18 who were first permanently disabled prior to age 22 (Kingson 1987; Kingson, Berkowitz and Pratt 1989).

For the elderly, survivors benefits are very important. Spouses age 60 and over (including divorced spouses) may be eligible for aged widow(er)s benefits on the death of the worker. They should be aware that such benefits are permanently reduced for each month they are accepted prior to the normal retirement age. Widow(er)s of any age caring for a child under age 16 (or an adult disabled child) may be eligible for a surviving parent's benefit. Benefits may also be available for surviving children under age 18 (in some cases 19) and to surviving adult disabled children. Very important, a widow(er) age 50 through 59 who is not caring for dependent children may be eligible for a reduced benefit (and, after a waiting period, Medicare) is s/he meets the Social Security disability test. It may also be worthwhile for a disabled widower aged 60 through 64 to apply for "disabled widow-Medicare only," status as a way of getting Medicare benefits prior to age 65.

Supplemental Security Income (SSI)

SSI is a means-tested program which provides cash benefits to approximately 4.5 million low-income elderly or disabled or blind people during each month of 1989—about 45 percent of whom were age

65 or over. For those meeting SSI eligibility criteria, the federal government provides a minimal income guarantee, $368 for a single person and $553 for a couple in 1989, which some states have elected to supplement. Application for federal SSI benefits and most state supplements is made through local SSA offices. Persons eligible for SSI are, with rare exception, also eligible for Medicaid—usually automatically—and for food stamps (except in California and Wisconsin, which increase state supplementation of SSI by cashing out food stamps).

Eligibility requires being aged 65 or over, or meeting SSA's disability criteria or blindness criteria (defined as 20/200 vision or less with the better eye after use of corrective lens or tunnel vision of 20 degrees or less) (U.S. House 1988). Additionally, restrictive income and assets tests must be met.

Benefits may be reduced by a number of factors including one-half of earnings in excess of $65 per month; dollar for dollar reductions for Social Security income in excess of $20 per month; other similar reductions for income from other sources; one-third reduction for living in the household of someone who provides in-kind support (e.g., free rent). Monthly SSI benefits are reduced to $25 for persons in a facility (e.g., a nursing home) in which Medicaid is paying a major part of their bill. The residents of public institutions are generally not eligible for SSI unless it is Medicaid approved and Medicaid is paying more than half the cost for the person. SSI payments can be made under certain circumstances to persons in small publicly operated community residences and to temporary residents of public emergency shelters for the homeless. Also, under certain circumstances persons who are temporarily in a public institution for psychiatric care can maintain eligibility for SSI benefits for up to 3 months so as to maintain their living situation in the community (U.S. House 1988). Similar provisions exist for persons who are temporary residents of nursing homes or other medical institutions.

Besides the 4.5 million persons who currently receive SSI benefits, many others are potentially eligible, but either do not know about it or have not applied. Because SSI eligibility almost always results in eligibility for Medicaid, it is in the interest of such persons to apply even if their cash benefits would be relatively small. Social workers and other service providers can play an important role in assisting potential beneficiaries in over-coming barriers (e.g., language, bureaucracy, lack of information) to receipt of SSI.

Medicare

Medicare provides partial protection against health care costs, especially hospital-based costs, for approximately 28 million elderly beneficiaries, 3 million Social Security disability insurance beneficiaries, and 100,000 persons with permanent kidney failure.[9] Although administered by the Health Care Financing Administration, applications are handled by local SSA offices. The program has two parts: Medicare Part A, the Hospital Insurance (HI) program; and Medicare Part B, the Supplementary Medical Insurance (SMI). Although HI provides substantial protection against the cost of hospital care and SMI provides considerable assistance with in- and out-patient physician and other services, it provides only very limited protection for the potentially catastrophic costs that can accompany long-term chronic illness in old age.

Work in employment covered by the Social Security and Medicare programs and premium payments establishes the right to benefits. Nearly everyone age 65 and over is eligible for HI. Persons entitled to Social Security disability benefits for 24 months are eligible as are persons with permanent kidney failure requiring dialysis and/or a transplant. Enrollment in SMI is voluntary, requiring payment of a monthly premium. Since it is highly subsidized by the federal government, elderly and disabled persons are well-advised to enroll.

The great bulk of Medicare expenditures goes to pay for hospital costs for aged and disabled beneficiaries. To be eligible for reimbursement for hospital costs, a beneficiary must need hospital care, have it prescribed by a physician, and be treated in a hospital that participates in Medicare. Nearly all hospitals do, but it is wise to check.

As this manuscript goes to press, it appears most likely that Medicare legislation will be passed, undoing many changes brought about by the enactment of the 1988 Catastrophic Coverage Act. Thus for an up-to-date overview of available benefits, the reader is encouraged to review the Medicare Handbook, available at no cost through local Social Security offices.

The 1988 Catastrophic Coverage Act added protections against some costs associated with: Medicare-funded hospitalizations exceeding 60 days, immunosuppressive drugs used following a transplant, some prescription drugs, some lengthened stays in skilled nursing facilities, respite care, and transfusions. The act also placed a yearly limit on the amount that Medicare beneficiaries would need to pay as a copayment for services covered under the SMI program. The program changes were to be funded by a modest increase in the monthly SMI premium payments of all Medicare beneficiaries and a special surcharge on the income taxes paid mainly by higher-income beneficiaries. It was this latter requirement—scheduled to cost some beneficiaries as much as $800 for 1989—which precipitated the political fire storm that appears to be resulting in repeal of many, perhaps all, of the new provisions. Just before this volume went to press, the House of Representatives voted to repeal nearly all the provisions of the act. The Senate, however, voted to eliminate the tax-surcharge, but to fund some benefits including long-term hospitalization protections, some respite care, home intervenous and some payments for immunosuppressive drugs via modest premium increases affecting all beneficiaries.

If the extended hospital protection remains unchanged, then Medicare HI beneficiaries would continue to be responsible for paying only one deductible per year for hospitalization—$560 in 1989. After that, Medicare, would pay the rest of the cost for inpatient hospital care including a semi-private room, meals, special care units (e.g., intensive care), operating and recovery room costs, x-rays, lab tests, radiation therapy, medical supplies, rehabilitation services, drugs provided by the hospital and blood (except for the first 3 pints) (Study Group 1988). Under certain circumstances, HI also covers a substantial portion of the costs of: 1) a limited number of days of rehabilitative inpatient care in a participating skilled nursing facility (SNF); 2) limited home health care; and 3) hospice care for dying persons. Reimbursement for medical costs under HI is fairly simple because the institution that treats the beneficiary and the *HI Intermediary*—the organization (usually Blue Cross) with whom Medicare contracts to handle claims—take care of all the paperwork.

For those enrolled in the SMI program, benefits provide for certain doctor's services; other medical and health services including many surgical services, outpatient hospital services; diagnostic procedures, and home health care.

SMI provides for limited home health services for persons who are not eligible for them under HI. Also, under certain circumstances up to 80 hours per year of respite care is provided to give unpaid caregivers who live with certain disabled Medicare beneficiaries relief from the very difficult job of providing on-going care. The future of this benefit is in question.

SMI will generally pay for 80 percent of approved charges for most covered services, after the beneficiary has paid the SMI deductible in a calendar year (the first $75 of approved charges). The deductible and coinsurance do not apply to certain services such as home health visits.

A Medicare beneficiary who has paid the SMI deductible must pay 20 percent of approved charges for covered services under the 1988 act Medicare was scheduled to pick up all recognized costs that exceeded catastrophic limit on costs—estimated as $1370 in 1990. SMI beneficiaries also must pay the portion of a medical bill that exceeds what Medicare calls "approved charges," as well as for services not covered by SMI. It is important to realize that doctors and medical suppliers who accept *assignment* agree to accept *approved charges* as payment in full. Thus, it is to the benefit of beneficiaries to take their business to persons accepting assignment. Otherwise they may be required to make much larger payments for health care services.

Service providers may, on occasion, need to assist elderly persons sort through Medicare billing procedures. Reimbursement under SMI is often more complex than under HI. If the provider does not accept assignment, not only is the cost of a service likely to increase substantially, but the amount of paperwork for a beneficiary is much greater. This is because the beneficiary often must take care of all the paperwork and correspondence with the *carrier*—the organizations (usually an insurance company or Blue Cross/Blue Shield) with whom medicare contracts to handle claims.

Medicaid

Medicaid is the means-tested federal/state program that provides access to health services each month to an estimated 23.6 million low-income Americans in 1987, including about 12.3 million children, 3.3 million persons age 65 and over, 3.0 million persons with disabilities, and 5.8 million other adults. States administer the program within federal guidelines. Thus there is much variation with respect to eligibility and benefits.

Applications for Medicaid are generally taken by local public assistance offices. Eligibility requires an applicant to meet income and assets tests and to be defined as either "categorically needy" or "medically needy." AFDC and SSI beneficiaries are always considered categorically needy, although some states use the more restrictive criteria for SSI recipients that were in effect in 1972. Some states extend categorical coverage to other groups (e.g. recipients of state-only SSI supplements; certain institutionalized persons). Some states also extend coverage to the medically needy, "aged, blind, disabled or members of families with dependent children whose incomes, after deducting medical expenses, fall below the state standard of need" (Kingson 1987). All states provide inpatient hospital services, outpatient hospital services, laboratory and x-ray services, skilled nursing care for adults, some home health services, health screening, diagnosis and treatment for those under 21, family planning services and physician services. Some states elect to provide services such as dentistry, eye glasses, and care in intermediate care facilities (Kingston, Berkowitz, and Pratt 1989).

Food Stamps

Although lodged in the Department of Agriculture and federally-funded,[10] the Food Stamps program is administered by the states. Applications are processed by local public assistance offices. However, SSI and Social Security beneficiaries can fill out applications for Food Stamps at local SSA offices. Applicants must meet income and assets tests. In general, the maximum monthly benefit in July 1989 (provided in the form of stamps which can be used to purchase food) was $90 for single persons, $165 for a couple and $300 for a family of four.[11]

Veterans' Benefits

Veterans discharged under other than dishonorable conditions and surviving dependents of these veterans are often eligible for veterans' cash or medical benefits.[12] In August 1986 the Veterans' Administration, the federal agency administering these programs, provided benefits to 662,000 veterans and 638,000 widows.

Veterans' compensation provides monthly cash benefits to persons whose disabilities or illnesses occurred or were aggravated during active duty. Payments are based on the degree of disability, ranging from a 10 percent disability to a total disability. Dependents' benefits are available for veterans with at least a 30 percent service-connected disability. There are no means tests and, under certain circumstances, spouses and dependent children can receive benefits.

Veterans' pensions are monthly cash benefits paid to low-income veterans who are totally and permanently disabled (or at least age 65 and not working). Such disabilities do not necessarily have to be service-related, although the veteran needs to have served during the Mexican border period, World War I, World War II, the Korean War, or the Vietnam War. The presence of a spouse and/or dependent children may increase the size of the pension as might the need for regular aid and attendance resulting from illness or disability. Survivors' pensions may also be available to widows or widowers, dependent children or adult dependent children who were disabled before age 18.

Veterans medical benefits include inpatient hospital treatment, outpatient treatment, nursing home care, home health services, alcohol and drug dependence treatment and domiciliary care. Spouses and dependent children are sometimes eligible for medical treatment.

Other programs

For information and referral purposes, service providers need to be aware of the many other public income security programs that might assist older Americans. They include: the state/federal Unemployment Insurance system which provides cash benefits to unemployed workers; Workers Compensation programs run by each state (and the federal government for its employees) which provide partial replacement of lost wages, medical and rehabilitation benefits and survivors' benefits for workers injured on the job; state and federal civil service retirement, survivor, disability and health protection; Railroad Retirement which provides covered employees with retirement, survivors and disability protection; the Black Lung Disability program which protects miners from income and medical costs resulting from black lung disease; military retirement and health programs; temporary disability programs in California, New York, Rhode Island, and Puerto Rico (and in the railroad industry); the means-tested General Assistance (also called General Relief) programs that many states and a few localities run as programs of last resort for selected groups of low-income persons who are not eligible for any federally-funded cash assistance; the refugee resettlement program; the Low Income Home Energy Assistance program. In many communities resource manuals have been developed by legal service and social service organizations which provide an overview of these services. If one is available, it can be an invaluable aid for information and referral.

CONCLUSIONS: THE FUTURE OF INCOME SECURITY POLICIES

There is little doubt that social insurance policies and, to a more limited degree, public assistance policies will continue to provide critical support to the elderly of the future. Budget data provide one indication of the nations' commitment to the elderly. In fiscal year 1988, 29 percent of the nation's federal outlays ($304 billion)[13] were for Social Security and Medicare, programs whose primary beneficiaries are the elderly (Ways and Means Committee, 1988). Federal and State expenditures on SSI and Medicaid totalled $13 billion and $49 billion, respectively, in fiscal 1987—much directed at the low-income elderly. Public opinion polls show strong support for Social Security among all age groups, even though the same polling data also show that nearly half of all persons, especially the young, lack confidence in its long-term future. The public, despite its skepticism, recognizes the critical importance of these programs to the entire family.

Social Security Financing

One of the best pieces of news of the 1980s was the success of the bipartisan compromise which resulted in the 1983 legislation that improved Social Security's financial status. Each year since the enactment of the 1983 amendments, revenues have exceeded outgo and are expected to continue to do so for about thirty years. These annual surpluses will result in very large reserves and are expected to largely offset the annual deficits that are projected to follow. The key point to note, however, is that — even under pessimistic assumptions about demographic and economic change — experts generally agree that Social Security can meet *all* its benefit obligations in a timely manner for *at least* the next 35 years.

The news, while generally good, does not mean that the need to make adjustments in the future has disappeared. Social Security's financing is sensitive to economic change implying, for example, that lower than anticipated economic growth could translate into financing difficulties or that higher than anticipated growth could result in large surpluses. Moreover, under the most-commonly-accepted assumptions about demographic and economic change, Social Security's actuaries forecast a small deficit (about 5 percent of expected revenues) over the next 75 years. But as the Trustees (1989) point out, the anticipated build-up of reserves "provides ample time to monitor the financial status of the program and to take corrective action at some time in the future," if needed. In fact, one of the great strengths of Social Security is its ability to adjust to changing social and economic conditions. For now, the program is adequately financed, and it seems extremely unlikely that changing economic or demographic circumstances could force a financing crisis such as those experienced during the mid- and late-1970s and early 1980s during the next thirty years. On the other hand, it is important to keep in mind that, as with all large institutions, over time, new problems will undoubtedly emerge, requiring new policy responses.

Other Policy Issues

There is also little doubt that policymakers and the general public will be confronted with other difficult decisions. The large federal deficit leads some to call for cuts in Social Security, most often by reducing cost-of-living protection. Concern for the large number of elderly persons who are poor and near-poor, leads naturally to proposals for liberalized income and asset testing in SSI, higher benefit levels and more effective outreach procedures (Villers 1985). Calls are also made for increased protection of other vulnerable groups—divorced women, women widowed in late middle age, and the very old. Increasing health care costs combine with the financing problems in the largest of the Medicare trust funds, Hospital Insurance, to guarantee the need to choose among tax increases, reduced protection and more generalized approaches to containing health care costs, or some combination thereof.

Today nearly all elderly persons are exposed to the potentially financially devasting risk of long-term care. Its emergence as a presidential campaign issue in 1988 is an indication of its growing significance. Although proposed solutions vary greatly, nearly all parties agree that it is a major problem. Some call for increased private savings and private insurance approaches, sometimes connected to expanded eligibility for Medicaid for the unprotected. Other proposals call for greatly expanded social insurance protection—perhaps through a Medicare Part C or through a new program. Other differences can be seen in whether such proposals are directed at protecting only the elderly, or respond to the need for protection against long-term care costs for other age groups.

Through direct contact with elderly persons and organizations, social workers and other human service providers are often in a position to document the need for improvements in income security and other social policies. Our work provides opportunities to assess whether legislative and regulatory change is beneficial or not and to use this information to shape the policy process via legislative advocacy, contact with the media, research, involvement with professional organizations and assistance to consumer organizations. By doing so, we can help clarify real and potential impacts, especially among the most vulnerable populations.

Increasingly, the politics of income security policy is being mistakenly cast in terms of trade-offs between the interests of young and old. Herein, perhaps, lies the most important challenge for social workers and other human service providers serving the elderly—one that requires the development of new educational strategies which clarify the benefits that accrue across generations, careful assessment of the trade-offs involved in various income security proposals, the willingness to accept certain policy changes that may place increased financial burden on some elderly persons, primarily those who are financially comfortable) and the development of a multigenerational agenda (Kingson 1988).

ENDNOTES

1. In 1987 the poverty threshold for single persons aged 65 or over was $5,447 and for married couples headed by a person aged 65 or over, it was $6,872. In 1986, the respective thresholds were $5,255 for elderly individuals and $6,630 for elderly couples. The poverty index seeks to measure "the adequacy of money income in relation to a minimal level of consumption (the poverty level)" (U.S. Senate, 1988). It measures pre-tax and post-transfer cash income, and adjusts for family sizes and changes in the consumer price index. It is based on a methodology which some have criticized as setting an unrealistically high poverty threshold because, for example, it does not account for the value of in-kind benefits such as Medicare and food stamps. Others, however, have criticized it as being unrealistically low because, for example, the methodology has never been adjusted to reflect the increased cost of housing and other commodities relative to food. It does, however, have the virtue of consistency over time, and consequently provides one good measure of the changing economic status of the elderly over time. For a good discussion of methodology behind the poverty index and summary of criticisms, see James H. Schulz of 1988. *Economics of Aging.*

2. The Bureau of the Census Current Population Surveys (CPS) provides data which serve as a basis of many reports on income and poverty which are issued by the Bureau on a regular basis and also used by the Social Security Administration in its series which reports on the income of the population age 55 and over. The CPS appears to be subject to under-reporting error (about 11 percent)—especially among higher income persons (Radner 1982). The under-reporting appears to be greater among the elderly, particularly higher income elders, primarily because property income and, second, earnings tend to be under-reported. Thus, some caution should be exercised in interpreting these data.

3. As noted elsewhere (see note 2), the data reported in table 10.1, probably overstate the importance of Social Security to aged units and understate the importance of assets and earnings.

4. For a good discussion of the impact of in-kind benefits on poverty and a

discussion of the various views concerning whether and how to include the value of in-kind benefits in poverty estimates, see Joseph Quinn (1986). Also see James H. Schulz (1988).

5. Derived from data presented in Schulz, p. 39.

6. Of course, in its absence rental or mortgage payments would have to be made, and so in this regard equity in a house does resemble income.

7. Even though up to one-half of Social Security income is now countable as taxable income for higher-income beneficiaries, Social Security income continues to receive favorable tax treatment.

8. This is one of the most important features of Social Security. It is the reason why, today, most elderly are well protected against inflation. Even so, it should be pointed out that Congress can amend the cost-of-living provision as it did in 1983 when it was permanently delayed for six months. Also, it should be noted that under certain circumstances the annual adjustment may be less than the rate of increase in inflation as measured by the Consumer Price Index. But this is unlikely to occur for decades.

9. Some of the material presented in the section is drawn with permission of the Save Our Security Education Fund from Kingson, Berkowitz, and Pratt, 1989.

10. States share the cost of administration with the federal government. The benefits are entirely federally-financed.

11. Maximum benefit levels are higher in Alaska, Hawaii, Guam, and the Virgin Islands, and lower in Puerto Rico.

12. The material on veterans' benefits is drawn with permission of the Save Our Security Education Fund from Kingson, E.R. Berkowitz, E.D., and Pratt, F. *Social Security in the U.S.A.: A Discussion Guide to Social Insurance with Lesson Plans. Teaching About Social Insurance* (Washington, D.C.: Save Our Security Education Fund, 1989).

13. Note that 6.5 percent of the nation's Gross National Product (GNP) is devoted to Social Security and Medicare, compared to 6.1 percent for national defense.

REFERENCES

Achenbaum, W. A. 1983. *Shades of Grey: Old Age, American Values, and Federal Policies since 1920*. Boston: Little, Brown.

Achenbaum, W. Andrew. 1986. *Social Security: Visions and Revisions*. New York: Cambridge University Press, 1986.

Atchley, R. 1971. *The Sociology of Retirement*. New York: Wiley/Schenkman.

Axinn, J. and H. Levin. 1982. *Social Welfare: A History of the American Response*. New York: Harper and Row.

Ball, R. M. 1978. *Social Security: Today and Tomorrow*. New York: Columbia University Press.

Berkowitz, E. D. 1987. *Disabled Policy*. New York: Cambridge University Press.

Board of Trustees, Federal Old-Age and Survivors Insurance and Disability Insurance Trust Funds. *1989 Annual Report of the Federal Old-Age and Survivors Insurance and Disability Insurance Trust Funds*. Washington, D.C.: GPO, April 1989.

Board of Trustees, Federal Hospital Insurance Trust Fund. *1989 Annual Report of the Board of Trustees of the Federal Hospital Insurance Trust Fund*. Washington, D.C.: GPO, April 1989.

Board of Trustees, Federal Supplementary Medical Insurance Trust Fund. *1989*

Annual Report of the Board of Trustees of the Federal Supplementary Medical Insurance Trust Fund. Washington, D.C.: GPO, April 1989.

Brown, J. D. 1972. *An American Philosophy of Social Insurance: Evolution and Issues.* Princeton: Princeton University Press.

Chen, Y. P. 1985. Economic status of the aging. In R. H. Binstock and E. Shanas, eds., *Handbook of Aging and the Social Sciences.* New York: Van Nostrand Reinhold.

Clark, R. L. and D. L. Baumer. 1985. Income maintenance policies. In R. H. Binstock and E. Shanas, eds., *Handbook of Aging and the Social Sciences.* New York: Van Nostrand Reinhold.

Clark, R. L., G. L. Maddox, R. A., Schrimper, and D. A. Sumner. 1984. *Inflation and the Economic Well-Being of the Elderly.* Baltimore: Johns Hopkins University Press.

Cohen, W. J. 1972. In W. J. cohen and M. Friedman, *Social Security: Universal or Selective?* Washington, D.C.: American Enterprise Institute for Public Policy Research.

Employee Benefit Research Institute. 1984, Individual retirement accounts: Characteristics and policy implications, *EBRI Issue Brief Number 32.* Washington, D.C.: Employee Benefit Research Institute.

Grad, S. 1988. *Income of the Population 55 or Over, 1986.* Washington, D.C.: Social Security Administration.

Graebner, W. A. 1980. *A History of Retirement.* New Haven: Yale University Press.

Kingson, E. R. 1987. *What You Must Know About Social Security and Medicare.* New York: Pharos Books.

Kingson, E. R. 1988. Generational equity: An unexpected opportunity to broaden the politics of aging. *The Gerontologist* 28 (6): 765–772.

Kingson, E. R., E. D. Berkowitz and F. Pratt. 1989. *Social Security in the U.S.A.: A Discussion Guide to Social Insurance with Lesson Plans.* Washington, D.C.: Save Our Security Education Fund.

Kingson, E. R., B. A. Hirshorn, and J. M. Cornman. 1986. *Ties that Bind: The Interdependence of Generations.* Cabin John, Md.: Seven Locks Press.

Kreps, J. M. and J. J. Spengler. 1966. The leisure component of economic growth. In National Commission on Technology, Automation, and Economic Progress. *Technology and the Economy.* Appendix 2. Washington, D.C.: GPO.

Latimer, M. W. 1932. *Industrial Pension Systems in the United States and Canada.* 2 vols. New York; Industrial Relations Counselors.

Lubove, R. 1968. *Struggle for Social Security.* Cambridge: Harvard University Press.

Myers, R. J. 1985. *Social Security.* Homewood, Ill.: Richard D. Irwin.

Munnell, A. H. 1987. The current status of our social welfare system. *New England Economic Review* (July/August), pp. 3–12.

Quinn, J. 1987. The economic status of the elderly: Beware of the mean. *The Review of Income and Wealth.* (March), 33(1): 63–82.

Radner, D. B. 1982. Distribution of family income: Improved estimates. *Social Security Bulletin* 45(7): 13–21.

Schulz, James H. 1988. *The Economics of Aging.* Dover, Mass: Auburn House.

Shapiro, I. and R. Greenstein. (1988). *Holes in the Safety Net.* Washington, D.C.: Center on Budget and Policy Priorities.

Social Security Administration. 1987. Social security programs in the United States. *Social Security Bulletin* 50 (4):5–70.

Storey, J. R. 1983. *Older Americans in the Reagan Era.* Washington, D.C.: Urban Institute Press.

Study Group on Social Security and the National Academy of Social Insurance (June 10, 1988). Congress passes major medicare expansion for catastrophic costs." Update #62 (New York, N.Y.).

U.S. Bureau of the Census. 1986. Money income and poverty status of families and persons in the United States: 1985. *Current Population Surveys: Current Population Reports.* Series P-60, No. 154. Washington, D.C.: GPO.

U.S. bureau of the Census. 1987. Money income and poverty status of families and persons in the United States: 1986. *Current Population Survey: Current Population Reports.* P-60, No. 157. Washington, D.C.: GPO.

U.S. House Committee on Ways and Means. 1988. *Background Material and Data on Programs within the Jurisdiction of the Committee on Ways and Means.* Washington, D.C.: GPO.

U.S. Senate. 1988. Special Committee on Aging in conjunction with the American Association of Retired Persons, the Federal Council on Aging, and the U.S. Administration on Aging. *Aging America: Trends and Projections.* 1987–88 ed. Washington, D.C.: U.S. Department of Health and Human Services.

Upp, M. 1983. Relative importance of various income sources of the aged, 1980. *Social Security Bulletin.* 46(1):3–10.

Villers Foundation. 1987. *The Other Side of Easy Street.* Washington, D.C.: Villers Foundation.

IV
COMMUNITY-BASED SERVICES

11

Services to Families of the Elderly

BARBARA OBERHOFER DANE, D.S.W.
Columbia University School of Social Work

American society is experiencing rapid changes which are certain to shape the lives of the elderly and their families as they approach the twenty-first century. Although there has been considerable speculation on how older people in general might be affected by current trends, the past decade has documented considerable research on the important role of the family in the care of the disabled elderly and dispelled the myth of family abandonment.

Troll and Smith (1976) have suggested that affective family relationships withstand distance, separation, and developmental changes. Similarly, Brody (1985) has emphasized that, although the relationship can be expected to change, the affective ties remain strong. Moss et al. (1985) have reported that parent and child share in familial structure, associations, affection, and values, as well as appropriate functional exchanges.

When assistance is needed, most elderly prefer turning to their families and friends rather than to the formal service system as their major providers of needed health care and social supports. In general, families demonstrate a pattern of reciprocal aid and assistance between older and younger relatives that continues throughout an individual's lifetime. However, as soon as elderly family members manifest a deterioration in their financial or health status they end up receiving more help than they give. Shanas (1979) showed that family members provide 80 percent of the services needed by disabled older adults, ranging from direct care (e.g., personal care, shopping, household help) to arranging and monitoring services from community agencies. The role that the family and other informal supports play in helping the frail elderly maintain themselves in the community is being scrutinized as a major source of care for the growing population of old people. The societal benefits of what is often full-time caregiving by family members are now widely recognized and appreciated. For example, the availability of family caregivers is seen as a major deterrent for early institutionalization.

However, the demands of caregiving and their impact on the caregiver and the family as a whole are increasingly becoming a cause for concern (Archbold 1982; Cantor 1983; Fengler and Goodrich 1979).

While families accept the responsibility to care for their members, the numbers of older persons needing at least minimal help is greater than ever before. The fastest growing segment of the older population are those age 85 and older. Since they had smaller families than in the past, the burden of care is potentially spread among fewer people. Add to that Brody's (1985) observation that many of the children who are potential helpers are themselves in their 50's, 60's, or even in some instances, 70's, and the magnitude of the problem is obvious.

There is a growing consensus to do a better job in meeting the needs of families who provide assistance, though there is still disagreement about the mix of services and support that would be best. Horowitz (1985) and Simmons et al. (1985) have suggested that a partnership between the formal and informal support networks can ensure effective care to the elderly person while also helping the caregiver.

This paper will summarize the state of the art of the informal family support systems providing a framework to understand the complexity and need for further development of formal services. A theoretical framework will provide an understanding of the functional and affective components of family caregiving. Special attention will be focused on services for families caring for a member disabled with Alzheimer's disease. Strategies for prevention and treatment of elder abuse and drug and alcohol usage by the elder person will be outlined.

FAMILY SUPPORTS AND THE NEED FOR FORMAL SERVICES

The complexity of families and their reactions to the demands of caregiving must be understood before relating to the formal services currently being provided. Both formal services and interventions can then be tailored to the family's unique situation.

Research concludes that the majority of persons aged 65 and older are married and live together in two-person households and major familial responsibility falls primarily on spouses. However, the likelihood of being married in old age differs markedly for men and women. Older men are more likely to be married, while older women are more likely to be widowed. This is especially evident among the oldest women, where less than 25 percent are married (Brotman 1982; Sangl 1983; Taeuber 1983). Only when spouses are unavailable or incapable of meeting extensive care needs do adult children take over as primary caregivers.

Adult children often are faced with competing time demands and role responsibilities. Those who do not live with their elderly parents may fulfill some filial responsibilities by serving as mediators between institutional bureaucracies and elderly relatives who are not too dependent (Sussman 1976). Divorce may have a detrimental effect on caregiving behavior. Adults with disrupted marriages were found to provide less help to elderly parents than adult children with intact marriages (Cicirelli 1983).

A squeeze on the time and resources of women in the middle generation has been documented. These women, who themselves are aging, are being called on to offer financial and emotional support to their adult children as well as their aging parents (Brody 1981; Brody 1985). Women traditionally have spent many hours in support of elderly persons in their families and in their communities. Changing sex roles, coupled with increased labor force participation among middle-aged women, place an additional burden on already strained family resources. With increasing numbers of women in the workplace, help will not be as readily available in the future. A major question is whether assistance to the elderly will decline as more women enter the labor force.

The family's ability and willingness to care for the growing numbers of older persons will, no doubt, be affected by some related demographic and social trends that are affecting the nature and stability of family support systems of aging relatives (Brotman 1982; Sangl 1983; Taeuber 1983).

In the next century, given current trends toward increased longevity, four- and five-generation families appears inevitable, resulting in increased need and demand for service to elders and their families. The escalating numbers of older impaired elders will need assistance from aged spouses or, if unavailable, younger caregivers who are themselves aging. It will become increasingly common for a 90-year-old widowed mother to be cared for by a 65-year-old adult child. Trends, such as declines in family size, high rates of divorce and remarriage, and increased geographic mobility, are likely to diminish the potential pool of people available to sustain older frail family members in the community.

ASSESSMENT

Assessment is a critical process in social work practice, for the nature of goals and the selection of relevant intervention. Assessment is an ongoing process that begins from the first contact with the elderly person and their family. Analysis of the problem within an ecological context involves the social worker considering the adequacy or deficiency, success or failure, strengths or weaknesses of salient systems in the environment that bear on the family and its older member. Problems which are particularly stressful for the family caregiver in determining the need for services are highlighted.

To understand how families respond to the demands of caregiving, it is necessary to assess the unique characteristics, resources and deficits of a given family. The complexity of the family in its organization is varied and differs on a number of dimensions that are likely to affect caregiving. These include size, geographic proximity, as in the case of the rural elderly, emotional closeness, values, ethnicity, differentiation of roles and past history of caregiving.

Social workers should identify the specific aspects of care that are burdensome and assess the following with the family. What are the physical demands of care? What amount of time must a caregiver devote? Is it temporary? Does caregiving result in job satisfaction? What are the associated burdens? Rakowski and Clark (1985) have demonstrated that pessimism on the part of caregivers occurs when their elders have significant impairments, need extensive assistance, and generate great amounts of stress.

Caregiving can range from minimal assistance with one or two tasks (e.g., transportation, management of finances) to around-the-clock assistance and supervision. There are also differences in the degree of emotional demands made by the impaired person, although these demands should not be regarded as necessarily correlated with physical needs for assistance. Clearly, the impact on families will vary, depending on the amount and type of assistance the impaired elder requires. Caregiver strain increases as the length of caregiving increases (Hoenig and Hamilton 1966; Johnson and Catalano 1983).

One distinction that may have major importance for understanding the impact on families is whether or not the impaired elder has dementia. Clinical experience suggests that there are major qualitative differences in caregiving of cognitively impaired and cognitively intact elders on their families. The dementia patient not only requires assistance and supervision as the disease progresses, but becomes increasingly impaired in language and social behavior. The result is that the usual interactions between dementia patient and caregiver that made the relationship mutually satisfying are disrupted. While relationships can suffer in any caregiving situation, the presence of dementia places greater strain on the family than with other problems. If the decline is rapid, families are more likely to consider nursing home placement than if the decline is slower. (Lund et al. 1988).

Even behaviors usually cited in the literature as extremely stressful, such as incontinence or agitation, are sometimes tolerated and managed effectively by specific caregivers (Zarit, Orr, and Zarit 1985). Some caregivers can cope more effectively with problem behaviors if they occasionally get help from other family members or from a service agency.

Caring for an older person is a unique combination of assistance and supervision, and is conditioned by the characteristics of the older person and his or her caregiver. Personality and coping styles of both patient and caregiver, the quality of their relationship prior to the need for caregiving, and other role demands are important lines of inquiry to be included in the assessment process.

Baseline information about the family system of the elderly should include a picture of the members of the family, where they live, their health and social status, predictable patterns of reaction to illness or other stress, and the quality of family relationships. Further information on an eco-map can simulate in a dynamic way the ecological system that encompasses the older person and family in their life space. This schematic representation of the family is an analytic tool that enables the family and social worker visualize the flow of resources, the nature of family environment exchanges, and highlights any lacks or deprivations which erode family strength in caring for the older person. The eco-map can be expanded to include significant non-family social relationships such as church groups, visiting nurses and other health professionals.

Mrs. Kane, a 76-year-old widow, was referred for discharge planning after sustaining a fractured hip. The initial visit by the social worker revealed that Mrs. Kane has one daughter who lived over 300 miles away but would spend two weeks with her mother commencing on Mrs. Kane's discharge date. The worker explored other social supports and community resources to alleviate Mrs. Kane's anxiety around receiving post-hospital care. An eco-map was drawn highlighting both neighbors and friends who may be available and community supports both private and public that would aid Mrs. Kane in her recovery process. The information obtained helped identify for the worker the next steps to undertake in contacting resources in Mrs. Kane's environment to strengthen and support her return home.

Remnet suggests attending to the following questions:

Is the family in a current state of crisis because of the failing capacities of one of its members?
Are other stresses impinging on the system?
Has the family system changed over the years to meet the needs of its members?
Is change acknowledged and accepted?

In relation to the older person:

1. Who is assuming responsibility for what?
2. Is the responsibility realistic?
3. Have all family members been involved in the plan?
4. Have the expectations of each family member been explored and defined?
5. Is the current plan considered permanent or temporary?

Further questions should include:

1. What services are needed to maintain the older person in the community?
2. Would access to day care, home care, and other respite programs strengthen the family and older person's needs? (1979:206–219)

A systems approach using an ecological model provides both the family and service provider with a solid plan of care, maximizing the family's strengths and coping capacities. If the problems call for services that are beyond an identified agency's function, referral to another agency should be undertaken.

FORMAL SERVICES CURRENTLY BEING PROVIDED

To strengthen the family support network to maintain the elder member at home, service providers have initiated and expanded home-based community programs such as home health care, adult day care and respite services to provide emotional support, advocacy and concrete services.

Old age leads to an increased utilization of acute care hospitals, long-term care institutions, and physician's services (McCally 1984). One of the most pronounced determinants has been the implementation, starting in 1983, of a prospective payment system under Medicare, by which hospitals are reimbursed a preset amount for each patient's care, according to the Diagnostic Related Grouping (DRG) of the patient's condition. Prospective payment works to encourage efficiency by providing incentives to hospitals and physicians to limit use of expensive procedures and to reduce length of stay resulting in a larger portion of recuperation occurring after the patient leaves the hospital. This calls for social workers and families to be more actively involved in managing post-hospital care and combining family-care with formally provided services.

In 1985, by conservative figures, over 2.1 million patients substituted home care for care in a hospital or nursing home. Home care implies in-home diagnosis, treatment, monitoring, rehabilitation, and supportive care for independent living (Nassif 1985). It is a holistic concept of care that strives to restore, maintain, and enhance the quality of life despite illness, infirmity, or even impending death, and includes social and other human services, not health services alone.

Home care patients or clients, as they are often called, as well as family caregivers are encouraged to participate actively throughout the plan of care. Home care providers teach self-care and other essential skills so that the individual or family unit experiences less stress and improved coping in daily life. Some home care providers render mainly home health services; others offer nonskilled and supportive services only. Many providers do both.

The burden on family caregivers is eased when the elder is a member of an HMO (Health Maintenance Organization) or SHMO (Social HMO) which provides case management services and a continuum of care. Professional health care varies with the extent and nature of family involvement. For a preset premium, HMO members receive comprehensive health services via the HMO at little or no additional cost.

The Nursing Home Without Walls program is the most innovative, viable and cost-effective alternative to long-term institutionalization and was operationalized in the summer of 1977. The program provides long-term care custom-tailored to the needs of the patient at home, without requiring the patient to fit into a fixed routine of an institution. The program assesses the need for, coordinates, and provides a broad range of health, social and environmental services managed on a 24-hour, seven-day-a-week basis.

The program's range of services, reimbursable by Medicaid, includes nursing, physical therapy, occupational therapy, speech pathology, medical social services, respiratory therapy, nutritional counseling, audiology, medical supplies and equipment, personal care, home health aide, homemaker, housekeeper, social day care, respite care, home-delivered meals, congregate meals, transportation, housing improvement, home maintenance, personal emergency response systems, and moving assistance.

Bereavement programs as integral components of hospice care are limited to post-death service assessment by a social worker and should be expanded to provide services to patients and families along the continuum of illness.

Since 1978 under the OAA's nutrition program, Meals on Wheels services, prepares, packages and delivers a nutritionally balanced noontime meal for the older shut-in person. Some programs also leave food for a cold supper and/or a breakfast. A minimal charge is usually requested. For caregivers who work it has reduced worry regarding lack of nutrition and unhealthy eating habits. For the older person it also provides a regular and predictable contact as well as daily nourishment.

The range of services provided for specific groups of elderly and their families vary from in-home services as well as community based services to reduce and relieve the demand and isolation caregiving can engender.

The National Council on the Aging's National Institute on Adult Daycare (Ranson and Kelly 1985) estimated that in 1985 there were over 1,000 adult day care programs in the United States which provide assistance to many semiambulatory and impaired elderly, while they continue to live with a spouse, family member or alone. For part of the day, in a group setting, maintenance, custodial care, and social activities are provided. In addition, the centers may supply limited medical assistance and rehabilitative/restorative services, such as physical, occupational, speech, reality therapy, social stimulation, as well as family counseling. Self-help and support groups have arisen spontaneously among families who are affiliated with social or health service centers.

Respite and support for family caregivers is a primary objective of adult day care programs. In adult day care, the social worker considers the family as a unit, recognizing the family's critical role in maintaining the disabled older person at home. Through their close and sustained contact with caregivers, social workers gain an understanding and appreciation of the day-to-day problems caregivers face. Social workers are in a unique position to take this information and form a partnership with caregivers and together effect change through advocacy.

One of the first steps in advocacy with and for caregivers is to raise public awareness about the existence and problems of these "hidden patients" in long-term care. To effectively engage caregivers in advocacy, their needs and limitations must be taken into account.

Day care programs are increasingly being developed which serve only demented adults (Panella and McDowell 1984; Ransom and Kelly 1985; Sands and Suzuki 1983). Although there are benefits to this approach in terms of programming and behavior management, it is unrealistic to believe that sufficient numbers of separate programs will be developed to adequately meet the demand for service.

Respite programs are used to relieve stress in family caregivers of patients with Alzheimer's disease and, secondarily, to keep patients in the community as long as possible so that scarce health care resources might be used by a larger number of individuals. Social workers assess the needs of the caregiver which have to be weighed against those of the patient, lest helping the caregiver have an adverse effect on the patient. Worsening of the patient's condition during respite might also lead ultimately to increased caregiver burden and earlier need for long-term hospitalization.

The cognitive and physical impairments of the dementia patients create the need for greater collaboration between the social worker, health care system and the family. Since the prognosis is one of variable but general decline, it is often thought that little can be offered the family once the diagnosis has been made. Social workers provide families with needed information about the illness, help with solving problems encountered in caregiving, render emotional support, and assistance with difficult decisions such as consideration of nursing home placement (Niederehe and Fruge 1984; Ware and Carper 1982; and Zarit and Zarit 1982).

In cases of dementia, the caregivers themselves have a series of major needs. Zarit (1979) suggests that social workers assist family members by providing: 1) information about the nature and prognosis of the patient's disorder; 2) give permission to attend to their own needs; 3) engage in problem solving about coping with the patient's behavioral problems; 4) develop strategies for maximizing the patient's level of functioning; and 5) connect them to supportive social and health services.

A number of social workers have recommended support groups for caregivers to strengthen their morale, provide emotional well-being, and coping skills, all of which are important factors in attaining optimal health and function of the patient with physical and cognitive disabilities. It is safe to assume that all self-help and support groups get their strength from the comfort of members' sharing their perceptions with others who are going through a similar experience. Participation reduces one's sense of being alone in the world. For many, it is only in this group that they feel they are really understood.

Professional social work interventions are certainly useful and needed by many families. It is also true that many families handle the emotional strain of caregiving remarkably well once they have adequate information about their relative's condition and ways of dealing with it. Several informative books are available focusing on a myriad of caregiving issues as well as publications to both educate and sensitize the family to the aging process. Other books are available, specifically for families caring for a member with dementia (Mace and Rabins 1981; McDowell 1980; Powell and Courtice 1983; Reisberg 1981). Families might also be instructed to call local chapters of the Alzheimer's Disease and Related Disorders Association, a self-help network for families dealing with problems and strains presented by relatives with dementia.

Although services to both the elderly disabled person and their families are available, dealing with agencies' inflexible rules and policies or rigid agency boundaries can often frustrate social work clinicians and families. Presently, none of the current or proposed programs adequately addresses the social trends of families as well as the number of caregivers who will be among the "young" and "middle old" age groups.

HELPING THE FAMILY WITH THE TRANSITION TO A NURSING HOME

Institutionalization has generally been viewed as the termination of family caregiving, as a transfer from self or family care to institutional care. Nevertheless, family involvement continues with elderly relatives in long-term care institutions and the data consistently suggests that close family relationships are likely to continue after institutionalization, whereas those that were strained or distant are likely to continue to be so (Chenitz 1983; Hook et al. 1982; Smith and Bengtson 1979).

Institutional placement is often preceded by deteriorating physical and mental status of the elderly person or of the caregiver, rather than deterioration in family ties (Bengtson 1978; Brody 1966; Brody and Spark 1966; Miller and Harris 1965). For many elderly persons and their families, nursing home placement leads to renewed or discovered closeness of familial bonds (Smith and Bengtson 1979). Nursing home placement can relieve relatives from the heavy burdens of physical care, leaving more time and energy for social and emotional care of the elderly relative (Chenitz 1983; Dobrof and Litwak 1977).

Despite family involvement the impact of the decision to place an older person in a nursing home constitutes a major life crisis for the applicant and the family. As Brody et al. state, "Placement of an older parent carries the overtones of the ultimate separation and in psychological terms is a preparation which stimulates the reactions associated with all separations from those in whom there is an emotional investment" (1974:74).

For adult children institutionalization is often experienced psychologically as tantamount to abandonment of a parent, though reality stresses may leave no option. Many families have difficulty discussing a plan of institutional care with the person needing such care. They try to circumvent the fact of permanent institutionalization by giving the relative some hope to relieve anxiety, i.e., "when you get better" or "when I feel better, you can come home."

The emotional problems are multiplied when a spouse is being considered for admission, with the guilt generated being even more intense. There may be social pressure from adult children, siblings, and other family members and friends, particularly if the wife is the caregiver. Often, the feeling expressed is that it is a wife's "duty" to care for her husband in illness and in health. There seems to be less expectation of the male spouse if he is the caregiver.

> Mrs. Elan, 70 years of age, cared for her husband since his onset with Alzheimer's Disease. As his condition began to deteriorate an increase of private homemaker services was obtained. Mrs. Elan had two days of respite when her husband participated in a nearby adult day care program. The Elan's children and grandchildren were emotionally supportive and assisted with household tasks. Although Mr. Elans' physical and cognitive functioning had declined gradually over a number of years, he was able with the assistance of his wife and supportive services to be maintained at home. When Mrs. Elan began to suffer from chronic hypertension, the doctor prescribed an increase of medication to control the illness and suggested she avoid heavy work and emotional excitement to minimize the chance of her having a stroke and heart failure. He further recommended she place her husband in a Nursing Home and referred her to a commu-

nity social worker. The first interview was arranged in the Elan's home and their two daughters were present. Although they recognized their father's worsened condition it was difficult to accept why their mother could not maintain him at home if they paid for additional private services. The worker enabled Mrs. Elan to discuss her feelings around placement and helped the family to consider how it would be with the additional help as well as listening to their fears, concern and anger regarding placement of their father and unrealistic expectations placed on their mother.

In working with a family the social worker must recognize the difficulties experienced by families and help the total family with problems of separation, moving to a strange setting and assuming an unfamiliar life style. Frequently, situations occur where the severely impaired older members no longer recognize family or confuse them with each other. The practitioner should provide emotional support and enable the family to express their sense of loss, depression, unhappiness and anger for the burden carried as well as guilt at their inability to care for the older person. A family that can make an appropriate placement decision with the elder's involvement will suffer less guilt and have more energy for the elder after admission. Questions, concerns and expectations the older person raises are helpful in their coping with a major life style change and reduces the traumatic effects of relocation to a nursing home. The social work clinician should discuss the need for the family and older person to be involved in the medical treatment decision-making process. Discussion of the implication of informed consent for the competent older person, and establishing proxy decision-making procedures for the legally incompetent is essential.

The nature of family involvement with nursing home residents has been the focus of very few studies. In general, it has been shown by the studies (Dobrof 1981; Dobrof and Litwak 1977; Fauerbach 1984; Litwak 1981; Reifler et al. 1981) that technical tasks involving physical or material care needs are performed primarily by the staff, whereas the nontechnical, emotional, or psychosocial care is more likely to be provided by families. In each of these studies variations of the division of technical and nontechnical care between staff and family, respectively, were described. It was emphasized in the studies that incongruence between staff and family perceptions about the division of these tasks may result in redundance and overlap of care. Further, overinvolvement of families in technical care may be seen by staff as interference, whereas overinvolvement of staff in nontechnical care discourages family involvement (Litwak 1981). Based on these findings, several researchers have recommended the development of a partnership between staff and family in which the type of care provided by each group is carefully distinguished. Such a clear division of tasks is intended to encourage family involvement in nontechnical care and to discourage family interference in technical care tasks (Litwak 1981).

Social workers can encourage family members to employ a number of tasks that can establish participation without interference. To compensate for the blandness of institutional food, they can establish a weekly routine of bringing in a home-cooked meal. Bringing in food is also a powerful way for family members to satisfy their need to nurture their relative, give them a sense of control and preserve some ties with home. Taking a family member to a restaurant, provides an opportunity to make choices and to consume foods normally not served in nursing homes. Another helpful practice is for family members to visit once a week on a particular day rather than intermittently or unpredictably. This routine allows their relative to anticipate that day: "Tomorrow is Saturday, the day my daughter comes" (Hooyman and Lustboder 1986).

Families can participate with their older member in a "newcomers" family group or self-help groups organized and run by families. The members have much to offer each other: support, information, and reassurance that they are not alone in their problems.

SERVICE NEEDS OF THE RURAL ELDERLY

One of the more enduring images of rural America is that of the family, self-reliant and caring for its own, especially the elderly. The presumed strength of traditional values particularly those of familial obligation, filial responsibility, and Christian duty thought to characterize rural populations has led to expectations of stronger, better integrated, and more extensive networks of familial support among the rural elderly (Deimling and Huber 1981; Heller 1970, Lee 1980).

Support for greater kin interaction has been provided by Fischer (1982), who found that rural informal support systems contained more relatives, and Antonucci (1985), who reported more extensive informal support networks among rural residents. Krout (1988) noted in his study frequent interaction between urban elderly parents and their children. In addition, Bultena et al. (1971) argued that lower rural population densities and the traditional outmigration of young adults from rural areas has led to a greater physical separation of the rural elderly and their children. The number of miles separating parent and child is a very crude measure of distance. Families with sufficient resources of money and time may be able to bridge the miles with more frequent visits and telephone contacts than can families with fewer resources.

Although for rural families financial assistance between parents and children is not affected by distance (Wilkening et al. 1972), certain kinds of help cannot be given when families are far apart. Regular personal care and daily housework necessitate continuous proximity.

Kivett (1985) and Mercier and Powers (1984) report that rural older adults have higher levels of interaction with friends and neighbors, which suggested that the rural elderly parents might have equal or greater levels of informal support without having more frequent contact with children. Rural elderly do not have more frequent in-person contact with their children and therefore the children may not be likely substitutes for formal service providers.

Although home health services have grown remarkably in recent years, rural areas have not benefited to the same extent as urban ones (Wozny et al. 1984). Cost, scarcity of funding, and shortage of trained personnel have led to an uneven distribution of formal in-home care services in a large number of rural counties (Coward 1983).

Even when such services have been available in rural communities, they have tended to be underutilized because of suspicion, lack of awareness, a strong sense of independence, and a greater reliance upon family, friends, and neighbors (Coyle 1982).

At the same time, in many rural areas little or no respite for family caregivers is available from the community because of the farm crisis (Breytspraak et al. 1986; Northwest Health Services 1986). Farm foreclosures have created a downward spiral in the economy of rural communities. Consequently, elderly person's home health services, normally available through county public health departments, have either been reduced or terminated for lack of funds (Breytspraak et al. 1986).

One response to the problems facing family caregivers is for social workers to use the well-established, accepted existing social networks and organizations in rural communities. Such networks and organizations can provide needed supporting services and help link the elderly and their caregivers to appropriate resources within the community's aging network (Coward 1979). Community social workers need to recognize the power structure within these networks and work within it to realize provision of nursing services to clients. A challenge to social workers is to train these grass roots networks and supply them with easily understood and usable information resources which enable them to help families deal with the stress of caregiving.

SERVICE NEEDS OF THE MINORITY ELDERLY

Ethnicity is an important dimension of differentiation among older people, and may be expected to have an impact on family relationships and supports. Interest in the social, economic and family supports among older minority groups has grown during the last ten years. Demographic trends of the 80's indicate that some older minority groups are among the fastest growing segments of the population. The minority family represents a strong social force in society. "Minority families rely much of the time on their own resources for the provision of social, economic and physical needs of the elderly. This is especially true as the elders' roles outside the family and their economic and physical status begin to decline" (Lockery 1985).

Valle et al. (1978) undertook a major cross-cultural study of minority elders in the San Diego area. They evaluated eight groups—the American Indian, Black, Chinese, Guamanian, Japanese, Latino, Filipino, and Samoan, for family help patterns. The study found that in times of need, the family network, both immediate and extended, was the major means of assistance in these groups.

Weeks and Cuellar (1981) reported that Hispanic elderly in San Diego were less likely to turn to family members in times of need despite the fact that those who live alone have an average of four times more extended kin in the area than nonminority elders. Other researchers have concluded, having kin nearby does not guarantee that sufficient help will be available to minority elders (Weeks and Cuellar 1981; Cantor et al. 1979).

Cantor (1979) examined the informal support system of black and Hispanic groups in New York. The Hispanic elderly tended to have extensive interactions with their children who provided a broad array of caregiving services. Cantor's (1979) study found that "black, Spanish-speaking, and other poor and working-class families are more likely to have highly developed patterns of child-parent interaction arising out of economic and social necessity than is the case among more well-to-do elderly" (1979:50–61).

Cultural beliefs and actual supportive behavior need not be congruent and Rosenthal (1986) has suggested that greater differences among ethnic groups will be found in cultural beliefs about the family rather than in actual supportive behaviors to older family members. Social work practitioners should be alert to the possibility that this lack of correspondence between beliefs and behavior may create problems for the elderly and their children, since people use cultural meanings to make sense of their family lives. The extent to which receiving help from children is perceived as dependency, and the degree of discomfort engendered by dependency, may well be related to a person's system of cultural meanings concerning aging and family relationships. Similarly, the extent to which an adult child perceives giving help to parents as culturally prescribed may affect experienced guilt and the extent to which aid is given without resentment. Cultural prescriptions usually affect the extent to which children expect to assist their parents in later life and may, therefore, be related to greater planning or preparation for the contingencies of the parents' old age.

Each group's cultural traditions have been influenced by their interaction, and the length of time of that interaction, with the dominant culture. Recent immigrants are more likely to try to adhere to traditional family values and functions. Long-term immigrants are more apt to move toward patterns and values of the nuclear family of the American society.

While family supports continue to play a primary role in keeping the minority older person in the community, outside supports are needed to bolster the stressful role of caregivers. Minority families can be strengthened by fully participating in public programs that give support to both the elderly and family members. Since minority elderly are relying more on public programs, all new policies, programs, and services should be developed with the understanding that minority families caring for the elderly will continue to be substantial users of services (Lockery 1985).

HELPING THE FAMILY WITH SPECIAL PROBLEMS

Families will often seek intervention with emotional and behavioral problems of an elder family member. The goal of intervention is to change symptoms into adequate coping, adaptation and growth attained through education and therapy. The social work clinician can redefine the presenting problems and target treatment to include family members, and other informal and formal supports in the older person's network. Some specific problems will be examined in this section.

Drug Misuse

Drug misuse in the elderly comprises two broad categories: self-medication and physician-induced drug misuse. In the first category, self-medication includes drug misuse that is primarily under the control of the older person. This includes under-medication and over-medication due to such behaviors as drug refusal, setting one's own dosages, doctor shopping, and self-treatment with nonprescription drugs (Solomon and Weiner 1983). The category of physician-induced drug misuse includes over-medication or under-medication by the doctor of the basically compliant person who experiences an adverse reaction, such as toxicity or therapeutic failure and, as a result, stops his medication (Giannetti 1983). This behavior is physician-induced because the doctor has failed to effectively monitor the dosage or educate the older person about the medication.

Clinical social work practice with the elderly is insufficient and involvement with the family members and the physician is essential. The desire to alleviate symptoms must be balanced by an approach that also considers complaints to be managed with medications. The design of an appropriate treatment plan for an older person requires comprehensive planning. The goals for treatment need to be clearly set forth and reevaluated at specified intervals. The elder and family members should be approached in a holistic manner by the social work clinician, and consideration given to the unique features of each person's situation.

> Mrs. George was visited by her daughter upon her return from a week's vacation with her family. Mrs. George, an alert, independent 80-year-old woman acted bizarrely and talked irrationally. Although confused Mrs. George responded "no" to any physical complaints. Within hours, the daughter brought her mother for an emergency visit to the out-patient geriatric clinic, where they were seen by a physician and social worker. After asking several questions, Mrs. George gave contradictory responses. When the doctor asked about the medication he prescribed it was evident that Mrs. George was taking a mixture of the new and old prescriptions. This combination could have resulted in exacerbating her cardiac condition, a possible stroke, and account for her current bizarre behavior. The social worker suggested to both Mrs. George and her daughter that they remove the old medications and color code the present medication or use 2 small paper cups and fill them with one capsule the night before. The worker

further requested the physician review with Mrs. George and her daughter why the change in medication and expected outcome. A follow-up call and visit was arranged to detect if the problem was only medication related.

Social workers should educate the elder and his family about his care needs, including the purpose and potential effects of his medications. For this education process to be effective, the elder must have the opportunity to ask questions, raise objections, and indicate his willingness to comply with the recommendations. In the process of talking and listening to each other, the elder person and physician build a partnership in which there should be freedom to communicate openly and honestly. Family members should also have the opportunity to ask questions, raise their own concerns, and offer suggestions.

Skilled social workers can offer a psychogeriatric assessment and linkage from hospital to community to achieve quality and consistency of care. Changing physician attitudes about the needs of the elderly and co-ordinated family and agency services create a better continuum of health care and reduces the elderly's drug mismanagement.

Alcohol Abuse

Aging is widely perceived as a time of stressful events such as retirement, widowhood, and illness. Alcohol use is a well-known and widely used adult strategy for reducing stress. Clinicians can expect some stressed older individuals to drink and to experience increased risk of self destructive behavior to themselves as well as family members suffering the consequences of their alcoholism. Alcoholism has been labeled "the family disease" (Steingloss 1980).

For social workers attending to older adults in clinics or congregate living situations, alcohol abuse, particularly if alcohol is used along with medications, is believed to increase the risk of accidents and unwanted medical side-effects.

These issues may take on special relevance with the elderly and clinicians may feel presumptuous or intrusive asking about it. We may have difficulty accepting the possibility that an older person may drink or get drunk. Our hopelessness about alcoholism in general may be magnified when we deal with the elderly, under the mistaken belief that the prognosis for change is poorer in this population. Finally, we may not understand that drinking to excess is not pleasurable. The belief that we should not deprive an older person of one of his or her "few remaining joys" is, unfortunately, still widely held (Willenbring and Spring 1988).

Routine assessment of alcohol use should be part of every intake evaluation. The social worker should identify a history of drinking as well as serious medical, behavioral and emotional problems that may compound alcohol abuse. Assessment requires a determination of the frequency and quantity of alcohol consumption. If early problematic drinking is identified interventions are most likely to be successful.

> Mr. Benjamin, 68 years of age, had recently been transferred from the hospital to Fairview Nursing Home for rehabilitation after he sustained a stroke. His wife was contacted by the social worker to assess the family situation for Mr. Benjamin's return home in six weeks. Mrs. Benjamin talked openly of the situation prior to her husband's stroke as well as her concern in having to quit her job as a home attendant which was very satisfying and provided supplemental income. As she spoke, she continuously clutched her pocketbook and the social worker noted and addressed the nonverbal behavior. Mrs. B broke into tears, and said she was worried about her husband returning home since the stroke was related to his twenty years of drinking. She felt if she continued to work, he would drink during the day and manipulate the homemaker to bring in alcohol as Mrs. B had sometimes done in the past to keep him home rather than in bars. The social worker suggested they meet with Mr. B and assess how rejoining the family on discharge would result in changes in the family system and his motivation to become active in A.A. and the family in Al-Anon. Detoxification was not suggested since no alcohol was ingested over the past six weeks.

It is important for the social worker to understand the environment in which the older person and their family members live and the importance of interactional factors. Through a clear understanding of "what it is like" in the family, the particular family dynamics can be understood, including the degree to which alcohol is the major organizing principle in the family. Understanding the environment is extremely important in working with the individual and family to plan treatment. The family must be helped to see how their actions promote drinking. Outlining family tasks that can aid the elder in changing this self-destructive behavior should be mutually agreed upon. The worker can confront the older person directly and clarify available options, which include an alcoholism treatment program, hospitalization, joining AA and the family should be encouraged to join Al-Anon.

Recognition that family members of the elder have treatment needs of their own, separate from the needs of the alcoholic members is an essential aspect of treatment. Family therapy, support groups and individual consultation enables abstinence for the elder and helps the family through the transition and new identity for the family with a recovering alcoholic member.

Elder Abuse

Elder abuse consists of the active physical abuse of an elderly dependent parent who is being "cared for" in the home of a relative, often an adult child (McCormack 1980). In its most common and less dramatic form, elder abuse includes exploitation, neglect, and psychological mistreatment (Pedrick-Cornell and Gelles 1982).

Families are the major support for older persons and as a consequence of ineffective coping and stress accumulation they are overtly responsible for abusive acts which include both passive and active neglect, mental anguish, financial exploitation, and the denial of medicines and medical care. Self-inflicted abuse can also occur.

According to Pedrick-Cornell and Gelles (1982), there is clear justification for social workers to consider acts and behavior beyond physical violence as being harmful to the elderly. The fear of being beaten or punished causes as much harm to the victim's functioning as the actual act (Legal Research and Services for the Elderly 1979). The deprivation of needed medicines and medical care can be injurious and life threatening. Financial exploitation, although not life threatening, is a criminal act and deprives the victim of independence, income, and assets.

Social workers can assess high-risk family systems in gathering information for a plan of care. The following characteristics are essential.

Lack of family support. If caregivers have no other relatives available to assist in the care of an older relative, or to provide periodic respite to the caregiver, the total burden of responsibility is placed on their shoulders.

Caregiver reluctance. Reluctance or hesitancy to provide care for an older person can possibly predict poor care and should prompt service providers to consider alternative arrangements for the care of the older person.

Overcrowding. Placement of an elderly person in the dwelling of a family which is already overcrowded may prove unfortunate not only for the older person but also for others in the family. Overcrowding and lack of privacy have been found to lead to intrafamily conflict and could result in anger toward the older person, who is seen as the cause of the inconvenience.

Isolation. Although isolation itself is not a cause of abusive behavior, families who are isolated from others place a vulnerable older person in an invisible position and abusive behavior may go undetected.

Marital conflict. Placement of an older person with a family undergoing marital difficulties should be avoided.

Economic pressures. Families faced with economic pressures resulting from unemployment or other economic problems may resent caring for an older person. Care may necessitate that one of the wage earners, often an adult daughter, quit work to care for the older person.

Intra-family problems. Some families are already subject to burdens, prior to placement of an older relative in their care. To add an additional burden could result in even greater family stress.

Desire for institutionalization. Any family which seeks institutionalization for an elderly relative rather than caring for the person in their own home should be carefully assessed. Clinicians should be cautious in urging family care and assess intergenerational conflicts that may stir up abuse.

Disharmony in shared responsibility. The availability of informal caregivers to share responsibilities does not guarantee the quality of interpersonal relationships in the helping process. There is some suggestion that disharmony between family caregivers can exacerbate the stress on the major caregiver of an elderly person (Kosberg 1988:47).

Elder abuse is one of the last types of family maltreatment to come to public attention. Some of the following interventions should be considered by social work practitioners:

1. Service providers to the elderly need to be educated about the problem of abuse and mistreatment by their children and care providers.
2. The elderly themselves need to be educated about spouse, familial, and formal caregiver abuse. Victims may be vulnerable to spouse abuse because they believe it to be acceptable. They need to be encouraged not to accept it, but rather to see it as a serious problem. Education can reduce the feelings of embar-

rassment and shame at being a victim and thereby make it easier to take action to stop the abuse.

3. Support groups and respite services need to be provided that are tailored to the problem of abuse among the elderly. It may be appropriate to establish safe apartments in congregate housing units where abused elders can take refuge. Consideration of the problem of abuse among the elderly can undoubtedly lead to a great many other policy and service innovations (Pillemer and Finkehor 1988).

Elder abuse will continue as long as ageism and violence exist (Kosberg 1986). Attention must be given to those factors which, although not causing abuse, contribute to its likelihood: poverty and unemployment, lack of community resources, intra-family cycles of abuse, and personal hedonism. Specifically proposed is the assessment of potential caregivers prior to the placement of an elderly person as one method for dealing with the problem of elder abuse.

THEORY

The theoretical work of Litwak (1978; 1985) provides a conceptual framework that permits classification of the functional and affective components of caregiving. With effectiveness as the desired goal, it is required by Litwak's Balance Model of Complimentary Tasks that formal organizations handle uniform tasks efficiently and that primary groups, such as families and neighbors, handle non-uniform tasks humanely. Service delivery is effected by a balance between the formal organization, which can concentrate technical knowledge, organize support services, and operate planfully, and the informal network, which can respond to crises and interact flexibly and personally with the elderly. When the system works, there is a balance between the efficient and the humane.

For the dispersed family, the service delivery continuum is out of balance and broken. The out-of-town relative often cannot provide the local attention required of the informal network and is not able to bridge the gap between the elderly person and the formal organizations in the community; frustration may increase for the caregiver and the elderly person and coping ability may diminish.

Litwak (1985) has further reported that, contrary to popular belief, formal organizations have not taken over the informal network and has suggested that it is the responsibility of the formal system to create a division of labor which allows for maximum service from both systems.

Several studies have noted a hierarchical nature to caregiving preferences and actual behaviors (Cantor 1983; Johnson and Catalano 1983; Sangl 1983). When care is needed, older persons prefer care from family and friends first, friends and neighbors second, and formal agencies and organizations only as a last resort.

Social workers providing services to the elderly should be sensitive to the family's involvement, recognize its value and work with the family and the agency to maximize the contributions of both parties. Linkage between the formal and informal support system should be done in a way that integrates both into a single effective care system. Most gerontologists agree that the integration of both informal and formal support systems foster the family's willingness and ability to care for its aged relative.

POLICY AND FUTURE DIRECTIONS

Caregiving has become one of the most important social and public policy issues of the '80s and beyond. With a greater percentage of the population living to old age and developing chronic impairments associated with advanced age, more and more families will provide care.

Many critics have noted that the United States has no family policy (Padberg 1979). What should be the governmental policy toward family care? What family members should be expected to contribute which goods and services to which relatives? When, if ever, should governments force or even gently persuade family members to provide care? How could public policy make it easier for those families who do provide care? When, if ever, should public policy be directed at helping family members relinquish caregiving tasks?

With the rapidly growing pressure for long-term care services in a time of declining public resources, policy makers are increasingly advocating greater private responsibility in meeting the elderly's needs. In fact, as Brody notes (1981), the informal support system, under the policy rubric of "preserving family ties," is being heralded as the primary resource for the aged. Policy initiatives such as various state Family Responsibility amendments to Medicaid exemplify how concern over spiraling costs has resulted in increased expectations on family caregivers to prevent or delay institutionalization of the elderly.

This issue of family caregiving responsibilities for the elderly has been conceptualized in terms of achieving a balance of responsibility between family and state. Litwak and Figueria (1968), for example, maintain that caregiving functions must be shared since families and bureaucracies are differentially effective in performing certain types of tasks. An "optimal sharing of functions" is achieved when families respond to their members' idiosyncratic, socio-emotional needs and bureaucracies deal with predictable or routine tasks.

Refining Litwak's model of "optimal fit," Nelson (1982) proposes that the state may compete with, complement, or substitute for the roles performed by the family system. He contends that more policies are needed which support the family's important role as a service delivery system for the aged.

The need for more community-based support services has been identified in public hearings, public documents, and publications dealing with gerontology. In pressing for public policy it is indisputable that recognition of the social, economic, and emotional costs of caring for the elderly are too great for the informal system to bear alone and that policies and programs are needed to complement or support the family's caregiving efforts. Through the provision of such services as meal preparation, laundry, house cleaning, transportation, and chore services, the intent would be to minimize the elderly's daily needs for care from informal support systems and, to prevent institutionalization. When such complementary services are reduced or eliminated, the burdens faced by families providing care will increase, resulting in negative consequences for both the informal caregiving system and the elderly.

In the last few years, some states have introduced tax deductions or tax credits for family members who give care. Some states directly pay family members who provide in-home support service. The amounts hardly compensate for a career forgone, but they may be a help, if not an incentive. The 1984 reauthorization of the Older Americans Act mandated training and support groups for the caregivers of persons with Alzheimer's disease. The official enthusiasm for the educational and support-to-the supporters approach may be linked to the inexpensive nature of this approach. But some public policies to assist the caregiver could substantially raise public long-term care costs (Kane 1985).

A new source of social pressure is growing rapidly. Policymakers are talking more and more about "the family" taking greater responsibility for care of frail elderly persons and of bearing a greater share of the financial burden. With increased longevity, more chronic illness and less government support for institutional care, the question of who will care for mom or dad will be asked more frequently.

Society is now poised at an important moment in the social history of the community's response to the dependent and frail elderly. Faced with a basic conflict of how to view the individual in the context of the family poses a dilemma facing service providers at the current time of social and demographic changes. Policies established in the seemingly narrow context of care for the elderly may have far-reaching implications for the fundamental institution of the family. Bayer (1986–1987) states that those who have taken the lead in bringing us to this juncture, have a special responsibility, a moral obligation, to so direct their efforts that the next generation will not look back in dismay at the fact that so many women and men of good intention could have collaborated in a process with so awful an outcome.

REFERENCES

Antonucci, T. C. 1985. Personal characteristics, social support, and social behavior. In E. Shanas and R. H. Binstock, eds., *Handbook of Aging in the Social Sciences.* 2d ed. New York: Van Nostrand Reinhold.

Archbold, P. G. 1982. All-consuming Activity: The Family as Caregiver. *Generations* 5(11):12–13, 40.

Bayer, R. 1986–87. Ethical challenges in the movement for home health care. *Generations* (Winter), pp. 44–47.

Bengston, V. L. 1979. You and your aging parents: Research perspectives on intergenerational interactions. In P. K. Regan, ed., *You and Your Aging Parent.* Los Angeles: University of Southern California Press.

Breytspaak, L., B. Halpert, and T. Sharp. 1986. Effects of Medicare's DRG implementation and the farm crisis on the health care of the rural elderly. Paper presented at meetings of the Gerontological Society of America, Chicago.

Brody, E. 1966. The aging family. *The Gerontologist* 6:201–206.

Brody, E. 1981. Women in the middle and family help to older people. *The Gerontologist* 21:471–480.

Brody, E. 1985. Parent care as a normative family stress. *The Gerontologist* 25:19–29.

Brody, E. and G. Spark. 1966. Institutionalization of the aged: A family crisis. *Family Process* 5:76–90.

Brody, E. et al. 1974. *A Social Work Guide for Long-Term Care Facilities.* National Institute of Mental Health. Washington, D.C.: GPO, 1974.

Brotman, H. B. 1982. *Every Ninth American: An Analysis for the Chairmen of the Select Committee on Aging, House of Representatives, Ninety-Seventh Congress.* Washington, D.C.: Publication No. 97–332, GPO.

Bultena, G. 1969. Rural-urban differences in the familial interaction of the aged. *Rural Sociology* 34:5–15.

Bultena, G., E. Powers, P. Falkman, and D. Frederick. 1971. *Life After Seventy in Iowa: A Restudy of the Aged.* Sociology report 95. Ames: Iowa State University.

Cantor, M. H. 1983. Strain among caregivers: A study of experience in the United States. *The Gerontologist* 23:597–604.

Cantor, M. H. et al., 1979. Social and family relationships of black aged women in New York City. *Journal of Minority Aging* 4:50–61.

Chenitz, C. 1983. Family involvement during institutionalization of an elder: Conflict and change. Presented at dissertation seminar, University of California, San Francisco.

Cicirelli, V. 1981. *Helping Elderly Parents: The Role of Adult Children.* Boston: Auburn House.

Cicirelli, V. 1983. Adult children's attachment and helping behavior to elderly parents: A path model. *Journal of Marriage and the Family* 45:815–824.

Comptroller General of the United States (1977a). *The Well-Being of Older People in Cleveland, Ohio.* Washington, D.C.: RD-77-70, U.S. General Accounting Office.

Coward, R. 1979. Planning community services for the rural elderly. *The Gerontologist* 19:275–282.

Coward, R. T. 1983. Cautions about the role of natural helping networks in programs for the rural elderly. In N. Stinnet, J. DeFrain, K. King, H. Longren, G. Rowe, S. Van Zand, and R. Williams, eds., *Family Strengths. Vol. 4: Positive Supports Systems.* Lincoln, Neb. University of Nebraska Press.

Coyle, J. 1982. Attitudes toward provisions of services to the elderly in rural communities. Paper presented at meetings of the American Public Health Association, Montreal. October.

Deimling, G. and L. Huber. 1981. The availability and participation of immediate kin in caring for the rural elderly. Paper presented at the Annual Meeting of the Gerontological Society of America, Toronto. November.

Dobrof, R. 1981. Guide to practice. In R. Dobrof and E. Litwak, eds., Maintenance of family ties of long-term care patients: Theory and guide to practice. Department of Health and Human Services Publication No. ADM 81-400. Washington, D.C.: GPO.

Dobrof, R. and E. Litwak. *Maintenance of Family Ties of Long-Term Care Patients,* Bethesda, Md.: National Institute of Mental Health.

Fauerbach, M. 1984. Nursing and family perceptions of the family's care task responsibility in the nursing home. Master's thesis, University of Wisconsin-Madison.

Fengler, A. and N. Goodrich. 1979. Wives of elderly disabled men: The hidden patients. *The Gerontologist,* 19(2):175–183.

Fischer, C. S. 1982. *To Dwell Among Friends: Personal Networks in Town and City.* Chicago: Chicago University Press.

Fischer, L. and N. Eustis. 1988. DRG's to family care for the elderly: A case study. *The Gerontologist* 28(3):383–389.

Giannetti, V. O. 1983. Medication utilization problems among the elderly. *Health and Social Work* 8:262–270.

Health Care Financing Administration. 1981. *Long-Term Care: Background and Future Directions.* Washington, D.C.: DHHS Publication No. 81-20047, GPO.

Heller, P. 1970. Familism scale: A measure of family solidarity. *Journal of Marriage and the Family* 32:73–80.

Hoenig, J. and M. W. Hamilton. 1966. Elderly psychiatric patients and the burden on the household. *Psychiatria et Neurologia* (Basel) 154(5):281–293.

Hook, W. F., J. Sobal, and J. C. Oak. 1982. Frequency of visitation in nursing homes: Patterns of contact across barriers in total institutions. *The Gerontologist* 22:424–428.

Hooyman, N. and N. Lustboder. 1986. *Taking Care.* New York: Free Press.

Horowitz, A. 1985. Sons and daughters as caregivers to older parents: Differences in role performance and consequences. *The Gerontologist* 25:612–617.

Johnson, C. I. and D. J. Catalano. 1983. A longitudinal study of family supports to impaired elderly. *The Gerontologist* 23(6):612–618.

Kane, R. 1985. A family caregiving policy: Should we have one? *Generations* (Fall), pp. 33–37.

Kivett, V. R. 1985. Aging in rural society: Non-Kin community relations and participation. In R. T. Coward and G. Lee, eds., *The Elderly in Rural Society.* New York: Springer.

Kosberg, J. 1986. Testimony before the U.S. Senate Subcommittee on children, family, drugs, and alcoholism. Domestic violence and public health. Washington, D.C.: GPO.

Kosberg, J. 1988. Preventing elder abuse: Identification of high risk factors prior to placement decision. *The Gerontologist* 1:43–49.

Krout, J. 1988. Rural versus urban differences in elderly parents' contact with their children. *The Gerontologist* 28:198–203.

Lee, G. R. 1980. Kinship in the seventies: A decade of review of research and theory. *Journal of Marriage and the Family* 42:923–934.

Legal Research and Services for the Elderly. 1979, Elder abuse in Massachusetts: A survey of professionals and paraprofessionals. Manuscript.

Litwak, E. 1978. Agency and family linkages in providing neighborhood services. In D. Thurz and J. Vigilante, eds., *Reaching People: The Structure of Neighborhood Services.* Beverly Hills: Sage.

Litwak, E. 1981. Theoretical bases for practice. In R. Dobrof and E. Litwak, eds., *Maintenance of Family Ties of Long-Term Care Patients: Theory and Guide to Practice.* Department of Health and Human Services Publication No. ADM 81-400. Washington, D.C.: GPO.

Litwak, E. 1985. *Helping the Elderly: The Complimentary Roles of Informal Networks and Formal Systems.* New York: Guilford Press.

Litwak, E. and J. Figueria. 1968. Technological innovation and theoretical functions of primary groups and bureaucratic structure. *American Journal of Sociology,* pp. 468–481.

Locker, R. 1981. Institutionalized Elderly: Understanding and Helping Couples. *Journal of Gerontological Social Work* 3:37–49.

Lockrey, S. 1985. Care in the minority family. *Generations* pp. 27–29.

Lund, D. A., M. A. Pett, and M. S. Caserta. 1988. Institutionalizing dementia victims: Some caregiver considerations. *Journal of Gerontological Social Work* 11:25–37.

Mace, N. 1984. Day care for demented clients. *Hospital and Community Psychiatry* 35:979–994.

Mace, N. and P. V. Rabins. 1981. *The 36-Hour Day: A Family Guide to Caring for Persons with Alzheimer's Disease, Related Dementing Illness, and Memory Loss in Later Life.* Baltimore: Johns Hopkins University Press.

McCally, M. 1984. Epidemiology of illness. In C. K. Cassel and J. R. Walsh, eds., *Geriatric Medicine.* New York: Springer.

McCormack, P. 1980. Battered elderly suffer at hands of loved ones. *Atlanta Journal,* 11, 11–17.

McDowell, F. H., ed. 1980. *Managing the Person with Intellectual Loss (Dementia or Alzheimer's Disease) at Home.* White Plains, N.Y.: Burke Rehabilitation Center.

Mercier, J. M. and E. A. Powers. 1984. The family and friends of rural aged as a natural support system. *Journal of Community Psychology* 12:334–346.

Miller, M. B. and A. Harris. 1965. Social factors and family conflicts in a nursing home population. *Journal of American Geriatrics Society* 13:845–851.

Moss, M. S., S. Z. Moss, and E. L. Moles. 1985. The quality of relationships between elderly parents and their out-of-town children. *The Gerontologist* 25:134–140.

Nassif, J. 1985. *The Home Health Care Solution.* New York: Harper and Row.

Nassif, J. 1986–87. There's still no place like home. *Generations* (Winter), pp. 5–8.

Nelson, G. M. 1982. Support for the aged: Public and private responsibility. *Social Work* 27:137–143.

Niederehe, G. and E. D. Fruge. 1984. Dementia and family dynamics: Clinical research issues. *Journal of Geriatric Psychiatry* 17(1):21–56.

Northwest Health Services. 1986. *Rural Health Crisis.* Kansas City, Mo.: Region 7 U.S. Public Health Services.
Padberg, W. H. 1979. Complexities of family policy: What can be done? *Social Work* 24(6):451–54.
Panella, J. and F. H. McDowell. 1984. *Day Care for Dementia: A Manual of Instruction for Developing a Program.* White Plains, N.Y.: Burke Rehabilitation Center.
Pedrick-Cornell, C. and R. Gelles. 1982. Elderly abuse: The status of current knowledge. *Family Relations* 31:457–465.
Pillemer, K. and D. Finkelhor. 1988. The prevalence of Elder Abuse: A Random Sample Survey. *The Gerontologist* 28:51–57.
Powell, L. S. and K. Courtice. 1983. *Alzheimer's Disease: A Guide for Families.* Reading, Mass.: Addison-Wesley.
Rakowski, W. and N. M. Clark. 1985. Future outlook, caregiving, and care-receiving in the family context. *The Gerontologist* 25:618–623.
Ranson, B. and W. Kelly. 1985. Rising to the challenge. *Perspective on Aging* 14:13–14.
Reifler, B., G. Cox, and R. Hanley. 1981. Problems of mentally ill elderly as perceived by patients' fantasies and clinicians. *The Gerontologist* 21:165–170.
Reisberg, B. 1981. *A Guide to Alzheimer's Disease: For Families, Spouses and Friends.* New York: Free Press.
Remnet, V. L. 1979. Alternatives in Health Care Services. In P. Ragan, ed., *Aging Parents.* Los Angeles: Andrus Gerontology Center, University of Southern California.
Rosenthal, C. 1986. Family supports in later life: Does ethnicity make a difference? *The Gerontologist* 26:19–24.
Sands, D. and T. Suzuki. 1983. Adult day care for Alzheimer's patients and their families. *The Gerontologist* 23:21–23.
Sangl, J. 1983. The family support system of the elderly. In R. Vogel and H. Palmer, eds., *Long-Term Care: Perspectives from Research and Demonstrations.* Washington, D.C.: Health Care Financing Administration.
Shanas, E. 1979. Social myth as hypothesis: The case of the family relations of old people. *The Gerontologist* 19:3–9.
Simmons, S., J. Ivry, and M. Seltzer. 1985. Agency family collaboration. *The Gerontologist* 25:343–346.
Smith, K. and V. L. Bengtson. 1979. Positive consequences of institutionalization: Solidarity between elderly parents and their middle-aged children. *The Gerontologist* 19:438–447.
Soldo, B. J. and J. Myllyluoma. 1983. Caregivers who live with dependent elderly. *The Gerontologist* 23(6):605–611.
Solomon, J. and A. Weiner. 1983. Drug misuse in the elderly. In L. A. Pagliaro and A. M. Pagliaro, eds. *Pharmacologic Aspects of Aging.* St. Louis: C. V. Masby.
Steingloss, P. 1980. A life history of the alcoholic family. *Family Process* 19:211–226.
Steingloss, P. 1980. Assessing families in their own homes, *American Journal of Psychiatry* 12: 1523–1529.
Stoller, E. P. and L. L. Earl. 1983. Help with activities of everyday life: Sources of support for the noninstitutionalized elderly. *The Gerontologist* 23(1):64–70.
Sussman, M. B., (1976). "The Family Life of Old People." In *Handbook of Aging and the Social Sciences.* New York: Van Nostrand Reinhold.
Taeuber, C. M. 1983. *America in Transition: An Aging Society.* US Bureau of the Census, Current Population Reports, Series P-23, No. 128, Washington, D.C.: GPO.
Tobin, S. S. and R. Kulys. 1980. The family and services. *Annual Review of Gerontology and Geriatrics* 1:371–399.

Townsend, P. 1968. The structure of the family. In E. Shanas, P. Townsend, et al., eds., *Old People in Three Industrial Societies*. New York: Atherton Press.

Troll, L. E. and J. Smith. 1976. Attachment through the life span: Some questions about dyadic bonds among adults. *Human Development* 19:156–170.

U.S. Senate Special Committee on Aging and American Association of Retired Persons. 1984. *Aging America: Trends and Projections*. Washington, D.C.: GPO.

Valle, R. et al. 1978. *A Cross-Cultural Study of Minority Elders in San Diego*. San Diego: Campanile Press.

Walsh, F. 1980. The family in later life. In E. A. Carter and M. McGoldrick, eds., *The Family Life Cycle: A Framework for Family Therapy*. New York: Gardner Press.

Ware, L. A. and M. Carper. 1982. Living with Alzheimer disease patients: Family stresses and coping mechanisms. *Psychotherapy: Theory, Research and Practice* 19:472–81.

Wasow, M. 1986. Support groups for family caregivers for patients with Alzheimer's disease. *Social Work* 31(2):93–97.

Weeks, J. R. and J. B. Cuellar. 1981. The role of family members in the helping networks of older people. *The Gerontologist* 21:388–394.

Wilkening, E. at al. 1972. Distance and intergenerational ties of farm-families. *The Sociological Quarterly* 13:383–396.

Willenbring, M. and W. Spring. 1988. Evaluating alcohol use in elders. *Generation* 4:27–31.

Wozny, M. C., S. F. Knapp, J. E. Burkhardt, M. J. Ramadel, L. Norton, and A. M. Lago. 1984. *Cost of Services to the Elderly*. Bethesda, Md.: Institute for Economic and Social Measurements.

York, J. L. and R. J. Caslyn. 1977. Family involvement in nursing homes. *The Gerontologist* 17:500–5.

Zarit, S. H. and J. M. Zarit. 1983. Families under stress: Interventions for caregivers of senile dementia patients. *Psychotherapy* 19:461–71.

Zarit, S. H., K. E. Reever, and J. Bach-Peterson. 1980. Relatives of the impaired aged: Correlates of feelings of burden. *The Gerontologist* 20:(6)649–55.

Zarit, S. H., N. K. Orr, and J. M. Zarit. 1985. *The Hidden Victims of Alzheimer's Disease: Families Under Stress*. New York: New York University Press.

12

Services to Widows and Elderly Women

BARBARA LEVY SIMON, PH.D.
Columbia University School of Social Work

The sixteen million women in the United States who are 65 years old or older are a highly heterogeneous lot, yet face common risks because of their gender, age, and single, or prospectively single, status (U.S. Census 1987). The resilience many of these elderly women have demonstrated over time is chronically tested in old age by financial and physical vulnerabilities; by the deaths of spouses, friends, relatives, and lovers; and by the continuing prejudices, discrimination, and neglect that they encounter in a society that has yet to assign adequate respect, roles, and resources to its older women and widows.

Most women in the United States become widows. Most women, consequently, endure the quadruple losses of widowhood: the loss of a key relationship, the loss of social and legal status, the loss of identity that stems from the loss of social role, and the loss of income (Lopata and Brehm 1986; Silverman 1986). Yet, widowhood is a transition that entails far more than these grievous losses; it is a process that requires the transformation of identity and daily life. As Lopata has noted, widowhood is a temporary stage of identity reconstruction with little social standing or meaning of its own (Lopata 1979). It is a way station on the journey to a new life after marriage.

Each widow undergoes three predictable phases, according to Silverman (1986). First, she endures the impact of the disequilibrating event of a spouse's death. This major phase of disruption is characterized by her numbness and disbelief in the face of the extreme stress of her loss. She tends to behave "as if" nothing has happened, relying on old roles and behaviors to get through the immediate aftermath of her husband's death.

The widow then moves into a phase of recoil (Silverman 1986). As her numbness wears off, the growing realization of the profundity of her loss brings her searing pain, grief, and, often, anger. She feels that she has lost part of her self and begins to glimpse the magnitude of change that has already occurred. Disruptions in sleeping and eating patterns frequently accompany this most painful of times.

Accommodation eventually follows recoil (Silverman 1986). As a widow's grief and despair gradually diminish over time, she develops a partial acceptance of her losses and the changes that attend these losses. She necessarily seeks to find a new sense of self, a new set of roles and initiatives, and relationships, both old and new, within which she can build an altered reality. Often, she finds support among other women who have also become widows.

Widows, together with still-married, never-married, divorced, and separated women who are among the very-old (85 years and older) make up the fastest growing segment of the elderly in the United States (Field and Minkler 1988). Their needs occupy one significant section of a continuum shared with old-old (75–84 years old) and young-old (65–74 years old) women. What are the contemporary needs of non-institutionalized women who are married and single? How do the salient needs of frail elderly women differ from those who are well? How do minority elderly women fare? Does rural, suburban, or urban residence affect elderly women's chances of receiving needed services? What gerontological services and policies respond to both shared and particular needs of the non-institutionalized female elderly?

NEEDS OF NONINSTITUTIONALIZED ELDERLY WOMEN AND WIDOWS

In contrast with American elderly men, three-fourths of whom are married and live with their wives, three-fifths of elderly women have no spouse. Most of these single elderly women are widowed; 5.2 percent are never-married; 4.4 percent are divorced; and a small remainder are separated. Not surprisingly, given the historic segregation of women in unpaid or poorly paid work and their consequent economic dependence upon men, many older women without spouses are in severe economic straits. Almost 90 percent of the elderly poor are drawn from this group of widowed, never-married, divorced, and separated women (U.S. Census 1987; Minkler and Stone 1985). As of

1983, 44.3 percent of women, compared with 18.2 percent of men in the U.S. 65 and older, had a total annual money income of $4,999 or less (Rix 1984). Black single women 65 years old or older lived on even less. They averaged only 70 percent of the total income in old age of their white single counterparts (Chen 1985).

Despite encouraging decreases in the poverty rate of the non-institutionalized elderly since 1960, a growing concentration of poverty is evident among elderly women living alone. By 1984, 52 percent of all poor elderly in the United States were single women living alone (Holden 1988). Dramatic increases over the past four decades in the proportion of elderly women living alone, from only 14 percent in 1950 to 41.3 percent in 1986, highlight this group as one requiring in-kind assistance, additional cash transfers, and more complete dependence on formal social services than do the married elderly (Holden 1988; U.S. Census 1987).

Social isolation, in addition to poverty, is a risk that accompanies the increasing proportions of older women who live alone. Though many single elderly women maintain vital networks of friends, relatives, and confidants, a significant percentage do not (Cohen and Syme 1985; Kendig et al. 1988; Rathbone-McCuan and Hashimi 1982; Silverman and Cooperband 1975; Simon 1987). Single elderly women who are at particular risk of isolation are those who belong to two or more of the following categories: the impoverished, those living in rural areas, those living in settings without a comprehensive public transportation system, the homebound, the mentally disabled, undocumented elderly immigrants, and the childless (Bender and Hart 1987; Rodeheaver and Datan, 1988). Prolonged social isolation among the elderly can contribute to physical inactivity, poor health, poor nutrition and weight loss, depression and other mental disorders, drug and alcohol abuse, and suicide (Bender and Hart 1988; Blazer, Hughes, and George 1987; Fellin and Powell 1988; Lopata 1987; Rathbone-McCuan and Hashimi 1982; Shifflett 1987).

Bereavement alone does not appear to place widows and other women who have lost long-term companions at appreciable psychological or physical risk (Blazer, Hughes, and George 1987; Neugarten 1987; Norris and Murrell 1987). Indeed, mourning is managed with "minimal mortality and morbidity by most people" (Norris and Murrell 1987: 611). However, widowhood does bring forth increased risks of diminished finances, reduced social contact and activity, and the loss of a home. (Lopata 1987; Rodeheaver and Datan 1988).

By contrast, caregiving by elderly women does constitute a major threat to their physical and mental health (Brody 1985; Horowitz 1985; Norris and Murrell 1987; Rodeheaver and Datan 1988; Simon

1988). More than a third of all primary caregivers of chronically and terminally ill Americans are elderly: 25.4 percent of primary caregivers are 65–74 years old; 10.1 percent are 75 years old and older (Stone, Cafferata, and Sangle 1987). Elderly caregivers are at great risk of "stress, anxiety, and, consequently, the use of psychotropic drugs" (Rodeheaver and Datan 1988:649). The needs of elderly caregivers encompass a wide range of financial, instrumental, and emotional domains that require an equally wide range of programmatic responses.

ASSESSMENT

The striking heterogeneity of need among elderly women, widows, and caregivers imposes on social workers and other geriatric and gerontological specialists an important challenge—that of developing assessment approaches that are, on the one hand, sufficiently nuanced to capture the particularities of a client's context, cultural and familial traditions, and psychosocial and physiological makeup, and, on the other hand, are coherent enough to identify the common needs of older people who come from diverse backgrounds.

Sophisticated assessment of elderly women requires the professional to sidestep three kinds of mistakes commonly made by diagnosticians. One frequent error of practitioners is to overlook significant and treatable mental and physical conditions that appear to be part of the normative aging process. For example, depression, alcoholism, drug abuse, and iatrogenic drug reactions are often ignored because their symptoms are misunderstood to be inevitable and irreversible dimensions of senescence (Rodeheaver and Datan 1988). A second common confusion in assessing older women is that of misdiagnosis: depression, alcoholism, and psychotropic drug abuse among elderly women are frequently misdiagnosed as Alzheimer's disease and therefore left untreated. A third frequent error is that of presuming that the physiological symptoms of menopausal and post-menopausal women are primarily psychological issues necessitating psychological treatment (Cowan, Warren, and Young 1985). In such circumstances, thorough exploration of physiological causes and medical remedies or palliatives is neglected.

Fortunately, practitioner alertness concerning these common mistakes in diagnosis can reduce markedly their incidence. Also encouraging is the growing availability, primarily in urban areas, of multidisciplinary assessment teams that combine geriatric medical evaluations; neuropsychological (cognitive) testing of attention, memory, reasoning, language, and visuospatial skills; detailed evaluations of competence in daily functioning; and psychosocial assessments of morale, environment, nutrition, and social and economic resources (Kapust and Weintraub 1988). The Home Visit Assessment, which combines systematic observation of daily functioning in people's own settings with a questionnaire completed by a clinician or family member who is a primary caregiver, has proved particularly useful to social workers working with older women (Kapust and Weintraub 1988). The Older Americans Resources and Services instrument (OARS), the Philadelphia Geriatric Center Morale Scale, and the Center for Epidemiological Studies Depression Scale (CES-D), also have proved helpful in assessing, respectively, personal functioning, subjective well-being, and levels of depression (Blazer, Hughes, and George 1987; Blazer and Williams 1980; Kozma and Stones 1987; Krause 1987; Liang et al. 1987). The Short Psychiatric Evaluation Schedule (SPES), a simple summative self-report that is a much-shortened version of the Minnesota Multiphasic Personality Inventory, constructs a usable index of mental health and psychopathology that encompasses anxiety, depression, suspiciousness, hypochondriasis, cognitive impairment, and many other common physical manifestations and emotional disturbances (Arling 1987).

INTERVENTION

Despite the diminution of federal funding for services to the aged during the Reagan years, geriatric services for noninstitutionalized elderly women and widows have mushroomed during the 1980s as mutual aid networks, state governments, Area Councils on Aging, profit-making geriatricians, and voluntary not-for-profit agencies responded to the exploding demand from the aged and their families for programs and services. From the most well to the most frail, from the 65-year-old to the centenarian, older women living in the community now may tap an elaborate continuum of informal and formal programs, provided that they have adequate knowledge, initiative, and literacy to demand those services for which they are eligible and proximate. Senior citizen centers, community centers, enriched housing projects, houses of worship, unions, workplaces, libraries, health and mental health organizations, and universities constitute the key sites of contemporary lay and professional programs for elderly women.

Mutual Help Groups

Mutual help groups, one of the fastest growing fronts of geriatric care, offer myriad informal supports to older and widowed women undergoing some form of transition in status (Silverman 1985). In the tradition of immigrant mutual aid societies and neighbors' self-help initiatives, groups of elderly widows; caregivers; hysterectomy, colostomy, and mastectomy survivors; divorcees; and retirees from diverse occupations meet regularly and provide reciprocal support, telephone reassurance, and detailed information and referrals. Some groups are without auspice; others are sponsored by area councils on aging, the American Association of Retired Persons, mental health associations, churches or synagogues, hospices, or hospitals (Silverman 1985). Many members of mutual aid groups find their way to them through the referrals of social workers, some of whom serve as consultants to self-help groups.

Assisting mutual aid organizations is one important dimension of the gerontological work that social workers and other geriatric professionals perform. Equally significant is their creation of a progression of more formal supports for noninstitutionalized elderly women, widows, and caregivers in community-based settings and in the women's homes. This set of formalized geriatric services for elderly women and widows currently has five essential parts: 1) preventive community support services for expanding the self-care capacities of well elderly women who are mobile; 2) in-home services for nonmobile elders who are minimally and moderately impaired; 3) special community services for the non-institutionalized frail elderly who require complements to their in-home care; 4) pre-retirement programs and services devoted to the enrichment of elderly women's health and welfare during retirement and the prevention of unnecessary mental and physical decline; and 5) gerontologic education and training of providers of concrete, health, and mental health services to the well and frail elderly living in the community. Each of these five segments of service merits separate attention below.

Community-Based Services for Well Elderly Women

An encyclopedic array of activities and material and emotional supports for well elderly women has sprung up over the past quarter century in senior citizen centers, unions, and other community institutions. Bereavement counseling, training and counseling for elderly family caregivers of the chronically and terminally ill, oral history projects, and medical self-help classes are four examples of newer forms of support that have become available in the 1980s in community agencies long accustomed to offering educational and cultural offerings, recreational workshops, health and nutritional aids, income supplements, information and referral services, crisis intervention, transportation, and case management services. Another notable innovation of the recent past is Elderhostel, a moderately priced series of noncredit, college-level seminars, short courses, and educational tours designed especially for small groups of the well elderly by universities and colleges in the United States and abroad.

At this point in time, the unimpaired elderly woman who is free enough from caregiving responsibilities to find time to walk into a program for the well aged would require herculean energy to take part in all or even most of the cultural and educational activities offered at any one site. Therefore, she would need to pick and choose among the cultural caravans, parties, exercise and dance groups, lecture series, discussion groups, structured reminiscing, creative writing worshops, arts and crafts activities, music lessons, courses at local high schools and colleges, and newsletters written by and for aged women.

In between cultural activities, she might choose to take in hot communal meals, training in advocacy and political participation, and health and nutritional screenings and workshops on subjects like osteoporosis and glaucoma. Like many well elderly women, she might engage in volunteer activity during some part of her week, punctuating this contribution with attendance in consumer education classes, crime prevention workshops, financial management classes, tax preparation seminars, and conversations with experts in legal aid, public assistance, Social Security, Medicare or Medicaid, or Supplemental Security Income. The enterprising well elderly woman might also attempt to supplement her income through participation in job training and placement, food coops, thrift shops, crafts shops, and workshops in auto and small appliance repair.

In-Home Services

In contrast, elderly women who are homebound have far fewer services available to them. Nonetheless, social workers and other geriatric professionals and paraprofessionals provide vital in-home supports without which institutionalization would be imminent for many moderately impaired women. Home-delivered meals, homemaker services, home health care, repair and winterization assistance, home safety audits, shopping services, escort help, friendly visiting, telephone reassurance, and televised educational programs are some of the programs delivered at home. In addition, social workers provide case management services, crisis intervention, and individual counseling to homebound women.

Special Services

In some suburban and urban communities, social workers and nurses offer adult day care and respite care programs for the moderately and severely impaired elderly. Such services aid elderly women caregivers as much as dependent elderly persons by giving the former temporary rest from the chronicity of long-term care. Both adult day care and respite care thereby address preventive and therapeutic goals simultaneously. Social workers also offer protective services for those elderly who are at risk of abuse or neglect. In a few areas of the United States, short-term, community geriatric hospitals offer medical services that preclude premature institutionalization of older people who are undergoing acute illnesses or difficult flare-ups of chronic diseases.

Since women make up 74 percent of all Americans 75 years old and older who have functional limitations due to chronic conditions, they constitute the overwhelming majority of the clientele of adult day care programs, respite care facilities, community-based geriatric hospitals, and geriatric wings of general hospitals (U.S. Census 1987;108–109). These services have become, de facto, programs for elderly women and widows by virtue of the demographic realities of the old and old-old. Discharge planning in respite care programs and hospitals, as a consequence, has emerged as a critical point in the delivery process of health care and social supports for aged women. As Medicare Diagnostic Related Groups (DRG's) force shorter and shorter stays in hospitals, despite the complex, multiple health problems of older people, discharge planners find themselves rarely able to consider the special needs of older women in the face of the scarcity of available family caregivers, of community-based programs for the frail elderly, of enriched housing for the aged, and of quality nursing homes.

Pre-Retirement Programs

Social workers and health educators, in increasing numbers of employer-based, union-sponsored, and senior center pre-retirement programs, address the needs of elderly women and widows long before program participants reach old age and widowhood. Mid-life women with access to such programs investigate concrete issues such as financial planning for retirement, part-time employment, job finding and job training, entrepreneurial possibilities in retirement, housing options, and relocation advantages and disadvantages. Many pre-retirement programs also help women explore health and mental health issues such as nutrition in old age, caregiving pressures, menopausal and post-menopausal effects, long-term care choices, the vicissitudes of widowhood, sex and sexuality in old age, and the prevention of such gender-specific diseases as osteoporosis, breast cancer, and uterine cancer.

Training of Providers

Since most elderly women and widows necessarily call upon the services of many kinds of professionals after, approximately, age 75, geriatric specialists have created educational modules and training segments for providers who are most likely to offer services to older people. These training projects are designed to sharpen the diagnostic and interventive skills of professionals by expanding their knowledge base concerning normative aging processes, the particular diseases of the aged, the socioeconomic realities of aged women, and cultural barriers that still confine old women.

An impressive variety of professionals and students in professional schools currently take part in training, among them: social workers, psychologists, physicians, nurses, chiropractors, pharmacists, allied health professionals, podiatrists, lawyers, and pastors. In a few regions, nonprofessional service providers such as gas meter readers, grocers, nurses' aides, beauticians, home health aides, mail deliverers, and apartment building supervisors are also systematically sensitized to the needs of the elderly (Fellin and Powell 1988). Training content includes such topics as detection of the initial signs of elder abuse, Alzheimer's disease, diabetic coma, stroke, depression, psychosis, suicidal moods, malnutrition, poly-drug abuse, and alcoholism. Participants also learn to offer information and referral services and to report suspected abuse or neglect.

Interventive Lacunae

As rich as contemporary geriatric programming has become since the late 1960s, many older women have yet to benefit from the abundant array of services described here. Like so many other resources of American society, services for elderly women are distributed differentially by race, class, geographic location, and legal status.

Black, Hispanic, Asian, and Native American women among the old and old-old continue to be significantly poorer, sicker, and shorter-lived than their white counterparts in the United States (Chen 1985; Die and Seelbach 1988; Fellin and Powell 1988; Ferraro 1987; Mahard 1988; Markides and Levin 1987; McDonald 1987; Pelham and Clark 1987; Taylor and Chatters 1988). As a result of limited educational opportunities, segregation into jobs with scant pay and no health benefits, and de facto exclusion from many unions and unionized jobs, minority and immigrant women over 65 years of age represent the population groups among the elderly at highest risk of ill health, early mortality, impoverishment, and malnutrition (Chen 1985; Jones 1985; Taylor and Chatters 1988). They are the least likely among American retirees to own a home, to have savings, to own a car, and to have a pension. Most elderly minority women who earned their living in domestic or agricultural labor rely in old age almost wholly upon their family, church, and community for retirement income and housing since they were uncovered by the Social Security system throughout all or most of their work lives. Immigrant retirees who are not citizens, ineligibles for Supplemental Security Income, Social Security, public housing, and Medicaid, similarly turn to informal social supports for survival. Geriatric professionals who have succeeded in attracting minority and immigrant elderly women into community-based formal services and in-home service networks have done so primarily through channeling resources and workers through church and neighborhood networks (Die and Seelbach 1988; McDonald 1987).

Six million rural old women constitute another impoverished, isolated, and underserved group. (Bender and Hart 1987; Krout 1988). Many services for the well and frail elderly now available to urban and suburbanites are far from the residences and consciousness of the rural elderly. Fortunately, a few model health promotion programs for the rural old have emerged at National Health Service Corps (NHSC) clinics. This prevention and advocacy work focuses upon health education and screening, nutrition, exercise, and safety programs for the old and very-old (Bender and Hart 1987). Regrettablly, the Reagan administration has dramatically cut funding for NHSC clinics for 1988–1989, leaving rural elderly women without public health service complements to family and church supports.

Emergent Services

A few, particularly promising projects that currently serve only a tiny proportion of the elderly may achieve the legitimacy and funding required to reach many more people in the 1990s. In some areas of the country, social health maintenance organizations (SHMOs) deliver pre-paid acute and chronic health care to Medicare beneficiaries (Fischer and Eustis 1988). Designed to reduce the costs and improve the quality of acute and chronic care for the elderly. SHMOs offer a continuum of health and mental health screening, assessment, care planning, case management, counseling, and care monitoring services.

Also in a pilot phase are aging resource centers for help (ARCHs), a program proposed by Robert Binstock (Binstock 1987). These centers, to be funded by Title III of the Older Americans Act, will create a nationwide network of resource centers responsible for assessment, planning, and information and referrals for the rural, suburban, and urban elderly. ARCHs will coordinate initial contact with the elderly, emergency responses, counseling, and material assistance without delivering direct services.

For more than a quarter century, life care communities, also known as continuing care retirement communities, have provided community, housing, and self-insured long-term care to those who have joined and paid the initial premiums and monthly fees. Several Quaker-run, life care communities near Philadelphia and the North Hill Community Care Retirement Center in Needham, Massachusetts, are thriving examples of voluntary, self-insurance entities (Branch 1987). These groups offer a five-part continuum of geriatric care that includes: 1) independent housing and physical maintenance; 2) community amenities, such as laundry and housekeeping services, social services, cultural activities, security, transportation, and one communal meal each day; 3) in-home support services as needed, including help with bathing, dressing, financial management, and household management; 4) in-home nursing services, both short and long-term; and 5) contractually guaranteed nursing home care in the same setting as the independent housing. Members of life care communities pay no added out-of-pocket expenses nor co-payments for long-term care received at home or in the community's health clinic or nursing home. Geriatric planners currently search for ways to extend the availability of this model in the future to low and moderate-income old people, as well as to larger numbers of middle- and upper-middle class elders.

TOWARD A SUBSTITUTION OF THEORIES

Nineteenth-century essentialist theory concerning gender has often informed the choices of planners, service deliverers, and social work clients in the past and in the present. Essentialism posits the premise that men and women are inherently different and complementary in emotional, moral, intellectual, and social capacities, as well as in physiological ones. Socialization processes, the essentialist thinker argues, only compound distinctions that are already inborn. A doctrine of separate spheres follows from essentialist theory—men are assumed to belong primarily in the public realm, and women in the private (Coward 1983).

The pervasiveness of this notion continues to have direct consequences for mid-life and elderly women and men, despite the obvious datedness of the theory. Women still view themselves as "natural" housekeepers and caregivers who will take charge of households and the care of loved ones over time regardless of their own health and welfare. Discharge planners and geriatric professionals count on the domesticity and altruism of mid-life and elderly women in devising long-term care strategies for male and female patients. Widowers are targeted as top priorities for in-home services and bereavement counseling because they are assumed to be far more at risk, constitutionally, for mental depression, home accidents, and malnutrition than are widows. In short, men's adaptiveness is taken for granted in the public sphere, yet derided in the private. Efforts on the part of churches and community groups to involve elderly women in volunteering during retirement appear to be far more energetic and systematic than campaigns to involve aged men.

Essentialism operates as much on the unconscious and preconscious levels of thinking and feeling as on the conscious. Consequently, it remains a potent theory and force for stereotyping and underestimating both men and women in old age.

A far more fitting theoretical construct for analyzing the complex needs and contributions of older Americans of the 1990s and beyond is that of social constructionism. Social constructionists assume that reality as we know it is constructed and interpreted by human beings who are using the language and categories of understanding of a particular tradition, time, and place (Conrad and Schneider 1980). According to this theoretical perspective, a person's "life chances," the choices and stable social bonds that together constitute his or her opportunities, are shaped much less by inherent individual attributes than by the niche one occupies in the social structure, a niche largely determined by generation, age, gender, nationality, regional affiliation, family of origin's social class, religion, and the nature of education and training available to one's parents and oneself (Dahrendorf 1979).

Any given society constructs in each historical period differential expectations, roles, rewards, and penalties for its members. Gender roles are one form of social construct; age-specific roles are another. Such roles, having been created by historical actors and forces, can be partially or totally reconstructed by others. So, for example, a culture that treats retired men and women over the age of 70 as superfluous beings can choose in the twenty-first century to become a culture that relies upon septuagenarian leadership in work, the family, and public life. Or, to use another illustration, a society that historically has rewarded men for protecting women and women for caring for men can evolve into one that requires each gender to perform both functions for each other.

POLICY ISSUES

Most discussions of policy concerning the noninstitutionalized elderly call for the increased integration of formal and informal service delivery systems. This essay will prove no exception, especially since women serve such a salient role in the provision of informal care. The urgency of developing a coordinated progression of services that extends from self-care for the most independent to nursing homes for the most dependent is never more evident than when examining the gaps in services and reimbursement for elderly women who deliver long-term care and for the old-old who receive such care.

Social Security reform is another policy domain in which elderly women and widows have special interest. Women homemakers and mothers still earn no Social Security benefits for their own labor at home. Widows' benefits continue to be calculated on the standard of living of a couple at the time of a husband's death, rather than at the time at which benefits were first paid. This practice poses a significant monetary disadvantage for survivors. Single women workers pay the same percentage of taxes to social security yet receive less retirement and survivor's coverage than do their married counterparts. Divorced women who were married fewer than ten years are entitled to no social security benefits in relation to their ex-spouses. Women with discontinuous labor histories, the vast majority of female retirees in the late 1980s, receive meager social security in their own right (Minkler and Stone 1985).

The Medicare DRGs have shortened hospital stays of elderly men and women without due regard for the complexity of their chronic and acute conditions or for the consequences for family caregivers. The development of a "severity or intensity index" in the official Medicare Diagnostic Related Groups would assist hospital staff in designating the duration of hospital treatment for the elderly based on individual need, without penalizing the hospital's reimbursements (NYS Task Force on Older Women 1986).

Finally, it behooves us as geriatric specialists who work with elderly women and widows to devise better collaboration between Area Agencies on Aging, community mental health centers, and physicians. Family caregivers require more help in understanding and responding to the multiple symptoms of their mentally or physically ill charges. Professionals, as well as voluntary care deliverers, would benefit from accessible consultation when trying to differentiate between the normative processes of aging and mental dysfunction brought on by organic disorder, alcoholism, poly-drug abuse, or iatrogenic drug reactions. Post-menopausal women and their providers would be less likely to "psychologize" physiological effects if aging, health, and mental health professionals worked more closely together.

As the feminization of poverty and the "graying of America" converge near the end of the twentieth century, increasing numbers of very old women are living longer lives with fewer dollars. Imagination, funding, and commitment must also converge if we are to devise programs and policies that will enable the noninstitutionalized old-old in our midst, most of whom are women, to do more than merely survive.

REFERENCES

Arling, G. 1987. Strain, social support, and distress in old age. *Journal of Gerontology* 42:107–113.

Bender, C. and J. P. Hart. 1987. A model for health promotion for the rural elderly. *The Geronotologist* 27:139–142.

Binstock, R. H. 1987. Title III of the Older Americans Act: An analysis and proposal for the 1987 reauthorization. *The Gerontologist* 27:259–265.

Blazer, D., D. C. Hughes, and L. K. George. 1987. The epidemiology of depression in an elderly community population. *The Gerontologist* 27:281–287.

Blazer, D. and C. D. Williams. 1980. Epidemiology of dysphoria and depression in an elderly population. *American Journal of Psychiatry* 137:439–444.

Branch, L. G. 1987. Continuing care retirement communities: Self-insuring for long-term care. *The Gerontologist* 27:4–8.

Brody, E. M. 1985. Parent care as a normative family stress. *The Gerontologist* 25:19–29.

Chen, Y. 1985. Economic status of the aging. In R. H. Binstock and E. Shanas, eds., *Handbook of Aging and the Social Sciences* 2d ed. New York: Van Nostrand.

Cohen, S. and S. L. Syme. 1985. *Social Support and Health.* New York: Academic Press.

Conrad, P. and J. W. Schneider. 1980. *Deviance and Medicalization: From Badness to Sickness.* St. Louis: C. V. Mosby.

Cowan, G., L. W. Warren and J. L. Young. 1985. Medical perceptions of menopausal symptoms. *Psychology of Women Quarterly* 9:3–14.

Coward, R. 1983. *Patriarchal Precedents: Sexuality and Social Relations.* London: Routledge & Kegan Paul.

Dahrendorf, R. 1979. *Life Chances: Approaches to Social and Political Theory.* Chicago: University of Chicago Press.

Die, A. H. and W. C. Seelbach. 1988. Problems, sources of assistance, and knowledge among elderly Vietnamese immigrants. *The Gerontologist* 28:449–452.

Fellin, P. A. and T. J. Powell. 1988. Mental health services and older adult minorities: An assessment. *The Gerontologist* 28:443–447.

Ferraro, K. F. 1987. Double jeopardy to health for black older adults? *Journal of Gerontology* 42:528–533.

Field, D. and M. Minkler. 1988. Continuity and change in social support between young-old and old-old or very-old age. *Journal of Gerontology: Psychological Sciences* 43:P100–106.

Fischer, L. R. and N. N. Eustis. 1988. DRGs and family care for the elderly: A case study. *The Gerontologist* 28:383–389.

Holden, K. C. 1988. Poverty and living arrangements among older women: Are changes in economic well-being underestimated? *Journal of Gerontology: Social Sciences* 43:522–527.

Horowitz, A. 1985. Sons and daughters as caregivers to older parents: Differences in role performances and consequences. *The Gerontologist* 25:612–617.

Jones, J. 1985. *Labor of Love, Labor of Sorrow.* New York: Basic Books.

Kapust, L. R. and S. Weintraub. 1988. The home visit: Field assessment of mental status impairment in the elderly. *The Gerontologist* 28:112–115.

Kendig, H. L. et al. 1988. Confidants and family structure in old age. *Journal of Gerontology: Social Sciences* 43:531–40.

Kozma, A. and M. J. Stones. 1987. Social desirability in measures of subjective well-being: A systematic evaluation. *Journal of Gerontology* 42:56–59.

Krause, N. 1987. Satisfaction with social support and self-rated health in older adults. *The Gerontologist* 27:301–308.

Krout, J. A. 1988. Community size differences in service awareness among elderly adults. *Journal of Gerontology: Social Sciences* 43:528–530.

Liang, J. et al. 1987. Cross-cultural comparability of the Philadelphia Geriatric Center Morale Scale: An American-Japanese comparison. *Journal of Gerontology* 42:37–43.

Lopata, H. Z. 1979. *Women as Widows: Support Systems.* New York: Elsevier.

Lopata, H. Z. 1987. *Widows: North America,* vol. 2. Durham: Duke University Press.

Lopata, H. and H. P. Brehm. 1986. *Widows and Dependent Wives: From Social Problem to Federal Program.* New York: Praeger.

McDonald, J. M. 1987. Support systems for American black wives and widows. In H. A. Lopata, ed., *Widows: North America.* Durham: Duke University Press.

Mahard, R. E. 1988. The CES-D as a measure of depressive mood in the elderly Puerto Rican population. *Journal of Gerontology: Psychological Services* 43:24–25.

Markides, K. S. and J. S. Levin. 1987. The changing economy and the future of the minority aged. *The Gerontologist* 27:273–274.

New York State Task Force on Older Women. 1986. *Older women: Strategies for action.* Albany: New York State Department of Social Services.

Minkler, M. and R. Stone. 1985. The feminization of poverty and older women. *The Gerontologist* 25:351–357.

Norris, F. H. and S. A. Murrell. 1987. Older adult family stress and adaptation before and after bereavement. *Journal of Gerontology* 42:606–612.

Pelham, A. O. and W. F. Clark. 1987. Widowhood among low-income racial and ethnic groups in California. In H. Z. Lopata, ed., *Widows: North America.* Durham: Duke University Press.

Rathbone-McCuan, E. and J. Hashimi. 1982. *Isolated Elders: Health and Social Intervention.* Rockville, Md.: Aspen Systems Corporation.

Rix, S. E. 1984. *Older women: The Economics of Aging.* Washington, D.C.: Women's Research and Education Institute of the Congressional Caucus for Women's Issues.

Rodeheaver, D. and N. Datan. 1988. The challenge of double jeopardy: Toward a mental health agenda for aging women. *American Psychologist* 43:648–654.

Silverman, P. R. 1985. Counseling widows and elderly women. In A. Monk, ed., *Handbook of Gerontological Services.* New York: Van Nostrand.

Silverman, P. R. 1986. *Widow-to-Widow.* New York: Springer.

Silverman, P. R. and A. Cooperband. 1975. On widowhood: Mutual help and the elderly widow. *Journal of Geriatric Psychiatry* 1:9–27.

Simon, B. L. 1987. *Never Married Women.* Philadelphia: Temple University Press.

Simon, B. L. 1988. Never-married women as caregivers: Some costs and benefits. *Affilia: Journal of Women and Social Work* 1(3):29–42.

Stone, R., G. L. Cafferata, and J. Sangl. 1987. Caregivers of the frail elderly: A national profile. *The Gerontologist* 27:616–626.

Taylor, R. J. and L. M. Chatters. 1988. Correlates of education, income, and poverty among aged blacks. *The Gerontologist* 28:435–441.

U.S. Bureau of the Census. 1987. *Statistical Abstract of the United States: 1988.* 108th ed. Washington, D.C.: GPO.

13

Multipuprose Senior Centers

LOUIS LOWY, PH.D.
Boston University

JOSEPH DOOLIN, PH.D., M.P.A.
Catholic Charities, Archdiocese of Boston

The multipurpose senior center is a community facility in which older people come together to fulfill many of their social, physical, and intellectual needs. The center can help expand their interests, tap their potentials, and develop their talents.

The center is also a bridge linking the senior community to the community at large. It is a bridge over which people and ideas, services, and resources can flow back and forth to the benefit of the entire community and which offers older people opportunities to create a special community of their own without isolating themselves from the larger community.

DEFINITION AND HISTORY

A multiservice senior center provides a single setting in which older people can take part in social activities as well as have access to essential services. A broad spectrum of activities and services is available at or through centers to those who come to the center as well as to the homebound through outreach. These activities and services include: nutrition, health, employment, transportation, social work and other supportive services, education, creative arts, recreation, and leadership, and volunteer opportunities. They are provided through a center's paid and volunteer staff, through social and community agencies that use the center as a base to provide their services, through service linkages and referrals to other agencies, and through outreach to older community residents unable to attend the center. Senior centers also serve as community resources for information on aging, for training professional and lay leadership and for developing new approaches to aging programs.

"Since time began, people have come together with others of their own age to exchange experiences common to their particular life stage, to shake their heads over or wonder at the generations younger or older than they are, to solve the problems of the world as seen from their vantage point" (NCOA 1962). The history of centers for older people begins in 1943 when the William Hodson Community Center was established in New York City by its welfare department. The idea of a center arose among social workers who noticed how desperately their older clients sought communication to escape the loneliness and isolation of their lives. At first the city merely provided the space, some refreshments, and games and then left the 350 or so original participants to fend for themselves. The hope was that somehow a program would develop; eventually it did, under the leadership of Harry Levine and Gertrude Landau. Subsequently the Sirovitch Center opened on Second Avenue in New York City to serve the older population in that neighborhood.

The next centers were established in San Francisco and in Menlo Park, California. Though each served a different type of community, both centers came to play an important role in the daily lives of the older people they served. The San Francisco Senior Center opened in 1947 as a result of the efforts of many community organizations. Though focused more on recreation and education that the Hodson Center, its programs were similarly supervised by professional staff, some detailed from various city agencies. Little House was designed to meet the needs of middle-class elderly in Menlo Park. This center was also sponsored by community agencies. Its distinctive feature was that most of its program was designed and directed by the elderly themselves. Among center services was a referral agency that furnished the members with the locations of places and people to contact when problems arose. In Bridgeport, Connecticut, a multiservice "leisure lounge" was developed in 1951 for late-middle-aged and older people to offer cultural, educational, and social support programs.

During the following thirty years the concept of a multiservice senior center was adopted by an ever-increasing number of communities across the country. The resulting growth can be seen in the following figures: in 1961, 218 centers were identified as operating; by 1965 the number had grown to 404; the National Council on Aging (NCOA) first directory, published in 1966, listed 360 centers; by 1969, another 754 centers had been founded, bringing the total 1,058; that same year, Anderson's major study on senior centers identified well over 1,000 centers; in 1970 NCOA's second directory listed 1,200 centers; from 1970 until 1973 another 1,169 centers were founded, and in 1974 NCOA identified 2,362 centers in its directory (NISC, 1974); in 1977 the Administration on Aging (AoA) estimated that there were 3,600 operational centers, and currently NCOA states that over 9,000 such centers are in operation.

Accompanying this growth in numbers was a diversification and consolidation of the internal structure of centers. Different models of center organization emerged. Interest groups were formed to create better voices for advocacy and research, and information programs developed to fill the increasing demands for data and evaluation. A perusal of the early literature on senior centers reveals the enthusiasm as well as the ad hoc nature of then-current practices.

A concrete measure of the internal differentiation can be found in the growing organization of the field. In 1959 the first state association (Ohio Association of Centers for Senior Citizens) was formed; it was soon followed by association in other states. At present most states and many regions and communities have their own organizations, providing representation of and communication within the center field. At the national level this evolution is equally noticeable: in 1962 an exploratory conference on senior centers was held, and, from 1964 on, the Annual Conference on Senior Centers got larger each year. Accompanying this trend was the establishment in 1963 of a National Institute of Senior Centers (NISC) as a permanent arm of the NCOA. In the following year the NISC Delegate Council was formed to widen the input structure from the centers representing various regions.

NEED FOR MULTISERVICE CENTERS

The rapid growth of the aging population has created a demand for societal responses and mechanism to deal with the differential needs of older people, be they biological, physical, economical, social, cultural, political, or spiritual. In the past fifteen years we have witnessed the emergence of federal, state, and local social policies, as well as programs that address some of the needs of a heterogeneous aging population to varying degrees. Three White House conferences have brought together older and younger people and have led to an exchange of ideas culminating in a number of recommendations on how to shape and design our social policies on aging.

At the 1981 White House Conference the following statement was adopted by delegates:

> Over the years, senior centers have demonstrated their ability to enhance the physical, social and emotional well-being of large numbers of older persons. Senior centers are an essential part of the community's continuum of care. The senior center is a community focal point which services the elderly with dignity and respect, supports their capacity to grow and develop and facilitates their continued involvement in the community. There must be support for senior centers at all levels of government as well as in the private sector. (White House Conference on Aging 1982 3:128).

Whether a senior center is needed in a community depends upon answers to these two questions: 1) Are the services that it offers needed by older persons? 2) Are these services currently available from other providers? At a national policy level, the issues of whether senior centers as a whole are a needed institution cannot presently be answered by specific criteria but only by indirect impressions.

Originally senior centers were established in response to grass roots, local initiatives in different communities. The expansion of the numbers of senior centers across the nation established their growing popularity, and their service record nationally indicates that senior centers are in demand and are being used. The experience of visiting a "good" senior center leaves many observers with quite a strong impression of their value. Indicators such as these can often be found in congressional hearings as the reason for a policymaker's endorsement of senior centers.

For example, during one of these hearings, one Senator opened his statement by recalling, "It's usually heart warming to visit a center; sociability and good works abound." Another felt that "The growth in number of such centers testifies to their increasing popularity and should be seen as a 'grass-roots' response to a clearly identifiable need." And others stressed the role of senior centers in the aging network of services and programs, and their capacity to become an "effective means of delivering social and other services to participants" (U.S. Congress 1978).

These observations are not direct measures of the need for senior centers, yet, in the absence of more accurate measures, they are a legitimate alternative. If for decades more and more people have been coming to senior centers, and if the number of such centers—even before availability of any federal funds—has been steadily growing, a senior center must possess significant utility to make both communities and center participants feel their efforts are worthwhile.

How many centers are needed? What kind of centers are needed? How shall centers be financed? How many centers should there be per 100,000 citizens? What does the average cost of operating a center amount to?

Looking closely at demographic data (number, education, income, and residence patterns of senior citizens) will yield an estimate of the number of centers needed during the next decades and also their approximate cost. Another approach to estimating the need for senior centers is based on the concept of target population, that is, the number and characteristics of people in a community or neighborhood that a senior center should serve. Here an assumption is made that the people to be served are in need of center services. The target population for most senior centers includes all the people over age 60 living in a particular geographic area. While a community institution should be accessible and open to all community residents, the just mentioned standard or target grouping is all-encompassing. The group of people it purports to want to serve is equal to the maximum conceivable number. Clearly no center could actually serve all the elderly in a geographic area, nor is it desirable that it should. A good number of elderly have neither wish nor need to be served by any center or social agency.

Another method of defining need is based on the number and characteristics of people who are already attending a center. To obtain a national estimate of need for senior centers, we can see how many people in a given community are attending a center and extrapolate this ratio. The average center reports over 500 older adults participating in program activities per month. If this statistic includes duplicated counts, the actual number of persons attending is likely to be smaller. If we contrast this figure with the average total population of a community (around 360,000, approximately 12 percent of whom are elderly), we see that the proportion of people actually served is quite small. Center staffs estimate that they serve about 30 percent of the elderly in their geographic areas. With well over two-thirds of the national sample having daily attendance numbers of less than 75 persons, this staff estimate is either overly optimistic or reflects a minimal level of service.

Although actual attendance figures at a multiservice senior center reflect both the supply and demand for services, the just quoted figures may be taken as a rough indicator of need. According to national census figures, in 1986 there were about 29 million people 65 or older.

If we assume that roughly one-third could utilize center services, this yields a possible service population of 8.6 million. The number of older people actually served at the present time is estimated to be approximately 4.4 million in approximately 9,000 centers. This averages 487 service recipients per center. If we project into the immediate future, the need for centers would increase. By the year 2000 it is estimated that there will be over 32 million people over 65 and, therefore, almost 5 million potential center users.

This estimate can be improved by recognizing that, even in communities that already have senior centers, not all people who would like to attend are actually able to do so. Therefore, attendance records probably understate the need. To reflect this need more accurately, we would want to add the number of nonusers who are interested in senior centers. According to the Harris data, almost 22 percent of those not currently attending a senior center would like to (Louis Harris and Associates 1981). Nationally this group may comprise more than a million people, a figure somewhat larger that the one extrapolated purely from attendance figures. Based on these calculations more that 11,000 new senior centers would be needed during the next decade. Whether these centers would be leased, purchased, or constructed, the establishment of such centers would require appreciable dollar outlays. Since it seems rather unlikely that the entire amount of money required to bring the country to these standards of service will actually be made available, another strategy is to forego the goal of broad national center availability in favor of developing a few model centers to illustrate the role senior centers could play in a properly developed aging-service network. This was the approach chosen in the aborted AoA initiative of 1977. In each state a minimum of two multipurpose senior centers were to be established that could meet professional guidelines as to range and volume of delivered services. In an environment of limited resources, such a selective approach does make sense but only if combined with a planning approach that calls for a nationwide inventory and assessment of the senior centers within each AoA Title III area, in order to determine a priority listing as to which communities are most in need of expansion or the establishment of a senior center.

PARTICIPATION IN CENTERS

For a number of years now, research findings have begun to attest to the multiple needs of the elderly. Sensory deterioration, self-concept decline, role changes, reduction of social reinforcement, income drop, growing isolation, physical infirmity, and external/internal stereotypes of aging—to name but a few—are cited as reasons for the special service needs of the elderly. It has been assumed that attendance at senior centers will meet some of these needs.

Actual comparison of user with nonuser profiles disproves some of these assumptions: no relationship between income and center attendance was found in several studies. In the NCOA sample, three-fourths of the users versus about one-half of the nonusers were retired. This probably indicates that center attendance is related to loss of the work role and increase in leisure time among the young old. (Anderson 1969; NCOA 1972; NISC 1974).

One might expect that older and generally needier people would join the centers. Again the data have not supported this assumption. The one factor that does distinguish members from nonmembers across a variety of studies is health. Indeed, health emerges as the key factor in predicting both service need and center utilization. It is the nonusers who are much more likely to have serious health problems. In the NCOA study, for instance, 22 percent of nonusers versus 13 percent of users had difficulty walking or climbing. Nonusers were also much more likely to rate their health problems as very serious. This is not to say that center members enjoy perfect health but that, of the two groups, nonusers have more serious health problems.

It is further suggested that older persons' decreasing social supports, their sense of isolation and loneliness, are major reasons for joining a center. For those isolated from meaningful social opportunities and detached from supportive relations, age-graded social clubs may provide relief from loneliness, while for those active in a variety of roles such groups may offer little attraction. Marital status shows little difference between members and nonmembers, although NCOA reports that more users are widowed, which supports the results of earlier studies that have viewed loss of a spouse as a major reason for center attendance.

And yet several other factors weigh against the social-isolation hypothesis. The vast majority of respondents in the NCOA study, irrespective of center attendance, did not view loneliness as a problem. In fact, studies have indicated that center participants enjoy good social relations and friendships. It is difficult to say to what degree social contacts and friendships preceded center attendance or resulted from it (Hanssen et al. 1978; Trela and Simmons 1971).

A different view holds that people don't join senior centers because they need to overcome loneliness and isolation but because they simply want to join. Since joining is viewed as continuation of a lifelong pattern of organizational membership, this perspective suggests that people who join a senior center are more likely to belong also to other social groups (Adams 1971; Graney 1975; Storey 1962; Tuckman 1967).

A related explanation of center attendance stresses people's lifestyles and preference patterns. Studies have found that senior center members enjoy recreation, socializing, and organizational participation to a greater degree than nonmembers. They do not care for passive activities but like to go places and do active things. Nonusers, on the other hand, are more likely to spend time at home, caring for a family member or "just doing nothing."

Finally, let us turn to the variable that has been used as an outcome measure in almost every study of senior centers—life satisfaction. The findings here are varied. Taietz (1976), for example, found no difference at all between the users and nonusers in his sample; Hanssen (1978) reported that senior center users were less depressed than those who didn't attend; and the NCOA (1972) study indicated that users showed a slightly greater degree of life satisfaction than nonusers.

Conspicuously absent as participants in multiservice centers are minority elderly, unless such centers are specifically geared to black, Hispanic, or other nonwhite populations. The number of aged minorities served by Older Americans Act Title III-B supportive services and senior center programs dropped by half a million in the first half of the eighties—from 2.0 million (21.9%) minority participants in 1980 to 1.5 million (16.5%) in 1985 (Older Americans Report, vol.12, no.35, August 26, 1988). Ethnically oriented programs address special white ethnic groups, notably Jews (via Jewish community centers) or Italian, Irish, and Polish elderly in areas where they are demographically concentrated. While centers make attempts to conduct activities across ethnic or racial boundaries, there is still an absence of ethnically and racially integrated program activities. Senior centers reflect pretty much the state of affairs in today's United States. More than a decade ago, Vickery (1972) argued that minority elderly were hard to reach mainly because they often reside in poor neighborhoods.

While lack of access may prevent their involvement, some aged subgroups, such as the black elderly, have shown a desire to be involved in senior centers. National data indicate that two in five blacks aged 55 and over do not currently attend senior centers but would like to. Lack of facilities and transportation are cited as the main inhibiting factors (Ralston 1982).

To adequately serve minority elderly, it is necessary to explore different models. One senior center model that has been implemented in some areas is the "neighborhood senior center." The neighborhood senior center is decentralized; it is located within the neighborhood to be served and incorporates programs that reflect the local, personal needs of the elderly. While there is hardly any literature concerning the effectiveness of the neighborhood senior center, several authors have suggested that neighborhood-based services are essential to take into account the heterogeneity and ethnicity of the aged population and to attract nonwhite elderly as participants.

In a study exploring the impact of the neighborhood senior center on the black elderly by determining their perceptions of senior centers (Ralston 1982), three groups of black elderly were interviewed: attenders of a neighborhood senior center, nonattenders in the same community, and nonattenders in a comparable community without a neighborhood senior center. A 29-item interview schedule was constructed that determined awareness of senior center activities and services. Significant differences were found among the three groups, with the attenders and nonattenders in the same community having the highest levels of awareness of senior center activities and services. Age, sex, and marital status were not found to influence perception of senior centers. These findings suggest that the neighborhood senior center needs to be further examined as a model for serving minority elderly.

Factors such as commitment to become involved in senior centers, expectation of significant others, and obstacles to senior center utilization may vary according to the background characteristics of older adults. For middle-class, white-collar elders, for example, lack of "interesting activities" is a major obstacle to senior center utilization. In addition, married males appear to be "encouraged" to attend senior centers by their spouses, but perhaps due to female-oriented programming, do not participate at the same rate as women. (Ralston and Griggs 1985).

The most frequently given reason for attendance at a center is the wish to meet others. Over half the sample in the NCOA study indicated that they came because the center provided them with opportunities for use of leisure time. These responses match with the view of centers as places for recreation and socializing, and most center users report that they have friends both inside and outside the center. This is the major reason why people are initially motivated to attend a center. Once they begin to come more regularly, their experience during the visit itself has an influence on why they come back.

In the NCOA study, members indicated identification with "their center." About two-thirds reported that they preferred "their" center to other similar ones, and over one-third said they would just stay home if their center closed instead of seeking out another one. Furthermore, feelings of loyalty to the center director was pronounced.

Groups of nonusers who have been studied fall into two categories: those who don't attend a center but would like to and those who don't wish to come at all. The chief reason for nonattendance given by the former is lack of a nearby facility, whereas the latter say they are just not interested, too busy with other activities or too sick to attend. Lack of a facility is a response given frequently by elderly in rural areas where fewer senior centers are available. But even within cities geographic distance and accessibility are key predictors of attendance. And, according to Krout (1987), centers located in metropolitan areas have a higher number of services, with metropolitan suburban senior centers offering the highest total number of services. The number of in-home services offered by senior centers increases in rural areas. Kim (1981) argues that this is another example of how federal government programs systematically discriminate against the rural elderly. Furthermore, there is scant evidence that most senior center programming is successful in targeting the most needy. Schneider (1985) found that they were attracting the "average" older person, and that church-going was strongly associated with senior center participation. Nor does there seem to be evidence suggesting that senior centers are achieving social intervention objectives, additionally program participation does not seem to result in attitudinal or behavioral change, nor in reduction of institutionalization.

A profile of a typical center user in the 1990s would describer her as a lower- to middle-middle class white woman in her mid-70s, socially oriented and not given to feelings of depression. She might not be perfectly healthy, but she is not greatly functionally impaired. She prefers going out and doing things with other people to staying around home working or resting. She belongs to several clubs or organizations and has friends in and out of the center. She is a low to middle-income person, has some high school education, and is interested in the world around her. To what extent this profile will change depends on the efforts of new initiatives to address the needs of minority, vulnerable, and frail elderly.

To summarize, senior center participation can be viewed as an outgrowth of life-style and activity preference. Some people enjoy active group experiences more than others. Some people are more socially outgoing than others. When these people become older, the senior center becomes one setting in which they can fulfill many of their needs and wishes. But the location of centers in neighborhoods and access to them does not have an influence on the actual as well as potential use by all elderly, particularly the minority aged and those with physical, emotional or mental disabilities.

THE PROGRAM OF THE SENIOR CENTER

What are the program goals of a multiservice senior center? Based on Morris Cohen's testimony before the U.S. Senate Special Committee on Aging in 1978, the following can be cited as major center goals:

For the individual, senior centers are to provide opportunities for:

1. Meaningful individual and group relationships.
2. Learning new skills for personal enrichment in the arts, languages, music, dramatics, nature, sports and games, dance and crafts.
3. Being useful and helpful to others through volunteer community service.
4. Assisting a person to maintain physical strength.
5. Promoting mental health through the use and development of creative abilities.
6. Developing a valued role in society.
7. Helping the individual to keep informed about changes in the community and the world.
8. Developing an individual's group-leadership skills and personal effectiveness in dealing with others.
9. Information and consultation on personal problems.

For the family, senior centers are to offer opportunities for:

1. Developing new skills and experiences to share with family members.
2. Helping older persons to be less dependent on family for activity and interests and appropriately dependent on family relationships for emotional support.
3. Helping people continue to contribute to the family's emotional well-being.

For the community, senior centers are to offer opportunities for:

1. Helping older people to remain in the community by assisting them to maintain their emotional well-being.
2. Helping the community to be aware of the needs of its older citizens, pointing up gaps and needed services.
3. Providing a resource of volunteer manpower from among the membership for public and private nonprofit community agencies and organizations.

Achieving these goals requires that a center's program be integrated and woven into the community fabric.

Lowy (1974) categorizes center programs into four groupings:

1. Direct services to older people.
2. Services offered to and through other institutions.
3. Community action with and on behalf of older people.
4. Training, consultation, and research activity.

Direct services include: recreational-educational programs (arts and crafts, nature, science/outdoor life, drama, physical activity, music, dance, games, social activities such as parties, literary activities, exercises, hobby/special interests, speakers, lectures, movies, forums, etc); social services (information; counseling and referral; protective services that are preventive, supportive, and therapeutic; friendly visiting; homemakers; telephone reassurance; day care; group work; etc.); nutrition services (congregate meals programs, meals on wheels, nutritional and dietary information); discretionary fund, home repair, and legal services; and respite care to relieve caretaking family members.

Services offered to and through other institutions, such as hospitals, housing projects, nursing homes, and rehabilitation centers, include: bringing together existing institutions for the delivery of services to older persons and setting up and arranging for homecare programs with appropriate community institutions and agencies.

Community action, transportation, and advocacy include planning for community projects and programs, coordinating facilities and making them accessible to older people near places where they reside, identifying new needs and new problems as well as representing the interests of older people as a group (e.g., at public hearings) through advocacy and setting up legislative information services.

Training, consultation, and research include: training volunteers and part-time staff for a variety of functions, consulting to community agencies and institutions related to needs and problems of the elderly, and serving as centers for research on needs and problems of older people in our society.

"A Senior Center should serve as a community facility to provide services on coordinated, continuous, and comprehensive basis and thereby reduce fragmentation to a minimum. Such a Center would be able to deliver services where they are needed and when they are needed" (Lowy 1974:8).

Another way of classifying services has been adopted by the NISC:

1. Individual services: counseling/referral, employment health maintenance, and screening services for the homebound, transportation
2. Group services: recreation, nutrition, education, social group work.
3. Community services: social services provided by older persons to community institutions, social action and advocacy.

Data collected by NISC/NCOA showed that most multipurpose senior centers offer at least three basic services: education, recreation, and information and referral/counseling. Presently most provide, in addition, volunteer opportunities and health and social services. Averaging across all types of senior group programs, the most frequently offered services are recreation (especially arts and crafts), information and referral (especially for health), participant and outreach counseling (mostly in areas of health), and education. Recreational activities (arts, crafts, games, and movies) are not only frequently offered but also draw very large attendances. Information and referral services are also much used. The largest turnout, however, is generated by nutritional programs on the premises. More than half of all centers serve hot lunches five or more days each week. Another one in five serve lunches between one and four times per week. While Title III-C of the Older Americans Act continues to be the cornerstone of elderly nutrition financing, part of the increase in service reflects funding also from states and localities. In addition to meals served at the center, almost a third of the centers report that they offer meals-on-wheels programs to homebound persons in the community.

Membership on governing groups, although encouraged by most centers, shows a markedly low use. Self-governance has declined since the 1960s and early 1970s. Now most senior center members are not active in any governance activity and rely on staff to govern and operate centers which is a serious problem since leadership development is a major objective of senior center programming.

The degree to which senior centers are linked with the community's service network is illustrated by the fact that most centers report contacts with local or county agencies, welfare departments, and local Social Security offices. Community health and welfare organizations are also seen as two-way contact points for referral and communication and as information and service resources for communitywide programs for the elderly. Centers assist other community agencies, cooperate in joint service delivery, or convene meetings of aging groups. Many centers provide training opportunities for college and graduate students and for agency personnel. Reality, however, often differs from the ideal. Krout's (1986) study of senior center linkage to the community found that a mere one-quarter of senior centers actually collaborated with nutrition sites, 10 percent with parks and recreation entities, 12 percent with other senior centers, and 10 percent with county and local offices on aging and legal aid. Fewer than 10 percent had linkages with employment commissions and day care centers. Not only was colocation found to be rare, but only one-quarter of the centers reported that they plan and coordinate with any other community organization. This would suggest that the majority of senior centers are not functioning as focal points in regard to interacting with other community organizations, e.g., fewer than one-third plan or coordinate with their local Area Agency on Aging!

Krout found that senior center administrators see the two greatest barriers to working with other agencies as lack of transportation (40%), and lack of time (35%). But, one-quarter of the centers also identified turf protection, lack of communication, and lack understanding the needs of elderly as problems.

Institutions most often contacted by senior center members are nursing homes, schools, and colleges. Outreach services are offered in over half the centers. Outreach is one of the methods most often used by centers to let the community, especially older residents, know about its programs. Other frequently used publicity channels include newspapers, newsletters, and posters. Television, radio spots, and community bulletins are also widely utilized.

PROGRAMS FOR IMPAIRED OLDER PERSONS

Today, about nine out of ten of the 9,000 centers nationwide are serving at-risk/frail, physically or mentally impaired, and chronically ill older people in some form or another. Since many center programs are oriented to recognize individual needs, they enhance the continuity of care for at-risk older people through coordination of services with community agencies and thereby facilitate access to a broad spectrum of health and social services. Strategies designed by senior centers to help at-risk older persons include encouraging self-help and mutual support, promoting integration of frail older adults with their more able peers, and drawing at-risk individuals into program planning and decision making (NISC 1980).

Centers, sporadically but increasingly, offer respite care to families; integrate the visually and hearing-impaired into group programs; link day-care clients to senior centers; reach out to the homebound and nursing-home patients; provide information, education, and support programs for families; and expand opportunities for access to services for the mentally impaired. Training programs sponsored by centers, often in concert with colleges, offer guidance to practitioners on serving and integrating the frail and impaired older person into the center's group program. The overall purpose of such training is to provide knowledge and skills required to meet special needs and to develop and strengthen linkages between center programs and other community-based service providers.

To what extent further inclusion of at-risk elderly will affect the attitudes, feelings, and participation of the "well elderly"—who have been the mainstays of the centers—and how such an integration of two groups of the elderly population on the health continuum will reshape the goals, purposes, operation, population on the health continuum will reshape the goals, purposes, operation, and organization of the centers is at this time unknown. Will the center become another competing institution on the aging network mainly oriented to serving the vulnerable, or will it maintain its original quality with a potential for the future as was expressed in the early 1970s.

> A Senior Center must become a core-institution (in the sociological sense of the term) which is truly identified and visible as an indigenous facility of the elderly. Children have their schools, young middle-aged adults have their institutions, whether in the world of work or in the world of leisure. Somehow, older people have become excluded from most of them and their world has become identified as the Nursing Home and the Old Folks' Home. The Senior Center can indeed become a community institution for all the older people whether "needy" or not. It is identified with wellness and not with debility. This can be enhanced by linking it with younger people through joint projects which have meaning to old and young. Youth would work with the elderly on their own "home ground" and they in turn could reciprocate by working with young people on their "home ground." Thus a base for identity would be established and intergenerational communication would be facilitated. This may lead to opportunities to develop new roles and a new status for the elderly simply by being aged in their own right. A Center can become a springboard for learning new roles such as making a contribution in new service roles such as home-health aides, foster grandparents, friendly visitors, and tutors to children, to name a few. Needed by our society, such roles can raise the status of the elderly on their own terms and would lead to the establishment of new relationships with the community. Instead of isolation and alienation, a sense of belonging would result because older people have a stake in the community again, which would be manifested to them by community acceptance (Lowy 1974:9).

In such a community institution older people can be hosts rather than guests and, thereby, achieve a more equitable symmetry in negotiating their status with the non-elderly. At the dawn of the last decade of the century, however, senior centers are under increasing pressure to function as day treatment centers of various kinds. Gelfand warns that, "In order to be effective as a focal point, the senior center needs to maintain its identity as a place where all older individuals come. Recent indications are that some older persons are beginning to view the senior center as a place exclusively for the frail and elderly. The ability to maintain its place not only as a multiservice provider but as a provider for all diverse groups of older persons will be a future challenge for senior centers" (1988:162–163).

MAJOR CHARACTERISTICS OF SENIOR CENTERS TODAY

Size and Location

Since there is no rigorous definition of a senior center, and since there are a great variety of senior group programs (many of them represent small local initiatives) and no registration or licensing standards are in force, one should not be surprised if neither an exact number of senior centers nor details about them are known. In 1986 Fowles (1987) found that an estimated 4.4 million older persons were being served in 9,000 centers throughout the country. Over half of all senior group programs are located in cities. In suburbs, senior clubs are far more prevalent than multipurpose senior centers, whereas in rural areas multipurpose senior centers can predominate.

Finances and Facilities

Over half the senior centers are funded by public funds, while less than a fifth rely exclusively on private dollars. The remaining numbers receive funds from both public and private sources, a trend that is likely to increase despite present economic and social policy directions.

The average center budget expanded from $17,652 in 1968 to $50,000 in 1974, and by 1989 it had crossed over the six-figure mark. These figures do not include in-kind contributions, which in some instances may represent a significant portion of a center's resources.

As the senior center is often the single most visible institution for a community's older residents, and as the type of facility in which senior centers are located is of considerable importance: a fourth of all centers operate out of their own facility; approximately a fifth operate from churches or synagogues; a third are located in recreation centers or local or county government facilities; approximately 10 percent meet in community centers of nonprofit organizations; and another 10 percent in Housing Authority buildings; and about 5 percent meet in private, commercial facilities.

As to the condition and appropriateness of these facilities, half of center facilities were renovated, presumably with the needs of senior members in mind. However, over a third of all centers operate in old buildings that have not been altered. On the other hand, a fourth of all present centers are located in new buildings, and roughly two-thirds are single-level facilities, eliminating the architectural barrier of stair climbing.

While facilities thus range from large, modern, well-designed centers to modest two- or three-room storefronts, several problems are shared by most of them. Two out of three centers are too small to function properly, which leads to all rooms being continually in use, often for purposes for which they were not designed. An important shortcoming is the frequency with which centers fail to provide adequate facilities for handicapped members. Parking ramps and bathrooms are often inadequate for members confined to wheelchairs. Even when accessibility has been assured, often the locations of phones, fountains, towel dispensers, and elevator call buttons are inconvenient. These physical shortcomings have a negative impact on a center's capacity to provide adequate services for vulnerable and handicapped elderly. With increasing numbers of at-risk elderly center members, concern about physical shortcomings of facilities has been mounting significantly.

Staffing

Staffing is perhaps the single most important organizational parameter. The nature, atmosphere, indeed the very success of a senior center is in large measure dependent on the size, attitudes, competence, skills, dedication, and creativity of its staff.

The average center staff is small. As many as a fourth of all multipurpose senior centers did not have a single full-time, paid staff person in 1975. Another third had only one full-time staff person, and about a fifth of the centers had a full-time staff of four or more. Many centers rely on volunteers and staff from other agencies for part of their regular programming. Also, over half of all centers are part of a larger network of multiple sites with personnel and services distributed throughout, so that the staff at any given site represents only a portion of the available manpower.

Although many centers have their staffs provide all services offered at the site, those that have time-sharing arrangements with other agencies concentrate their own activities mostly on information and referral, arts and crafts, and recreation. They are unlikely to provide educational programs, home-delivered meals, or health, legal, employment, and library services that require special skills. Staff from other agencies are utilized to provide these services.

Volunteers (including members) in many centers contribute substantially to the program. Center participant volunteers usually assist with serving meals and with arts and recreation activities; community volunteers generally help with delivering meals to people's homes and with conducting educational programs.

The educational level of center directors is diverse. According to 1975 data, most had at least some college experience and approximately a fifth had attended graduate schools, chiefly schools of social work; a fourth had no post-high-school training. One explanation for the small size of center staffs and their modest educational levels can be found in the low salaries; only a fourth of all center directors received salaries over 20,000 in 1980. More recently however, increasing professionalization of senior center staff is reflected in the NISC (1987) study of senior center personnel practices. Among other things, it found that in 1987 dollars the average senior center staffer was paid \$21,000—with a range from \$5,720 to \$41,000!

Seminars, on-the-job training, and paid attendance at professional meetings are offered by about half of all centers, whereas paid tuition for attending institutes and workshops has markedly decreased in recent years.

Representative Centers

The following brief profiles describe four representative multiservice centers of varying size and type.

H Center is open five days a week and offers a variety of social, educational, and physical activities. The center has bowling lanes and a swimming pool. Its members assist the staff with all the programs, including the therapeutic swim program for Stroke Club members.

P Center was built with capital improvement funds in 1967 on an eighteen-hole golf course. The center has lawn bowling, tennis, shuffleboard courts and has both men's and women's choruses. It is the home of Senior Adults, Inc., publishers of *News* since 1968, and the home of an extensive travel program serving more than its 3,000 members. Numerous other activities are offered during the hours of operation each week. Programs are funded by public and private sources, including federal, state, county, and city agencies, the board of education, as well as the United Way, unions, churches, and schools. The center includes special programs for the physically and mentally handicapped.

E Retiree Center serves a rural community, using a converted residence. Volunteers (there is no paid staff) oversee the center's operation. Open five days a week, it provides recreation and social services and is funded through the municipality as a special project of state government.

K Center, housed in a converted furniture store in the main shopping district of a large, integrated, low-income neighborhood of a northeast city, this center is an example of the senior center as a provider agency. Open seven days, serving two meals each day plus a light breakfast, the center program integrates the well elderly with those needing the on-site day care and respite programs. It is the area-wide provider of congregate and meals-on-wheels nutrition services, operating twenty-three satellites including three ethnic sites (Chinese, Haitian, and Hispanic), and a day center and mobile outreach program for homeless elders citywide. A geropsychiatric outpatient clinic, alcoholism program, homemaker/home health aide, home repair program, and extensive transportation system are in addition to the usual recreation-leisure time programs available through the center, its nutrition satellites, or at the several public housing sites in which the agency runs mini-centers. K Center's mid-seven-figure annual operating budget comprised of 90 percent public-sector grants contracts, and reimbursements, includes no categorical senior center funding.

The diagram in figure 13.1 is an illustrated concept of the potential services and activities provided by and/or through a multipurpose senior center.

STANDARDS FOR MULTISERVICE SENIOR CENTERS

For many years the NISC has sought to develop standards for senior centers. In 1975 the AoA of the U.S. Department of Health, Education and Welfare provided funds to the NCOA to develop program guidelines and standards of practice for senior centers.

The need for standards was documented by the findings of a two-year comprehensive national study of community-based senior group programs. The findings supported the senior center's function as a focal point for services, providing opportunities for older persons and serving as a community resource for all age groups. It also revealed that there were no evaluation criteria or even clear definitions for senior center programs. While some senior center programs were the focal point for a community's concern for its older citizens, others were functioning in a limited manner and not serving segments of the older population who could benefit from a more adequate center program. While some of the weaknesses revealed in the study could be attributed to limited resources, there was evidence that they were

FIGURE 13.1. Multipurpose Senior Center. An illustrated concept of the potential services and activities provided by or through the efforts of a multipurpose senior center.

SOURCE: Adapted from *Bridge to the Community* (Indianapolis: Central Indiana Council on Aging, 1975)

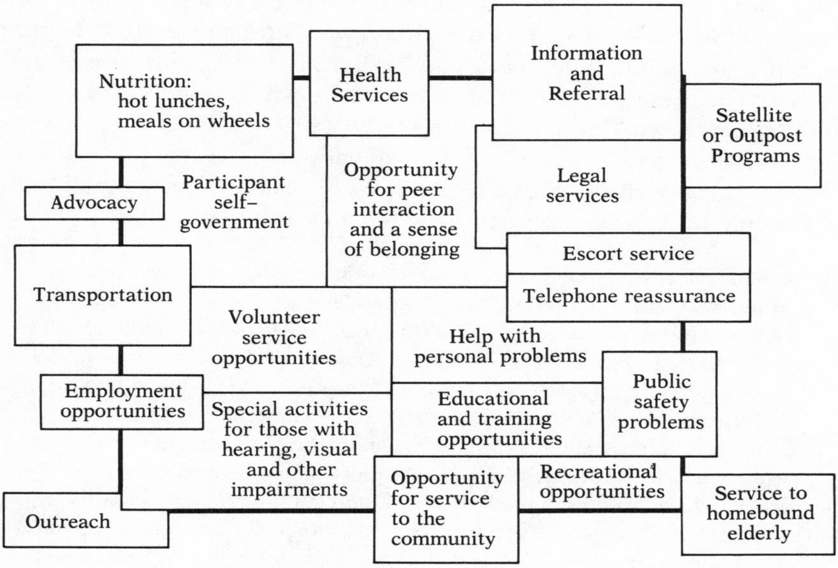

▬ = The walls of a multipurpose senior center. Some activities occur completely within the walls, some completely outside the walls, and still others occur both within and without.

also related in important ways to an inadequate understanding of good center practices and sound administration.

A Standards and Guidelines Steering Committee and five subcommittees of the NCOA developed guidelines and standards in areas related to management, operation, programming, facility, and community relations. These subcommittees were made up of recognized authorities reflecting not only the several professions and disciplines that underlie center programming and operation, but also the diversity of facilities that function as or sponsor senior centers.

In addition to providing general information input, center directors and others related to centers participated in pilot testing of the standards and the self-assessment instrument developed by the committee, reviewed the guidelines, and made recommendations regarding their dissemination and utilization. The resultant standards are contained in NISC (1978).

Senior Center Philosophy

Through the years, the senior center field has evolved a philosophy that provides a perspective concerning the place of a senior center in the community's network of human services and an associated value orientation about older persons. Whereas other organizations and groups focus their attention upon health, housing, economic stability, and other more limited aspects of the older person's existence, a senior center has a commitment to all aspects of living. Its program, providing opportunities and alternatives for enhancing the quality of life of the later years, is called "The Senior Center Philosophy."

> A senior center seeks to create an atmosphere that acknowledges the value of human life, individually and collectively, and affirms the dignity and self-worth of the older adult. This atmosphere provides for the reaffirmation of creative potential, the power of decision making, the skills of coping and defending, the warmth of caring, sharing, giving, and supporting. The uniqueness of the senior center stems from its total concern for older people and its concern for the total older person. In an atmosphere of wellness, it develops strengths and encourages independence, while building interdependence and supporting unavoidable dependencies. It works with older persons, not for them, enabling and facilitating their decisions and actions, and in so doing creates and supports a sense of community that further enables older persons to continue their involvement with and contribution to the larger community.
>
> The philosophy of the senior center movement is based on premises

> that aging is a normal developmental process; that human beings need peers with whom they can interact and who are available as a source of encouragement and support; and that adults have the right to have a voice in determining matters in which they have a vital interest.
>
> In accordance with these premises and on the basis of experience, the senior-center field adheres to the following beliefs:
>
> Older people are individuals and adults with ambitions, capabilities and creative capacities.
>
> They are capable of continued growth and development.
>
> They, like all people, need both access to sources of information and help for personal and family problems and the opportunity to learn from individuals coping with similar experiences.
>
> They have a right to make choices and to be a part of decision-making processes.
>
> Senior center staffs are obliged to create and maintain a climate of respect, trust, and support, and to provide opportunities for older people to exercise their skills and to develop their potential as experienced adults within the context of the whole community to which they belong and to which they bring their wisdom, experience and insight. (NISC 1978:5)

As senior centers evolve and adapt to meet the changing needs and interests of older persons, so the philosophy will continue to evolve until positive images of age have become a general perception of reality and senior centers are regarded as a regular community facility serving the older population. Then senior centers will truly be "social utilities," as freely available and generally supported as libraries, parks, and beaches.

Senior Center Principles

The standards are organized into nine sections, each enunciating a basic principle: purpose, organization, community relations, program administration and personnel, fiscal management, records and reports, facility, and evaluation (NISC 1978:17).

> I. Purpose—A senior center shall have a written statement of its purposes consistent with the Senior Center Philosophy and a written statement of its goals based on its purposes and on the needs and interest of older people in its service areas. These statements shall be used to govern the character and direction of its operation and program.

Major subject areas include: philosophy, goals, and program objectives and their uses.

> II. Organization—A senior center shall be organized to create effective relationships among the participants, staff, governing body and the community in order to achieve its purposes and goals.

This section deals with legal sanctions; documents related to the constitution and bylaws of the center; information about the organizational structure role, functioning and composition, and responsibilities of the governing and advisory body; and involvement of the membership in governance.

> III. Community Relations—A senior center shall form cooperative arrangements with community agencies and organization in order to serve as a focal point for older people to obtain access to comprehensive services. A center shall be a source of public information, community education, advocacy and opportunities for community involvement of older people.

Linkages with community, involvement of other agencies of the aging network, coordination and planning mechanisms, and creation of volunteer and employment opportunities are part of this section.

> IV. Program—A senior center shall provide a broad range of group and individual activities and services designed to respond to the interrelated needs and interests of older people in its service area.

This section addresses the two ways in which the needs of older persons are taken into consideration in program planning, in setting of priorities, and in the operation of activities and services. It looks at program scope, diversity, atmosphere, accessibility, outreach efforts, engagement and participation by members, quality of program, and use of staff.

> V. Administration and Personnel—A senior center shall have clear administrative and personnel policies and procedures that contribute to the effective management of its operation. It shall be staffed by qualified, paid and volunteer personnel, capable of implementing its program.

The deployment of personnel, staffing patterns and responsibilities, job descriptions, personnel policies and practices, staff development programs, use of volunteers in relation to nonvolunteers, interaction of staff, and emergency arrangements are included in this section.

> VI. Fiscal Management—A senior center shall practice sound fiscal planning, management, record keeping, and reporting.

Securing of financial resources, fiscal planning and reporting, risk, protection (insurance), fiscal management and purchasing procedures as well as inventory control belong in this section.

VII. Records and Reports—A senior center shall keep complete records required to operate, plan and review its program. It shall regularly prepare and circulate reports to inform its board, its participants, staff, sponsors, funders, and the general public about its operation and program.

To what extent participant records and reports related to programs and administrative records and reports related to operations, are kept is at the heart of the maintenance of confidentiality and necessitates appropriate safeguards.

VIII. Facility—A senior center shall make use of appropriate facilities for its program. Such facilities shall be designed, located, constructed or renovated and equipped so as to promote effective access to and conduct of its program and to provide for the health, safety, and comfort of participants staff and public.

Responsibilities for building, grounds and equipment and assurance of physical comfort, safety and quality is the concern of this part of the assessment and planning guide.

IX. Evaluation—A senior center shall have adequate arrangement to monitor, evaluate, and report on its operation and program.

A senior center shall have or be part of an evaluation system that will assist to determine the extent to which the center is achieving its purposes, goals, and objectives, is truly meeting the needs and interests of its participants, and is efficient and effective in the operation of the center and its program.

The formal and informal evaluation arrangements, the basic elements of an evaluation system, and its sources and results to be used and disseminated are the essential aspects of this criterion.

Based on these criteria, a "self-assessment instrument" has been developed (NISC 1979). The emphasis is on self-assessment and not on accreditation, though the idea of accrediting centers has been entertained by the NCOA for some time. So far no concrete plans have emerged that would place accreditation function in the hands of NCOA or any other organization. Standard setting and upgrading center quality is predicated upon voluntary compliance rather than upon mandatory review.

Whether the advent of these standards and the use of the self-assessment instrument has contributed to a more uniform quality of practice of center operation is as yet unknown. The practice principles guiding each of these nine sections are criteria not only to assess prevailing standards of a multiservice center but also serve as prescriptive tools to plan and operate such a facility. The self-assessment instrument can assist a center in a number of ways:

1. It can help assess the extent to which a senior center's policies, procedures, and program conform to the standards of good practice.
2. It can help a center systematically prepare and plan responses appropriate to growth in the program, changes in the demographic composition of older people in the community, and changes in available resources.
3. Through its use, a center can systematically collect information about its operation and program, showing how each component of the center is interrelated.
4. It can help recognize areas where further training and technical assistance may be needed to improve a center's operation and program.
5. Its use can promote the development of skills related to planning, evaluation, and program development and provide opportunities for all those involved in the process to exchange ideas about a center.

SOCIAL WORK AND SENIOR CENTERS

Historically, social work has played a significant role in the creation, design, and operation of senior centers. Names associated with the center movement such as Landau, Mathiason, Levine, Eckstein, Maxwell, Lowy, Tarrell, Cohen, Schreiber, Marks, Dobroff attest to this fact. And social workers have continued to play an important part in the provision and administration of a variety of services to older persons in and through multiservice centers as part of genrontological social work. Social action to bring about changes on the community level, and human growth and development through group participation on the individual and family levels, have been the twin focuses of social work and the senior center movement.

Social workers have assumed major functional responsibility for counseling, information/referral, and case-management function. Techniques of psycho-social support, crisis intervention, problem identification, assessment and resolution are essential ingredients of many direct service programs offered in or through a senior center. The role of case manager as a link to other services calls for social work competencies.

Brandler underscores the informal style of most senior center social workers, and the camouflaging of therapeutic goals in group activities. This is her view of social work and senior centers

The social worker in the senior center plays many parts. In some centers, she/he is responsible for everything from maintenance to budget, from meal planning to policymaking, performing all the traditional roles, and standing in lieu of family for some center participants. All tasks relate to two basic objectives, to provide older people with needed support and to assure that older people maximize independence. These are the major concerns of the social worker whether as administrator, as group worker, or as caseworker. The objectives must be achieved with a consciousness of the group interests as well as those of the individual. (1985:205)

The role of the social worker in the senior center, whether it is related to administration, work with groups or work with individuals, is to give a sense of strength, meaning and joy to center participants. Ideally, center participation should be broadening, should encourage spiritual, emotional, and intellectual productivity and health. One participant, in a letter to the social worker in her senior center, sums it up by writing, "You give ma a reason to wake up in the morning. Thank you." (1985:210)

Self-help and mutual support groups rely on the skills of social workers to get them started and to be available as consultants and backup persons. Advocacy functions demand commuinty organization skills that are made accessible and available in a variety of ways. Social workers also conduct training programs (in-service or orientation) for staff, volunteers, and board members, and frequently offer supervision to staff members (paid and volunteer) and students in field training.

Senior centers have a diversity of staffing patterns; this is reflected in the use and distribution of social workers. Although centers are not an exclusive domain of social-work activity, social workers are engaged in planning and providing services as well as in management functions at many centers. The inclusion of at-risk elderly as a result of the implementation of the NISC study has led to an increased infusion of social workers as well as other mental health professional into the staffing patterns of senior centers.

THEORETICAL BASES OF SENIOR CENTERS

Senior centers base their efforts on a philosophy of human growth. A humanistic belief in the creative potential of people emphasizes that older people are individuals in their own right. They are adults with capabilities, creative capacities, and aspirations. They have the capacity for continuing development. They may need access to information and services. They may need help for personal or family problems. They may need opportunities to learn from individuals coping with similar experiences. Yet most of all, they may need support for being themselves to affirm their identity in dignity and with respect. These beliefs bear unmistakable resemblance to the humanistic psychology of Maslow and the therapeutic theory of Rogers.

Most centers prefer an activity rather than a disengagement view of aging. They believe that aging is a natural part of life and that adults have a right to make their own life choices. One major assumption of centers is that human beings need peers for interaction and support. Senior-center staff are expected to create an atmosphere that acknowledges the value of human life and affirms the self-worth of the older person through projecting an attitude of respect, trust and mutual support. To help older people actualize their potential, centers provide opportunities for decision making, service to others, and creative activity. To support ego maintenance, opportunities for exercising coping skills are combined with interpersonal support and warmth. The concern for vulnerable older people and their needs and problems requires further theoretical articulation that has not yet occurred.

Two conceptual models of senior centers can be contrasted: the "social agency model," which views the senior center as a collection of programs designed to meet the needs of elderly and predicts that the poor and disengaged are the most likely candidates for participation in senior centers; and the "voluntary association model," which views the senior center as a joinable community group and predicts that those elderly will join who are more actively involved in voluntary association and who manifest a stronger interest in the community (Taietz 1976).

Senior centers fulfill a useful function under either model. But if center representatives wish to stand by the social agency-model, intervention efforts can be directed to more isolated or at-risk target groups with attendant consequences for membership, program, and image.

PUBLIC POLICY

Since senior centers have been, for the most part, born out of local initiative and are supported by local government, private nonprofit organization, or civic unit they have developed their own priorities and their own place in the community and will continue even without federal money. In the early 1960s there were attempts to support the growth of senior centers with federal funds. In 1964, for instance Congressman Claude Pepper introduced H.R. 4055 and H.R. 4056. In the same year the Smothers-Mills Bill (H.R. 5840, S. 1357) proposed to secure funding for both the construction and operation of senior centers. No action was taken then.

The Older Americans Act

In 1965 the Senate considered a bill entitled the Senior Citizens Community Planning and service Act of 1965 that would have covered 50 percent of center construction costs. The House then considered a more comprehensive bill (H.R. 4409), the Senior Activity Centers and Community Service Act of 1965, which would have supported both construction and operational expenses. The act that finally passed both houses and was signed by the President was the Older Americans Act of 1965. It contained no separate title for senior center funds, but Title IV was devoted to "Research and Development Projects," and it specified in section 401(2) that the Commissioner on Aging could provide funds for the purpose of "developing or demonstrating new approaches, techniques, and methods (including the use of multipurpose activity centers) which hold promise of substantial contribution toward wholesome and meaningful for older persons." Yet the same act also stated explicitly that, with respect to establishment of new programs or expansion of existing programs with Title III funds, "No costs of construction, other than for minor alterations and repairs, shall be included in such establishment or expansion." Thus senior center applications were limited to the relatively smaller funds in Title IV. In 1972 a major revision of the Older American Act provided an explicit title for senior centers. This bill was pocket vetoed by President Nixon. However, in the following year the 1973 amendments to the Older Americans Act (P.L. 93-29) resulted in a major revision of the entire Act. These amendments (incorporated mainly in the revised Title III) overshadowed the incorporation of another new title called Multipurpose Senior Centers, known as Title V.

The purpose of Title V was "to provide a focal point in communities for the development and delivery of social services and nutritional services designed primarily for older persons." The strategy through which this purpose was to be achieved consisted of making available grant or contract funds to pay up to 75 percent of the costs of acquiring, altering, or renovating existing facilities to serve as multipurpose senior centers. The title vested with authority for application approval and fund disbursement directly in the a Commissioner on Aging.

With the 1978 amendments to the Older Americans Act, another overhaul took place. Title III was expanded by consolidating the social services, nutrition, and multipurpose-center provisions of the act and thereby eliminated Title V. (Since 1978, the Senior Community-Service Employment Program has been Title V.) Funding for multiservice centers was now included as part of funding for supportive social services and congregate and home-delivery nutrition services. Through grants to states, which award monies to Area Agencies on Aging for community planning, these funds are used in accordance with a state-approved area agency plan.

Since the amendments of 1978 require the development of specified services (states are to spend at least 50 percent of social services on three categories: access, in-home, and legal services), senior centers have found it necessary to develop such specified services in order qualify for federal funding. The impact of federal dollars on the goals, directions, and programming of senior centers is quite evident.

Reauthorization of the Older Americans Act was passed by Congress in the fall of 1981, and again in the fall of 1984. The Act retains language to continue separate authorizations under Title III, as under the 1978 amendments. Senior centers have to compete with other Title III programs for funding; this means a loss of identity for them with attendant consequences for goals, programs, membership composition, and philosophy as well as organizational context. Only during 1977 and 1978 were separate funds for senior centers appropriated ($20 million and $40 million, respectively). Now centers have to compete again for funds via budgets of Title III and other federal programs besides the Older Americans Act. Both the Nixon and Ford administrations argued that no money should be authorized for Title V, since there already existed sufficient other programs (e.g., under the Housing and Community Development Act of 1974) that could fund senior centers. A look at the record of the Department of Housing and Urban Development indicates that the overall impact of grants made by this department has been small: few dollars actually reached senior centers. In times of inflation and local tax revolts, many communities have difficulties financing even their basic services (school, fire department, criminal justice system), and the proportion of federal tax receipts continues to decrease. That is why senior centers find it increasingly difficult to compete effectively for a share of the shrinking dollar base. When they are successful, it is primarily for those activities that are "fundable" under the federal guidelines.

Funds from nongovernmental sources continue to be sought by NCOA as well as by individual senior centers. Service contract agreements with federal programs, matching funding from private foundations, and creative fund-raising activities are the fiscal underpinnings of multiservice centers today.

Policy Issues and Future Directions

At least three major policy issues can be identified dealing with program membership and functional emphasis.

1. PROGRAM EMPHASIS: EDUCATION/RECREATION VS. TREATMENT

Senior centers started as places for older people to gather for enjoyment and relaxation. As the multiple needs of older people became more apparent, however, social and health services began to be offered along with recreational activities in many centers. In these budget-conscious times, paying millions of dollars for "fun and games" is seen by many as frivolous. In a climate of inflation, tax revolts, and curtailment of social programs as against expansion of military programs, the federal government has taken the position that its resources must address the most basic needs of the most destitute elderly, "the truly needy." Senior center advocates support offering more services because their location in a senior center makes them more acceptable to the elderly client. But to "help impaired older persons maintain independent living" requires a major shift in program focus and staffing patterns.

Faced with such a shift, many members of a center may feel alarmed and even resentful. While it is true that, as an expression of concern at the national policy level, senior citizens strongly support the goal of independent community living, this does not mean that member of a local senior center would support having their facility turn into a major health service institution.

And what will distinguish a senior center from another type of social/health service agency in competition for scarce resources? How will the vision of a center as an indigenous social host institution for the well older person fare?

2. MEMBERSHIP EMPHASIS: MAINSTREAM VS. IMPAIRED ELDERLY?

Since senior centers started as a grass-roots movement in local communities, they were initiated by and designed for people with fairly adequate economic resources. As a result, current data reflect under-representation of the less economically privileged and the minority elderly.

With increased federal involvement and new grass-roots awareness in senior centers, the emphasis on serving low-income and minority elderly at a center now serving white, middle-class people can be increased. But the federal commitment to minorities—old or young—considerably abated during the 1980s and establishing new centers in areas where minority members reside so far achieves only program availability, not integration of elders with different backgrounds.

Another issue concerns the elderly's health status. The new emphasis on attracting "at-risk older persons" will invariably bring about not only shifts in service and program directions but also lead to new membership composition. Will membership status become client status, and will a "social utility" become a "case-service" facility?

3. FUNCTIONAL EMPHASIS: DIRECT SERVICES VS. COORDINATION

Since 1973, state and area agencies have been viewed by the AoA as the cornerstone of the aging network. Senior centers had emerged long before the Older Americans Act, at a time when the aged were first discovered as a group with special service needs. Indeed, many of what we now consider aging services can be said to have originated around senior centers. During the past thirty years, senior centers have become in many communities the symbol of services to the aged, the outward and visible focus for the community's concern for its elderly residents. As such centers are already involved in or informed about many aspects of community activities that would be of interest to their members. Centers do perform direct program and coordinating functions.

With the advent and maturation of state and area agencies, the relationship of senior centers to the aging network needs further study and analysis. Generally, centers will acknowledge the area agencies as the central planning and administrative agencies. In return, they want to be acknowledged as the community focal point for aging services. In this model a community would have two focal aging institutions: the area agency would be responsible for fund administration and area-wide planning; the senior center would be the delivery site for these services and programs. Developments so far have not supported the practical implementation of such a model. Despite the intent of Title III to coordinate various social, nutrition and senior center services within their planning and service areas, such coordination was not very successful, and fragmentation is still the order of the day. Given the political and economic climate of the 1990s, centers are unlikely to become major coordinating mechanisms; in fact, they will more likely move more and more toward direct service provisions and, if any coordinating takes place at all, leave this to state and area agencies or councils on aging. The reflection of the 1977 AoA's Multiservice Senior Centers Initiative introduced by then Commissioner Arthur Flemming, to designate centers as focal points for meeting needs of the elderly in a community in 1978, made the trend quite clear. This does not suggest that individual centers in individual communities may not fulfill some coordinating functions.

Future Options

At this juncture of our social policy, a number of major questions must be addressed and research must be undertaken to bring data to bear on the social process of social-policy shaping.

1. What are the demographic trends in specific states, areas, and communities? Who are the most likely target groups for senior centers? Will we move toward a family orientation and eventually toward a family policy?
2. What are the political trends in the field of aging? How will aging policy be shaped following the 1991 White House Conference on Aging, and how will this policy affect senior centers?
3. What are the economic trends affecting the social, health, and educational priorities in the United States? How will these trends influence income, health, housing, and social service policy and their implementation in the aging network? What will be the place of centers in this network within the context of supply-side economic?
4. What are the sociocultural trends in our society and how will the high-technology revolution affect not only the social and cultural macrostructure but also the microstructure of four-

generation families and their individual members? Will senior centers be able to respond to newly emerging needs, problems, and crises? Will they become instrumental in designing programs that serve the differential needs and aspirations of a heterogeneous aging population and the "sandwich generation"? Will they become "host" institutions, with identities of their own, as sociocultural centers for older people and serve as "guests" of others? Will they be hammer or anvil, leaders or followers, in the redesign of social institutions to respond to demographic, political, economic and sociocultural changes.

Penetrating analytical thinking will produce more refined and differentiated questions, which in turn must be examined and studied. A research strategy that concentrates on such an agenda is likely to yield answers not only for the future role of multiservice senior centers, but also for the population as a whole.

REFERENCES

Adams, D. L. 1971. Correlates of satisfaction among the elderly. *The Gerontologist* 11(4):64–68.

Anderson, N. 1969. *Senior Centers: Information from a nationwide survey.* Minneapolis: American Rehabilitation Foundation.

Brandler, S. M. 1985. The senior center: informality in the social work function. *Journal of Gerontological Social Work* 8(3/4):195–210.

Conrad, W. R. Jr., and W. E. Glenn. 1976. *The Effective Voluntary Board of Directors: What It Is and How It Works.* Chicago: Swallow Press.

Fowles, D. G. 1987. The use of community services. *Aging* no.355, pp. 36–37.

Gelfand, D. E. 1988. *The Aging Network: Programs and Services.* 3d ed. New York: Springer.

Gelwicks, L. S. 1975. The older person's relation to the environment: The effects of transportation. In E. J. Cantilli and Schmelzer, eds., *Transportation and Aging: Selected issues.* Washington, D.C.: GPO.

Graney, M. J. 1975. Happiness and social participation in aging. *Journal of Gerontology* 30(6):701–706.

Hanssen, A. M. et al. 1978. Correlates of senior center participation. *The Gerontologist* 18(2):193–199.

Jacobs, B., ed. 1974. *Social Action: Expanding Role for Senior Centers.* Washington, D.C.: National Council on the Aging.

Jacobs, B. 1976. *Working with the Impaired Elderly.* Washington, D.C.: National Council on the Aging.

Jacobs, B., P. Lindsley, P. and M. Feil. 1976. *A Guide to Intergenerational Programming.* Washington, D.C.: National Institute of Senior Centers, National Council on the Aging.

Jordan, J. J. 1975. *Senior Center Facilities: An Architect's Evaluation of Building Design, Equipment and Furnishings.* Washington, D.C.:National Institute of Senior Centers, National Council on the Aging.

Jordan, J. J. 1978. *Senior Center Design: An Architect's Discussion of Facility Plan-*

ning. Washington, D.C.: National Institute of Senior Centers, National Council on the Aging.

Kim, P. K. 1981. The low-income elderly: Under-served victims of public inequity. In P. K. Kim and C. Wilson, eds., *Toward Mental Health of the Rural Elderly*. Washington, D.C.: University Press of America.

Krout, J. A. 1987. Rural-urban differences in senior center activities and services. *The Gerontologist* 1(27):92–97.

Kubie, S. H. and G. Landau. 1953. *Group Work with the Aged*. New York: International Universities Press.

Leanse, J., M. Tiven, and R. B. Robb. 1977. *Senior Center Operation: A Guide to Operation and Management*. Washington, D.C.: National Institute of Senior Centers, National Council on the Aging.

Louis Harris and Associates. 1981. *The Myth and Reality of Aging in America*. Washington, D.C.: National Council on the Aging.

Lowy, L. 1955. *Adult Education and Groupwork*. New York: Whiteside/Morrow.

Lowy, L. 1974. The senior center: A major community facility today and tomorrow. *Perspective on Aging*, 3(2):5–9.

Lowy, L. 1979. *Social Work with the Aging*. New York: Harper and Row; 2d ed., Longman, 1985.

Maxwell, J. 1973. *Centers for Older People*. Washington, D.C.: National Council on the Aging.

National Council on the Aging. 1972. *The Multi-Purpose Senior Center: A Model Community Action Program*. Washington, D.C.: The Council.

National Council on the Aging. 1978. *Fact Book on Aging: A Profile of America's Older Generation*. Washington, D.C.: The Council.

National Institute of Senior Centers. 1974. *Directory of Senior Centers and Clubs*. Washington, D.C.: National Council on the Aging.

National Institute of Senior Centers. 1975. *Senior Centers: Report of Senior Group Programs in America*. Washington, D.C.: National Council on the Aging.

National Institute of Senior Centers. 1978. *Senior Center Standards: Guidelines for Practice*. Washington, D.C.: National Council on the Aging.

National Institute of Senior Centers. 1979. *Senior Center Standards: Self-Assessment Workbook*. Washington, D.C.: National Council on the Aging.

National Institute of Senior Centers. 1980. *Senior Centers and the At-Risk Older Person: A Project Report*. Washington, D.C.: National Council on the Aging.

Ralston, P. A. 1982. Perception of senior centers by the black elderly: A comparative study. *Journal of Gerontological Social Work* 4(3/4):127–137.

Ralston, P. A., and Griggs, M. B., 1985. Factors affecting utilization of senior centers: Race, sex, and sex and socioeconomic differences. *Journal of Gerontological Social Work* 9(1):99–112.

Schneider, M. J., D. D. Chapman, D. E. Voth, 1985. Senior center participation: A two stage approach to impact evaluation. *The Gerontologist* 2(25):194–199.

Storey, R. T. 1962. Who attends a senior activity center? A comparison of Little House members with non-members in the same community. *The Gerontologist* 2(4):216–222.

Taietz, P. 1976. Two conceptual models of the senior center. *Journal of Gerontology* 31(2):219–222.

Trela, J. E. and L. W. Simmons. 1971. Health and other factors affecting membership and attrition in a senior center. *Journal of Gerontology* 26(1):46–51.

Tuckman, J. 1967. Factors related to attendance in a center for older people. *Journal of the American Geriatrics Society* 15(5):474–479.

U.S. Congress. Senate Special Committee on Aging. 1978. *Senior Centers and the Older Americans Act*. Washington, D.C.: GPO.

Vickery, F. E. 1972. *Creative Programming for Older Adults: A Leadership Training Guide.* New York: Associated Press.
Weiss, C. H., ed. 1972. *Evaluating Action Programs.* Boston: Allyn and Bacon.
White House Conference on Aging. 1982. *Final Report: The 1981 White House Conference on Aging.* 3 vols. Washington, D.C.: The Conference.

14

Services to Older and Retired Workers

❖

JUDITH WINEMAN, M.S.W., C.S.W.
International Ladies' Garment Workers' Union, New York

The provision of social services by unions antedates the large and complex social service bureaucracy we know today. In recent years, the parallel interests of unions and employers have given rise to a rapidly expanding field of industrial social work under private auspices, such as unions. Fifty or sixty years ago, these "parallel interests" were nowhere to be found. Trade unions were young and struggled for recognition. The concept of people working together meant people helping each other, too. The union representative whose initial task was to help members with job-related issues soon became the basis of "social unionism," the belief that the union is a way of life rather than an economic organization whose sole purpose is to improve wages and and working conditions.

The trade unions' commitment to their retired members stems from this philosophy of social unionism. This chapter describes union retiree service programs with particular reference to the International Ladies' Garment Workers' Union (ILGWU), the Amalgamated Clothing and Textile Workers' Union (ACTWU), and District 65 of the United Automobile Workers (UAW). The members of these unions have not participated in the trend toward early retirement characteristic of the U.S. labor force as a whole that is due in part to the institution of private pension plans that supplement workers' Social Security benefits. In the steel and auto industries (at least until the difficult times for these industries in the late 1970s) a major retirement period was between ages 60 and 62. In the public employee unions—police, fire, and government—the trend has been toward even earlier retirement, for example, between the ages of 50 and 55.

The workers described here are at the opposite end of the scale in terms of skills and wages. For example, there has never been a mandatory retirement age in the women's apparel industry. The major incentive to retire is eligibility for full Social Security benefits at age 65. Pensions in the industry are low, and the seasonal nature of the work builds in a certain amount of "forced unemployment" over a person's work history that may delay eligibility for a full pension. The retired workers served by the ILGWU, ACTWU, and District 65 are therefore older and, in most cases, retired from industries that are themselves rapidly aging: apparel, textile, and light manufacturing. The population is overwhelmingly female, part of the huge immigrant wave of the first quarter of the twentieth century. They are multilingual, multiethnic, multiracial: Jews, Italians, Irish, Hispanics, blacks. They worked as sewing machine operators, weavers, milliners, shipping clerks, and packers. Their wages were low and their work often seasonal.

Many of these people view social work as charity for poor people; the image of "welfare worker" still often attaches to the name social worker. Furthermore, they perceive the social-agency system as alien and difficult to negotiate. By contrast, the social services provided by their unions are familiar, the system is negotiable, and access is assured. Many elderly retirees will not accept service unless it is from their union because to do so would (in their eyes) mean accepting charity. Retired union members feel they have earned their right to union services. They paid dues and struggled to make their unions strong. The unions, in turn, promote this concept and take pride in their relationship to retired workers. Unions mandate services to retired workers in recognition that their responsibilities to them do not end with retirement. Retired workers are encouraged to turn for services to their unions first, and unions are committed to serving their retired members from within the organization. Union retiree departments are not mere referral systems.

Services to retired workers may be the agenda of the unions' social service department but these services are not the main priority of the union. "The world of work is an adversarial setting where the parallel interests of the individual and those of the organization may not be readily apparent" (Akabas and Kurzman 1982). It is essential for social workers practicing in union settings to understand the structure and functions of the union and the background of its members.

Visiting a "shop" (the work site), for example, enables the social worker to catch a glimpse of the worker's life before retirement and thus to establish valuable reference points for future interaction. Reading the union constitution will help the social worker understand the union's complex organizational hierarchy: the election process for officers and staff, the nomenclature of administrative units, the responsibilities of elected officials to their constituencies, and the rights and benefits of the members themselves. Effective delivery of social services to retired union members depend upon social workers in these settings broadening their knowledge of both the "nontraditional" auspices in which they work and the industry in which their clients have spent nearly a lifetime.

TYPES OF SERVICES

Direct Services

Direct services to union retirees include one-time services such as completion of an application form for a union benefit; longer-term, often task-centered casework involving more than one presenting problem; and long-term service continuing over several years. Wherever possible, the union expects its social workers to resolve retirees' problems "in house." When referral to a community agency like a hospital or nursing home is necessary, the union social worker coordinates and monitors the delivery of these external services.

The services requested of their unions by retirees involve transportation (assistance to shopping, doctors' offices, banks); counseling (for individual and family problems); eldercare (locating resources for adult children providing care to elderly family members); legal problems (wills, estates); union and government benefits (applications, appeals); medical and hospital bills (assistance with Medicare, Medicaid, and health insurance claims); homecare arrangements; nursing home placement (for retirees or family members); housing (help in relocating, landlord/tenant issues); and crime (victim compensation, safety courses). The actual provision of services is affected by the size of the retiree population and the priorities of the union. For example, a request by a District 65 retiree for transportation from the borough of Queens to a union dental clinic in Manhattan would be handled by the dispatch of a van maintained specifically for such purposes. For the much larger ILGWU, the provision of actual transportation would not be cost-effective; instead, their retiree service department would provide a companion to assist the retiree on public transporta tion.

Mrs. B., a 92-year-old retired garment worker, lives alone in a decaying inner-city neighborhood. She has vision and hearing impairments, and an operation on her knee two years ago has greatly restricted her mobility. Mrs. B. has no family nearby. She has a brother overseas and two nieces, to whom she is closest, in her native country in the West Indies.

Mrs. B. initially came into contact with her union retiree services program through her participation in a union-sponsored retiree club. At one club meeting, she approached the social worker who was present that day to speak about a new health insurance benefit for retirees. Mrs. B. wanted to apply for food stamps. The social worker and Mrs. B. arranged for a meeting later in the week at the retiree services office to give Mrs. B. time to gather the necessary documents. While completing the food stamp application, the social worker noticed that Mrs. B's rent seemed abnormally high. An appeal for a city-sponsored rent abatement was initiated.

Mrs. B came to see the social worker regularly over a period of about six months after the initial consultation. She was very depressed over her inability to secure visas for her two nieces in the West Indies to come to the United States. She wanted her relatives to live with her in New York but, although they were eager to do so, a complex and already long-standing problem with the immigration authorities had developed. Mrs. B asked the social worker for help in bringing her nieces to America. The social worker turned first to the union legal department for assistance in securing an attorney if necessary. The social worker also contacted a local agency specializing in immigration problems. This task, which unfolded over a period of two years, ultimately involved city and state agencies, Mrs. B's congressman, the office of the union president, and religious agencies as well as an immigration attorney and the U.S. Department of State. Mrs. B's nieces were finally able to visit their aunt but have not yet been permitted to remain permanently in the United States.

The social worker also helped Mrs. B with linkage to a neighborhood nutrition center and with appeals for new housing and energy assistance from the city, and she supplied a union paraprofessional to visit Mrs. B at home regularly to assist her with light shopping and transportation to doctors.

Retiree Clubs

Retiree clubs are another way in which unions preserve their ties with retired members. For the retirees, the clubs are important sources of support, socialization, and leisure, educational, and political activities. For the unions, they provide forums by means of which the unions can readily communicate with retirees on issues of concern to them and also mobilize the retirees' efforts on issues of concern to the union.

Retiree service departments serve the clubs in a number of ways. They often provide technical assistance in beginning a new club—site selection, fund raising (often from union sources), mailings to potential members, and program development. Union social workers may assist the clubs in arranging events and in some cases accompany groups on outings. They often address clubs, bringing information about union and government benefits and receiving feedback from members about the effectiveness of union retiree programs. They also make use of these opportunities to reach out to retirees who may need the direct services provided by the retiree service department.

Their numbers and locations will, of course, determine how retirees are organized. When retirees are widely scattered, a club may meet at a central union office. When retirees are concentrated in a particular community, community-based clubs are appropriate. Community-based clubs are desirable for their potential for heightened involvement in community affairs and greater networking with community agencies.

District 65 holds meetings in areas of heavy retiree concentration, both to publicize the programs offered at its headquarters in downtown Manhattan and to recruit volunteers for its home-visiting program. Social work students are then assigned to organize retirees into community self-help networks. Large international unions may have clusters of retirees living in areas quite removed from any union activity. The ILGWU, with International headquarters in New York City and one of its regional offices in Chicago, has a retiree club in the upper peninsula of Michigan.

Legislative and Political Action

Union retirees may be mobilized for legislative and political action on two fronts: issues of primary concern to the aged (e.g., Medicare) and issues of concern to the labor movement (e.g., trade agreements with foreign nations). These areas may overlap (e.g., Social Security concerns), and the mutual interests of active and retired workers will be the force behind legislative and political action.

Preliminary to legislative and political action must be education. Staff social workers may address gatherings of retirees, the retiree club being the natural vehicle through which to begin the educational process. Their purpose at these gatherings is to describe the issue at hand and to elicit retirees' initial impressions and concerns relative to the issue.

Legislative and political action are not unfamiliar to retired trade unionists. Through their years as active workers, members responded to as well as initiated calls to political or legislative action on behalf of their union. Social workers who represent and service retirees must be particularly sensitive to their impressions. Likewise, the resultant action should reflect a balance between the social workers' agenda and those impressions and concerns. One may explain an entire legislative campaign only to have a retiree ask why he or she should care in the first place. Clear, nontechnical language in presentation is critical to motivate retirees to take action. Social work training provides outreach and community organizing skills that can be readily transferred to political action with retiree groups.

The education process may include the development of "fact sheets" and "action guides" for retirees and their organizations. Fact sheets can look like glossaries—they help to visually sort out technical terms and concepts. They are perhaps most useful when kept separated from action guides. Their purpose is to supplement materials presented orally or in newsletters and union newspapers when an issue is exceptionally complex or critical.

Action guides tell retirees what to do. The following is an outline workers may find helpful in developing this sort of literature.

1. A concise statement of the issue at hand. If more than one issue requires action, separate pieces should be used. Example: "Reduced fare transportation is in jeopardy. Those of you 65 and older may now obtain an I.D. card free of charge to use our local transportation facilities. The county wants to charge you for this card, payable on a yearly basis."
2. Explain why retirees should be for or against the issue. Example: "This charge will impose undue hardship for you, our retired members living on fixed incomes."
3. Recommended action. Example: "We must oppose this charge and take action immediately. Write to your county legislators. Tell them . . ." Here a short sample letter can be inserted. Long

letters are not necessary; it's what is being said and the signature that has an impact.

4. The social worker's (or department's) name, phone, and address so retirees can obtain additional information.

Letter-writing campaigns may be most effective when explained and carried out simultaneously. Retiree clubs often have on hand paper, envelopes, stamps, and legislators' addresses. The social worker may address the club on an issue, distribute sample letters, and then help club members with their letters.

To better acquaint a target group with the legislative process at different levels of government, workshops may be held in which union staff and outside experts participate. Our hypothetical transportation issue might justify a workshop at which county legislators and retirees discuss the problem as each group sees it. The goal of preventing the imposition of a fare increase may be better achieved by the retirees themselves, not the union staff, describing their concerns.

Retraining and Employment

THE LABOR FORCE PARTICIPATION OF OLDER WORKERS

Four out of every ten workers 55 and older say they would prefer to continue working part-time after retirement (Sheppard and Mantovani 1982). In 1982, 20 percent of older employed men and women were employed part time on a voluntary basis, while only 10 percent of workers aged 20 to 54 were employed in this manner.

The 1981 Harris Poll for the National Council on Aging (on which the Sheppard study was based) concluded that the preference for part-time work, particularly in the same field as prior to retirement, was even more marked among those aged 55 to 64 (79 percent) and among those 65 and older (73 percent). Schulz (1980) noted that almost all older workers who work part time do so by preference to supplement income. In addition, he offered three other reasons why older workers prefer to work part time: 1) health concerns limit full-time employment; 2) the individual is participating in a phased retirement program; 3) the individual may "want more leisure but still value[s] highly the various social and monetary benefits arising from some amount of labor force attachment."

Thus, the Harris report noted: "The American labor market, and employers in particular, should anticipate extended participation of older workers in the world of work." The Work in America Institute

(1980) went beyond the "anticipatory references" of the Harris report to set out minimal guidelines for options to extend labor force participation:

> Employers should introduce and continue programs, where practicable to provide new options for employees such as job sharing, part-time jobs, job redesign, new work schedules, phased retirement.
>
> The reemployment of retired workers offers an opportunity that may benefit both workers and the organization. Therefore, management and unions should try to resolve the problems that presently prevent retired employees from returning to work on a full-time, part-time, or temporary basis, where practicable.
>
> Areas in which these retirees can benefit the company [or industry] include (1) contributing to the needs of the organizations, (2) filling in for employees on vacation or leave, (3) assisting the organization during peak work loads, and (4) assisting in training present employees. (pp. 3–4)

Before we examine the possible role of unions, and of social workers employed by unions, in developing training and employment programs for older and retired workers to facilitate reentry into the labor force, we must look at what motivates people to retire, to leave the work force in the first place. Subsequently, we must look at why those who have left the work force seek to return.

"The decision to retire is one of the major job-related *choices* people make and, once made, is usually not reversed. Among the factors affecting this decision are: health limitations, retirement income sources, the state of the economy and the demand for older workers" (Rivlin 1982). Yet what happens if the decision to retire is *not* voluntary? Health-related concerns are most often cited by Social Security studies as the reason for increasingly early retirement. The second major reason for early or "forced" retirement that these studies cite, however, is layoff or discontinuance of jobs. Among the workers is the unions described here, the realities of unemployment too often displace well-laid plans for a secure and voluntary retirement.

As workers reach their late 40s and early 50s, joblessness increases. The duration of unemployment is also greater for older workers. Kirkland states: "Once unemployed, the older worker runs the greatest risk of being without work for long periods of time. Official statistics do not include labor force "drop outs." Millions of older men and women have withdrawn from the labor force unwillingly because they simply could not find jobs and eventually gave up looking for them" (1982:12).

Long-term unemployment of older workers erodes savings earmarked for retirement. If and when these workers return to their original jobs, pension benefits may have been irreversibly reduced.

There are many disincentives, from an employer's point of view, to the hiring of older workers. (Kirkland reminds us that unions are rarely involved in the hiring of *any* new employees.) For example, hiring older workers adds costs to health and welfare benefit packages because older people use more health care services. Since 1982, the changes in the Medicare program have only exacerbated this particular situation by requiring for example, employers to provide their regular health insurance package for workers 65–69 should the worker so desire. In this case, Medicare becomes the secondary payor (or supplemental insurer) instead of the primary insurer as is generally the case for individuals over 65. Thus the employer has a disincentive to hire an older worker because the employer and not the government could be responsible for providing the bulk of that individual's health benefits.

Studies have shown that older workers seem to be less willing (or able?) to shift from looking for one type of work to looking for another. Finally, the skills developed by the current pools of older workers in labor-intensive industries such as auto, steel, apparel, and textiles are not readily transferable to today's "high tech" marketplace.

Many questions arise as to the role unions can or should take in the retraining and employment of older workers: Should unions establish training programs for workers 55–65 still on the job or—particularly in the industries described here—should they focus on employed workers in the same age group? Should unions develop reentry programs for already retired workers 65 and over? Is reemployment in the same industry they formerly worked in a realistic or suitable goal for older unemployed or retired workers? Should unions seek to train their workers for entry into other industries? Is is fair to younger workers when jobs are scarce in labor-intensive industries to introduce added competition for the same few jobs? Finally, what are the psychological realities relevant to these age groups and the lack of employment? Have the already retired done so voluntarily and made the necessary adjustments away from full-time employment? Can they cope with many added hours a day without a routine or regular schedule? Have their relationships with spouse and family become tense and strained? Haven't the unemployed been forced, unprepared, into a traumatic and vulnerable state and shouldn't their unions, therefore, attend to these unprecedented stresses before those of the retired group?

Organized labor has been active both nationally and locally in responding to the needs of the unemployed and the older worker.

Congressional action has resulted from labor advocacy in the areas of extended unemployment benefits and health care for the unemployed. Local unions have conducted seminars on stress and family problems arising from both short- and long-term unemployment. District 65 and the ILGWU have begun such programs under the auspices of their Member Assistance or Personal Service units. These units are, for the most part, distinct from programs in the same union that offer services to retired members (i.e., unless a worker is actually receiving a pension check, the aforementioned programs and *not* retiree service departments will be responsible for the delivery of services).

When possible, collective-bargaining agreements have also included the concerns of older workers. They have sought to provide, for example, stronger seniority systems in an effort to protect older workers from arbitrary layoffs caused by economic instabilities or changing technology.

FRIENDLY VISITING AS AN EMPLOYMENT PROGRAM

Social workers in union retiree service programs may be required to develop retraining or employment programs for *retired* workers 65 and older. A model program of this sort is the ILGWU's Friendly Visiting Program established in 1967.

The ILGWU Friendly Visiting Program employs retired garment workers in the service of their fellow retirees. Friendly visitors (FVs) are trained by the professional social work staff of the union's retiree service department to assist retired members with support, guidance, companionship, and in an advocacy capacity with matters such as benefit application procedures, nursing home placement, and linkage to community resources such as health clinics, nutrition programs and eldercare services.

FVs meet every three weeks for two hours with their supervisors. Small groups of five or six FVs meet together following individual supervision to share information and discuss cases. Social workers are responsible for overall supervision of FV cases and for assuring FVs of current and comprehensive information on procedures, case handling, and government, community, and union benefits. FVs are also required to attend quarterly in-service training meetings on topics such as nursing home placement and elder abuse.

The essence of the FV contact with a retiree is the home visit. (Regular phone contact is also maintained.) Each time a FV meets with a retiree (appointments are arranged in advance), he/she must fill out a report sheet describing the visit. FVs must be able to supply the following information for each contact:

1. Does the retiree live alone or with spouse, family?
2. How does the retiree manage? Can the retiree do his or her own cooking, shopping, cleaning?
3. Does the retiree have Medicare parts A and B? Does the retiree have supplemental health insurance to Medicare?
4. Does the retiree qualify for a city rent abatement?
5. Does the retiree know about: reduced fare benefits; neighborhood senior centers; union retiree clubs; union drug, eyeglass, health clinic benefits; other community services; direct deposit of Social Security and other benefit checks?

These reports are the basis for the supervisory session between the social worker and FV. Follow-up is conducted by both social worker and FV in many cases where a retiree requires sustained, coordinated services. Almost all direct services of the retiree service department are delivered through this collaborative model. Friendly visiting is a preventive service. The program does not wait until a retiree asks for a visit or is ill and in need of help. The program mandates that each new retiree be visited within the first year of retirement. Case histories illustrate the value of this program:

> A widowed retiree mourning the death of her only daughter is comforted by the FV's shared experience of a similar loss.
>
> A retiree is crippled with arthritis and struggling to use crutches. The FV suggests she consult her doctor for a walker, accompanies the retiree to her doctor's office, and assists with the purchase of the walker, which the retiree receives in two weeks.
>
> A retiree living comfortably with his daughter is desperately lonely for friends from the "old days." The FV introduces the retiree to the retiree club in his union local.

FVs are paid at the prevailing minimum wage and are entitled to specific sick and vacation benefits arranged through their employer, the union. Expenses such as transportation, postage, and telephone calls are reimbursed. A FV may set his or her own work schedule, but each month he/she will receive an "assignment" of twenty or thirty retirees to be visited. FVs work in their own neighborhoods, where they are familiar with helping networks available to older persons.

A friendly visiting program developed and sponsored by a union enables retirees to reenter the world of work through involvement with their own union and their contemporaries from the shop. Dressmakers, cutters, and pressers are retrained in a battery of new skills.

With retiree numbers increasing, unions and their service departments can provide a dual service with the establishment of a friendly visiting program: training and employment for one, outreach to many.

EMPLOYMENT IN RETIREE SERVICE DEPARTMENTS

Union retiree service departments may also directly employ retired workers as part-time clerical and support staff. These individuals may be retired union staff as well as members. Tasks may include secretarial work, reception, computer operation (for which the retiree would be trained), and special projects such as developing recreational programs or a pilot project for housekeeping assistance under the direction of a professional social worker.

The incorporation of retirees as staff in retiree service departments is a natural outgrowth of a philosophy that unions have held for years: to build the organization through the ranks, from within. There should be no question of appropriateness or age discrimination or turf struggles in the employment of retirees in union service departments. Retired trade unionists have organizing skills. The protection of their rights as active workers depended on their abilities both to initiate and to respond collectively to a call for action. The hiring of retirees as staff in union service departments offers an exemplary model for the training and employment of older and retired workers in less "age related" sectors of the economy.

EMPLOYMENT OUTSIDE THE UNION

What is the role of the social worker in helping retired workers to find employment outside the union? The focus here shifts, of necessity, to that of information specialist and technical adviser. The social worker must ask: What skills and strengths do retirees already have? Can they be retooled and, if so, how?

Employment agencies and services in both the public and private sectors geared specifically to older workers are rare at best. Hiring and training practices remain tainted by stereotypes of the elderly as lacking the motivation and skills to cope with modern technology. Sandell (1987) noted that older workers experience difficulties remaining in and reentering the labor force which

> stem from three distinct, but not mutually exclusive, sources: 1) factors totally unrelated to age, such as living in an economically depressed area or being subject to racial discrimination; 2) factors correlated with age—poor health and low levels of formal education are more common

among older workers and, in turn, are associated with low earnings; and 3) age discrimination.

Intervention is necessary, therefore, to promote elderly workers in a more realistic light to move away from generalizations such as those stated above. This is not an easy task in a society that is geared to the image of the perpetual "Pepsi generation."

Sheppard (1971) noted that society and its organizations (family, school, church, etc.) does little to prepare its members for "multi-careers prior to entry into the labor force." He further stated: "Our popular mentality . . . Is dominated by the single career concept, the notion that an individual should have a single lifetime occupational role-identity." We even have stereotypes that say: Blue-collar workers don't have careers, they have jobs. Our increasingly specialized professionalization allows this label to be attached only to the white-collar world. However, the labor force is graying, and increased longevity and better health should force a revision of this damaging type-casting.

In the area of employment, social workers' strategies should be to help clients set new goals for second careers: Can on-site training programs be set up? For example, if a computer system is available, will training retirees to use it facilitate their reentry into the labor force outside the protective auspice of the union? Can those interested be evaluated and referred to community-sponsored training and employment programs? Economic contingencies, in both the public and private sectors, will impact heavily on social workers' abilities to advocate retraining programs for older workers. In industries with an older work force and a shrinking market, such as the American garment industry, (average age of the unionized work force in the apparel industry is 45), social workers should look to developing specialized programs targeted to displaced and older workers who are likely to have been laid off well prior to the customary retirement ages of 62 or 65. Programs for displaced older workers should explore a wide range of issues and services including unemployment compensation and pension counseling as well as training and relocation strategies.

Post Retirement Programs

Pre-retirement programs are designed to help workers anticipate and plan for life in retirement. A post-retirement program (a single seminar may be enough) offers additional help from the vantage point of six months or a year after retirement. One's outlook and thus the assistance required may be vastly different once the transition from work to retirement has been completed.

The union social worker conducting a post-retirement program asks: "What is it like now that you have retired?" The social worker encourages exploration of that "state" from several perspectives: What is the retiree's relationship with family now that he or she has retired? How, if at all, have roles changed? How does a retiree feel about himself or herself in the midst of all these changes? Has the retiree noticed changes in attitude as the first year of retirement progresses? Aging stereotypes must be carefully discussed and worked through.

A post-retirement program can also be a refresher course on company and union benefits, health insurance, and community services. The focus here is on specific coping strategies so that if a particular service is required the retiree will know where, how, and when to apply. Retirees will probably have been exposed to this information at their pre-retirement programs, but the post-retirement program gives the social worker a chance to review this material and also to update it. Distribution of packets of information on Social Security, Medicare, senior discounts, and community resources is particularly important at this time.

Post-retirement programs can encourage retirees to remain active and to do so through their union, reconnecting them to the union through retiree clubs, classes, and social services. "Reconnection" serves two purposes: For the retiree, it increases options for activities, usually at little or no cost. For the social worker, it enhances the credibility of the retiree service department by assuring retirees' utilization of available union services.

Finally, post-retirement programs provide a good opportunity to evaluate the union's own preretirement programs. Through observation, discussion, and written evaluations with post-retirement attendees, service providers can gauge the strengths and weaknesses of their preretirement programs.

POLICY

The union retiree and older-worker programs reviewed here fall within the private sector. That is, the unions are private entities, and the workers they represent are not engaged in city, state, county, or federal government jobs.

Unions mandate and, for the most part, fund their retiree services. Shortly after its inception in 1967, the ILGWU Retiree Service Department received a state grant to underwrite a portion of its program. Although unions continue to solicit government funding for a variety of projects, basic funding is provided by the unions themselves. For example, UAW retirees voluntarily contribute one dollar from their monthly pension checks toward the support of retiree programs. District 65 retirees pay dues to a retiree local. The ILGWU offers yearly contributions to its retiree clubs.

On the other hand, public social welfare policies impact broadly on the delivery of retiree services, and union social workers must be knowledgeable about both the theory and the application of these policies in order to provide quality service to their constituents.

Unions and their workers are highly politicized. Labor legislation is the direct result of the struggles of workers and their representatives for government recognition and protection. The social worker's task will as often be to "translate" for a client the implications of a certain public policy (e.g., a chance in Medicare reimbursement regulations) as it will be to alert the organization to that policy's importance to retirees. Similarly, social workers must be ready to relate current union legislative goals to retirees, frequently in the quest for retiree support and assistance. Social workers may use their knowledge of policy to bridge what seems to be a rapidly widening gulf between the perceptions of active and retired members of their respective interests. The debate surrounding the current and future status of the Social Security system is illustrative of this gulf as it consistently pits the interests of today's elderly against those of tomorrows.

The intent of this section is to increase the social worker's awareness of public social welfare policy as it affects their roles as service providers. Detailed descriptions of programs such as Social Security and Title V can be found in handbooks published by the government. Unlike specific legislation mandating home-health care or legal services, for example, public policy on services to older workers can only begin to be described by a review of particular acts and regulations.

Social Security

The Social Security Act of 1935 recognized, for the first time, a compact between government and the citizenry to provide for income adequacy in old age. The original intent of the Act was to provide for a "floor of protection" for workers in retirement. Workers began paying into the Social Security System in the form of a payroll deduction (FICA) in 1937. The first benefit check was issued in 1940. Congress added benefits for survivors and dependents in 1939, and disabled workers became eligible for benefits in 1956.

The 1978 *Social Security Handbook* describes the program as one that has the "basic objectives of providing for the material needs of individuals and families, protecting aged and disabled persons against the expenses of illnesses that could otherwise exhaust their savings, keeping families together, and giving children the opportunity to grow up in health and security." Programs under the Social Security Administration include Retirement Benefits, Disability and Survivors Benefits, Medicare, and Supplemental Security Income.

Approximately 38 million persons in the United States in 1988 were receiving monthly Social Security checks. These were primarily retired workers (but also the disabled and survivors of deceased workers). Social Security retirement benefits are available to workers retiring as early as 62, although at reduced levels. Full Social Security benefits are available at age 65. The 1983 amendments to Social Security changed the popular American definition of retirement age for those born from 1943 to 1960 to 66 years and for those born after 1960 to 67 years. For each year that an individual over 65 works and does not collect Social Security, the benefit may be increased. This delayed retirement credit was revised in 1983 to follow a scale of increases. This system, however, will only benefit those retiring at normal eligibility age after 1989.

Workers contribute to Social Security through payroll tax deductions (7.51 percent in 1988–89). Employers pay an equal tax for employees. Work performed in a covered employment (almost all American workers are covered by Social Security) is "credited" to an individual's work record for eventual eligibility for Social Security benefits. Thus the concept that Social Security is an earned right.

Social Security credit is measured in what is known as "quarters of coverage." A worker's actual benefit is figured by means of a complex formula reflecting actual earnings and adjustments for national changes in average wages. Workers with high incomes receive higher benefits. On the average, benefits equal 42 percent of earnings just before retirement. For example, the maximum monthly benefit in 1988 was $822 for an individual retiring at age 65. The average monthly payment for an individual who retired with full benefits at age 65 in 1988 was $513. Social Security benefits are adjusted for inflation.

Eligibility for Social Security benefits is limited by an earnings test for those under age 70. In 1988, retired persons aged 65 to 70 drawing Social Security benefits could earn up to $8,400 ($6,120 for persons under 65) before losing $1 in benefits for each 42 of additional earnings. Beginning in 1990, the earnings test will result in a $1.00 reduction in Social Security benefits for every $3.00 over exempt earnings amounts. Until the 1983 amendments to the Social Security Act, all Social Security income was tax free. The 1983 amendments placed a threshold on nontaxable income of $32,000 yearly for a couple and $25,000 yearly for an individual.

In considering Social Security, special attention must be paid to the situation of women, particularly in view of the fact that most of the constituency of the union retiree programs discussed in this chapter are women. These women are most likely to be single. In 1980, 67 percent of all single women 72 and over were almost totally dependent on Social Security for income. Therefore, problems of elderly female retirees stemming from income inadequacy are frequent concerns of union social workers. They must often assist these clients in negotiating the Social Security bureaucracy on matters ranging from lost checks to retrieval of benefits. Other benefits such as rent exemptions, energy assistance, and food stamps may have to be obtained for clients with low Social Security benefits. Applications for Supplemental Security Income (SSI) may also be necessary. (SSI, although administered by the Social Security Administration, is not financed by payroll taxes and is not, therefore, a part of the Social Security system. It was designed to provide a minimum monthly income to needy individuals 65 and over or blind or disabled. An individual must have limited income and assets to qualify.)

Medicare

Medicare is Title XVIII of the Social Security Act, passed in 1965. Parts A and B of the Title mandate hospital and medical insurance, respectively. Medicare is available to most individuals over 65 and in some cases to persons under this age. Administration of Medicare is assigned to the Department of Health and Human Services. The Health Care Financing Administration (HCFA) is the agency within that department with jurisdiction over Medicare.

Medicare Part A (hospital insurance) covers inpatient hospital care. The Medicare beneficiary is responsible for the payment of a deductible, since Medicare is not designed to cover 100 percent of health care costs for the elderly. Supplemental insurance policies—"medigap" plans—are available from private insurance carriers to assist in payment of healthcare costs not covered by Medicare.

An individual should apply for Medicare three months before his or her sixty-fifth birthday, whether or not he or she intends to retire at that time and begin collecting Social Security benefits.

Medicare Part B (medical insurance) helps to pay for doctors' services, outpatient care, and home health care. Part B requires both a monthly premium (deducted from the beneficiary's Social Security check) and a yearly deductible that must be satisfied before Medicare will begin reimbursement.

Medicare reimbursement rates are based on 80 percent of the "reasonable and customary" charges for health care services. Beneficiaries are responsible for the remaining 20 percent plus whatever difference exists between the doctor's actual charge and the amount approved by Medicare for reimbursement. While eligibility for Part A is automatic, Part B coverage is optional. Most retirees elect to purchase Part B as well as a "medigap," or supplemental policy to Medicare.

Union social workers are often called upon to help clients negotiate the Medicare and related health-care service systems. If a beneficiary is not satisfied with a decision on a claim, social workers should be cognizant of the Medicare appeals process and be able to take the client through it (or seek assistance from trained advocates in fair-hearing procedures). In July 1988, the first major amendments to the Medicare system since its enactment were signed into law. The Medicare Catastrophic Coverage Act of 1988 was designed to help beneficiaries protect themselves from the devastating costs of unexpected illnesses. The Medicare Catastrophic Coverage Act was repealed in September 1989 before most of its provisions went into effect.

Title V of the Older Americans Act

Title V of the Older Americans Act of 1965 (Section 502) authorizes the establishment of programs for part-time community service employment of low-income individuals 55 years of age or older with "poor employment prospects," including, for example, the unskilled and women. Employment sites include hospitals, day care centers, and nutrition and energy projects.

The Administration on Aging contracts with agencies and organizations for the delivery of training to workers and for employment. In 1982, the Title V budget of $277 million provided an estimated 54,000 jobs. Also in 1982, the Congressional Budget Office reported that two-thirds of the participants in Title V programs were female, more than half were 65 or older, and the average hourly wage was $3.50.

Union social workers should be aware of these opportunities when assisting appropriate clients to reenter the labor force. Davis (1980), however, describes Title V as a "quasi-employment program which emphasizes income transfer to the eligible elderly poor participants as much or more so than it does mainline employment. It lacks the training, job development and appropriation essential for an employment program."

Employee Retirement Income Security Act (ERISA)

ERISA, passed in 1974, was the culmination of a decade of legislative work in the area of pension reform. Its basic intent was to set minimum standards for pension rights protection. It applied to all pension and welfare plans in existence on September 24, 1974, and those established thereafter. ERISA's impact was felt nationwide in almost every private pension plan since it required a step-by-step reevaluation of pension funding, finance, and administration.

ERISA has played a major role in establishing and redefining minimum vesting requirements for pension eligibility. Schulz (1980) defines vesting as "the provision [of a pension plan] that gives a [plan] participant the right to receive an accrued benefit at a designated age regardless of whether the employee is still employed at that time. Thus, vesting removes the obligation of the participant to remain in the pension plan until the date of early or normal retirement." As an example of the application of vesting to pension rights, consider the union member who, in order to qualify for a full pension, needed twenty years of employment covered under the plan. Before ERISA, if the worker left the industry or retired with only fifteen years, all contributions to the plan in his or her name would have been lost and the pension forfeited. ERISA set up requirements for all pension plans to provide minimum vested benefits based on at least one of three options for benefit accrual. Although the most prevalent plans following the enactment of ERISA were those that provided for vesting of 100 percent of accrued benefits after ten years of service, the Tax Reform Act of 1986 intended for most workers to attain vested status sooner than the schedule in the original ERISA legislation. Since 1986, some workers qualify for 100 percent vesting after five years of employment. Thus, our hypothetical union member above would, under ERISA, be eligible for a pension reflecting his/her fifteen years of service. Suppose seven of those fifteen years had been spent as a sewing machine operator in one factory and eight as an operator in another. Would that influence eligibility for a vested pension? In the garment industry, the answer would be no, because of the "portability" of pension rights for garment workers. Portability is "a type of vesting mechanism that allows employees to take their pension credits with them when they change jobs" (Schulz 1980). Although in theory portability should reduce erosion of benefits for workers who change jobs, "the administrative, financial, and actuarial complexities of setting up such arrangements have discouraged any significant action in this area" (Schulz 1980:134) and thus the positive effects of portability on workers have been minimal thus far.

Age Discrimination in Employment Act (ADEA)

ADEA was originally passed in 1967 and amended as of January 1, 1979. In it 1967 form it focused on age discrimination against employees between 40 and 65 only (thereby defining an older worker as one 40 or older.) The 1978 amendments made it illegal for a nonfederal employer to force workers to retire before the age of 70. Since 1978, the age 70 limit has been removed entirely by federal legislation. ADEA applies to most work sites with more than twenty employees.

ADEA represented a major step toward a national policy on older workers. Yet stereotypes of older persons' ability to perform on the job, their perceived health concerns, and the notion of increased costs of their employment persists some fifteen years after enactment. Realistically, of course, the major thrust of ADEA should be to combat mandatory retirement as a form of age discrimination. Kingson (1982) summarizes the potential impact of ADEA in relation to current retirement trends as follows: "Faced with projections for increased pension costs, longer life spans, and future declines in the number of younger workers relative to older workers, there is a clear need to begin to readjust our expectations concerning retirement age. The passage of this legislation [the 1978 Amendments to ADEA] may well be the beginning of the legitimization of later retirement (or, to put it another way, the beginning of the delegitimization of early retirement)."

The expected broad impact of the 1978 amendments to ADEA has not materialized. This is attributed in the literature to several factors, including: stereotypical attitudes that older workers are recalcitrant, untrainable, and unreliable; high rates of unemployment, and preference for younger workers when jobs become available; and weak administration and enforcement procedures of the Act. (Originally administered by the Department of Labor, ADEA is now under the jurisdiction of the Equal Opportunity Employment Commission.)

Union social workers will not find their primary role to be the enforcement of ADEA. This is the domain of a government agency. However, when working with clients who have recently lost jobs and are seeking new ones, social workers should be aware of the existence of ADEA and be able to help client negotiate its systems.

THE FUTURE OF RETIREE SERVICES

In the spring of 1983 the AFL-CIO established a new committee of its Executive Council known as the Committee for Retiree Affairs. A similar committee had been established in 1958 under the late AFL-CIO president George Meany, but its success had been negligible. Why would the AFL-CIO reestablish such a committee?

Demographics has much to do with the answer. Since 1958 the number of people 65 and over in the United States has increased from some 16 million to well over 28 million. Further, older Americans are more likely to vote and exercise their political clout than any other age cohort. One out of every five people who voted in the 1986 midterm elections was over age 65. (U.S. Senate 1987:147)

The growing ranks of the elderly include thousands of retired trade unionists. Thus the establishment of a Committee on Retiree Affairs signified organized labor's recognition both of its continued responsibility for these retired workers and of the contributions these retired workers can continue to make to the labor movement. Organized labor can speak out on issues of concern to its retirees: Social Security, Medicare, housing. In turn, retirees can assist organized labor with its social, educational, and political agenda. Active and retired workers can work together for their mutual interests.

In times of limited financial resources, some unions may regard retiree social services as luxuries they can no longer afford. Social workers in union retiree service departments are in a position to help retirees prove their value to the union as a whole. A legislative education program in a retiree club can enable retirees to help the union lobby a bill to protect strikers; a "foster grandparent" type of program in which retirees spend time with children of active workers in a city where day-care programs are costly and scarce will help the union to take care of its own. It is in the continuing interests of retirees, active workers, organized labor, and social workers in industrial settings that such options for reciprocity be well explored.

REFERENCES

Akabas, S. H. 1977. Labor: Social policy and human services. In *Encyclopedia of Social Work*. 17th ed. Washington, D.C.: National Association of Social Workers.

Akabas, S. H. and P. A. Kurzman, eds. 1982. *Work, Workers, and Work Organizations: A View from Social Work.* Englewood Cliffs, N.J.: Prentice-Hall.
Akabas, S. H., P. A. Kurzman, and N.S. Kolben, eds. 1979. *Labor and Industrial Settings: Sites for Social Work Practice.* New York: Columbia University/Hunter College/Council on Social Work Education.
Amalgamated Clothing and Textile Workers Union. 1982. *Social Services: Department Profile.* 2d ed. New York: Union.
American Association of Retired Persons. 1988. Special Report on the Medicare Catastrophic Coverage Act of 1988. *AARP News Bulletin,* vol. 29, no. 10.
Brodsky, J. and W. Robinson. 1981. Current employment programs: NCOA/TVA senior energy counselor program. *Aging and Work* 4(1):58–60.
Buck Consultants, Inc. 1983. *For Your Benefit . . .* New York: Buck Consultants.
Burkhauser, R. V. and G. S. Tolley. 1978. Older Americans and market work. *The Gerontologist* 18(5):449–453.
Clague, E., B. Palli, L. Kramer. 1971. *The Aging Worker and the Union.* New York: Praeger.
Copperman, L. F. and A. M. Rappaport. 1980. Pension and welfare benefits for older workers: The preliminary impact of the ADEA amendments. *Aging and Work* 3(2):75–87.
Davis, T. F. 1980. Toward a national policy on older workers. *Aging,* nos. 313–314, pp. 12–19.
District 65. 1982. *Programs for Retired Members.* New York: The Union.
Doctors, S. I. et al. 1980. Older worker employment services. *Aging and Work* 3(4):229–237.
International Ladies' Garment Workers' Union. 1971. *After a Life of Labor.* New York: The Union.
International Ladies' Garment Workers' Union. 1982. *Retiree Service Department.* New York: The Union.
Keizer, J., and M. Habib. 1980. Working in a labor union to reach retirees. *Social Casework* 61(3):180–183.
Kieffer, J. A. and A. S. Fleming. 1980. Older Americans: An untapped resource. *Aging,* nos. 313–314, pp. 2–11.
Kingson, E. R. 1982. Current retirement trends. In M. H. Morrison, ed., *Economics of Aging: The Future of Retirement.* New York: Van Nostrand Reinhold.
Kirkland, L. 1982. Employing the older worker: A labor perspective. *Generations* 6(4):12–13.
Korn, R. 1976. *A Union and Its Retired Workers: A Case Study of the UAW.* Ithaca, N.Y.: New York State School of Industrial and Labor Relations, Cornell University.
Kurzman, P. A. and S. H. Akabas. 1981. Industrial social work as an arena for practice. *Social Work* 26(1):52–60.
Louis Harris and Associates. 1981. *Aging in the Eighties: America in Transition.* Washington, D.C.: National Council on the Aging.
Meier, E. L. 1980. New ERISA agency considered an pension issues of women and minorities. *Aging and Work* 3(2):135–139.
Morrison, M. H. 1982. Economics of the older worker: A national perspective. *Generations* 6(4):18–19,65.
Morrison, M. H., ed. 1982. *Economics of Aging: The Future of Retirement.* New York: Van Nostrand Reinhold.
Rivlin, A. 1982. *Work and Retirement: Options for Continued Employment of Older Workers.* Washington, D.C.: Congressional Budget Office.
Sandell, S. H. 1987. *The Problem Isn't Age: Work and Older Americans.* New York: Praeger.
Schulz, J. H. 1980. *The Economics of Aging.* 2d ed. Belmont, Calif.: Wadsworth.

Sheppard, H. L. 1971. *New Perspectives on Older Workers.* Kalamazoo, Mich.: Upjohn Institute for Employment Research.
Sheppard, H. L. and R. E. Mantovani. 1982. *Part-Time Employment After Retirement.* Washington, D.C.: National Council on the Aging.
Social work and the workplace. 1982. *Practice Digest* 5(2):3–31.
Stein, L., ed. 1977. *Out of the Sweatshop: The Struggle for Industrial Democracy.* New York: Quadrangle/New York Times.
U.S. Administration on Aging. 1970. *Older Americans Act of 1965, as Amended.* Washington D.C.: GPO.
U.S. Department of Health, Education, and Welfare. 1979. *Social Security Handbook.* 6th ed. Washington, D.C.: GPO.
U.S. Department of Health and Human Services. 1987. *Your Medicare Handbook.* Washington, D.C.: GPO.
U.S. Department of Labor, Bureau of Labor Statistics. 1988. *Monthly Labor Review* 3(8):20–24. Washington, D.C.: GPO.
U.S. Senate. 1987. Special Committee on Aging. *Aging in America: Trends and Projections.* Washington, D.C.: Department of Health and Human Services.
Weiner, H. J., S. H. Akabas, and J. J. Sommer. 1973. *Mental Health Care in the World of Work.* New York: Association Press.
Work in America Institute. 1980. *The Future of Older Workers in America.* Scarsdale, N.Y.: The Institute.

15

Pre-Retirement Planning Programs

ABRAHAM MONK, PH.D.
Columbia University School of Social Work

Retirement marks the transition from productive maturity to a non-occupational status in later life. It is the focal point that triggers a confrontation with aging and its concomitant economic and social deficits. With mandatory retirement already sanctioned as a major national policy in the United States, the current forecast is that by the year 2030 there will be over 50 million persons 65 and over with an average of fifteen to twenty years of retirement living. Will their transition into retirement be a stressful one, marred by anxiety and uncertainty, or will they find security, meaningful opportunities for growth and even improve the quality of their lives? Much will depend on the extent of "anticipatory socialization," a conscious and systematic preparation that these prospective retirees have undertaken in midlife or in the years that precede their impending retirement.

Although most workers concede that there is a need to plan for their retirement, it is estimated that only about 10 percent of the labor force have actually gone through such programs. Moreover, a 1983 study conducted by the U.S. General Accounting Office revealed that 40 percent of workers included in pension plans offering early retirement were not aware of, or were incorrect about, their eligibility for that benefit. Only 11 percent of the workers knew about their prospective benefits (*Productive Aging News* 1988)

Pre-retirement planning programs have emerged only during the last three decades and remain, for the most part, in their experimental stages. Federal legislation fostered their implementation over ten years ago with the 1973 amendments to Title III of the Older Americans Act. A variety of programs for retirement preparation were launched during the last twenty years by a new professional cadre of pre-retirement counselors. The main objective of their efforts usually consists of providing information and planning skills that will enable individuals to make adequate choices concerning their post-retirement lives. The program content invariably includes financial planning, health maintenance, nutrition, changing roles and attitudes, volunteer roles, leisure-time activities, and housing alternatives. Most focus only on tangible "nuts and bolts" issues. A few venture into more sensitive psychological concerns.

As preparation for retirement is being recognized as a legitimate public priority, there is reason to wonder whether the programs that resulted from pioneer efforts of the 1960s and 1970s are suited to the needs of the swelling ranks of retirees of the 1980s and 1990s. What features of the present "first generation" pre-retirement programs have worked and should be continued in the future? Which ones will have to be discarded? What new directions should future programs follow in terms of format, auspices, and content? What will be their central themes? How will they account for emerging realities such as inflationary pressures, postponement of the retirement age, loss of confidence in the Social Security system, high health care costs and rapid occupational obsolescence? What role will corporate employers and unions play in the sponsorship, design, and implementation of such programs? As these questions are answered, the very nature of a "second generation" of pre-retirement programs more responsive to the 30 million retirees of the 1990s may begin to unfold.

Employers, personnel counselors, and industrial social workers entering this field of service are confronted with two central questions:

1. Do pre-retirement preparation program actually work? What service do they render?
2. What shape will these program adopt in the next generation, and how can they become attractive to cost-conscious sponsors?

Before these questions are answered, it is befitting to observe the field at large. A review of the literature and its main issues will provide the proper perspective to this critical service.

THE RETIREMENT SYSTEM IN TRANSITION

Retirement has become an established institution in modern societies for those nearing the seventh decade of life. The right of older people to continue working if they so desire, irrespective of overall manpower, mobility, or efficiency considerations, is being advocated, however, at a time when large numbers of workers opt to retire *before* the 65-year age limit. There is an unmistakable trend among males toward shortening their work lives. According to a report issues by the Hoover Institution (1988), 87 percent of all males retire before age 65. While poor health was the predominant reason for the early retirements of the 1960s and 1970s more recent studies quoted by the Hoover report link this early trend to the better financial status of older workers.

While policymakers speculate about the age at which American workers will opt to retire, it is a fact that more people than ever are retiring today. A threefold retirement pattern is likely to evolve: first, the present trend toward early retirement (ages 60 to 62) may continue as larger numbers of workers begin drawing income supports from private pensions; second, conventional retirement at 65 will probably attract occupationally stable and financially cautious workers; and, third, late retirement at 70 will probably appeal to healthy, achievement-oriented older workers.

Regardless of the option selected, retirees can expect to spend an increasing number of years in retirement. As stated by Greenough and King (1977), in 1935 a male retiree of 65 could expect to live about thirteen years in retirement. Today, the life expectancy of a male aged 65 is eighteen years. Moreover, the labor-force participation of older workers has been steadily declining over the past twenty-five years. It reached a low of 19.1 percent in 1980 for men 65 and over, compared to 27 percent ten years earlier. It is worth mentioning that working older women held their ground during the same period, but they constituted a small minority of their cohort (U.S. Congress 1981). True, this trend may slow down even reverse because the work force itself is aging. In the course of the next decade employees between the ages of 35 and 54 will be the fastest growing labor force segment. By the year 2030, the median age of the work force is expected to rise from the present 32 to 42 years (AARP 1987). The relative decrease in the number of younger workers, coupled with declining unemployment rates may spearhead a new manpower strategy aimed at enticing older workers to actually delay retirement, or similarly, to bring back the retirees with the promise of flexible and individualized schedules that take into consideration their health, leisure interests, etc. (U.S. Senate 1985). This will constitute a fundamental turn around from labor practices that, until recently tended or discourage gradual transitions from work to retirement, or cycles of departures and reentries of varying flexibility and duration. Instead of a drastic separation between work and retirement, the American workforce may be heading toward a gradual blurring of their boundaries.

THE NEED TO PLAN

The retirement transition usually involves a loss of income, an alteration of familial and social relationships, increased leisure time, and, for many, the loss of status and of meaning derived from one's work. Each of these areas, when unforeseen or unplanned for, can create obstacles to a successful adjustment.

Sheldon, McEwan, and Ryser (1975) have identified lack of preparation for retirement as a major obstacle to its success. Such preparation, they suggest, should include the development of financial and social alternatives to employment, the anticipation of change, and the planning of a response to that change that will lead to a positive accommodation to one's newly developed life-style.

The extent to which planning for retirement is altogether feasible was questioned, however, by Schulz (1980), who stated that the individual preparing for retirement cannot establish with certainty when he will die, what his basic retirement needs will be, nor what life-style he will ultimately prefer for that period. Moreover, he cannot anticipate the future rate of inflation, which may depreciate the value of those retirement assets that do not adjust fully and reduce the buying power of income from those assets. Ultimately, he cannot predict the rate of economic growth, which is likely to affect his economic position relative to that of the wage-earning population. Pre-retirement planning programs are called for, however, to help the potential retiree shape expectations and spell out realistic personal goals, not to engage in guesswork about future events. Yet the majority of employers do not offer systematic or comprehensive preretirement programs. Morrison and Jedrziewski (1988) surveyed all members of the American Society of Personnel Administration and found that while more than half—55 percent—of the employers offered early retirement preparation information, only 33 percent of these programs encompassed specially designed features to meet individual needs. Hayes (1987) sought information about programs specially attentive to middle-aged female workers and found that only 8 out of 300 surveyed organizations did offer them.

Ossofsky (1980) reported that a survey of the nation's largest corporations revealed a heightened awareness among corporate leaders of the grave financial ramifications of inflation for retirees. There is also an increasing sense of corporate responsibility for the welfare of older workers and an interest in developing retirement planning programs. Retirement programs, however, remain the exception rather than the rule among survey participants. The absence of programs can be attributed to their low priority status and the lack of personnel to implement them. Respondents agreed that the responsibility for planning should be shared by the individual and the employer.

THEORETICAL PERSPECTIVE

Retirement constitutes for some the advent of a leisured life-style, the reward for long years of work, and a liberation from boring and draining routines. For others, it is a painful transition because it terminates status-enhancing roles without replacing them adequately. Moreover, it demotes most individuals to standards of living below those they were used to most of their lives. Both views concur, however, that anticipatory socialization can facilitate an adaptation to the impending transition. Anticipatory socialization, in the form of pre-retirement planning, thus serves to reorient the individual and to give continuity to a series of role positions. It softens the abruptness of change and makes the future more manageable. Cumming and Henry (1961), postulating that retirement is part of the natural and universal process of disengagement, gave advocates of the first perspective their long-awaited theoretical justification. Disengagement is a social process that occurs even in the absence of a psychological urge to sever ties from society. It serves to functionally minimize the disruptive consequences of the ultimate disengagement—death—and, in all circumstances, it is the basic prerequisite for "successful" aging, here conceived as a stage when society no longer places obligatory demands on the individual and the individual responds by withdrawing from dominant, producing roles. Rosow (1973) did not agree with the alleged naturalness of the disengagement process and viewed the cessation of the work role as affecting the person's sense of self-esteem. "The process of role loss," he stated, "steadily eats away at these crucial elements of social personality and converts what is to what was. . . . If the social self consists of roles, then role loss erodes self-conceptions and sacrifices social identity" (p. 83). Through every other stage of the life cycle, individuals have managed to cope with crises and develop ways to substitute and even improve upon the losses they experienced. Retirement, however, constitutes entrance into a stage devoid of socially prescribed roles. It throws individuals into a limbo of rolelessness. Lacking any sense of purpose, many retirees feel, as Rosow added, "oppressively useless and futile."

The notion that retirement is a "stressor" that negatively impinges upon the central component of the person's identity was challenged by Streib (1958), who discovered that the alleged psychological trauma was not as profound as had been assumed and could be caused by other factors besides retirement. Personal circumstances such as poor health and low socioeconomic status may depress the morale of the older worker more than retirement itself. Simpson and McKinney (1966) similarly found that the adjustment patterns that evolve after retirement depend heavily on previous lifelong coping behaviors and the kind of work from which the individual retires.

Theoretical interpretations have expanded into a more diversified array of conceptual systems, and preretirement programs based on their premises have followed course. While often similar in structure or content, programs differ in their underlying philosophical orientations. Monk (1977) identified five theoretical models of pre-retirement planning programs. The first four models correspond to Schein's (1980) four sets of images of humankind: rational-economic; social; humanistic; and complex. The fifth model centers on crisis theory. The following is a summary of these five models:

1. The *rational-economic* model assumes that economic self-interest and, therefore, work-oriented values are the bases of all human motivation. Life after retirement must therefore involve a rechanneling of the achievement motive into hobbies and voluntarism. The focus of programs founded on this premise is to help prospective retirees remain active and seek rewards in civic or community oriented volunteer roles.
2. The *social* model identifies man's need to belong and to be accepted by others as the major human motivator, more important than financial motives. Programs that reflect the social perspective rely primarily on group peer support. The content of such programs emphasizes:
   a. *Role flexibility* or the capacity to take on new life roles which were not typical of the middle years.
   b. *Interpersonal competence.* Group dynamics, sensitivity training, encounter groups, and transactional analysis are emphasized in some programs to promote better self-awareness, communication skills, and the ability to handle conflict, ambiguity, and dissidence in human interaction.
3. The *humanistic-existential* model assumes that man primarily strives for meaning in life and that pride and self-esteem are enhanced when creative capacities are developed. It sees retirement as an opportunity for human liberation through increasing

self-awareness and encouraging individual growth and self-exploration of one's potential. This humanist trend seeks to promote the concept of "lifelong learning," continued personal growth, and self-renewal.

4. The *complex-systemic* model starts from the premise that man is complicated and highly variable system. Each individual is unique in terms of interests, concerns, and motivational patterns. Variance exists not only between people but also within the individual at different points in his/her life. Therefore, in order to fully appreciate these personal differences, individualized preretirement counseling must be provided, rather than any kind of standardized program. This includes case diagnosis, planning, and the provision of information based on an assessment of each person's situation and needs.
5. The *crisis model* is not independent of the four preceding archetypes, since there is a crisis component in each of them. All programs must contend with emotional turmoil, anxiety, and fear. This model emphasizes that retirement is a loss that must be grieved. The ego sustains an injury as a result of this loss which creates a high risk of depressive reactions in retiring workers. Programs are therefore designed to foster a life-review process including the recognition of the successes one has achieved as well as one's strengths and assets. Preparation for grief work and reconciliation with impending losses are primary goals.

These five models do not represent strict or pure categories. Many programs incorporate features or attributes of more than one model. However, they identify trends and central ideas within the new and growing field of preretirement and life planning.

THE PROVISION OF SERVICES

The designation "retirement preparation programs" refers, according to Olson, to "formally organized interventions so that an employee . . . can gain information about, and begin to prepare for his or her impending retirement" (1981:176). Olson inventories the various names given to such programs: pre-retirement assistance, pre-retirement counseling, pre-retirement planning, pre-retirement education, etc. Of more recent vintage, however, are broader, euphemistic labels such as "life transitions counseling," "life-long learning," "life planning," "personal growth," etc. In a more recent paper Olson and

Koslovski (1988) deplore the confusion between "life planning" which encompass many age-related changes, retirement included, and the more specific retirement planning programs. If the latter are conceived to assist with the transition from work to retirement, the relation between retirement and other areas of human experience require a more carefully differentiation.

The designing and implementation of retirement planning programs was initially the province of education specialists. Counseling personnel, industrial psychologists, and social workers made subsequent claims of competence and expertise and by and large succeeded in validating them over a couple of decades of trial and error. Most programs are offered by private corporations and public employers as an employee benefit. It is not unusual, however, for unions to fill the vacuum. More recently, community colleges, continuing education programs, public libraries, senior citizen organizations, life insurance companies, savings and loan associations, chambers of commerce, and Area Agencies on Aging have assumed a share of the task. It is virtually impossible to establish which is a better or more successful sponsor as each may be appealing to a different constituency.

Almost thirty years ago Wermel and Beideman (1961) altered that most programs are "limited" in scope because the information they provide does not exceed pension and Social Security benefits. Only a few are "comprehensive"—that is, include housing, health, legal, and leisure issues and even some psychological concerns. The picture may have been reversed. A survey by Research and Forecasts (1980) indicated a substantial trend toward increasing comprehensiveness.

However, pre-retirement planning programs have consisted for the most part of an employer's providing last-minute, one-shot presentations of the company's pension program. Corporate or management initiatives have often been motivated by a desire to encourage employees to utilize early retirement options and to improve the corporate image, or by the belief that such programs would enhance worker morale and thereby increase productivity. Glamser and DeJong (1975) found the effectiveness of these programs to be relatively minimal. As case examples reported by the *50 Plus* retirement newsletter of comprehensive programs, it is worth mentioning one started by the Westinghouse Electric Corporation of Pittsburgh in 1980. This program consists of seven weekly, two-hour sessions covering the following topics: Planning for Your Successful Retirement; Your Home; Health; The Law; Leisure; Money; and The Company's Benefits. It recruits resource speakers from the community and usually includes ten to fifteen couples in each seminar. The program offered by the International Minerals and Chemical Corporation of Northbrook, Illinois, is structurally similar but the sessions are lengthier, up to three hours. It is occasionally offered in the evening, preceded by dinner, and includes, as an incentive, a special education-assistance bonus of $500 for pursuing hobbies or specialized training.

Fitzpatrick (1980) reported that the National Council on Aging had developed a program structured for middle-aged workers ranging from blue-collar employees to middle-level executives. The program included eight planning areas: life-style planning, financial planning, new careers in retirement, leisure time, health, personal relationships, living arrangements, and community services.

The American Association of Retired Persons (AARP), the largest grass-roots membership organization of older persons has recently come up with a new program called "Think of Your Future" (1986). It replaces A.I.M., an earlier product named after Action for Independent Maturity, AARP's special retirement division.

The AARP program touches all conceivable topics, from the more instrumental and concrete like financial security, housing, investments, legal arrangements and estate planning, to the more subjective ones like roles and attitudes, choice of life-styles, family relations, etc. The program's content can be taught and discussed in a seminar or may be presented for group discussions. The main pedagogical strategy is to affirm that there are no prescribed normative solutions and that each participant must consequently explore the alternatives that are more suitable to his/her life circumstances and aspirations. Moreover, the Program underscores the developmental theme of growth and exploration of new life opportunities. Rather than limiting itself to systematize the information and outline the range of alternatives, the program adopts an exhortational tone aimed at motivating people to begin planning.

THE EVALUATION OF PROGRAM EFFECTIVENESS

Almost simultaneously with the design and implementation of program models, pre-retirement counselors pondered whether their initiatives actually accomplished their stated objectives. Initial evaluation efforts have shown some promising results. Charles (1971) studied workers who participated in pre-retirement planning at the Drake University Pre-Retirement Planning Center and found that there was an increase in awareness and involvement in many aspects of retirement—financial concerns, health, life-styles, etc. The National Council on the Aging (1973) surveyed participants before and after a retirement preparation program given by United Airlines and concluded that participants had a more positive attitude toward retirement as well as possessing more accurate information about its various aspects.

Ash (1966) also compared those who completed a course in pre-retirement planning with a comparable group of retirees who were not involved in such a program. The experimental group was more favorably disposed toward post-retirement life. Three years after retirement, the group members retained a higher sense of purposefulness compared to the control group. Tornquist et al. (1988) compared five companies that offered AIM's "Think of Your Future" program with 5 that did not have a retirement planning program. Participants in the first group had a higher gross annual family income after retirement than nonparticipants. Given the fact that individuals with high pre-retirement incomes were not more likely to participate than those with low income, the researchers presume that the AIM's strong emphasis on financial planning could partially explain those findings. It is interesting to note that participants with lower income and poorer health found the program very beneficial. Their satisfaction was much higher than that of nonparticipants with higher income and better health.

What did the employers gain from offering the program? Tornquist et al do not feel that they accrue many benefits other than that of promoting a better image of corporate responsibility and compliance with ERISA's requirements. In their conclusions they add the emphasis on financial planning is the key to the program's success, and they recommend that employees should begin these programs much earlier in their careers.

Overall, the evidence to date suggests that pre-retirement preparation programs are helpful to the preretiree in planning activities and in easing the transition from work to retirement. Relationships have been established between exposure to programs and successful retirement factors (e.g., acceptance of retirement transition, sound financial plans, realistic view of retirement, disbelief in the stereotypes and myths of retirement, retirement activities, good health, etc.). However, it is important to mention the possibility of selective bias in research findings. As Kasschau (1974), Monk (1977), Heidbreder (1972), and others have suggested, those who are most likely to experience problems in retirement are the least likely to plan for it, while those who do participate in planning may already be mindful and positively inclined toward retirement. For instance, Heidbreder studied factors the retirement of blue- and white-collar workers and reported that poorly adjusted retirees were twice as likely to have engaged in little or no planning.

Comparative program evaluations are beginning to shed some light on the controversies surrounding the relative effectiveness of various program models. Kasschau had delineated programs in terms of "planning" functions and the "counseling-adjustment" approach. In view of the fact that the majority of people arrive at retirement without realistic plans, the "planning" perspective seeks to help one develop reasonable expectations about retirement life and to anticipate and prepare for income loss. Since adjustment is correlated with health and income, the ideal program should emphasize the planning function. Kasschau suggests that counseling programs based on the view of retirement as a transition crisis are successful in promoting planning.

Many programs emphasize group processes, human growth, and consciousness-raising approaches as instructional strategies as opposed to the more traditional methods of instruction. Bolton (1976), at the University of Nebraska, evaluated a humanistic program entitled Planning and the Third Age. He reported that 74 percent of the participants thought the program was useful and 94 percent were favorably disposed to the humanistic (affective) group processes. Glamser and DeJong (1975) compared a group-discussion model to an individual-briefing model using an experimental control-group research design. The group-discussion method was reported more effective in increasing knowledge of retirement issues. Participants felt better prepared for retirement, were less uncertain about the future, and showed significant increases in the number of preparation activities undertaken. The individual-briefing program was relatively ineffective, suggesting the need for comprehensiveness in pre-retirement program design. Boyack and Tiberi (1975) reported the findings of the first phase of a project comparing three approaches: a group counseling model; a lecture discussion model; and an information media model. The following results were cited:

1. There were significant differences between each program and the control group in regard to attitudes, behavior, and information growth.
2. The group counseling approach indicated the greatest degree of positive change on attitudinal and behavior variables.
3. The lecture discussion approach indicated the greatest degree of change in information growth variables.
4. The information media approach indicated the greatest degree of change in one financial information variable.

Thus research to date on techniques and program formats implies that a variety of methods are effective on different outcome measures related to the major objective of pre-retirement planning.

ROLE OF THE SOCIAL WORKER COUNSELOR

Social workers involved in preretirement counseling usually perform three major tasks:

1. *Developmental.* This consists of "selling" the idea of preretirement preparation, of generating self-awareness and involving as many people as possible, and of assuring that these programs are offered on a continuing basis in a variety of settings. The organizational task is manifold and ranges from planning and implementation through the evaluative stage.
2. *Educational.* The transition into retirement implies an adjustment to new life conditions. Retirees need to discover where they can find satisfaction for their needs, interests, and expectations. Assessing the person's personal needs, determining the most suitable and gratifying sources, and facilitating the connection with such services resembles the information, referral, and monitoring functions of classical case management. The role- and skills-learning process operating at the retiree's end makes the task indistinguishable from adult-education models.
3. *Therapeutic.* When the impending transition is negatively experienced and the person harbors unrealistic expectations, the ensuing conflict may require therapeutic assistance. It may lead to a better sense of self-awareness and a new sense of direction like the one he/she possibly experienced in past work roles. As stated by Schlossberg, Troll, and Leibowitz (1978), it is the responsibility of the therapist "to help clients regain a sense of control by pointing out to them expanded alternatives, by offering them guidance in narrowing down options, and by making them aware of existing resources."

In a more schematic fashion, the range of social work tasks may be outlined as follows:

1. *Developmental*
   a. *Research.* Surveying workers' needs and interests and problem formulation. Inventorying benefits, entitlements, an resources. Implementing a process and impact evaluation.
   b. *Organization and Planning.* Negotiating auspices and support

for the program. Securing staff, speakers, and consultants. Designing the format and course content. Training volunteers or professional staff. Developing training course content, evaluative instruments, and advertising materials. Reaching out to potential participants and promoting program objectives.

2. *Educational.* Gathering information about participants. Obtaining sources of information and negotiating consultative participation from major sources (pension administrators, health-insurance administrators, Social Security officials, etc.). Delivering course content in lecture format, group discussions, and individual tutoring sessions. Referring participants to specialized sources and monitoring the linkage process. Eliciting feedback.
3. *Therapeutic*
   a. *Individual:* Casework counseling; individual assessment; crisis intervention; problem solving and setting of life goals.
   b. *Group:* Resocialization; problem solving, task-oriented and self-help groups.

Many of the tasks in reference are generic requirements of any information and referral service, but no other aging-related service may require such a vast arsenal of information sources. Social workers delivering preretirement training and counseling must become aware of the potential inputs of

Area Agencies on Aging
Social Security Administration
Consumer protection agencies
Adult- and continuing-education programs
Life insurance companies
Investment consultants and estate planners
Bank trust officers
Tax attorneys
Health-insurance carriers
Interstate service commissions
State real-estate commissions
Better Business Bureaus
Transportation departments and public transit authorities
Internal Revenue Service
Local bar associations
Local bank managers
Crime and fire-protection agencies
Health maintenance organizations
State lawyers referral services

Legal-aid services for the elderly
Local hospitals
Nutrition programs for the aged
Physical-fitness programs
Blindness, arthritis, heart, cancer, and Alzheimer's disease prevention organizations
Franchise organizations
Departments of Commerce
National Park Service and Forest Service
National Center for Voluntary Action
Service Corps for Retired Executives
Multiservice senior centers
Utility companies
Chambers of Commerce
Private employment agencies
University extension and career-training programs
Recreation programs
Self-help organizations
Veterans Administration and veterans organizations
Homecare services

The list, obviously, is a partial one and keeps expanding. Pre-retirement counselors cannot be expected to master in detail what each of these resources offers, but they should know how and whom to turn to for the pertinent information on a one-time basis or even for a continuous advisory relationship.

ASSESSMENT

Assessing pre-retirees' needs also transcends the generic psychosocial inventories of the social work profession and requires additional fine tuning and in-depth exploration in the following areas:

Age, race, sex.
Marital status. Length of marriage, onset of widowhood, presence of children and extent and quality of interaction with them, presence of living elderly parents and responsibilities toward them.
Educational advancement. Educational level reached, continuing education record, retraining and updating occupational skills, initiation and possible completion of a second career.
Health status. Onset of chronic conditions, functional ability and

history of work-related disabilities, health maintenance, prevention and fitness practices.

Housing and interregional move. Status of possible home ownership, equity, outstanding debts, condition of house and extent of needed repairs, local taxes, access to services, amenities, and possible employment; future housing and regional preference, incidence of climate on health, and proximity to relatives and friends.

Labor force participation. Career patterns, job security, and advancement prospects if remaining in the labor force; labor force demand in present occupational sector.

Financial resources and assets. Savings, Social Security credits, and vesting in private pension plans; estate planning.

Use of time. Leisure interests, skills, hobbies, physical activities, and cultural interests

Social participation. Volunteer experience and community participation; networks of same cohort friends and intergenerational involvement.

Life goals. Formulation of postretirement objectives based on personal interests and a realistic appraisal of available resources

IMPLEMENTING THE PROGRAMS

The actual presentation of the instructional material in lecture, group, or tutorial fashion is usually based on fairly standardized and professionally reliable guidelines and handbooks, issued by specialized organizations, universities, and private corporations. The most widely used are those published by the American Association of Retired Persons through its AIM division, the National Council on Aging, the Industrial Relations Center of the University of Chicago, the University of Michigan, the Ethel Percy Andrus Gerontology Center of the University of Southern California, and private corporations like Hearst (Retirement Advisers Inc.). The International Society of Pre-Retirement Planners—a membership organization of individual counselors, designers of packaged programs, and corporate providers—acts as a clearinghouse of most ready-made instruction resources.

Because none of the instructional kits are tailor-made for the needs of a specific group of learners, social workers must make proper adaptations, combine elements of several such programs, and experiment and invest their ingenuity in innovative departures. The instructional series of meetings is, however, only the first stage. It serves to create awareness, but it must be followed by problem-solving tasks in a collaborative group atmosphere. It is ultimately intended that participants will feel stimulated to actually formulate a set of objectives, a plan, and begin working toward its implementation. On occasions, the plan will be tested in a group situation through role playing, simulations, and self-analysis. In a more realistic sense, the implementation phase will be a lengthy one, during which the social worker, possibly in conjunction with the group, will provide feedback and encouragement and assist in the reexamination of the objectives and in acquiring the necessary skills for their realization. To this end, preretirement counselors are often inspired by the andragogical method (Ingalls and Arceri 1972). Andragogy is defined as the art of leading adult learning. Learners are committed to a process of self-diagnosis in a facilitative group environment and learn a problem-solving orientation. Individuals go through a sequence that includes:

1. *Needs assessment.* Identification of personal lags and problems that require resolution.
2. *Competency model building.* Inventorying the person's potential abilities and actual preferences, identifying the actual gap between the two and what may be required to overcome the gap. The gist of the method consists precisely in working on that gap, between what the person can do and what he or she wishes to do.
3. *Decision-making model.* Individual reeducation starts from the above-mentioned gap and assumes the form of a commitment, a sense of purpose with a definition of priorities or a rearrangement of existing priorities. The trainer assists in creating a learning climate, provides clarification, helps discerning between realistic and unrealistic aspirations, encourages mutuality, and acts as a consultant in the formulation of personal measurable objectives.

FUTURE DIRECTIONS

Programs presently in operation have obvious weaknesses. Most fear touching upon psychological issues because they regard that as an intrusion into the private lives of the participants. They tend to begin too late, when retirement is practically around the corner. Few really venture into painful concomitants of old age such as disability, widowhood, and death. Finally, most programs are too short, covering, at best, eight sessions of one to two hours each, and little attention is given to reinforcing previously acquired skills.

The future character of pre-retirement counseling programs will depend on the sequencing patterns between work, leisure, and education. Work, according to Hirschorn (1977, 1979), is undergoing a change from the fixed linear pattern of schooling and job scheduling of classical industrialism to a more flexible or cyclical pattern of interspersing work and education. It will also include a more subtle interpenetration of work requirements and personal life-styles. Initial symptoms of the transition are in early retirement, alienation from job ladders, more restlessness and career switching in middle life, more flexible time schedules, and dual careers in families that need to be coordinated. New organizational forms are emerging in the more advanced sector of the economy, based on temporary, task-centered teams, like "throw away" organizations rather than fixed job hierarchies.

Programs will then be geared to facilitating gradual retirements and periodical reentries to occupational roles. It is possible that present-type programs will give way to "life planning," "second-careers programs," planning for life transitions throughout the life span, or more specific forms of leisure education. "Second-career" programs, however, are too often euphemisms for volunteer recruitment. At times, they capitalize on the retiree's technical experience and seek suitable assignments in the service sector like the Second Careers Volunteer Program of New York and the Los Angeles Second Careers Program reported by Shackman (1980).

However, there are very few employment programs directed to older workers. As reported by Root and Zarrugh (1982), the few in operation are targeted to specific categories of workers and tend to exclude unskilled blue-collar workers. Sheppard and Mantovani (1982) found pervasive interest in post-retirement, part-time employment precisely among Hispanics, blacks, women, and low-income older workers. Both studies suggest that planning for post-retirement employment should occur prior to retirement and that proper incentives must be offered to employers to generate work opportunities. Coberly, Bentsen, and Klinger (1983) list such possible incentives: hiring subsidies, tax credits of up to 50 percent on the first $6,000 of an employee's first year's wages, training subsidies, Social Security waivers, tax credit for health-insurance costs, and placement and screening services. In a study of a *Fortune 500* sample and smaller southern California companies, they found a positive disposition to hire older workers if such inducements were sanctioned by public policy. Long-range initiatives tend to underscore the policy inadequacies in current retirement practices and advocate the provision of partial retirement options in public-pension systems, abolition of work disincentive provisions in Social-Security benefits, and tax incentives for experimenting with retirement options such as shorter work weeks, sabbaticals, extended vacation periods, part-time employment, job sharing, educational leaves, phased retirement, "flextime" systems, etc.

Many of the above initiatives remain, for the moment, in a hypothetical stage. It is not known how effectively they would respond to the challenge of demographic trends, economic realities, and personal value aspirations of the emerging adult cohorts. Increasing life expectancy and escalating costs of Social Security have already resulted in the gradual postponement of the mandatory retirement age.

In the more immediate future, there is moderate evidence of increasing employer concern with older workers' needs, including retirement preparation. Employers are beginning to assist workers with their elder care responsibilities. The Elder Care Referral Service (ECRS) created to that effect by IBM received nearly 6,000 inquiries in its initial five months. It is available to the corporation's 270,000 employees, retirees and spouses but it will be eventually extended to other companies. IBM estimated that 30 percent of its employees are involved in the care of adult dependents. (AARP-Working Age, 1988) Aetna Life and Casualty similarly assists its employees with information on long term care facilities, home care services, housing and community programs (Retirement Advisers 1988). Employers are also creating data banks on part-time or temporary employment for retirees, others are launching well targeted recruitment drives, particularly in areas where younger workers are hard to find. Even in the case of disability, employers are investing in retraining and job redesign which reduce the physical demands on partially incapacity workers. Putting in place more benefits for older workers, retirement planning included will result in greater operational costs. Yet not all employers are willing to bear such costs, nor are workers going out of their way to demand the provision of pre-retirement counseling as an employment benefit. Employers may eventually realize that such programs enhance workers' morale and may lead to higher productivity. Workers, in turn, may ultimately find that they increase their life options. At the end, advocates of pre-retirement programs will have to demonstrate that, by designing new retirement life patterns, they can prevent or postpone many of the costly problems of old age. It is possible that only then will society commit itself to a steadfast sponsorship of pre-retirement preparation programs.

REFERENCES

AARP (American Association of Retired Persons). 1988. *Working Age* (July/August), 4(1):4.

Ash, P. 1966. Pre-retirement counseling. *The Gerontologist* 6(2):97–99, 127–128.
Bolton, C. R. 1976. Humanistic instructional strategies and retirement education programming. *The Gerontologist* 16(6):550–555.
Boyack, V. L. and D. M. Tiberi. 1975. A study of pre-retirement education. Paper presented at the 28th Annual Meeting of the Gerontological Society, Louisville.
Charles, D. C. 1971. Effect of participation in a pre-retirement program. *The Gerontologist* 11(1:1):24–28.
Coberly, S., E. Bentsen and L. Klinger. 1983. *Incentives for Hiring Older Workers in the Private Sector: A Feasibility Study*. Los Angeles: Andrus Gerontology Center, University of Southern California.
Cumming, E. and W. E. Henry. 1961. *Growing Old: The Process of Disengagement*. New York: Basic Books.
Fitzpatrick, E. W. 1980. An introduction to NCOA's retirement planning program. *Aging and Work* 3(1):20–26.
Glamser, F. D. and G. F. DeJong. 1975. The efficacy of pre-retirement preparation programs for industrial workers. *Journal of Gerontology* 30(5):595–600.
Greenough, W. C. and F. P. King. 1977. Is normal retirement at age 65 obsolete? *Pension World* 13(6):35–36.
Hayes, C. 1988. Few women plan for retirement. *The Aging Connection* (December 1987–January 1988), 8:2.
Heidbreder, E. M. 1972. Factors in retirement adjustment: White-collar/blue-collar experience. *Industrial Gerontology*, no. 12, pp. 69–79.
Hirschhorn, L. 1977. Social policy and the life cycle: A developmental perspective. *Social Service Review* 51(3):434–450.
Hirschhorn, L. 1979. Post-industrial life: A U.S. perspective. *Futures* 11(4):287–298.
Hoover Institution. 1988. *Issues in Contemporary Retirement*. Stanford: Stanford University Press.
Ingalls, J. D. and J. M. Arceri. 1972. *A Trainers Guide to Andragogy*. Washington, D.C.: U.S. Social and Rehabilitation Service.
Kasschau, P. L. 1974. Reevaluating the need for retirement preparation programs. *Industrial Gerontology* 1(1):42–59.
Louis Harris and Associates. 1975. *The Myth and Reality of Aging in America*. Washington D.C.: National Council on the Aging.
Monk, A. 1977. Pre-retirement planning models: Social work inputs and applications. Paper presented at the 5th Professional Symposium of the National Association of Social Workers, San Diego.
Morrison, M. and M. K. Jedrziewski. 1988. Retirement planning: Everybody benefits, *Personnel Administrator* (January), pp. 5–10.
National Council on the Aging. 1973. *Preparation for Retirement: A Comparison of Pre- and Post-Tests*. Washington, D.C.: The Council.
Olson, S. K. 1981. Current status of corporate retirement preparation programs. *Aging and Work* 4(3):175–187.
Olson, E. A. and K. D. Koslovski. 1988. Retirement planning programs: Are they still relevant? Paper presented at the 41st Annual Scientific Meeting of the Gerontological Society of America, San Francisco.
Ossofsky, J. 1980. Retirement preparation: Growing corporate involvement,. *Aging and Work* 3(1):14–17.
Productive Aging News. 1988. The Center for Productive Aging, Mount Sinai Medical Center, New York. February.
Research and Forecasts. 1980. Retirement preparation: Growing corporate involvement. *Aging and Work* 3(1):1–13.
Retirement Advisers. 1988. *Insights* (Fall), p. 2.
Root, S., Lawrence and L. H. Zarrugh. 1982. Innovative employment practices for

older Americans. Paper prepared for the National Commission for Employment Policy. Washington, D.C.

Rosow, I. 1973. The social context of the aging self. *Gerontologist* 13(1):82–87.

Schein, E. H. 1980. *Organizational Psychology*. 3d ed. Englewood Cliffs, N.J.: Prentice-Hall.

Schlossberg, N. K., L. Troll, and Z. Leibowitz. 1978. *Perspectives on Counseling Adults: Issues and Skills*. Monterey, Calif.: Brooks/Cole.

Schulz, J. H. 1980. *The Economics of Aging*. 2d ed. Belmont, Calif.: Wadsworth.

Shackman, D. 1980. Second career volunteer program. *Sharing* 4(6):5–6.

Sheldon, A., P. J. M. McEwan, and C. P. Ryser. 1975. *Retirement: Patterns and Predictions*. Rockville, Md.: National Institute of Mental Health.

Sheppard, H. L. and R. E. Mantovani. 1982. *Part-Time Employment After Retirement*. Washington, D.C.: National Council on the Aging.

Simpson, I. H. and J. C. McKinney eds. 1966. *Social Aspects of Aging*. Durham, N.C.: Duke University Press.

Streib, G. F. 1958. Family patterns in retirement. *Journal of Social Issues* 14(2):46–60.

Tornquist, P. H., W. B. Newsom, and D. S. Cochran. 1988. More than a gold watch: Pre-retirement programs can make an employer look good. But do they really help workers build rewarding post-career lives? *Personnel Administrator* (April), pp. 54–56.

16

Legal Services

❖

JULIA C. SPRING. M.S.W., J.D.
Columbia University School of Law

NANCY H. KUEHN, M.S.W., J.D., L.L.M.
Prudential Insurance, Newark, New Jersey

The "graying" of the American population has had effects on the need for legal services to the elderly that are greater than the actual population changes themselves. One effect has been an increasing number of persons who, because of problems in mobility, access, finances, communication, or comprehension, are unable to avail themselves of legal help for the problems adults of all ages have. The same population has additional legal problems because of its statistically greater vulnerability to fraud and abuse. But most important, for the infirm and firm elderly alike, a whole new area of legal problems has emerged because of the reliance of the middle-class elderly on Social Security and Medicare and of the elderly poor and near-poor on SSI, Medicaid, food stamps, and other government income and in-kind entitlement programs. A large body of substantive law, as well as law regarding the administration of these programs, has developed. Because there is no constitutional right to benefits, and because there are strong cost-containment pressures, many programs for the elderly have become adversarial despite their original beneficial intent. Although some of the fiscal pressures pre-date 1980, they have become worse, especially for the poor elderly, since the start of the Reagan administration (Storey 1986; Tolchin 1988). Thus even clearly entitled elderly clients often need assistance for mere initial access to those government benefits. As Nathanson summarizes it:

> More than any other group, the elderly depend upon complex public and private institutions for their daily subsistence. Therefore, their legal problems frequently relate to the policies and actions of government agencies and private corporations, both of which often present themselves as bureaucratic mazes.
>
> Superimposed upon the lives of the low-income (and especially the lives of the frail) elderly is a vast array of complex statutory, regulatory and decisional law. Their shelter may be provided or secured under federal and state public and subsidized housing laws, and zoning laws. Their health is often dependent upon Medicare, Medicaid, laws regulating nursing homes, and laws relating to the advertisement of prescription drugs. Their nutrition is often secured by the food stamp program and nutrition programs established by other federal laws. The source of their income may be Social Security, Supplemental Security Income, civil service or railroad retirement programs or private pensions. Their dignity, personal freedom and control of property are subject to the vagueness of the law of guardianship, conservatorship and involuntary commitment.
>
> Since they enter into contracts, own property, and have family relations, the elderly also have many of the same legal concerns as the rest of the population. (1982:37)

However, as front-line gerontological services agency workers know well, this upsurge in legal needs of the elderly has not been matched by an upsurge in legal services. On the contrary, the political and cost-containment pressures that have made access to government entitlement programs more difficult have also made access to legal services more difficult. In addition, historically the law of government entitlements is "welfare" law and as such is not a crucial domain of private lawyers who earn their livings from client fees, nor of the law schools that train them. An attempt on the part of the American Bar Association since 1979 to activate the private bar to provide more free and low-cost legal assistance to the elderly has been only partly successful (ABA Commission 1988). Among government-funded legal services, those of the Legal Service Corporation (LSC) are for the poor of all ages and cannot serve those whose income and resources fall above certain amounts; in fact, proportionately fewer of the poor elderly than of other age groups are served by LSC grantees. Additional legal services for those 60 and over have taken up only some of the slack since being funded under the Older Americans Act in 1975. Furthermore, the number of elderly served by both programs has decreased in the 1980s, due to political and economic pressure to limit government-paid legal assistance for the poor and elderly (U.S.AoA. 1982; Golick, Spring, and Bograd 1986).

OBTAINING LEGAL ASSISTANCE

The Role of Social Work in Linking the Elderly Client to Legal Services

Given the many areas (listed in appendix 16.1) where the elderly need legal assistance, and the fact that the elderly remain legally underserved, the gerontological social worker has a particularly important role both in facilitating referrals to available legal resources and in using other means to resolve legal problems when possible.

Social workers are uniquely qualified to serve as links between elderly clients and legal professionals (Brieland and Lemmon 1985). Social workers have a commitment, held by no other profession, to their clients' overall ability to cope with life and whatever problems life may present. Whatever the treatment approach, the social worker's role is to recognize psychological or environmental barriers, including legal ones, to effective functioning and to assist the client in overcoming these barriers. Further, gerontological social workers are frequently the clients' primary social contacts since many elderly clients served by social agencies are isolated: institutionalized in medical or nursing facilities; homebound for psychological, physical, or environmental reasons; impaired in communication ability. This commitment to, and contact with, the elderly client can be used to help the client overcome threshold difficulties in asserting legal rights —depression, mistrust of lawyers, often-realistic fears of futility or reprisal in "fighting city hall" (Bernstein 1980). The social worker's ability to help a client overcome such fears and hesitations is as important when the underlying source of the problem is legal as in any other area.

To do so, the worker may have to put aside his or her own reluctance to deal with the legal system and lawyers. Clients and workers share the general societal perception of lawyers as inadequately responsive to human concerns and therefore not to be sought out except in acute and specific instances—for example, an imminent eviction. In addition, social workers and lawyers tend to draw rigid boundaries separating legal problems from social or emotional problems and to have doubts about collaboration (Ehrlich and Ehrlich 1979; Weil 1982). Just as lawyers are often unwilling to recognize or deal with the emotional aspects of a legal concern, so too social workers often do not recognize the legal dimensions of a client's problem. This difference is exacerbated by the fact that in practice it is usually social workers who must adapt to the language and patterns of the higher-status professions, medicine as well as law, in order to secure the services that their clients need (Foster and Pearman 1978).

In summary, gerontological social workers must recognize both their ability and their responsibility to deal with the legal concerns of the elderly. Gerontological service agencies also must recognize this responsibility and provide front-line workers with the time, training, and other supports to perform this technical and time-consuming work. The social worker's role in regard to legal problems is the same problem-solving role as always: providing objective information about rights, remedies, and resources; activating the elderly client by working through the client's anxieties and fears that interfere with getting help; and assisting the referral or outside resource—the lawyer—in understanding the client's problem.

Identifying Legal Issues and Deciding Whether Referral to a Lawyer Is Necessary

To decide whether or not legal referral is required, the gerontological social worker must have basic information about the function of law, specific substantive areas of law relevant to the elderly, and due-process concepts (Jankovic and Green 1981; Miller 1980).

Law in our society is intended to structure the behavior of citizens toward one another and between the government and individuals by providing a set of rules generally regarded as mandatory. The law involves both rights and responsibilities. The fact that something is called a "right" does not mean it is a legal right unless a court or a legislative body has assigned reciprocal rights and responsibilities on the topic. The "human right" not to be hungry, for example, is much broader than the legal right to food in congregate feeding programs or to food stamps.

However, the fact that a problem is identified as "legal" does not automatically mean a lawyer is needed or that a lawsuit is involved. In fact, whenever a client asks what can be expected in the way of health-care coverage or income supplement from the government, he/she is raising a legal concern—for example, what rights under the law does this client have? Thus every social worker in a specialized area is wise to become conversant with the law regarding that area, as well as with the structure of the legal and court system. The Brieland and Lemmon 1985 text *Social Work and the Law* contains excellent background materials. While no social worker—and no lawyer—can possibly master all substantive areas of law affecting the elderly, he/she should be aware of the general areas in which laws have been enacted and the sources of legal authority in those areas (appendix 16.1).

Two specific problems should be noted about learning the law in a particular subject area. First, a general manual or handbook such as those cited in the References list usually becomes outdated rapidly; one small change in a statute (passed by a legislature) or a regulation (put into effect by an executive agency) may make it inapplicable to a particular client's situation. Lawyers usually use "reporter" (subscription) services to keep up to date on the law; a worker without such resources must always check out with those who have them whether the general law stated in a manual or handbook is still in effect. Second and similarly, many laws vary from one geographical area to another; a federal law (Social Security, SSI, Medicare) will generally be uniform across the country, while a law that has federal and state components (Medicaid, taxes) or is entirely state (mental health, guardianship) varies from state to state. The monthly *Clearinghouse Review* (National Clearinghouse for Legal Services) and *NSCLC Weekly* (National Senior Citizens Law Center) are two periodicals that are good sources of the changes in law affecting the elderly. Appendix 16.2 lists relevant advocacy organizations.

In addition, there are procedural aspects of law that cut across the different substantive areas—analogous to the processes of working for and with social work clients that cut across the particular problems that are being addressed. Most of the procedural laws regulating government action are defined by federal and state statute and regulation; in addition, they must conform to constitutional "due process" principles (Brieland and Lemmon 1985; Dickson 1976; Stone 1978). As one of the most fundamental constitutional concepts, due process in the government entitlement context refers to "what process is due" at all stages of the government's interaction with a person who applies for or receives an entitlement. The process due starts with the requirement that the government accept the application of every person who wishes to receive a benefit. The government must then determine whether or not that person is eligible and give the individual written notice and an opportunity for a hearing to contest a finding of ineligibility. Similarly, once a person is receiving a benefit, the government may decide that he/she no longer qualifies and may ultimately reduce or discontinue benefits—but only after notice and an opportunity for a hearing at which the individual may present his/her side of the story.

Although specific procedural safeguards vary depending on the context, in essence due process is a requirement that the government be "fundamentally fair" in its dealings with an individual by informing him/her of its proposed actions and the reasons for those actions, and letting the person tell an impartial decision-maker of reasons for disagreement with that action. It does not stop the final action if legally justified—eviction, termination of benefits—but it protects the client from arbitrary or premature action. A worker with the elderly may well find that his/her intuitive reaction to whether an elderly client has been treated fairly comports with due-process requirements. Thus a client may come in with a letter stating that Medicaid recertification has been denied because the client failed to document eligibility. The client says he gave the agency everything asked for, but that he didn't know he had to submit those papers by a certain date or the application would be rejected. If the worker's reaction is "That's not fair, how can they do that—they didn't even give him a chance to comply," he/she would be focusing on exactly the right legal issue.

With a basic knowledge of procedural concepts and substantive areas of law relevant to the elderly, a worker is prepared to identify legal problems of the elderly. It is crucial to note that the questioning necessary for a potential legal referral should be keyed as closely as possible to the specific legal issues involved (Binder and Price 1977; Shaffer 1987). Thus, for example, a social worker might need to question an elderly client about her living arrangements for a possible challenge to an SSI reduction after she has moved in with her sister. Although the social worker would usually focus on whether or not the elderly sisters are adapting to life together, in the SSI context the concern would be to determine whether the client is paying her share of the rent in order to establish legally that she is still entitled to maximum "living alone" benefits. Such specific legal-issue fact-finding is crucial either for referral of a client to a lawyer or for representation of the client by a nonlawyer. In addition, the worker may also be serving a valuable social work function by assisting the client in sorting out fact from fantasy, for example, that the Social Security worker was following regulations in this matter rather than simply giving the client a hard time.

Thus a gerontological social worker has a three-step process: 1) identifying the relevant area of law and, if possible, its specific provisions; 2) gathering the facts of the situation as relevant to the specific law; 3) deciding whether to assist the client directly in coping with the problem or to seek legal assistance.

In many areas related to the elderly, there is no definite line separating the role of a social work advocate from that of a lawyer. As discussed in the next section, social work representation at an administrative hearing may well be the best advocacy route. When is a lawyer needed, then? The following are rough guidelines for seeking a lawyer:

1. When a catastrophic result is imminent without court intervention (e.g., eviction or surgery the client opposes);
2. When the client has been served with legal papers;
3. When other administrative remedies have been tried and failed to get the desired result (e.g., denial of a Social Security claim up through the Appeals Council level);
4. When the client wants to achieve a goal that must comply with certain legal requirements in order to be valid or enforceable (e.g., divorce, will, general power of attorney);
5. When the client needs information about legal options in order to decide what course of action to take (e.g., eligibility for Medicaid if money is transferred to a child or an action for age discrimination).

If the decision is made that the client's situation requires a lawyer, private and public resources should be pursued with all the networking skills social workers employ in other situations. If the decision is made that the situation does not so require, there are various modes of proceeding without a lawyer.

Proceeding Without a Lawyer

There are three routes for acting without a lawyer: the client acts on his/her own; the client acts with the assistance of a nonlawyer (often a relative or a social worker); and the client or worker uses nonlegal dispute-resolution mechanisms.

First, some proceedings are set up with the intention that cases will be handled by the aggrieved person himself/herself. Small-claims courts, for example, are set up by many civil court systems to handle the noncriminal, small dollar-value grievances of one person against another or against a business (the person whose dry cleaner has lost laundry, or whose landlord has not returned a security deposit). Self-help books found in many bookstores and those listed in the References contain resources for handling these procedures alone, although it is wise to check what is useful in each particular state of locality.

Other proceedings permit a person to act on his or her own, to be represented by a lawyer, or to be assisted by a nonlawyer. Usually, when the government has an obligation to provide certain services or benefits generally or to specific population groups—often through state and federal agencies dealing with income, health, housing, tax, employment, and discrimination—due process requires a hearing to contest a decision not to grant such benefits. In these hearings an individual may choose whether and how to be represented. In an administrative hearing (i.e., the meeting that is the final step of an agency's review of objections to decisions it has made), nonlawyers are often as skilled as lawyers. Thus this is a crucial arena for social workers to exercise advocacy skills. This is particularly true if the nonlawyers are well versed in the relevant law, or if the problem is not so much one of disagreement about the law as confusion about the facts, as often is true in agency proceedings. Then the hearing may be viewed as an opportunity to present an organized, clear view of the facts (and supporting documents or spoken testimony) to someone (called a judge but really a hearing officer) who comes to the situation without the bias of having dealt with the particular case previously. Various organizations have manuals about lay hearing representation in general or in specific substantive areas; some of these manuals are listed in the References (e.g., Fried 1985; Young Lawyers Section of the New York State Bar Association 1986).

In addition, there is a general legal principle that even in a court that permits representation by another person only if that other person is a lawyer, an individual can still represent himself/herself entirely alone *(pro se)*. How this general legal principle is carried out varies according to specific state and federal laws. However, claimants who carry out all prior Social Security, Medicare, or SSI appeals steps and still receive unfavorable decisions, or individuals who believe their civil rights have been violated, may go on their own to the *pro se* clerk of the nearest federal district courthouse. An individual who goes to state or federal court on his/her own and who also files a "poor person's" *(in forma pauperis)* petition indicating that he or she cannot pay court fees, will often (although not necessarily) have a free *(pro bono)* lawyer appointed by the court. A poor client who is charged with a crime will also usually have a free lawyer appointed by the judge.

Finally, over the last decade or so there has been an increasing interest in nonlegal dispute resolution—either mediation, in which an impartial person simply helps the antagonists revolve the dispute, or arbitration, in which the antagonists agree ahead of time that the impartial person will make a decision to which they will adhere (ABA Special Committee on Legal Problems of the Elderly and Standing Committee on Dispute Resolution 1988). Such conflict resolution may be particularly useful to individuals who might otherwise attempt to sue to settle something that's not really a legal matter, or where legal expenses and procedures are out of proportion to the dollar value of the actual issue—for example, disputes between relatives or neighbors, or between a client and a small business.

Government-Funded Legal Services

If referral to an attorney is needed, many gerontological agency social workers will first contact local legal services (often called legal aid) funded by the Legal Services Corporation (LSC) and/or the Administration on Aging (AoA) of the U.S. Department of Health and Human Services. The LSC, established by Congress in 1974 as a quasi-governmental entity and successor to the legal-services programs under the 1964 Economic Opportunity Act (the Kennedy-Johnson "War on Poverty"), provides free civil legal assistance to all poor persons, not just the elderly. LSC-funded legal assistance is for those who have incomes below 125 percent of the federal Office of Management and Budget poverty line. The original 1965 Older Americans Act (OAA) did not provide specifically for legal services. The 1975 amendments to Title III of the OAA introduced legal services (usually called "Title III" legal services), free for those 60 and over. These services are not targeted specifically for the poor, although in 1980 over half the clients served were low income. Rather, the OAA requires preference for older persons with the greatest economic and social need without imposing a means test. This preference is most often manifested by targeting issues relevant to the elderly poor (income, health care, housing, protective services) or geographic areas where the poorest are concentrated. A main problem with legal services under Title III is that no specific amount has been appropriated, but, rather, potential legal services providers must compete annually for funds from the local Area Agency on Aging with providers of other critical services, like nutrition, transportation and health care (Coleman 1988).

Both LSC and AoA legal services are forbidden to take fee-generating cases (i.e., ones where the individual is suing for money) and have many other limitations. On the whole they specialize in civil, not criminal, cases having to do with income maintenance, health benefits, consumer complaints, and family, and housing law. Some specialize even further—particularly in these days of cost containment—in order to use their resources most effectively for their target population.

An urban legal services program, whether funded by AoA or LSC or funds from both, might have three or four lawyers, possibly assisted by paralegals and law students. It might have a social worker, but probably would not. Each attorney might well have a caseload of over one hundred, typically involving landlord-tenant disputes, protective services and home care issues, and question of eligibility for government income and medical care programs. Frequently, more than one legal issue would be involved. For example, a client might be referred because he or she had received an eviction notice for nonpayment of rent. Upon investigation, the attorney might discover the client's nonpayment of rent to be related to a problem caused by the Social Security Administration or to a cognitive inability to manage his or her funds.

Elderly clients would first come in contact with this office by telephone or by referral of family, social agencies, or other lawyers. Home visits might occasionally be made. At the initial contact, some brief information about the client and his or her problem would be taken. If the client seemed appropriate for government-funded services in terms of broad characteristics such as age, financial status, and type of problem, the client would be given an appointment for more thorough intake interview. In an emergency, a client would be scheduled for an initial interview as soon as possible.

After the initial interview, the supervising attorney would determine whether the office would handle the problem. If another referral were more appropriate, it would be made. At all stages of this process and subsequent legal representation, a social worker or family member might well be involved if the client so desired; the lawyer would probably wish to see the client alone at least once to ascertain the client's wishes. Such assistance would be particularly crucial if the client had some diminished ability to understand the legal proceedings or to carry out necessary actions.

Legal services offices for the elderly take other forms around the country. As AoA funding must be given to the best possible provider, in 1981 one-third of the AoA funds went to other than LSC grantees; for example, the New York City Office on the Aging each year since 1978 has awarded funds to one law school clinic, one social service agency, and two different LSC grantees. In small communities and rural areas, AoA legal services are often provided by contract with local private lawyers.

Both AoA and LSC legal services are frequently under federal and state political and economic attack. In 1981 the Reagan administration tried to abolish the LSC; it only accomplished a 25 percent cutback, which by 1988 is equivalent to a 40 percent funding reduction (Coleman 1989). Title III legal services are additionally vulnerable to local political pressure since, unlike LSC funding decisions (made federally and with the obligation that all allotted funds go to legal services or administration), the decisions on allocating AoA funds to legal services are made by the local Area Agency on Aging (AAA). An AAA is required only to spend "some funds," no amount specified, on legal services—and indeed since 1982 it is required not to spend any funds if it finds the legal needs of the elderly in the community are already being met. Since the AAA is usually a branch or a neighbor of the state human services/welfare agency, many AAAs are reluctant to fund legal services that may represent clients against these agencies especially when the block grant must also fund homecare and access services. Thus many AAAs resolve this political dilemma by allocating negligible resources, primarily for information and referral, not direct representation to legal services. In 1982 proportionately fewer dollars were spent on legal services by AAAs than the previous year: an average of less than $20,000 per AAA, ranging from 1.5 percent to only 22.6 percent of the total state Title III grant.

A more recent approach has been for an LSC grantee or another organization to seek funding from other government sources. Title XX Social Security Act funds are to be used by states for services to prevent or reduce economic dependency and inappropriate institutional care, and thus may be used for legal services to prevent such care. States are mainly interested in using such finds for legal assistance in areas where an elderly person who has been denied a federally funded benefit (Medicare or SSI) is currently being cared for at least partly at state expense (Medicaid or general welfare assistance). As an example, a Connecticut LSC grantee called LAMP (Legal Assistance for Medicare Patients) has received major Title XX funding since 1977, and Medicaid funding since 1982, to carry out both major lawsuits and highly replicable administrative appeals of denials of Medicare reimbursement for skilled-nursing care in hospitals and nursing homes. Since 1983 a number of states (including Illinois, Massachusetts, New York, and Pennsylvania) have paid legal services programs to pursue federal Social Security and SSI disability claims, again with the primary motivation being to get such "dual eligibles" off state welfare rolls. A description of a number of such programs is contained in a 1988 *Clearinghouse Review* article (Stein 1988).

To maximize the chances of getting free legal assistance for a client in these days of restricted public funding, workers should keep several factors in mind. First, as already discussed, the worker should have a clear statement of the legal problem in order to facilitate referral to the appropriate, probably overworked office and lawyer. Second, the possibility that a private attorney would be more appropriate, or necessary, should have been examined, as discussed in the next section of this article. Third, as the presence of income and population restrictions implies, both AoA and LSC legal services are themselves entitlement systems, like the government bureaucracies against which they often act for their clients; this means that only some individuals, who meet certain criteria, are entitled to free legal services. Further, neither system has any procedure for a person who has been denied representation to appeal that decision. Thus, knowing what kinds of cases and clients are served by a particular office is crucial to client advocacy. Information is available from the federal Legal Services Corporation on all grantees nationwide; each state's office on aging has information on Title III services for the state, as does the federal Administration on Aging. A question to the local Area Agency on Aging or to the state office on aging should reveal whether a particular LSC grantee is also receiving Older Americans Act funds; these grantees are precluded from using a rigid means test, although services may be targeted for those with the greatest economic need (Landrum 1982; U.S. AoA 1982; Coleman 1988).

Private Lawyers and Bar Associations

Many workers with the elderly avoid the use of private attorneys on the assumption that a private lawyer is likely to be too costly and not attuned to the psychosocial needs of older clients. However, at times private attorneys can and should be used. First, some elderly clients despite low fixed incomes, do have savings and other assets; these resources will make them ineligible for LSC-funded legal assistance and most AoA-funded assistance. In turn, the clients' possession of economic resources may necessitate taking legal precautions to ensure that these resources will be transferred or managed well in case of death, or decreased mental ability; these areas of law that are often well known by private attorneys. An elderly person with money and facing institutionalization—or the spouse to remain in the community—will also probably need to use a private attorney, but that lawyer is likely to need additional information about how Medicaid eligibility interacts with traditional financial planning methods (e.g., Special Committee on Legal Problems of the Aging 1986; Reagan 1985).

Second, in some areas of law there are provisions for lawyer payment if the client wins. In such cases, a prepayment of fees (retainer) is usually not required. For example, up to 25 percent of a retroactive Social Security benefit won in a hearing by an attorney may be paid directly to the attorney. This is not applicable to SSI, although at least one state, Illinois, has enacted comparable payment provisions (Stein 1988). It may well be worth that payment for an elderly client to receive denied past benefits as well as future ones (Sweeney and Lyko 1980). Or, a client's case might result in a money settlement (out of court) or judgment (in court)—for example, when a physically injured client wishes to sue the person who caused the injury for money (a fee-generating case LSC and AoA grantees cannot take). An attorney may be willing to take on such cases on a "contingency fee" basis, meaning that the lawyer will get a preestablished proportion (usually one-third) of whatever is won. Obviously, a lawyer is usually willing to take on a case without a retainer only when there is a good chance of winning.

It should be noted that if a client, or a relative, is contemplating such a suit or other legal action, it is worth a consultation with a private lawyer on the probable outcome of such a case, potential contingency fee, and willingness to take the case. In fact, such a consultation is necessary in order to decide whether to proceed. It is standard in legal practice to ask when setting up the appointment what the consultation fee (if any) for a specified length of time is. The consultation does not imply a commitment to employ that lawyer. During the consultation, discussion should include both the fee for the lawyer's services and the fee for court and other costs. This process and what an employment agreement should contain are detailed in one advocacy manual. (HALT 1983).

How to find a private attorney? Networking is critical. With an elderly person, it might be wise to check first whether there is a lawyer friend or relative who would be willing to handle the particular problem, if put in touch with relevant legal manuals or a specialist in this kind of law. Other workers or clients might know private attorneys who are skilled in the particular substantive law. The local LSC- or AoA-funded legal services office might refer a client to a private attorney; because of the recent decrease in federal legal assistance funding, as well as because the legal problems of the elderly cut across all economic classes, some legal services attorneys have recently moved into private practice with a partial specialization in legal problems of the elderly.

Another source is a bar association, which may be organized by municipality, county, state, or, in urban areas, by particular groups of attorneys (women, blacks, etc.). Since the mid-1970s a number of bar associations have developed special programs for the elderly that may either provide or refer for the services needed. These elderly-specializing private bar services tend to be of two basic types: pro bono (volunteer), usually in a few legal areas, like wills; and reduced-fee referrals for the elderly with fixed incomes. Prepaid "judicare" programs, once seen as the wave of the future, have not generally been successful. In addition, many bar associations have a general telephone-referral service in which attorneys are listed by areas of law they practice in return for agreeing to see referred clients for an initial consultation at a flat fee that is somewhat below the market rate. Legal Counsel for the Elderly, a program of the American Association of Retired Persons, has a call-in service in Pennsylvania and the District of Columbia; the attorney who answers the phone attempts to resolve the problem with phone advice, and if necessary refers to a lawyer who has agreed ahead of time to the total and reduced price (Coleman 1989). Every referral lawyer must be a member of good standing of the local bar, but the amount of screening and attorney monitoring varies considerably among bar referral services. A consultation should provide necessary data to decide on the costs, necessity, and feasibility of pursuing a particular legal course, as well as the skills of the particular lawyer. Again the worker's or client's network may be needed to confirm that impression.

Advertised "legal clinics" have developed since the mid-1970s, particularly in urban areas. For highly repetitive legal problems (for example, a simple will or an uncontested divorce that does not involve property, alimony, or child support), a clinic may have low fees because the case-handling can be replicated on a volume basis, often by paralegals. A clinic should not be used if there are any complications in a problem, and its reputation should be checked through the client's or social worker's network.

A final approach is to look around for lawyers or law-related groups that have a particular interest in the issues the client is concerned with (employment discrimination, mental illness), the population your client is a member of (retirees of a particular union, Masons), or the kind of case (Social Security appeal, immigration problem). A local law school may have a practice component (also called a "clinic") handling one of the above, in which students represent clients who are unable to pay, under the supervision of a faculty member/attorney. Most schools select only a few categories of cases that have been determined to be both educationally useful and where students can offer significant services to clients (Harbaugh 1976; Nathanson 1982).

Last, if ever a lawyer's service, whether public or private, to a client is unsatisfactory, it is possible to complain about that lawyer, usually through a local, county, or state bar association (ABA 1982). An investigation and response to a written complaint will usually be made. If a court has appointed a lawyer to represent a client or a guardian *ad litem* (obligated in a particular lawsuit to represent the client's best interest, not his or her choice), a complaint may also be made to that court. Finally, it is possible, although more difficult, to consult another attorney about a legal malpractice suit if there has been harm to a client as a result of the first attorney's failure to act by the standards of the legal profession.

DEVELOPING LEGAL SERVICES FOR THE ELDERLY

Direct Provision of Legal Services to Agency Client

In most cases, direct provision of legal assistance by a gerontological services agency is not financially possible. However, putting aside the question of money, there is the difficulty in many social service agencies in persuading top executives and board members, whether social workers or lawyers, of the need for legal services for the elderly. Although those with direct client contact know the importance of law-related areas to the daily lives of the elderly, those not in direct practice often do not realize that the problems of the elderly cannot be managed simply by information, referral, and counseling but require intensive and costly advocacy. Lay and even gerontologist board members may not recognize that client law problems usually cannot ethically be handled by the same lawyers who handle legal questions for the organization itself (like, for example, those of its tax-exempt or incorporation status). Lawyer board members unfamiliar with entitlement law are probably not aware of the adversarial nature of government benefit systems.

If this threshold obstacle were surmounted, two primary organizational problems would have to be dealt with. First, the overhead costs for legal services are higher than those for social services and would not be covered by the usual sliding fee scale. Costs include both the higher salary of the lowest-paid attorneys, as well as that of a legal secretary. Legal supplies will be needed, funds for court fees and transcripts, malpractice insurance, and expensive books and subscription reporter services in crucial areas of the law. Donations of or access to some legal materials can perhaps be arranged, but without basic materials immediately at hand the lawyer will be unable to work efficiently and effectively.

Second, the gerontological-services agency must consider how to handle conflicts between the lawyer's and the social worker's goals in working with a shared client (Malick and Ashley 1980). Preparation for such conflicts includes mutual education that the differences between the professional stances are just that—differences, not right or wrong in any absolute sense. Equally important is establishing guidelines for what cases will be handled and a way to make decisions if consensus breaks down on those cases that are handled.

Lawyers and gerontological social workers are often in harmony on their work with clients. However, at times there will be conflict between the ways that each profession regards as essential to assist a client, consistent with its professional theory, ethics, and practice. For example, social workers in a gerontological agency might decide, as a matter of professional judgment, that an elderly person is unable to manage Social Security benefits and therefore needs a representative payee to receive and spend those checks on behalf of the actual beneficiary. The in-house lawyer might be called in to obtain the representative payee but perceives his/her professional obligation as representing the client's expressed desire to continue to receive benefit checks and spend them, however inappropriately. Social workers and lawyers might also find themselves in conflict when the professional confidentiality obligation of one precludes sharing certain information with the other (Bernstein 1977; Weil and Sanchez 1983). These areas become increasingly important as demographic changes push gerontological agencies into work with the isolated elderly who may have diminished mental capacity. There is a tendency for lawyers to accuse social workers of practicing commitment without a license, and of social workers to accuse lawyers of obstructing needed care. In fact, the tensions between protection of the vulnerable and preservation of civil rights are immense and must continue to be worked out by both professions (Coleman 1989; Hayes and Spring 1988).

The Lawyer's Code of Professional Responsibility or the Model Rules of Professional Responsibility (available from state bar associations) require the lawyer to make legal decisions with the individual client, not allowing agency or other interests to control these decisions. Even a lawyer board of directors can set only broad policy guidelines, for example on the kinds of cases that may be taken, not specific directions on what course of action may be taken in a specific case. Most gerontological service agencies would be reluctant to pay for an in-house lawyer who would have ultimate say in such conflicts. Consequently, it is critical to establish, as part of the development of a legal assistance program, what kinds of cases will be handled (e.g., only administrative hearings or more costly court appeals). These guidelines can be made clear to an attorney being hired as well as to agency clients and workers. Because of the practical and ethical problems of one profession supervising another (Barton and Byrne 1975;

Ehrlich and Ehrlich 1979) it is probably best to have the legal services unit of a social-service agency operate within those guidelines but somewhat separately from the usual agency lines of authority.

An alternative would be for a gerontological services agency to use available funds to pay an outside lawyer, lawyers, or firm to handle clients' cases, which would avoid in-house professional conflict on how to assist an elderly client. If the arrangement were with just one or a few attorneys, it would be possible to select one who has knowledge of legal and interpersonal issues relevant to the elderly, which would be less possible if the referrals were to large a firm where the case might be assigned to one of a number of lawyers.

It would again be important to discuss service issues fully, in an atmosphere of mutual education, before the agreement is reduced to a written document. These issues would include fee, unit of service, case preferences or limitations, referral mechanisms, and reciprocal confidentiality concerns. Defining the unit of service and payment for it is particularly important because of the different professional assumptions on what is appropriate service. Finally, it would be advisable to have an ongoing review of the terms of the agreement, as both social workers and lawyers develop a fuller sense of what the working arrangement actually entails.

Expansion of Legal Services Available to Elderly Clients in the Community

A gerontological services agency might choose to expand legal services in the community through a small- or large-scale mobilization of the community bar association. A connection with the private bar should help institutionalize legal services in the locality rather than having them depend on one agency's fiscal choices. The skills required for such mobilization are those social workers use in other community organization tasks, with due attention to particular strategy issues raised by the formal and informal authority structure of local bar groups as well as the status difference between social workers and lawyers. Such an effort would capitalize on recent interest in the private bar's involvement in provision of legal services to the elderly. This movement, born in the mid-1970s, has come partly from within the organized bar itself. Since 1976 the American Bar Association (ABA) Young Lawyers Division has been active in encouraging state and local bar associations to supply legal information and services to the elderly; since 1979 the ABA has had an interdisciplinary Commission on Legal Problems of the Elderly (ABA Commission 1988) with the delivery of legal services to the elderly as one of its priorities. The movement can be traced to a recognition that many of the elderly who are too poor to pay private attorneys still have middle-class legal needs, including the need for wills, trusts, and other arrangements that care adequately for the older generation, in the community and in institutions, as well as their offspring. The result is that when some attorneys decide to fulfill their ethical obligation to do legal work *pro bono publico* (volunteer; literally "for the public good"), the elderly are an appealing section of the public to assist (ABA Commission and Private Bar Involvement Project 1987). Pressure to mobilize the private bar has also come from the government-funded legal services sector. Since 1978, AoA grantees have been required to foster involvement of the local private bar to provide reduced-fee and pro bono services to those over 60, while since 1982 LSC grantees have been mandated to expend 10 percent of funding on involvement of private attorneys in provision of legal services to the poor.

The potential for such service must not be overestimated, since in the current straitened economy there is much competition for scarce pro bono resources. However, since even slight assistance from local lawyers may be of major assistance to elderly clients, it is an approach worthy of consideration. The most modest approach—and the most common nationwide—would be for the bar association to provide a number of limited (in time and scope) services of the kind the member attorneys are already likely to be expert in—for example, executing a number of wills or providing brief consultation on consumer or other issues, perhaps at a senior citizens' center. The New York City Bar Association Committee on Legal Problems of the Elderly recently coordinated a project among legal service offices receiving Title III funds, a volunteer law firm, and Department on Aging transportation services through which about twenty wills are executed each month for poor elderly New Yorkers (Abrandt 1988). The essence of this general approach is that the volunteer attorney incur limited obligations, only a specific task; the lawyer does not become the client's more general legal representative. If the client's social worker can ensure that the client will get to the appointment with relevant documents and facts, this will help the success of such a project.

There are, of course, other examples of private bar legal assistance to the elderly of varying degrees of complexity. Many of these examples are described in state bar association publications (Schmidt 1980). A project in rural Colorado sponsored by the state bar association and run by a nonlawyer director uses 120 pro bono attorneys to serve clients spread out over eleven counties (Paine 1982). Volunteer lawyers through the Cleveland Bar Association aid that city's Hospice Council. The large-scale Volunteer Lawyers Project in Boston uses lawyers and paralegals with background in special areas of law to provide technical assistance and close working relationships with volunteer attorneys who handle a variety of cases for low-income clients (Lardent 1980).

Another way that pro bono attorneys may be helpful, perhaps through a state or local bar association committee on legal issues of the elderly, is in the development of legislation that might increase funding for legal services, whether or not specified for the elderly. Four states (Massachusetts, Ohio, Oregon, and Wisconsin) mandate and four states (Arizona, Georgia, Florida, and Nevada) permit a filing fee proportion or surcharge which goes toward legal services. More dollar-generating are the Interest on Client Trust Fund (IOLTA) programs in forty-seven states, a mechanism for pooling the trust funds that lawyers must secure for their clients, but the interest from which lawyers may not ethically use (nor, practically, apportion to each individual client). Starting with California and Florida in the late 1970s, administrative entities were set up to pool the interest and distribute it, generally for civil or criminal legal services to the indigent. Although many of the states' programs are voluntary it is still estimated that over $42 million was raised in this fashion in 1987—close to 15 percent of the federal budget for the Legal Services Corporation (Coleman 1988; Stein 1988).

Several issues should be kept in mind as more models for raising funds and for delivery of services are considered. First, because much law related to the elderly, particularly government-benefit law, is specialized, private attorneys will need training and on-going technical assistance in order to do high-quality work and feel comfortable in the process. Similar requirements emerge as the representation becomes larger scale, more complex, or of longer duration. Related is the problem of monitoring the quality of representation either when a project becomes large scale or when the referral system means that the lawyer may perceive ongoing communication with the referral source as a breach of confidentiality or of decision control. Those who have developed successful large-scale pro bono projects indicate that the best way to maintain volunteer attorney investment and quality performance is to key the work to the volunteer's particular interests, with substantial ongoing technical assistance for areas of law in which private lawyers are not expert (ABA Commission 1988; Lardent 1980; Lardent and Coven 1981; Paine 1982).

Obviously, these additional needs would require a director to coordinate, train, and monitor volunteers, as well as to raise funds. Another important function would be close coordination between this service and other available legal resources, including LSC- and AoA-funded projects, and perhaps attempts to utilize funds from these sources. Ways to raise funds for payment of lawyers have different political and legal constraints in different states; the recent *Clearinghouse Review* article (Stein 1988) details benefits and risks of a number of fund-raising approaches. To enter the competition engendered by scarce funds is, of course, possible as the local AAA is mandated to locate the best possible provider. Better, however, might be to develop a community consortium of gerontological service agencies, the private bar, and government-funded legal services. In such a way might the legal and social service resources of a community pull together to use their energy to improve the status of the country's legally underserved elderly.

APPENDIX 16.1. Basic Legal Issues for the Elderly, Sources, and Agencies

Subject Matter	*Statute*
1. Income maintenance	
(a) Old age, survivors, and disability insurance ("Social Security")	42 U.S.C. §401 *et seq.*
(b) Supplemental security income (SSI)	42 U.S.C. §1381 *et seq.*
(c) General assistance (home relief, welfare)	State public assistance statutes
(d) Food stamps	7 U.S.C. §2011 *et seq.*
(e) Railroad retirement benefits	45 U.S.C. §231 *et seq.*
(f) Veterans benefits	38 U.S.C. §301 *et seq.*
(g) Private pensions	Employee Retirement Income Security Act of 1974 (ERISA), 29 U.S.C. §1001 *et seq.*; Internal Revenue Code of 1954, as amended, 26 U.S.C. §401 *et seq.*
(h) Age discrimination in employment	Age Discrimination in Employment Act of 1967 (ADEA), 29 U.S.C. §621 *et seq.*; state fair employment practice laws; state human rights laws
2. Health Care	
(a) Medicare	42 U.S.C. §426 *et seq.*, 42 U.S.C. §1395 *et seq.*
(b) Medical assistance program (Medicaid)	42 U.S.C.A. §1396 *et seq.*; state medical assistance statutes
(c) Veterans benefits	38 U.S.C. §601 *et seq.*

Regulations	*Agency Responsible*
20 C.F.R. §404 *et seq.*	Social Security Administration (SSA), U.S. Dept. of Health and Human Services
20 C.F.R. §416 *et seq.*	Social Security Administration, U.S. Dept. of Health and Human Services
State public assistance regulations	State assistance agencies (e.g. Dept. of Social Services)
20 C.F.R. §27 *et seq.*, regulations of state	State public assistance agencies under the direction of the U.S. Dept. of Agriculture
20 C.F.R. §200 *et seq.*	Railroad Retirement Board (federal)
38 C.F.R. §3 *et seq.*	Veterans Administration (federal)
29 C.F.R. §2560 *et seq.*	Labor Management Service Administration, Pension Benefit Guaranty Corp.; Internal Revenue Service
29 C.F.R. §5 *et seq.*	Equal Employment Opportunity Commission (Federal)
State regulations	State agencies (e.g., State Division of Human Rights)
42 C.F.R. §405 *et seq.;* 20 C.F.R. §405 *et seq.*	Health Care Financing Administration (HCFA) and Social Security Administration (SSA), U.S. Dept. of Health & Human Services (HHS)
42 C.F.R. §430 *et seq.;* state regulations	State public assistance agencies under the direction of HCFA and SSA of U.S. Dept. of Health & Human Services
38 C.F.R. §17.30 *et seq.*	Veterans Administration (Federal)

APPENDIX 16.1. (*Continued*)

Subject Matter	*Statute*
(d) Nursing homes (licensing, patients' bill of rights, abuse reporting)	42 U.S.C. §1395; §1395 X(j)(SNF); 42 U.S.C. §1396 d(c)(ICF); state public health laws
3. Social Services	Social Services Block Grant Act (Title XX of the Social Security Act) 42 U.S.C. §1397 *et seq.*
4. Housing	
(a) Public housing	42 U.S.C. §5301 *et seq.*
(b) Housing subsidy	Section 8 of the U.S. Housing Act of 1937, 42 U.S.C. §1437c
(c) Housing loans (rural housing loans and grants to the elderly to improve/repair homes)	§504 of the Housing Act of 1949, 42 U.S.C. §147 *et seq.*
(d) Adult homes	See SSI#1(b)
(e) Rent control, exemption from increased rent, protection from eviction in a condo/co-op conversion	State housing statutes; local housing statutes
5. Consumer Affairs	
(a) Consumer fraud	Federal Trade Commission Act. 15 U.S.C. §2301 *et seq.*; Magnuson-Moss Warranty FTC Improvement Act. 15 U.S.C. §2301 *et seq.*; state unfair trade practices and consumer protection acts
6. Legal Services	
(a) Legal services	Legal Services Corporation Act. 42 U.S.C. §2996 *et seq.*
(b) Older Americans Act	Title III of the Older Americans Act. as amended. 42 U.S.C. §3021 *et seq.*

Regulations	*Agency Responsible*
42 C.F.R. §405.1120 *et seq.* (SNF); §442.250 *et seq.* (ICF); state public health regulations	U.S. Dept. of Health & Human Services; state depts. of health
45 C.F.R. §1397 *et seq.*	State agencies under the direction of the U.S. Dept. of Health & Human Services
24 C.F.R. §860.1 *et seq.*	U.S. Dept. of Housing & Urban Development (HUD) with local public housing authorities
24 C.F.R. §882 *et seq.*	U.S. Dept. of Housing & Urban Development with local public housing authorities
7 C.F.R. §1904; 1904.301 *et seq.*	Farmer's Home Administration (Federal)
See SSI#1(b)	See SSI#(b)
State and local housing regulations	State agencies; local housing boards
16 C.F.R. §700 *et seq.;* state consumer protection regulations	Federal Trade Commission; state consumer affairs agencies
45 C.F.R. §1600 *et seq.*	Legal Services Corporation; local grantee corps.
45 C.F.R. §1321 *et seq.*	Federal Administration on Aging; state aging agencies; areas agencies on aging

APPENDIX 16.1. (*Continued*)

Subject Matter	*Statute*
7. Protective Services	
(a) Conservatorship (of property)	State mental hygiene/mental-health statutes
(b) Committee/guardian (of the person)	State mental hygiene/mental-health statutes
(c) Commitment (involuntary)	U.S. Constitution; state mental health/mental-hygiene statutes
(d) Power of attorney (durable)	State statutes (e.g., N.Y. General Obligations Law)
(e) Surrogate payees	Social Security Act
8. Property Transfers	
(a) Wills, trusts, lifetime gifts	State statutes (e.g., N.Y. Estates, Powers & Trusts Law)
(b) Probate; living wills	State probate statutes (e.g., Uniform Probate Code)
9. Tax Relief	
(a) Income tax	Internal Revenue Code of 1954 as amended. 26 U.S.C. §151
(b) Property tax/utility rates	State/local statutes

Regulations	*Agency Responsible*
State mental health/mental-hygiene regulations	State mental health/mental-hygiene agencies; state courts
State mental health/mental-hygiene regulations	State mental-hygiene agencies; state courts
State mental health/mental-hygiene regulations	State mental health/mental-hygiene agencies; state courts
Not applicable	Not applicable
20 C.F.R. §§404 and 416	Social Security Administration (Federal)
Not applicable	Not applicable
Rules of the state court	Surrogate's court/probate court (state)
26 C.F.R. §1.151-1(c)	Internal Revenue Service (Federal)
State/local regulations	State/local tax commissions

Appendix 16.2. National Organizations Dealing with Issues Relevant to the Elderly

American Bar Association
750 North Lake Shore Drive
Chicago, Ill. 60611

ABA Commission on Legal Problems of the Elderly
1800 M St., N.W.
Washington, D.C. 20036

Center on Social Welfare Policy & Law
95 Madison Avenue, Room 701
New York, N.Y. 10016

Food Research and Action Center (FRAC)
1319 F St., N.W.,
Washington, D.C. 20004

H.A.L.T., Inc.
1319 F St., N.W.
Washington, D.C. 20004

House Select Committee on Aging
712 House Office Bldg. Annex No. 1
Washington, D.C. 20515

Institute on Law and Rights of Older Adults
Brookdale Center on Aging/Hunter College
425 East 25th Street
New York, N.Y. 10010

Legal Assistance to Medicare Patients (LAMP)
P.O. Box 258, 902 Main St.
Willimantic, Conn. 06226

Legal Counsel for the Elderly
American Association of Retired Persons/National Retired Teachers Association
P.O. Box 19269-K
Washington, D.C. 20036

Legal Services Corporation/Office of Field Services
733 15th Avenue, N.W.
Washington, D.C. 20005

Legal Services for the Elderly
132 West 43d Street
New York, N.Y. 10036

National Bar Association Black Elderly League Assistance Project
1225 11th Street, NW
Washington, D.C. 20001

National Clearinghouse for Legal Services
407 S. Dearborn, Suite 400
Chicago, Ill. 60605

National Consumer Law Center
11 Beacon Street
Boston, Mass. 02108

National Health Law Program
2639 South La Cienega Boulevard
Los Angeles, Calif. 90034

National Housing Law Project
1950 Addison Street
Berkeley, Calif. 94704

National Institute for Dispute Resolution
1901 L Street, N.W.
Washington, D.C. 20036

National Organization of Social Security Claiment Representatives
19 East Central Avenue
Pearl River, N.Y. 10965

National Senior Citizens Law Center
1302 18th Street, N.W.
Washington, D.C. 20036

Appendix 16.2. (*Continued*)

or
1636 West 8th Street
Los Angeles, Calif. 90017

Pension Rights Center
918 16th Street, N.W.
Washington, D.C. 20006

Practising Law Institute
810 Seventh Avenue
New York, N.Y. 10019

Senate Special Committee on Aging
Room G-225 Dirksen Senate Office Bldg.
Washington, D.C. 20510

Volunteer Lawyers Project
73 Tremont Street, Suite 1001
Boston, Mass. 02108

REFERENCES

Abrandt, J. 1988. Nyc-Bar pro bono wills project serves the elderly. *BIFOCAL.* 9(1):6.

ABA (American Bar Association). 1982. *Grievance Referral List of Lawyers Disciplinary Agencies.* Chicago: ABA.

ABA. Commission on Legal Problems of the Elderly. 1985. *Doing Well by Doing Good: Providing Legal Services to the Elderly in a Paying Private Practice.* Washington, D.C.: ABA.

ABA. Commission on Legal Problems of the Elderly and Private Bar Involvement Project. 1987. *Pro Bono Seniorium: Volunteer Lawyers Projects for the Elderly.* Washington, D.C.: ABA.

ABA. Commission on Legal Problems of the Elderly. 1988. *Legal Services for the Elderly: Where the Nation Stands.* Washington, D.C.: ABA.

ABA. Commission on Legal Problems of the Elderly and Standing Committee on Dispute Resolution. 1988. *Mediation: The Coming of Age—a Mediator's Guide to Serving the Elderly.* Washington, D.C.: National Institute of Dispute Resolution.

ABA. Commission on Legal Problems of the Elderly and the Committee on Delivery of Legal Services. 1989. *The Law and Aging Resource Guide.* Washington: ABA.

Barton, P. N. and B. Byrne. 1975. Social work services in a legal aid setting. *Social Casework* 60:226–234.

Bernstein, B. 1980. Lawyer and social worker as an interdisciplinary team. *Social Casework* 65:416–422.

Binder, D. and S. Price. 1977. Legal interviewing and counseling: A client-centered approach. St. Paul: West.

BIFOCAL. ABA Commission on Legal Problems of the Elderly, Washington, D.C. (quarterly).

Brakel, S. J., J. Parry, and B. A. Weiner. 1985 The mentally disabled and the law. Chicago, American Bar Foundation.

Brieland, D. and J. Lemmon. 1985. *Social Work and the Law.* St. Paul: West.

Clearinghouse Review. National Clearinghouse for Legal Services, Chicago, Ill. (monthly).

Coleman, N. 1989. The delivery of legal services to the elderly in the United States.

In J. Eekelaar and D. Pearl, eds., *Aging World: Dilemma and Challenges for Law and Social Policy*. Oxford: Clarendon Press.

Dickson, D. 1976. Law in social work: Impact of due process. *Social Work* 21:274–278.

Drew, E. 1982. A reporter at large: Legal services. *New Yorker*, February 27.

Ehrlich, I. and P. Ehrlich. 1979. Social work and legal education: Can they unite to serve the elderly? *Journal of Education for Social Work* 15(2):87–93.

Foster, M. G. and W. A. Pearman, 1978. Social work, patient rights, and patient representatives. *Social Casework* 59(2):89–100.

Fretz, B. and N. Dudovitz. 1987. *The Law of Age Discrimination: A Reference Manual.*

Fried, B., ed. 1985. *Representing Older Adults: An Advocates Manual.* Washington, D.C.: National Senior Citizens Law Center.

Golick, T., J. C. Spring, and H. Bograd. 1986. The need for legal services for the Jewish poor in New York City. A report prepared for Federation of Jewish Philanthropies, New York City.

HALT. 1986. *Citizens' Legal Manual: Using a Lawyer.* Washington, D.C.: HALT, Inc.

Handler, J. 1979. *Protecting the Social Services client.* New York: Academic Press.

Harbaugh, J. D. 1976. Clinical training and legal services for older people: The role of the law school. *The Gerontologist* 16(5): 447–450.

Hayes, C. and J. C. Spring. 1988. Professional judgment and clients' rights. *Public Welfare*, pp. 22–28.

Health Advocate. National Health Law Program, Los Angeles, Calif. (quarterly).

Hemphill, C. F. Jr. 1981. *Consumer Protection Handbook: A Legal Guide.* Englewood Cliffs, N.J.: Prentice-Hall.

Jankovic, J. and R. D. Green. 1981. Teaching legal principles to social workers. *Journal of Education for Social Work* 17(3):28–35.

Kaufman, E. 1987. Social Security disability claims. New York City: Practising Law Institute.

Komlos-Hrobsky, P. 1988. An advocate's guide to home care for the elderly. Chicago: National Clearinghouse for Legal Services.

Krauskopf, J. M. 1983. *Advocacy for the Aging.* St. Paul: West.

Landrum, R. 1982. *Report of the Legal Services Corporation Conference on Legal Services and the Elderly.* Washington, D.C.: Legal Services Corporation.

Lardent, E. F. 1980. Pro bono that works. *NLADA Briefcase.* 37:54–71.

Lardent, E. F. and I. M. Coven. 1981. *Quality Control in Private Bar Programs for the Elderly.* Washington, D.C.: American Bar Association.

Malick, M. D. and A. A. Ashley. 1980. Politics of interprofessional collaboration: Challenge to advocacy. *Social Casework* 62(3):131–137.

McCormick, H. L. 1983. *Social Security Claims and Procedures.* St. Paul: West.

Miller, J. 1980. Teaching law and legal skills to social workers. *Journal of Education for Social Work.* 16(3):87–95.

Nathanson, P. 1982. An innovative approach to elders' unmet legal needs. *Generations* 6(3):37.

NSCLC Washington Weekly. National Senior Citizens Law Center. Washington, D.C.

New Jersey Institute for Continuing Legal Education. 1983. *Counseling the Elderly.* Newark: The New Jersey Institute for Continuing Legal Education.

1988 Medicare Explained. 1988. Chicago: Commerce Clearing House.

1988 Social Security Explained. 1988. Chicago: Commerce Clearing House.

Nursing Home Law Quarterly. Natural Senior Citizens Law Center. Washington, D.C.

Paine, K. 1982. Stretching resources for legal services: Nontraditional approaches in two settings. *Clearinghouse Review* 16(6):559–565.

Regan, J. 1985. *Tax, Financial and Estate Planning for the Elderly Client.* New York: Matthew Bender.

Schmidt, L. 1980. *Bibliography of Selected Materials: Private Bar Involvement in Legal Services Delivery.* Washington: Legal Services Corporation.

Schuster, M. R. 1985. *Disability Practice Manual for Social Security and Supplemental Security Income.* Washington, D.C.: Legal Counsel for the Elderly.

Shaffer, T. L. 1987. *Legal Interviewing and Counseling.* St. Paul: West.

Slonim, S. 1982. *Landlords and Tenants: Your Guide to the Law.* Chicago: American Bar Association.

Social Security Forum. National Organization of Social Security Claimants' Representatives. Pearl River, N.Y. (monthly).

Special Committee on Legal Problems of the Aging. 1986. Six issues critical to older Americans: A checklist of topics that should be discussed by lawyers with their older clients. New York: Record of the Association of the Bar of the City of New York 41:786–807.

Stein, J., moderator. 1988. Management column: New funding for legal services. *Clearinghouse Review* 22(3):255–263.

Storey, J. R. 1986. Policy changes affecting older Americans during the first Reagan administration. *The Gerontologist* 26:27–31.

Stone, L. M. 1978. Due process: A boundary for intervention. *Social Work* 23(5):402–405.

Striker, J. M. and A. O. Shapiro. 1981. *How You Can Sue Without Hiring a Lawyer: A Guide to Winning in Small Claims Court.* New York: Simon and Schuster.

Tolchin, M. 1988. Federal aid for destitute reaching just half of those eligible. *New York Times,* May 10, 1988.

U.S. Administration on Aging. 1982. Legal services programs under Title III of the Older Americans Act. Washington Office of Field Services, Legal Services Corporation.

Weil, M. 1982. Research on issues in collaboration between social workers and lawyers. *Social Service Review* 56:393–404.

Weil, M. and E. Sanchez. 1983. The impact of the *Tarasoff* decision on clinical social work practice. *Social Service Review* 56:112–124.

Young Lawyers Section. 1986. *Senior Citizens' Handbook: A Guide to Programs and Laws Affecting Older New Yorkers.* Albany: New York State Bar Association.

17

Assistance to Victims of Crime and Abuse

JORDAN I. KOSBERG, PH.D.
University of South Florida, Tampa

Those in the helping professions are in vantage points to detect, prevent, and treat elderly who are victimized by the criminal or abusive behavior of others. Whether in hospital emergency rooms, in family service agencies, in mental health centers, or other such settings, professional care providers should be sensitized to detect cases of elder abuse and victimization, trained to help the victimized elderly person, and committed to needed social policy changes to better protect the elderly, especially the most dependent and vulnerable.

This paper deals with the victimization of the elderly on the street and in the home by strangers and with the abuse of elderly by informal care providers—family members, friends, and neighbors. Explanations of the problems are followed by suggestions for prevention of victimization and abuse and for treatment of the elderly victims. Because of my background of study in the area of elder abuse and the "invisibility" of this problem, I will emphasize the problem of abusive behavior against the elderly.

GENERAL VULNERABILITY

The following examples of elder abuse, elicited in hearings before the Subcommittee on Retirement Income and Employment of the House Select Committee on Aging (U.S. Congress 1981), reflect the variety and severity of the abuse to which the dependent elderly are peculiarly vulnerable:

> The North Carolina County Department of Social Services reported finding a 91-year-old widow lying on her bed. She had multiple severe bruises on her face, hands, arms and chest. She was incoherent and very confused. She was assessed to have been beaten approximately a week before. The daughter of the elderly woman had been beaten by her own son, also, and that was why she had not reported her own mother's condition. The elderly woman was transported to an emergency room where she eventually died. Her grandson is being held on charges of murder. (p. 171)
>
> Caseworkers in West Virginia were alerted that an 80-year-old couple might be having problems. Upon investigation they found the husband ill to the point of being comatose. The man was described as "unable to respond, barely breathing with eyes glazed." The wife was exhausted and distraught from trying to care for her husband to the point where her mental condition was unstable. The wife would not allow authorities to remove the man to a hospital for treatment. She charged them with engaging in a plot to take her husband away from her. Caseworkers contacted the couple's daughter to assist them in persuading the wife that the man needed attention. They were unsuccessful and the husband died two days thereafter. (p. 174)
>
> California officials report that an 87-year-old widow in frail health and generally confined to a wheelchair, unable to to care for her day-to-day needs, as allegedly the victim of physical and financial abuse from 1974 through 1980. A nurse companion who was also her conservator and three children depleted her financial resources by more than $300,000 while depriving the woman of proper medical attention, food, and clothing. Caseworkers helped the woman to institute legal proceedings. (p. 175)
>
> In California, an 87-year-old woman in ill-health, confined to a wheelchair, and unable to care for her daily needs, was repeatedly and systematically abused by her family and nurse companion. The mental and physical torture lasted six years. During this time, the woman was threatened, held prisoner, deprived of all contact with the outside world, not permitted to see friends and family, and battered. (p. 176)

> In Washington, an 84-year-old woman terminally ill with cancer was refused proper medical attention by her grandson who did not want the woman's property and income dissipated by doctor and hospital payments. The woman was found in tremendous pain living in truly wretched conditions. The victim was transferred to a nursing home where she died a few weeks later. (p. 177)

There are many reasons why the elderly are especially vulnerable to criminal or abusive behavior (Kosberg 1983). Some pertain to social values and attitudes toward the elderly, and others pertain to their physical and economic needs. Still other reasons for the vulnerability of the aged are related to their social and psychological losses.

The elderly are likely to live alone, which is especially true for elderly women. This fact combined with residence in a high-crime-rate area increases the vulnerability of the elderly and the probability of isolation (through fear of leaving one's dwelling) or the actual commission of crime against the elderly.

Because of their diminished physical strength and stamina, older people are less able to defend themselves or to escape from threatening situations (Goldsmith and Tomas 1974). Related to this is the fact that they are likely to suffer from physical disabilities and have impairments affecting hearing, sight, touch, and mobility. The result is a lessened ability to resist crimes of a physical nature, whether the aggressor is a stranger or a relative.

There is a likelihood that the elderly will be additionally vulnerable to crime because of residence in neighborhoods with high crime rates where they are in close proximity to groups likely to victimize them—the unemployed and teenage dropouts (Goldsmith and Tomas 1974). There are at least two reasons why the elderly often live in high-crime areas. First, low incomes may necessitate moving to low-rental areas. Second, there is a reluctance to leave the neighborhood (and home) where one has lived for many years, even when the neighborhood has greatly changed. The economic, social, and psychological meaning of one's dwelling may be more important than the extent of crime or incongruity of population in one's neighborhood.

Many elderly persons rely on walking or on public transportation to get around in the community. Accordingly, they are visible and vulnerable. Walking to and from public transportation, waiting at stops, getting on or off a bus or subway, and being in crowded situations all have ramifications for the possibility of accidents as well as for victimization.

Given low fixed incomes, the elderly are especially vulnerable to fraudulent promises and quick-wealth schemes (Butler 1975; Pepper 1983). Poor health conditions, with little if any hope for improvement, can make an elderly person vulnerable to health care quackery or schemes to evoke anxiety about health or economic security. Expensive or excessive health insurance, funeral arrangements, cemetery plots, and health devices are but a few of the many gambits to part the elderly from their financial resources. In addition, the loneliness of elderly persons makes them vulnerable to overly friendly and solicitous clerks, salespersons, or strangers. Many elderly have had their savings "stolen" by a variety of confidence games and unscrupulous salespersons.

The dates when monthly pension and benefit checks are received in the mail are widely known. Such knowledge results in mail boxes being broken into and checks stolen, robberies, and purse snatchings. These crimes are especially frequent around banks, shopping malls, and grocery stores.

Beside these reasons for the vulnerability of the elderly to criminal activity, there are also reasons why the elderly are especially vulnerable to abusive behavior by members of their informal care system.

Elder abuse by family members occurs within the home, outside of public scrutiny. If a problem is detected by outsiders, it is considered a "family affair." Even professionals are reluctant to intervene. Finally, the informal care system has been used as a panacea by those in the legal, social service, and health care systems; yet such individuals turned to for care of ill and dependent elderly may be ill-suited, ill-prepared, and unmotivated to provide necessary care or may be motivated for all the wrong reasons (e.g., exploitation). "In the eagerness to find an easy and inexpensive solution to care for an elderly person, those making referrals . . . may turn too quickly to family members without assessing the appropriateness of the family or pressures on the family to be caused by having to care for an elderly relative" (Kosberg 1983:267). Brody (1985) has discussed that many families take on the caregiving role out of guilt; not wanting to shirk from their responsibilities for their elderly relatives.

In addition to these factors associated with vulnerability of the elderly to criminal or abusive behavior is the social perception of the elderly in society as worthless. Such a negative view of the elderly can result, it is believed, in aimless and senseless crimes against them. Too often one reads about muggings, beatings, psychological abuse, killings, etc. with no apparent motives. The only conclusion is that the criminal or abusive behavior was based upon thrills, taking out aggression on a defenseless scapegoat, or seeking out a (perceived) valueless individual. It is further believed that if an elderly person is also perceived as a deviant (e.g., alcoholic, drifter, handicapped, mentally ill, etc.), the greater the likelihood of his/her becoming a victim. In American society, being dependent is also an undesirable status. Katz (1979–80) has suggested that ageism and bias against the handicapped can result in the creation of abusive situations.

DIMENSIONS OF THE PROBLEM

According to the Senate Special Committee on Aging, of 1,000 persons aged 65 and over studied, 22 had been victims of theft (19 of personal larceny without contact); 8 had been victims of violent crimes, including 5 instances of robbery and 3 of assault (U.S. Congress, 1978).

Research findings on the most prevalent forms of elder abuse are inconclusive and reflect variations in the definitions of elder abuse as well as the methods by which abuse is measured and reported. The House Select Committee on Aging found that physical trauma was the most prevalent type of abuse in a Massachusetts study, psychological abuse in a Maryland study, passive neglect in a Michigan study, a lack of personal care in an Ohio study (U.S. Congress 1981).

It is difficult to know the exact extent of criminal victimization of the elderly and abusive behavior against the aged. First, the elderly may fail to report their victimization. Second, the problem of criminal or abusive behavior may not be detected or correctly identified.

Criminal activity by strangers against the elderly has been rather widely studied (Malinchak and Wright 1978). While elderly individuals are victims of personal larceny (e.g., purse snatching) more so than younger persons, the elderly have much lower rates of homicide, robbery, rape, assault, burglary, larceny from the household, and motor vehicle theft than younger persons (Hindelang and Richardson 1978). Tomas (1974) concluded that, for several cities, the rates of victimization for robbery with injury, personal larceny, and fraud of the elderly were equal to or higher than that of younger age groups. In a national crime survey, Hirschel and Rubin (1982) found that the elderly are more likely than others to be victimized by personal larceny, fraud, confidence games and medical quackery. Certain groups of elderly were found to be more likely to be victimized. For example. Liang and Sengstock (1983) found the risk of criminal victimization among the elderly higher for urban dwellers, the young-old, those who are not married, nonwhite persons, and men.

Often the fact that the aged do have lower levels of crime committed against them is interpreted to mean that the problem is not a significant one. Such a conclusion glosses over important considerations. First, the consequence of crime may be an injury from which convalescence is slow or may result in institutionalization; the loss of possessions or financial resources may greatly affect the quality of life; and damages to property cannot be repaired or replaced. Second, the older person is more likely to be victimized repeatedly—often by the same offender (Goldsmith and Tomas 1974). Third, low crime rates reported for the elderly may result, in part, from the failure of the elderly to report the commission of a crime (such as theft or fraud) because of embarrassment, fear or intimidation, or because they believe the reporting of a crime to be futile. Liang and Sengstock (1983) found that 45 percent of aged victims failed to report the commission of the crime.

The fourth, and final, consideration glossed over by crime statistics is fear. As insidious as being the victim of a crime is the anticipation of becoming a victim. Fear of crime has been found to be a more prevailing emotion for the elderly than for younger persons (Clemente and Kleiman 1976). Braungart et al (1980) analyzed National Opinion Research Center data and found that fear of crime among the elderly was greatest for women; particularly for those who live alone, were in poor health, or who had been previously victimized. Whether the fear is based upon real or imagined danger of crime, the results limit the comings and goings of elderly persons and adversely affect the quality of their lives by being, in many cases, an all-consuming preoccupation. Finley (1983: 22), however, notes that fear of crime is not all bad, for it has "an important role in reducing actual victimization [of the elderly], as it does for all age groups." Yin (1985), too, has alluded to fear as a factor in lowering the exposure of the aged to criminals.

Less empirical work has been done on elder abuse, although the problem has increasingly received attention in the mass media. (For example, a front page article in the *Wall Street Journal,* by Ansberry (1988), was entitled, "Abuse of the Elderly by Their Own Children Increases in America.") Given the invisibility and underreporting of the problem, coupled with methodological difficulties and differing definitions (Johnson 1986; Kosberg 1979), the limited number of studies on elder abuse preclude definite conclusions about the scope of the problem. This author has concluded that a comprehensive definition of elder abuse should include the following:

1. *Passive Neglect.* Characterized by a situation in which the elderly person is left alone, isolated, or forgotten. The abuser is often unaware of the neglect or the consequences of the neglect, due to the abuser's lack of intelligence or lack of experience as a care provider.

2. *Active Neglect.* Characterized as the intentional withholding of items necessary for daily living, such as food, medicine, companionship, and bathroom assistance.
3. *Verbal, Emotional, or Psychological Abuse.* Characterized by situations in which the older person is called names, insulted, infantilized, frightened, intimidated, humiliated, or threatened.
4. *Physical Abuse.* Characterized by the older person being hit, slapped, bruised, sexually molested, cut, burned, or physically restrained.
5. *Material or Financial Misappropriation.* Characterized by actions including monetary or material theft or misuse (when not being used for the benefit, or with the approval, of the elderly person).
6. *Violation of Rights.* Characterized by efforts to force an elderly person from his or her dwelling or to force him or her into another setting (most often a nursing home) without any forewarning, explanation, opportunity for input, or against the older person's wishes.

Self-abuse is a special problem and, since it is mainly done without assistance, is not included for discussion. When, however, informal care providers are cognizant of the self-abuse and either do not intervene or, indeed, knowingly assist in the self-abuse (e.g., by buying alcohol or filling prescriptions, not seeking professional assistance), then the problem can be considered an example of neglectful behavior. Currently being debated is the question of whether or not the definition of elder abuse ought to include maltreatment of residents/patients within long-term care facilities. While some see commonalities of abuse dynamics occurring in the community and in institutional settings, the fact that a perpetrator is a paid staff member (and not a relative) and that the dynamics can include administrative policies for the care of large numbers of impaired older persons and administrative opportunities for lower echelon aides and orderlies (who are most likely to be the offenders), it is believed that merging discussions may diffuse the unique dynamics which result in adverse treatment of the elderly in both types of settings.

Several studies on elder abuse were undertaken during the late 1970s. Rathbone-McCuan (1980) presented information on the existence of intergenerational family violence and neglect affecting elderly relatives. Steinmetz (1978) was also one of the first to identify and discuss the maltreatment of the elderly by their families. The University of Maryland's Center on Aging undertook a study of battered elderly persons (Block and Sinnot 1979) and found that 4.1 percent of the elderly respondents in their study reported abuse. If projected to a national population of elderly, the researchers concluded that there would be nearly 1 million cases of elder abuse each year. Other estimates of elder abuse range from 500,000 to 2.5 million cases per year (Rathbone-McCuan and Hashimi 1982).

In an exploratory study of professional and paraprofessional encounters with abuse in Massachusetts (Legal Research 1979), it was found that 55 percent of the respondents knew of at least one incident of abuse in an eighteen-month period. A study in Michigan (Hickey and Douglass 1981) was based upon recollections of care providers (i.e., police, social workers, physicians) in five study areas. While they found little or no direct physical abuse, 50 percent reported contact with passive neglect. Finally, in a study of abuse of elderly clients at the Chronic Illness Center in Cleveland, Ohio (Lau and Kosberg 1979), it was found that 10 percent of all clients had been abused. Informal care providers, mainly relatives, were the abusers.

The flurry of empirical research findings of abusive behavior by family and friends of elderly persons produced hearings by the U.S. House of Representatives Select Committee on Aging in June 1979, and in 1980 a Senate-House joint hearing took place. In 1981 a National Conference on Abuse of Older Persons was held and experts' testimonies were presented to the House of Representatives Select Committee on Aging. The Committee (U.S. Congress 1980:xiv–xv) concluded that "some four percent of the nation's elderly may be victims of some sort of abuse from moderate to severe. In other words, one out of every twenty-five older Americans, or roughly one million elder Americans may be victims of such abuse each year." The report went on to indicate that abuse was most likely to be a recurring event rather than a single incident, and that elderly victims were likely to be the very old, women, and those dependent on others for care and protection. Generally, the abused older person lives with the abuser, who is most often a relative. Finally, the research studies concluded that no aged person is immune to the possibility of abuse, for it is not associated with social class, educational level, race or nationality, or geographic location.

More recent studies, reported by Callahan (1988) and Hudson (1986), indicate that seldom do studies and surveys of the extent of elder abuse exceed 5 percent of the older population. In a recent study, Pillemer and Finkelhor (1988) found that 3.2 percent of a random sample survey of 2,020 elderly persons had experienced physical violence, verbal aggression, or neglect. Even while acknowledging the possibility of gross underreporting, Callahan has stated that "from the standpoint of society actual abuse affects few of our fellow citizens" (1988:455). He goes on to speculate why elder abuse has become the source of concern, at this point in time, and identifies several possibilities: the involvement of the media, professional concern with employment opportunities, and the need to justify the funding of programs and services.

While such a point of view is provocative, indeed, one could quibble with efforts to minimize the concern about elder abuse (due to the small proportion of elderly found to be abused). As stated elsewhere (Kosberg 1988), elder abuse is a very invisible problem because it occurs out of sight in private dwellings, it is seen as a family affair, the abused victims seldom report the problem, professionals may not correctly assess the cause of a problem, and few of those in the helping professions who are required to report suspected cases of elder abuse do so. The U.S. House of Representatives Select Committee on Aging (U.S. Congress 1980) estimated that while one out of every three cases of child abuse are reported, only one out of six cases of elder abuse are reported. Finally, regardless of the actual number or percentage of elderly who are currently abused, it is suspected that the problem will grow. Reasons include the fact that the number of the old-old (the most impaired and, thus, the most vulnerable) is growing, the fact that more women are employed outside the home (and, therefore, more likely to have the dual pressures of career and caregiving), and the fact that caregivers, spouses and children, will be old and less likely to give necessary and appropriate care and attention to an impaired relative. Thus, the problem of elder abuse should remain an area of concern.

EXPLANATIONS

Crime against the elderly is, of course, a reflection of the pervasive nature of crime in general. The elderly are victimized for the same reasons that younger persons are victimized. And the motivations of those who victimize the elderly are the same for those who victimize younger persons. Yet the characteristics of the elderly do make them especially visible, vulnerable, and defenseless.

The causes of abuse and maltreatment of the elderly by informal care providers are complex and varied. Those in the helping professions should be aware of differing explanations for the abuse of elderly persons (mainly by family members), so that appropriate intervention and treatment can be provided. The following is a summary of the major theoretical explanations for elder abuse (or those explanations extrapolated from research on child or spouse abuse).

Psychopathology Model

Elderly individuals may be maltreated by individuals who exhibit abnormal or deviant behavior, including drug addiction, alcoholism, mental illness, and senile dementia, among others. Steele and Pollock (1968) found child abusers to be impulsive, immature, and depressed; abusive behavior displaced aggressive and sadistic inclinations. Parents may have cared for schizophrenic, retarded, or alcoholic children who became adults. "As aged parents weaken and need care, their adult children become abusing and neglectful caregivers because of an inability to make appropriate judgments and perceptions" (Lau and Kosberg 1979:13).

Sociological Approach

Gelles (1973) discussed sociological interpretations of child abuse that have, it is believed, application to elder abuse. Vulnerability of children to abuse was explained as due to their lack of physical ability to withstand physical force, and the fact that they are not capable of much meaningful social interaction, resulting in parent frustration. Further, the infant (or elderly person) may create stress by imposing economic hardships or interfering with professional, occupational, or educational plans.

Intrafamily violence may be caused by stress-producing conditions. An overrepresentation of abusing fathers have been found to be unemployed (O'Brien 1971). Another contextual factor is that child abuse is often associated with an unwanted pregnancy, often the parents had to get married, were ill-prepared to become parents, or the unwanted child caused stress in the family. "The child may be a financial burden, an emotional burden, or a psychological burden" (Gelles 1973:618). So, too, might the elderly parent be an unwanted or unexpected responsibility.

Social Exchange Theory

Edwards and Brauburger (1973) studied the exchange system between parents and their adolescent children. They found that when exchange between them breaks down, conflict develops. This exchange incorporates a system of rewards, power, the costs of compliance, and reciprocity. Conflict was found related to coercive control techniques used to resolve problems. While, for adolescents, increased independence from parents can produce tension and conflict, it may well be that increased dependence of elderly parents upon grown children can result in conflict. The conflict, in turn, may result in maltreatment or abuse.

Adding to the understanding of exchange phenomena, Richer suggested that the greater the availability of resources and alternative sources of rewards available to children "the less likely parental dictates are to be followed and the more conflict-ridden the relationship with parents will be" (1968:464). It is interesting to speculate whether the relationship problems of earlier times are reproduced in the old age of the parents, or whether a role reversal occurs whereby the elderly parent is expected to comply with the directions of the adult children. In this latter case, the earlier social-exchange relationship is altered, if not reversed.

Life Crisis Model

Justice and Duncan (1976) discussed stress resulting in child abuse. They focused upon life-changing events that require readjustment in the life-style of a person or family. When an excessive number or magnitude of such life-change events occur, a "state of life crisis" may be said to exist. The researchers found such "states" associated with abusing parents. They utilized the forty-three events requiring some readjustment by the person or family to whom the event occurred (Holmes and Rahe 1967). These events include physical illness, occurrence of an accident or injury, and personal, social, economic, or interpersonal changes. Such a multicausal model of abuse focuses upon life crises caused by excessive change, as predisposing factors. The life crises, a series of change events rather than situational day-to-day problems that are often unpredictable, result in abuse:" [T]he end state of the life crisis is a stage of exhaustion, of decreased ability to adjust, and increased risk of losing control" (Justice and Duncan 1976:112).

Social-Structural Theory of Family Violence

The social-structural theory of conflict focuses, in part, upon the socialization of aggression. "The theory states that parents who punish more severely produce children who are more aggressive" (Lystad 1975:330). This socialization of violence is seen for certain groups with lower educational achievements and lower socioeconomic status as well as among broken families.

The power structure of the family is also considered in relationship to family violence. Each family has a hierarchy of interpersonal relationships with superordinate and subordinate roles. Each family has different structures, values, and beliefs regarding power relationships. Moreover, the power structure of the larger society affects violence in the family. Societal abuse of children (through hunger, poverty, poor education)—or any dependent population (including the aged)—can be seen to be more serious than individual abuse (Gil 1971). Cultural values support the view that the aged are unimportant, and cultural norms toward dependent populations (use of physical force) may sanction abusive behavior.

Finally, the social-structural variables of race and ethnic subcultures have been discussed as "cultures of violence." It is suggested by some that such systems of values justify and support violent behavior (Lystad 1975), although Cazenave (1983) believes that the "culture of violence" is more an impression than an empirical fact.

Intergenerational Conflict

Less empirically based are efforts that focus specifically upon the intergenerational problems between the elderly and their grown children. Tensions between older mothers and adult daughters have been discussed in terms of personality conflicts that are worsened by the passing of years (Farrar 1955). Failure to redefine family roles with the passing of years has been seen to result in either hostility (Blenkner 1965) or overt violence (Glasser and Glasser 1962). It has been suggested that conflict between family members and aged relatives is more likely in situations where the family, as individuals or a unit, has difficulty coping with an elderly parent suffering from a chronic disease (Maddox 1975). Miller (1981) has written about the stress to adult children, facing their own aging process and the needs of their own children, of having to care for elderly parents. Conflict between generations has also been viewed as reflecting a lack of normative definition with regard to the rights and responsibilities of middle-aged children vis-à-vis their aged parents (Cavan 1969).

ASSESSMENT

As Rathbone-McCuan states: "Identification of and intervention in cases of physical abuse and purposeful neglect of the elderly within the context of the family are rare; because professionals in the field seem unaware that the phenomenon exists, they fail to recognize cues of willful abuse and neglect" (1980:296). Indeed, to discuss assessment and, especially, intervention without first alluding to the need to address sensitivity to the possible existence of criminal or abusive behavior against an elderly person is rather meaningless.

Those working with and for elderly persons should not expect elderly persons to necessarily verbalize their adversities. As has been discussed, elderly victims are often reluctant to report the criminal action against them because of embarrassment, fear, or belief that it would be futile. Research on elder abuse has found that abused elderly, too, do not report their adversities. In their study of elder abuse, Lau and Kosberg (1979) found that denial was the most prevalent reaction of elderly persons, followed by resignation. Failure to report abusive behavior or denial of its existence by an elderly person may arise from the following reasons (Kosberg 1983): fear of reprisals by the abuser, embarrassment about the behavior of a family member who is the abuser, anticipation that the solution to the problem will be worse than the problem (e.g., removal from one's home, institutionalization), fear that legal and criminal action might be taken against the abusing family member, belief that the problem is a family affair that should remain within the confines of the family, or feelings of guilt in being dependent and causing tensions and pressures on informal care providers.

If there is a reluctance to report criminal and abusive behavior by the elderly, then those in the helping professions have a special responsibility for detecting and assessing such problems. The consequences of certain types of adverse action are obvious, if proper assessment is undertaken: injuries, bruises, burns, etc. Other consequences are more subtle to discern and can be best identified through assessment of a person's affect and demeanor. Depression, fear, confusion, anger, withdrawal, etc. may result from a variety of causes. Criminal or abusive behavior can be one such cause and should not be overlooked. Physical assessments to determine elder abuse (Falcioni 1982) or criminal activity against the elderly seem further developed than more subtle social or psychological assessments for such problems. Yet, several screening protocols have been developed to identify physical and behavioral symptoms of elder abuse (Sengstock and Hwalek 1986; Quinn and Tomita 1986).

Ideally, those in the helping professions who are in contact with elderly persons who might be victims should be able to establish a relationship with an elderly person in a quiet and private location. (For a comprehensive discussion of diagnosis and intervention strategies, see Quinn and Tomita 1986.) The interviewer's role should be clarified, and the appropriate use of information should be mentioned. Emphasis should be placed on assistance and support, not on criminal charges against an individual. Especially in cases of suspected abuse, there should not be anyone else present (such as a family member who brought the older person to the hospital emergency room, social service agency, etc.). The relative should be interviewed separately, and the explanations for what happened to the older person should be compared to the report by the older person. When there is incongruence in stories, or suspected collaboration in a fabricated story, there is reason to further pursue the actual events leading up to a problem situation (whether of a long-term or episodic nature). The skills and personality of the professional or paraprofessional will determine the success in securing factual information about the older person and the occurrence of criminal or abusive behavior.

In assessing the problem of criminal or abusive behavior, there is a danger in viewing problems too simplistically. Assessment should include information on the type of criminal or abusive behavior, the frequency and duration of such behavior, and the sequence of events leading to the adversity. In addition, the elderly person (or witnesses to events) should be questioned about events surrounding the adversity in terms of the time and place of occurrence and number of offenders and characteristics. For abusive behavior, information should be obtained as to the conditions under which the abuse occurred and the motivation of the abuser. (While the results of the action on an older person may be similar, intervention with one who abuses out of ignorance is different than with one who abuses out of hostility.) Also, it is important to learn whether there was more than one abuser and whether the abuse took place with the knowledge or in the presence of others.

Finally, the interpretation by the elderly person to the adverse actions of another, or others, is important. Some elderly persons may see the criminal or abusive behavior to be a result of their own actions, limitations, or needs: "I was too interested in getting something for nothing" or "I was desperate for a cure" in cases of fraud; "I was a burden to my daughter" or "I beat my son when he was a child" in cases of abuse. In other situations, the older person does not see the problem in the same way as the professional: "There was no maltreatment. My family has always been very physical and emotional with one another." And, in cases of elder abuse, the assessment of the abuser's explanation of the problem is vital to the type of recommended treatment plan. Some abusers remain hostile and deny any wrongdoing in their treatment of an older person; some are confused and do not understand what they have done; and some are embarrassed and saddened by events and situations that erupted in their abuse of an elderly relative.

INTERVENTIONS

Activities to assist the elderly include both prevention before and treatment after abuse or criminal victimization has occurred. There are prodigious roles for those concerned with the vulnerability of the elderly to criminal and abusive behavior. A variety of direct, programmatic, and policy interventions follow.

With Crime Victims

As has been discussed, research findings have helped identify high-risk elderly and situations related to the commission of crime. "When older persons can learn to identify criminal opportunities in their environment and assess their risk, they can then take simple precautions to divert the criminal's behavior" (Jaycox and Center 1983: 319). Community care providers can assist the elderly in preventive activities. Jaycox and Center (1983) have identified individual and collective crime prevention activities. The former include home inspections by trained individuals to determine the security status of the home and particular risks, property-marking programs for the identification of possessions, improved precautionary activities (e.g., using locks, leaving lights or radios on), and increased precaution on the street (e.g., sensitivity to one's appearance and the environment). Collective activities include block clubs, neighborhood watch, building patrols, escort service, and telephone assurance programs, among others.

Curtis and Kohn (1983) have discussed preventive activities in age-segregated settings for the elderly and emphasized the importance of environmental design as a detriment to criminal activity against the elderly. Such preventive strategies can include access controls that create barriers for visitors, formal surveillance, programs to increase prevention awareness, and fostering protective behaviors.

Those working with aged who have been victimized (whether by personal attacks, theft of possessions, fraud, or exploitation) or immobilized by fear need a special sensitivity and skills to deal with the trauma of the criminal act and its aftermath on the older person. While the clinical skills of those working with the elderly are covered elsewhere in this volume, public policy is needed to create victim-assistance programs for the elderly. "Programs which are primarily concerned with helping people recover from their crime-induced stress usually offer counseling and social services, and may lobby for sensitive handling of victims by social agencies and criminal justice professions" (Jaycox and Center 1983:323). Examples of victim-assistance efforts are rape crisis centers and shelters for battered women. Organizational efforts concerned with victimized elderly include the National Victim Center, in Fort Worth, Texas, the National Council of Senior Citizens' Criminal Justice and the Elderly Program, and the American Association of Retired Persons' Criminal Justice Services.

Jaycox and Center (1983) have identified three main objectives of victim-assistance programs for older crime victims. First, there is the need to assist the elderly to recover from the psychological and emotional impact of being a victim. This necessitates clinical skills as well as providing support and empathy. Second, assistance should be provided to get whatever benefits are available as compensations for losses. For example, some states have victim-compensation programs. Third, assistance is needed to provide either directly or indirectly (through referrals) services needed by the older person to recover from the criminal act (e.g., medical care, transportation, homemaker services, etc.) and to participate in the criminal justice process (e.g., assistance and support in dealing with the law enforcement and judicial bureaucracies). The setting for such victim-assistance activities can be located within police departments, social service and health care resources, or the court system.

With Abuse Victims

Those working with older persons, in whatever the setting, should be sensitive to the possibility of abusive behavior. Research and practice experience has identified high-risk elderly persons: the old old, the impaired and dependent, and women. Findings from research studies and conclusions from social science theory in the areas of child and spouse abuse extrapolated to an elderly population have identified individual or situational conditions that are associated with abusive behavior. Kosberg (1988) has developed a High Risk Placement Worksheet to assist professionals in the placement of older persons who might be at-risk to abusive behavior. The Worksheet focuses upon the characteristics of 1) the older person (e.g., impairments, provocative behavior, advanced age); 2) the caregiver (e.g., problem drinker, caregiving inexperience, stressed); and 3) the family system (e.g., family support, intra-family problems, isolation). Pillemer (1986) has also discussed risk factors related to elder abuse.

From a preventive perspective, there are several mechanisms that can be used to preclude placing an elderly person in a situation that could well lead to abuse. Social workers and other professionals in social and health service systems should make a careful assessment of the appropriateness of an informal care provider. "Designating a relative a guardian, placing an elderly client with a child, or discharging an elderly patient to the family without adequate assessment may be viewed as a panacea by service providers but may result in great problems for the elderly person" (Kosberg 1983:271). Those who care for dependent elderly persons should be mentally, socially, physically, and economically able to provide the needed care and attention. Additionally, the perceptions of potential and actual caregivers of impaired elderly, regarding the anticipated or actual caregiving experiences, need to be determined. Kosberg has developed the Cost of Care Index (reported in Kosberg and Cairl 1986), which assesses the anticipated, or actual, experience resulting from care provision in five areas: personal and social restrictions, physical and emotional health, value of providing care, older person as provocateur, and economic costs. It is believed necessary to include both subjective and objective information in the overall assessment of a caregiver. Further, the informal care system should be assessed. This refers to the number, location, and health of family members and friends who can either share in the care of an elderly person or who can be available to relieve the major care provider from ongoing responsibilities.

Inasmuch as there are often economic pressures on those caring for elderly persons, those in the helping professions should advocate social policies that seek to relieve some of the economic burdens of such care. Among various proposals are those for tax incentives, direct subsidies, or direct cash payments through a family allowance program. Such proposals may encourage family members to share in the care of an elderly person and can reduce the economic burden of such care. The enactment of policies need, however, some mechanism to ensure that the motivation for care is not an economic one.

Supporting community services for those caring for elderly persons is important for preventive reasons. Especially for those caring for elderly relatives who do not have extensive informal support systems, formal supporting services are vital to relieve family members from the constant and demanding care of a dependent elderly relative. Such needed community services include adult day care, day hospitals, friendly visitors, respite care, homemaker and home health aides, and chore services, among others. The existence of these supporting services can assist in precluding the institutionalization of an elderly relative by a family that can no longer cope with the constant demands for care and can relieve some of the pressures and tensions upon the family that could result in abusive behavior.

The areas of prevention and treatment of elder abuse are not mutually exclusive, and each has elements of the other. Protective services have elements of both prevention and treatment. In 1980, twenty-five states had some type of protective services legislation (Salend, Satz, and Pynoos 1981). Only three state units indicated that they have no laws addressing elder abuse (APWA and NASUA 1986). All states should have protective-service legislation that would permit social workers and other professionals entry into private homes (to investigate cases of suspected abuse), provision of services, legal intervention, and authority for the removal of an elderly person (being abused) without the consent of family members. Of course, removal of an elderly person from the home should be the last resort and would follow 1) efforts to work with family members to resolve problems, and 2) the mobilization of supporting community services or informal resources in the effort to assist the family in the care of their elderly relative (Hooyman and Lustbader 1986).

Counseling or casework with the elderly person and family is another area that embraces elements of both prevention and treatment. As for prevention: "Counseling should be available during the time a family is making decisions regarding care for [an] elderly person. Families endure enormous social pressure to care for their own, and the professional's role should be to aid the family to make an intelligent decision, not on social values of guilt, but on what they want or are able to do" (Steuer 1983:245). Kosberg (1988) has also advocated the need to counsel those who are considering the taking on of care-giving responsibilities, so as to identify those who are overly optimistic or pessimistic, or who seem to be motivated for the wrong reasons.

Steuer (1983) suggests that once abusive behavior has been identified, intervention with the abuser and the entire family is necessary to work out feelings of conflict and guilt. Rathbone-McCuan and Hashimi (1982) have indicated that clinical intervention in cases of elder abuse was both "ill-defined" and in need of evaluation. Rathbone-McCuan, Travis, and Voyles (1983) have attempted to fill this practice gap in their discussion of a task-centered model for family intervention in cases of elder abuse. If social or psychological interventions do not resolve the problem and elder abuse continues, legal action should be taken. Removal of the elderly person from the customary dwelling should always be the last resort, after all else fails. It is hoped that, as a result of the publicity given to the existence and causes of elder abuse, those caring for the dependent elderly persons will voluntarily seek out professional guidance to deal with their feelings or the consequences of excessive demands upon them prior to an eruption of abusive behavior. But in cases of identified elder abuse, those who mistreat elderly persons should be required to seek professional intervention, at the very least.

Professionals need to consider legal protection against irate relatives who are either elder abusers or are under suspicion of being elder abusers. Given the difficulty of securing conclusive evidence of abusive behavior by a family member, accusations or confrontations may result in actions against the professional. Certainly, personal professional liability insurance is needed; often an agency's policy covers individual professional staff. Professionals need to be protected as well from false accusations of abusive or unprofessional behavior by the elderly client, who may be suffering from delusional or distorted perceptions. In this regard, it is necessary for those working with elderly persons to judge very carefully the accuracy and validity of any charges of abusive behavior. Such accusations need to be substantiated by a very careful assessment of the elderly person's cognizance of reality, at the least, and by the statements of others whose testimony corresponds to that of the older person.

It has been found that 43 states are operating mandatory, statewide reporting systems for elder abuse. Although there is variation between states, such legislation requires those from the helping professions to report, to a central state agency, suspected cases of adult or elder abuse. However, such a mechanism for identifying cases of abuse can hardly be viewed as a panacea. "The reluctance to report child abuse by professionals (who fear legal action by alleged abusers, time spent in the criminal justice system, or who are uncertain whether abuse has occurred) may be characteristic of professional responses to mandatory reporting laws for elder abuse" (Kosberg 1988:44). Many fail to report cases of abuse by erroneously assuming privileged communications with a patient or client to take precedent over the reporting requirement. Finally, O'Brien (1986) has found that not all professionals in states with mandatory reporting legislation are aware of their responsibilities.

Foster Care as a Preventive Measure

Foster care for the elderly has come to be considered a viable alternative to independent living, on one hand, and to institutional living, on the other. However, foster care has been subject to the criticism that elderly persons can be quite vulnerable to abusive behavior at the hands of foster-care providers. Brody (1977), for example, questions the motivations of foster care:

> Discussions of foster home care constantly refer to the family, to the family setting and to participation in normal family activities as essential ingredients. . . . If six people or 10 people . . . are in such a home, is it really a "family residence"? Or, is it a congregate facility of some type such as the many "Mom and Pop" boarding homes that almost invariably are without a "Pop"? Or, is it an unlicensed nursing home? Are these really "families" as we know them, with a variety of motivations for providing foster care? Or, are they small business concerns?

A report of the Senate Special Committee on Aging concluded that foster homes are less capable of meeting the needs of discharged mental patients:

> Most often, they are converted residences but they may also be new high rise buildings or converted hotels, in some cases they may be converted mobile homes or renovated chicken coops. What they have in common is that they offer board and room but no nursing care and that most States do not license such facilities. (U.S. Congress 1976b)

Lack of licensure pertains both to the characteristics of the foster home and the characteristics (training, motivation, and suitability) of the foster care providers. Further, there has seldom been any mandated professional surveillance or follow-up to a foster care placement of an elderly person. The possibility of abuse of a vulnerable elderly person in a foster home is thus great and may continue undetected. As Dr. Robert N. Butler testified to a joint hearing of the House Subcommittees on Long-term Care and on Health of the Elderly, "From the perspective of civil liberties, as well as health care, of the two sides of the right-of-treatment concept, such facilities as foster care homes have even less protection than do mental hospitals" (U.S. Congress 1976a).

Upgrading foster care homes for the elderly can be achieved by educational or training requirements for care providers as well as by assessment of their backgrounds, commitments, and motivations. The homes themselves should be subject to licensing standards pertaining to issues of safety, sanitation, and privacy, as well as limitations on the number of foster care recipients within each home. How many individuals can be cared for in a foster home before it is no more a "family" but an institution or "small business concern?" Sherman and Newman point to a perplexing paradox: regulations will drive out small foster homes. "The advantage of these homes is their small size, but if the regulations are made too stringent, there will not be sufficient incentive for the small homes and they simply may become unfeasible" (1977:519).

CONCLUSIONS

Crime and abusive behavior against the elderly are, ultimately, affected by social values and attitudes toward dependency and the importance of older persons. Accordingly, professionals have a role to play not only in assessment and intervention but also in influencing changes in public education, the mass media, and efforts by the aged themselves to challenge popular myths, stereotypes, and negative perceptions of the old, the ill, and the dependent. In addition to safeguards for the elderly, which will minimize their chances for being victims of crime and abuse, these more elementary and pervasive changes of attitudes and values are needed. Such changes are the first steps in true and lasting prevention of adverse behavior against the aged.

REFERENCES

American Public Welfare Association and National Association of State Units on Aging. 1986. A comprehensive analysis of state policy and practice related to elder abuse. Washington, D.C.: APWA and NASUA.

Ansberry, Clare. 1988. Abuse of the elderly by their own children increases in America. *Wall Street Journal,* February 3, 1988, pp. 1 and 5.

Blenker, M. 1965. Social work and family relationships in later life with some thoughts on filial maturity. In E. Shanas and G. F. Streib, eds., *Social Structure and the Family: Generational Relations.* Englewood Cliffs, N.J.: Prentice Hall.

Block, M. and J. Sinnot, eds. 1979. *The Battered Elderly Syndrome: An Exploratory Study.* College Park: Center on Aging, University of Maryland.

Braungart, M. M., R. G. Braungart, and W. J. Hoyer. 1980. Age, sex, and social factor in fear of crime. *Sociological Focus* 13(1):55–66.

Brody, E. M. 1977. Comments on Sherman/Newman paper. *The Gerontologist* 17(6):520–522.

Brody, E. M. 1985. Parent care as normative stress. *The Gerontologist* 25(1):19–28.

Butler, R. M. 1975. *Why Survive? Being Old in America.* New York: Harper and Row.

Callahan, James J., Jr. 1988. Elder abuse: Some questions for policymakers. *The Gerontologist* 28(4):453–458.

Cavan, R. 1969. *The American Family.* 4th ed. New York: Crowell.

Cazenave, N. A. 1983. Elder abuse and black Americans: Incidence, correlates, treatment, and prevention. In J. I. Kosberg, ed., *Abuse and Maltreatment of the Elderly: Causes and Interventions.* Boston: Wright-PSG.

Clemente, F. and M. B. Kleiman. 1976. Fear of crime among the aged. *The Gerontologist* 16(3):207–210.

Curtis, L. A. and I. R. Kohn. 1983. Policy responses to problems faced by elderly in public housing. In J. I. Kosberg, ed., *Abuse and Maltreatment of the Elderly: Causes and Interventions.* Boston: Wright-PSG.

Edwards, J. N. and M. B. Brauburger. 1973. Exchange and parent-youth conflict. *Journal of Marriage and the Family* 35(1):101–107.

Falcioni, D. 1982. Assessing the abused elderly. *Journal of Gerontological Nursing* 8(1):208–212.

Farrar, M. S. 1955. Mother-daughter conflicts extended into later life. *Social Casework* 36(5):202–207.

Finley, G. E. 1983. Fear of crime in the elderly. In J. I. Kosberg, ed., *Abuse and Maltreatment of the Elderly: Causes and Interventions.* Boston: Wright-PSG.

Gelles, R. J. 1973. Child abuse as psychopathology: A sociological critique and reformulation. *American Journal of Orthopsychiatry,* 43(4):611–621.

Gil, D. G. 1971. Violence against children. *Journal of Marriage and the Family* 33(4):637–648.

Glasser, P. H. and L. N. Glasser. 1962. Role reversal and conflict between aged parents and their children. *Journal of Marriage and the Family* 24(1):46–51.

Goldsmith, J. T. and N. E. Tomas. 1974. Crimes against the elderly: A continuing national crisis. *Aging,* nos. 236–237, pp. 10–13.

Hindelang, M. J. and E. H. Richardson. 1978. Criminal victimization of the elderly. In U.S. Congress, House Select Committee on Aging. *Research into Crimes Against the Elderly,* part 1. Washington, D.C.: GPO.

Hirschel, J. D. and K. B. Rubin. 1982. Special problem faced by the elderly victims of crime. *Sociology and Social Welfare* 9(2):357–374.

Holmes, T. H. and R. H. Rahe. 1967. The social readjustment rating scale. *Journal of Psychosomatic Research* 11(2):213–218.

Hooyman, N. R. and W. Lustbader. 1986. Taking care: Supporting older people and their families. New York: Free Press.

Hudson, M. F. 1986. Elder mistreatment: Current research. In K. A. Pillemer and R. S. Wolf, eds., Elder abuse: *Conflict in the Family.* Dover, Mass.: Auburn House.

Jaycox, V. H. and L. J. Center. 1983. A comprehensive response to violent crimes against older persons. In J. I. Kosberg, ed., *Abuse and Maltreatment of the Elderly: Causes and Interventions.* Boston: Wright-PSG.

Johnson, T. 1986. Critical issues in the definition of elder mistreatment. In K. A. Pillemer and R. S. Wolf, eds., *Elder Abuse: Conflict in the Family.* Dover, Mass.: Auburn House.

Justice, B. and D. F. Duncan. 1976. Life crisis and precursor to child abuse. *Public Health Reports* 91(2):110–115.

Katz, K. D. 1979–80. Elder abuse. *Journal of Family Law* 18(4):695–722.

Kosberg, J. I. 1979. Family conflict and abuse of the elderly: Theoretical and methodological issues. Paper presented at the 32d Annual Scientific Meeting of the Gerontological Society of America. Washington, D.C.

Kosberg, J. I. 1983. The special vulnerability of elderly parents. In J. I. Kosberg, ed., *Abuse and Maltreatment of the Elderly: Causes and Interventions.* Boston: Wright-PSG.

Kosberg, J. I. 1988. Preventing elder abuse: Identification of high risk factors prior to placement decisions. *The Gerontologist* 28(1):43–50.

Kosberg, J. I. and R. E. Cairl. 1986. The cost of care index: A case management tool for screening informal care providers. *The Gerontologist* 26(3):273–278.

Lau, E. E. and J. I. Kosberg. 1979. Abuse of the elderly by informal care providers. *Aging,* nos. 299–300, pp. 10–15.

Legal Research and Services for the Elderly. 1979. *Elder Abuse in Massachusetts: A Survey of Professionals and Paraprofessionals.* Boston: Legal Research and Services for the Elderly.

Liang, J. and M. C. Sengstock. 1983. Personal crimes against the elderly. In J. I. Kosberg, ed., *Abuse and Maltreatment of the Elderly: Causes and Interventions.* Boston: Wright-PSG.

Lystad, M. H. 1975. Violence at home: A review of the literature. *American Journal of Orthopsychiatry* 45(3):328–345.

Maddox, G. 1975. Families as context and resource in chronic illness. In S. Sherwood, ed., *Long-Term care: A Handbook for Researchers, Planners, and Providers.* New York: Spectrum.

Malinchak, A. A. and D. Wright. 1978. The scope of elderly victimization. *Aging,* no. 281/282, pp. 10–16.

Miller, D. A. 1981. The "sandwich" generation: Adult children of the aging. *Social Work* 26(5): 419–423.

National Association of State Units on Aging and American Public Welfare Association. 1988. *Adult Protective Services: Programs and State Social Service Agencies and State Units on Aging.* Washington, D.C.: NASUA and APWA.

O'Brien, J. E. 1971. Violence in divorce prone families. *Journal of Marriage and the Family* 33(4):692–698.

O'Brien, J. E. 1986. Elder abuse: Barriers to identification and intervention. Paper presented at the meeting of the Gerontological Society of America, Chicago, Ill.

Pepper, C. D. 1983. Frauds against the elderly. In J. I. Kosberg, ed., *Abuse and Maltreatment of the Elderly: Causes and Interventions.* Boston: Wright-PSG.

Pillemer, K. A. 1986. Risk factors in elder abuse: Results from a case-control study. In K. A. Pillemer and R. S. Wolf, eds., *Elder Abuse: Conflict in the Family.* Dover, Mass.: Auburn House.

Pillemer, K. and D. Finkelhor. 1988. The prevalence of elder abuse: A random sample survey. *The Gerontologist* 28(1):51–57.

Quinn, M. J. and S. K. Tomita. 1986. *Elder Abuse and Neglect: Causes, Diagnosis, and Intervention Strategies.* New York: Springer.

Rathbone-McCuan, E. 1980. Elderly victims of family violence and neglect. *Social Casework* 61(5):296–304.

Rathbone-McCuan, E. and J. Hashimi. 1982. *Isolated Elders: Health and Social Intervention.* Rockville, Md.: Aspen.

Rathbone-McCuan, E., A. Travis, and B. Voyles. 1983. Family intervention: Applying the task-centered approach. In J. I. Kosberg ed., *Abuse and Maltreatment of the Elderly: Causes and Interventions.* Boston: Wright-PSG.

Richer, S. 1968. The economics of child rearing. *Journal of Marriage and the Family* 30(3):462–466.

Salend, E., M. Satz, and J. Pynoos, 1981. *Mandatory reporting legislation for adult abuse.* Los Angeles: UCLA/USC Long-Term Care Gerontology Center.

Sengstock, M. C. and M. A. Hwalek. 1985. *Comprehensive Index of Elder Abuse.* Detroit: SPEC.

Sherman, S. R. and E. S. Newman. 1977. Foster-family care for the elderly in New York state. *The Gerontologist* 17(6):513–520.

Steele, B. and C. Pollock. 1968. A psychiatric study of parents who abuse infants and small children. In R. E. Helfer and C. H. Kempe, eds., *The Battered Child.* Chicago: University of Chicago Press.

Steinmetz, S. K. 1978. Battered parents. *Society* 15(5):54–55.

Steuer, J. L. 1983. Abuse of physically disabled elderly. In J. I. Kosberg, ed., *Abuse and Maltreatment of the Elderly: Causes and Interventions.* Boston: Wright-PSG.

Tomas, N. E., ed. 1974. *Reducing Crimes Against Aged Persons.* Report of the Mid-Atlantic Federal Regional Council Task Force Workshop, U.S. Department of Health, Education, and Welfare.

U.S. Congress. 1976a. House. Select Committee on Aging. *Mental Health Problems of the Elderly.* Washington, D.C.: GPO.

U.S. Congress. 1976b. Senate. Special Committee on Aging. *Nursing Home Care in the United States: Failure in Public Policy.* Washington, D.C.: GPO.

U.S. Congress. 1978. Senate. Special Committee on Aging. *Developments in Aging, 1977,* part 2. Washington, D.C.: GPO.

U.S. Congress. 1980. House. Select Committee on Aging. *Elder Abuse: The Hidden Problem.* Washington, D.C.: GPO.

U.S. Congress. 1981. House. Select Committee on Aging. *Physical and Financial Abuse of the Elderly.* Washington, D.C.: GPO.

Yin, P. 1985. *Victimization and the Aged.* Springfield, Ill.: Thomas.

V
HOME-BASED SERVICES

18

Housing

SUSAN R. SHERMAN, PH.D.
The University at Albany
State University of New York

The focus here will be on housing services to individual clients and their families. Much of the material may also be used by social workers involved in policy development and program planning for the elderly.

Although my concern is with housing, housing cannot be considered in isolation. Thus there are many linkages between topics covered here and topics covered elsewhere in this handbook. Housing for the elderly, whether age-segregated or age-integrated, must be considered as part of the elderly's wider environment. This environment includes, for example, transportation, medical and social services, shopping, recreation and activity centers, potential social networks, vulnerability to crime—all components whose impacts extend beyond the individual dwelling unit. Housing for the elderly must be considered in the context of service provision, both hard services and social networks.

My major premise is that the client must be given a *choice* of housing, that is, available alternatives and the information necessary to make a wise decision. While this should not need to be stated in a handbook for social workers, it is far from realization in the case of housing for the elderly. Many types of housing alternatives are described. Unfortunately, a complete continuum of housing is unavail-

I am grateful for the valuable contributions to the second edition made by Vera Prosper of the New York State Office for the Aging.

able to a large number of elderly, sometimes because of financial restrictions and at other times because of local gaps in service.

Not only at the macro policy level of making a broader choice of housing available, but at the micro level, choice is the issue. The client must be involved in the decision about his/her housing (including preoccupancy visits and possibly temporary stays). No one type of housing is best for all.

NEED

In order to analyze the issue of housing need, we must first subdivide the population of elderly persons. Among persons aged 65 and over, about 5 percent live in institutions. That group is discussed elsewhere in this handbook and will not be considered here. Estimates of those living in specialized planned housing range from 4 percent (Lawton 1980) to 10 percent (AARP n.d.)—the latter figure based on a 1986 survey of persons 60 and over. This leaves about 85 to 90 percent living in the community. The present chapter discusses both the 5 to 10 percent in special planned housing and the 85 to 90 percent in ordinary housing dispersed in the community. It is likely that social workers will have contact with both groups.

Housing need may be described in terms of household composition to understand the need for social support; in terms of housing tenure to assess the security and flexibility of the current situation; and in terms of housing quality to understand the need for relocation to different housing arrangements.

Household Composition

Among men 65 to 74, about 80 percent live with their spouse and about 10 percent live alone or with a nonrelative. Among men 75 and older, nearly 70 percent still live with their spouse and about 20 percent live alone. By contrast, among women 65 to 74, less than 50 percent live with their spouse and about 35 percent live alone. Among women 75 and over, only 20 percent live with their spouse and 50 percent live alone (or with a nonrelative) (Atchley 1985). These differences have important implications for social work with older persons. Although the myth that families abandon their older members has been dispelled time and time again, the overwhelming number of older persons prefer not to live with their children. If there is need for support and supervision, and if no alternatives are available, some older persons may have to live with their children. Indeed, about 15 percent of persons 65 and older live with adult children or other relatives (Harris et al. 1986). But despite sentimental revisions of history, three-generation family households have never been the norm.

Housing Tenure

Seventy-three percent of all household heads 65 and over own their homes (a higher proportion of men than of women), and 80 percent of these homes are mortgage free (Jacobs 1986; Solan 1987). Although for many this represents an element of security, both psychological and financial, for other elderly this may be more of a "trap." The unit may be too large, there may be unnegotiable stairs, the house may be located in a high-crime neighborhood, and taxes and fuel costs may be consuming too large a share of the person's monthly income. Additionally, the owner may not be able to afford maintenance of the house. Struyck (1984/85) estimated that in 12 percent of older households modifications were needed because of the resident's health or disability. Real-property-tax exemptions have been applied unevenly. However, the sale of the house may be difficult and may not bring enough money to ensure a secure future in rental housing. Furthermore, the older person may be reluctant to leave a familiar setting and friends.

Because of all these factors, there is a growing interest in Home Equity Conversion, an arrangement in which the older owner remains in her home and borrows against or sells a share of the equity (Fish 1985; Jacobs 1986; Solan, 1987). These plans do not require regular monthly loan repayments (Scholen 1987). The variety of such home equity conversion programs, as well as guides for the consumer are described in detail by Scholen (1987) and by Solan (1987).

Sometimes housing tenure, rental or owned, is threatened by forced relocation due to urban renewal, conversion to condominiums, or "gentrification." The lack of affordable rentals affects the medium-income elderly as well as the poor elderly (N.Y. Leg. 1982). Renters aged 65 and over spend nearly one-third of their incomes on housing costs.

Housing Quality

According to a survey by the U.S. Department of Housing and Urban Development, 9 percent of units with household heads 65 and holder had physical deficiencies or flaws; the rate for the population as a whole was 9.7 percent (Allan and Brotman 1981). Struyck (1985) estimated that almost one-third of household units headed by older persons have physical deficiencies and increasing costs. It has been found that housing deficiencies are more prevalent in rented than in owner-occupied dwellings.

Despite these deficiencies, Carp (1976) cited several studies reporting favorable assessment, by residents, of housing that investigators rated as poor. She suggested that if persons have no choice, a positive assessment may be a defensive reaction. When residents were given a choice, Carp found that housing evaluation became more negative. Ward, LaGory, and Sherman (1988) found that despite objective neighborhood problems, respondents expressed high neighborhood satisfaction. This partly reflected limited options.

Groups who are most deprived with respect to housing include inner-city elderly, farm dwellers, Hispanic-Americans, Asian-Americans, blacks, and Jewish slum dwellers (Carp 1976; Lawton 1980). A growing need exists for those who are aging in the suburbs. These persons who bought their homes after World War II are now aging-in-place. Their needs have changed, but many services to meet these needs are lacking. Transportation is a related and serious need. Logan and Spitze (1988), however, in analyzing the 1984 Supplement on Aging of the National Health Interview Survey found few differences, overall, between city and suburban elderly residents in services used. They comment that there might be differences among metropolitan areas, or in smaller districts, which were not shown in the aggregate level of analysis they used.

ASSESSMENT

A good conceptual tool for assessment is the Lawton/Nahemow adaptation model described more fully in the "Theory" section. In essence, this model indicates that, for a given environment, a person of a specified level of competence will be optimally adjusted. Likewise, for a given level of competence, an environment of a given level of demand will be optimal. This necessitates a careful understanding of the client's capabilities and of the environment's requirements. When various options are described below, they will be arrayed roughly in terms of decreasing environmental demand. Although clients will be described who are particularly appropriate for each modality, such guidelines should be used with caution. There is much overlap between optimal types for each housing alternative, depending on client's wishes and coping style and the availability of other formal and informal supports. Many housing facilities have experienced an "aging-in" of their residents. That is, when the facility was new, residents may have averaged 65–70 years of age. Now the modal age may be in the 80s. This means that a facility which began in the more independent range of the continuum below, can now be offering services more typical of the less independent range of the continuum. Thus there is an increasing blurring across categories.

A particular agency or housing counseling program may devise its own assessment tool. See, for example, Pastalan's assessment schedule in Lawton (1975). This survey, derived from Pastalan (1972), asks respondents about what type of housing they would prefer, where they would prefer the housing to be (in terms of rural/urban continuum, access to services and to friends), what services they wish provided within the building, important neighborhood and dwelling-unit features, plans to move, causes for move, current housing arrangements and cost, transportation, need for in-home services in current home, health problems and perceived need for housing and other services in the community.

Because the array of housing types is so diverse, it would be difficult to have an all-purpose instrument to match a specific client with a specific housing alternative. Moos and his colleagues (Lemke and Moos 1987; Moos and Lemke 1984) have developed a set of scales to measure four sets of environmental features of a housing facility: physical, organizational structure and policies, suprapersonal, and the social climate. It is unlikely that an individual seeking housing would find that the facilities of her choice had been rated on these dimensions. However, a worker in a given setting, or a case manager who links clients to many settings might find the scale items useful as a guide in planning. Since the first edition of this book, it is becoming increasingly apparent that a continuum of services is preferable to rigid levels of care. That is, because of the aging-in of residents in every type of housing described in this chapter, we find an increasing need for any level to offer a flexible "package" of services, either by the management itself or by facilitating access to services brought in by other providers. Residents and their families should be able to draw upon these services as needed, rather than having to move from rung to rung in an array of rigidly defined types of housing. One must think of long-term housing needs, and the extent to which the option chosen can be adapted to changing needs (Lawton, Moss, and Grimes 1985). This increases the need for social workers to be involved in assessment and intervention.

Clearly, one type of housing assessment is that of determining what interventions are necessary in current housing. Are repairs necessary? Are there services that need to be brought in? Another kind of assessment is required for relocation (perhaps involuntary) to an institution. For this, a medical assessment is required. The emphasis here, however, is on moves that are relatively voluntary and that are to other types of relatively independent housing.

As in all good social work assessment, the client should be asked his/her preferences in housing, and involved in the decision-making process. Some of the major dimensions that need to be decided are:

Age-segregated or age-integrated housing.
Need and desire for services, for example, meals, housekeeping, and activities.
Maximum distance willing to move, that is, increasing (or decreasing) distance from relatives, friends, and familiar places.
Type of location.

When persons in the community are asked whether they would prefer age-segregated or age-integrated housing, the large majority prefer age-integrated. For example, Sherman et al. (1985) found that 22 percent of a sample of persons 60 and over would prefer to live in housing limited to people their own age. On the other hand, when persons already living in age-segregated housing are queried, a large majority report being satisfied (Lawton and Nahemow 1975). Eighty percent of Sherman's (1972) sample of persons in retirement housing said that it is better for retired people to live in special housing.

Social workers need to be concerned with being sure that older persons considering a move relocate so as to be near needed resources and that transportation for older persons to services is available. But a further question is what services, for example, medical, meals, should be available at the housing facility itself. The issue of providing services at the setting is somewhat controversial. On the one hand, a major advantage of special housing for the elderly is the efficiency of providing centralized services within the housing setting, since a population with relatively high need is concentrated there. On the other hand, there are those (both consumers and providers) who fear that the provision within housing of too many services will generate an institutional atmosphere. Perhaps even more crucially, this argument proceeds, if too much is provided too early, over-dependency might be encouraged, leading to further loss of function and negative change in self-concept (Carp 1976). Lawton (1980) cites some findings that indicate the possibility of some reduction in engagement with the external environment, but suggests that considerably more research is needed to settle the question definitively. Prosper's (1987) review concludes that there is no relationship between availability of services and increased usage. She further suggests an emphasis on preventive services as promoting rather than reducing the client's independence. If we wish to make it possible for older persons to "age-in-place," whether in special housing or in neighborhood housing, and to avoid further relocation, it is important to design a flexible environment in which the resident can increase her use of services when necessary over time.

Lawton (1980) describes two developmental models of planned housing:

Constant: The housing maintains the same level of capability among the residents. The residents must leave as soon as they cannot maintain themselves at that level of demand.

Accommodating: The housing is able to maintain a resident as his or her capability changes, up to twenty-four-hour nursing. The facility changes its programs, physical space, and requirements for new tenants.

Whether a facility is constant or accommodating is important for the social worker to consider when he or she is counseling a client who is making a move.

The provision of recreational activities may be beneficial for those to whom this is an important part of their life-style. However, for some this would represent an intrusion.

A related question is how much modification is needed or desired in the housing unit itself. For example, some special housing facilities offer emergency call buttons, easy to reach electric outlets and cupboards, elevators or single-level facilities, walk-in/sit-down showers, and grab bars. Ideally, these features would be useful for a person of any age.

> In recent years, there has been a growing emphasis on the development of new technology, furniture, and design elements that can be unobtrusively incorporated into the design of all senior housing, including single family homes and independent apartments, enhancing the accommodating nature of the senior housing environment. Such technology and features (for example adjustable kitchen work space; increased, balanced, indirect lighting; lever style faucets and door handles; building layout, interior path systems, and decor designed to maximize way-finding and compensate for vision/hearing loss; computer-based home command and control systems that conserve energy use) extend the time that the resident can competently and independently manage daily activities. This reduces or avoids a resident's need for external supportive aid, delays or avoids the need for involuntary relocation, and main-

> tains the resident's personal sense of competence and self-esteem. (Prosper, personal communication, 1988).

These options are not widely available at the present time, but offer promise for the future.

A further question to be considered when deciding whether one would be satisfied in retirement housing is how much dislocation would be required. There was some alienation found at the one site studied by Sherman (1972) where a substantial proportion (30 percent) had recently moved from out of state. Relocation does not necessarily mean an increase in distance from children. For example, at a retirement hotel and an apartment building studied by Sherman (1975b), residents had actually decreased the distance from their children by making the move. These findings are not unlike those of Bultena and Wood (1969), who established that only one-fourth of the migrants (from Wisconsin to Arizona) they studied had had a child located in their home community. Furthermore, a disproportionate number of old persons who seek special housing are childless (Bultena and Wood 1969; Carp 1966; Sherman 1975b).

Finally, probing must be conducted as to the type of location desired: urban, suburban, rural, and in what part of the country. Even the types of facilities commonly associated with the Sunbelt, for example, retirement villages, are available in other parts of the country as well. Clients must be clear in their minds as to the priorities given climate and social networks.

The most essential step in assessment is to arrange for the client to visit the prospective housing. This means not only an inspection of the facility but a more extended stay—a meal, an activity, even an overnight stay. If the client is moving to a different climate or community, a longer visit is necessary—perhaps two or three visits at different times of the year. Visits are important not only to determine if the client likes the site but to determine if he or she is compatible with the other residents. Before buying into a retirement community, some clients may be offered an opportunity to rent a unit temporarily.

Before leaving the topic of assessment, some mention should be made of the issue of relocation stress. Most of the research on relocation stress has been on the move within institutions or from community to institution, and that will be covered by Irene Gutheil in this handbook. With respect to relocation in the community, Lawton (1980), in summarizing several studies, notes a risk of deterioration in physical health with relocation (but not in social and psychological functioning or in mortality), but this is dependent on preparation, the quality of the new environment, and perceived choice in the situation.

In Schulz and Brenner's (1977) review of within-community relocation, both choice and the quality of the new environment appeared to be important determinants of positive outcome. Finally, it should be recognized that, for some people, change or novelty is enhancing, such as is predicted by the Lawton/Nahemow model described below.

INTERVENTION

Unlike some programs discussed elsewhere in this handbook, housing is not a specific "program." Rather, it is a disparate collection of environments, some of which have arisen out of specific governmental policies, others of which have emerged "in the marketplace." Because housing is not one specific program, there is not a well-defined path nor a typical sequence for social work intervention. The role of the social worker will be defined below as each modality is described. A useful role for social workers, rarely realized at the present time, is as part of a housing counseling service. There is an increasing need for case management; this is described [in another contribution to this book] by White and Steinberg, this volume.

Range of Services

The first division that needs to be made when discussing the range of housing services is between independent, unplanned housing in the community and special, planned housing. As was explained previously, about 85 to 90 percent of all persons age 65 and over live in housing dispersed in the community, and about 70 percent of all household heads 65 and over own their homes. The housing may be too large, old and run-down, in high crime areas, and subject to rising property taxes and fuel costs, leaving little money for maintenance and repairs. If the person desires to move, he or she may not be able to make enough from the sale of the house to be able to afford future rents. Furthermore, many people are reluctant to leave a familiar community with well-established social networks. Thus, the vast majority of older persons prefer to age "in place," but to receive supportive services (Pastalan 1985).

Unplanned, dispersed community housing, whether owned or rented, is particularly appropriate for independent, healthy elderly with available social networks or for more dependent elderly who have strong family support, usually a spouse (Lawton 1981).

Social workers will be involved with persons who live in unplanned housing as needs for additional services arise, either those specifically related to housing, such as home repairs, or those concerning in-home social and medical services, described elsewhere in this handbook. Referrals for information on tax benefits or rent increase exemptions may be part of a case management package. The social worker may also be involved in helping to make a decision to relocate and sell a house, and must consider accessibility to shopping and medical services. In protective-service cases, the older person may have to move when he or she can no longer live alone safely or maintain the dwelling. This suggests a further role for the social worker when the elderly person is reluctant to leave and needs to be assisted in handling this crisis (Schooler [1976] and Fried [1963], discuss grief engendered by involuntary moves.) While not considered in detail here, it is important for the social worker involved in helping to plan a relocation to understand the importance to the client of bringing cherished objects from home, even if it is only some favorite pieces of jewelry, photographs, etc. (Sherman and Newman 1977–78).

The other general category of housing for the elderly is that of special planned housing. The impetus for special planned housing has come primarily from nonprofit organizations, private enterprise, and the federal government. A few types could be described more accurately as having evolved into senior housing rather than having been planned as such. Sherman (1971) found that reasons given for moving to retirement housing included easy maintenance, health and personal needs cared for, change in physical strength, wish to be with own age group, quality of the dwelling, proximity to facilities and services, proximity to children, relatives, or friends, and provision of meals. In summarizing a number of studies, Lawton (1980) concluded that low-intensity medical services are most highly valued, while meal services are lower in priority.

We shall array planned housing according to the amount of *independence* required by the *typical* occupant. This is a very rough ordering, not only because the names of the types vary from locality to locality but because each category itself includes a range of housing, and a particular facility may house a range of occupants. Some staff in comparable sites offer more assistance than others. Thus, in terms of independence, there is much overlap between categories; the requirements may not be visible on the outside; much depends on what goes on inside the facility. Three other dimensions upon which to order planned housing are financial arrangement, type of dwelling unit, and government program. Financial arrangements include purchase, rental, cooperative, condominium, and life-care. Type of units include detached houses, apartments—either high-rise or garden-type—

mobile homes, single rooms. Government programs are described in the section entitled "Policy." There is a certain degree of correlation among these four dimensions, and financial and dwelling arrangements will be described when they typify one of the categories below.

RETIREMENT VILLAGES

Although retirement villages have received the most publicity in sunbelt areas, they appear in many parts of the country. They frequently offer hundreds of units, either apartments or detached houses or both. Some have congregate housing and institutional care on the premises, in which case they could serve throughout the independence continuum applied here (Lawton 1981). (See Continuing Care Retirement Communities discussed in a later section.) They are usually for purchase, including cooperatives and condominiums (Walkley et al. 1966a, 1966b). Some were designed to be self-contained "new towns" (Marans, Hunt, and Vakalo 1984). The advantages of retirement villages are:

1. They may have a complete package of on-site services, such as shopping, medical clinics, activity programs, social clubs, golf course, swimming pools, and arts and crafts rooms.
2. They may offer on-site maintenance of the dwelling, both inside and outside. Frequently a great deal of care is given to maintenance of very attractive grounds.
3. They may have special security arrangements, such as a gate, guard, etc.
4. There is the potential for an extensive network, offering both instrumental and expressive support.

The disadvantages of retirement villages are:

1. Usually the resident is dependent on an automobile, either within the site or off-site. Some retirement villages have their own transportation systems, but they are not usually extensive enough to make the person completely self-sufficient. Transportation may only be within the village, but shopping, entertainment, hospital, etc. may be off-site at some distance. When the person is no longer able to drive, a move may be necessary.
2. Many villages are oriented to married couples. When a person become widowed, he or she may be left out of social networks.
3. Most villages are expensive.
4. Some villages are isolated from an urban area, from services, and from previous social networks. There may be reduced con-

tact with families (although significant possibilities for new friendships).

5. Many retirement villages are constant rather than accommodating environments, as in Lawton's designation, and the resident may have to move again if, for example, his or her health declines.

Retirement villages are particularly appropriate for financially well-off, independent, healthy elderly, who can drive an automobile, and who are interested in an extensive opportunity for activities. If involved at all, it is most likely that a social worker would be involved in this type of housing primarily with helping a client with a decision to move. However, although designed for the well-elderly, retirement villages also are experiencing the "aging-in-place" of their residents. The residents have aged, do not wish to move, and now need services. At some retirement villages, managers have been hired with social work backgrounds, and social workers are part of the housing package (Prosper, personal communication, 1988). This then resembles the Continuing Care Retirement Communities to be described below.

MOBILE HOMES

While most mobile-home parks are not exclusively for the elderly, some have a policy of adults only, and some specifically have programs for the elderly. In 1986, 7 percent of all persons 60 and older lived in mobile homes (AARP n.d.). Most parks have the spaces for rent while the mobile homes are owned by the individuals. Mobile-home subdivisions are those with a mobile home placed on a permanent foundation; the owner of the mobile home owns the space as well.

The advantages of mobile-home living are:

1. Low cost.
2. Informality.
3. Active social life and sense of community (Johnson 1971) in some mobile-home communities.

The disadvantages of mobile-home living are:

1. Possible lack of privacy.
2. Lack of space.
3. Lack of accessibility to the community and services.
4. Nonaccommodating.
5. Necessity to drive an automobile.
6. Limited tenants' rights.

7. Limited re-salability of the mobile unit.
8. Cost of repairs may be prohibitive.

Mobile home parks are particularly appropriate for healthy elderly who like the opportunity to combine independence with the availability of informal support in time of need. Again, it is unlikely that a social worker would be involved with this type of housing other than in assisting the client to make a decision to move in, or helping to decide when the client needs a greater degree of support. However, assistance may be needed in the areas of tenants' rights (e.g., being forced to move).

RETIREMENT HOTELS AND SINGLE ROOM OCCUPANCIES (SROs)

Retirement hotels can range from expensive to inexpensive. Some older hotels in central cities, in order to maintain reasonable occupancy, have specialized as senior-citizen hotels. This ordinarily involved little adjustment, since by that time the hotel had already become occupied primarily by senior citizens. In some cases, meals are provided. There may be a few activity rooms and a few organized activities such as cards and bingo.

A type of housing that has been receiving increasing attention is the SRO. The number of elderly who choose SROs appear to be increasing (Siegal 1978). SRO housing is found in large commercial hotels, specialty retirement hotels, rooming houses, and converted apartment buildings. These facilities contain furnished rooms, usually without kitchens, and frequently without bathrooms. The facilities may be old and deteriorated, and they are usually in or near transitional or commercial inner-city locations, thus accessible to services (Blackie et al. 1983; Eckert 1979). They may be used by welfare clients and discharged mental patients as well as by the elderly. "Contrary to commonly held assumptions, the majority of SRO residents are not vagrants or social deviants . . . [they] have simply chosen this type . . . Because of its affordability" (Blackie et al. 1983:37). Developers have begun constructing senior citizen SROs which include a common dining hall as a means of providing affordable housing to low income elderly and homeless elderly.

Thus while there is overlap between the categories of retirement hotels and SROs, there are some more luxurious hotels with meal plans that would not share many of the characteristics of SROs, and some SROs that are not in hotels. Many of the advantages, however, are the same.

The advantages are:

1. For a relatively reasonable cost, provision of services—for example housekeeping and/or meals.
2. Accessibility to the services of the city, including restaurants, and to transportation.
3. Privacy and the ability to continue a life-style of independence (what others might call isolation) and autonomy (Erickson and Eckert 1977; Plutchik, McCarthy, and Hall 1975; Stephens 1975).
4. Sociability and some limited support provided by the other residents, when desired.
5. Sense of security provided by twenty-four hour staff.

The disadvantages are:

1. The hotels are frequently located in high-crime areas.
2. The units may be unattractive.
3. Space is limited.

Hotels are particularly appropriate for self-reliant elderly who wish to continue a life-style of independence. They are appropriate for those who wish to be near the amenities of a city and who need public transportation, or for those who simply prefer the urban life-style. For the more affluent elderly who prefer to have meals prepared, specialized retirement hotels would be appropriate. But more generally, this type would be for people who do not desire housekeeping responsibilities.

A caseworker in a local social services department might very well be involved in placing an elderly client in a hotel. The worker would need to know the availability of such residences, whether meals are offered, and the availability of localized services. It is also more likely that a social worker would be involved in housing placement for hotel clients, as they tend to represent a disproportionate share of the childless.

INDEPENDENT APARTMENTS

Apartment complexes that provide meals and other more intensive services will be discussed under congregate housing; in this section, I refer to a relatively common type of housing in which meals are not provided, requiring an intermediate degree of independence on the part of residents. (Some may require more independence than do some retirement hotels, discussed previously.) There may be some common rooms for social activities. Some facilities may offer some meals through a nutrition program operating in the building. Project sizes vary widely. Much of this housing has been built under government programs, such as public housing, Section 202, or Section 236. This category presently houses a wide range of income groups.

The advantages are:

1. Quality and affordability of the dwelling unit. Frequently this is of a quality much higher than the residents had ever hoped to have.
2. Central location. While this is not intrinsic to the housing type, much of such housing is in urban areas, if not in central cities.
3. The opportunity to form social networks.
4. The availability of on-site activity programs.

Independent apartments are particularly appropriate for persons who want the privacy of their own apartment, who want to and are capable of preparing their own meals, and who seek the opportunity to have new friends available when needed for either instrumental or expressive support. It may be an economical way to achieve an attractive living environment. These arrangements are quite popular, and many facilities have long waiting lists.

The social worker could be involved in helping the client find such housing, and perhaps in negotiating the system of eligibility requirements, waiting lists, etc. The "aging-in" process mentioned above has caused an increasing number of "independent" facilities, proprietary and non-profit, to offer social work services and in some cases a services package, which might be optional and selected by only a portion of the residents.

CONGREGATE HOUSING

While buildings in this category may look like those in the previous category, congregate housing has a special meaning: a multi-unit or shared housing environment, combining private apartment living and supportive services. It is the combination of housing and services that distinguishes congregate housing from independent apartments described in the previous section. Sponsors may be private proprietary, private nonprofit, and public. Services generally include congregate meals, housekeeping, 24-hour emergency response, and transportation. Also included may be personal care, social services, and case management (Prosper 1987). These services are part of the effort to enable the growing population of frail elderly to age in place, as they prefer, and avoid costly institutionalization. Both the federal and state governments have become involved. In 1988, the U.S. Department of Housing and Urban Development passed legislation to make their 1978 demonstration congregate housing program permanent

(Prosper, 1988, personal communication). Chellis, Seagle, and Seagle (1982) describe planning, development, design and services issues involved in implementing the congregate housing model. Nachison (1985) cites demonstration projects that indicated that services attributed to the Congregate Housing Services program were less costly than the same services delivered through community agencies.

A modified version of congregate housing is the Continuing Care Retirement Community, described later. It should be noted that the distinction between congregate housing and adult homes has lessened. Some developers are now building upscale adult homes that include apartments rather than just private bedrooms, while congregate housing sponsors are extending their services to include the availability of personal care and 24-hour on-site staff or emergency coverage. Therefore, the services provided can be the same and the resident profile can be the same. A major distinction between congregate housing and adult homes is the requirement for licensure in the latter but not in the former (Prosper, personal communication, 1988).

The advantages of congregate housing are:

1. The provision of nutritious meals.
2. The sociability of eating together.
3. The opportunity to form social networks.
4. The accessibility to coordinated services.

A disadvantage might be that the housing could take on an institutional atmosphere.

Congregate housing is particularly appropriate for older persons who need some support in order to remain on their own in the community. This housing offers a range of services that may be used when needed.

Social workers may be part of the staff in congregate housing. More generally, they could be involved in helping a client determine if this is the level of support needed and then locating a facility.

SHARED HOUSING

Shared housing recently has received increasing attention (Blackie et al. 1983; N.Y. Leg. 1982; NYOFA, n.d.; Streib 1978). "Shared housing refers to a household of two or more unrelated persons residing in one dwelling unit. The members of the household share in the financial responsibilities as well as in household duties such as cooking and cleaning" (Blackie et al. 1983:1), although in the managerial model staff take care of such tasks as cooking, cleaning, shopping, laundry, and transportation. "The kitchen, bathroom, and other public areas of the unit are shared, while each person maintains a private area, such as a bedroom" (Blackie et al. 1983:1).

At a November 1981 Congressional hearing on shared housing, three models were identified as shared-living environments: residences of individuals who open their homes to others, groups of unrelated individuals who live in a single housekeeping unit, and single-occupancy apartments with common dining areas. (A related form is intermediate housing in which residents share only a living room, but have some support from the sponsoring long-term care institution [Lawton 1981].) The formation and operational structure of shared homes fall into three categories: naturally occurring shared homes, generally accommodating three to five persons; agency-assisted; and agency-sponsored, generally serving two to twenty persons (Blackie et al. 1983; N.Y. Leg. 1982). The first and sometimes the second type are not sheltered or supported housing and would belong earlier in the independence continuum. The "enriched housing" program in New York state, for example, serves up to seven unrelated elderly living in a single housekeeping unit. Congregate meals, homemaking, shopping, transportation, personal care, and social support services are provided in the program. Public assistance for shared housing has come from such programs as Section 8, Community Development Block Grants, Title XX, Older Americans Act monies, and state, city, and county governments.

The advantages of shared housing are:

1. Companionship and social support.
2. Maintenance of ties with the community.
3. Income for the homeowners.
4. Sustained involvement in the household.
5. Safety and protection from crime.
6. In some cases supervision with activities of daily living.
7. Financially efficient.

The disadvantages are:

1. Difficulty for strangers to share living quarters, kitchens, etc., problems with territoriality.
2. Loss of privacy.

Shared housing is particularly appropriate for someone who needs support in order to prevent institutionalization, for someone who wishes to have the opportunity to form social networks, and for those who want someone to share expenses or maintenance. Good interpersonal skills are important. This model may not be appropriate for persons who are used to living alone.

The social worker will be involved in screening and matching clients and in case management. Matching is absolutely critical to the success of this program. Additionally, such housing requires ongoing follow-up to be sure residents receive necessary services and to provide counseling when conflicts arise among residents.

LICENSED BOARDING HOMES/ADULT FOSTER FAMILY CARE

The licensed boarding home is an old form of assisted housing for the elderly. These homes are generally licensed by state or local social welfare departments or the Veterans Administration to provide personal care and services (Walkley et al. 1966a, 1966b). This category may overlap with the following category. (Some elderly, of course live in boarding homes that are not licensed and that might be placed higher on the independence continuum.) Meals are provided. A subcategory of boarding homes is foster-family-care homes (Sherman and Newman 1988), generally housing no more than six residents and usually fewer. Frequently a part of the mental-health system, these homes provide some supervision for the residents. This is an option that has not been sufficiently explored for the frail elderly who are not in need of institutionalization but who need some supervision. Over the past several years, there has been a slowly increasing interest in the use of this model.

The advantages are:

1. Permits a person needing a protective setting to live in the community, perhaps delaying institutionalization.
2. Offers the possibility of a family atmosphere, although research has indicated that the clients themselves may be what constitutes a family, rather than being introduced into some model family form (Sherman and Newman 1988).
3. Offers the possibility of greater participation in the community.

The disadvantages are:

1. May be of poor quality because of lack of regulation.
2. May lack stimulation.
3. May increase dependency.

Licensed boarding homes or foster family care homes are particularly appropriate for persons in need of a protective environment but not requiring institutionalization. They are appropriate for persons who have lost contact with their own families and who have limited social networks.

Caseworkers in local social services departments are responsible for the recruitment, initial evaluation, visitation, and continued supervision and evaluation of small foster family homes. Caseworkers would also be involved in helping clients find such homes, in matching clients and homes, and in providing training for caretakers (Sherman and Newman 1988).

HOMES FOR THE AGED/ADULT HOMES/DOMICILIARY-CARE FACILITIES/PERSONAL-CARE RESIDENCES

These homes, both nonprofit and proprietary, provide supportive services on a twenty-four-hour basis for aged, frail, or disabled adults (Snider, Pascarelli, and Howard 1979). Services include room and board, housekeeping, personal care, supervision, and other nonmedical services. The homes tend to be more institutional than congregate housing. The National Center for Health Statistics defines a domiciliary-care residence as offering one or two of eight personal-care services, while a personal-care residence is one that offers three or more such services (Lawton 1981). As part of the long-term care continuum offering a lower level of care than health-related or skilled nursing facilities, these homes are described in more detail elsewhere in this handbook. Facilities are diverse, ranging in size from under a dozen beds to a few hundred. In some institutions, life-care arrangements are available. These facilities tend to be more luxurious and offer a greater diversity of services. In other homes, recreation facilities may be no more than a TV room. This is such a diverse category that it is difficult to specify general advantages and disadvantages. Homes for the aged are particularly appropriate for persons requiring support services but not a formal medical component.

Caseworkers would be involved in determining that this is the proper level of care, in locating a facility, and in making the referral. In some large homes, there could be a social worker on staff, involved with admission, activities, etc.

CONTINUING CARE RETIREMENT COMMUNITY

These settings offer "a specialized housing and supportive services environment with a medical component (skilled nursing facility). It is a congregate campus community accessible to higher income elderly which incorporates contractual lifetime tenancy and care" (Prosper 1987:7). A range of housing options are offered at one site, from independent living to skilled nursing services. In 1985, Prosper reported that 90,000 elderly were residing in 276 continuing care (life care) communities.

The advantages are:

1. An accommodating environment.
2. Guarantee of long-term care.
3. Affordable health care rates (Prosper 1985).

The disadvantage is that they are generally priced for middle- and upper-middle class elderly and not affordable by working-class elderly, whose needs may be greater (Rohrer and Bibb 1986).

Other alternatives, which deserve further examination but which will not be discussed in great detail here, include:

An accessory apartment. "Also referred to as a single-family conversion, is a small, self-contained unit within a larger building, most often a single family home. Approximately 2.5 million accessory apartments were built into existing buildings between 1970 and 1980, many in homes owned by an elderly person. After the conversion, the elderly homeowner may reside either in the accessory apartment or in the remaining part of the home . . . Benefits [are] extra income . . . [and] increased security" (Blackie et al. 1983:2).

Elder cottage housing opportunity (ECHO). [Also called "Granny Flats"] "refers to the concept of a small, temporary, self-contained housing unit which is placed in the yard of an existing host house. The elderly person resides in this unit in close proximity yet independent of his/her child or relative" (Blackie et al. 1983).

Client Contact with Services

Client contact would depend greatly on the type of housing. For example, retirement villages advertise privately. Mobile-home parks are listed in various directories, as are shared-housing programs. Retirement hotels are listed in telephone directories. Social service departments have lists of licensed boarding and foster family care homes. Some aging-related agencies also have lists of available housing. We are beginning to see case management as part of housing services. Case managers may be part of agency staff, or may work privately, providing housing referrals and assisting with placement.

Effectiveness of Current Forms of Intervention

Most research on the effectiveness of special planned housing has been either on housing for the economically advantaged elderly or on public housing. Neither group is particularly representative of most older persons, and the results may not be generalizable. Some of the studies cannot be conclusive because of design problems, such as self-selection. Furthermore, when we discuss special planned retirement housing, we include a number of characteristics besides age segregation, such as new construction, service access, etc. The literature has tended to equate the study of age segregation with the evaluation of planned housing (Carp 1976). However, the issues need to be distinct; Sherman (1971) found that for many persons who moved to retirement housing, a wish for easy maintenance and having health and personal needs cared for were more salient than a wish to be with their own age group.

Early research on retirement housing focused on dilemmas such as maximization of friendship networks but separation from the larger society; promotion of a leisure life style but reduction of privacy; and service provision but creation of dependency. After much research, it would appear that these controversies do not have a simple answer. The reason is that the persons who move into these settings are fairly successful at finding an environment that would suit their needs, or perhaps at adjusting their needs to fit the characteristics of the environment—at least for the moment.

A few of the studies of planned housing programs may be summarized here, keeping in mind that they are not studies of age segregation per se, but of a special type of environment with many diverse features, only one of which is age segregation.

Sherman, Newman, and Nelson (1976) found that among elderly in public housing, there was less fear of crime and less crime experienced in age-segregated buildings than in age-integrated buildings. Sherwood, Greer, and Morris (1979) found among movers to a medically oriented public housing project as compared to matched controls, greater housing satisfaction, participation in formal social activities, and likelihood of being admitted to an acute care hospital; but less likelihood of becoming institutionalized, less time spent in a long-term care facility and a lower death rate.

Lawton, Moss, and Grimes (1985) studied five federally assisted housing projects for the elderly where residents' health had declined as they aged in place. They concluded that the introduction of services by community agencies which was arranged by the facilities was working reasonably well. In their studies of adult foster family care, Sherman and Newman (1988) investigated both integration into the foster family and integration into the community. Their measures of familism indicated that family integration and participation did occur and that in the majority of cases the homes could be termed surrogate families. Both care providers and residents reported generally friendly, though superficial, interactions with neighbors and others in the community. The more the provider used the resources of the community and socialized in the community, the more the residents did the same (Sherman and Newman 1988).

Lawton and Cohen (1974), in comparing movers to controls who had not applied for such housing, found that movers rated higher on housing satisfaction, involvement in external activities, and satisfaction with the status quo. However, there was no change due to new housing in morale or breadth of activities, and there was a decline in functional health. Prosper (1987) cites findings by Malozemoff, Anderson, and Rosenbaum (1978) indicating that among congregate residents, participation in programs and activities increased in number and frequency compared to their previous participation while in the general community.

Sherman (1975c) found that, with respect to caring for health needs, desire for counseling services and expected support in crises, a good match between personal need and environmental provision was reported at five of the six retirement housing sites studied. During a two-year period (both interviews after the move to retirement housing) there was an increase in leisure-activity scores for retirement-housing residents and a decrease for community residents (Sherman 1974). Sherman (1975b) also found that retirement housing residents had more new friends and visited more with neighbors and with age-peer friends. There was little test-control difference in sufficiency of contact or in assistance patterns (Sherman 1975a). In a study of seventy women, Adams (1985) found that age-segregated housing fostered the development of emotionally close, local friendships because residents were aware of the things they had in common, were motivated, and had the opportunity to make new friends.

On the other hand, Ward, LaGory, and Sherman (1988) found that age concentration in neighborhoods was much less influential than that found in specially planned retirement housing. Although neighborhood age concentration was associated with greater presence of age-peer neighbors in support networks, it had little relation to interaction or mutual assistance with neighbors in general, feelings of neighborhood satisfaction, general availability of helpers and confidants within informal networks, perceived well-being, or age-based activism (Sherman, Ward, and LaGory 1985). Some reasons suggested to explain the divergence included an insufficient number of older persons in these neighborhoods to constitute a critical mass; the fact that community residents have not chosen to live in age-concentrated neighborhoods; the absence of special social structures that give age-segregated housing its supportive advantage; and the realization that relocation to special settings sets up a sensitivity to age peers. These differences suggest a sense of caution for policy formulation and planning (Sherman 1988).

It is evident that persons who study special housing for the well elderly sometimes develop their theories in isolation from those who study nursing homes and from those who study the environment in age-integrated settings. The danger in this is that the data bases and the theories are disjunctive. One has one set of conclusions based on one type of setting and another set based on another type. It is necessary to fill in the continuum and extend theory based upon highly age-segregated settings through an array of age-integrated environments.

THEORY

During the 1980s there has been a resurgence of interest in developing and extending theory in environment and aging (Schooler 1982). The most useful theories in considering housing for the elderly use an ecological or person-in-environment approach; that is, an emphasis on the dynamic interaction or transaction between the older person and the environment. This means both that the person is affected by the environment and that the person affects the environment (Elder 1981; Sherman 1988). Most generally, it is critical to seek a good match between the person and the environment. The person-in-environment approach also means that an environment that formerly met the person's needs may be unsatisfactory as the person's abilities decline (Lawton 1980). This framework encourages us to look at the change with age in the interaction between the person and the environment. The person-environment interaction has special meaning in the later years: one characteristic of aging can be a decreased ability to modify one's environment, due to decreasing health or to economic deprivation. A few theories or models that are particularly relevant to housing selection will be summarized here.

Lawton and Nahemow's (1973; Lawton 1982) adaptation model is perhaps most useful for the social worker. This model characterizes two dimensions: environmental press, referring to the demands of the setting, and individual competence, including such dimensions as biological health, sensorimotor functioning, cognitive skill, and ego strength. The social worker can attempt to maximize adaptive behavior and positive affect either by improving the individual's competence level or by adjusting the demands of the environment. In practice, this frequently means assessing the competence of the client and helping to determine that he/she needs a less demanding environment —for example, one with no stairs, one that offers meal service, etc.

Lawton and Simon's (1968) environmental docility hypothesis asserts that the less competent the individual, the greater the impact of environmental factors on that individual which would suggest that the choice of housing is particularly important for the vulnerable client who is most likely to come to the attention of the social worker. It also means that it is the vulnerable client who is most likely to be affected by even a small change in environment, either positively or negatively. Contrastingly, elderly who are healthy and economically secure would be least likely to have aspects of their behavior dependent on external conditions of the housing environment. Sherman (1974) found that moving to retirement housing did not increase the leisure-activity level for persons of high economic and health status relative to community residents. Persons in the community group had the economic means and health to maintain an activity level as high as that of their counterparts who chose to move into special housing.

In Kahana's theory of person/environment congruence (Kahana 1982; Kahana, Liang, and Felton 1980), a person may be characterized by the types and relative strengths of his or her needs; the environment may be characterized by the extent to which it is capable of satisfying these needs. Kahana stresses that environments do not have a uniform effect; a given environment is not good for all persons. It is the role of the social worker to enhance adjustment by matching the individual's needs with the environment in question. An aid to this match may be found above, in the discussion of assessment, and the descriptions of clients who can benefit the most from each housing type.

Dowd's (1975) exchange theory has relevance for issues of housing for the elderly. Since the bargaining position of older persons is weakened because of devalued status, an age-segregated environment may be strategic to minimize the costs inherent in ordinary social exchange. In such an environment, exchange networks will be formed within age categories rather than between categories, and the older person will not be at such a disadvantage.

Schooler's (1982) stress-theoretical model enables the worker who is helping an older person planning a move to separate the effect of residential relocation from actual change in the environment. The model also has confirmed the buffering effect of the confidant relationship. These factors should be considered seriously by housing managers, as a guide toward intervention.

In Kuypers and Bengtson's (1973) social reconstruction model, housing is viewed as an intervention that can help to reverse a cycle of social breakdown. By improving housing conditions, dependence will be reduced and self-reliance will be increased. This will lead to self-labeling by the client as able, and to an internalization of an effective self-image. The social worker can be a critical catalyst for such a reversal.

In analyzing the effect of planned retirement housing facilities, Sherman (1979) employed the concept of site permeability. Retirement housing facilities can vary from a relatively closed community (i.e., low site permeability) to one that allows for frequent penetration and movement in and out of its boundaries (i.e., high permeability). In Sherman's model, perceived community support in crises is a joint function of site permeability and service availability: given a situation of good service availability, the lower the site permeability, the greater the perceived community support; given a situation of poor service availability, the lower the site permeability, the less the perceived community support. The social worker thus needs to look beyond the dimension of service availability to the dimension of site permeability. Those elderly who prefer and select a site with low permeability may be in greater need of service augmentation and supportive assistance at times of crisis, for example, of illness or bereavement, than those elderly who select a site with high permeability. At those sites where services are present, the less permeable the boundaries, the less is the need for additional support during crises. Once a threshold of services is available, the very sense of enclosure provides security.

O'Bryant and Wolf (1985) introduce the concept of subjective "attachment to home." They found that this was more important in predicting homeowners' satisfaction than were personal demographic variables or housing characteristics, whereas physical housing characteristics were more important for renters. It has been suggested (Golant 1984; Karp and Yoels 1982; Lawton 1983; Ward, LaGory, and Sherman 1988) that we need to look not only at the objective environment, but particularly for the vulnerable older person with limited options, the subjective environment. High levels of neighborhood satisfaction in the face of limited options may be explained in this way.

POLICY

The major federally assisted housing programs are the Section 8 program, the Section 202 program, and the low-rent public housing program.

The section 8 program provides "subsidized housing to households with incomes too low to obtain decent housing in the private market. Under the program, HUD enters into assistance contracts with owners of existing housing . . . for a specified number of units to be leased by households meeting Federal eligibility standards" (U.S. Congress 1982:214). "HUD makes up the difference between what a low- and very low-income household can afford and the fair market rent for an adequate housing unit. . . . Project sponsors may be private owners, profit-motivated and nonprofit or cooperative organizations, public housing agencies and State housing finance agencies" (U.S. HUD 1984: 35). Some section 8 assistance is tenant based and other assistance is project-based, i.e., a certain number of units in a project are allocated as section units (Bergwall 1988).

"The section 202 program is the primary Federal financing vehicle for constructing housing for older persons that will enable them to remain self-sufficient and independent" (U.S. Congress 1982:216). The program provides "long-term direct loans to eligible, private nonprofit sponsors to finance rental or cooperative housing facilities for occupancy by elderly or handicapped persons. Section 8 funds are made available for 100 percent of the Section 202 units" (U.S. HUD 1984:36).

Under the low-rent public housing program, locally established, nonprofit public housing agencies develop, own, and operate low-income public housing projects, financing them through the use of HUD-sponsored grants (Roaldi 1988). "HUD furnishes technical and professional assistance in planning, developing and managing the projects and gives two kinds of financial assistance: debt service annual contributions to pay principal and interest costs on obligations issued by public housing agencies to finance development or acquisition of projects and annual contributions for operating subsidy" (U.S. HUD 1984:66). Also provided is comprehensive improvement assistance funding to cover the major cost of capital improvements or repairs (Roaldi 1988).

Other federal programs include rural housing loans, rural rental housing, mortgage insurance, Indian housing, community development block grants, urban development block grants, rehabilitation loan programs, energy assistance programs, and monies obtained from Title III of the Older Americans Act or from Title XX of the Social Security Act. It should be noted that several of the programs also serve persons who are not elderly. Social workers will also need to be familiar with state or local assistance programs, which cannot be covered in this book. The worker should contact the local or State unit on Aging, particularly because both Federal and State programs are subject to change.

There are many gaps in our public policies regarding housing for the elderly. First, there is insufficient housing offered in an intermediate range between independent housing and an institutional setting, which makes the job of the social worker working with a frail but not seriously impaired client far more difficult.

Second, federal housing policy has been primarily that of construction of rental housing (NYOFA n.d.). Since 70 percent of all elderly heads of households own their homes, it is clear that this cannot possibly be sufficient to address fully the housing needs of older persons. It is only with drastic federal cutbacks that increased attention is being paid to more innovative programs, primarily at the local level.

According to Lawton: "The overriding policy issue in the area of housing for the aged concerns the relative lack of federal programs designed to aid the more than 90% of all older people who live in ordinary, unplanned communities" (1980:72). It is generally agreed that federal policy has paid insufficient attention to programs for maintenance/rehabilitation and weatherization of existing housing, much less to offering housing counseling services. Other programs that also have been used only sparsely are local property tax rebates. According to an analysis by the N.Y. State Senate Committee on Aging: "HUD's 1983 budget emphasis on preservation and protection of existing housing stock is indicative of a policy shift from new construction to rehabilitation" (N.Y. Leg. 1982:11).

All of the programs described above together do not approach meeting the housing needs of older Americans. The theory is that new programs can serve a wider population. Whether they do, remains to be seen. Again, we see the importance of case management to advocate for the individual client. Social workers can also be involved at the policy level in helping to advocate for more innovative and widespread housing programs.

REFERENCES

AARP (American Association of Retired Persons). n.d. *Understanding Senior Housing: An American Association of Retired Persons survey of consumers preferences, concerns, and needs.* Washington; D.C.: American Association of Retired Persons, Consumer Affairs Section.

Adams, R. G. 1985. Emotional closeness and physical distance between friends: Implications for elderly women living in age-segregated and age-integrated settings. *International Journal of Aging and Human Development* 22:55–76.

Allan, C. and H. Brotman, comps. 1981. *Chart Book on Aging in America.* Washington, D.C.: White House Conference on Aging.

Atchley, R. C. 1985. *Social Forces and Aging.* 4th ed. Belmont, Calif.: Wadsworth.

Bergwall, H. 1988. Personal communication.

Blackie, N., J. Edelstein, P. S. Matthews, and R. Timmons. 1983. *Alternative Housing and Living Arrangements for Independent Living.* Ann Arbor: National Policy Center on Housing and Living Arrangements for Older Americans, University of Michigan.

Bultena, G. L. and V. Wood. 1969. The American retirement community: Bane or blessing? *Journal of Gerontology* 24(2):209–217.

Carp, F. M. 1966. *A Future for the Aged: Victoria Plaza and Its Residents.* Austin: University of Texas Press.

Carp, F. M. 1976. Housing and living environments of older people. In R. H. Binstock and E. Shanas, eds., *Handbook of Aging and the Social Sciences.* New York: Van Nostrand Reinhold.

Chellis, R. D., J. F. Seagle, Jr., and B. M. Seagle. 1982. *Congregate Housing for Older People.* Lexington, Mass.: Lexington Books.

Dowd, J. J. 1975. Aging as exchange: A preface to theory. *Journal of Gerontology* 30(5):584–594.

Eckert, J. K. 1979. The unseen community: Understanding the older hotel dweller. *Aging,* nos. 291–292, pp. 28–35.

Elder, G. 1981. History and the life course. In D. Bertaux, ed., *Biography and Society: The Life History Approach in the Social Sciences.* Beverly Hills, Calif.: Sage.

Erickson, R. and K. Eckert. 1977. The elderly poor in downtown San Diego hotels. *The Gerontologist* 17(5):440–446.

Fish, G. S. 1985. On home equity conversion mortgages for elderly homeowners. *Journal of Housing for the Elderly* 3:51–64.

Fried, M. 1963. Grieving for a lost home: Psychological costs of relocation. In L. J. Duhl, ed., *The Urban Condition.* New York: Basic Books.

Golant, S. 1984. *A Place to Grow Old: The Meaning of Environment in Old Age.* New York: Columbia University Press.

L. Harris and Associates. 1986. *Problems Facing Elderly Americans Living Alone.* Conducted for the Commonwealth Fund, Commission on Elderly People Living Alone. New York: Louis Harris and Associates. Mimeo.

Jacobs, B. 1986. The national potential of home equity conversion. *The Gerontologist* 26:496–504.

Johnson, S. K. 1971, *Idle Haven: Community Building Among the Working-Class Retired.* Berkeley: University of California Press.

Kahana, E. 1982. A congruence model of person-environment interaction. In M. P. Lawton, P. G. Windley, and T. O. Byerts, eds., *Aging and the Environment: Theoretical Approaches.* New York: Springer.

Kahana, E., J. Liang, and B. J. Felton. 1980. Alternative models of person-environment fit: Predictions of morale in three homes for the aged. *Journal of Gerontology* 35(4):584–595.

Karp, D. and W. Yoels. 1982. *Experiencing the Life Cycle: A Social Psychology of Aging.* Springfield, Ill: Thomas.

Kuypers, J. A. and V. L. Bengston. 1973. Social breakdown and competence: A model of normal aging. *Human Development* 16:181–201.

Lawton, M. P. 1975. *Planning and Managing Housing for the Elderly.* New York: Wiley.

Lawton, M. P. 1980. *Environment and Aging.* Monterey, Calif.: Brooks/Cole.

Lawton, M. P. 1981. Alternative housing. *Journal of Gerontological Social Work* 3(3):61–80.

Lawton, M. P. 1982. Competence, environmental press, and the adaptation of older people. In M. P. Lawton, P. G. Windley, and T. O. Byerts, eds., *Aging and the Environment: Theoretical Approaches.* New York: Springer.

Lawton, M. P. 1983. Environment and other determinants of well-being in older people. *The Gerontologist* 23:349–357.

Lawton, M. P. and J. Cohen. 1974. The generality of housing impact on the well-being of older people. *Journal of Gerontology* 29(2):194–204.

Lawton, M. P., M. Moss, and M. Grimes, 1985. The changing service needs of older tenants in planned housing. *The Gerontologist* 25:258–264.

Lawton, M. P. and L. Nahemow. 1973. Ecology and the aging process. In C. Eisdorfer and M. P. Lawton, eds., *Psychology of Adult Development and Aging.* Washington, D.C.: American Psychological Association.

Lawton, M. P. and L. Nahemow. 1975. *Cost, Structure, and Social Aspects of Housing for the Aged.* Philadelphia: Philadelphia Geriatric Center.

Lawton, M. P. and B. Simon. 1968. The ecology of social relationships in housing for the elderly. *The Gerontologist* 8(2):108–115.

Lemke, S. and R. H. Moos. 1987. Measuring the social climate of congregate residences for older people: Sheltered care environment scale. *Psychology and Aging* (2). 20–29

Logan, J. R. and G. Spitze, 1988. Suburbanization and public services for the aging. *The Gerontologist* 28:644–647.

Malozemoff, I., J. Anderson, and L. Rosenbaum. 1978. *Housing for the Elderly: Evaluation of the Effectiveness of Congregate Residences.* Boulder, Colo.: Westview Press.

Marans, R. W., M. E. Hunt, and K. L. Vakalo. 1984. Retirement communities. In I. Altman, M. P. Lawton, and J. F. Wohlwill, eds., *Elderly People and the Environment.* New York: Plenum Press.

Moos, R. H. and S. Lemke, 1984. Supportive residential settings for older people. In I. Altman, M. P. Lawton and J. F. Wohlwill, eds., *Elderly People and the Environment.* New York: Plenum Press.

Nachison, J. S. 1985. Congregate housing for the low and moderate income elderly: A needed Federal State partnership. *Journal of Housing for the Elderly* 3:65–80.

New York State Legislature. Senate. Standing Committee on Aging. 1982. *Shared Housing for the Elderly.* Albany.

New York State Office for the Aging. n.d.. *Innovative Housing Programs for the Elderly in New York State.* Albany: New York State Office for the Aging.

O'Bryant, S. and S. M. Wolf, 1983. Explanations of housing satisfaction of older homeowners and renters. *Research on Aging* 4:349–363.

Pastalan, L. 1972. *Retirement Housing Study.* Madison: Methodist Hospital of Madison, Wisc.

Pastalan, L. 1985. From the editor. *Journal of Housing for the Elderly* 3(3/4):1–2.

Plutchik, R., M. McCarthy, and B. H. Hall. 1975. Changes in elderly welfare hotel residents during a one-year period. *Journal of the American Geriatrics Society* 23(6):265–270.

Prosper, V. 1985. Continuing care retirement communities: A background report. Albany: New York State Office for the Aging.

Prosper, V. 1987. A review of congregate housing in the United States. Albany: New York State Office for the Aging.

Prosper, V. 1988. Personal communication.

Roaldi, D. 1988. Personal communication.

Rohrer, R. L. and R. Bibb. 1986. Marketing: The CCRC challenge. *Contemporary Long-Term Care* (May). 9(5):41–58.

Scholen, K. 1987. *Home-Made Money: Consumer's Guide to Home Equity Conversion.* Washington, D.C.: American Association of Retired Persons.

Schooler, K. K. 1976. Environmental change and the elderly. In I. Altman and J. Wohlwill, eds., *Human Behavior and Environment: Advances in Theory and Research,* vol. 1. New York: Plenum.

Schooler, K. K. 1982. Response of the elderly to environment: A stress-theoretical perspective. In M. P. Lawton, P. G. Windley, and T. O. Byerts, eds., *Aging and the Environment: Theoretical Approaches*. New York: Springer.

Schulz, R. and G. Brenner. 1977. Relocation of the aged: A review and theoretical analysis. *Journal of Gerontology* 32(3):323–333.

Sherman, E. A. and E. S. Newman. 1977–78. The meaning of cherished personal possessions for the elderly. *International Journal of Aging and Human Development* 8(2):181–192.

Sherman, E. A., E. S. Newman, and A. D. Nelson. 1976. Patterns of age integration in public housing and the incidence of fears of crime among elderly tenants. In J. Goldsmith and S. S. Goldsmith, eds., *Crime and the Elderly: Challenge and Response*. Lexington, Mass.: Lexington Books.

Sherman, S. R. 1971. The choice of retirement housing among the well-elderly. *International Journal of Aging and Human Development* 2(2):118–138.

Sherman, S. R. 1972. Satisfaction with retirement housing: Attitudes, recommendations, and moves. *International Journal of Aging and Human Development* 3(4):339–366.

Sherman, S. R. 1974. Leisure activities in retirement housing. *Journal of Gerontology* 29(3):325–335.

Sherman, S. R. 1975a. Mutual assistance and support in retirement housing. *Journal of Gerontology* 30(4):479–483.

Sherman, S. R. 1975b. Patterns of contacts for residents of age-segregated and age-integrated housing. *Journal of Gerontology* 30(1):103–107.

Sherman, S. R. 1975c. Provision of on-site services in retirement housing. *International Journal of Aging and Human Development* 6(3):229–247.

Sherman, S. R. 1979. The retirement housing setting: Site permeability, service availability, and perceived community support in crises. *Journal of Social Service Research* 3:139–157.

Sherman, S. R. 1988. A social psychological perspective on the continuum of housing for the elderly. *Journal of Aging Studies* 2:229–241.

Sherman, S. R. and E. S. Newman. 1988. *Foster Families for Adults: A Community Alternative in Long-Term Care*. New York: Columbia University Press.

Sherman, S. R., R. A. Ward, and M. LaGory. Socialization and aging group consciousness: The effect of neighborhood age concentrations. *Journal of Gerontology* (in press).

Sherwood, S., D. S. Greer, and J. N. Morris. 1979. A study of the Highland Heights apartments for the physically impaired and elderly in Fall River. In T. O. Byerts, S. C. Howell, and L. A. Pastalan, eds., *The Environmental Context of Aging: Life-Styles, Environmental Quality, and Living Arrangements*. New York: Garland STPM Press.

Siegal, H. A. 1978. *Outposts of the Forgotten*. New Brunswick, N.J.: Transaction Books.

Snider, D. A., D. Pascarelli, and M. Howard. 1979. *Survey of the Needs and Problems of Adult Home Residents in New York State: Final Report*. Albany: Welfare Research.

Solan G. 1987. Home equity conversion: Background paper. Albany: N.Y. State Office for The Aging. April.

Stephens, J. 1975. Society of the alone: Freedom, privacy, and utilitarianism as dominant norms in the SRO. *Journal of Gerontology* 30(2):230–235.

Streib, G. F. 1978. An alternative family form for older persons: Need and social context. *Family Coordinator* 27(4):413–420.

Struyck, R. J. 1984/85. Housing-related needs of elderly Americans and possible federal responses. *Journal of Housing for the Elderly* 2:3–26.

U.S. Congress Senate. Special Committee on Aging. 1982. *Developments in Aging, 1981*, vol. 1. Washington, D.C.: GPO.

U.S. HUD (Department of Housing and Urban Development). 1984. *Programs of HUD*. Washington, D.C.: GPO.

Walkley, R. P., W. P. Mangum, Jr., S. R. Sherman, S. Dodds, and D. M. Wilner. 1966a. The California survey of retirement housing. *The Gerontologist* 6(1): 28–34.

Walkley, R. P., W. P. Mangum, Jr., S. R. Sherman, S. Dodds, and D. M. Wilner. 1966b. *Retirement Housing in California*. Berkeley: Diablo Press.

Ward, R. A., M. LaGory, and S. R. Sherman. 1988. *The Environment for Aging: Interpersonal, Social, and Spatial Contexts*. Tuscaloosa: University of Alabama Press.

19

Home Care

❖

CAROLE COX, D.S.W.
The Catholic University of America, Washington, D.C.

Home care programs are based upon the philosophical tenet that ill and disabled persons have the right to be card for, whenever possible, in their own homes rather than in institutions. Within the continuum of long-term care services, home care has been regarded as either a substitute or an alternative to nursing homes with the latter view presently tending to dominate.

The shifting interest toward home care for the elderly may be traced to the 1965 Medicare legislation (Title XVIII of the Social Security Act) which resulted in the rapid expansion of home health agencies. The number of such agencies increased from 252 in 1966 to an estimated 10,000 in 1986 with the advent of this legislation (American Bar Association, 1986).

NEED FOR HOME CARE

Several factors have led in recent years to renewed interest in community care. The proliferation of nursing homes, which began in the 1960s, is now giving way to a more balanced consideration of home-based services. The growing realization that institutional care is reaching prohibitive cost levels coupled with the relentless demographic expansion of the elderly, particularly those 85 and older, have stimulated the promotion of home care services.

About 5 million chronically ill elderly living in the community typically need at lease minimal assistance in performing their activities of daily living (GAO, December 1986). By the year 2000, over 15 million older persons will suffer from a chronic illness that will limit their functioning, a 50 percent increase over 1980s estimate (Spiegel 1987). While studies continue to demonstrate that most assistance is provided informally by family and friends, changes in family structure, the simultaneous aging of the family members along with their frail relatives, and the reduced availability of women caregivers contribute to a need for more formal home care services. This is confirmed by the fact that in fiscal year 1985 Medicare paid about $1.7 billion for home health care services, more than six times the amount spent in 1976 (GAO 1986).

Another key factor impacting the home care industry has been the recent changes in hospital discharge policies. A year-long study by the Senate Special Committee on Aging revealed that Medicare's Prospective Payment System (PPS) provides incentives to hospitals to discharge patients "quicker and sicker," placing an additional stress on post-hospital services (U.S. Senate 1986).

New Jersey, a state which has had the Prospective Payment System in effect since 1980, shows the total admissions to home health agencies increasing by 48 percent between 1980 and 1983 (Taylor 1986). National data on the utilization of home health services similarly reveals a substantial growth in use following the implementation of the PPS policies. Visits per user, total number of visits and visits per 1,000 Medicare enrollees rose from 17 per 1,000 in 1974 to 46 per 1,000 enrollees in 1983 (Leader 1986).

It is not surprising that the home care industry has been simultaneously expanding to meet the demand for services. In the twenty-year period between 1967 and 1987, the number of Medicare certified home health agencies rose from 1,753 to 5,877 (National Association for Homecare 1987). With this phenomenal rate of growth, expenditures by Medicare on home health care, doubled between 1980 and 1983, from $772 million to $1.5 billion, growing at an annual rate of approximately 34 percent per year (Doty, Liu, and Weiner 1985). It is important to note, however, that this increase is not keeping up with the presumed need. Denials by Medicare for home health services have also multiplied. Medicare covered visits rose an average of 19 percent between 1980 and 1983 but slowed to only 8 percent in 1984 despite the fact that the demand for services under the PPS system continued growing (Heinz 1986). As a result, many consumers must pay for the services themselves or do without care.

THEORETICAL FOUNDATION FOR HOME CARE

Two conceptual frameworks are pertinent to an understanding of the importance of home care services. Continuity theory (Bultena 1969) views old age not as a distinct phase of life but as a natural continuation of earlier periods. Persons, therefore, seek to maintain their earlier life-styles, roles, and activities as long as possible. This occurs even in the face of opposing social forces which seek to discourage this continuation.

Bengston's social breakdown and reconstruction theory (1976) suggests, in turn, that many factors in the environment act to both threaten and destroy the older person's competence. As abilities become less acute with age, the person is labeled deficient and impaired, thus becoming vulnerable to dependency, a label which tends to be fostered by existing services. Using a social reconstruction framework, practitioners can break this vicious circle by rebuilding the confidence and coping skills of the older person, thus preventing the social breakdown.

Both of these theoretical frameworks can assist in understanding the role played by home care. As the service maintains persons in the community, it assists in helping them to continue in their established roles. At the same time, as it provides essential, rather than total assistance, it works to strengthen skills and enhance autonomy.

In working toward the individual's right to remain independent, home care attempts to minimize the negative consequences and effects of the client's illness or disability. Decisions regarding care are made in accordance with the wishes of the client and the family with the home care worker acting as an adviser. The final decision regarding services rests with the client. The role of the agency is to serve as a resource for the client regarding appropriate community supports which will strengthen his abilities, and, if necessary, to serve as a link with them.

TYPE OF SERVICES AND AGENCIES

There is considerable variation in the types of services provided by home care agencies and among the agencies themselves. Services can range from high technological care, usually offered by a hospital, to assistance with household tasks such as cleaning and shopping. The scope of services provided includes personal care with medical supervision and assistance, personal maintenance, rehabilitation, and social and emotional counseling. Ancillary community services, such as meals on wheels and transportation programs, may also be considered a part of home care or as coordinates to it.

Home care is provided by four general types of agencies: public, nonprofit, proprietary, and a mixed type of dual sponsorship. All public agencies operated by state or local governments are primarily located in health and welfare departments. Non-profit agencies are organizations such as the Visiting Nurse Association, programs sponsored by religious groups, and other nonprofit programs such as hospitals, nursing facilities, and rehabilitation programs. Proprietary agencies are privately operated for profit, while combined agencies are those operated with dual sponsorship by a governmental and voluntary unit as in the contractual merger of a health department and a Visiting Nurse Association.

The wide array of services that an individual may require and the assortment of providers that may be involved in the provision of care can be confusing. It is not always clear as to what services are essential to insure the independent functioning of the individual and who should be responsible for providing and coordinating them.

INTERVENTION

Entry into the Home Care System

Referrals for home care services may come from many sources. Most commonly, they are made by hospital discharge planners, physicians, social service agencies, families, or the clients themselves. However, if services are to be reimbursed under Medicare, it is required that the persons' need for service be documented by a physician.

Assessment in Home Care

Home care begins with an assessment of the needs and capabilities of the client. Initially, this evaluation determines eligibility under policy provisions and the type of services required. Periodic assessments are made subsequently to determine the changing status of the person, the quality of the services provided, and the overall standard of care.

Since hospitals are a primary source of referrals to home care, the physicians, nurses, discharge planners and social workers, are often the ones who make the initial assessments regarding need for services. The inherent problem in these hospital based assessments is that they seldom take into account the home environment or the availability of preexisting community supports.

CAAST is an example of a patient assessment method commonly used by attending physicians to determine the need for home care (Glass and Weiner 1976). It covers the following five areas:

1. *Continence.* Fully continent/incontinent for two days to one month/ incontinent for more than one month
2. *Ambulation.* Fully ambulatory/unable to move independently more than 20 feet two days to one month/unable to move for more than one month
3. *Age.* Younger than 65/65-79/older than 79;
4. *Social background.* Admitted from home and likely to return home/admitted from an extended care facility and likely to return there; admitted from home and likely to be discharged to an extended care facility; admitted from extended care facility and likely to be discharged to another;
5. *Thought processes.* Fully oriented/disoriented for more than one month.

Each of these items is scored from 0 to 2 based on severity and weighted for chronicity. A higher total score indicates greater dependence with posthospital care and the need for more extensive posthospital arrangements. The assessment is based closely on a medical orientation and therefore, does not collect data on social functioning, emotional needs, or wishes of the patient. These are often the precipitating factors in the institutionalization of the elderly.

Home care programs have also developed their own assessment instruments but they are not without their own shortcomings. According to Kaye (1985) these instruments tend to be provider-oriented rather than client-oriented as they are influenced by the available resources of the agency, the interests of the dominant service profession, and financial eligibility criteria rather than the actual needs of the older person.

Bulau's (1986) assessment form for use by home health agencies, in addition to medical information, records the type of equipment required in the home, the type of specific home health care services required, financial information and the following factors:

1. Applicant is homebound;
2. Applicant is under care of a physician.
3. Applicant needs part-time or intermittent skilled nursing services and at least one other therapeutic service, e.g., physical or occupational therapy;

4. Reasonable expectation exists that the applicants medical, nursing, and social needs can be met adequately by the home health care agency in the applicant's place of residence;
5. The home health care services are necessary and reasonable to the treatment of the applicant's illness or injury;
6. The applicant is 16 years of age or older.

One of the most thorough assessment forms has been developed by the Office of Continuing Care in Manitoba, Canada, which uses the same standardized form to assess for admission to either home care or nursing home care (Continuing Care Program Manual, 1983). The assessment identifies:

1. Those activities basic to household, health, personal and social needs and essential to remaining at home in the community which the person can perform and those which the person cannot, or should not, perform.
2. Those activities which others in the household or which family members living within a reasonable distance are performing or could realistically perform.
3. Those activities for which resources exist in the community or through other government programs.

These assessments provide the basis for the home care services. However, they are not static and reassessments are made periodically to ensure that services remain consistent with needs. Although some programs routinely reassess every 90 days, it is usually necessary to make them based on the level of services and needs of the client.

An area of concern in the assessment of the quality of the service is the workers' qualifications. Unfortunately, much home care is provided by unlicensed paraprofessionals working in the roles of homemaker/home health aids. These persons work under the auspices of many agencies including welfare departments, public health departments, and for profit agencies. They typically receive little, if any, training, work at below minimum wages without employee benefits, and have little opportunity for advancement. Often these paraprofessionals have no direct supervision while, at the same time, there is a lack of uniform standards to measure the quality of their work.

The Omnibus Budget Reconciliation Act of 1987 has attempted to rectify some of the issues associated with the quality of care. It has included provisions to protect the rights of recipients of services of home health agencies, to strengthen certification procedures and to specify training requirements for personnel.

Care Plan

Once the assessment has determined that the individual's needs can be adequately met through the home care program, a care plan is developed. This plan indicates the types of services, the amount and duration of each service, and the required informal and formal care providers. The objective here is to insure a minimum amount of service required to maintain the person at home.

Care plans also provide the framework for monitoring both the client and the quality of care and are, therefore, critical to a program's effectiveness. The Home Care Quality Assurance Act of 1987 requires that agencies develop care plans which identify services to be provided, provide a means for identifying additional client needs, and include coordination mechanisms with other service agencies.

Service Delivery

As previously mentioned, there are several types of personnel involved in providing home care services. Descriptions of the roles played by these primary service providers include the following personnel:

The home health care *registered nurse* makes the initial and subsequent evaluations of nursing needs. She also is responsible for providing specialized nursing services and for informing the homecare agency and physician of changes in the client's status. The nurse, in most instances, is the usual supervisor of the other homecare staff.

The tasks performed by *the home health aides* include assistance with personal care and toileting, bathing, simple medical procedures, ambulation and exercises. They may also supervise the administration of medications.

Homemakers are generally responsible for housekeeping, meal preparation, laundry, grocery shopping and assistance in other household duties. The work may also entail companionship to the older person but it does not encompass personal care that must be provided under nursing supervision.

Other skilled services commonly offered through home care include speech therapy, physical therapy, and occupational therapy. These are provided through contracts with the agencies with the home care supervisor responsible for monitoring their work.

Social Workers in Home Care

As home care has evolved out of medical institutions, hospitals, and visiting nurse associations, it is not surprising that it has maintained a medical orientation. This orientation is strongly reinforced by the Medicare Conditions of Participation for the home health agencies which require skilled nursing care as a condition for reimbursement. There is no equivalent requirement for nonmedical personnel including social workers who continue to play secondary roles in most agencies. This medical emphasis ignores the fact that many of the problems and needs of the elderly are complex and could be most appropriately met by social work counseling and intervention.

Social workers have the potential to play significant roles in home care programs. They are skilled in analyzing problems, defining alternative solutions, and developing appropriate options for care. These skills are recognized and utilized in home care programs in other countries where the social workers act as key workers in assessing the individual and coordinating care (Shapiro 1987). The social worker's further ability to understand the psychosocial aspects of the problems of the elderly and their relations to individual needs and functioning can further contribute to a program's effectiveness.

The role of the social worker in the home care agency has been characterized as having three related components: direct service to the patient; consultation service to other staff members; and being a part of the community resource system (Auerbach et al, 1984). The social worker can also identify missing but needed community resources, coordinate services for clients, manage cases, and review policy. When performing these tasks as a team member the social worker enacts the roles of counselor, enabler, advocate, planner, and educator. Moreover, the social worker can assist other team members to understand the social and emotional factors associated with health problems, and assist in the development of the care plans which recognize these factors.

Coordination of Service

Considering the wide array of services in the home care field, the need for coordination is evident. However, coordination is hampered by variations in agency philosophies regarding service provision, differences in the assessment of patient's needs, separate and often conflicting plans for care, differing perspectives on the kind and amount of services required and the type of personnel best suited to provide those services (Trager 1980).

The inherent problem is deciding who is to be the service coordinator among the personnel of the fragmented programs. A lack of service coordination can result in duplication of services and manpower, poor service accessibility, and the underutilization of services.

Case managers are increasingly stepping in to assist in the coordination of services. The role of the case manager is to ensure that proper services are provided and to keep track of the various providers. This can involve explaining the total plan to the patient and the family, monitoring daily activities, evaluating services, solving problems, and acting as a liason between client and agencies. However, the effectiveness of this person is limited to the extent that the providing agencies remain independent and are under no mandate to accept the manager's plans.

Again, looking at the experiences in other countries can help to illustrate the roles that various professionals, such as case managers, can play in home care. The home care program in Kent, England, is directed by case managers (Davies and Challis 1986). In this system the case manager, a social worker, is employed by the local social service departments to arrange and coordinate all of the home care services of each client. The worker has the authority and flexibility to develop a package unique to each client from a wide range of usually fragmented resources. In addition, the case manager develops viable home care support networks and monitors their effective functioning.

THE EFFECTIVENESS OF HOME CARE

Measuring the effectiveness of home care services is as intricate an issue as the very nature and organization of the programs themselves. Criteria as to what constitutes effectiveness vary according to the philosophies and interests of the participating agencies. However, under current government funding and restrictions, the cost savings or efficiency criteria become the overriding concerns when comparing home care to other forms of care.

A recent study (Bergner et al. 1988) of home care for patients with chronic lung disease found that after one year there was no difference in survival, pulmonary functioning, or every day functioning for those receiving care from respiratory home care nurses, standard home care, or those getting care in the physician's office. However, the cost of the respiratory home care was significantly higher than the other modes of treatment.

A study comparing home dialysis provided by home health aides with traditional hospital-based dialysis also casts doubt about the cost effectiveness of providing specialized technical care at home (Sparer et al 1983). The results found no differences in hospitalization or mortality rates between those receiving home care dialysis and those receiving traditional hospital dialysis. However, the training of the dialysis aides brought the cost of the home care to a level comparable to the cost of hospital dialysis in half of the experimental clients. These findings tend to indicate that if cost-effectiveness and savings are the main objectives of home care, it may be necessary to target services on persons requiring less costly care.

Another criterion used in evaluating home care is to examine its effect on institutionalization. An evaluation of a comprehensive coordinated home care program in Chicago found that an experimental group receiving home care had a significant reduction in nursing home admissions compared to controls who did not receive the service (Hughes 1984). The experimental group also had an increase in the sense of well-being and a decrease in their unmet needs for community services. However, the mortality and hospitalization rates for the two groups did not differ.

An extensive descriptive comparison between nursing home and home care patients based upon samples from 20 home health agencies and 46 nursing homes in twelve states was made by Kramer, Shaunessy, and Pettigrew (1985). Their findings indicated that the two populations differed with homecare patients being younger, having shorter lengths of care, and being less functionally disabled than nursing home patients. Among the Medicare patients in each program, the home care patients were less proficient in independent living skills. In considering the cost effectiveness of home care, the authors concluded that home care may be more cost-effective as a substitute for acute care following a hospital stay.

Capitman (1986) reviewed the extensive evaluations of five demonstration projects in long term care sponsored by the Health Care Financing Administration (HCFA). The five projects were the New York City Home Care Project, the Long-Term Care Project of North San Diego County, Project OPEN, the South Carolina Community Long-Term Care Project and the On Lok Community Care Organization for Dependent Adults. All of the demonstrations offered 1) expanded case management; 2) paraprofessional home health services to meet needs associated with activities of daily living, instrumental activities of daily living and mental status disabilities; 3) multidimensional assessment and reassessment and service arrangement and management.

The programs differed in both their target populations and objectives. The South Carolina Program attempted to divert nursing home applicants to home care while On Lok provided a consolidated package of care to individuals who would otherwise be admitted to nursing homes. The other three projects upgraded, through additional services, the home care packages provided to Medicare recipients.

The results of the evaluations suggested that expanded home care services and case management may only impact on nursing home use when they are offered to persons who have made nursing home applications, having no noticeable effect on equally frail persons who have not made such applications.

Other outcome measures that have been used in evaluating the effectiveness of home care programs include patient satisfaction and degree of dependence on the service. Bass and Noland (1983) studied two home care programs in the Boston area which provided general homemaking and domestic services. The data collected from 750 clients, with an average age of 78 years, showed a high satisfaction with the service although the degree of dependence on it was less certain. Only one-third felt that they would be unable to live independently without it.

The satisfaction with a professional home health care team has also been examined (Zimmer, Groth-Trencher, and McCluster 1985). The team composed of a physician, geriatric nurse practitioner, and social worker served only clients who were seriously or terminally ill. The findings on the clients indicated that the group had fewer hospitalizations, nursing home admissions, and outpatient visits than the controls not visited by the team. Although the clients did not differ from the controls on morale, both they and their caregivers were more satisfied with their care than those not receiving home services.

Conclusions regarding the effectiveness of home care services are difficult to make on the basis of these studies. However, even with diverse clienteles, home care appears to be associated with higher client satisfaction and a reduction in the use of nursing homes. The issue of cost-effectiveness, particularly for those requiring highly specialized technological care needs to be more closely examined and perhaps, balanced with other evaluative criteria when serving the frail elderly. A specific factor which needs to be more closely studied is the effect of home care on caregiver stress and burden, and its relationship to the caregivers ability to continue maintaining the person in the community.

POLICY AND HOME CARE

The diversity found in the myriad of services and providers in the home care field reflects, to a large extent, the inconsistency in the government's policy toward home care. Although the federal government aims to reduce health care costs by means of earlier discharges from hospitals, this has not resulted in increased funding for home care. The lack of a comprehensive policy in this area has resulted in confusion in both agencies and consumers. Both groups remain unsure as to their payments or entitlement to services.

The passage of the catastrophic insurance bill (H.R. 2941) extended home care benefits under Medicare but not to the degree needed to implement a policy which substantiates community care as an alternative to institutionalization. Moreover, its continued focus on the medical diagnosis as essential for benefits continues to ignore many of the problems associated with prevention, maintenance, chronic illness, and social and emotional needs which afflict the elderly. Four federal programs provide the major funding for home care: Medicare, Medicaid, Title XX, and the Older Americans Act.

Medicare

Although home health care constitutes only about 3 percent of total Medicare expenditures, this program is the largest source of public funding for home care. Moreover, the home health care benefit is the fastest growing benefit in the program but this growth has not been easy. Sections 1814 and 1861 of the Social Security Act require Medicare Part A reimbursement for the care of homebound Medicare-eligible beneficiaries: in need of part time or intermittent skilled nursing, physical therapy, speech therapy, occupational therapy, medical social services under the direction of a physician, medical supplies and equipment, part-time or intermittent services by a home health aid as permitted by regulations and medical services of interns and residents under an approved teaching program of a hospital.

Problems with the program immediately arise over the definitions of the regulations. There are no standardized definitions for "medically reasonable and necessary," the basic requirement for establishing care. This has resulted in many claims for service not being paid. With the Omnibus Budget Reconciliation Act of 1987, clear definitions were given to "homebound" and "intermittent care." Homebound is defined as not being bedridden but needing assistance or support to leave home because of an illness. Intermittent care is care provided to a maximum of 38 days, 7 days a week. Services may be extended under "exceptional circumstances," a concept that remains undefined.

Bills for payment of home care services are processed for Medicare by ten fiscal intermediaries throughout the country. These intermediaries consult with the home care agencies, do billing, audits, and evaluations. They are also under a mandate to "administer the program in a manner that achieves maximum savings and cost avoidance for the Medicare trust funds" (*Federal Register,* December 1986). This places the intermediaries in a position in which they are almost forced to become restrictive rather than balanced in their reimbursements to agencies.

The issue of cost control is most clearly shown in the denials of claims made to the home health agencies. Since the initiation of the prospective payment system in 1983 the number of denials rose from 1.2 percent to 8.3 percent in 1987 (National Association for Home Care, 1988). At the same time the Health Care Financing Association (HCFA), which administers the program, attempted to eliminate the "waiver of liability" under which the home health agencies were given flexibility in interpreting Medicare rules and regulations. The waivers allowed persons whose eligibility was questionable to receive services. Under the waivers, an agency with fewer than 2.5 percent of its visits disallowed in a quarter is permitted to be reimbursed for services found not to be covered at a later time. HCFA was unsuccessful in its effort and these waivers have now been extended to 1990.

The increasing attention being paid to long-term care insurance and extended health coverage may begin to reshape the government's attitude and policy toward home care benefits under Medicare. Changes likely to occur are the inclusion of other than medical or skilled nursing care, the coverage of homemaker services, dietary, and prevention counseling, respite care, and case management. The coverage of these services would expand the role of home care to meet many of the pressing and chronic needs of the elderly.

Medicaid

Medicaid, Title XIX of the Social Security Act, is a joint federal/state program that provides medical assistance for low income persons. Each state administers its own program subject to federal guidelines which mandate that it be provided to all recipients of Aid to Families with Dependent Children, most beneficiaries of Supplemental Security Income, and those in programs for the blind, disabled, and aged. However, states have the latitude to determine the scope of benefits and the level of reimbursement.

Medicaid must cover home health care physician services. It must also provide intermittent or part-time nursing care, home health aid services, and medical supplies and equipment. As in the Medicare program, these services can be provided only after the written recommendation of a physician with the plans being reviewed every sixty days.

Under the system of Medicaid waivers, the states are able to provide community and home services to persons who would otherwise be in an institution. The waivers broaden the types of services that can be provided, including social and personal services and case management. States are also permitted to offer homemaker, home health aid and chore services, rehabilitation, day health care, and respite care. However, the costs of these home care services must not exceed the cost of Medicaid care in an institution.

The waivers are a small part of the Medicaid program. In requesting waivers states have to provide assurances showing decreased state expenditures for home care services under Medicaid. This type of requirement, combined with the government's interest in cost containment, have restricted the growth of the program. It is difficult to always prove that the fiscal costs of home care are less than a nursing home or that the recipient would have to be in an institution without the home care services.

Social Service Block Grant-Title XX

Title XX, the Social Services amendment to the Social Security Act, is the major social service program funded by the federal government. Under this grant states are permitted to provide funds for services that would prevent or reduce inappropriate institutional care by providing community care, home care, and other forms of less intensive care. Title XX authorizes home health, homemaker, chore, home health aid, and home management assistance. It also provides for adult day care, home delivered meals, transportation, counseling and prevention, and social support services. States, however, can use the Title XX funds on any of these services they select. Funds are allocated on the basis of population within a federal budget ceiling. Because competition for funds within the states' programs may be great, its impact on home care services has been limited.

Older Americans Act

Under Title III of the Older Americans Act, grants are given to state agencies on aging that are responsible for funding the local area agencies on aging in their planning, coordinating, and advocating of services for older persons. Congress has given priority under Title III to in-home services such as homemaker and home health aid, friendly visiting, and telephone reassurance. Case management, assessment, adult day care, and respite care may also be provided. Many states coordinated these programs with those of Title XX.

FUTURE DIRECTIONS

As the demand for comprehensive long-term care services increases, home care services are expected to similarly expand. The primary issue is to develop a coherent federal policy which provides a framework for this expansion. To date the program has tended to be fragmented and one of reaction rather than planned action.

The active involvement and participation of consumers, interest groups, and providers of services will be required in the formulation of directions for a new policy. Data which carefully documents needs and costs, including "unmet needs" and persons not being served, its effects on delaying institutionalization among comparable groups of elderly, and its effects on caregivers must be collected to influence that policy. While it is true that expensive hospital-type services may not be cost-effective when provided at home, it is important to realize that this type of care is not required by the majority of persons needing home care services. Most could benefit from simple domestic assistance that would foster their independence and help to maintain them in the community. Once home care is viewed not only as a means of reaching a humanitarian goal but also as a means of reducing unnecessary health care costs associated with institutionalization, its role in long-term care policy and services may be more firmly established.

REFERENCES

American Bar Association. *The Black Box of Home Care Quality*. A Report presented by the Chairman of the Select Committee on Aging, House of Representatives, 96th Congress, August 1986.

Auerbach, D., D. Bann, and D. Davis. 1984. The social worker in home health care. *Caring* 3(10):71–76.

Bass S. and R. Roland 1983. *Client Satisfactions and Elderly Homemaker Services: An Evaluation.* Boston: Gerontology program, College of Public and Community Service, University of Massachusetts.

Bengston, V. 1976. *The Social Psychology of Aging.* Indianapolis: Bobbs-Merrill.

Bergner, M. L. Hudson, D. Conrad, and C. Patmont. 1988. The cost and efficacy of home care for patients with chronic lung disease. *Medical Care* (June 6), pp. 566–579.

Blue Cross Association. Home Health Care, Model benefit program and related guidelines, Chicago, June 1978.

Bulau, J. 1986. *Administrative Policies and Procedures for Home Health Care.* Minneapolis: Aspen.

Bultena G. 1969. Life continuity and morale in old age. *The Gerontologist* 9:251–53.

Capitman, J. 1986. Community-based long-term care models, target groups, and impacts on service use. *The Gerontologist,* 4:389–398.

Challis, D. and B. Davies. *Case Management in Community Care,* Brookfield: Gower, 1987.

Davies, B. and B. Challis. *Matching Resources to Needs in Community Care,* Brookfield: Gower, 1986.

Doty, P., K. Levis, and J. Wiener. An overview of long-term care. *Health Care Financing Review (Spring),* 6(3)70.

Epstein, W. 1980. The social work planner in long-term home care: A case study of institutional geriatric care in the veterans administration. *Social Work in Health Care* 6(1):23–25.

Federal Register. 1986. Medicare program: Criteria and standards for evaluating intermediary and carrier performance during fiscal year 1987. December 10. Nos. 44525, 44527.

Glass, R. and M. Weiner. 1976. Seeking a social disposition for the medical patient: CAAST, a simple and objective clinical index. *Medical Care* 14:637–641.

Hedrick, S. and T. Inui. 1986. The effectiveness and cost of home care: An information synthesis. *Health Services Research* 20(6):851–880.

Hughes, S., D. Cordray, and V. Specer. 1984. Evaluation of a long-term home care program, *Medical Care* 22:460–475.

Kaye, L. 1985. Home care. In A. Monk, ed. *Handbook of Gerontological Services.* New York: Van Nostrand.

Kramer, A., P. Shaughnessy, and M. Pettigrew. 1985. Cost effectiveness implications based on a comparison of nursing home and home health care mix. *Health Services Research* 20(4):387–405.

Leader, S. 1986. AARP, home health benefits under Medicaid: A working paper. Washington: American Assn of Retired Persons, July 21, p. 234.

Manitoba. 1983. Department of Health, Office of Continuing Care. *Policy Guidelines and Program Manual.*

National Association for Home Care. 1987. *Basic Statistics on Homecare* (August).

National Association for Home Care. 1988. What is home care? (January)

National League for Nursing. 1978. *Prospectives for a National Homecare Policy,* New York.

Omnibus Budget Reconciliation Act of 1987 (P.L. 100–203), 101 STAT. 1330, (1987).

O'Shaughnessy, C., R. Price and J. Griffith. 1985. *Financing and Delivery of Long-Term Care Services for the Elderly.* Washington, D.C.: Congressional Research Service, Library of Congress, 85–1033 EPW.

Shapiro, E. 1987. Multidisciplinary health assessments of the elderly in Manitoba, Canada. Paper presented at the International Work Group Meeting on Multidisciplinary Health Assessments of the Elderly, Goteburg, Sweden, May.

Sparer, G., G. Cahn, G. Robbins, N. Sharp. 1983. The paid aid demonstration: Summary of Operational Experiences. *AANNT* (American Association of Nephrology Nurses and Technicians) *Journal* 10:19–29.

Spiegel A. 1987. *Home Health Care.* 2d ed. Owings Mills: Rynd Communications, 1987.

Taylor, M. 1986. Home Health Agency Assembly: Letter to the editor. *Pride Institute of Long-Term Health Care* (Spring), 5(2):24.

Trager, B. 1980. Home health care and national policy. *Home Health Care Services Quarterly* 1(2):1–103.

U.S. Government Accounting Office. 1986. Medicare, need to strengthen home health care payment controls and address unmet needs. Washington, D.C.: GPO.

U.S. Health Care Financing Administration. 1980. Medicare: Participating health facilities 1979. Health Care Financing Program Statistics. Washington, D.C.: GPO.

U.S. Senate. Special Committee on Aging. 1986. *The Crisis in Home Health Care: Greater Need, Less Care:* A Staff Report, July 28, 1986.

Zimmer, J., A. Groeth-Juncker, and J. McChester. 1985. Effects of a physician led home care team on terminal care, *American Journal on Public Health* 75:1340–144.

VI

LONG-TERM CARE AND INSTITUTION-BASED SERVICES

20

Long-Term Care Institutions

❖

IRENE A. GUTHEIL, D.S.W.
Fordham University, New York

When people develop infirmities or disabilities that impair their capacity to function independently, they may require health care, personal care, and other supportive services. The ongoing provision of these services is referred to as long-term care. The majority of long-term care for frail older persons is provided by families in the community. Families usually perform heroicly in their efforts to care for dependent aged family members. Generally, it is not until a family's emotional or physical resources are overwhelmed that an institutional placement is pursued. The institutional setting for delivery of long-term care services is commonly referred to as the nursing home. The distinctive feature of nursing homes is the potential for provision for all of the residents' needs within the institution itself. Although in the ideal situation, the boundaries between institution and community are highly permeable, even nursing homes that are well integrated into the surrounding community cut residents off from the outside world to a considerable degree. Because of this, the nursing home is most appropriately thought of as a self-contained world, providing or arranging for the range of services people need to live.

Despite its insular nature, the nursing home is an integral part of the continuum of long-term care services. Residents may be admitted to the facility during a process of recovery, returning to community residence once a new level of functioning is achieved. In addition, long-term care institutions can and increasingly do offer services to people living in the community. Nursing homes are especially well suited to administer programs such as day care and home care because of their facilities and pools of health care providers. An example of an institution based program for impaired community residents is the respite care program at the Veterans Administration Hospital in Menlo Park, California. Eight nursing home beds are available for periods of 3 to 28 days to provide relief to primary caregivers (Scharlach and Frenzel 1986).

HISTORY OF NURSING HOMES

In the past, as today, the bulk of long-term care was provided by families. The nursing home industry did not actually develop until 1935 with the enactment of the Social Security Act. Prior to that time, poor, frail older people without family to provide care generally went to county poorhouses, as there were no public institutions specifically for the dependent aged. These poorhouses were, on the whole, dreadful places where inmates lived in squalid conditions and were vulnerable to a range of abuses. The 1935 Social Security legislation reflected a rejection of the poorhouse as an unsatisfactory means of providing care to the dependent aged and direct assistance was therefore denied to people living in government supported institutions. As a consequence, the clear need arose for more private homes for the aged. The real turning point, however, came in the 1960s with the enactment of Medicare and Medicaid, which provide federal funds to care for sick older people. The opportunity to make a profit providing nursing home care spurred an accelerated growth of the nursing home industry (Achenbaum 1978).

Waldman (1985) identified two important characteristics of the evolution of federal legislation on nursing homes. First, the bulk of publicly funded nursing home care has been provided through the welfare system. Second, nursing homes have been seen as part of a broader medical care program. The ongoing influence of these two characteristics continues to impact on nursing home residents today. Residents frequently must become impoverished in order to qualify for government financing of care, and the influence of the medical model at times makes it difficult to properly attend to residents' social and emotional needs.

NURSING HOMES TODAY

According to data from the 1985 National Nursing Home Survey (which did not include Alaska and Hawaii), there are 19,100 nursing homes in the United States with 1,624,200 beds. Nursing homes can be owned privately and operated for profit, or owned and operated by nonprofit organizations or the government. The overwhelming majority (75 percent) are proprietary homes. Of the remaining facilities, 20 percent are nonprofit and 5 percent government homes. Since the 1970s, there has been a substantial increase in the number of chain homes operating under one general authority or ownership. Even though less than half of the nation's facilities are chain homes (41 percent), they account for more total nursing home beds than do independently owned facilities because they tend to have a higher average number of beds (Strahan 1987).

In addition to type of ownership, nursing homes are currently classified by level of care. Homes can be federally certified as skilled nursing facilities (SNFs) or intermediate care facilities (ICFs), sometimes called health related facilities (HRFs). SNFs provide 24-hour skilled nursing care; ICFs are less intensive and are reimbursed at a lower rate. Objective assessment procedures such as New York's Patient Review Instrument (PRI), which must be filled out by a trained assessor, have been used to determine level of care need. After October 1990, the distinction between ICFs and SNFs will be eliminated as a result of the 1987 Nursing Home Quality of Care Amendments (NASW 1988).

THE NEED FOR NURSING HOMES

Nursing homes are part of the lives of a significant number of older people. At any given time, well over one million older persons live in such facilities. Although this figure represents approximately 5 percent of the elderly population, it does not reflect the real rate of nursing home utilization. Viewing the situation over time rather than at any given moment in time, as many as 36 percent of this country's older people may spend some time in a long-term care facility during the latter part of their lives (Liang and Tu 1986). From the perspective of increasing age within the older population, the percentage of people using nursing homes rises sharply. Among persons 65 to 74 years of age, one in every one hundred lives in a nursing home. The number increases to seven out of one hundred among persons 75 to 84, and over one fifth by 85 and older (Eustis et al. 1984). Data from the 1985 National Nursing Home Survey show that residents aged 85 and over comprise 45% of the aged nursing home population (Hing 1987). The 85 and older group is the fastest growing segment of our population; a 91 percent increase is anticipated by the year 2000 (Wolff et al.

1988). Consequently, the demand for nursing home beds is bound to increase. According to current projections, the nursing home population will reach 2 million by the year 2000 and 4.6 million by 2040 (U.S. Senate 1987–88).

Use of nursing homes by minority groups differs from that of whites. While 5 percent of the white elderly reside in long-term care facilities, fewer (4 percent) of the black aged, and only 2 percent of the aged of other races are nursing home residents (Hing 1987). Residents are typically female, reflecting the facts that women live longer than men and that persons without a spouse are more likely to enter nursing homes. The two most powerful predictors of nursing home placement are being 85 or older and living without a spouse at home. However, when considering clusters of characteristics rather than individual predictors, even for those persons in the younger 65–74 age group the probability of institutionalization is over 50 percent when this constellation of risk factors is present: no spouse at home, recent hospital admission, residing in retirement housing, at least one problem with basic activities of daily living, and mental impairment (Shapiro and Tate 1988).

POLICY

Nursing home care is paid for primarily through private resources (50 percent) and public sources (48 percent). Only about 1 percent is paid for by private insurance (Wolf and Weisbrod 1988). Public sources include Medicare and Medicaid. Medicare, which covers nearly all persons 65 or older, provides limited coverage for nursing home care, available only if strict criteria are met. Until recently, Medicare, which does not cover custodial care, covered up to 100 days of skilled nursing care after a hospitalization. The Catastrophic Coverage Act of 1988 would have increased the maximum number of days Medicare covered to 150 per year and eliminated the prior hospitalization requirement. Because this legislation was repealed in 1989, the future of nursing home benefits is unclear at the time of this writing. Medicaid, the primary source of public funds for nursing home care provides coverage only after a person has exhausted his or her other resources. Because eligibility is based on ability to pay, savings must be spent down to the qualifying level in order to receive benefits. Eligibility standards do vary somewhat from state to state because Medicaid is a federal and state program. Private long-term care insurance generally follows the Medicare model, focusing on skilled nursing rather than custodial care. Policies are expensive and persons considered to be high risk can be excluded. Consequently, private long-term care insurance cannot realistically be seen as a viable option for financing nursing home care (Wiener et al. 1987).

In the past, nursing homes were generally reimbursed on the basis of flat per diem rates. Recently many states have changed to some form of prospective payment or payment according to a case-mix formula (Kane and Kane 1987). For example, in New York, a system called Resource Utilization Groups (RUGs) was developed to deal with the impact of case-mix on nursing home costs. A score is computed for each resident, taking into account requirements for nursing and activities of daily living care. A facility's case-mix index is derived by averaging the residents' scores. A higher case-mix index translates into more Medicaid reimbursement (Selikson and Ellsworth 1987).

Changes in reimbursement for hospital care under Medicare are assumed to have impacted on nursing home admissions. Under the prospective payment system introduced in the 1980s, a hospital patient is identified by a diagnosis related group (DRG) and reimbursement is paid at a fixed rate determined by that DRG. As a consequence, hospitals have a strong impetus to discharge patients quickly. Older people who at one time stayed in the hospital to recover or to die, are now being discharged when acute care is no longer necessary. Because people are being discharged with greater needs for care than in the past, nursing homes are likely to be affected in several ways. Residents may enter nursing homes with more intensive medical needs or more need for intensive rehabilitation services. In addition, more people may be transferred to nursing homes for the final stages of dying, when acute care is no longer indicated (Peterson 1986). One study in Portland, Oregon, found that the total number of nursing home deaths increased by over 20 percent after the introduction of DRGs (Lyles 1986). An added complication of efforts to discharge patients from hospitals as early as possible is the tremendous pressure on patients and their families to make difficult decisions about nursing home placement in a short period of time.

THE OMBUDSMAN PROGRAM

Older people living in nursing homes are a vulnerable population for two primary reasons: their increasing frailty or cognitive impairment and their dependence on facility staff. Frailty and infirmity make it difficult for residents to monitor or protest infringement of their rights. In addition, feelings of powerlessness and the fear of retaliation engendered by being dependent on institutional caregivers frequently prevent residents from speaking up in their own behalf. These factors, together with the alarming history of abuse in some nursing homes, underscore the need for someone to advocate for and protect the rights of residents of long-term care facilities. The federal government's response to this need has been the nursing home ombudsman program.

Throughout the 1970s and 1980s, the ombudsman program was developed, refined, and strengthened. In 1972 and 1973, as part of initiatives to improve nursing homes, ombudsmen were included in seven demonstration projects. The 1975 amendments to the Older Americans Act provided for grants for state ombudsman development. The 1978 amendments mandated state ombudsman services for all nursing homes (Litwin 1985). Most recently, the 1987 amendments strengthened the program, and the 1987 Nursing Home Reform Quality of Care Amendments guaranteed ombudsmen immediate access to any nursing home resident and, with the permission of the resident or his or her legal guardian, an opportunity to examine clinical records.

Ombudsman programs operate at the state and local levels. At the state level, the focus is on five major functions: "complaint investigation, technical assistance and training, advocacy including coordination with other state agencies, public education, and program management and development" (NASUA 1988, p.i). Local ombudsman programs deal directly with nursing homes, handling individual residents' complaints and working to resolve these complaints within and in cooperation with the facility. Organization and administration at the local level varies from state to state. Some states rely primarily on paid staff to provide direct ombudsman services while others make extensive use of trained volunteers.

Local ombudsmen visit nursing homes in order to receive, investigate, and resolve complaints made by or on behalf of residents of the facility. After receiving a complaint, the ombudsman makes an investigation in order to verify and fully assess the grievance before determining the best way to proceed. Ombudsmen often turn to nursing home social workers for information about or verification of residents' complaints. Social workers are frequently involved in the resolution process as well. For the most part, grievances are resolved within the nursing home in collaboration with the administrator and staff. In situations where an appropriate outcome cannot be reached at the facility level, the ombudsman will make use of outside resources such as the state health department.

Generally, ombudsmen work closely with nursing home social workers, seeing them as important allies in the advocacy process. It is sometimes more difficult for social workers to view ombudsmen in an equally positive way. Social workers may feel that ombudsmen, in mediating and advocating for residents' rights, are infringing on a role that has traditionally been theirs. In addition, professional social workers may have reservations about the expertise or judgment of paraprofessional advocates. However, nursing home ombudsmen do make a difference, especially in highlighting quality of care issues that go beyond the minimum required by law (Litwin and Monk 1987). When social workers recognize this advantage to residents' quality of life, they are motivated to overcome their reservations and see ombudsmen as valuable allies.

SOCIAL WORK IN NURSING HOMES

The federal code requires that nursing homes arrange for someone to be responsible for providing social work services. This person need not have professional training. When a facility employs someone without a professional degree, arrangements must be made for consultation by a professional social worker. There is no minimum number of hours for professional consultation. Although individual states can mandate more stringent requirements, this is not always the case. Some nursing homes do opt to set higher standards themselves and employ professional social workers on their staffs. Nonetheless, the complex and demanding job of the nursing home social worker is frequently performed by people without specialized training and with limited consultation from a professional. This problem will be alleviated to some extent by the 1987 Quality of Care Amendments, effective October 1990, which require at least one full time professional social worker (having at least a bachelor's degree in social work or similar professional qualifications) for facilities with more than 120 beds (NASW 1988).

Theoretical Foundation for Practice

Because nursing homes have always been part of a broader medical care program, they have been strongly influenced by the medical model. Even facilities that actively strive to avoid the use of a medical model must combat the ongoing subtle influence of this perspective. The medical model focuses on eradicating disease and is predicated on the idea of individual deficiency. The model is grounded in a belief that because professionals have specialized knowledge, they are the agents of change. The client bows to the professionals' greater expertise, is expected to passively submit to and has no say in the treatment process (Weick 1983).

Because the medical model deals with people on the basis of their deficits rather than their strengths, it is easy for a nursing home to become entrapped in this view. This is partly due to stereotypes that perpetuate a picture of old people as dependent and incapable of managing their own lives. Of greater impact, however, is the reality that residents are in a nursing home precisely because they have many deficits, frequently including cognitive impairment. According to the 1985 National Nursing Home Survey, 63 percent of elderly nursing home residents were disoriented or memory impaired (Hing 1987). Well meaning staff members often assume a paternalistic attitude toward cognitively impaired residents, unwittingly supporting a medical model of care.

In contrast to the medical model, nursing home social work practice is grounded in a psychosocial model, based on an ecological perspective which recognizes the complex interplay between people and their environments. Maluccio's discussion of ecological competence is particularly pertinent to social work practice in nursing homes:

> In traditional formulations, competence is generally considered a property or trait of the person; the burden of competence is placed primarily on the person. In contrast, in the ecological approach, competence becomes a transactional concept; it is defined as an attribute of the *transaction* between the person and the environment. (1981:7)

An environment that deals with people on the basis of their deficits undermines their competence. Rather than focusing on deficits, the social worker focuses on identifying and nurturing remaining strengths. The social worker frequently serves as an advocate for this perspective in the facility, helping the staff see that even residents with severe cognitive impairment retain residual abilities. A prerequisite to uncovering and tapping these abilities is the recognition that, as Edelson and Lyons (1985) point out, "the impaired person's environment is . . . as puzzling to him as his seemingly irrational behavior is to us" (p. 5). It is essential to understand that behavior has meaning and can be an effort to communicate. This effort to communicate is a strength. Social work in nursing homes reflects a commitment to attend to residents' psychosocial as well as physical needs with a focus on remaining strengths or assets. Residents are seen as capable of taking meaningful action on their own behalf, even if this action is simply repetitive banging on a table to signal distress.

Social Work Intervention

Social work practice in nursing homes consists of three general phases of service delivery: admission, living in the facility, and discharge, transfer, or death. Because the nursing home social worker assumes several roles in the course of providing services, a review of these roles is woven into the following discussion, illustrating how they are performed throughout the process of service delivery. The social worker may assume the role of counsellor, educator, mediator, and advocate, as well as interdisciplinary team member and resource person.

ADMISSION

Admission to a nursing home is an emotional, painful process. The potential resident, already dealing with loss of health and functioning, must now face the loss of home, familiar surroundings, and a good deal of control of his or her own life. In making the difficult decision to pursue nursing home placement, well meaning family members may offer false reassurance in the hope of making the process easier by avoiding direct discussion of painful or frightening feelings. Potential residents may be excluded from the planning because family members are concerned that they will become upset or will not understand (Bogo 1987). The very ways families often try to protect their loved ones may compound the loss of control and make the infirm older person feel incompetent and powerless.

The social worker must, from the beginning, be sensitive to families' desires to protect their elders from pain, while working to include the potential resident in the planning to the fullest possible extent. The social worker may assume an educator role at this time, helping family members understand the relationship between being part of the decision making process and later adjustment to nursing home living.

Ideally, the social worker meets with prospective residents and their families prior to the final decision for admission. During this period the social worker acts as a counselor, providing support, and an educator, familiarizing everyone involved with the nursing home and the admission process. When placement is the end result of a relatively long period of planning, this can be the case. Unfortunately, when need for placement is determined by a crisis, there may be little time for preadmission contact. In addition, when placement results from pressure for discharge from the hospital, both resident and family may feel they have little control of the process. Some people may feel they have been pressured into a nursing home placement that could have been avoided altogether with a longer hospital stay. In these situations, the social worker is an essential source of support on and after admission. It is crucial that the social worker help residents and families recognize and deal with the anger, frustration, and fear that can result from admission to a nursing home without adequate preparation. If these feelings are not attended to, they may be misdirected at the facility, making adjustment very difficult.

The actual admission to a nursing home can be a shock even for the best-prepared resident. It is impossible to anticipate the full impact of such changes as sharing a room with a stranger, adapting to an institutional schedule, or giving up so much privacy on a long-term basis. At the same time, however, nursing home living can offer positives beyond the assurance of provision for basic physical needs. There is some empirical evidence that impaired older people in nursing homes have higher life satisfaction than those receiving health care in their own homes (Salamon 1987). A nursing home offers a potential social environment, something often lacking for older persons confined to their homes. Families, relieved of the burdens of caregiving, may be able to spend more quality time with their elders. A resident who is seriously ill or in need of a great deal of assistance may find comfort in the accessibility of staff members. Social workers can help residents and families recognize and work through both the positives and negatives of nursing home living.

From the first contact, the social worker begins collecting information to develop a full, individualized picture of the resident and an assessment of his or her current life situation, level of functioning, and capabilities. Special attention is given to identifying strengths, assets, and residual abilities that can be nurtured in the facility. The social worker plays a crucial role in educating staff members by providing the psychosocial information necessary to fully understand and individualize each resident. At times, the social worker may need to mediate between the resident and facility staff in order to ensure that individual strengths are recognized. For example,

> Mr. Moore was very protective of his possessions and struck out at anyone who attempted to move his books or toilet articles, even to clean them. He was labled as cantankerous by staff members. They dealt with the problem by coming to clean when he was out of the room, which only upset him more. The social worker reframed the situation by suggesting that Mr. Moore was a very organized man who took pride in his possessions. A clean-

ing schedule was worked out so that he would know when to expect the housekeeper and could "supervise" her work.

Family members may have considerable difficulty dealing with nursing home placement. In addition to grieving the loss of a loved one as they once knew him or her, families generally feel guilty for placing a relative in a nursing home. When family members feel relieved to be freed of caregiving responsibilities, they must deal with the additional guilt that accompanies this relief. Overwhelmed by painful, confusing feelings, sometimes family members become over involved in day-to-day nursing home life or become increasingly withdrawn from the resident. Families often benefit from social work services during this difficult period, to deal with their painful feelings and reach an acceptance of the nursing home placement.

The social worker carefully observes family patterns of coping and interacting, as these will impact on the relationship between family members and the institution as well as between family and resident. The social worker may help families work through difficulties that interfere with positive adjustment. In the case of long-standing difficulties that are played out in the nursing home situation but go far beyond it, a referral to community resources for counseling may be indicated. However, some family members will not be receptive to social services, and their wishes must be respected.

It is vitally important to support the maintenance of residents' family ties. Research had shown that continued family involvement after nursing home placement is important to resident well-being (Harel 1981; Greene and Monahan 1982). Families should be viewed as a resource, in partnership with the facility in providing care to the aged (Solomon 1982). Family and nursing home staff should work together in carrying out realistic plans to meet residents' needs.

When admission to the facility is expected to be time-limited as for rehabilitation or recovery from illness, resident and family may need help determining the extent to which to maintain previous living arrangements during placement. The social worker can help resident and family avoid precipitous decisions by assuming a supportive, educative role, focusing on the consequences of potential changes and the full range of available alternatives.

LIVING IN THE NURSING HOME

As in any living situation, some people find nursing home living easier than do others. For some residents or families, there may be little need for contact with the social worker once they have settled in to the facility. For others, the need may be considerable. The social worker's involvement with residents and families is determined by their individual circumstances.

Frequently, change is the key factor in determining the need for social work services. Residents may experience change in family visitation patterns, a new roommate, death of a friend or loved one, problems with a staff member or another resident, and so on. The social worker can often be instrumental in helping residents deal with these upheavals. For example, residents should be fully prepared for a change in room or roommate. The social worker works directly with the resident, helping him or her anticipate the impact of the change, and may also have to advocate with other staff members to ensure that the resident is as fully involved in the process as possible. When a change must be made quickly with little time for preparation, as when a roommate dies and a new one is immediately admitted, the social worker deals not only with the resident's reaction to the change, but his or her sense of powerlessness and lack of control as well. In situations where administrative decisions appear to conflict with a social work orientation, it is helpful to bear in mind that administrative priorities such as keeping beds filled reflect an agenda that, although different from social work's, is essential to keeping the institution operating productively.

Just as residents sometimes need assistance dealing with changes in their lives, families may turn to the social worker when struggling with such issues as their elders' complaints about nursing home living or their physical or mental deterioration. The social worker can be helpful to families through supportive counseling or education about, for example, the anticipated progression of an illness. In addition, the social worker may mediate between families and staff members when difficulties develop.

Often, a particularly helpful intervention is linking family members with other families in the facility (Brubaker and Schiefer 1981). Such linkages will often lead to a support network which enables family members to draw upon their own strengths and resources in providing support to each other. For example,

> Several families were struggling with their elders' increasing cognitive impairment. Some family members privately shared with the social worker their questions about how to make visiting more enjoyable. The social worker invited these families to join a new group which would focus on dealing with this concern. In the first meeting, participants actively shared not only

their concerns, but their relief that others were having the same experience as well. Over the next two sessions (the group had contracted for three sessions), group members shared effective ways they had found for improving quality of visits. When the group ended, two of the members had decided to visit at the same time so that they could support one another. Two others had agreed to keep an eye on each other's mother when one was not able to visit.

As this example demonstrates, groups are often an effective way of providing services. This holds true of work with residents as well as families. Groups not only make optimum use of the social worker's time, they afford people the potential of being helpful to others. For residents, who are generally in the position of being helped, being able to provide something of value to another is empowering and nurtures strengths. The crucial factor is that the social worker make the decision to provide group services based on best serving the needs of residents and families. Some people are unable to make use of group services and some problems are best dealt with on an individual basis.

Because the bulk of care to nursing home residents is provided by nursing aides, who may have limited training or experience working with the frail elderly, social workers can play a crucial role in educating staff members about residents' psychosocial needs through the facility's in-service program. To achieve maximum effectiveness, the social worker should tailor programs to reflect current concerns or problems in the facility rather than presenting arbitrarily chosen topics. In addition, utilizing techniques such as role play can heighten staff engagement in the learning process (Gutheil 1985). The advocacy role at times overlaps with that of educator, when the social worker uses in-service to present the resident or family point of view.

As part of an interdisciplinary team, the social worker takes the interests of both clients and facility into consideration. This role is constantly challenging because representatives from other disciplines bring their own perspectives and priorities to the team. These differing approaches can lead to strikingly different ideas about the best way to achieve the same goals.

Social workers also serve as links between residents and resources outside the facility. Every effort should be made to keep members of the community such as volunteer visitors, students in local schools, entertainment groups, and so on involved with residents. In nursing homes with strong activities departments, social workers are less involved in many of these linkages. However, responsibility for connecting residents with certain resources such as mental health services in the community generally remains the social worker's domain.

DISCHARGE, TRANSFER, OR DEATH

Transferring or being discharged from the facility generally reactivates feelings of loss and fear. The nursing home environment is familiar and predictable. Patterns of living have been established and new relationships formed. Even the resident who is eager to return home is likely to experience some fear about being able to "make it" with less help. Residents who are being transferred to another facility because they require a higher level of care must mourn loss of functioning at the same time they are wondering if the new institution will be better or worse than what they are leaving. In addition, any major change in physical environment can be stressful and may distress both residents and families (Greenfield 1984).

As soon as transfer or discharge becomes a possibility, the social worker begins preparing residents and families for this change. Reasons for the move should be clearly explained and questions encouraged. Some fears, such as the quality of another institution, can be allayed through providing information or arranging a preadmission visit. Families and residents should be involved in the discharge planning to the fullest possible extent, although a resident's impairment may severely curtail his or her ability to participate.

During this period, the social worker generally combines the counseling and educative roles. It is important to anticipate with the resident and family the kinds of alterations the discharge or transfer will make in their lives. If a resident is returning home, family members may need to provide care or supervise caregivers. Helping family anticipate and plan for the accompanying changes in their own lives can help prevent problems later on. Similarly, helping family members predict the impact of factors such as greater travel distance to a new facility can foster advance planning and may prevent later stress. Sometimes in the tumult of a major change, details such as these may be overlooked. However, it is often these details that cause problems later.

In preparing for discharge, the social worker assesses the need for community resources and ensures that services are in place when the resident leaves the facility. When a resident transfers, the social worker contacts appropriate staff members in the new facility to effect the best possible transition to the new environment.

Many residents will die in the nursing home. When death comes quickly or unexpectedly, family members may need help dealing with the fact that they never had a chance to say goodbye. When dying is more clearly a process, both resident and family experience a range of painful emotions, but also have an opportunity to put closure on the relationship. The dying resident who is aware and alert will need special attention as he or she faces death. Reminiscing is often a great comfort at this time. Residents with severe cognitive impairment can benefit from gentle touch or reassurance that they are not alone. Other residents in the facility may need support as they struggle with their own reactions to another's death.

Some families prefer to rely on their own resources for dealing with death while others gratefully accept the social worker's offer of support. For families, as with residents, reminiscing can be of considerable therapeutic value. Family members struggle with many intense and painful feelings during this period and can benefit from reassurance that their reactions are normal. When a loved one has suffered or become severely demented, family members may feel that death is a blessing. They must then deal with the guilt that accompanies such feelings. For this reason, many families can benefit from social work contact for a brief period after the resident's death. If the nursing home social worker is not able to provide this service, referral to a community resource may be indicated. Finally, it is important to bear in mind that not everyone feels grief upon the death of a family member or wants help in dealing with grief. People need the opportunity to react to death in their own way, in a nonjudgemental environment.

CURRENT CONCERNS

There are several areas of special concern in nursing homes that spring primarily from institutions' responses to the growing needs of residents. This section addresses these concerns.

Because providing quality care to people with Alzheimer's Disease requires a special environment and carefully trained staff, a number of nursing homes have created specialized units for residents with severe mental impairment. These units generally segregate the demented residents and work to create an environment that is geared to their unique needs. Because these residents tend to have difficulty adapting to their environment, a major goal of the unit is to prevent either overstimulation or understimulation (Peppard 1985/86). Every effort is made to provide consistency in programming and staffing. Whenever possible, programs are brought to the unit to reduce resident anxiety about leaving a familiar place. Staff members receive special training to help them fully understand residents' needs and efforts to communicate. Social workers play an important role in helping staff members understand the special needs of demented residents and their families and in supporting staff members who must work tirelessly to create a specialized environment (Grossman et al. 1985/86).

Two factors have combined to compel nursing homes to consider the Do-Not-Rescusitate (DNR) issue: the increasing number of acutely ill residents being admitted and increasing attention to residents' rights. Many nursing homes are in the process of formulating DNR policies. One study found that almost half the facilities surveyed had formal or informal policies to address the DNR issue (Longo et al. 1988). In homes that do not have policies in place, there may be mounting pressure as staff members increasingly face difficult treatment decisions with no advance directives from residents or families (Levenson et al. 1987). One way to deal with formulation of DNR policies is to establish an institutional ethics committee to create a forum for discussion and planning. Although ethics committees are not common in nursing homes, their numbers are increasing. Typically, the social worker serves on the committee (Brown et al. 1987). As DNR policies demand increasing attention, social workers are likely to become involved either through participation in discussions establishing facility policies, educating staff members about the purpose and value of such policies, or direct work with residents and families during the period of decision making.

Increasing attention has been directed in recent years to the impact of the physical environment on people's lives. Because residents generally spend most of their time in the nursing home, the physical environment of the facility has a continuous, powerful impact on their lives. Social workers, with their understanding of the interrelatedness of people and their environments, are especially well suited to studying and working to improve the nursing home's physical environment. The kinds of things social workers should be attuned to include mechanisms that promote resident privacy and the availability of special areas in resident rooms so that each occupant has his or her own space. There are many other aspects of the physical environment social workers should be aware of. For example, color-coded halls and room numbers or name signs in large letters at wheelchair height help residents remain as oriented and independent as possible. Social interaction between residents can be encouraged by seating them at corners or across from each other rather than side by side (Sommer 1959). A prized possession or pictures of family can help individualize a room and create familiar surroundings. In observing the physical environment of the nursing home, social workers can play an important advocate role, working to achieve an environment that is supportive of residents' strengths and dignity.

Documentation requirements make tremendous demands on staff time in nursing homes. Social workers in particular frequently feel frustrated by the time documentation takes away from their direct contact with residents and families. Since documentation is mandated, social workers have no choice but to adapt to this requirement. It is helpful, however, to remember that documentation has some real benefits. It is a way to systematically convey vital psychosocial information to other staff members so that resident care can remain sensitive and individualized. In addition, having to record work with residents and families ensures that social workers take the time to formulate clearly thought out assessments, goals, and treatment plans. Finally, documentation provides a formal record of the social worker's work with residents and families, demonstrating the impact and value of the psychosocial perspective.

The final concern to be discussed here is burnout. Nursing home social work is a demanding, complex job. Workers frequently feel there are not enough hours in the day to attend fully to all of their responsibilities. At times, the social work perspective is at odds with others in the facility and the worker may feel frustrated in his or her attempts to foster an environment that recognizes and promotes residents' strengths and recognizes families as valuable resources. This frustration can be demoralizing, and prevent social workers from experiencing the many satisfactions their job offers. The importance of support in counteracting this effect should not be underestimated. Nelsen notes that: "Social workers should . . . be aware that when they do not receive support within their professional settings, they may be less able to offer support to their clients" (1980:390).

In facilities with two or more social workers, there is a ready source of support. Regularly scheduled department meetings or informal get togethers offer an opportunity for social workers to air frustrations and be supportive of one another. When there is only one social worker in the facility, he or she may find other staff members with whom to develop this kind of relationship. Many localities have organizations that bring together social workers in nursing homes or health care settings in general. These associations are of great value because they often provide educational forums and advocacy as well as organized support networks. Like support, ongoing education can help prevent burnout.

Ongoing education or professional training can contribute significantly to the nursing home social worker's ability to do his or her job effectively. Social workers play a crucial role in the provision of services to nursing home residents and their families. They assure that psychosocial needs will be recognized and attended to. Their job encompasses an array of roles which call upon a wide variety of skills. The skills required to perform this complex job must not be underestimated. The more trianing nursing home social workers have, the better able they will be to provide quality services.

REFERENCES

Achenbaum, W. A. 1978. *Old Age in the New Land.* Baltimore: Johns Hopkins University Press.

Bogo, M. 1987. Social work practice with family systems in admission to homes for the aged. *Journal of Gerontological Social Work* 10(1/2);5–20.

Brown, B. A., S. H. Miles, and M. A. Aroskar. 1987. The prevalence and design of ethics committees in nursing homes. *Journal of the American Geriatric Society* 35(11):1028–1033.

Brubaker, E. and A. W. Schiefer. 1987. Groups with families of elderly long-term care residents: building social support networks. *Journal of Gerontological Social Work* 10(1/2):167–175.

Eustis, N., J. Greenberg, and S. Patten, 1984. *Long-Term Care for Older Persons: A Policy Perspective.* Monterey, Calif.: Brooks/Cole.

Green, V. L. and D. J. Monahan. 1982. The impact of visitation on patient well-being in nursing homes. *The Gerontologist* 22(4):419–423.

Greenfield W. L. 1984. Disruption and reintegration: dealing with familial response to nursing home placement. *Journal of Gerontological Social Work* 8(1/2):15–21.

Grossman, H. D., A. S. Weiner, M. J. Salamon, and N. Burros. (1985/86). The milieu standard for care of dementia in a nursing home. *Journal of Gerontological Social Work* 9(2):73–89.

Gutheil, I. A. 1985. Sensitizing nursing home staff to residents' psychosocial needs. *Clinical Social Work Journal* 13(4):356–366.

Harel, Z. 1981. Quality of care, congruence and well-being among institutionalized aged. *The Gerontologist* 21(5):523–531.

Hing, E. 1987. Use of nursing homes by the elderly, preliminary data from the 1985 National Nursing Home Survey. *Advance Data From Vital and Health Statistics.* National Center for Health Statistics. No. 135. DHHS Pub. No. (PHS) 87-1250. Public Health Service. Hyattsville, Md., May 14.

Kane, R. A. and R. L. Kane. 1987. *Long-Term Care: Principles, Programs, and Policies.* New York: Springer.

Levinson, W., M. A. Shepard, P. M. Dunn, and D. F. Parker. 1987. Cardiopulminary resuscitation in long-term care facilities: A survey of do-not-resuscitate orders in nursing homes. *Journal of the American Geriatrics Society* 35(12):1059–1062.

Liang, J. and E. J. Tu, 1986. Estimating lifetime risk of nursing home residency: a further note. *The Gerontologist* 26(5):560–563.

Litwin, H. 1985. Ombudsman services. In A. Monk, ed. *Handbook of Gerontological Services.* New York: Van Nostrand Reinhold.

Litwin, H. and A. Monk. 1987. Do nursing home ombudsmen make a difference? *Journal of Gerontological Social Work* 11(1/2):95–104.

Longo, D. R., R. Burmeister, and M. Warren. 1988. Do not resuscitate: policy and practice in the long-term care setting. *The Journal of Long-Term Care Administration* 16(1):5–11.

Lyles, Y. M. 1986. Impact of medicare diagnosis related groups (DRGs) on nursing homes in the Portland, Oregon metropolitan area. *Journal of the American Geriatrics Society* 34(8):573–578.

Maluccio, A. N. 1981. Competence-oriented social work practice: an ecological approach. In A. N. Maluccio, ed., *Promoting Competence in Clients.* New York: Free Press.

NASUA (National Association of State Units on Aging). 1988. *Comprehensive analysis of state long-term care ombudsman offices.* Washington, D.C.: GPO.

NASW (National Association of Social Workers). 1988. The 1987 nursing home reform legislation, the agenda for social workers. *Social Work Practice Update.*

Nelsen, J. 1980. Support: a necessary condition for change. *Social Work* 25(5): 388–392.

Peppard, N. R. 1985/86. Special nursing home units for residents with primary degenerative dementia: Alzeheimer's Disease. *Journal of Gerontological Social Work* 9(2):5–13.

Peterson, K. J. 1986. Changing needs of patients and families in long-term care facilities: implications for social work practice. *Social Work in Health Care* 12(2):37–49.

Salamon, M. J. 1987. Health care environment and life satisfaction in the elderly. *Journal of Aging Studies* 1(3):287–297.

Scharlach, A. and C. Frenzel. 1986. Evaluation of institution-based respite care. *The Gerontologist* 26(1):77–82.

Selikson, S. and B. Ellsworth. 1987. Resource utilization groups: a clinical dilemma. Letters to the Editor. *Journal of the American Geriatrics Society* 35:11:1034–1035.

Shapiro, E. and R. Tate, 1988. Who is really at risk of institutionalization? *The Gerontologist* 28(2):237–245.

Solomon, R. 1982. Serving families of the institutionalized aged: the four crises. *Journal of Gerontological Social Work* 5(1/2):83–96.

Sommer, R. 1959. Studies in personal space. *Sociometry* 22(3):247–260.

Strahan, G. 1987. Nursing home characteristics; Preliminary data from the 1985 National Nursing Home Survey. *Advance Data From Vital and Health Statistics.* National Center for Health Statistics. No. 131. DHHS Pub. No. (PHS) 87-1250. Public Health Service. Hyattsville, Md.

U.S. Senate. 1987–88. Special Committee on Aging. *Aging America: Trends and Projections.* Washington, D.C.: U.S. Department of Health and Human Services.

Waldman, S. 1985. A legislative history of nursing home care. In R. J. Vogel and H. C. Palmer, eds., *Long-Term Care: Perspectives from Research and Demonstrations.* Rockville, Md.: Aspen.

Weick, A. 1983. Issues in overturning a medical model of social work practice. *Social Work* 28(6):467–471.

Wiener, J. M., D. A. Ehrenworth, and D. A. Spence. 1987. Private long-term care insurance: Cost, coverage, and restrictions. *The Gerontologist* 27(4):487–493.

Wolff, N., B. A. Weisbrod, and S. Stearns. 1988. Summary proceedings long-term care for the elderly: issues and options. *Journal of Aging Studies* 2(1):83–94.

21

Respite and Adult Day Services

❖

ELOISE RATHBONE-MCCUAN, PH.D.
University of Kansas, Lawrence

The purpose of this paper is to offer practical information about two distinct but related social service programs utilized by older persons and their families. Both are of growing importance in the United States as the population of frail elderly and their primary caregiver's age. The first service, respite care, is temporary and supportive, offered to caregivers; the second, adult day care, provides longer term health and social services to older community residents. Each is designed and operated as a component of community service systems. Unfortunately, seldom is either service available or accessible at the community level in proportion to need.

Each service may be valuable for elderly persons unable to perform essential activities of daily living or to experience meaningful social interactions without assistance. Those who utilize one service often benefit from the functions provided through the other service. An elderly day care center participant, for example, may receive respite care through a home health agency because his spouse, who is the primary caregiver, is hospitalized. He continues to participate in the center while she receives respite support. The wife's illness and need for respite in no way reduces the importance of day care for the elderly husband and in fact reduces the number of hours each day that respite is needed.

Sections of the paper will address the need for respite and day care service, the composition and structure of both, and the development and delivery of each service. Social service practitioners assume numerous and diverse roles in the delivery of these services such as functional assessment, direct service referral, care plan management, service eligibility determination, and service monitoring. Additionally, practitioners may accept responsibility for developing or expanding the availability of services or improving the quality of existing resources. Social service expertise is central to the success of respite services and day care center programming.

Increasingly, social service practitioners desire to provide services to the elderly in a manner that supports the caregiving efforts of families. The outreach of formal care sources to the informal care network is a pattern relevant in many social service systems to reduce discontinuities in care. Family and others in the informal care network receive the brunt of providing in home services for very disabled elderly. This help far exceeds the amount of service available for elders through arrangements such as nursing homes, day centers and other programs. A family perspective is applied throughout, however, the author recognizes that nonfamily caregivers also need opportunities for respite and that persons without a family support system use day care services to great advantage.

RESPITE CARE AS A CORE SERVICE

Studies of actual caregiving situation involving frail elderly contribute evidence for the need to structure and provide respite functions in a manner that meets the expectations of both the person who is in need and the caregiving network members for whom temporary assistance is sought (Silverstone 1982). The connection between care provided by the family and an elder's ability to stay at home is well documented. Research demonstrates relatively comparable levels of function between old persons in nursing homes and those receiving in home care (Moore 1987). In the beginning of this decade, federal policy defined respite care as temporary services for an individual who is unable to care for himself on a full time bases because of the absence of the person who typically cares for the individual (U.S. Congress 1980). As more respite resources have been created that limited definition has been expanded to include preventive concerns for the stresses of the caregiver.

Stress among caregivers has become a "spotlight" issue in connection with the widespread concern about the consequences of Alzheimer's disease and its prevalence that ranges from 1.5 million to 2.0 million with every indication that greater numbers of people will become its victim. The victimizing impact of Alzheimer's disease is shared between the ill person and their caregivers (Lund, Pett, and Caserta 1987). Other chronic diseases where the potential of major rehabilitative gains are lessened by preexisting health conditions, level of cognitive impairment, severity of medical conditions, and ability to tolerate intensive therapy (Becker and Kaufman 1988) create situations of burdening care.

Respite care is not a single mode of care but an array of different patterns that will be explored in the following section. Some respite care is organized through volunteer efforts of caregivers who exchange help and other sources are more formalized as a component of comprehensive efforts to maintain community residence. A nationwide example of respite services being integrated with home care, outpatient clinics, and geriatric assessment is developing within the Veterans Administration medical care system. That system, like others, place respite care under the category of extended rather than acute care. That view is reflected in the following discussion of different respite care delivery models.

Models of Respite Care

Gerontological practitioners often define very narrowly and loosely the sources of respite care. The concept gets joined with very specific categories of special care arrangements now popular in other countries. Night care, weekend care, vacation care, and floating beds, for example, are approaches built into the approved and financed use of institutional and quasi-institutional settings. These represent the "bed space strategies" that rely on out-of-home resources for respite care as a way to avoid the costs of empty beds. Only limited use has been made of these strategies in the United States. Respite strategies employed in this country must fit into restrictive third-party cost regulations that may ignore the less visible costs of empty extended care space.

Social service providers should view respite for caregivers of frail elderly as broadly defined and diversely provided. One useful specification of respite service alternatives identified from the field of developmental disabilities continues to illustrate current alternative models that are more or less available for geriatric care. Kinney (1979) described five models of respite care valuable to the parents of handicapped children. These models, with their various strengths and limitations, are all potentially applicable to some segment of the aged population requiring respite care:

1. *In-Home Respite Care.* Specifically trained respite providers (preferably persons who already know the family) go into the home while the caregiver is away.
2. *Out-of-Home Respite Care.* The impaired person moves into the home of the respite provider which serves as a temporary foster home.
3. *Respite Group Home.* The impaired person moves into a setting specifically planned to be a respite facility for multiple persons who need respite care and approximates the permanent residential environment.
4. *Group Home Respite.* The impaired person moves into a permanent residence group home that is equipped with the capacity to accommodate a short-term stay person living in another permanent residence.
5. *Institutional Respite.* The impaired person moves into space designated for short-term respite use in a twenty-four-hour care facility that is devoted primarily to ongoing institutional services to patients.

Table 21.1 presents service characteristics that illustrate the variety of ways in which respite care can be organized and delivered for the elderly. Although the listing is not exhaustive, it suggests that elder respite care is not a unidimensional program. Some models are more popular, but it is important to continue to demonstrate the appropriateness of these and other variations as options for respite care.

IN-HOME RESPITE

Although there are similarities, the in home respite arrangement should not be confused with an elder companion service. This form typically involves care for a length of time that exceeds the brief period available from a companion program. Given the current limits of resources in most communities, the practitioner attempting to create respite alternatives may begin by contacting an agency that coordinates companion personnel or at least maintains a register of independent individuals available to provide such services. Examples of agencies where companions might be identified include home health agencies, visiting nurses, and senior citizen employment referrals. Through programs funded by ACTION, such as RSVP or Senior Companions, it is sometimes possible to identify older persons who will come to the home and provide care for another elder for a weekend or longer. Listings from agencies vary widely on such factors as: the extent to which the listing is current, the types of situations acceptable to the person who comes into the home, the references or other indicators of competency for the respite provider, the geographical area within which the respite provider is willing to travel, and the liability or insurance arrangements. The positive features of in-home respite arrangements include a lower cost than other forms of respite, less disruption to the older person because he/she remains in personal surroundings, and it is more quickly arrangeable than some other respite forms that require that space be available at the needed time. A negative feature of in-home respite is the discomfort that can be felt by both the aged person and family if the provider is a stranger. Also, unanticipated behavioral problems can arise because of a lack of familiarity between the individuals or with the caregiving procedures.

Families, independent of any agency assistance, find and utilize in-home respite providers. Some rely on the friendship network to iden-

TABLE 21.1. Critical Characteristics of Respite Care for Elders: The Beginning of a Typology

Respite Care Characteristics	*Alternative Program Approaches*
Location	Respite care can be delivered either in the home of the elder or by transporting the elder to a location where respite care is available. *In-Home Respite Care* is when specially trained respite providers travel to the home of the elder to provide care. *Out-of-Home Respite Care* is characterized by three primary approaches: (1) a *Respite Home* is where the elder temporarily moves into the home of the respite care provider; (2) a *Respite Group Home* is a facility that can accommodate more than one elder at a time for respite care; and (3) *Institutional Respite* is where public and private institutions (e.g. hospitals and nursing homes) maintain a few beds that are used for respite care on a rotating basis.
Timing	The need for respite care is sometimes a consequence of an *emergency*. The primary caregiver may be suddenly hospitalized, incapacitated, or overwhelmed by a personal crisis and unable to meet the needs of the

tify help or turn to the church or similar organization to identify a reliable person (Rathbone-McCuan and Hashimi 1982). They also will utilize word-of-mouth or advertise to generate a list of potential helpers. Others fulfill this need through their contacts with "caregiver support groups"—self-help support groups formed by individuals who are the primary source of care for an elder. Many families, however, would not consider contacting a professional service to find a suitable individual or, if they wanted to do, would not know what sources to contact. Getting families access to appropriate respite provider sources is an ongoing problem as the number of profit and nonprofit geriatric care agencies expand.

OUT-OF-HOME RESPITE

The concept of a respite home may reflect many similarities to foster home care for the elderly. It is a concept that has begun to be con-

TABLE 21.1. (*Continued*)

Respite Care Characteristics	*Alternative Program Approaches*
	elder. At other times, the timing of the respite care may be *planned*. Plans for a necessary business trip, vacation, or visit to kin may be made well in advance and respite care arranged for the dependent elder.
Arranging for respite care	In many instances, the *family* or *primary caregiver* makes all of the necessary arrangements for respite care—identifying providers, checking references arranging for transportation, and negotiating fees. In other cases, these details are handled by a formal *social-service agency*.
Service orientation	Most respite-care services are focused exclusively on providing for the physical, safety, and social needs of the elderly *individual*. Recently, however, there have been a growing number of services that use respite care as a vehicle for attending to the distinct needs of the entire *family*.

sidered for the elderly as family groups, service advocacy organizations, and citizen participation and demand increases. As applied to handicapped children, it is considered to be a relatively inexpensive approach that can be modified during emergency periods of crisis or illness (Kinney 1979). The adaptation of this form of respite as a model adopted for the elderly requires strong family advocacy networks to sustain the volunteer respite resources. While such a self-helping cadre is desirable, reliance on volunteer organized elder respite is of limited applicability because of the limited volunteer pool. When a fee is attached to the out-of-home model, the accessibility drops for many families.

RESPITE HOME

The respite home is a variation of the foster home because respite is not intended to be more than a brief stay arrangement. Many foster home care providers prefer that the resident care be very stable. Therefore, these providers may not desire to use their homes as respite resources because payment would be less predictable. Often it is difficult to identify the rare foster home that will accept a respite client. The invisibility of those that do often relates to the confusing systems that categorize foster homes, unreliable community lists, and the parameters of licensure and regulations (Steinhauer 1982).

If communities lack quality foster homes willing to offer respite placement, practitioners can initiate an effort to increase availability. There are several benefits to that process. First communities can expand their resources and second provide a more readily available referral list for families. It is important, however, that foster home providers be prepared for respite stay care, perhaps through special training that allows providers to qualify for a special certificate indicating they have received respite care preparation.

GROUP HOME RESPITE

Some of the features of foster home respite are similar to group home respite. The group home alternative has lagged behind other approaches in the evolution of noninstitutional alternatives for the aged. Nationwide, there is a limited supply of placement opportunities in geriatric group homes. Of those that exist, few are designed to serve as a source of respite. Lack of space and skill to help a respite stay elder integrate into the routine of other permanent residents in the setting are two problems that have received little attention. An expansion in the number and quality of the group home model requires more than the mere designation of a few existing group home placements reserved for respite. Also the cost of vacant space, beds reserved for respite care but not in use, is prohibitive to the overall operation. More effort is needed to experiment with the logistics of financing and staffing geriatric respite group homes as unforeseen family needs may extend the needed respite period and/or the rapid health decline of the person in the respite may create a medical crisis. These facilities would need to be integrated with emergency admission procedures at local hospitals that now often create a crisis for elders who need emergency admissions (Shepard, Mayer, and Ryback 1987).

INSTITUTIONAL RESPITE

Institution based respite, utilizing existing extended or long-term beds, has received the greatest attention in U.S. geriatric care. Until the implementation a national DRG linked acute hospital reimbursement system, there was a practice of admitting elderly people to an acute hospital for what was essentially caregiver respite. This practice was not an optimal means of offering respite, but it was often made available to family members by physicians concerned about the caregiver. In some cases this arrangement was a transition to institutional care. That option is no longer present in an era of utilization review and prospective reimbursement.

As noted earlier, the Veterans Administration has taken steps to establish respite care as a resource for qualified veterans. Respite care, while still considered an innovative approach under evaluation, must be designed to match the resources of local VA medical centers. Individual facilities must establish policies, procedures, and criteria for respite. It is mainly available to offer relief to a primary caregiver of a chronically ill veteran who is being managed and cared for at home.

There is a definite need to create institutional based respite as a component of a system of community long-term care. Their is no greater need among those who care for elderly with dementia conditions, but there are also disadvantages to institutional respite. For many elders and their families, a short stay institutional admission is unacceptable because it is perceived as contrary to their goal to prevent institutionalization. Furthermore, if there is no third party reimbursement the cost of even a short stay can be a substantial burden on resources. However, the most important drawback to use of institutional respite is the potential negative effect on the aged person who must endure a series of disruptions associated with entry and discharge. Their personal and emotional difficulties of hospital or nursing home admission are sufficiently great for the individual and family even when institutionalization is necessary.

Counseling as a Component of the Respite Process

Social workers and other professionals have made significant advancement in the extension of counseling as a resource for the respite care process. It is recognized as a multidimensional process involving significant social exchange within the caregiving network and requires coordination between family and community. The respite service models described here are seriously underdeveloped, but the demand will hopefully drive an increase in the diversity and quality of respite options.

Additional services have been recommended as valuable to at-risk families caring for the elderly. In the first version of this paper written several years ago, there was much literature discussing what might benefit caregivers. For example, Archbold (1982) was among the first to suggest that stress-related health screening be available to the caregiver, coping skills be fostered as part of the caregiving process, accurate and comprehensive information on referrals be readily available, and social and emotional support be extended.

Measurements of objective and subjective dimensions of caregiver burden are now in use widely to estimate the potential risks to caregivers (Gallo, Reichel, and Andersen 1988; Zarit, Todd, and Zarit 1986; Zarit and Zarit 1986) and data about information needed by caregivers is also a major service provided (Simonton 1987). Understanding of the real and anticipated consequences of burdening parental care has also been considered in assessing those risks that could be a focus of family concern (Cicirelli 1988).

Family therapy, either individual or group, adds to the array of professional services that can address needs associated with respite. Problems such as coping with parental caregiving and communication among the aged and younger family members are all situations that can be lessened through family therapy especially when counseling addresses the broader scope of problems created from the interaction with environmental resources (Bogo 1987; Zarit 1980).

Families always have the option of defining their own respite needs and locating appropriate resources to meet those needs without the involvement of a formal service agency. When families approach an agency for help in locating a source for respite no other social services may be requested or required. When additional services are needed and sought by the family short term counseling to facilitate service selection and utilization may be appropriate. Practitioners need to be aware that counseling efforts can be directed toward assisting families to map their own service priorities as a function of their assessment of the support needed to continue to offer care without undue and dangerous stress to the family. Even practitioners whose primary function is to provide therapeutic counseling should have a working and updated knowledge of community resources and to best explain to families their complexities of accessing those resources.

ADULT DAY CARE

Adult day care is a service delivery approach that offers community based long-term care support to the elderly and their caregivers. The continuous evolution of U.S. geriatric day care services has been influenced by many factors including the complex and restrictive policy environment governing its status as a legitimate care approach. As a long-term care service it has been evaluated consistently under the rubric of determining whether it is a viable alternative to institutional care and/or prevents institutionalization by a person's participation in a center program.

The growth of adult day care services has been slow yet consistent over the past twenty years. While it has developed unevenly in different states, the place of adult day care has become an increasingly important resource in the long-term care continuum. In spite of negative reimbursement policies for adult day care, there has been major expansion. There are approximately 1,400 day care programs listed in the most recent edition of the National Day Care Directory, which represents almost twice the number listed in the early 1980s (National Institute on Adult Daycare [NIAD], 1982, 1988). The purpose of this section is to describe the concept of adult day care from an historical perspective, discuss its current programmatic status and discuss some of the new interest in linking respite care into day care programming. Since the beginning of the adult day care movement social workers and nurses have played instrumental roles in planning, administering and staffing these programs. Despite the challenges faced in the creation and operation of adult day care programs, the dedication and quality of center staff continue to remain an outstanding characteristic of this service.

Overview of Adult Day Care Service Development

Day care first evolved as an alternative to mental hospitalization in Russia in the 1920s. Eventually the concept spread to this country and was used in programs for both the psychiatrically ill and the mentally retarded. The use of the concept in programs for the elderly took much longer to develop. Lionel Z. Cousin introduced the idea at the Oxford Hospitals in 1950, and a separate facility with its own staff was established in 1958 (Padula 1981). The concept of day care for the elderly grew successfully in England as part of that country's effort to develop a comprehensive system of geriatric care (Farndale 1961). It minimized institutionalization and coordinated and integrated hospital and community resources for the elderly (Brockelhurst 1973).

One of the persistent dilemmas faced by those who develop adult day care services is to formulate a definition of the service that can be useful in planning a program, developing policy, devising a reimbursement strategy, conforming to regulations, and educating the community to the goals of the program. The difficulty in defining adult day care is a function of the extent to which the concept is flexible, therefore, subject to programmatic variations. The lack of a uniform definition has been a point of frustration to policymakers with responsibilities for generating operational and reimbursement regulations.

Throughout the 1970s and 1980s there has been a systematic attempt to distinguish between programs that qualify as health oriented and those dominated by a social service approach. In the early 1970s when day care was still a new and very scarce resource a broad designation was common, but between 1976 and 1986 the distinction between a health and social emphasis became central to the initial design of programs. For the purpose of this discussion a general definition is applied and reflects the definition established in the 1984 Standards for Adult Day Care from the National Institute of Adult Daycare:

> Adult day care is a community-based group program designed to meet the needs of functionally impaired adults through an individual plan of care. It is a structured, comprehensive program that provides a variety of health, social and related support services in a protective setting during any part of a day but less that 24-hour care. Individuals who participate in adult day care attend on a planned bases during specified hours. Adult day care assists its participants to remain in the community, enabling families and other caregivers to continue caring for an impaired member at home. (NIAD 1984:4).

The most consistent variation from this definition, the one most generally accepted by professionals in the adult day care field, involves statement of the medical orientation and the level of disability among participants. For example, the one applied by the Veterans Administration states that the major purpose of adult day health care must be for the program to provide a substitute for nursing home care. This implies that a veteran who utilizes this form of care either at an adult day health program operated in a VA facility or through a contract arrangement must have a disability profile sufficiently complex to warrant institutional care.

As the concept of adult day care expanded and diversified there was an increased recognition of the family or caregiver as part of the client system (Rathbone-McCuan 1976; Weiler and Rathbone-McCuan 1978). To accommodate to the influences of third-party reimbursement, demands for client outreach, and organizational sponsorship, new aspects were added to differentiate the focus each enter (Rathbone-McCuan and Elliott 1976; Robins 1981). Issacs (1981) noted that programs likely to qualify for Medicaid were going to reinforce the medical/health service aspects while those receiving funds from Title XX of the Social Security Act or Title III of the Older Americans Act were going to at least balance the health focus with equal priority being given to health and social services. This pattern has remained consistent as these continue to be important for funding.

The diversity among programs was sometimes more a matter of internal description rather than variation in the scope and pattern of service provision. Centers that determined their goal to be restoration concentrated on rehabilitation so staffed centers with certified specialists or consultants that could provide the appropriate therapies. Screening of possible clients included in-depth attention to medical status and the need for rehabilitation that could be predicted to improve client function. Other programs were clear to educate the community that their centers emphasized the social service aspects necessary to assure that the highest level of a participant's potential for social functioning was sought and that social isolation among participants was decreased through individual and group programming (Issacs 1981).

Summary of Current Center Characteristics

The most current information available about adult day care is presented in the preliminary analysis of data gathered from a national survey conducted by the National Council on Aging beginning in 1985

(NIAD 1988). A report was prepared from the sample of 834 centers with the far greatest number of them qualifying as private nonprofit agencies. Only 10 percent of the centers were operated by private for-profit organizations. As previously implied, day care center care is not evenly distributed throughout the United States. Some states such as California, Massachusetts, Minnesota, and Florida are "day care service rich" by comparison to states such as Idaho, Mississippi, Montana, New Hampshire, and West Virginia that had no centers contributing data to the national survey. States leading the way in the creation of many centers and diversification among them have found it useful to create formal state associations or something comparable to share information and provide advocacy for beneficial legislation and progressive policies supportive of adult day care.

Over the past decade licensed day care has increased. Centers are licensed under different categories predominantly under the adult day health or social day care auspice. But some qualify under nursing home, outpatient, or rehabilitation clinic status, depending on the sponsoring organization. According to the survey summary, "certification is a process of requiring a center to meet certain standards usually to become eligible for Medicare and Medicaid" (NIAD 1988:9). There is a dramatic difference between the proportion certified for Medicaid as compared to Medicare. Medicare reimbursement continues to be a very limited source of financing for adult day care and is available only to those programs that have a strong medical and rehabilitation service.

The importance of referrals to the operation of an effective day care program continues to be important both for the program to be financially viable and linked into the community service network. It is common for centers to have many channels of referral, but the most active referral sources include social service agencies, health programs, and through the community grapevine (NIAD 1988). Even with much staff time spent with other community agencies and spending significant time speaking in local settings, many citizens remain confused about the concept of adult day care.

The predominant living arrangements among the group of the U.S. elderly who are formal participants in adult day care programs continues to be with another person. While there is no accurate estimate of the actual total number of people enrolled in adult day care, the survey reported that 64 percent of day care center participants represented by the centers in the study lived with someone (NIAD 1988). This one characteristic is strong support for the importance of links between the day care center and the family or care provider as a part of the client system. Data available from the survey reinforce the position taken by the early advocates in the day care movement that a center approach is very appropriate for adults with both physical and/or mental disabilities. On the other hand, day care centers are not for everyone. The two criteria identified most frequently as reasons for excluding an applicant were general incontinence and disruptive behavior. It is interesting to note that despite the strong health orientation among many programs, the delivery of services from a physician or psychiatrist are handled mainly through referrals while the majority of social services and nursing care is provided by staff (Table 21.2).

The final and most complex of factors analyzed from the day care survey involves costs and funding for service provision and program operation. The average annual budget of the 642 centers that reported

TABLE 21.2. Services Provided in Adult Day Care Centers (n=816)

Services	*% Staff*	*% Contract*	*% Referrals*
Social services	74	8	16
MD (assessment)	9	11	54
MD (treatment)	5	7	60
Psychiatry	5	12	59
Podiatry	3	18	56
Dentistry	3	9	59
Nursing	70	7	13
Diet counseling	57	18	14
Physical therapy	19	31	41
Occupation therapy	22	28	37
Speech therapy	10	30	42
Recreational therapy	98	4	1
Art therapy	61	8	3
Music therapy	63	9	3
Exercises	95	5	<1
Reality therapy	85	3	1
Transportation (home–center)	56	32	10
Transportation (other)	38	19	16
Meals (at center)	62	35	1
Dressing/grooming/toileting	73	3	8
Bathing	34	3	20
Laundry	18	3	20
Other	12	5	2

SOURCE: Adult Day Care in America: Summary of a National Survey, Washington, D.C.: National Council on Aging, Institute on Adult Daycare, 1988, p. 25.

budget data, the average annual budget was $137,085. The unsubsidized average per diem cost was reported to be $27.00 and with the addition of subsidies the cost increased to a $31.00 per diem. The pattern of mixed funding sources is an almost universal characteristic of all day care centers. Sources of funding contributing to 25 percent or more of most day care budgets include: participant fees, Medicaid, Title II, mental health funds and other special categories of state and local funds.

The information provided in this section benefited from the data released this year by the National Council on Aging, thus, it is important to note the qualifications made by the senior project staff, "Although we have summarized the average characteristics of participants and centers, there is great diversity in Adult Day Care programs" (NIAD 1988:25).

Presented here is a checklist of services included in a very comprehensive adult day care program. This listing might serve as a useful tool for practitioners to assist elderly persons or concerned family members to choose a day-care service or to select from among several programs. The indicators are organized into eighteen program dimensions.

1. Counseling
   a. Is there counseling available to individuals and families?
   b. Are mental-health referrals and linkages readily available?
   c. Do program participants receive encouragement to discuss personal issues in a relaxed and informal context?
2. Education
   a. Have program staff received appropriate training to provide care to the mentally or physically impaired elderly?
   b. Are education programs made available to program participants in a stimulating and appropriate format?
   c. Does the day care center serve as an educational training site for student or have a linkage with an educational program?
3. Exercise
   a. Is there adequate space for program participants to safely exercise?
   b. Is exercise a part of the daily program?
   c. Are appropriate devices and instructions available to program participants with special exercise needs or limitations?
4. Group and Individual Activities
   a. Are there a combination of both group and individual activities available for each program participant every day?

b. Are group and individual activities recorded and monitored as part of an individual care plan?
c. Are the special needs of each program participant recognized within the scope of group activities?

5. Health Care
   a. Is health care provision a major goal of the program?
   b. What is the health care expertise of the program staff or consultants?
   c. How are the health needs of individual program participants assessed?
6. Health Screening
   a. Is health screening required before an individual is accepted into the program?
   b. Is general health screening done at the program?
   c. Is there a policy for follow-up if health-screening results indicate the existence of a problem?
7. Information and Referral
   a. Is the program known to local information and referral services in the community?
   b. Are information and referral functions performed by the day care service staff for individual program participants?
   c. Are information and referral functions performed by the day care service staff for family member or other caregivers connected to individual program participants?
8. Meals
   a. Are there resources to provide for special diets?
   b. Do program participants enjoy the food served at meal times?
   c. Are meals and eating treated as a dignified personal and meaningful social activity?
9. Medical and Social Evaluation
   a. Is medical and social information required and/or gathered at the time of admission?
   b. Is evaluation information used for initial and ongoing individual care planning?
   c. If requested, will important information be available to other agencies serving program participants?
10. Occupational Therapy
    a. Is occupational therapy available in the program?
    b. Is occupational therapy included in the assessment of the needs of the program participant at the times of admission and discharge?
    c. When appropriate, is occupational therapy introduced as part of the individual care plan?

11. Physical Therapy
    a. Are there resources to provide physical therapy to program participants?
    b. Are the physical therapy services integrated into a larger rehabilitation care plan?
    c. Are program staff skilled at dealing with the potential problems of program participant resistance?
12. Reality Orientation
    a. Is there a range of reality orientation techniques that are used according to the individual needs of program participants?
    b. Are program staff trained to employ other complementary behavior-modification approaches as needed?
    c. Are program participants who do not need reality orientation given the option not to participate?
13. Recreation
    a. Is recreation conceived and offered as a special part of the daily program?
    b. Is recreation programming planned with the ongoing input of program participants?
    c. Are opportunities for recreational events available outside the daycare setting?
14. Remotivation Therapy
    a. Is motivation therapy offered in the program based on individual assessments of need?
    b. Does an atmosphere of general program-participant motivation dominate throughout the program?
    c. Are efforts made to have continuity of remotivation efforts supported in the program participant's residential environment?
15. Speech Therapy
    a. Is speech therapy available at the center from an appropriately trained person?
    b. Can speech therapy consultation be used for program participants with special communication problems?
    c. Are program staff prepared to assist and provide consistent support of speech improvement goals?
16. Socialization
    a. Are the socialization needs of a program participant objectively assessed at admission?
    b. Are the goals of socialization clearly distinct from recreation?

   c. Are the opportunities for socialization matched to individual backgrounds and preferences?
17. Supervision
   a. Is supervision available for program participants throughout the daily regime of the program?
   b. Does the program provide for an individualized plan of supervision that varies according to the functional disability and specific daily program schedule or program participants?
   c. Are all day care staff and volunteers provided with some overall training and supervision related to their service?
18. Transportation
   a. Is transportation a stable and dependable component of the day care program?
   b. Is there a means of accommodation for participants with special transport problems?
   c. Are there consistent policies regarding a transportation emergency or breakdown?

As more day care programs have reached a point where there are some special state regulations that control or at least guide the staffing pattern, it is possible to identify a typical staffing with qualifications. Table 21.3 is adapted from the Isaacs (1981) study overviewing day care.

CONVERGENCE OF RESPITE AND DAY CARE

In the early 1980s it was important to keep the discussion of respite and adult day care separate as day care did not exist for the primary benefit of care providers, rather the elder participants. There is now increasing concern, however, about how day care centers might develop greater capacities to deal with clients with more advanced stages of dementia and thereby offer a more comprehensive respite function. With that goal, the Alzheimer's disease and Related Disorders Association (ADRA) and the Administration on Aging (AoA) co-funded the Dementia Care and Respite Service Program to begin August 1988. This large research and demonstration project will provide grants of up to $300,000 to nineteen day care centers over a period of four years under a deficit-financing arrangement. The average amount of money awarded to participating centers was $262,000. Each of the co-funding organizations will contribute $625,000 with the balance of support being provided by Robert Wood Johnson (Reifler and Smyth 1988).

This funding will allow the participating day care centers to take leadership to develop new ways of serving the needs of dementia clients while at the same time greatly intensifying direct work with caregivers. Case coordination with other community resources and active training to anticipate care problems as well as diagnostic and treatment facility identification to the mutual benefit of the caregiver and the client are some of the service goals.

Like other large research projects funded in the late 1970s and early 1980s involving the analysis of day care services in the United States (U.S. Health Care Finance Administration 1982), this project

TABLE 21.3. Day Care Staff Qualifications

Staff	*Qualifications*	*Functions*
Activity recreational specialist	Training in therapeutic recreation and one or more years in an adult social or recreational program	Plans leisure events, works with residents in planning and preparing for events, conducts socialization groups, and designs individual plans for participants with special needs.
Social worker	Training at master's level and one or more years of work experience, preferably with programs for disabled and elderly	Does in home assessments, participates in the admission and treatment planning, may do individual, group, or family counseling as well as case management and possible program administration
Program nurse	A registered nurse with current state licensing and at least one year of experience in a health care setting	Evaluates intake health data, plans health care component of individual's plan, does treatments and medication supervision, may do health education, and connects with physicians as well as program administration

involves the expectation that the new respite day care center capacity will prove cost-effective. Through this major project there will be an opportunity for creative experimentation to encompass the needs of clients and their caregivers. Assuming that many of the day care centers in the project will provide valuable and timely assistance the question remains, how will such respite services be sustained in the future without shifting the burden of payment onto the caregiver system? It remains important to revamp the very fragmented and incomplete sources of long term care funding that have plagued day care and other home based services since their introduction into the U.S. health and social service delivery system for older Americans and chronically disabled adults.

TABLE 21.3. (*Continued*)

Staff	*Qualifications*	*Functions*
Medical consultant	Licensed to practice medicine by the state	Reviews adequacy of medical data at intake and may consult participant's physician, reviews policy and procedures in the program, may do staff consultation and provide emergency medical backup as required
Rehabilitative therapist	A bachelor's degree from an accredited program and licensed, registered, or certified in accordance with state standards	Does individual assessment and treatment planning and implements the therapy, does preventive work in group programs and may work with families to handle special in home needs
Dietary aide	Training in food handling and one year experience in meal preparation and serving	Does meal planning, reviews special diets, involves participants in nutrition interests, and may prepare and or coordinate food service

SOURCE: B. Issacs, A description and analysis of adult day care standards in the U.S. Monograph National Council on the Aging, Washington, D.C. 1981.

REFERENCES

Archbold, P. G. 1982. All consuming activity: The family as caregiver. *Generations* 6(2):12–13.

Becker, G., and S. Kaufman. 1988. Old age, rehabilitation and research: A review of the issues. *The Gerontologist* 28(4):459–468.

Bogo, M. 1987. Social work practice with family systems in admission to homes for the aged. *Journal of Gerontological Social Work* 10(1/2):5–19.

Brockelhurst, J. C. 1973. Role of day hospital care. *British Medical Journal* 4(3):223–225.

Cicirelli, V. G. 1988. A measure of filal anxiety regarding anticipated care of elder parents. *The Gerontologist* 28(4):478–482.

Farndale, J. 1961. *The Day Hospital Movement in Great Britain.* New York: Pergamon.

Gallo, J. J., W. Reichel, and L. Andersen. 1988. *Handbook of Geriatric Assessment.* Rockville: Aspen Systems.

Issacs, B. 1981. A description and analysis of adult day care standards in the United States. Research report for the National Council on the Aging, Washington, D.C.

Kinney, M. 1979. *A Handbook for Home-Based Services.* New York: Educational Resources Information Center.

Lund, D. A., M. A. Pett, and M. S. Caserta. 1987. Institutionalizing dementia victims: Some caregiver considerations. *Journal of Gerontological Social Work* 11(1/2):119–136.

Moore, S. T. 1987. The capacity to care: A family focused approach to social work practice with the disabled elderly. *Journal of Gerontological Social Work* 10(1/2):79–98.

National Institute on Adult Daycare. 1982. *Why Adult Day Care?* Washington, D.C.: National Council on the Aging.

National Institute on Adult Daycare. 1984. *Standards for Adult Day Care.* Washington, D.C.: National Council on Aging.

National Institute on Adult Daycare. 1988. *Summary of a National Day Care Survey.* Washington, D.C.: National Council on Aging.

Padula, H. 1981. Toward a useful definition of adult day care. *Hospital Progress* no. 3, pp. 42–45.

Rathbone-McCuan, E. 1976. Geriatric day care: A family perspective. *The Gerontologist* 16(6):517–170.

Rathbone-McCuan, E. and M. W. Elliott. 1976. Geriatric day care in theory and practice. *Social Work in Health Care* 2(2):153–170.

Rathbone-McCuan, E. and J. Hashimi. 1982. *Isolated Edlers: Health and Social Interventions.* Rockville: Aspen Systems.

Reifler, B. V. and R. S. Smyth. 1988. Dementia care and respite services program: Program summary. Paper from the Department of Psychiatry at the Bowman Gray School of Medicine in Winston-Salem.

Robins, E. G. 1981. Adult day care: Growing fast but still for lucky few. *Generations* 5(3):22–23.

Shepard, P., J. B. Mayer, and R. Ryback. 1987. Improving emergency care for the elderly: Social work interventions. *Journal of Gerontological Social Work* 10(3/4):123–141.

Silverstone, B. 1982. The effects on families of caring for impaired elderly in residence. *Benjamin Rose Institute Bulletin,* no 3, pp. 1–2.

Simonton, L. J. 1987. Assessing caregiver information needs: A brief questionnaire. *Journal of Gerontological Social Work* 10(1/2):177–180.

Steinhauer, M. B. 1982. Geriatric foster care: A prototype design and implementation issues. *The Gerontologist* 22(3):293–300.
U.S. Congress. Senate 1980. Comprehensive community based noninstitutional long term care service for the elderly and disabled (Senate Bill 2809). Washington, D.C.: GPO.
U.S. Health Care Financing Administration. 1982. Research and demonstration in health care financing 1980–1981. Baltimore.
Weiler, P. G. and E. Rathbone-McCuan. 1978. *Adult Day Care: Community Work with the Elderly*. New York: Spinger.
Zarit, S. H. 1980. *Aging and Mental Disorders: Psychological Approaches to Assessment and Treatment*. New York: Free Press.
Zarit, S. H., T. A. Todd, and J. M. Zarit. 1986. Subjective burden of husband and wives as care givers: A longitudinal study. *The Gerontologist* 26(3):260–266.
Zarit, S. H. and J. M. Zarit. 1986. Dementia and the family: A stress management approach. *Clinical Psychologist* 39(4):103–105.

22

Protective Services

❖

ELIAS S. COHEN, J.D., M.P.A.
Community Services Institute, Narbeth, Pennsylvania

Improvements in mortality rates have brought about an unprecedented blessing of very old age on large numbers of people. The blessing is not unmixed. The increase has brought with it an ever-increasing number of very old people who are unable to protect themselves, unable to give effect to their choices and their preferences, and—for reasons of physical impairment, mental impairment, severe social and environmental obstacles, or poverty—who are at risk or potential risk of serious harm.

For purposes of this paper, protective services are defined in terms of services that assist individuals to voluntarily alter *legal relationships* or which provide for the imposition of services involuntarily. However, that is not all of it. There are too many situations in which the legal solutions are inadequate or in which the legal guidelines may lead to an unjust solution. In such instances, ethical analysis may be required. Ethical analysis and legal analysis are not antithetical. Indeed, it is precisely ethical analysis that has brought about current advanced *legal* positions in such areas as informed consent by third parties, advance directives (e.g., durable powers of attorney, living wills, trusts, etc.), and revisions in guardianship statues.

Furthermore, current "legal" solutions may not be "solutions" at all. For example, there are an estimated 500,000 to 750,000 persons in America's nursing homes who suffer from a dementing illness. For the vast bulk of these it can be assumed that the dementia is of sufficient severity that they would meet any standard of legal incompetency. In point of fact, only a tiny percentage of them have been subjected to court proceeding, findings of incompetency, and the appointment of a guardian. Others (often family, but sometimes nursing home personnel "next best friends") are making decisions for them—important decisions such as those concerning medical treatment, medications, placement in a facility, permissions to go on field trips, clothing purchases, application of physical or chemical restraints, and so on.

From a strictly legal perspective, those third parties have no legal rights that empower them to make these decisions. And clearly, the demented do not have the power to do so.

Does this mean that those of us concerned with right, fairness and justice should undertake the filing of 500,000 to 750,000 petitions for the appointment of guardians? Would this accomplish the result of more and better treatment in the right place at the right time? Would we be assured of a better life for this group of patients?

For some number of them, the answer is undoubtedly, "Of course!" But for the bulk of them, the actual result would be an unequivocal "No!" The reasons for this are complex: First, such a flood of petitions would produce a torrent of hearings even more routine than those we witness in traffic courts—judicial hearings in our system are most effective when there is vigorous search for truth, a vigorous contest. Neither courts nor the probate bar are equipped for this pursuit now; second, courts have neither the resources nor the experience for the supervision of the varied interests that such patients present—they would neither require nor could they exercise surveillance if they did require the kinds of reports reflecting protection of the interests; and third, guardianships necessary to protect those interests require guardians with training and sensitivity to those issues—and such guardians are simply not available.

This is not to say that guardianships are neither necessary nor effective. Rather it is to point out that when we view protective services from the broad applied social policy perspective it may be necessary to seek to influence other applied value foci—in this instance, the ethical issues confronting a wide array of professions, occupations and social institutions—to achieve the desired result.

Although we can trace the historical antecedents of adult protective services, and particularly protective services all the way back to the fourteenth century,[1] it is largely within the last twenty years that adult protective services for the elderly, have received specific attention. Since 1963, scholars and practitioners have wrestled with definitions of protective services that attempted to define them in terms of the characteristics of the recipients of the services, in terms of the nature of the service, or in terms of the objectives the services were intended to achieve. Those definitions are not always helpful because they encompass too much and confuse *protective services* with the broad array of social services in general. Nonetheless, those early definitions are useful because they explicate the intent, the techniques, the populations, and the kinds of services that are frequently called into play.

In addition to these early definitions, more recent attempts have been made in such volumes as *Protective Services for Adults*, a 1982 publication of the U.S. Department of Health and Human Services, and in various state statutes that have established protective services by law. The following definitions are drawn from materials presented in *Protective Services for Adults:*

1. The federal definition set forth in 45 CFR 222.73 pursuant to Title XX of the Social Security Act:

> Protective services means a system of services (including medical and legal services which are incidental to the service plan) which are utilized to assist seriously impaired eligible individuals who, because of mental or physical dysfunction, are unable to manage their resources, carry out the activities of daily living, or protect themselves from neglect or hazardous situations without assistance from others and have no one available who is willing and able to assist them responsibly.

2. The Administration on Aging, in a "Guide on Protective Services for Older Persons," set forth in an appendix to *Protective Services for Adults* defines protective services as follows:

> Protective service is a social service with medical and legal aspects provided to an older person, who, as a result of physical or mental dysfunction (or both), abuse, neglect or extreme social or economic need is at risk of harm to self or to others. The purpose of protective services is to protect that older person from such harm, by stabilizing his (or her) situation in order to maintain him in the least restrictive setting, or by providing institutional care where it is needed. Community protective service involves case work services and occasionally medical and legal intervention. Medical interventions are needed to identify the type and severity of functional disability and abuse and neglect (physical, emotional, mental). Legal interventions to protect the individual's money or his person may be required when the older individual appears unable or incompetent to use judgement or unable to make decisions for himself. These legal procedures may include conservatorship, guardianship, admission to a chronic care institution or commitment to a mental institution in the case of a seriously mentally impaired individual. Such legal procedures are necessary to authorize Protective Service intervention when an older person is unable or incompetent to authorize or consent to protective service intervention himself.

3. New York State offers the following definition:

> Protective services for adults is a system of care which includes the availability of a constellation of services bearing individually or in concert upon a problem situation of an adult requiring a planned approach of intervention. As a preventive, supportive and surrogate service, it is aimed at maintaining individuals in the community as long as feasible rather than institutionalizing them, though, in some cases, the latter may be necessary. More specifically it can be stated that a protective service system aims at the prevention, reduction or elimination of neglect, exploitation or crisis breakdown through the provision of services appropriate to the individual's needs which will strengthen his capacity to function and maximize his ability at self direction.

Most such definitions, however, are either so broad as to include virtually all medical and social services or so narrow as to include only services brought into being through the use of formal judicial interventions. In fact, most social, medical, psychiatric, and legal services may be regarded as "protective services" since an individual may require them in order to avoid extraordinary vulnerability. On the other hand, to suggest that protective services are those that come into being in conjunction with, or immediately following, judicial intervention is to avoid an important middle ground that both law and practice envision.

It is the premise of this paper that protective services are those that are invoked or that accompany as a natural result the alteration in legal relationships undertaken to protect and preserve the best interests of the adult individual including the interests associated with self-determination.

This definition admits to the array of services under the rubric of *protective services* any and all of the traditional social services provided to adults, *provided that these services emerge following recognition and action on the recognition that an individual's decision-making power has been altered through legal means by the individual himself or by judicial intervention.* Similarly, it excludes from the definition all those services that may in some way "protect" or "serve" the best interest of the client" without any deliberate effort or action to alter legal relationships. Furthermore, the definition encompasses a wide array of legal devices ranging from those that are "preventive" in nature and entirely under the control of the adult individual to those that are involuntary, massively intrusive, and involve entirely the judgments of others that an individual is incompetent and unable to make decisions for himself/herself. Thus, protective services may include assisting an individual to understand and execute a power of attorney (including a "durable power"), establishing a trust for oneself, assisting the attorney-in-fact with providing certain services or amenities, doing the same for a trustee, on up to petitioning for guardianship, conducting the investigation, responding to requests for assistance in dealing with an alleged incompetent, assisting a guardian, assisting an alleged incompetent to secure representation, and many other activities. The common thread in all these services is the alteration of legal relationships that, in some way, permits—on a temporary and revocable basis or on a more "permanent" court basis —the transfer of the client's decision-making power to another person or persons.

Critical to the definition is the notion that the interests to be served are first and foremost those of the client, subject only to the limitations customarily invoked in the exercise of the police power to protect individuals from their own actions. These limitations do not usually justify intervention to protect individuals from their own willful, rationally arrived at, though foolish, decisions. The right to folly is reasonably well preserved in both law and, hopefully, the philosophy of protective services.[2] It is too often honored in the breach— a breach more difficult to close than usual because it derives, in general, from beneficent motives.

LEGAL STATUS AND THE RIGHT TO BE PROTECTED

Given a definition that has at its heart the alteration, voluntarily or otherwise of legal relationships, the question of *legal status* is an important consideration.

The legal status of elderly people is determined by a great many things. First and foremost, however, is the status conferred by having reached adulthood, however defined and for whatever purposes.[3] In addition to status achieved through adulthood, older individuals also receive special status as taxpayers; Supplemental Security Income beneficiaries; social-services beneficiaries; users of public transportation, social services, educational and recreational programs; renters or home owners; and workers. Furthermore, "old age" may grant special protection, and hence special status, relative to mandatory retirement or other discrimination in employment based on age. These special statuses all give rise to interests to be protected. In addition to these interests that grow out of age, there are the usual interests that grow out of adulthood, namely, the interests arising from our status as parties to contracts, as renters, home owners, taxpayers, citizens, residents of particular jurisdictions, and so on.

On the other hand, there are some "negative" statuses that may be conferred by law (however wrongheaded they may be) and that are of significance here because they frequently concern the basis for invading the rights of older people. There continue to be, in too many states, definitions contained in statutes setting forth standards for determination of incompetency that incorporate negative stereotypes of old age. Just a few of these might be cited here (emphases added):

> Incapacitated person means any person who is impaired by reason of *advanced age* . . . to the extent that he lacks sufficient understanding or capacity to make or communicate responsible decisions concerning his person (Arizona Rev. Stat. 14-5101).

> An "incompetent" . . . is a person who is incapable by reason of . . . *senility* . . . *old age*, or other incapacity, of either managing his property or caring for himself or both (Indiana Stat. Ann. 29-1-13-1(c)(2)).

> "Person of unsound mind" means . . . one whose mind, because of . . . *old age* has become imbecile or unsound as to render him incompetent to manage his estate (Kentucky Rev. Stat. Ann. 387.010).

> A guardian may be appointed for . . . any person who, by reason of extreme *old age* . . . is mentally incompetent to have the charge and management of his property (Nebraska Rev. Stat. 38-201).

> The Supreme Court and the County Courts outside the City of New York have jurisdiction over the custody of a person or his property, if he is incompetent to manage himself of his affairs by reason of age . . . (New York Standard Civil Practice Service—Mental Hygiene 78.01).

WHAT ARE THE INTERESTS TO BE PROTECTED?

Virtually all the interests to be protected can be grouped under the overarching interests of the older individual, indeed of all adults, in maintaining and maximizing autonomy—the exercise of self-determination, of making preferences and choices operational, of controlling one's destiny and fate in both short-and long-range time frames. This translates into choosing where and how one lives, where and how one eats, imbibes, dresses, recreates, associates, votes, contracts, maintains personal hygiene, withholds or gives consent for medical procedures, and otherwise engages with (or without) the rest of society.

Related to the interests of autonomy are the interests associated with property currently or potentially available, that may give meaning to those interests associated with autonomy and the exercise of free choice. Thus, an interest in a potential money benefit is an interest to be protected since it may give rise to the exercise of more choice if secured than if not.

One interest deserves special mention because of the frequency with which it appears to arise, its apparent relationship to the rights of privacy arising from the Fourth Amendment, and the very recent emergence of "recognition" of this interest—namely, the interest or right to be left alone. This interest will be discussed in greater detail below in the so called "right to die" cases or similar situations like *Northern v. State.*[4]

Interest analysis is crucial in any approach to protective services, whether theoretical or clinical. Key questions to be raised *always* are:

What interests are involved?
Whose interests are involved?
What limitations are being considered for which party?
Whose autonomy is being limited?
Who will bear the burden if particular remedies are imposed?
Who will bear the burdens if the remedies are not imposed?

It is out of this kind of interest analysis that the paradox and dilemma of protective services arises, particularly for social workers. The paradox in which the social worker finds himself/herself is: How can limitations on free choice in decision making increase the range of autonomy for the objective of the protective service? Viewed obversely, the question becomes: If no benefits accrue to the increased autonomy of the individual, what justification exists for limiting freedom and autonomy?

TYPICAL LIFE SITUATIONS APPEARING TO CALL FOR PROTECTIVE SERVICES

There is an array of older people—whose numbers are increasing at a furious pace—for whom protective services appear to be required:

The old man with a severly impaired memory who can't recall what he did with his funds, where his money comes from, what amount he gets, or what he has spent it for. He manages somehow to have a little bit of food in the cupboard. He sometimes forgets to cash checks or spend money, and at other times spends it foolishly and comes down to the end of the month without enough to provide himself with food. Somehow neighbors and a few friends step in, although he lives on the verge of starving, suffers leg ulcers and may be filthy and bewildered.

The old man or lady constantly moving from place to place, unable to stay rooted very long, frequently without funds.

The wanderers, street people, "vent men," bag ladies, and others who have no permanent living quarters but who use bus stations and other public places in which to live.

The dischargee from the mental hospital, disoriented as to time and place, living in a boarding home, foraging for scraps in garbage cans, wandering in the street, shouting obscenities, dressing bizarrely, and appearing to neglect himself/herself.

The bedridden, crippled, or arthritic individual dwelling in a building he/she owns that is full of rubbish and infested with vermin, refusing hospitalization for treatment of infection, seclusive and fearful.

The recluse living in an apartment using a portable kerosene heater and a hot plate for cooking, living in filth and regarded as something of a danger because he or she set a fire accidentally nine months before while cooking a meal.

The mildly forgetful, physically well busybody who is intrusive, garrulous, mildly paranoid, an unabashed beggar, often demanding food or money, living in his or her own home that is packed with the "treasures" accumulated over the years including both valuable paper ephemera as well as collections of old milk bottles (now grown valuable) and pure unmitigated junk that represents a horrendous fire hazard.

The 55-year-old mentally retarded individual never adjudged incompetent and, in fact, never institutionalized. Such individuals may have lived with parents all their lives and may find that they are alone following the death of parents and in possession of very considerable amounts of property.

The neatly dressed old man in good shape physically but forgetful and confused who continues to operate a small neighborhood store with his business affairs hopelessly tangled. He may be heavily in debt, but his entire life is wrapped up in his business. He is without known relatives or friends to whom he can turn.

The proud and independent old lady in imminent danger of sustaining serious personal injury by reason of her infirmity who refuses to consider leaving her home and who will not accept any help in the home.[5]

These are the people into whose lives social workers may be called upon to intervene. They may be well-to-do or they may be poor. They may be alone or they may have family. They may be wise or they may be foolish. And they may or may not meet the tests the law prescribes for incompetency.

HISTORICAL LEGAL ANTECEDENTS OF PROTECTIVE SERVICES

The legal antecedents of protective services are to be found in the laws and decisions concerning the mentally ill. The historical evolution has moved from the seizure of the individual who was "furiously mad" in order to protect the public to protection of the individual himself and subsequently his estate. In more recent years, courts have modified the powers of the state to intervene and have imposed (or relaxed) strictures concerning the need for and meaning of informed consent, while legislatures have been busy tinkering with the uniform probate code, with durable power of attorney statutes, and with natural death or right-to-die acts. Protective services have their roots both in the police power (narrowly construed) and in the state's power as *parens patriae.*

Under the police power, the state has authority to confine dangerous individuals so that the health and safety of others may be protected. The most familiar exercise of this power is under the criminal law. However, in some instances, as in the exercise of mental-health commitment laws, the police power may be exercised to commit to mental institutions individuals who are dangerous to others and who are, by reason of mental illness, unable to control their activities.

However, where the harm that the individual might visit is not upon others but rather upon himself or herself, the power the state exercises is that of *parens patriae.* It grows out of the notion that the sovereign, as the political father and guardian of the kingdom, has a special obligation to care for those who, because of their lack of mental capacity, are unable to take care of themselves.[6]

An 1845 Massachusetts Supreme Judicial Court decision in *Re Josiah Oakes* blended the police and *parens patriae* powers.[7] Josiah Oakes, it was alleged, was mentally deranged, the evidence of which was that he had become engaged to a young woman of questionable character shortly after the death of his wife. There was no indication in the report of the case that he was violent and it wasn't clear whether his involuntary confinement was for his benefit or for the safety of the community. Nonetheless, it represents the earliest case in which involuntary confinement was used to justify therapeutic benefit for the patient as well as a measure to protect the safety of the community.[8]

There is now little question that states have the power to confine mentally ill or mentally retarded persons for therapeutic purposes, although that power has been moderated somewhat to require that, if individuals aren't confined to protect the public or to protect themselves, then they must be confined for therapeutic purposes *(O'Connor v. Donaldson).*[9] The ruling in this case is a far cry from a right to treatment. The court held only that a nondangerous patient was entitled to release if he received no treatment.

Courts have not been imaginative in dealing with the issues presented by protective services. It is only recently that some states have begun to develop specific statutory bases for intervening in cases of vulnerable, potentially incompetent individuals in ways that will not necessarily and inevitably lead to the violent act of imposing a guardianship—violent because it strips an individual of his personhood in virtually every relevant facet of his life.

Protective services, as we are beginning to know them, are a recent phenomenon for a variety of reasons. It is less than half a century since the Social Security Act radically altered the way in which vulnerable people in society were provided for. Prior to 1935, "indoor relief" was a common mode of care. The idiot, the insane, the derelict, the alcoholic, the ne'er-do-well, the unemployed, and the inadequate were housed together in the county home or almshouse. The Social Security Act made clear that the preferred method of "treatment" was to provide economic relief in the community. Federal relief was not available for those in institutions. This beginning was followed some thirty years later by the so-called Services Amendments added to the Social Security Act in the 1960s that made further provision for the delivery of a wise variety of social services to past, present, and potential dependents. At that point, the federal government reimbursed the state for 75 percent of expenditures for services in behalf of such persons. The appropriation was open-ended. In the late 1960s the Community Mental Health Act reinforced that declaration with the development of community mental-health centers. It was no accident that the National Council on Aging, the American Public Welfare Association, and other organizations began to look at the issue of protective services in a serious way.[10]

The issue, however, was not informed by very much research in the area. Alexander and Lewin's landmark study, *The Aged and the Need for Surrogate Management,* pointed out that, in examining over 400 cases in which guardians were appointed for certain mental-hospital patients, not a single case could be found in which any benefit accrued to the incompetent person.[11]

The U.S. Senate Special Committee on Aging commissioned a paper on protective services for the elderly by John J. Regan and Georgia Springer (1977). Once again, the issues were well explicated and an attempt was made to present a model guardianship, conservatorship, and power-of-attorney legislation.

That relatively little progress has been made is attested by the persistence of statutes and probate-court practices that make guardianship easy to obtain, make no provision for intermediate remedies, and provide minimal due-process protections for those who need help and assistance in altering legal relationships.

BASIC LEGAL CONCEPTS IN PROTECTIVE SERVICES

Underpinning any development of protective services are two fundamental concepts: First is the presumption of competence on the part of the impaired individual. To be sure, the presumption is a rebuttable one, but all efforts must be made to support the basic presumption. One must raise this presumption even for those who are uncommunicative and who appear not to understand or to be unresponsive. One must inquire whether they need an interlocutor because they are not conversant in English, may be hard of hearing, may suffer aphasia, or may not understand the questions being put. A presumption of competence requires an inquiry into a determination of precisely what areas of behavior are impaired and what areas are unimpaired. It requires a determination of those areas in which the individual can express or articulate preferences, choices, and wishes and whether the impairment is limited to the ability to give effect to those wishes. The bedridden patient who cannot visit a benefit office, who may not have a phone, who certainly can't go shopping, and who is utterly dependent on others is not necessarily incompetent. Incompetence is not synonymous with dependence. Quadriplegia renders one almost totally dependent but does not deprive one of competence.

The second legal concept crucial to protective services is the Doctrine of the Least Restrictive Alternative. The doctrine was perhaps best articulated in *Shelton v. Tucker* as follows: "Even though the governmental purpose be legitimate and substantial, that purpose cannot be pursued by means that stifle fundamental personal liberties when the end can be more narrowly achieved. The breadth of legislative abridgement must be viewed in the light of less drastic means for achieving the same basic purpose."[12] What this means in protective services terms is that guardianship must not be imposed if conservatorship will do as well; a total guardianship must not be imposed if a limited guardianship will achieve the result; involuntary processes must not be used if such voluntary processes as the use of agency or power of attorney or a joint bank account or trusteeship will serve as well.[13]

The least-restrictive alternative has been most directly applied to the elderly in Judge David Bazelon's opinion in *Lake v. Cameron.*[14] While this was a commitment proceeding, the least-restrictive-alternative principles are well laid out. In this particular situation, Ms. Lake was detained as she was leaving a government building where she had gone to inquire about a tax matter. She appeared to be confused. She was taken into custody and subsequently committed to St. Elizabeth's Hospital. Judge Bazelon held that the presence of "mental illness" without more was insufficient to deny basic freedom rights to an individual. He pointed out that it was the way in which an individual functioned and the alternatives that would least impinge upon civil rights that mattered most. Thus, confronted with a petition for commitment to an institution, the court held that there must be an inquiry as to the possibility of employing less restrictive measures to compensate for the functional problems that were present.

As a matter of law, the Lake case has no real precedential value. It was grounded primarily in District of Columbia law and, while it has been cited as support for similar issues (deservedly so), it cannot really govern. There is little evidence that the kind of inquiry suggested by Judge Bazelon is routinely made. And there is little to suggest that options for less-restrictive alternatives are presented to the court or that services in the community are ordered for the mentally impaired elderly.

In the Lake case, Judge Bazelon ordered the District of Columbia Department of Public Welfare to explore and secure less-restrictive alternative services (i.e., alternatives to commitment to St. Elizabeth's Hospital) in order to avoid institutionalization. The issue here was to find services that would help Ms. Lake with her shopping and activities of daily living in her home. While the decision and the decree were admirable, the results were less so. Ms. Lake ended her days in St. Elizabeth's Hospital because the District of Columbia could not fashion a program of less-restrictive alternatives for her. Among other things, the lesson here may be that the judicial forum, despite its power to issue orders and decrees, is very frequently at the mercy of the executive branch of government for implementation.

Of course, in addition to these less-restrictive-alternative considerations, it goes without any further explication that due process protections normally available in criminal and involuntary commitment cases are no less important in involuntary protective services proceedings.

Less fundamental, but no less important to the development of a gamut of protective legal devices ranging from voluntary and revocable transactions to involuntary transactions is an understanding of the law of agency. The law of agency does *not* govern what social agencies or organizations can or can't do, nor does it deal with such agencies' behavior. The law of agency concerns the duties, obligations and privileges that arise when one person, an *agent,* undertakes to carry out the orders of another, the *principal.* In such an arrangement, the agent, having agreed to the undertaking, agrees to carry it out and to exercise no more discretion and to do no more or less than the undertaking calls for (if possible). The principal will be liable for the acts of his/her agent carried out within the scope of the duty. A principal may change his/her mind at any point. The authority given to an agent is always revocable (except in a durable power of attorney as described below). The law of agency is the basis of all powers of attorney. It is a venerable doctrine of high utility in protective services that has not been utilized appropriately.

While there are some other legal concepts that come into play in the course of protective services (such as those embodied in the law of trusts), it is not necessary to review those here. Suffice to say that a starting point of presumptive competence, the knowledge and application of the doctrine of least-restrictive alternative, and some understanding of the law of agency will provide a basis for assisting in the resolution of the paradox of liberating through intrusion and may assist social workers as they attempt to understand the role they play in relationship to their clients and the duties they owe to the agencies for which they work.

LEGAL DEVICES FOR PROTECTIVE SERVICES

Voluntary Devices

Legal devices for protective services for adults are at an early stage of conceptual development, although the devices discussed here have, as noted, ancient origins. The adoption or rejection of any of them is predicated upon the employment of sensitive assessment mechanisms that take into account not only the psychological and physical capabilities of an individual but also his or her social situation and how he or she has been able to adapt to it. The question of which legal device to employ is not and cannot be a matter of precise formula or scoring system that produces a computerlike response. The legal devices noted below are nothing more than available patterns that social workers, together with lawyers, can utilize to tailor-make a solution for any given individual and any given set of problems.

AGENCY

Agency, as noted above, is the shorthand description for a relationship between a principal and an agent. Agents are utilized in those situations where the client is sufficiently well-oriented to be able to make choices, express preferences, and enjoy the benefits of a degree of autonomy. Agents can be advantageously utilized even where clients suffer a degree of impairment such that they may not be completely oriented to time, may suffer some short-term memory loss, and may even have some difficulty in managing money. Nonetheless, such a person might sincerely enjoy the utility of an agent if one were provided. An agent might help the client pay his bills, deposit his funds in the bank, and assist in many ways in giving effect to the client's preferences and wishes. One analogy might be that of a beneficent son or daughter, son-in-law or daughter-in-law, brother or sister who has undertaken to assist a relative whose powers are somewhat diminished but who, nonetheless, has preferences, expresses them, and needs help in bringing those preferences to fruition.

An agent is something more than an informal helper and something different from a friend who drops in occasionally and gives the client a ride to the senior citizens center. An agent is one who owes a fiduciary duty to the client. He is bound to carry out his or her principal's instructions and exercises judgment only to the extent that the principal has delegated such power to the agent. This authority is spelled out in some detail in writing. The written instrument is called a power of attorney. Control of the scope and duration of the relationship is squarely in the hands of the principal. It is not unusual for some impaired persons to terminate agency relationships with some degree of frequency, especially if the impairment is accompanied by even a mild paranoia. That a principal may change his or her mind with what may be maddening frequency is not necessarily an indication that the principal is too demented to utilize an agent. It may be an indication of fickleness, frustration over the loss of capabilities, or one of the last gestures of authority that a diminished older person can exercise. Agents are, after all, agents. They are not "friends," they are not "relations," and they are not "angels of mercy." Their function is to proceed at the direction of their principal and to give effect to his/her preferences and decisions.

"Agents" have not yet found their way into the array of social services. There are a few very limited experiments and demonstrations utilizing agents in the way described here. Some Senior Companion Services and RSVP programs have made some attempt at this, and there is at least one demonstration program funded by the Administration on Aging through a grant to the South Orange, New Jersey, section of the National Council of Jewish Women. Beyond that, however, social agencies, Area Agencies on Aging, and other organizations that serve older people must fashion and train (not to mention provide legal, medical, psychiatric, and social work back-up to) their own cadres of agents.

POWER OF ATTORNEY

A power of attorney is a legal instrument through which a principal grants power to an agent to act for him or her. Powers of attorney may be very broad and general and provide for the agent to buy and sell property, make investments, enter into contracts, receive and disburse funds, sue, receive service in suit, defend the principal, and expend funds in either suit or defense thereof, and otherwise act for the principal. On the other hand, the power of attorney may be extraordinarily narrow, authorizing the agent only to expend funds from the principal's bank account for the sole purpose of paying the principals' rent, which shall not exceed for example $227.50 per month. Powers of attorney are what we give to stockbrokers who execute orders on our behalf, real estate agents who undertake to sell our homes, and attorneys-at-law who undertake to represent us. Many people execute a power of attorney when they are going into a hospital or when they take a vacation out of the country where they may not be reached easily in the event that their business or personal affairs require some immediate action.

A power of attorney is revocable at will by the principal. As long as it is not revoked, it is said to be renewed at each and every moment that the principal has the capacity to renew it. This represents a serious limitation on the use of the ordinary power of attorney. If, for example, a principal is ill and slips into a coma, the power of attorney he executed would automatically expire and would be invalid while he was in that coma. Similarly, if a power of attorney were executed and the principal became incompetent, or so demented that he could not properly extend the power to his attorney-in-fact (the term used for an agent named in a power-of-attorney instrument), the power of attorney would automatically expire.

There has now developed in all but about four states a device intended to overcome this problem. It is commonly known as a "durable power of attorney." A durable power of attorney is a special instrument, authorized by state statute, that permits a power of attorney to endure beyond the incapacity of the maker of grantor of the power. Depending upon the particular state law, a durable power of attorney must declare the intent of the maker of the power for it to endure beyond his incapacity, may require special witnessing or notarization of signatures, may require that the attorney-in-fact be a relative of the maker of the power, and may have other special requirements.

Durable powers of attorney typically govern powers involving the acquisition, disposition and management of real and personal property. Four states (California, Colorado, North Carolina, and Pennsylvania) recognize durable powers of attorney for health care decisions. Durable powers of attorney for health care decisions can, depending upon state law, make very broad grants of power. More importantly, such instruments, when well drafted, can and do give important guidance to the attorney-in-fact as to what the principal wants. Such guidance is binding upon the attorney-in-fact. Thus, a principal may say, "In the event that I become comatose or fall into what appears to be a persistent vegetative state, and regardless of the prognosis by physicians attending me, I wish to receive such treatment as will sustain my life as long as it is possible providing me with as much freedom as possible from physical pain", or conversely, may provide language authorizing the withdrawing or withholding of treatment or nourishment.

In many ways, the durable power of attorney is a major breakthrough in what we might call "preventative protective services." In a manner of speaking, it permits an individual while still competent to select someone to manage his affairs at some future time when he (the principal) is no longer able to do so, In some ways, it is almost like selecting one's own guardian. If the durable power of attorney is sufficiently broad, it can cover virtually all eventualities.

"LIVING WILLS"

"Living will" is a generic term used to represent a legislatively authorized advance directive addressed to physicians and caregivers instructing them in matters concerning the prolongation or termination of life when the maker of the instrument is comatose, persistently vegetative, is sustained only by artificial techniques that assist respiration, cardiovascular functioning, kidney function or nutrition. Such directives are variously grouped under legislative designations as "Right to die," "Natural death," and/or "Death with Dignity" statutes.

Thirty-nine states have adopted Living Will legislation as of 1988. Provisions vary significantly from state to state. Typically, statutes authorize the execution of document by an individual instructing physicians as to what they are to do relative to prolongation or termination of life in certain circumstances. The "living will" exculpates the physician (and sometimes others) from civil or criminal liability for carrying out such instructions. The physician is obliged to carry out such instructions, although few states provide penalties for failure to do so. Most states have special witnessing requirements, and permit revocation or modification of the document so long as the maker is competent to do so. Virtually all states require confirming consultation and written certification of terminal condition. About two-thirds of the states address the issues of providing or terminating nutrition and/or hydration specifically. Very few explicitly recognize similar documents from out of state. About one third of the states provide for giving the power to instruct physicians to a proxy—almost like a special kind of durable power of attorney.

There is a growing body of case law interpreting the statutes. This area, like virtually all of the protective services legislation and common law is governed by *state* law and thus may vary considerably from state to state. The important thing to remember about living wills is that they are designed to deal only with very narrow situations. Thus, a living will may guide a physician whose patient requires a respirator to sustain life and direct him to disconnect it or to avoid it altogether. It does *not* deal with the penultimate situation where the patient contracts a pneumonia which *can* be treated successfully with antibiotics which treatment will avoid the life threatening situation altogether. In this latter situation, virtually all states would not permit the denial of the antibiotics in order to produce the life-threatening circumstance that *would* invoke the living will direction.[15]

JOINT BANK ACCOUNTS

Another method of determining in advance who will have control over liquid financial assets is through joint bank and stock accounts or other jointly held property in which either party is permitted to deposit, withdraw, expend, invest or liquidate accounts, funds, securities, and real or personal property jointly held. This, like the power of attorney, permits an individual to make plans in advance of incapacity so that funds can be managed. It provides, however, only for management of property and, unlike the power of attorney, does not permit application for public or private benefits that might accrue, as for example through public or private pension plans, disability plans, and similar matters.

TRUSTS

A trust is a legal device whereby an individual (technically known as the settlor) transfers title of property to another, known as the trustee, for the explicit purpose or purposes of being used for the benefit of a beneficiary. The beneficiary may be the settlor himself and the trust may be limited to particular purposes. The beneficiary may be one or more persons and the settlor may designate residual beneficiaries who will acquire an active interest in the trust upon the death of the named primary beneficiary(ies). Beneficiaries can be named to enjoy benefits during their lifetimes or for a term of years (or months). Trusts can be created that are either revocable or irrevocable. The trustee is bound to carry out the terms of the trust, and the trust can be enforced through state courts. Trustees can be surcharged for mismanagement, and they are bound to a high-level duty to manage the property in the way that the settlor intended. Here again is a device that can be used by an individual or individuals to provide for the management of property in advance of incapacity. Trusts can be established that will become effective upon the occurrence of a certain event, such as a determination of incapacity. Trusts may be formed during an individual's lifetime or may be established upon death as a part of the devolution of one's estate. That is to say, one may leave a portion of one's estate to a trust to be administered by a trustee for the benefit of one or more beneficiaries.

Involuntary Devices

The preceding devices are those that one would term "voluntary." All require action and volitional expression by a competent adult. With the exception of the irrevocable trust, the individual maintains absolute control and can withdraw any powers or participation that he or she may have authorized or entered into. The two following devices, conservatorship and guardianship, are, for the most part, involuntary. In some states that provide for conservatorships, there may be provision for application for a conservator by an individual himself. This, however, is rare, and accordingly conservatorship and guardianship are treated here as involuntary devices.

California has introduced an interesting and perhaps important semantic distinction along with the substantive improvements noted below. The California statute focuses on *incapacity* rather than upon *incompetence.* This requires courts, then, to zero in on limiting the powers of surrogates (i.e., conservators) solely to those matters identified as areas in which the incapacitated individual cannot function and no others.

CONSERVATORSHIP

Conservatorship is generally a procedure that is involuntary, involving a petition to a court, an investigation, a hearing, and a court finding. Conservators are appointed by the court, typically (but not always) to manage the estate (i.e., the property) of the conservatee. Conservatorships do not typically require a finding of incompetency. That is generally said to be the value of a conservatorship. Being a device that manages only the property, it leaves the conservatee's control of his or her person in tact. Conservatorships, however, have left unanswered in too many instances questions of who determines where the conservatee lives, what control a conservatee may have over any allowance he or she may receive, what control a conservative may have over wages or salary earned, and similar matters.

Recognizing the importance of being able to tailor-make protective arrangements, the California legislature modified the California probate code to provide for conservatorships that do, in fact, take account of the variations that may arise between and among people with different disabilities. In California, conservators may be appointed for both the person or for the estate. The state's probate code provides for appointment of a conservator of the person for one "who is unable properly to provide for his or her personal needs for physical health, food, clothing, or shelter" (Sec. 1801). A conservator of the estate may be appointed for a person who is substantially unable to manage his or her own financial resources or resist fraud or undue influence. The statute also provides that substantial inability may not be proved by isolated incidents of negligence or improvidence (Sec. 1802).

Most important, however, for our purposes are the explicit provisions that address the rights that a conservatee may retain. The new probate code provides that the court may limit the powers of the conservator and reserve those powers to the conservatee. The court may do so in accordance with the capacity and abilities of the conservatee (Sec. 2351). The court may grant the conservatee certain explicit rights (Sec. 187). And the statute explicitly grants the conservatee the right to control an allowance or any wages or salary, the right to make a will, and the right to enter into transactions to provide necessaries. It is possible, under the California statute, for the conservatee to retain powers to grant or withhold informed consent for medical treatment if the court so finds (Sec. 1880). The appointment of a conservator does not affect the right to marry *ipso facto*. The right to marry is determined independently of whether a conservator was appointed or not; the law that would apply would be that which is applied to the validity of all marriages. And finally, a conservatee may retain the right to vote if the court does not determine that he or she is unable to complete the necessary affidavit for voting.

Conservatorship in the California context attempts to provide surrogate authority that comports with the doctrine of least-restrictive alternatives. It provides safeguards through court investigation, court follow-up, and court review. The statute, however, is nothing more than the legal framework on which social services must be placed in order to achieve the hoped for results for the individual, namely, assistance with the management of one's property and personal affairs in a way that maximizes autonomy and free choice and minimizes the frustrations imposed by physical or mental disability.

GUARDIANSHIP

Guardianship is the most intrusive of the so-called protective services. It is the ultimate exercise of *parens patriae* powers. Guardianship follows a finding of incompetency and effectively replaces the personhood of the incompetent with that of the guardian. The ward (i.e., the incompetent) is bereft of virtually all rights. He or she cannot vote, drive, marry, contract, sue or be sued, or manage his or her affairs in any way. He or she is not entitled to manage any allowance, cannot give or withhold informed consent for medical treatment, and may not be able to resist "voluntary" admission to a mental hospital, nursing home, or other institution where such arrangements have been made by the guardian.

In some jurisdictions, provision has been made for the office of public guardian. The public guardian is a public official who is named as the guardian for persons found to be incompetent who do not have sufficient estates to pay for the services of a private guardian. Public guardians tend to have bureaucratized offices with assignments of wards to staff on a caseload basis. Caseloads are typically in excess of forty or fifty wards per staff member, a level that makes it impossible for the fiduciary duty of the guardian to be carried out. Wards thus tend to be neglected. No satisfactory system of oversight for public guardians has yet been designed and, for the most part, offices of public guardians rely on institutionalization and more restrictive measures of intervention rather than less.

THE ROLE OF SOCIAL WORKERS AND LAWYERS IN PROTECTIVE SERVICES

Protective-services cases begin with the identification of a problem by family members, friends, neighbors, police, landlords, physicians, emergency-room personnel, or social service personnel from within or outside the agency.

Too often, the life situation presented is one that has persisted for a long time and where, at the point of reporting, perhaps the life and certainly the well-being of the prospective protective-services client is severely threatened.

The nature of the problem that protective-services clients present typically calls into question the safety of an at-risk individual unless some intervention in his or her life is undertaken. The intervention may be of a medical nature, of a housing nature, of an institutional nature, or some other control over the autonomous conduct of the individual, since it is the autonomous conduct (or the absence of help in the case of someone who is physically or mentally impaired) that has created the risk. This places into conflict the values of safety and freedom.

It is the resolution of that conflict that requires substantial judgment. In an excellent guide series, "Improving Protective Services for Older Americans," published recently by the Center for Research and Advanced Study of the University of Southern Maine, Mary Collins offered a heirarchy of "solutions":

> Freedom is more important than safety: safety at home with informal support is preferable to safety with formal interventions: safety with formal kinds of help is preferable to involuntary care: involuntary care in the least restrictive setting with specified time limits and restrictions are preferable to full guardianship or institutional placement. Thus, workers should strive to assist people with their safety and care needs without disrupting their lifestyle or removing their freedom of choice.
>
> If you cannot provide safety in appropriate care at home, you should seek the least restrictive alternative. The formulation suggests the disruption of lifestyle is *more* important than *level* of care. Marginal help near the home may be far better than sophisticated care far away.

> Likewise, freedom of choice is more important than safety, except possibly when involuntarily ordered medical treatment has a high probability of restoring the person to health and safety.
>
> The worst possible outcome is one in which the person is made safe but suffers total loss of freedom and maximum lifestyle disruption. This is the case when a public guardian places a person in a distant nursing home or institution.

Within this generalized framework, the social worker is frequently the key "manager" who is expected to do something about the "problem." The process is essentially a four-stage one: The first stage is problem identification. Problem identification breaks down into two parts: First, is this a *prima facie* protective-services case? And second, what is the precise nature of the problem?

The second stage is the stage of solution identification, which is further broken down into the following questions:

What legal relationship appears to be most appropriate in terms of the strengths, capacities, incapacities, and disabilities of the client?

What social, medical, legal, or other services represent specific remedies to meet the precise problems identified in the first stage?

What outcomes are anticipated if the social, medical, legal, and other services are made available for the client, and what time frames can be postulated for the achievement of those goals?

The identification of solutions is further informed by an understanding of the client's desires and preferences, the conflict between safety and freedom, and judgment as to what represents the best interests of the client.

The third stage involves program delivery. Protective services cases frequently require the aggregation of a variety of services coming from different agencies, organizations, and formal and informal resources, each with a different funding stream and frequently with different eligibility requirements. In this respect, protective-services delivery is little different from the delivery of services for elderly long-term care patients who, more often than not, present clusters of problems served by different categorical agencies with differing eligibility and funding characteristics.

The final stage is that of assessment to determine whether problems were correctly identified, solutions correctly identified and applied, and hoped-for goals achieved. The assessment process is also utilized to determine the extent to which change has occurred in the life situation, introducing new or modified problems that require adjustment in solutions identified and programs enlisted.

In terms of casework services and case-management services, protective services for the elderly are distinguished by the issue of legal relationships and the resolution of the freedom/safety conflict. The case management or service-provision model is essentially a common one.

Because assessment of the problem is at the heart of this process, some aids and examples are provided here.

As noted above, stark determinations of legal competency often do not satisfy. Family members fret about the safety of a loved parent who is indeed forgetful, but who is *not* incompetent by any legal standard. A lonely old man "purchases" the friendship of companions, feeding their and his own drinking habits. An old lady refuses medical care but, in fact, she has *always* refused medical care. Situations like these produce ethical dilemmas—conflicts between what is beneficent and what is respectful of the individual; conflicts between principles of just distribution of burdens and benefits and principles of beneficence.

The resolution of such dilemmas requires ethical analysis—a listing and weighing of the relative good and harm that might arise from any particular course of action, the assessment of who will reap the benefits and who will carry the burdens—and what those benefits and burdens really are; and, of course, always the difficult measure of respect for persons—how much autonomy will we cede to a foolish or an unwise person. In a word, our understanding and approach to law must be tempered with an appreciation of that which is morally compelled or prohibited.

Assessment in protective services situations is frequently difficult. The prospective client may be uncommunicative, fearful, debilitated, and in need of emergency services. The protective services worker must develop for himself/herself criteria that make very clear imminent danger to the safety of the individual or to others. If the individual is completely debilitated, demented, lying in filth, etc., emergency intervention procedures are apparently justified. The situation becomes difficult when, despite apparent dementia and filth, the individual has some ability to get along and wants no part of any intervention. Different jurisdictions make different provisions for emergency detention of mentally deranged individuals. These detentions should be known and sparingly used, but where the emergency is palpable and the danger imminent, workers should not and need not shrink from some form of emergency detention, followed up swiftly with a determination of what less-restrictive alternatives might be available.

For those situations that are not urgent, it is important to focus on behavior; the person's wants and preferences; the strengths available through the individual, his family, neighborhood, friends, and other possible supports; and the potential resources that might be available to ameliorate the situation.

Figures 22.1 and 22.2 are two assessment forms, one developed by the Connecticut Department of Social Services and the other by the New York City Human Resources Administration (Project Focus). The Project Focus form is preliminary and has not yet been thoroughly tested and validated. Nonetheless, it is offered here as the result of careful study.[16]

Obviously, the assessment of the potential protective-services client may involve other disciplines, including medicine, psychology, and possibly law.

Where the conclusion is that the problem is not a *prima facie* protective-services case, that is, where no effort will be made to affect legal relationships, the case should no longer be dealt with as a protective-services case. This is not to say that counseling; supportive efforts; the furnishing of homemaker service, chore service, medical service, and housing assistance; or a host of other services should not go forward. It is only to say that protective-services units should not be cluttered up with situations that are service cases for older individuals.

Dealing with the protective-services client calls into conflict the roles that social workers may have identified with. Social workers at one and the same time may find themselves serving as a client's advocate, "protecting his rights," and respecting his or her wishes and preferences. On the other hand, the worker may also be making judgments about what is "in the best interest of the client" and may actively pursue legal interventions that may severely limit the client's range of choices and freedoms. The activity may well represent directions to which the client is opposed. The social worker, for better or for worse, is *not* the client's agent. The social worker may seek involuntary, coercive procedures through judicial intervention that the client may perceive as adverse to his or her interests.

Sometimes, in order to gain access or to obtain consent, social workers may utilize what has been called "authoritative casework" or "professional authority." Caseworkers may "bargain" or use moral persuasion where possible. There are, of course, ethical and legal limits. Workers may seek to persuade but must avoid coerciveness. Workers may seek to assist in management but must avoid decision making. Covert manipulation is to be avoided, and professional authority can never be used to violate civil rights or to act against demonstrated or known wishes. Full disclosure of the worker's activities in behalf of a client should always be made, and the client should provide, at the very least, tacit permission.

These are the bare bones of ethical considerations which arise in the course of the social worker/client relationship. Frequently, the situations test our understanding of the principle of Respect for Persons. One quails at the risks some older people are willing to take and which we feel we ought to prevent.

There are few formulas for proceeding in many of these difficult cases.[17]

SPECIAL ISSUES

Special issues that should be dealt with include clients who are abused, violent, or whose condition requires emergency intervention. Each of these situations is intimately entwined with legal considerations. How and when to intervene as well as who can intervene are frequently spelled out in statutes dealing with emergency detention, emergency commitment, and temporary detention. Each of these situations has a common thread in the need for emergency action. To be prepared for such eventualities, workers should determine what the law is in their respective jurisdictions, who has the authority to intervene, the nature of the information that must be filed and where it must be filed for emergency intervention, and the most effective ways of securing that intervention. Knowing the law and the procedures, however, is probably not enough. Arrangements should be made in advance through contact with mental-health authorities, Area Agencies on Aging, and the police in order to get to know the personnel involved, what material and information they need, and what is the best way to secure a result.

At the same time, social workers must be cognizant of the extraordinary potential for invasion of clients' civil rights and ought to be prepared to take steps to assure that those civil rights are protected either through location of counsel or some sort of advocate. In some jurisdictions, public defenders are responsible for representing persons confronted with civil commitment, while in other jurisdictions it may fall to community legal services, legal-aid societies, or some element of the private bar. In any event, this area needs coverage as well.

In working with attorneys, keep in mind that they are accustomed to viewing problems of all sorts in a highly structured fashion. In seeking help or advice from an attorney, it is useful to formulate for

STATE OF CONNECTICUT DEPARTMENT OF SOCIAL SERVICES
Protective Services for the Elderly

CLIENT EVALUATION AND FUNCTIONING

Client's Name ______ Age ___ Sex ______

Client's Address ______ Race ______

PHYSICAL ENVIRONMENT

Neighborhood: ______

Shelter: Sound___ Deteriorating___ Dilapidated___
Water ___ Electricity___ Heat___ Toilet___
Food ___ Stove ___

Housekeeping: ______

Hazards: ______

Other Observations: ______

SOCIAL ENVIRONMENT

Isolated ___ Known & visited by neighbors ___

Relatives: ______

Household Composition: ______

PERSONAL APPEARANCE

Dress: ______ Facial Expressions: ______
Gait: ______ Gestures: ______
Posture: ______ Speech: ______

PHYSICAL HEALTH

Client-defined problems: ______

(Indicate duration of problems.)
Malnourishment ___ Open sores ___
Lumps ___ Sudden weight loss ___
Persistent cough ___ Severe chest pain ___
Severe headaches ___ Shortness of breath ___
Vomiting ___ Change in bowel habits ___
Blood in urine ___ Vision impairment ___
Vaginal bleeding ___ Hearing impairment ___
Dizziness ___ Other ___

Most recent visit to a doctor ______

Next medical appointment ______

Recent medical problems ______

Medications ______
Comments ______

MENTAL HEALTH

Client-defined problems: ______

(Indicate duration of problems.)
Loss of appetite ___ Delusions ___
Insomnia ___ Thought distortion ___
Loss of interest ___ Confusion ___
Hypochondria ___ Impaired judgment ___
Suspiciousness ___ Memory lapses/loss ___
Hallucinations ___ Orientation ___
Feelings of Worthlessness ___ Other ___
Hazardous behaviors ______
Alcohol or other drug use ______
Recent losses of family or close friends ______
Past mental health problems ______

Capacity to consent ______
Other comments ______

CLIENT MOBILITY		PHYSICAL COMPETENCE	
Bedridden	___	Feeds self	___
Partially bedridden	___	Bathes self	___
Wheelchair	___	Dresses self	___
Housebound	___	Uses toilet	___
Able to get to yard	___	Gets out of bed	___
Neighborhood	___	Climbs stairs	___
Public transportation	___	Goes outdoors	___
Drives car	___	Cooks	___
Other	___	Shops	___
Comments	___	Light housework	___
		Heavy housework	___

ECONOMIC SITUATION

Income ______ Resources ______
Expenses ______

Affairs managed by ______
Comments ______

Other helping persons or agencies involved (specify involvement): ______

Client's perception of problems: ______

Worker's perception of problems (specify nature of protective problem): ______

Recommended action: ______

Obstacles: Does client consent? ______
Is client's ability to consent questioned? ______
Other: ______

EMERGENCY: ______

______
Worker's Name

______
Date Completed

I, ______, authorize the Department of Social Services to provide the services they may deem necessary to insure my safety. I agree to reimburse the Department if it is later determined that I am to pay for the services provided.

______ Witness's Name ______ Applicant's Name ______ Date

FIGURE 22.1. Assessment Form Developed by the Connecticut Department of Social Services.

Client's name____________________ Case number [____]
Date____________________

PROTECTIVE SERVICES RISK ASSESSMENT

SECTION I—ENDANGERING CONDITIONS
Instructions: Check all conditions known to be present, then rate the client on each dimension using the scales located along the right hand margin. If the client's life is not endangered on a given factor, circle "0 - no life threat." If the set of conditions is immediately life threatening, circle "3 - immediate life threat." Note less hazardous conditions by circling "1" or "2."

RISK FACTORS

1. Neglect

specify whether by:
[] self
[] other(s)
[] both

conditions include:
[] dirt, fleas, lice on person
[] skin rashes
[] bedsores
[] ulcerated sores
[] malnourished or dehydrated
[] doesn't get/take medications
[] inadequate clothing
[] fecal/urine smell
[] untreated medical conditions
[] other (specify)____________________

0.......1.......2.......3
no life threat — immediate life threat

2. Abuse

[] words or gestures that put client in fear of harm
[] multiple or severe bruises or burns
[] restrained, tied, swaddled, locked in
[] broken bones or wounds
[] rope marks
[] injuries in odd places
[] injuries at several stages of healing
[] other (specify) ____________________

0.......1.......2.......3
no life threat — immediate life threat

3. Self endangering behaviors

[] suicidal acts
[] wandering
[] frequenting dangerous place (specify) ____________________
[] life threatening behaviors (specify) ____________________
[] refuses medical treatment
[] other (specify) ____________________

0.......1.......2.......3
no life threat — immediate life threat

FIGURE 22.2. Assessment Form Developed by the New York City Human Resources Administration (Project Focus)

FIGURE 22.2. (continued)

-2-

4. Environmental hazards

[] homeless
[] no toilet facilities
[] no food storage facilities
[] no heat
[] animal-infested living quarters
[] other utilities lacking
[] other poor housing condition (specify) ______
[] threatening weather condition (specify) ______
[] other (specify) ______

0.......1.......2.......3
no life threat — immediate life threat

5. Intellectual impairments

[] faulty reasoning
[] can't follow instructions
[] incoherent speech
[] inappropriate or no response
[] disoriented to time and place
[] confusion
[] memory failure
[] loses things constantly
[] other (specify) ______

0.......1.......2.......3
no life threat — immediate life threat

6. Exploitation

[] extortion
[] parasitic relationship
[] unexplained disappearance of funds or valuables
[] servitude
[] other (specify) ______

0.......1.......2.......3
no life threat — immediate life threat

MANAGEMENT OF DAILY ACTIVITIES

1. Activities of daily living (Check if client does not do)

[] transferring from/to bed or chair
[] bathing
[] grooming
[] dressing
[] eating
[] toileting
[] other (specify) ______

0.......1.......2.......3
no life threat — immediate life threat

FIGURE 22.2. (continued)

-3- Client's name________________

2. Instrumental activities (Check if client does not do)

[] shop for food
[] shop for other things
[] drive car
[] use public transportation
[] do housework
[] do laundry
[] prepare meals
[] take medications properly
[] other (specify) ____________________

0.......1.......2.......3
no life threat ... immediate life threat

3. Capacity to manage finances (check if characteristic of client)

[] hoarding
[] squandering
[] failure to pay bills
[] many credit purchases
[] uncashed checks
[] large amounts of cash
[] inaccurate/no knowledge of finances
[] giving money away
[] other (specify) ____________________

0.......1.......2.......3
no life threat ... immediate life threat

****

ACTION NEEDED

a) If all of the scales in Section I are rated "0 - no life threat", Sections II and III need not be completed. Skip to Section IV— "Action Taken," on page 6.

b) If any scales in section I are rated "1" or "2", but none are "3 - immediate life threat", agency policy and the assessor's judgement will determine whether further assessment is required.

c) Sections II, III and IV should be completed for all clients with any ratings of "3 - immediate life threat" in Section I and for other clients for whom further assessment is required.

****

FIGURE 22.2. (continued)

-4-

SECTION II—AGGRAVATING AND MITIGATING SOCIAL FACTORS
Instructions: Check all conditions known to be present.

1. At the present time, does the client depend for essentials on an unreliable caregiver?

   [ ] no (skip to question 2)
   [ ] yes, specify why unreliable below:

      [ ] sometimes neglects responsibilities
      [ ] sometimes is incapacitated because of alcohol or drugs
      [ ] is physically or mentally unable to provide needed care
      [ ] other______________________________
      ____
      ____

2. Is any person who lives in the client's household, or has ready access to the client, responsible for any risk factor in Section I— items 1, 2, or 6 (neglect, abuse, or exploitation)?

   [ ] yes
   [ ] no

3. Is the client living in unusually isolated circumstances?

   [ ] yes
   [ ] no

4. Has a recent change in the client's social environment contributed to the client's endangerment?

   [ ] no (skip to question 5)
   [ ] yes, specify changes below:

      [ ] loss of caregiver
      [ ] loss of other major social support
      [ ] move to new environment
      [ ] other______________________________
      ____
      ____

FIGURE 22.2. (continued)

-5- Client's name____________________

5. How much help will the following social supports provide?

	Will Provide: All help necessary	Will Provide: Partial help	Not a potential source of help
a) persons living in the client's household	[] 1	[] 2	[] 3
b) other persons— neighbors, friends, and relatives	[] 1	[] 2	[] 3
c) other agencies, churches, temples, and organizations	[] 1	[] 2	[] 3

If no potential sources of help, skip to Question 6. If help available:
Identify the social support(s)______________________________

State how the social support(s) will help______________________________

State the limitations of the social support(s)______________________________

6. Generally, how willing is the client to accept help?

[] totally willing
[] somewhat willing
[] refuses all help

SECTION III—ASSESSMENT OF CLIENT'S NEED FOR PROTECTIVE INTERVENTION

1. Does the client understand the risk(s) he or she is facing?

[] yes
[] partially
[] no

2. Taking into consideration the client's endangering conditions, social resources, and understanding of the risks he or she faces, assess whether the client needs protective intervention. Use the following criteria:

a) If the client has social supports that are available, able, and willing to provide all necessary help and he or she will accept this help, the client does not need additional protective intervention (although other forms of help may be required).

b) If the overall level of endangerment is immediately life threatening, and the client does not have social supports to provide sufficient help or he or she is unwilling to accept such help, the client requires protective intervention.

c) If you are unable to make either of the above decisions, further assessment is required.

Does the client require protective intervention?

[] yes
[] no

FIGURE 22.2. (continued)

-6-

SECTION IV—ACTION TAKEN
Instructions: Complete this section for all clients.

[] case not opened
[] case referred for service elsewhere
case referred to:____
____
[] case opened for protective services
[] case opened for other services but not for protective services

If case has been opened, complete the following:

1. Case assigned to:
worker________________________________
unit__________________________________

2. Has an offer of service been made to the client?

[] yes (answer question 3)
[] no (skip questions 3 and 4)

3. Does the client accept the offer?

[] yes (skip question 4)
[] no (answer question 4)

4. Is the client likely to become voluntary with further casework?

[] yes
[] no

5. Types of assistance likely to be provided include:

[] food	[] money	[] money management
[] shopping	[] transportation	[] housekeeping
[] personal care	[] shelter	[] medical aid
[] psychiatric aid	[] other (specify________________________________)	

yourself in advance what you see as the problem or problems and what you believe the remedies are for those particular problems. Lawyers will want to know as precisely as possible what the issues are that the protective-services worker can deal with, what services will right the wrong the client is confronting, who has the resources or authority to deliver what is necessary to right the wrong, and what special attributes of the client may give rise to an entitlement. The lawyer's contribution may take the form of designing a strategy to secure that which is necessary. It must also be clear to the lawyer whom he is representing. The lawyer's advocacy is total. If he is representing the client, he will view the situation through the client's eyes and will look on every effort at restricting the client's freedom of choice in an adversarial way. If he is the social agency's attorney, he will view the situation from the standpoint of the duties and obligations that the agency owes the client, the local, state, or federal agency that provides it money to do certain things, and so on.

The relationship with the courts can be facilitated through a similar understanding of the court's role and range of activity. In protective services, courts play several roles. In the first instance they may be asked to decide upon the competency of an individual or the need for intervention on an emergency of conservatorship basis. While court proceedings are highly ritualistic and heavily surrounded with procedural requirements, they are nonetheless well equipped to decide questions on brief notice, provided they have adequate and sufficient information concisely presented, supported wherever possible by objective evidence. Judges and their clerks are more readily available than is commonly assumed. Protective-services workers above all should not be cowed by the mystique that surrounds the judicial process or the judicial persona. Where emergencies arise, a protective-services worker need not shrink from calling the judge's chambers and asking to speak to the judge's clerk. Good preparation in identifying the problem you wish to solve through judicial intervention, the remedy you are seeking from the court, and the justification for emergency will help immeasurably. Where no emergency exists, courts will appreciate clearly presented petitions outlining all the facts and subsequent support in a hearing by well-presented evidence. Court intervention is an extreme measure. Courts are increasingly disinclined to exercise their power in these situations unless the evidence is compelling. Given the array of legal devices that fall short of court intervention, recourse to the courts should be limited.

Finally, under the rubric of special issues, are those occasional cases that arise among clients who are ill and who refuse to give informed consent for life-saving measures. Where a client is competent and is aware of the consequences of his or her refusal to give informed consent, virtually all jurisdictions will honor that refusal and permit the patient to expire. The social worker's role in situations where the client is apparently aware of the consequences and is sufficiently well-oriented so that he or she can process the information being given to him or her is to support the client in his decision and protect him or her from what may be coercive, if beneficent, behavior on the part of physicians or other providers and to help him or her defend against an incompetency petition.

The more difficult cases are those where the client's orientation and awareness may be less apparent but where nonetheless the expressed wish to forgo treatment is consistent with values held when abilities were less diminished. Here the worker will have to be more sensitive and focus on the discovery and protection of values of individuals of declining or diminished capacity. This may require the search for a "prior explicit statement" by the patient before capacities were diminished or the explication of what Nancy Neveloff Dubler has termed the "sedimented life values of patients," those values being the ones that emerge through the fog of memory loss and even dementia and that are consistent with earlier behaviors, wishes, and preferences.[18]

A number of cases begin to explore the issue of competence and the right to die; knowledge of these cases will undoubtedly be useful to the protective-services worker who confronts such a situation. The courts are stepping gingerly around this issue, which is truly a vexing one. Some are "pull the plug" cases like *In Re Quinlan*. More frequently, however, cases also incorporate the issue of third party consents authorizing termination of treatment or the withdrawal of nutrition or hydration. Examples of such cases include *In the Matter of Nancy Ellen Jobes, In the Matter of Helen Peters;* and *In the Matter of Kathleen Farrell,* three carefully reasoned New Jersey Supreme Court Cases and *In Re Earl Spring.*[19] Others concern decisions to grant or withhold consents for treatment to retarded or severely demented patients like the *Saikewicz* and *Dinnerstein* opinions.

None, however, is more vexing than the case of Mary Northern, an elderly lady brought into a hospital against her wishes for treatment of a respiratory infection. Following her admission, it was discovered that her feet were frostbitten. Ms. Northern was advised that gangrene had set in and that if her legs were not amputated she would certainly die. Ms. Northern, who was well-oriented to time, place, and person, demurred. She protested that her legs were not that badly infected, that she knew they would get better, that she had no wish to die, and that the issue was not that she preferred dying to having her legs cut off. It was her firm position that there was nothing wrong with her legs. A petition was filed to have her found incompetent. Despite testimony by examining psychiatrists that she was not incompetent, a court found her to be so and appointed the superintendent of the hospital her guardian. There was additional testimony in this case that if her legs were not amputated she would have only a 10 percent chance of survival. There was further psychiatric testimony that if her legs *were* amputated, there was a 50–50 chance that she would retreat into a psychotic fugue from which she might never emerge. Within a space of two weeks, this case was heard by the Tennessee Supreme Court, which affirmed the decision of the lower court to appoint a guardian but which further required that no action be taken to amputate her legs unless two named physicians asserted that she was in imminent danger of death. In this case, the court appeared to waltz around the problem. Mary Northern was never operated on. She survived for some months after the decision and died before any surgery took place. Some commentators have suggested that this case is a "right to be left alone case." It undoubtedly presents the most difficult kind of problem that social workers, attorneys, and courts can possibly confront.

FINDING SOLUTIONS

Problems that social workers have encountered in the protective-services arena grow largely out of the lack of clarity, the conflicts between safety and freedom, the ethical dilemmas involved in attempting to help but knowing that precious liberties may be eliminated, and an absence of proper and sufficient services to meet the needs of the physically and mentally impaired who may require what we have come to know as protective services. The solutions are both legislative and nonlegislative. Legislative solutions must be significant alteration of statutes defining incompetency and providing for the imposition of guardianships. John Reagan has outlined an agenda in this area.[20] He suggests first and foremost the narrowing of the criteria for determining incompetency so as to assure that the autonomy of alleged incompetents is maximized by determining whether or not an individual has any recognizable premise for his decisions and whether any reasonable purpose can lie behind the individual's decisions and behavior, however foolish they might appear. While this may appear extreme, given the tendency of courts to permit even single instances of irrational behavior to become the basis for findings of incompetency, modification of criteria in the direction suggested here may well be appropriate.

Second, he suggests requiring behavioral evidence of recent conduct exhibiting inability to manage one's affairs or to give direction to others to carry out that management and threatening vital personal interests. The causes of disability should be eliminated from any evidence since they are irrelevant to determining whether a person has the competence to act on his own behalf or whether his legal capacity should be transferred elsewhere.

Third, Reagan suggests that total guardianship be abolished and that all guardianships be tailor-made to the specific disabilities and impairments of the alleged incompetent. This would mean that all guardianships would be limited and specific and that powers not transferred to a guardian would reside with the ward.

Fourth, Reagan recommends the abolition of public guardianships precisely because they are nonresponsive and, more often than not, harmful to the individual.

And fifth, he recommends that procedural safeguards be assured particularly through the mandatory provision of counsel in all guardianship proceedings.

Provision for protective services and emergency intervention has been vexing state legislators throughout the country. Numerous provisions surface each year. One bill put before the Pennsylvania senate in 1983 is the result of several years' study by the state and others. It makes provision for emergency involuntary intervention, imposes obligation to report on findings, severely limits the interventions that courts can authorize, and provides for assuring due-process rights.

Although Reagan's recommendation to eliminate total guardianships would appear to cover the situations provided for by California's conservatorship statute, the steps taken by California appear to provide for some surrogate service without a finding of incompetence and to explicitly assure a number of civil rights to the conservatee. This section of California's probate code deserves attention by other jurisdictions.

While the majority of the states have enacted durable power of attorney statutes, it is recommended that this provision become universal, particularly in the light of America's mobile elderly population and their migration to Sunbelt states.

The durable power of attorney statutes are fine as far as they go (and most only go to issues of property), but provision for durable powers of attorney for health care decisions would be the single most important step in moving toward some solution to the problems presented by the growing numbers of demented people in and out of nursing homes who have never been adjudicated as incompetent but who cannot give legal consent for treatment or its cessation. To be sure, durable powers cannot be executed *after* one is demented, but authorizing advance directives for health care might encourage their use more generally.

Finally, protective services would be enhanced by the universal adoption by state legislatures of so-called "Right to Die" or "Natural Death" statutes. While some thirty-nine states *have* some form of the statute, there is a lack of uniformity and a seeming reluctance to honor explicitly statutes of a state in which the Living Will was executed if different from the state in which the individual resides.

Nonlegislative solutions necessarily include the revision of service systems so that services can be requisitioned by protective-services workers much as physicians requisition services in a hospital. This is not unlike the concept operationalized in the Channeling Project on Long-Term Care and currently being demonstrated in sites around the country. Protective-services agencies frequently are unable to secure appropriate housing, counseling, homemaker services, chore services, money-management services, friend/advocates (agents), and similar accommodations for their clients. They are left in an impossible situation, attempting to protect the rights of their clients, avoiding excessive intervention, institutionalization, guardianships, or the like, and are utterly without the social service resources necessary to give effect to the treatment of choice determined in an adequate assessment. Subsumed under that general heading of revised service systems, it is clear that mental health systems that have traditionally been unresponsive to the needs of deranged, demented, and distressed elderly clients must revise their orientation, services, and relationships with other social agencies serving the elderly.

Finally, some provision must be made either through voluntary organizations or through public social services to develop a cadre of agents who can serve as friend/advocates for those elderly who require assistance to give effect to their wishes, decision, and preferences.

NOTES

1. *De Praerogative Regis,* 17 Edward 2 c.9 (1324), established in statute law the duty of the sovereign as *parens patriae* to carry responsibility for protection and care of the person and property of mentally disabled people.

2. See, for example, *Bryden's Estate* 211 PA. 633, 636, 61 A. 250, 251 (1905), cited with approval in *Urquhart's Estate* 431 PA. 134, 245 A. 2d 141, 142 (1968) and *In Re Estate of Porter* 345 A. 2d 171, 173 (1975): "A man may do what he pleases with his personal estate during his life. He may beggar himself and his family if he chooses to commit such an act of folly."

3. Adulthood has various benchmarks depending upon context. It may be achieved at age 14 in some jurisdictions for determining contributory negligence, 16 for criminal responsibility, 18 for voting, 21 for purchase of alcoholic beverages, or no chronological age at all for consent to abortion in the case of a pregnant female.

4. 575 S.W. 2d 8946 (Tenn. 1978).

5. This list of cases draws heavily (although not entirely) from L. Bennett, "Protective Services for the Aged," in Pennsylvania Conference on Protective Services for Older People, 1964, *Proceedings* (Harrisburg: Pennsylvania Citizens Council, Commission on Aging, 1965).

6. L. Shelford, *A Practical Treatise of the Law Concerning Lunatics, Idiots and Persons of Unsound Mind* (London: S. Sweet, 1833).

7. 8 Law Reporter 122 (Mass. 1845).

8. For a fuller discussion of guardianship and *parens patriae,* see P.M. Horstman, "Protective Services for the Elderly: The Limits of Parens Patriae," 40 *Missouri Law Review* 215 (1975).

9. 95 S.Ct. 2486 (1975).

10. See Seminar on Protective Services for Older People, Arden House, 1963, *Proceedings* (New York: National Council on the Aging, 1964): National Council on the Aging, *Guardianship and Protective Services for Older People* (New York: NCOA Press, 1963).

11. G. J. Alexander and T. H. D. Lewin, *The Aged and the Need for Surrogate Management* (Syracuse: Syracuse University, 1972).

12. 364 U.S. 479, 488 (1960).

13. For a fuller discussion of the least-restrictive alternative doctrine, see D. L. Chambers, "Alternatives to Civil Commitment of the Mentally Ill: Practical Guides and Constitutional Imperatives," 70 *Michigan Law Review* 1108 (1972). Chambers' discussion of the application in a variety of contexts is important because it imparts historical legitimacy to the concept. From the standpoint of legal argument this may be significant in some courts.

14. 364 F 2nd. 657D.C. Circ. (1966).

15. A complete review of Living Will Laws can be found in *Handbook of Living Will Laws* (New York: Society for the Right to Die, 1987).

16. For fuller explication of the Project Focus material, see S. Daiches, *Risk Assessment: A Guide for Adult Protective Services Workers* (New York: New York City Human Resources Administration, 1983) and S. Daiches, *Protective Services Risk Assessment: A New Approach to Screening Adult Clients* (New York: New York City Human Resources Administration, 1983).

17. An excellent review of protective services worker roles and relationships with courts can be found in *Guide on Improving Protective Services for Older Americans: Social Worker Role* (Portland: University of Southern Maine, 1982).

18. Outline by Nancy Neveloff Dubler distributed at a seminar entitled Legal and Ethical Aspects of Health Care for the Elderly sponsored by the American Society of Law and Medicine. Washington, 1983.

19. Important right to die cases include: *In Re Quinlan* 70 NJ 10, 335 A. 2d 647 (1976); *In Re Earl Spring* 405 N.E. 2d 115 (1980); *Superintendent of Belchertown State School v. Saikewicz* 373 MASS. 728, 370 N.E. 2d 417 (1977); *In Re Dinnerstein* 380 N.E. 2d 134 (Mass. App. 1978); *In Re Eichner* (Brother Fox) Ct. of App. 52 N.Y. 2d 363, 20 N.E. 2d 64, 438 N.Y.C. 2d 266 (1981); *Northern v. State* 575 S.W. 2d 8946

(Tenn. 1978); *In the Matter of Nancy Ellen Jobes,* 108 NJ 394 (1987); *In the Matter of Helen Peters,* 108 NJ 365 (1987); *In the Matter of Kathleen Farrell,* 108 NJ 335 (1987).

20. J. Reagan, "Adult Protective Services: An Appraisal and a Prospectus," in National Law and Social Work Seminar, Improving Protective Services for Older Americans, *Proceedings and Prospectus* (Portland, Me: 1982)

23

Services for the Dying

THEODORE H. KOFF, ED.D.
The University of Arizona, Tucson

A paper on services to the dying in an earlier edition of this book was written by Richard A. Kalish, Ph.D., a social psychologist who had published extensively on the subjects of death and dying. His work on the cultural aspects of dying opened new vistas for understanding differences among different cultural groups and his clear yet always provocative presentations served to stimulate my thinking as well as that of many others in the field. Unfortunately Dick was afflicted with cancer at the time he was preparing a new version of his earlier essay and died before he was able to put his thoughts into writing or communicate what he would have wanted to say to us in this presentation. Dick took with him his thoughts for this chapter, but more importantly, we lost the wisdom, warmth, and friendship of a dear friend. It seems fitting that I quote from the final thoughts of his earlier chapter in beginning my thoughts for this new approach. "It then seems obvious that our capacity to improve services for the elderly in general and for the dying in general may accomplish all that is necessary to improve services for the elderly dying" (Kalish 1985:545). Dick argued for a just and humane society for all, irrespective of age or proximity to the end of life. Such a society would provide appropriate services to older people who are dying. This was Dick's goal and it is mine as well.

With this goal in mind I dedicate this paper to the memory of Dick Kalish.

Kalish traced the evolution of writing and thinking in the area of services for the dying and noted a shift in emphasis over the years:

> from innovation and exploration to institutionalization and bureaucratization. The period from the mid-1950s to the mid-1970s laid the groundwork by challenging the taboos and pointing out potential paths for possible services; from the mid-70s to the present, the emphasis has been on planning, developing, and funding improved services. In 1967, Cicely Saunders began St. Christopher's, the first facility in the modern hospice movement; within fifteen years, with an unknown number of hospices in varying stages of development, the major issue in the United States has become the potential for third-party payments. (1985:531–532).

Having demonstrated the hospice concept and institutionalized hospice through its acceptance by Medicare and private insurance programs, the focus of attention shifted to issues of adequacy of payments. This process illustrates what Kalish observed as a transition from innovation to bureaucratization, with the clear implication that attention has slipped away from the person in need to larger societal issues. Some of the same thoughts are presented by Siegler (1985) when he talks about the stages of medicine, commenting that we have entered what he calls the "third age of medicine." The first age was paternalistic, the second was the age of autonomy and the current one is the "age of bureaucratic parsimony," in which decisions will be made on the basis of cost benefit analysis. This point of view is, in fact, analogous to Kalish's issues of institutionalization and bureaucracy and serves to illustrate that much of the thinking about services for the dying has indeed shifted away from concerns about the dying person to the societal issues of dealing with dying in our society today. Thus we see the tension between innovation and bureaucratization, the intersection of concerns about the individual and the larger societal needs, and the challenge of improving the quality of living and dying that may be in conflict with attempts inappropriately to continue life when such attempts may result in death with indignity.

Here, I will explore, in the contexts of Siegler's age of autonomy and Kalish's periods of innovation and bureaucratization, several themes critically relevant to a person's dying. Among these themes are the revitalization of the role of the family in providing services to the dying and issues dealing with the autonomy of the dying person as it relates to the continuity or discontinuity of life near the end of life, and opportunities for societal intervention on behalf of the dying person and family members.

DEATH WITH DIGNITY

Among these new themes are those dealing with the concept of death with dignity, which refers to the respective roles of the dying person and the care providers in the dying process; issues related to the continuity of treatments when it no longer is in the best interests of the patient; issues about the rationing of health care and its impact on the continuity or discontinuity of life; issues of suicide and the cost of sustaining life for the old in our society; and issues of euthanasia or the ability to assist a person to reach death at a time selected by the person. In a sense, services for the dying lie in a continuum that begins before death and continues after death. These services are related to the economic status of the dying person and family members as well as to the presence of family, whether or not there have been earlier opportunities to have communicated preferences about continuity of medical care and what services are desired during the dying process, and the relationship between the physician and the patient and family. In addition, "one rarely dies on one's own" (Roy 1988:137); dying has become a team activity that often takes place in the presence of technology and technologists. In a sharp departure from the past, when most Americans died at home, an estimated 80 percent now die in hospitals or nursing homes (Wallis, 1988). Yet while dying has become a team activity for the providers of services, the older person may die alone—although not on his or her own. This is especially true in the absence of family and friends.

Today dying often is surrounded by decisions and frequently the decisions are to be made on behalf of the dying person. Therefore decisions about dying are likely to be shared decisions directed by the dying person, if competent, and/or the family, if family is available. Too often the dying person and/or family members are alienated from the dying event and the decisions associated with that event. Compliance with decisions made by the dying person and family is what Roy (1988) refers to as the "deprofessionalization of dying" or giving back to the dying person opportunities for decision-making regarding life.

The older person can draw strength from the relationship with the health professional, especially when that relationship is what Kalish refers to as open communication with the health care provider. "The closer these relationships are and the more opportunity for personal interaction that exists, the greater will be the capacity of the dying person to draw strength from the relationship" (Kalish 1985:539). It is open awareness in the clinical relationship that generally precedes the ability to deal with death and dying. "It is not the task of the health or social work professional to force a person to accept his or her own death . . . our obligation is to give the individual enough information so that he or she can ask relevant and intelligent questions if he or she wishes to ask them" (Kalish 1985:541). It is in the framework of open awareness that the social worker or health care worker can communicate the important message that, although the disease cannot be cured, continuing caring will be available and the person will not be abandoned.

It also happens that very often people do not just die; their dying requires decisions about the sustenance or curtailment of life, the payment for care, the quality of life. In earlier periods people simply died and others watched. We usually cannot predict where we will die, under what circumstances and in whose company. Consider the difference in the way one may die in a situation in which he or she has a heart attack in the midst of a well-equipped medical center and a situation in which a life-threatening event is experienced by someone alone in a mountain retreat. How often is death announced by the accumulation of mail in a mailbox or a pile of newspapers at the door of an isolated person?

The alternative to the depersonalization of dying is dying with dignity, or as Roy states, helping the person "live or die in a fashion that honors his or her dignity and ours as well" (1988:144). The call for dignity is a call for the skillful use of relationships with those who are dying in order to serve their needs and those of the family. Social workers can employ their special skills in the use of relationships and supporting open communication to provide this assistance. In some ways the dying person can no longer be seen only as a victim of death itself but rather as the victim of a system that seriously fails to care for and about the individual, a system that ignores the needs and values of the dying person, with patients becoming objects with no right to assert their beliefs or express their wishes (Glasse and Murray 1984). And at the end of life, "at the moment when a patient is most likely to want to exercise his autonomous right to die, he will often pass out of consciousness or competency" (Dickey, Gaylin, and Safar 1987:123). What constitutes the ability to die with dignity is subjectively defined by the dying person's perception of his or her quality of life, both when near death and in earlier periods. Decisions regarding the intervention of treatment or the continuation of treatments often hinge upon the physician's perception of the quality of life.

Pearlman and Jonsen studied quality-of-life issues in the making of medical decisions and found that most medical decisions were made on the basis of the physician's perception of the quality-of-life issues involved. However, "the term 'quality of life' has no obvious meaning; it is not clear to which empirical states the term refers, nor is it manifest how any particular person will evaluate those states" (Pearlman and Jonsen 1985:348). In the study, they found that "a significant minority of the physicians studied considered the patient's quality of life sufficiently poor to withhold additional treatments, whereas most physicians considered it sufficiently good to justify implementing additional therapy. These results highlight the inherent ambiguity of the term 'quality of life' " (1985:348) and the authors caution against its use as a determinant of the provision of services. There are some individuals who as patients reject the quality of life issue as being of any consequence. These individuals consider life to have intrinsic worth and regard prolongation of life as the overriding determinant of the utility of an intervention. Therefore "responsible use of the inherently ambiguous concept of quality of life occurs when clinicians attune their interactions with patients to the values and goals of the patient" (Pearlman and Jonsen, 1985:349).

Getting to know how the person chooses to die, the person's values, religious beliefs, ethics, and family considerations all become important to care providers when they are faced with helping an individual die with dignity. Here again, the social worker can be especially helpful by raising important questions for the family to discuss and resolve. It is not the caregiver's belief system that should be the determinant unless the caregiver's belief system is based on a commitment to demonstrate complete support for the wishes of the dying person. Usually the most trying circumstances occur when care providers must attempt to reconcile known wishes of the patient and family with their own or the institution's beliefs and policies.

ROLE OF THE FAMILY

The issue of the quality of life is expressed by Gadow as related to the freedom of self-determination. "It is based on the principle that freedom of self-determination is the most fundamental and valuable human right and therefore is a greater good than any health care can provide. This means that the right to self-determination ought not to be infringed even in the interest of health, perhaps not even in the interest of life itself" (Gadow, 1980:390–391) It is the patient's decisions that are truly his or her own and they need to be arrived at after consultation with the health care providers and family members. While health care providers will always be on the scene, family members frequently may not be present or may be there without having received clear communication of the preferences of the patient or the patient's best interests. When a patient cannot exercise self-determination, whose wish prevails?

Is it that of the physician or the family? In a recent "right to die" decision, the New Jersey Supreme Court ruled that a patient's right to self determination can supersede the treatment policies of medical institutions. The court determined that a family's request to withdraw artificially given food and fluids from a 31-year-old woman who had been in an irreversible coma state since 1980 was ethical and appropriate (Armstrong 1987). The court did not involve itself in the nature or appropriateness of the treatment but concentrated on the importance of selecting the right proxies for making such decisions, should the patient be incompetent. Fletcher adds that "whatever is done to a patient against his or her will is a battery, an assault, and (if surgical) mayhem" (1987:679).

The following statement was issued in March 1986 by the Council on Ethical and Judicial Affairs of the American Medical Association as a guide to physicians in determining when life-sustaining interventions may be abandoned.

> The social commitment of the physician is to sustain life and relieve suffering. Where the performance of one duty conflicts with the other, choice of the patient, or his family or legal representative if the patient is incompetent to act on his own behalf, should prevail. In the absence of the patient's choice or an authorized proxy, the physician must act in the best interest of the patient (Dickey 1986:471).

The President's Commission for the Study of Ethical Problems in Medicine and Biomedical and Behavioral Research (1983) stresses the importance of the family's involvement in decisions related to the care of the dying person and recommends that patients be enabled to give directions about their preferences for care prior to becoming incompetent. While a family approach to dying seems reasonable and rational it is not yet supported by public policies that determine under what circumstances public funds will be utilized in providing services for the dying person's family or to enable care providers to honor the wishes of family regarding the continuity of services. For example, public funds are available to support programs to keep alive a person who is near death or to support someone who is dying; the same funds are not available to support the family after the death of the individual, even though the family members may require bereavement or other health services stemming from the effects upon them of that death. A comparable issue is raised for the family that is prepared to make life-determining decisions on behalf on a non-competent individual, yet is not permitted to act on behalf of the family member because of the confusion surrounding issues of ethics and liability, or the intervention of health care providers or the government. What should evolve is an orientation to the importance and value of the family in the process of dying or a paradigmatic shift that considers services for the dying to be services to the family of the dying and recognizes members of the family unit as appropriate recipients of dying-related services at any particular time. How family is to be defined (i.e., the biological family, marital family, or organized friendships supportive of the patient), how roles and responsibilities of the family are to be defined and how government, health care providers and insurers are to relate to the family unit are questions requiring further consideration in order to evolve a theoretical framework that structures our thinking, research and policy formation related to services for the dying. In essence the issues of death with dignity can be framed in the context of death in a family setting.

These are also issues requiring advocacy for changes in the way the family unit is viewed by governmental agencies. Social workers, as change agents, could be leaders in advocacy efforts to recognize family services as an important component of services to the dying.

Fulton (1987) introduces his discussion of "The Many Faces of Grief" by reviewing an obituary of a man who died in the Sunbelt, having left the northwest twenty years before. A memorial service was held for him in his home town, with people attending who probably had not seen him for twenty years, and his burial in the Sunbelt community was attended by a small group of friends who knew very little about his earlier years. The man had four children, each living in a different city distant from where he had settled. He died in a nursing home and was separated from family and friends at the time of his death and for some time prior to his death. Was the life of this man made less remarkable because of the separation from his family and old friends? Was his dying depersonalized and perhaps lonely? Was his family denied opportunities to relate to the man during this important period of his life? This event is certain to happen with greater frequency as family sizes diminish and more and more children live in cities distant from their parents. Opportunities to unite families have to be explored and policies that encourage families to be involved with their dying relatives have to be implemented.

The issue of family is especially critical when family members become surrogate decision-makers for a seriously ill individual who is not capable of communicating preferences regarding issues of the continuity of special care treatments, the initiation of some aspects of care, or the desire to discontinue some care. If the family members have not had the opportunity to review these care issues with the patient and/or cannot rely upon a living will or durable power of attorney to assume responsibility for implementing the patient's preferences, a period of indecision or a delay in the implementation of a decision that would have been supported by the patient may occur. The issues of self-determination in dying in contrast to the imposition of the will of the care providers as well as the issues of life sustaining treatments, the living will and the durable power of attorney, are all of current concern and are being dealt with in the literature (Kalish 1982, 1985; Hirsh 1986; Pearlman and Jonsen 1985; Powills 1985; Berger 1988; Wass 1977; Brody 1985; Dickey 1986; Osterweis 1985; Fahey 1987; Germain 1984; Fletcher 1987; Bodnar 1987; Michel 1984). All these issues can be dealt with in the framework of the family, where family exists, or can be developed wherever the public policies recognize the importance of the family in maintaining a quality of life in dying in order to assure the continuation of the wishes of the dying person throughout the dying process. Decisions about dying are meant to be shared decisions involving the family members and the providers of care (Roy 1988).

SUICIDE AND EUTHANASIA

Another issue of quality and dignity of life is related to the individual's ability to determine if and when it is the appropriate time to end one's own life. It has been noted that the incidence of suicide increases greatly among the very old (Wass 1977; Wass and Myers 1982; Siegler 1985; Osgood 1987; and Caplan 1987) and that some persons seek support from family, friends, and physicians to relieve them of their pain and suffering. Yet society frowns upon and imposes penalties upon its members who provide assistance in ending a life before it has been determined that death is appropriate and that nothing else should be done either to preserve life or to assist in its coming to an end. We consider maintaining the status quo or permitting a natural ending of the life to be quite different from actively helping the person end the final stage of life in the quickest and most painless manner. The issue of choosing when a life is to end, whether by deciding when it might be appropriate to intervene to terminate the life or by assisting in the completion of the life, has constituted a major portion of the writings concerning death during the past five years.

The suicide rate for the elderly is high and Osgood (1987) reports that even though the 60 and over age group comprises only 12 percent of the population, they account for fully 17–25 percent of all suicides.

Even if these figures are underreported, due to the ease with which suicide is disguised by taking overdoses or mixing drugs, failing to take life-sustaining drugs, or starving oneself to death, suicide has become one of the ten leading causes of death in the United States. Osgood also says that unlike the young who attempt suicide as a call for help the elderly are more likely to be serious in their effort and successful in their attempts: 80 percent of the elderly who threaten suicide follow through. Therefore each sign of suicide has to be taken seriously if it has been determined that suicide is to be avoided. It is important that older people, especially those in crisis, have access to mental health services that fully understand the needs of the elderly, are supportive to the client and family, and can minimize the stigma older persons often associate with mental health services.

The presence of depression has been correlated highly with suicide. The biggest problem with depression according to Bernstein (1987) is access to service. "Due to the current reimbursement system most mental health agencies have so many exclusion factors in their criteria for accepting clients, many older people can't be treated. A couple of major factors which cause depression and can lead to suicide are loss of occupational role and bereavement. The death of a spouse can account for true clinical depression up to one year after death in up to 20 percent of the widowed population" (Bernstein, 1987:9). With approximately 800,000 new widows and widowers each year, up to 160,000 older persons are suffering clinical depression (Osterweis 1985). These older persons may be subject to acts of suicide unless suitable intervention is provided in response to the depression.

Some older persons may seek help in dying because they accept the end of their life and want to avoid prolonged suffering and pain. Earlier research has identified that the elderly generally do not want to be kept alive by artificial means (Wass 1977) and that as a group the elderly are less fearful of death than younger age groups (Wass and Myers 1984). In a sense they may paraphrase the statement of Lamm, "the tragedy of life is not death; it is dying unfulfilled, not having loved, without accomplishments" (1987:xiv). What is the right intervention in the life of a dying person and how should the appropriateness for that individual be determined?

Caplan (1987) has asked why he, as a physician, with the concurrence of the family and an independent medical panel, shouldn't be allowed to "quickly and painlessly end" the suffering of a patient of his. Essentially, he advocates for the legalization of euthanasia in order to achieve what he believes is a proper or humane death that relieves prolonged suffering. There are, of course, many arguments against the legalization of euthanasia. Some are related to the decision-making authority of a physician to determine when a life is to end, some to memories of the arbitrary extermination of people in Europe in the 1930s and 1940s, some to reluctance to legalize killing people for medical reasons, and some to concern lest a person's right to euthanasia could become a duty to accept euthanasia if the continuation of the life burdened the family or if the continuity of the life were to be too costly for the family and the society. There also is reluctance to establish a precedent for euthanasia in any form for fear that it would justify its broader use in subsequent years.

Acts of direct euthanasia or deliberate ending of a suffering person's life are almost universally not sanctioned. However, although not formally sanctioned, acts of passive euthanasia, in which some action is not taken that could have prolonged a person's life, are probably more common and are perhaps frequently practiced (Seguine 1985). Seguine makes a strong moral distinction between euthanasia, which is killing out of mercy, and murder, which is killing from malice. Yet courts have ruled that mercy killing was an act of murder and found a spouse guilty of murder for relieving his wife of suffering.

Issues related to euthanasia, while long-standing, have come once again to the forefront because of the current debate about economic pressures to thwart efforts that sustain life. Foremost among those who have introduced this debate is the former governor of Colorado, Richard D. Lamm. He says that "when we start using machines that do not cure or heal, that do not prolong life, but merely extend dying, then we are trying in vain to stop the irreversible. We have abdicated our role as ethical human beings. We are making sacrifices to that secular god 'technology' that are profoundly wrong. Our priorities are misplaced. If we do not succeed in reorienting them, we will indeed cheat our children and generations to come" (Lamm, 1984:xv).

When is it appropriate to discontinue a lifesaving intervention or to avoid the use of such intervention when the person's life may be at risk? It is argued by Dickey, Gaylin, and Safar (1987) and Fletcher (1987) that there is no ethical difference between discontinuing a process already in place and deciding not to intervene at all. Roy (1988) points out that courts in three states have ruled that there is no legal difference between artificial feeding and any other medical treatment and that there is ethically no difference between stopping treatment and never starting it. But care providers "may experience an intolerable discord between a principled justification for discontinuing life-prolonging treatment and the personal perception that one has become a killer in so doing" (Roy 1988:142). Enter Callahan and his thesis that "our common social obligation to the elderly is only to help them live out a natural life span; that is, the government is obliged to provide deliberately life-extending health care only to the age which is necessary to achieve that goal . . . I believe an age-based standard for the termination of life-extending treatment would be legitimate" (1987:116) He argues further that the "aged would need only those resources which would allow them a solid chance to live that long and, once they had passed that stage, to finish out their years free of pain and avoidable suffering. I will, therefore, define need in the old as primarily to achieve a natural life span and thereafter to have their suffering relieved" (1987:135)

Has the discussion by Callahan moved the debate directly toward endorsement of a society-approved program that supports suicide or euthanasia in order to assure that when the appropriate time arrives, the older person will leave on cue? Well, even if such a position does not sanction euthanasia, it is rationing and it implies the propriety of determining when health care of an older person should be terminated. Rationing can be compared with simultaneously pulling the plug and failing to initiate any health care service and is intended only to help society rid itself of persons considered too old to be supported by the health care system. The ethical distinction between killing the pain and killing the patient is as clear as the distinction between killing out of mercy and killing from malice.

Stollerman says that "the right of 'benign neglect' of the disease, but never the patient, is defended as 'not tantamount to negligence,' " (1986:173) that decisions to limit treatment when made out of respect and love (for the patient) do not equal crass abandonment. In fact, it may not only be fair but also accurate to characterize such decisions as "loving"—by patient, family, and physician—if not by society as a whole.

With so many opportunities to be misunderstood (i.e., killing the pain but not the patient, limiting treatment out of love not negligence), occasions occur when the intervention is not directed to the wishes of the patient but are modified by the uncertainty of how an action will be treated in a court of law.

Churchill joins in the debate, agreeing that there is the need for rationing of health care in our society but arguing that there is no justification for rationing by age. "Any morally justifiable age-rationing scheme will have to be lodged in a more just overall health care system. Rationing aimed specifically and exclusively at the aged will make them scapegoats and will wrongly exonerate the rest of us" (1988:646)

The debate about health care issues related to the older population is certain to persist through the next decade as we continue to be concerned about enabling the older person to die with dignity and try to deal humanely with that group of older persons who, because they are ill and near death, make disproportionate demands upon the health care system.

Among the many individuals and groups who are concerned about how we as a society deal with the final stages of life and dying with dignity, one group deserves special mention for its long-standing efforts to educate the public about these issues. It is the Concern For Dying organization; its credo includes the following:

> Society must indicate convincingly that it wants physicians to be humanitarians as well as skilled technicians.
>
> Life-supportive measures should not be used to prolong dying in cases of terminal illness with intractable pain or irreversible brain damage.
>
> Medication should be given to the dying in sufficient quantity to eliminate pain, even if tending to shorten life.

The stages of institutionalization and bureaucratization in the literature of the dying raised by Kalish become quite evident when we hear talk about the need to set some limits on the extent to which life should be maintained, especially because of the financial burdens imposed on society by sick old persons. Yet we as a society penalize spouses or physicians who in an act of mercy assist in bringing a life to its end instead of permitting it to be dragged out indefinitely. Somehow, the complexity of the issues has led to reluctance to acknowledge the significance of the events associated with dying to the individual and family.

It should be clear that in the institutionalization of the processes of dying the states should "establish a clear, legal opinion for those who choose to refuse or limit life-sustaining medical care" (Glasse and Murray 1984:326) and to determine the instrumentation required to assure that the expressed wishes of the patient are honored, thereby giving families the option of discontinuing treatment when health care providers find doing so to be inappropriate.

REPLACEMENT PARTS

A radical new approach to altering the process of dying has been introduced through the advanced medical technology of organ transplants. A person near death because of the failure of one of the essential organs is advised that death may be postponed if a donor organ of an appropriate match can be found in time. A decision to try to proceed with an organ transplant signals a race against time and against death. In this unusual circumstance the survival of the recipient is dependent upon the death of a donor. One prays for the availability of the organ but not necessarily for another person's death (hopefully, with dignity) so another person may live. The issue of living with replacement parts will become an increasingly important aspect of the process of dying. A recent report in *Newsweek* (Mair 1988) showed that 1,182 liver transplants, 1,512 heart transplants, and 8,967 kidney transplants were performed in 1987. (The kidney transplants also included kidneys from living donors.)

Because, in general, too few replacement parts have been available, the decision about who will receive a part has become an additional complication for contemporary ethics of medical technology and therefore of society's attitude toward dying. At present, an available donor part usually goes to the sickest person on the waiting list. Is this criterion appropriate when the sickest tend to have the least chance of surviving? We are increasingly being faced with decisions regarding the possible rationing of organs by the recipient's age or income. Will heart transplants be provided to persons in their 60s and 70s or to an even older person or a person on Medicaid? Will we have to redefine death with dignity or make an exception for the dying person who knows that a replacement part would have been available, and with that the continuity of life, if only he weren't poor.

The issue of replacement parts, especially of the high cost of the replacement process, requires a continuing examination of the ethical issues confronting our health care system. Binstock says "the rationing of high-cost technology and procedures, and the evolution of the two-class health care raise ominous prospects for the elderly. Such developments will begin to make manifest the latent ethical issues concerning the value of one life compared with another" (1985:11). Issues of rationing the availability of health care by age were raised earlier in a discussion of Lamm and Callahan. Binstock says "that rationing issues are customarily framed with a bias against older persons. Especially when the underlying issue is so-called 'cost-effectiveness,' the policy analysis is customarily framed to weight the answer in favor of those who can be presumed to have a longer potential life span" (1985:11)

What if the decisions for allocation of replacement parts were to be framed in a context not of age per se but in relation to the value of this person's contribution to society or ability to continue to contribute regardless of age?

DEATH OF AN ADULT CHILD

An additional complication created by the successful prolongation of life results in increasing numbers of aged parents outliving their adult children. In our society it is expected that we will grow old and that our children will outlive us. In addition, as we age and become more dependent on others for assistance it is to our children that we initially turn for help. Normative or on-time losses can be expected as we age and may be acceptable because they fit into the overall societal schema. However, "the addition of off-time losses such as the death of a child may significantly increase the risk of psychological or medical disorders. Thus, with the loss of an adult child, aged parents must learn to cope with the death of their child as well as with normative-age graded losses" (Moss, Lesher, and Moss 1986:211). Death of an adult child may leave the parent with increased vulnerability to institutionalization because it represents loss of a potential care provider. Such a loss of a supportive relationship may therefore symbolize the loss of independence. Singly or in combination, these can complicate emotional recovery from the trauma of the loss itself (Brubaker 1985; Osterweis 1985). As any person lives and ages there is increased exposure to death and loss. Loss of an adult child is but one illustration of a new phenomenon that has been added to the loss of spouse and friends that have been ever-present upsetting events in the lives of survivors. Losses, for some, become more painful as life progresses, because opportunities to replace lost loves and friendships are increasingly restricted.

A valuable resource for aged parents needing assistance in handling the trauma of loss of an adult child is participation in a support group of others in a similar situation. These groups should become part of the services of local social work, health, and aging programs.

HOSPICE

Hospice programs are a specific response to the needs of dying patients and their families. These programs were developed out of a concern that dying was not being dealt with openly but was being disguised in institutional settings and that family interpersonal relationships were neglected in the concealment of dying.

The needs of the dying person and family members are very personal and the care of the dying has to be removed from a depersonalized organizational structure, returned to the family and home setting, and provided with the support of an integrated team of health care professionals in a personalized relationship. These are the essential ingredients of hospice care (Koff 1980). The social worker, whose training and experience emphasize the importance of human interaction, is a key member of the care team.

The concept of hospice is, then, of a caring system, not cure oriented, with services provided by a comprehensive team of practitioners. Care is offered to patient and family in a choice of environments, but especially in the home (Koff 1980). And caring is no less demanding, no less sophisticated than any other aspect of a quality care program. While the presence of volunteers has been an important component of hospice care, especially as it provides a highly personal response to the unique needs of each patient, volunteerism has not meant a reduction in the quality of the response. It has meant the enlargement of the scope of caring for the dying person. The principles underlying the concept of hospice include death with dignity, or a response to the values and concerns of the patient. The emphasis is on palliative rather than curative care and the aggressive reduction of pain and other adverse symptoms, knowing that cure is not possible. The entire family is considered to be the patient, with concern for the emotional and physical needs of family members making it possible for them to stay together and support one another.

Developing internal support structures and educational programs is important to enable hospice staff to meet the unusual demands of a specialized population of the dying. The National Hospice Organization and the hospice group in the National Home Care Organization represent two national organizations interested in the development of hospice programs.

EDUCATION PROGRAMS IN CARE OF THE AGING

It becomes especially important that significant content related to death be included in the education of health care providers. Students need to learn about how to deal with the death of patients and with issues of their own mortality (Dickinson, Sumner, and Durand 1987). Important also is the ability to deal with the family of a dying patient in an understanding way, helping the family to provide support for the patient and to convey to the patient the values related to the issues of prolongation of life versus the termination of treatments at the appropriate time. And certainly education in health care should include content in health care ethics and in helping the student to understand the differences that may exist between the ethics of the patient, those of the physician, and those of the society in which both reside.

CONCLUSION

In this paper on the issues of dying in our society I started with the premise of Kalish that dying had moved into a phase of institutionalization and bureaucratization and away from issues of innovation and exploration. Implicit in this premise is that a move away from an emphasis on personal compassion for the dying individual toward institutionalizing the dying process can only have inevitable adverse consequences for our society.

Upon reflection and review of the Kalish chapter, I feel that we may have reached a plateau in the process he described and that there is a resurgence of concerns about the dignity of dying and the importance of respecting the wishes of the dying person when confronted by decisions about the continuation of life-sustaining activities in the face of a severly impaired quality of life. Concurrently, the debate mounts regarding the rationing of health care services and its impact on attitudes toward the continuation of life, whether these be related to the wishes of the patient or to the bureaucratization of decisions regarding access to health care.

It is Siegler's characterization of our times as being the age of bureaucratic parsimony that is particularly troublesome, because it suggests the increasing possibility that health care services will be allocated on the basis of age or income in order to maintain some level of control over the national cost of health care. With increased bureaucratic intervention and court decisions that sustain the right of the individual to stop receiving treatment in order to permit death in a timely manner, will the issues surrounding euthanasia assume greater weight in the debate over prolongation of life versus termination of life?

Compassion and concern for the quality of life have led us to accept benignly motivated withholding or withdrawal of treatment when there is no hope for the restoration of health or the absence of suffering. This position has not come any more easily than the rulings in several court cases. Active intervention by assisting a life to come to its end has not yet found approval in either the courts or the ethics of our society, although some organized groups advocate for the legalization of euthanasia. No matter who makes the decision to discontinue or withhold active treatment of a dying person, selection of this option should not be a responsibility assumed by care providers. Nor should the decision not to treat be misinterpreted as not caring.

Discussion of whose responsibility it is to determine when active treatment should be curtailed ultimately leads us back to consideration of the role of the family. Much more attention needs to be paid to understanding the events leading up to a person's death and to discovering how family members can be given the support they need when they must deal with someone's death. Some families may fully understand the moral and ethical values of their relative; some may not. Some families may have had sustained contact with the dying person and been able in advance to discuss plans in the event their relative becomes incompetent. They may even have received written instructions in the form of a living will or durable power of attorney. Some families may not be prepared to make this crucial decision.

The "family" may, in fact, be a biological family or one constituted through marriage or some other form of bonding. What matters is the acceptance of the family structure as the patient and the ability to communicate the interests of the patient. We need to know much more about how a family manages under the stress of impending loss of a loved one, how a family functions during extended periods of stress related to the incompetence of a loved one, what enables a family to avoid the pitfalls of unusual stress. What are the influences upon patient and family stress levels of the presence of a strong support system, the presence of professional counselors, the availability of respite services, feeling confidence in the authority of their decisions rather than confusion arising from diverse interpretations of the situation by varied players, or some other force or forces?

"But death, like aging, is universal, and legislators—along with everyone else who wishes the final phase of life to be worthy of all that preceded it—must ask themselves from time to time whether public policy is exercising positive or negative influence on the conditions surrounding death in our nation" (Oriol 1984:309).

Oriol echoes the sentiments of Kalish when he says that our nation should engage in serious debate about final care for the terminally ill and should recognize the dangers of building a "separate but equal" system rather than incorporating services "for the chronically or terminally ill into a more humane, less institutionalized, and much more flexible system, which in meeting the growing needs of the elderly, is likely to serve other age groups as well to the greater satisfaction than is now the case" (Oriol 1984:320). The issues revert back to the importance of establishing policies that recognize the dignity of the human being, the responsibility of care providers to honor the requests of the patient and, when the patient lacks the capacity to act, the honoring of a decision conscientiously made by family. Death with dignity certainly includes all of these issues as well as contributing to the dignity of a society that understands the needs of its members and acts accordingly.

Death can be beautiful when,
Full of years, ripe with good works,
A parent, among his children, says his last words
And turns to the wall.

REFERENCES

Armstrong, P. W. 1987. Patient's right to refuse care affirmed. *American Medical News* (July 3/10), p. 30.

Berger, S. 1988. Hospital takes up life-and-death issue. *Modern Healthcare* (July 15).

Bernstein, R. 1987. As quoted in Nearly 25% of all suicides in U.S. are older adults. by Weindi Middleton *Aim* (Aging in Michigan) (July/August), Lansing: Michigan Office of Services to the Aging. 13(4):8–9.

Binstock, R. H. 1985. Health care of the aging: Trends, dilemmas, and prospects for the Year 2000. In C. M. Gaitz, G. Niederehe, and N. L. Wilson eds. *Aging 2000: Our Health Care Destiny, Vol. 2: Psychosocial and Policy Issues.* New York: Springer.

Bodnar, A. 1987. Living Wills. *Harvard Medical School Health Letter.* (February), 12:4–6.

Brody, B. A. 1985. The interaction between ethics and economics in planning health care for the aged. In C. M. Gaitz, G. Niederehe, and N. L. Wilson, eds. *Aging 2000: Our Health Care Destiny,* Vol. 2: Psychosocial and Policy Issues. New York: Springer.

Brubaker, E. 1985. Older parents' reactions to the death of adult children: Implications for practice. *Journal of Gerontological Social Work* (Fall), 9(1):35–48.

Callahan, D. 1987. *Setting Limits: Medical Goals in an Aging Society.* New York: Simon and Schuster.

Caplan, H. 1987. It's time we helped patients die. *Medical Economics* (June 8), 64:214–227.

Churchill, L. R. 1988. Should we ration health care by age? *Journal of the American Geriatrics Society* 36(7):644–647.

Dickey, N. W. 1986. Withholding or withdrawing treatment. *Journal of the American Medical Association* 256:471.

Dickey, N. W., W. Gaylin, and P. Safar. 1987. Ethical issues in life support. *Patient Care* (March 30), 21:120–133.

Dickinson, G. E., E. D., Sumner and R. P. Durand. 1987. Death education in U.S. professional colleges: Medical, nursing, and pharmacy. *Death Studies* 11:57–61.

Fahey, C. 1987. Corporate ethical decision making in health care institutions. *Hospital Administration Currents*. 31(4) 19–26.

Fletcher, J. 1987. Medical resistance to the right to die. *Journal of the American Geriatrics Society* 35(7):679–682.

Fulton, R. 1987. The many faces of grief. *Death Studies* 11:243–256.

Gadow, S. 1980. Caring for the dying: Advocacy or paternalism. In *Death Education*. Washington, D.C.: Hemisphere,

Germain, C. B. 1984. The elderly and the ecology of death: Issues of time and space. In M. Tallmer, E. R. Prichard, A. H. Kutscher, et al., eds. *The Life-Threatened Elderly*. New York, Columbia University Press.

Glasse, L. and D. R. Murray. 1984. Limiting life-sustaining medical care for the terminally ill. In M. Tallmer, E. R. Prichard, A. H. Kutscher, R. Debellis, M. S. Hale, and I. K. Goldberg, eds., *The Life-Threatened Elderly*. New York: Columbia University Press.

Hirsh, H. L. 1986. The living will in action. *Nursing Homes* (May/June), 35:31–32.

Hirsh, H. L. 1985. Who may eat and who may starve? *Nursing Homes* (July/August), 34:9–10.

Kalish, R. A. 1982. Death and survivorship: The final transition. *The Annals of the American Academy of Political and Social Science* (November), 464:163–173.

Kalish, R. A. 1985. Services for the dying. In A. Monk ed. *Handbook of Gerontological Services*. New York: Van Nostrand Reinhold.

Koff, T. H. 1980. *Hospice: A Caring Community*. Boston: Little, Brown.

Lamm, R. D. 1987. Ethical health care for the elderly: Are we cheating our children? In T. M. Smeeding, M. P. Battin, L. P. Francis, and B. M. Landesman, eds., *Should Medical Care be Rationed by Age?* Totowa, N.J.: Rowman and Littlefield.

Maier, F. A second chance at life. *Newsweek*, September 12, 1988, pp. 52–61.

Michel, V. 1984. An approach to the preservation of self-determination in health care decision-making. *Linkages* (Spring/Summer).

Moss, M. S., E. L., Lesher, and S. Z. Moss, 1986–87. Impact of the death of an adult child on elderly parents: /Some observations. In *OMEGA* 17(3):209–219.

Oriol, W. E. 1984. Public policy questions related to death with dignity. In M. Tallmer, E. R. Prichard, A. H. Kutscher, et al., eds., *The Life-Threatened Elderly*. New York: Columbia University Press.

Osgood, N. J. 1987. The alcohol-suicide connection in late life. *Postgraduate Medicine*, 81(4):379–384.

Osterweis, M. 1985. Bereavement and the elderly. *Aging* 348:8–13, 41.

Pearlman, R. A. and A. Jonsen 1985. The use of quality-of-life considerations in medical decision making. *Journal of the American Geriatrics Society* 33(5) 344–352.

Powills, S. 1985. Coalition asks, "Life at any price?" *Hospitals*, May 16, 1985.

President's Commission for the Study of Ethical Problems in Medicine and Biomedical and Behavioral Research. 1983. *Deciding to Forego Life-Sustaining Treatment: A Report on the Ethical, Medical and Legal Issues in Treatment Decisions*. Washington: GPO.

Roy, D. J. 1988. Is dying a matter of ethics? *Death Studies* 12:137–145.

Seguine, A. 1985. Euthanasia—a death warrant or a rite of passage? In O. S. Margolis et al., eds., *Loss, Grief, and Bereavement; A Guide for Counseling*. New York: Praeger.

Siegler, M. 1985. How are the elderly to die? *The Christian Century* 102:68–69.

Stollerman, G. H. 1986. Lovable decisions: Re-humanizing dying. *Journal of the American Geriatrics Society* 34(2):172–174.

Wallis, C. 1988. To feed or not to feed? *Time*, March 31, 1988.

Wass, H. 1977. Views and opinions of elderly persons concerning death. *Educational Gerontology* 2:15–26.

Wass, H. and J. E. Myers. 1984. Death and Dying: Issues for educational gerontologists. *Educational Gerontology*, pp. 65–81.

VII
SPECIAL ISSUES

24

The Ethnic Factor in the Delivery of Social Services

❖

REGINA KULYS, P.H.D.
The University of Illinois at Chicago

The ethnic elderly, especially minority elderly, increasingly are becoming the focus of gerontological interest. Whether ethnicity makes a difference over and above socioeconomic class in such areas as interaction with family and friends, life satisfaction, living arrangements, support systems, expectation of help and assistance, as well as attitudes toward death and dying, is investigated by different disciplines and professions.

Service delivery to the ethnic populations reflects a growing recognition, particularly by professional members of various ethnic groups, that minorities are not being provided with culturally sensitive services. For the elderly, the barriers hindering effective provision of social services are being identified but except where services are provided by ethnic agencies, little progress has been made to ensure that ethnic elderly are made aware of existing services and that those services are accessible and culturally relevant.

How important is ethnicity in the delivery of social services to the elderly? The answer to this complex question depends on many factors. To be considered are: whether one is or is not an immigrant, if an immigrant, whether one came as a refugee or entered as an illegal alien, the age at immigration, the country of origin and its level of development, whether the move to the United States was perceived as permanent or temporary, education and occupation at the time of immigration, the congruence of cultural values between the country of origin and the dominant values in the United States, length of time one has lived in the United States, the type of community or neighborhood in which one settled and now lives, the mastery of English, and racial distinctiveness of the ethnic group. If native born, factors include whether one lives or does not live on a reservation, the tribe to which one belongs, governmental supports available for schooling, and work related opportunities, education and socioeconomic class, number of generations since ancestors came to America, racial distinctiveness of the group and the severity of discrimination.

Above factors are related to acculturation defined as "change of cultural patterns to those of host society" (Gordon 1964). Overall the lower the level of acculturation the greater the need in the organization of social services to pay special attention to the ethnic factors. This in turn means that service providers need to expend additional efforts and resources in providing services to less acculturated elderly if they are to benefit equally from services that should be available to all elderly in America without reference to race or national origin.

The focus in this paper is on the provision of social services to ethnic elderly who find themselves at various points in the acucltura-tion process, who are not able at will "to turn ethnicity off" (Holzberg 1982), and who experience barriers in the utilization of services. The focus, furthermore, is on:

1. The identification of barriers that impede utilization of services;
2. Organizational strategies that service providers can employ to reach the elderly; and
3. Assessment and intervention methods that facilitate the provision of services.

Since understanding of the immigrant and minority group experience is an integral part in the provision of social services, immigration policy and the ethnic community will also be discussed.

ETHNICITY DEFINED

Ethnicity and ethnic groups have been defined in various ways. Isajiw (1974) analyzed over twenty definitions. Gordon (1964:27) defines ethnic groups as groups that are distinguished "or set off by race, religion or national origin or some combination of these categories." The notion of self and other identification with the group is introduced by

Shibutani and Kwan, who state that "an ethnic group consists of those who conceive themselves as being alike by virtue of their common ancestry, real or fictitious or are so regarded by others" (1965:47). To stress that for members of minority groups, ethnic group membership is involuntary, Isajiw states that ethnicity refers to "An involuntary group of people who share the same culture or descendants of such people who identify themselves and/or are identified by others as belonging to the same involuntary group" (1974:122).

Thus, ancestry, race, and religion, the perception of self and others and the idea of involuntary membership have been identified as elements characterizing an ethnic group. Based on the characteristic of race, blacks, whites and Asians constitute an ethnic group. While this basic distinction may be useful for comparative purposes in such areas as income, education, and longevity (Markides 1982), the categories are too broad if the focus is on the delivery of social services. Thus it is useful to view race as a broad category containing several ethnic subgroups (Jackson 1975).

The concept of minority group is also pertinent to this discussion. According to Shibutani and Kwan, minority groups are "The underprivileged in a system of ethnic stratification" and "people of low standing—people who receive unequal treatment and who therefore come to regard themselves as objects of discrimination" (1965:35). The dominant group is known as the majority even though it may not have numerical majority. The dominated group is the minority despite the fact that it may constitute numerical majority. Power, status, and privilege differentiate the minority from majority. Minority group concept has also been applied to non-ethnic groups such as women, homosexuals, or the aged, but in this discussion, it refers to ethnic groups viewed as having low status.

IMMIGRATION POLICY IN HISTORICAL PERSPECTIVE

A brief description of immigration policy will provide a background for understanding the changing patterns of immigration to the United States. The fact that many of the immigrants are refugees and come from non-Western cultures has important implications for the delivery of social services.

Policy

Immigration to the United States was unrestricted with respect to country of origin until 1882 when Chinese Exclusion Act was passed. In 1917 virtually all immigration from Asia was banned. The National Origins Act in 1924 created a quota system designed to allow immigration that reflected the distribution of national groups as established in the 1890 Census, which subsequently was changed to the 1920 Census. This restriction was partly a response to the popular belief that immigrants from Northwestern Europe were most desirable (Higham 1965).

Towards the end of World War II, all Chinese Exclusion Laws were repealed. After the Second World War the Displaced Persons Act authorized the issuance of visas to World War II refugees. Subsequently, the Refugee Relief Act of 1953 provided for the immigration of refugees and escapees form Iron Curtain countries.

Amendments to the Immigration and Nationality Act in 1965 abolished the national origins quota, fixed an annual ceiling for immigration of 290,000 persons per year, and established a preference category for refugees. In 1980 the Refugee Act removed refugees as a preference category, reduced the world-wide limit to 270,000 immigrants, allocated 50,000 visas for "normal flow" refugees and permitted the President, after consultation with Congress, to increase this annual allocation.

The Immigration Reform and Control Act of 1986 created a mechanism for giving legal status, or amnesty to perhaps milions of illegal aliens who could prove that they resided continuously in the United States since before January 1, 1982. It also requires employers to verify that all newly hired people are legally authorized to work in the United States.

Immigration Data

As a result of the abolition of national origin quota, immigration from continents other than Europe is rapidly increasing: 62 percent of all immigrants from Asia arrived in the last two decades (1961–1981); in contrast 95 percent of immigrants from Europe came before 1961 (Statistical Yearbook 1984).

In the twenty-five-year period (1961–1986), 1,410,699 refugees were admitted as permanent residents to the United States. Cubans were the largest group admitted from one country (445,862) followed by

Vietnamese (390,282). Close to three quarters of a million (725,446) refugees came from Asia, outnumbering the refugees from all other continents (U.S. Dept. Commerce 1988).

Different waves of refugees are composed of different socioeconomic classes. The earliest wave of Cuban refugees who settled in Miami represented the top layer of pre-revolutionary society (Boswell 1985). In contrast the refugees from Laos were rural settlers with limited education.

In 1980, United States population included 14,079,000 foreign born people (U.S. Census 1983a), a conservative estimate since foreign born are under-represented and illegal immigrants usually not included in the Census.

In 1970, a third of foreign-born immigrants were 65 years and older (U.S. Census 1973). In constrast, new immigrants are primarily young as only 3.2 percent of 5,560,363 people immigrating between 1970–1980 were 65 years and over (U.S. Census 1983b). However, 175,000 elderly arriving in one decade is not a negligible number with respect to delivery of social services.

Ethnic Groups

BLACK AMERICANS

Black Americans constitute 11.6 percent of the United States population with elderly comprising 7.8 percent of the total black population. Almost 60 percent of blacks reside in central cities and only 19 percent live in non-metropolitan areas. Slightly over half reside in the South (U.S. Census 1982a; U.S. Dept. Commerce 1985).

HISPANIC AMERICANS

Hispanic Americans make up 6.4 percent of the United States population. Mexican-Americans (60 percent) predominate among the 14 million persons of Hispanic origin, followed by Puerto Ricans (14 percent), and Cubans (6 percent). Only 4.6 percent of Hispanics are 65 years and older. Almost 90 percent reside in urban areas and over 40 percent live in the West (Census 1982b, 1984).

ASIAN AMERICANS

Asian Americans are a fast-growing minority. In 1980 there were 3.7 million Asians and Pacific Islanders in the United States comprising approximately 1.7 percent of the population. The category of Asian Americans include Japanese, Chinese, Vietnamese, Filipinos, Koreans, Asian Indians, Samoans, and others. Six percent of Asian Americans in 1980 were 65 years and over. Asian Americans are most highly urbanized as 92 percent live in urban areas with 60 percent residing in the West (U.S. Census 1984; U.S. Dept. Commerce 1985).

NATIVE AMERICANS

The term Native Americans includes American Indians, Eskimos and Aleuts. The 1980 Census indicates that the Native American population numbered approximately 1.5 million people, 5.1 percent of whom were 65 years and older. At present there are over 250 federally recognized tribes. Almost two-thirds (63 percent) live off reservations and other designated tribal areas. The majority (51.6 percent) of Native Americans live in non-metropolitan areas (Census 1983c).

EURO-AMERICANS

Guttmann (1986), using 1971 and 1972 census data, estimated that Euro-Americans, 65 years and over, constitute over 7 million people. While most of the European ethnic groups have done well economically, an undetermined number of the elderly are in poverty and have difficulty with English. The ethnic neighborhoods in larger cities contain a high percentage of these elderly.

Income

In all racial groups, higher percentages of the elderly live in poverty than the total population (table 24.1). Whites and Asians have the lowest rates of poverty, and American Indians, Eskimos, Aleuts, and blacks the highest. However, the poverty rate for black elderly is almost three times as high as for white elderly. High poverty rates among black, Native American, and Hispanic populations also mean that children and kin of the elderly are economically less able than whites and Asians to provide the elderly with help and support.

It is ironic and devastating to observe that in America, the land of freedom and opportunity, two groups with the highest rates of poverty consist of descendants of inhabitants who lived in America before the coming of the white men or those who were forcefully brought as slaves.

ETHNIC COMMUNITIES AND NEIGHBORHOODS

In this section the meaning and the role of the ethnic community-neighborhood will be discussed. An understanding of the ethnic community is an important element in the provision of services (Cantor 1979; Biegel and Sherman 1979; Berger and Neuhaus 1977). Knowledge about the ethnic community helps to understand the social world of the elderly including patterns of interaction among families and friends and the provision of informal supports (Kalish 1986; Biegel and Naparstek 1982). It also enables service providers to assess both the ability and willingness of ethnic communities to assist in the provision of social services by such actions as legitimation, approval, provision of information, and willingness to cooperate, since ethnic

TABLE 24.1. Persons Below Poverty Level in 1979 for Selected Racial Groups in the United States

Selected Racial and Ethnic Groups	*Total*[a]	*% 65 and over*	*1979 Income Below Poverty Level Percentage*
U.S. total	220,845,766		12.4
65 and over	24,154,364	10.9	14.8
White total	184,466,900		9.4
65 years and over	21,691,260	11.8	12.8
Black total	25,622,765		29.9
65 years and over	1,988,887	7.8	35.2
Spanish origin, total[b]	14,339,387		23.5
65 years and over	654,740	4.6	25.6
Asian/Pacific Islander total	3,643,966		13.1
65 years and over	216,382	5.9	14.5
American Indian, Eskimo, and Aleut, total	1,484,059		27.5
65 years and over	76,259	5.1	32.1

SOURCE: U.S. Bureau of the Census (1984). Data are estimates based on sample.

[a] Exclude inmates of institutions, persons in military group quarters, and in college dormitories, and unrelated individuals under 15 years.

[b] Persons of Spanish origin may be of any race.

communities often are instrumental in enabling the elderly to use services.

Meaning of Ethnic Neighborhood

Immigrants, transplanted from one culture to another, have to reconstruct their interpersonal networks by establishing a new community of personal affiliations (Eisenstadt 1952). For most newcomers the ethnic community, defined as "an area of common life" both territorial and social (MacIver 1970) provides this connectedness and a sense of security in a strange and sometimes hostile land (Chen 1979; Die and Seelbach 1988). For the newcomer, the ethnic community performs many functions ranging from provision of information necessary for immediate survival such as stores, housing and jobs, to help at the time of death and sickness, to world news and information about life "back home" (Rumbaut and Rumbaut 1976). For newer immigrants from Asia such as Koreans, lack of well-established ethnic communities into which they can be absorbed creates additional stress and may contribute to the development of serious psychological problems (Kiefer et al. 1985). The ethnic community also serves as a reference group against which members measure their own status, achievement and well being (Lopata 1976; Rogg 1971).

Most immigrants pass through ethnic communities. While some stay only temporarily, others, such as Italians or Mexicans, reside in the same neighborhood for generations (Vecoli 1978). Sometimes entire neighborhoods move to more prestigious areas as did Chicago Jews (Rosenthal 1960). In instances, where by public policy an attempt was made to disperse the group throughout various regions within the United States as in the case of Vietnamese, secondary migration takes place and people regroup in ethnic neighborhoods (Montero 1979).

Comunities with a large number of ethnic residents develop an array of institutions such as benevolent associations, newspapers, ethnic churches, economic, political, and even professional organizations (Light 1972; Fishman et al. 1985). Some communities attempt to recreate the social world of their home country, where members vie for positions of power and prestige. The ethnic community also enables people, especially older refugees who experienced downward occupational mobility (Rogg 1971; Haines 1985) to live in two worlds. In the outside world a person may be a janitor or a painter, while in the world of their ethnic neighborhood they continue to be known as "judge," "professor," or "general." Often such people assume important organizational positions within their neighborhoods.

Breton (1964) found that the higher the number of institutions available in the ethnic community the more the members tended to interact with each other, to develop cohesiveness and to exclude others. He also reported that higher institutional completeness was associated with inability to speak English.

Ethnic neighborhoods and communities are important sources of security and support not only for immigrants but also for blacks and Native Americans (Solomon 1976). Black church has traditionally been a very meaningful institution in the black community providing the elderly with both spiritual and material sustenane (Taylor and Chatters 1986; Heisel and Faulkner 1982).

A given neighborhood often contains a number of ethnic groups with each group having an institution such as a church or a club to serve as a symbol of ethnic identity. Some neighborhoods, particularly in the inner city such as the area surrounding Jane Addams Hull House in Chicago, have been a home for a succession of ethnic groups. When transition takes place the elderly are often "left behind" mostly because they cannot afford to move. Such elderly run a risk of isolation as the familiar supports—churches, ethnic stores, as well as ethnic professionals—disappear. These isolated elderly are frequently not reached by service providers as was discovered by a service program called "Senior Ethnic Find" (Hayes 1986).

Elderly living in changing and inner city ethnic neighborhoods, especially minority elderly, are concerned about crime (McAdoo 1979; Bild and Havighurst 1975). Fear of crime and victimization inhibit such activities as church attendance, interaction with friends, relatives, participation in social groups (Sundeen and Mathieu 1976; Clements and Kleiman 1976; Goldsmith and Tomas 1974) and may also interfere with the older person's ability to get to services such as senior centers.

Not all ethnic elderly live in ethnic communities, some are scattered in suburbs, small towns, and even rural areas. How much contact they maintain with the ethnic neighborhood, provided an ethnic neighborhood is within reach, is not known. Furthermore, there are no data to indicate how ethnic elderly who live in nonethnic neighborhoods fare in the use of social services, particularly those who have difficulty communicating in English.

While many factors influence acculturation, the ethnic community has to be considered both as a facilitator (Rogg 1971) and a deterrent to acculturation (Lieberson 1961).

NEED FOR SERVICES

The elderly's needs for social services such as mental health, senior centers, and services to families are discussed in the relevant sections of this book. Does minority status intensify these needs?

Minority status is associated with low income, minimal education, poor housing, discrimination, and lack of opportunity. People who live under these conditions not only experience more stress but have fewer psychological, social and economic coping resources (Kessler and Cleary 1980; Varghese and Medinger 1979). Markides and Mindel state that the "social stress" or "social causation." perspective is "commonly evoked to account for greater psychopathology among the lower social classes, a finding documented in a variety of community surveys and other studies of psychiatric epidemiology". (1987:123)

The hypothesis that ethnic minorities experience more distress than majority Americans has been separated by Mirowsky and Ross (1980) into three arguments and further elaborated by Liu and Yu (1985).

The first argument states that minorities suffer from prejudice and discrimination. Minority group members in comparison to majority whites of the same education have less pay, less prestigious jobs, fewer advancement opportunities, are less likely to live where nonminorities live. In essence the racism experienced by minority group members in a society that subscribes to individual advancement may create a dissonance between expectation and achievement leading to higher psychological distress.

The second argument asserts that low social class to which most minorities belong rather than racism per se generates psychosocial distress. When social-economic class is controlled for, differences between minority groups and whites tend to disappear in many but not all areas.

The third perspective states that since ethnic minorities differ in values, beliefs and behaviors from the majority and since the majority represent the dominant culture, this difference creates alienation and tension. The greater the gap between the minority and the majority culture the more problematic the process of adaptation and the more exhausting the coping process.

The factors identified in these three arguments are interrelated in that social class, racism as well as different cultural values and beliefs operate together to create psychosocial distress.

The needs of ethnic and minority elderly for services and the barriers preventing utilization have been identified and discussed by many authors, among them: Salcido 1979; Bell et al, 1976; Lum et al. 1980; Chen 1970; Li et al. 1972; Kim 1973; Jackson 1980. These arguments and data support the premise postulated by the Federal Council on Aging that "older minorities constitute the bulk of the elderly population most in need" (1979:45).

UTILIZATION OF FORMAL SERVICES

Social Services

Empirical data on the utilization of formal services by ethnic elderly, except in the area of mental health, are scarce and inconclusive. Data, moreover, are usually reported for blacks, whites, and Mexican-Americans without further ethnic specificity of the inclusion of other Hispanic groups. Part of the difficulty also relates to lack of clearly established criteria to measure utilization. What is to be considered underutilization, overutilization, or just adequate utilization with respect to a given service? Is utilization to be determined by need, by need combined with social class, by some other criteria or by parity considerations? Parity is reached when the percentage of an ethnic group who receive a service is the same as the group's percentage in the population (Meinhardt and Vega 1987). The parity criterion is also questionable because it does not take into consideration the possibility that minority needs might be greater than the needs of the white majority. To overcome this problem, Meinhardt and Vega (1987) developed a weighted parity measure to reflect the need factor. This kind of analysis is lacking in areas other than mental health.

Fujii (1976), after reviewing several studies in which elderly Asians were asked what services they had utilized, concluded that Asian-Americans fail to use social services. Fourteen social service agencies in Seattle assisted Asian elderly only 643 times out of an estimated 205,156 times equivalent to .03 percent. Blau et al. (1979) and McCaslin and Calvert (1975) however report that blacks were higher users of services than whites.

Findings also suggest that Hispanics underutilize social services (Lacayo 1982; Guttmann and Cuellar 1982). Greene and Monahan, after examining use of service among Hispanic elderly enrolled in a comprehensive case management system in Arizona conclude that "Hispanic elderly tend to consume fewer social service resources than do Anglo elderly, even in this case when they are enrolled in a program designed to provide access to a variety of services" (1984:33). Data on nursing home use consistently show that the white utilization rate is higher than the rate for other ethnic groups (National Center for Health Statistics 1981; National Nursing Home Survey 1981; Eribes and Bradley-Rawls 1978). Douglass et al. (1988), however, based on a study conducted in 1981 report no major under-representation of the black elderly in nursing homes in the Detroit area. Participation in senior centers by minority elderly has also been low unless such centers are specifically geared to blacks, Hispanics, or other nonwhite populations (Lowy 1985; Ralston 1984).

Guttmann (1979) gathered data from 720 elderly from eight white ethnic groups about utilization of ten services ranging from counseling to escort service. Jews were the most frequent and Polish from Baltimore the least frequent users. Less than 1.4 percent of the respondents had used counseling, homemaker or escort services. Guttmann concluded that formal services either do not reach a large segment of the ethnic elderly or that the elderly in these ethnic groups have less need for government offered services. Gelfand (1986), however, reports that Soviet Jews use formal services. Even in the case of the personal problems, agencies were used more extensively as a source of assistance than children and other family members.

Mental Health

Outpatient mental health services are underutilized by elderly in general and ethnic minority elderly in particular (Flemming et al. 1986; McNeil and Wright 1983; Becerra and Shaw 1984; Berk and Hirata 1973). Szapocznik et al. (1979) indicate that in Dade County Mental Health Center, only 3.6 percent of Hispanic elderly clients were seen although the Hispanic elderly comprised 16 percent of the elderly population. White ethnic elderly also often fail to utilize mental health services (Giordano and Giordano, 1977). Markson (1979) reports that for the white ethnic elderly, inpatient psychiatric hospitalization is sometimes used as solution for lack of other alternatives such as nursing homes. This may be even truer for black elderly whose rate of inpatient admission to state and county mental hospitals was, in the 1970s, twice as high as the rate for white elderly (President's Commission on Mental Health 1978).

BARRIERS HINDERING USE OF SERVICES

McKinley (1972), after reviewing health and social service literature, identified the following dimensions as determinants of utilization behavior: economic, socio-demographic, geographic, social psychological, sociocultural and organizational. Several dimensions correspond to "barriers" hindering use of social services by ethnic elderly (Gelfand 1982; Newton 1980; Stanford 1974). These barriers include:

1. lack of knowledge and information;
2. unfamiliarity with social services and social workers;
3. location of service;
4. language and culture;

Lack of Knowledge and Information

For all elderly, lack of information about services is related to utilization as people are not able to use services if they do not know about them. Krout (1983a) after reviewing literature focusing on the knowledge and use of services by the elderly, reports that research findings on the degree of knowledge of medical and social services vary considerably from study to study and from service to service. Silverstein (1984) indicates that fewer than a quarter of 706 respondents in Boston showed a high level of service awareness. Other studies report similar results (Ward et al. 1984; Snider 1980).

Empirical data are scarce about ethnic and minority elderly's knowledge and awareness of services. Die and Seelbach (1988) report that in a Texas study of sixty Vietnamese immigrants, over 90 percent were aware or used major service categories such as Medicaid or Food Stamps but only 3 percent knew about or utilized mental health services, and 1 percent home health services. Since most of these elderly were involved with a resettlement program, knowledge about health and economic programs may be the result of such contacts. For elderly who did not have resettlement services available, even such basic knowledge may be lacking.

Harel (1985) reports that among 701 nutrition site users, white aged had more knowledge about and access to services than blacks. McCaslin, after reviewing four studies (Mindel and Wright 1982; Starrett and Decker 1986; Krout 1983b; and McCaslin 1989), concluded that "A relatively large amount of variance in service use can be explained by the extent of older persons' awareness of available services and their perception of those services as sources of assistance for their own current of potential needs" (1988:597). Furthermore, both the Mindel and Wright (1982) and Starrett and Decker (1986) studies indicated that "the influence of knowledge is somewhat greater for minority than for majority elderly individuals" (McCaslin 1988:597).

Walmsley and Allington (1982) examined 126 documents related to information regarding such essential services as Medicare, Medicaid, food stamps, public assistance, Social Security, Blue Cross/Blue Shield and Supplemental Security Income. They concluded that, because 98 percent of the documents tested required reading ability of ninth grade or higher, a sizable percentage of elderly have difficulty reading documents that are important to gain access to services.

If the elderly in general have limited knowledge of services, and difficulty understanding documents, it is reasonable to expect that ethnic elderly, particularly those who do not read English will be far less knowledgeable about services. Knowledge that services are available while necessary, however, is not a sufficient condition of service use. Services have also to be perceived as culturally relevant and accessible. That people are often "ping-ponged" from agency to agency further discourages use (Jackson 1980). Data from National Conference on Social Welfare show that "60 percent of the people who seek social services are turned away from agencies" (Hayes and Guttmann 1986). Data are also needed on ethnic elderly who are either turned away or referred to other agencies.

Unfamiliarity with Social Workers and Social Services

Many foreign-born people are unfamiliar with social workers or what social workers do (Timberlake and Cook 1984; Ryan 1981). Some languages do not even have a word for social work (Dorf and Katlin 1983). Lack of familiarity with the type of services provided, particularly services that are treatment oriented, makes it difficult for elderly to understand what benefit is to be achieved by talking about problems, especially when personal problems are not to be discussed with strangers and when the perceived need is for concrete service. Dorf and Katlin (1983) report that even for Soviet Jews the traditional insight-oriented problem-solving approach is completely foreign. Moreover, ethnic elderly, particularly those who are refugees, are often mistrustful of bureaucrats and fearful of any involvement with the government (Ho 1976; Chen 1979; Brodsky 1988). They are also often suspicious and mistrustful of researchers (Montero and Levine 1977; Sue and Sue 1972).

Location of Service

The physical location of the service is an important element in its utilization (Stanford 1977; Bell et al 1976; Arroyo and Lopez 1984). Traveling to an unfamiliar area outside the ethnic neighborhood not only means venturing into strange surroundings but also negotiating inside strange and often complex buildings. Transportation difficulties and additional expenses have also to be considered. Philippus (1971) described a newly decentralized mental health program in a Hispanic neighborhood in Denver that was successful in attracting Hispanic patients. The services were located in a housing unit where, upon opening the front door, one immediately stepped into the "living room." A Spanish-speaking receptionist met and registered the patient. Subsequently the service was moved to a new location, little more than a block away, placed on a second floor and made a part of a larger health complex where patients were processed through an admission procedure similar to the average hospital routine. Within the first month the proportion of Hispanic patients fell from 70 to 50 percent and continued to decrease to 35 percent. The staff made some readjustments and eventually moved the service into a separate area on the street level, reinstituting the informal registering procedure by the receptionist. Within a short time the percentage of Spanish-speaking patients increased to 65 percent of the total visits.

This example illustrates the importance of providing services in familiar surroundings without complex intake procedures. Such inconsequential strategies as locating the office on the first floor and simplifying admission procedures can mean the difference between attaining or not attaining a service.

Language and Cultural Barriers

LANGUAGE

Census data indicate that 23.060 million people in the United States use a language other than English in everyday communication. Of those, 14.2 percent are 65 and over, or 3.273 million people (Census 1983d). While a substantial number of elderly who use another language at home may speak English, inability to communicate in English is a serious barrier to service utilization (Chen 1973; Arroyo and Lopez 1984; Lum et al. 1980; Li et al. 1972; Fujii 1976). Garcia (1971) charges that most agencies continue their punitive practice of helping only those clients who can communicate in English.

Even though many foreign-born elderly are adept in "getting along" in English at work, or paying bills, they are more likely to experience difficulties in communicating personal problems involving the expression of feelings and emotions (Westermeyer 1987). Furthermore there is evidence to suggest that under severe stress or physical illness people may lose the secondary language but retain their mother tongue (Marcos and Alpert 1976). Communication problems can also be experienced between native-born lower-class minority elderly and middle-class service providers (Kadushin 1972; Hollis and Woods 1981; Cormican 1976, 1978; Cooper 1973). Some social workers use unnecessary jargon, do not understand the clients' dialect, or are unfamiliar with common English expressions employed by a particular ethnic group. Because of provider perceived communication difficulties, lower-class minorities of all ages are often seen as less likely candidates for psychotherapy than more verbal middle-class patients (Garfield 1971; Lorion 1973, 1974; Acosta 1979).

Clients can also "choose not to understand" when understanding is anxiety provoking or requires activities that are perceived to be difficult or unnecessary (Arroyo and Lopez 1984; Sotomayor 1971). In a large urban hospital, for example, a social worker reported that a 75-year-old patient did not understand anything she had to say. When, however, a bilingual, bicultural social worker went to see the patient the old lady clutched the worker's hands and said "there was a woman here to tell me that I have to go to a nursing home. You won't let that happen to me, will you?" The expectation expressed in the last sentence can be problematic to a worker of the same ethnic group because it implies a special relationship based on ethnicity and a special type of obligation. The dilemmas faced by ethnic and minority workers when they find themselves in situations where: a) their own ethnic community rejects them; b) they have to choose between allegiance to their ethnic group or the employing institution; and c) they have to struggle with internal conflicts related to ethnicity and having "made it" have been discussed: Wintrob and Harvey 1981; Kane and McConatha 1975; Munoz 1981; and Maykovich 1977.

CULTURE

If they are to be used, services have to be culturally meaningful; they need to "make sense" to the recipient (Rosenfeld 1964). Newton (1980) states that to Mexican-Americans, the system of "personalismo" where individuals relate to each other as whole persons and not in an impersonal or contractual manner is important. Dignity, pride, and respect are values embedded in this system. According to Aguilar (1972) it is often necessary to spend time just interacting on a personal level before it is appropriate to discuss problems. Toupin (1980) reports that Japanese, even though they disagree will "nod in agreement so as not to risk any embarrassment to the 'other' by disagreeing" (p. 83). Noninterference, an important Native American value, has many implications for the provision of services (Good Tracks 1973; Lewis and Ho 1975). Szapocznik et al. (1980), however, report that Cuban elderly in their interactions with counselors and physicians, prefer hierarchical authority relationships.

Attitudes about mental health, illness, and the experience of pain also vary among different ethnic groups (Press 1978; Snow 1974; Harwood 1977; Zborowski 1952; Zola 1966). In many cultures, there is no dichotomy between physical and mental illness and mental distress is often communicated through physiological symptoms. Beliefs that illness is caused by such supernatural forces as witches, departed ancestors, spirits, or "evil eye" also exist in some cultures. Protection resides in talismans and amulets and help is sought from such healers as root doctors, curanderos, spiritualists, or herbalists (Harwood 1971; Rocereto 1973; Kleinman et al. 1978; Kreisman 1975). While such practices may be limited (Snyder 1984; Edgerton et al. 1970), and while people often seek help from both folk healers and physicians, the use of healers may be higher among old people (Tripp-Reimer 1983). Snyder (1984), who studied folk healing practices among older Asian Americans and Hawaiians in Honolulu, states that information about an individual's health beliefs and customs is important in providing appropriate health and welfare services, especially for older people.

Different cultures, thus, have preferred ways of interaction, of deference, of showing respect, of defending pride and integrity, of role differentiation between men and women, of deciding when and under what circumstances and from whom it is appropriate to seek help. If the strangeness existing between the help seeker and help provider from different cultures is not overcome, if the "invisible wall" remains (Brown 1979), the social services probably will not be used. Effective intervention clearly has to include strategies to overcome these barriers.

ASSESSMENT AND INTERVENTION

The provision of services to ethnic elderly consists of two distinct yet interrelated stages. First the elderly have to be made aware that services are available and then encouraged to either contact the service providers or to respond to referrals or outreach efforts. During the second stage, which begins with the initial contact, services have to be delivered in a culturally meaningful way to insure utilization. Failure to continue with services, particularly in counseling and mental health, is a serious problem for ethnic populations (Padilla et al. 1975; Abad et al. 1974; Overall and Aronson 1963).

Assessment with respect to the provision of services occurs at two levels: the organizational-administrative level and at the individual client level or the case.

Organizational level

Ethnic agencies will not be included in this discussion because despite similarity of concerns between ethnic and nonethnic agencies, many issues facing the two types of agencies are different. Furthermore, since many ethnic communities do not have the capability, interest, or resources to provide services directly, this responsibility rests primarily with public, and to some extent private, agencies. However, the question of what should be the role of the ethnic community in the provision of services to ethnic populations and whether such services should be funded by public monies remains a controversial issue (Kim 1973; Aguilar 1972; Jackson 1980; Jenkins 1981).

Nonethnic agencies, first of all, need to know the minority/ethnic composition of the elderly in their catchment or service area (Fellin and Powell 1988). If an ethnic concentration exists what percentage of the elderly from the different minority ethnic groups use a given service? Based on these and other relevant data such as the level of need, if minority elderly are underrepresented, the agency has to decide if it will engage in special outreach efforts. If the answer is yes, they have to decide what strategies to employ to increase utilization. The choice of strategies depends on the type of service as well as on geographical, political, economic, legislative, social, and professional factors. Strategies include attempts to increase utilization of existing services, decentralization of services to ethnic neighborhoods, creating outposts in churches or storefronts, cooperative arrangements with other agencies, and formation of multi-ethnic, multi-agency coalitions (Kim 1973; Barg 1972; Lum et al. 1980; Li 1972; Colen and Soto 1979; Szapocznik et al. 1979).

Inherent in all these strategies is the need to inform the elderly either directly or indirectly about the availability of services. A variety of direct methods, such as ethnic newspapers, radio, and television, non-English printed material and outreach workers have been used with varying success (Szapocznik et al. 1979; Abad et al. 1974; Heiman et al. 1975). Indirectly, the elderly can be reached through their informal networks as families, friends, neighbors, and churches can be instrumental in providing linkages with service providers (Ward et al. 1984; Sussman 1976; Bell et al. 1976; Taietz 1975).

Overall policymakers, service providers, and researchers recognize that in geographically concentrated ethnic neighborhoods, the involvement of the ethnic community in the service delivery system is a key element in the provision of services (Chen 1973; Lum et al. 1980; Bengston et al. 1977; Hayes and Guttmann 1986). The involvement of the community can take many forms: partnership, membership on boards or advisory committees, employment as professionals, paraprofessionals, or indigenous workers, volunteer work, or interpretation. The main functions of the ethnic community in its role as an intermediary with respect to the elderly are legitimation, provision of information, approval, facilitation of access and outreach. The main contributions for the service providers are advice, education, provision of information, supply of personnel, and cultural interpretation. Since there may be discrepancy between the service providers and the elderly both as to what needs exist and how to meet them, ethnic organizations can also be helpful in this conflict.

It is also important to recognize that ethnic leaders and representatives of the various organizations may not be knowledgeable about the needs of the elderly or may deny their existence. Moreover, since ethnic communities do not consist of homogeneous individuals, disagreements, in-fighting, and competition for status and prestige between organizations and among influential individuals are not uncommon (Chen 1970; Vecoli 1978; Stanford 1974). Awareness of this complexity in planning services is important.

Involvement or contact with ethnic organizations is not always possible. Many catchment or service areas do not have a concentration of ethnic elderly. Likewise not all ethnic elderly live in ethnic communities, have contact with ethnic organizations or wish to associate with their ethnic group. Because of confidentiality or shame, or perceived competency, some may prefer to receive services from mainstream agencies.

SUMMARY

At the organizational level the agency is responsible for:

a) Assessing whether or not the ethnic elderly have reached parity in the utilization of services;
b) Deciding how to overcome location barriers, if they exist;
c) Devising strategies to inform the elderly of the availability of services;
d) Employing culturally sensitive service providers if bicultural-bilingular workers are not available;
e) Developing relationships with ethnic communities.

Case Level

Assessment and treatment at the level of the individual case or family unit requires the application of all social work skills and knowledge necessary to work with non-ethnic elderly. Special emphasis, however, needs to be placed on:

a) awareness of one's own ethnicity and the development of cultural sensitivity;
b) knowledge of the client's culture, patterns of family support and the meaning of the neighborhood; and
c) understanding client's patterns of interaction and preferred ways of communication, including the use of an interpreter.

Since the importance of culture, the neighborhood, and communication has already been discussed the focus will be on cultural awareness and the use of an interpreter. Specific suggestions regarding assessment and intervention will also be made.

CULTURAL AWARENESS

Devore and Schlesinger (1981) discuss four levels of understanding needed to work with people in a culturally sensitive manner. First relates to basic knowledge of human behavior. The second to workers' self-awareness, including insights into one's own ethnicity and how it may influence professional practice. Questions such as "who am I in the ethnic sense? what it means to me?" and "how it shapes my perception of persons from different ethnic backgrounds?" serve to begin this process. Awareness of one's own ethnicity, or the realization that there is no specific ethnic identification, helps workers to understand how ethnicity can impact professional and personal behavior.

The third level relates to the impact of ethnicity upon the daily life of the older person in such areas as deference to authority, role differentiation between men and women, interaction with adult children, and expectation of help and assistance. Knowledge about the client's ethnic group, patterns of immigration, cultural values, and behavioral expectations are also important. The last level permeates the whole helping process as various aspects of practice—assessment, interviewing, intervention—are adapted to the client's cultural reality. Moreover, the social work principle of starting where the client is has to become an intrinsic part of the helping process.

The President's Commission on Mental Health (1978) identified similar areas as requiring attention to prepare helping professionals to work with ethnic minorities. Hayes et al. (1986) developed a model for training practitioners to provide services to ethnic elderly. Social work has likewise recognized the need for such training, how effectively it is being translated into practice is questionable (Ryan 1981; Pinderhughes 1979; White 1984; Longres 1982). Preparing practitioners to work with ethnic elderly in a culturally sensitive way through inservice workshops, or by educational institutions needs to be a high priority. While it is not necessary to possess knowledge about every ethnic group, it is essential to understand the meaning of ethnicity in the lives of people and to be familiar with the cultures of the ethnic groups for whom services are provided. Sources such as *Harvard Encyclopedia of American Ethnic Groups* by Thernstorm, ed. (1980), provide historical and immigration data on many ethnic groups.

INTERPRETERS

While bilingular-bicultural workers should provide services to non–English-speaking elderly, often this is not possible because of a shortage of professionally trained ethnic workers (Liu and Yu 1985). As a result interpreters are necessary. Social work through interpreters, however, can be problematic if careful attention is not paid to their selection and training.

Marcos (1979) reports that when the content of eight audiotaped interpreter-mediated psychiatric interviews were analyzed, distortions were discovered relating to interpreter language competence, lack of psychiatric knowledge and to interpreter attitudes. Interpreters who were relatives tended either to minimize or to emphasize psychopathology depending on their own investment. Also they tended to answer questions intended for the patient without asking them.

Freed (1988) states that the use of relatives as interpreters should be avoided. Others problems noted for the client involve issues of confidentiality and embarrassment. Embarrassment was also an issue for interpreters particularly when questions related to sex, finances, or suicidal tendencies (Marcos 1979). Baker (1981) recommends the development of a pool of carefully selected and trained interpreters to ensure sensitivity, accuracy and ability to interpret cultural content.

Practice Suggestions

Several techniques and suggestions need to be considered in working with the ethnic elderly:

1. Older people are first and foremost individuals with the result that they may adhere to all or none of the cultural values associated with their ethnic group. Finding out what values are important constitutes part of the assessment process.
2. Learning how to pronounce the older person's name correctly is important as one's name is a very meaningful personal attribute. If the name is "difficult" asking the older person's help communicates not only interest but also a willingness to learn and be taught. In general, an expressed interest to learn from the elderly about their culture enhances the relationship.
3. It is always important to ask the older person how they prefer to be addressed. In some cultures it is impolite and disrespectful to refer to the older person by first name, particularly when the worker is younger. In others the use of first name denotes informality and diminishes the social distance. Likewise some older people may chose to address the worker by the first name.
4. In some cultures there is the expectation that the worker share with the client some personal information, such as whether they are married, have children, etc. Workers need to decide how they prefer to respond to such situations and the impact on the relationship if there is unwillingness to interact on this level.
5. Elderly from some ethnic groups are very reluctant to give information about finances, as financial information is most private. When financial information has to be obtained it is helpful to verbalize one's understanding of how uncomfortable the older person may be made by this request.

6. Confidentiality is essential. If services are provided by paraprofessionals, community workers, or interpreters it is extremely important to ensure that this information will not be shared with anyone else in the community. Failure to protect confidentiality will result in distrust and betrayal. Also it is important to assure the older person that confidentiality will be protected.
7. If the request is for concrete services, whenever possible, it is helpful to provide them. If referrals to other agencies are needed it is necessary to make linkages with other agencies by either contacting the agency and giving the older person appointment information including time, date, and the worker's name, or by having the other agency initiate the contact. Merely telling the older person where to go or whom to contact may not be enough.
8. Since many elderly, especially refugees or illegal aliens, are fearful of signing documents or giving financial information, it is helpful if the older person can take home a copy of the form before it is completed. If the client cannot read English, a brief explanation in client's own language should be attached to the form. Likewise a copy of the completed form provides tangible proof of the type of information provided.
9. Attention needs to be paid to the physical set up of the office. Official behind-the-desk seating arrangements may be expected by some clients but perceived as frightening and formal by others. A tangible symbol representing the client's culture may also add comfort and connectedness. A worker located in the middle of a multi-ethnic community has a number of pictures on the office wall representing images such as shrines or monuments familiar to the different ethnic groups. He finds this very helpful as different ethnic groups recognize their own symbols and relate to them.
10. If the problem or issue involves health care and the people use indigenous healers it is important to communicate an informed and non-critical attitude towards such practices. For some ethnic elderly the most effective form of treatment involves both the indigenous and Western medicine.
11. Recognize that men in some cultures feel uncomfortable about discussing personal problems with social workers who are women. Likewise women in some cultures view men as having more authority and as professionally more knowledgeable than women.

THEORY

The impact of American society on ethnic groups and in turn the impact of ethnic groups on American society gave rise to a number of theories to explain both the process of interaction between the groups and the eventual sociopolitical position of the various ethnic groups vis-à-vis the larger society. Models are also advanced on how acculturation and assimilation take place. Postiglione's (1983) succinctly synthesizes and summarises the theoretical perspectives to be discussed.

Melting Pot

The melting pot theory asserts that the immigrant groups will interact with the dominant host society and through this process a new synthesis will be created representing the "best" traits of each of the culture. Thus people will cease identifying themselves with ethnic groups and melt into the newly created dominant culture. Israel Zangwill, a Jewish immigrant, popularized the melting pot idea in the early twentieth century through a play first performed in 1908. Turner (1920) was one of its proponents.

Cultural Pluralism

The cultural pluralism theory contends that groups with different status retain their unique individual character and traits. Each group maintains its identity while at the same time society creates conditions for a peaceful co-existence among the groups. Moreover, each group while retaining its own identity interacts with other groups and through this process takes on common traits. Kallen (1970) and Berkson (1920) advocated this point of view.

Emerging Culture

The notion behind emerging culture is that the immigrant group interacting with the host society group forms a new culture that is a combination of both groups. In this process a Greek becomes a Greek-American and a Japanese, a Japanese-American. Although each group remains different from another, the group is also different from the original group in the sense that an Italian-American is different from an Italian and a Mexican-American from a Mexican. In the context of this theory the culture of the United States becomes different, its values are somewhat modified. The American way of life is somewhat altered by each new immigrant group. As this process occurs over and over again, each group moves toward the others in some respect. "The image presented is a dynamic one, constantly changing and evolving as new immigrant groups enter the 'emerging American culture' " (Postiglione 1983:20). Contributors to this perspective are: Glazer and Moynihan 1970, 1975; Greeley 1974; Novak 1972; Yancey et al. 1976.

Policy Implications

While at the present time there is no agreement which model of ethnicity best interprets those processes that occur when people of different ethnic groups come together, the theoretical perspective to which one subscribes influences one's views how ethnic groups should behave in relation to the larger society and how the larger society should act with respect to ethnic groups. Public policy decisions related to bilingual education, preferential treatment of certain ethnic groups, quota systems, prohibition of discrimination based on race or national origin even the type of questions asked at census time are manifestations of how the larger society, through official policy, responds to ethnic groups concerns. Thus public policy decisions have been and are potent instruments in influencing the life chances and opportunities of various minority and ethnic groups. In the area of aging, for example, the singling out in the Older Americans Act of minority groups for special attention, support or lack of support of research focused on minority or ethnic aged and the support or lack of support with public monies of ethnic-group specific social services for the elderly are public policy decisions containing a message about the importance of ethnicity. Since the messages are often unclear or contradictory, depending on the issue and the level and unit of government involved, they are interpreted differently by various interest groups. Canada, on the other hand, has clearly identified its stance with respect to ethnicity by enacting a public policy of "bilingualism within a framework of multi-culturalism" supporting at different government levels through money and other resources the maintenance of ethnic group identity. In the absence in the United States of a clearly articulated public policy regarding ethnic groups and especially at the level of service delivery to the elderly, it is essential to strive to provide services in a manner that recognizes their dignity, heterogenity and ethnic diversity.

Future Directions

Concerted efforts are being made by organizations such as National Center and Caucus of the Black Aged, National Association for Spanish-Speaking Elderly, National Indian Council on Aging, and National Pacific/Asian Resource Center on Aging to advance research and to advocate on behalf of the minority elderly. The Council of the Gerontological Society of America established a Task Force on Minority Affairs which in 1988 prepared a plan of action to accomplish the following three goals:

1. To increase the quantity and quality of gerontological research on minority aging questions;
2. To increase the number of minority researchers in gerontology; and
3. To increase the number of minority members in the Society.

Undoubtedly all of these activities will have an indirect but a significant impact on service delivery to ethnic and minority elderly.

A more direct approach is to increase the number of ethnic and minority professionals such as social workers to work with the elderly. Furthermore, it is necessary to develop various models concerning collaboration and cooperation between mainstream social service agencies and the ethnic communities. Such models have to specify the essential components of collaboration and to identify the strategies needed to make this collaboration possible. Development and empirical testing of such models would advance our knowledge of how to deliver social services to the ethnic elderly.

REFERENCES

Abad, J., J. Ramos, and E. Boyce. 1974. A model for delivery of mental health services to Spanish-speaking minorities. *American Journal of Orthopsychiatry* 44(4):584–595.

Acosta, F. Y. 1979. Barriers between mental health services and Mexican-Americans. *American Journal of Community Psychology* 7(5):503–530.

Aguilar I. 1972. Initial contacts with Mexican-American families. *Social Work* 17(3):66–70.

Arroyo, R. and S. Lopez. 1984. Being responsive to the Chicano community: A model for service delivery. In B. White, ed., *Color in White Society*. Silver Spring, Md.: National Association of Social Workers.

Baker, N. 1981. Social work through an interpreter. *Social Work* 26(5):391–397.

Barg, S. 1972. A successor model for community support of low-income minority group aged. *Aging and Human Development* 3(3):252–253.

Becerra, R. M. and D. Shaw. 1984. *The Hispanic Elderly: A Research Reference Guide*. Lanham: University Press of America.

Bell, D., P. Kasschau, and G. Zellman. 1976. *Delivering Services to Elderly Members of Minority Groups: A Critical Review of the Literature*. Santa Monica, Calif.: Rand Corporation.

Bengston, V., E. Grigsby, E. Corry, and M. Hruby. 1977. Relating academic research to community concerns: A case study in collaborative effort. *The Journal of Social Issues* 33(4):75–92.

Berger, P. L. and R.J. Neuhaus. 1977. *To Empower People: The Role of Mediating Structures in Public Policy*. Washington, D.C.: American Enterprise Institute for Public Policy Research.

Berk, B. and L. Hirata 1973. Mental illness among Chinese: Myth or reality? *Journal of Social Issues* 29(2):149–166.

Berkson, I. 1920. *Theories of Assimilation*. New York: Columbia University Press.

Biegel, D. E. and A. J. Naparstek, eds. 1982. *Community Support Systems and Mental Health*. New York: Springer.

Biegel, D. E. and W. R. Sherman. 1979. Neighborhood capacity building and ethnic aged. In D. Gelfand and A. Kutzik, eds. *Ethnicity and Aging*. New York: Springer.

Bild B. and R. Havinghurst. 1975. Senior citizens in great cities: The case of Chicago. *The Gerontologist* 16(1):47–52.

Blau, Z., G. Oser, and R. Stephens. 1979. Aging, social class, and ethnicity. *Pacific Sociological Review* 22(4):501–525.

Boswell, T. 1985. The Cuban-Americans. In J.O. McKee, ed., *Ethnicity in Contemporary America: A Geographical Appraisal*. Dubuque, Iowa: Kendall Hunt.

Breton, R. 1964. Institutional completeness of ethnic communities and the personal relations of immigrants. *The American Journal of Sociology* 70(2):193–205.

Brodsky, B. 1988. Mental health attitudes and practices of Soviet Jewish immigrants. *Health and Social Work* 13(2):130–136.

Brown, J. A. 1979. Clinical social work with Chicanos: Some unwarrented assumptions. *Clinical Social Work Journal* 7(4):256–266.

Cantor, M. H. 1979. The informal support system of New York's inner city elderly: Is ethnicity a factor? In D. Gelfand, and A. Kutzik, eds. *Ethnicity and Aging*. New York: Springer.

Chen, P. N. 1970. The Chinese community in Los Angeles. *Social Casework* 51(10):591–598.

Chen, P. N. 1973. Samoans in California. *Social Work* 18(2):41–48.

Chen, P. N. 1979. A study of Chinese-American elderly residing in hotel rooms. *Social Casework* 60(2):89–95.

Clements, F. and M. B. Kleiman. 1976. Fear of crime among the aged. *The Gerontologist* 16(3):207–210.

Colen, J. N. and D. Soto. 1979. *Service Delivery to Aged Minorities: Techniques of Successful Programs*. Sacramento: Sacramento State University, School of Social Work.

Cooper, S. 1973. A look at the effect of racism on clinical work. *Social Casework* 54(2):76–84.

Cormican, J. 1976. Linguistic subcultures and social work practice. *Social Casework* 57(9):589–592.

Cormican, J. 1978. Linguistic issues in interviewing. *Social Casework* 59:145–151.

Devore, W. and E. Schlesinger. 1981. *Ethnic-Sensitive Social Work Practice*. St. Louis: C. V. Mosby.

Die, A. and W. Seelbach. 1988. Problems, sources of assistance, and knowledge of services among elderly Vietnamese immigrants. *The Gerontologist* 28(4):448–452.

Dorf, N. and F. Katlin. 1983. Soviet immigrant client: Beyond resettlement. *Journal of Jewish Communal Service* 60(2):146–154.

Douglass, R., E. Espino, M. Meyers, S. McClelland, and K. Haller. 1988. Representation of the black elderly in Detroit metropolitan nursing homes. *Journal of National Medical Association* 80(3):283–288.

Edgerton, R. B., M. Karno, and I. Fernandez. 1970. Curanderismo in the metropolis: The diminished role of folk psychiatry among Los Angeles Mexican-Americans. *American Journal of Psychotherapy* 24(1):124–134.

Eisenstadt, S. N. 1952. The process of absorption of new immigrants in Israel. *Human Relations* 5:222–231.

Eribes, R. and M. Bradley-Rawls 1978. The underutilization of nursing home facilities by Mexican-American elderly in the southwest. *The Gerontologist* 18(4):363–371.

Federal council on Aging. 1979. *Annual Report to the President, 1979*. Washington, D.C.: GPO.

Fellin, P. A. and T. J. Powell 1988. Mental health services and older adult minorities: An assessment. *The Gerontologist* 28(4):442–447.

Fishman, J. A., M. H. Gettner, E. G. Lowy, and W. G. Milan. 1985. *Ethnicity in Action*. Binghamton, N.Y.: Bilingual Press/Editorial Bilingue.

Flemming, A. S., J. G. Buchanan, J. F. Santos, and L. D. Rickards. 1986. *Mental Health Services for the Elderly: Report on a Survey of Community Mental Health Centers. Action Committee to Implement the Mental Health Recommendations of the 1981 White House Conference on Aging,* vol. 3 Washington, D.C.: American Psychological Association.

Freed, A. O. 1988. Interviewing through an interpreter. *Social Work* 33(4):315–319.

Fujii, S. 1976. Elderly Asian Americans and use of public services. *Social Casework* 57(3):202–207.

Garcia, A. 1971. The Chicano and social work. *Social Casework* 52(5):274–278.

Garfield, S. L. 1971. Research on client variables in psychotherapy. In A.E. Bergin and S.L. Garfield, eds., *Handbook of Psychotherapy and Behavior Change: An Empirical Analysis*. New York: Wiley.

Gelfand, D. 1982. *Aging: The Ethnic Factor*. Boston: Little Brown.

Gelfand, D. 1986. Assistance to the new Russian elderly. *The Gerontologist* 26(4):444–498.

Giordano, J., and G. P. Giordano. 1977. *The Ethno-Cultural Factor in Mental Health: A Literature Review and Bibliography*. New York: Institute on Pluralism and Group Identity of the American Jewish Committee.

Glazer, N., and D. Moynihan. 1970. *Beyond the Melting Pot*. 2d ed. Cambridge: MIT Press.

Glazer, N., and D. Moynihan. 1975. *Ethnicity: Theory and Experience*. Cambridge: Harvard University Press.

Goldsmith J. and E. Tomas, 1974. Crimes against the elderly: A continuing national crisis. *Aging* 236–237:10–13.

Good Tracks, J. G. 1973. Native American noninterference. *Social Work* 18(6):30–34.

Gordon, M. 1964. *Assimilation in American Life*. New York: Oxford University Press.

Greeley, A. 1974. *Ethnicity in the United States*, New York: Wiley.

Greene, V. and D. Monahan, 1984. Comparative utilization of community based long term care services by Hispanic and Anglo elderly in a case management system. *Journal of Gerontology* 39(6):730–735.

Guttmann, D. 1979. Use of informal and formal supports by white ethnic aged. In D. Gelfand and A. Kutzik, eds., *Ethnicity and Aging*. New York: Springer.

Guttmann, D. 1986. A perspective on Euro-American elderly. In C. Hayes, R. Kalish, and D. Guttmann, eds., *European-American Elderly*. New York: Springer.

Guttmann, D. and J. Cuellar. 1982. Barriers to equitable services. *Generations* 6:31–33.

Haines, D. 1985. Toward integration into American society. In D. Haines, ed., *Refugees in the United States*. Westport, Conn.: Greenwood Press.

Harel, Z. 1985. Nutrition site service users: Does racial background make a difference? *The Gerontologist* 25(3):286–291.

Harwood, A. 1971. The hot-cold theory of disease. *The Journal of American Medical Association* 216(7):1153–1158.

Harwood, A. 1977. *Rx: Spiritist as Needed: A Study of a Puerto Rican Community Mental Health Resource*. New York: Wiley.

Hayes, C. 1986. Resources and services benefiting the Euro-American elderly. In C. Hayes, R. Kalish, and D. Guttmann, eds., *European-American Elderly*. New York: Springer.

Hayes, C., J. Giordano, and I. Levine. 1986. The need for education and training. In C. Hayes, R. Kalish, and D. Guttmann, eds., *European-American Elderly*. New York: Springer.

Hayes, C. and D. Guttmann. 1986. The need for collaboration among religious, ethnic, and public service institutions. In C. Hayes, R. Kalish, and D. Guttmann, eds., *European-American Elderly*. New York: Springer.

Heiman, E., G. Burruel, and N. Chavez. 1975. Factors determining effective psychiatric outpatient treatment for Mexican-Americans. *Hospital and Community Psychiatry* 26(8):515–517.

Heisel, M. and A. Faulkner. 1982. Religiosity in older black population. *The Gerontologist* 22(4):354–358.

Higham, J. 1965. *Strangers in the Land*. New York: Atheneum Press.

Ho, M.K. 1976. Social work with Asian Americans. *Social Casework* 57(3):195–201.

Hollis, F., and M. Woods. 1981. *Casework: A Psychosocial Therapy*. 3d ed. New York: Random House.

Holzberg, C. S. 1982. Ethnicity and aging: anthropological perspectives on more than just the minority elderly. *The Gerontologist,* 22(3):249–57.

Isajiw, W. 1974. Definitions of ethnicity. *Ethnicity* 1:111–124.

Jackson, J. 1975. Some special concerns about race and health: An editorial finale. *Journal of Health and Social Behavior* 16(4):342, 428–429.

Jackson, J. 1980. *Minorities and Aging*. Wadsworth.

Jenkins. S. 1981. *The Ethnic Dilemma in Social Services*. New York: Free Press.

Kadushin, A. 1972. The racial factor in the interview. *Social Work* 17(3):88–98.

Kalish, R. 1986. The significance of neighborhoods in the lives of the Euro-American elderly. In C. Hayes, R. Kalish, and D. Guttmann, eds., *European-American Elderly*. New York: Springer.

Kallen, H. 1970. *Culture and Democracy in the United States*. New York: Arrow Press.

Kane, R. L. and P.D. McConatha, 1975. The men in the middle: A dilemma of minority health workers. *Medical Care* 13(9):736–743.

Kessler, R. C. and P. D. Cleary, 1980. Social class and psychological distress. *American Sociological Review* 45(3):463–478.

Kiefer, C. W., S. Kim, K. Choi, L. Kim, B. L. Kim, S. Shon, and T. Kim. 1985. Adjustment problems of Korean American elderly. *The Gerontologist* 25(5):477–482.

Kim, B. L. 1973. Asian Americans: No model minority. *Social Work* 18(3):44–55.
Kleinman, A., L. Eisenberg, and B. Good, 1978. Culture, illness and care. *Annals of Internal Medicine* 88(2):251–258.
Kreisman, J. 1975. The curandero's apprentice: A therapeutic integration of folk and medical healing. *American Journal of Psychiatry* 132(1):81–83.
Krout, J. A. 1983a. Knowledge and use of services by the elderly: A critical review of the literature. *International Journal of Aging and Human Development* 17(3):153–167.
Krout, J. A. 1983b. Utilization of services by the elderly. *Social Service Review* 58:281–290.
Lacayo, C. 1982. Triple jeopardy: Underserved Hispanic elders. *Generations* 6(5):25–58.
Lewis, R. G. and M. K. Ho. 1975. Social work with Native Americans. *Social Work* 20(5):379–382.
Li, F. P., N. Y. Schlief, C. J. Chang, and A. C. Gaw. 1972. Health care for the Chinese community in Boston. *American Journal of Public Health* 62:536–539.
Lieberson, S. 1961. The impact of residential segregation on ethnic assimilation. *Social Forces* 40(1):52–57.
Light, J. 1972. *Ethnic Enterprise in America: Business and Welfare Among Chinese, Japanese, and Blacks*. Berkeley: University of California Press.
Liu, W. T. and E. Yu. 1985. Ethnicity, mental health, and urban delivery system. In L. Maldonado and J. Moore, eds., *Urban Ethnicity in the United States*. Beverly Hills, Calif.: Sage.
Longres, J. 1982. Minority groups: An interest group perspective. *Social Work* 27(1):7–14.
Lopata, H. Z. 1976. *Polish Americans: Status Competition in an Ethnic Community*. Englewood Cliffs; N.J.: Prentice-Hall.
Lorion, R. P. 1973. Socioeconomic status and traditional treatment approaches reconsidered. *Psychological Bulletin* 79(4):263–270.
Lorion, R. P. 1974. Patient and therapist variables in the treatment of low-income patients. *Psychological Bulletin* 81(6):344–354.
Lowy, L. 1985. Multipurpose senior centers. In A. Monk, ed., *Handbook of Gerontological Services*. New York: Van Nostrand Reinhold.
Lum, D., L. Cheung, E. R. Cho, T. Tang, and H. B. Yau. 1980. The psychosocial needs of the Chinese elderly. *Social Casework* 61(2):100–106.
MacIver, R. M. 1970. *Community: A Sociological Study*. 4th ed. London: Frank Cass.
Marcos, L. R. and M. Alpert. 1976. Strategies and risks in psychotherapy with bilingual patients: The phenomenon of language independence. *American Journal of Psychiatry* 133(11):1275–1278.
Marcos, L. 1979. Effects of interpreters on the evaluation of psychopathology in non-English-speaking patients. *American Journal of Psychiatry* 136:171–174.
Markides, K. 1982. Ethnicity and aging: A comment. *The Gerontologist* 22(6):467–470.
Markides, K. and C. Mindel. 1987. *Aging and Ethnicity*. Newbury Park, Calif.: Sage.
Markson, E. 1979. Ethnicity as a factor in the institutionalization of the ethnic elderly. In D. Gelfand and A. Kutzik, eds., *Ethnicity and Aging*. New York: Springer.
Maykovich, M. 1977. The difficulties of a minority researcher in minority communities. *The Journal of Social Issues* 33(4): 108–119.
McAdoo, J. L. 1979. Well-being and fear of crime among the black elderly. In D. Gelfand and A. Kutzik, eds. *Ethnicity and Aging*. New York: Springer.
McCaslin, R. 1988. Reframing research on service use among the elderly: An analysis of recent findings. *The Gerontologist* 28(5):592–599.

McCaslin, R. 1989. A new look at service utilization. *Journal of Gerontological Social Work,* in press.
McCaslin, R. and W. R. Calvert. 1975. Social indicators in black and white: Some ethnic considerations in the delivery of service to the elderly. *Journal of Gerontology* 30(1):60–66.
McKinley, J. 1972. Some approaches and problems in the study of the use of services: An overview. *Journal of Health and Social Behavior* 13:115–152.
McNeil, J. S. and R. Wright. 1983. Special populations: Black, Hispanic and Native Americans. In J. W. Callicutt and P. J. Lecca, eds., *Social Work and Mental Health.* New York: Free Press.
Meinhardt, K. and W. Vega. 1987. A method for estimating underutilization of mental health services by ethnic groups. *Hospital and Community Psychiatry* 38(11):1186–1190.
Mindel, C. H. and R. Wright. 1982. The use of social services by black and white elderly: The role of social support systems. *Journal of Gerontological Social Work* 4:107–125.
Mirowsky, J. and C. Ross. 1980. Minority status, ethnic culture, and distress: A comparison of blacks, whites, Mexicans and Mexican Americans. *American Journal of Sociology* 86:479–495.
Montero, D. 1979. Vietnamese refugees in America: Toward a theory of spontaneous international migration. *International Migration Review* 13:624–648.
Montero, D., and G. Levine. eds. 1977. Research among racial and cultural minorities: Problems, prospects and pitfalls. *Journal of Social Issues* 33(4):1–132.
Munoz, J. 1981. Difficulties of a Hispanic-American psychotherapist in the treatment of Hispanic American patients. *American Journal of Orthopsychiatry* 51(4):646–653.
National Center for Health Statistics. 1981. No. 51. DHHS Publication, No. (PH5) 81–1712. Hyattsville, Md.
National Nursing Home Survey. 1981. *Characteristics of Nursing Home Residents, Health Status, and Care Received,* 1977. Hyattsville, Md.: U.S. Department of Health and Human Services, Public Health Service, Office of Health Research, Statistics and Technology, National Center for Health Statistics.
Newton, F. C. 1980. Issues in research and service delivery among Mexican-American elderly. A concise statement with recommendations. *The Gerontologist* 20(2):208–213.
Novak, M. 1972. *The Rise of the Unmeltable Ethnics.* New York: Macmillan.
Overall, B. and H. Aronson. 1963. Expectations of psychotherapy in patients of lower socioeconomic class. *American Journal of Orthopsychiatry* 33: 421–430.
Padilla, A., R. A. Ruiz, and R. Alvarez. 1975. Community mental health services for the Spanish speaking/surnamed populations. *American Psychologist* 30(13):892–904.
Philippus, M. J. 1971. Successful and unsuccessful approaches to mental health services for an urban Hispano American population. *American Journal of Public Health* 61(4):820–830.
Pinderhughes, E. B. 1979. Teaching empathy in cross-cultural social work. *Social Work* 24(4):312–316.
Postiglione, G. A. 1983. *Ethnicity and American Social Theory.* New York: University Press of America.
Presidents Commission on Mental Health. 1978. *Task Panel Report.* vol. 3: *Appendix.* Washington, D.C.: GPO.
Press, I. 1978. Urban folk medicine: A functional overview. *American Anthropologist* 80:71–84.
Ralston, P. 1984. Senior Center utilization by black elderly adults: Social attitudinal and knowledge correlates. *Journal of Gerontology* 39(2):224–229.

Rocereto, L. 1973. Root work and the root doctor. *Nursing Forum* 12(4):415–426.
Rogg, E. 1971. The influence of a strong refugee community on the economic adjustment of its members. *International Migration Review* 5(4):474–481.
Rosenfeld, J. M. 1964. Strangeness between helper and client: A possible explanation of non-use of available professional help. *Social Service Review* 38(1):17–25.
Rosenthal, E. 1960. Culturalization without assimilation? The Jewish community of Chicago, Illinois. *American Journal of Sociology* 66:275–283.
Rumbaut, R. D. and R. G. Rumbaut. 1976. The family in exile: Cuban expatriates in the United States. *American Journal of Psychiatry* 133(4):395–399.
Ryan, A. S. 1981. Training Chinese-American social workers. *Social Casework* 62(2):95–105.
Salcido, R. 1979. Problems of the Mexican-American elderly in an urban setting. *Social Casework* 60:609–615.
Shibutani, T. and K. Kwan. 1965. *Ethnic Stratification*. New York: Macmillan.
Silverstein, N. M. 1984. Informing the elderly about public services: The relationship between sources of knowledge and service utilization. *The Gerontologist* 24(1):37–40.
Snider, E. 1980. Awareness and use of health services by the elderly: A Canadian study. *Medical Care* 18(12):1177–1182.
Snow, L. 1974. Folk medical beliefs and their implications for care of patients. *Annals of Internal Medicine* 81:82–96.
Snyder, P. 1984. Health service implications of folk healing among older Asian Americans and Hawaiians in Honolulu. *The Gerontologist* 24(5):471–476.
Solomon, B. 1976. *Black Empowerment*. New York: Columbia University Press.
Sotomayor, M. 1971. Mexican American interaction with social systems. *Social Casework* 52(5):316–324.
Stanford, E. P. 1974. *Minority Aging*. Proceedings of the second institute on minority aging. San Diego: San Diego State University, Center on Aging, School of Social Work.
Stanford, E. P. 1977. *Comprehensive Service Delivery Systems for the Minority Aged*. San Diego: University Center on Aging, San Diego State University.
Starrett, R. A. and J. T. Decker. 1986. The utilization of social services by the Mexican-American elderly. *Journal of Gerontological Social Work* 9:87–101.
Statistical Yearbook. 1984. *Statistical Yearbook of the Immigration and Naturalization Service*. Washington, D.C.: GPO.
Sue, D. W. and S. Sue. 1972. Ethnic minorities: Resistance to being researched. *Professional Psychology* 3:11–17.
Sundeen, R. A., and J. Mathieu. 1976. The fear of crime and its consequences among the elderly in three urban communities. *The Gerontologist* 16(3):211–219.
Sussman, M. 1976. The family life of old people. In R. Binstock and E. Shanas, eds., *Handbook of Aging and the Social Services*. New York: Van Nostrand Reinhold.
Szapocznik, J., D. Santisteban, W. Kurtines, and O. Hervis. 1980. Life enhancement counseling for Hispanic elders. *Aging* 305–306:20–29.
Szapocznik, J., J. Lasaga, P. Perry, and J. R. Solomon, 1979. Outreach in the delivery of mental health services to Hispanic elders. *Hispanic Journal of Behavioral Sciences* 1(1):21–40.
Taietz, D. 1975. Community complexity and knowledge of facilities. *Journal of Gerontology*, 30(3):357–362.
Taylor, R. J. and L. M. Chatters. 1986. Church-based informal support among elderly blacks. *The Gerontologist* 26(6):637–642.
Thernstorm, S. ed. 1980. *Harvard Encyclopedia of American Ethnic Groups*. Cambridge: Belknap Press, Harvard University Press.

Timberlake, E., and K. Cook. 1984. Social work and the Vietnamese refugee. *Social Work* 29(2):108–113.
Toupin, E. S. 1980. Counseling Asians: Psychotherapy in the context of racism and Asian-American history. *American Journal of Orthopsychiatry* 50(1):76–86.
Tripp-Reimer, T. 1983. Retention of a folk-healing practice (Matiasma) among four generations of urban Greek immigrants. *Nursing Research* 32(2):97–101.
Turner, F. 1920. *The Frontier in American History*. New York: Holt.
U.S. Bureau of the Census. 1973. *1970 Census of the Population. Subject Report: National Origin and Language,* table 10. Washington, D.C.: GPO.
U.S. Bureau of the Census. 1982a. *Current Population Reports*. Series, P-20, no. 374. Washington, D.C.: GPO.
U.S. Bureau of the Census. 1982b. *Current Population Reports*. Series P-20, no. 396. Washington, D.C.: GPO.
U.S. Bureau of the Census. 1983a. *1980 Census of the Population.* Vol. 1: ch. C, table 254. Washington, D.C.: GPO.
U.S. Bureau of the Census, 1983b. *1980 Census of the Population.* Vol. 1: ch. C, table 255. Washington, D.C.: GPO.
U.S. Bureau of the Census. 1983c. *1980 Census of the Population.* Vol 1, ch. B, table 48. Washington, D.C.: GPO.
U.S. Bureau of the Census. 1983d. *1980 Census of the Population.* vol 1, ch. C, table 256. Washington, D.C.: GPO.
U.S. Bureau of the Census. 1984. *1980 Census of the Population.* vol 1, ch D, table 304. Washington, D.C.: GPO.
U.S. Department of Commerce. 1985. *Statistical Abstract of the United States,* table 20. Washington, D.C.: GPO.
U.S. Department of Commerce. 1988. *Statistical Abstract of the United States*. Washington, D.C.: GPO.
Varghese, R. and F. Medinger. 1979. Fatalism in response to stress among the minority aged. In D. Gelfand and A. Kutzik, Eds., *Ethnicity and Aging: Theory, Research, and Policy*. New York: Springer.
Vecoli, R. J. 1978. The coming of age of the Italian Americans: 1945–1974. *Ethnicity* 5:119–146.
Walmsley, S. and R. Allington 1982. Reading abilities of elderly persons in relation to the difficulty of essential documents. *The Gerontologist* 22(1):36–38.
Ward, R., S. Sherman, and M. LaGory, 1984. Informal networks and knowledge of services for older persons. *Journal of Geronotology* 39(2):216–223.
Westermeyer, J. 1987. Clinical considerations in cross-cultural diagnosis. *Hospital and Community Psychiatry* 38(2):160–164.
White, B., ed. 1984. *Color in a White Society*. Silver Spring, Md.: National Association of Social Workers.
Wintrob, R. M. and K. Y. Harvey. 1981. The self-awareness factor in intercultural psychotherapy. In P. B. Pedersen, J. G. Draguns, W. J. Lonner, and J. E. Trimble, eds., *Counseling Across Cultures*. Honolulu: University Press of Hawaii.
Yancey, W., E. Erickson, and R. Juliani. 1976. Emergent ethnicity: A review and reformulation. *American Sociological Review* 41(3):391–403.
Zborowski, M. 1952. Cultural components in response to pain. *Journal of Social Issues* no. 8, pp. 16–30.
Zola, I. 1966. Culture and symptoms: An analysis of patients' presenting complaints. *American Sociological Review* 31(5):615–630.

25

Ethical Issues in Services for the Aged

HARRY R. MOODY, PH.D.
Hunter College of the City University of New York

Human Service professionals in the field of aging are today confronted with ethical dilemmas that arise in practice and demand the most thoughtful attention. Some of these ethical issues in services for the aged are familiar and arise with younger age groups as well, while others are particularly associated with distinctive characteristics of the last stage of life. These issues are discussed briefly here.

Some of the dilemmas in services for the aged are already clear and well recognized. These are issues that have surfaced in the area of health care and medical technology and have dramatically captured public attention. Foremost here are ethical dilemmas of death and dying, for example, to prolong life or to hasten dying for persons of advanced age. Because more than two-thirds of deaths now occur among those over age 65, these dilemmas are disproportionately associated with elderly patients. What in previous generations might have been part of the natural course of events—the timing of death—now becomes increasingly a matter of human choice and ethical deliberation.

But exercising choice depends on the capacity to choose and here the process of aging often brings other obstacles to full deliberation. It would be a mistake to equate aging itself with loss of decisional capacity. But there is no denying the increasing frequency of conditions that may impair decision-making abilities in old age. For example, Alzheimer's disease and other forms of mental impairment occur overwhelmingly among older people, raising questions about informed consent under conditions of diminished mental capacity.

Even when mental capacity is clear, other problems are often manifested. Living at home and in the community, the frail elderly are vulnerable to threats of many kinds. But it is not always easy to know when protective intervention is justified. In addition, policies of cost-containment have already raised serious problems about justice and the allocation of resources in an aging society. With 11 percent of the population, the elderly today consume more than 30 percent of expenditures on health care and that figure is likely to grow in the future. Finally, as we devote more resources to prolong the lives of the very old, we confront deeper questions that have no easy answer. How do we define what quality of life consists of? All of these questions are relevant to the ethics of providing services for the aged.

The meaning of "ethics," as I shall use the term here, simply describes the disciplined effort to reflect on the questions that arise for those who bear the responsibility of choice. There is, of course, a second meaning of the term "ethics": namely, those issues of clear-cut "professional ethics" that come to the fore when we confront clear cases of fraud, abuse, or exploitation. In this discussion I will not be much concerned with this second meaning of ethics. Instead, the attention will be on the ethics of *ambiguity* and uncertainty in the midst of responsibility for choice.

Even when our ethical principles lead to clear duties or imperatives, what is to be done is not always clear. These ethical imperatives are not always easy to achieve, partly because of material circumstance (e.g., lack of staff or funding) and other practical obstacles, but also because attempting to put one ethical principle into practice sometimes involves a conflict with other principles. Ethicists commonly cite three primary principles: beneficence (promoting welfare), autonomy (respect for self-determination), and justice (fairness in distributing resources). But the three principles can obviously conflict among themselves and, in a particular case, the result may be a dilemma with no easy answer. The task of framing and analyzing ethical principles is the responsibility of philosophical ethics.

RECENT PHILOSOPHICAL BACKGROUND

Since the late 1960s there has been a revival of work in normative ethics as a sub-discipline within philosophy. This development signaled a dramatic change from the style of analytic philosophy that grew to influence in the middle of this century. With the revival of normative ethics and applied ethics, philosophers no longer confined themselves to examining the logical basis of moral discourse (metaethics). Instead, they became interested once again in substantive ethical theories about society and human action. A landmark here was John Rawls' theoretical treatise, *A Theory of Justice* (1971), but major stimulus also came from controversies about war and peace, racial discrimination, and advances in biomedical technology. For the first time in this century, philosophers in large numbers ventured outside the academy and promoted "applied ethics."

During the late 1960s and early 1970s a new discipline of biomedical ethics burst upon the scene and quickly captured public attention. The late '60s were the years of the first heart transplant and other new technologies of medical care that posed difficult questions for medicine and biology. A benchmark for the arrival of a new discipline of bioethics was the founding of the Hastings Center and its interdisciplinary journal, the *Hastings Center Report* in 1969. Somewhat later, the field of social work began to witness more systematic reflection on ethical dilemmas of practice, often successfully using the analytic methods of biomedical ethics as a model (Reamer 1982; Yelaja 1982). By the late '70s issues in the field of aging began to attract attention (Cassel and Meier 1986), and work has progressed rapidly in recent years (Kapp, Pies, and Doudera 1985; Moody 1982).

Ethical issues in services for the aged can be analyzed both in terms of the structural or social setting for decisions—for example, senior centers, home care, long-term care, and so on—and also in terms of the conceptual issues that cut across different settings—for example, autonomy and paternalism, inter-professional collaboration, access and entitlement to services, etc. In this discussion we first look at cross-cutting conceptual issues and then examine how those issues are understood in specific institutional settings.

AUTONOMY AND PATERNALISM

A recurrent issue in services for the aged is the matter of autonomy and respect for individual self determination (Cohen 1985). The issue arises in many settings but debate on this subject is furthest developed in the field of health care. For example, for persons with normal mental capacity, under principles of both law and ethics there is a clear right to informed consent in accepting or rejecting medical treatment. For those with significantly diminished mental capacity, there are a variety of interventions including surrogate decision-making (proxy consent), durable power of attorney, and court-appointed guardianship, for those declared legally incompetent. As a matter of practice, declarations of legal incompetency are rare, but informal psychiatric or medical determination of diminished capacity is very common. The discussion of this subject by lawyers and philosophers, particularly in life-and-death matters of termination of treatment, has been vigorous in recent years.

While the debate has been strong, the results may be viewed differently by human service professionals than by lawyers and physicians. Simply extrapolating ideas from biomedical ethics may not prove effective. In fact, human service professionals in the field of aging often find these debates unrealistic and unsatisfactory for a variety of reasons. In the first place, there is the point that "mental competency" is not a single or univocal term. Ethicists have been quick to note that a patient may be incompetent, say, to manage his financial affairs but quite capable of making a decision about medical treatment. Instead of a global standard of mental competency, bioethicists have urged a more differentiated, functionally specific standard of competency.

In the second place, there is the troubling matter of fluctuating competency. Whether we view mental competency in global or in functional terms, clinicians know quite well that a patient's decision-making capacity will vary depending upon fatigue, medication, time of the day, emotional stress, physical illness, and many other factors. For example, decision-making capacity for those with dementia can fluctuate from day to day or week to week. What happens if a patient gives knowledgeable consent but than recants that consent a day or two later? Or what about the case when a patient gives willing consent but then forgets that he has given consent, perhaps even forgets the whole conversation? What happens if the patient remembers and affirms the earlier consent but entirely forgets all the information provided on behalf of the decision?

A related point concerns the phenomenon of so-called proxy decision-making. As a matter of practice, it is family members who act as the surrogate when a frail or marginally competent patient, for example, someone with advanced Alzheimer's disease, can no longer make decisions. Without the go-ahead of the family, social agencies or health care providers are reluctant to take definitive action for fear of lawsuits. Professionals or institutions may be mistaken, but the fear persists. The family as a group becomes the proxy. Whatever legal sanction this arrangement may or may not have, it does have the advantage of avoiding complicated or time-consuming petitions for a court-appointed guardian.

One big ethical problem here is that family members may well disagree among themselves. When the cost of life-prolonging measures conflicts with concern for inheritance by survivors, there are real conflicts of interest in family decision-making. Whenever money and power are involved, conflicts are to be expected. What seems to be needed is an intermediate-scale solution: something more formal than inter-professional or intra-family surrogates but less formal than full-scale court proceedings. We need to develop legal instruments offering multiple levels of consent for clear and explicit delegation of decision-making powers: for example, Living Wills, durable power of attorney, guardianship, etc. The task of applying legal principles in ways that safeguard autonomy without creating undue red-tape is one of the greatest challenges in aging services today.

It should also be noted that in settings furthest removed from the health care system, for example, in senior centers or home care programs, the application of ideas formal competency or proxy consent is almost entirely informal. Take the case of a frail, reclusive older person who appears undernourished but refuses a meals-on-wheels service that is offered. Closer involvement in the situation may disclose fear of crime in the neighborhood, a history of intermittent family support, perhaps cultural reluctance to use the formal service system. Typically, social workers intervene in complex situations and make the best of the situation, often without clear authority or guidelines. The solution is not necessarily to rely on a more formalized procedure but rather the kind of skillful intervention that could be called "negotiated consent" (Moody 1988). Certainly respect for client self-determination remains a paramount value. But this kind of case illustrates some of the ways in which ethical issues in services for the aged need to be addressed in terms different from the bioethical model of autonomy and paternalism.

INTER-PROFESSIONAL COLLABORATION

Providers of services for the aged rarely work in isolation from other professionals. But collaborating in teams or in institutional settings can raise issues for human service professionals who try to honor both the imperative of collaboration and doing what is best for the patient. For example, one ethical dilemma involves truth-telling: how much to disclose to patient or family about disagreements in the professional team, how much to "fudge" the facts in order to obtain reimbursement or eligibility for medically defined services. Other ethical dilemmas focus on relationships among professionals and toward institutions: for example, the dilemma of loyalty or "carrying out orders" versus dissent and disobedience. Here the status of the psychologist (as employee or consultant) may be a significant factor in the way the dilemma is framed. The ethical dilemma of the "professional-as-employee" is a familiar one with no clear-cut answers (Abramson 1985).

JUSTICE AND ALLOCATION OF RESOURCES

Another important set of issues involves social justice and the allocation of scarce resources, such as time, personnel, funding, and access to services. A good example of the allocation problem can be found in the case of Title XX of the Social Security Act where different age groups are to be served and trade-off decisions may have to be made (Gilbert 1981). Another example is the implementation of the Older Americans Act itself, where services are directed toward the elderly but priority is to be given to those in greatest social and economic need.

At the local or organizational level, issues of access to services commonly arise. Who will gain admission to high quality nursing homes and who will be directed toward less desirable facilities? Hospital discharge planners face this kind of issue every day, often without clear ethical guidelines. All too often, they must make decisions without full consultation or disclosure to the patients involved in the decision. The impact of cost-containment measures, such as Medicare's Diagnostic Related Groupings, has been to increase the pressure to move elderly patients quickly out of hospitals and into less intensive settings, such as home care or nursing home care.

Human service professionals have increasingly been moving into "gate-keeping" roles as the politics of cost-containment clashes with an historical commitment to serving the elderly. So for example troublesome ethical issues can also arise in the context of case management where a human service professional undertakes to help clients identify and gain access to needed services. When the case manager is an employee of a publically funded agency, it is impossible to avoid questions about the ultimate independence of the case manager. How far, we may wonder, can advocacy be pressed in these circumstances?

These issues are familiar enough to practitioners in the human services. But in the mass media recently more provocative questions have been raised about justice between generations. Since the mid-1980s there has been a vocal public debate on the subject of "generational equity:" namely, the idea that perhaps the elderly, as a group, are gaining too many public resources at the expenses of other groups, such as needy children. This debate has naturally seemed unwelcome to human service professionals in the field of aging who in their daily practice are in direct contact with needy elderly clients. Debates about "generational equity" seem to call into doubt the legitimacy or at least the priority of aging services in comparison to the needs of other groups.

These debates have been troublesome to many professionals in the aging network, which has grown to maturity in recent years. Gelfand and Olson (1984) have described the growth and diversification of the aging services network over the past two decades. The historical growth of the aging network took place during a period when resources and services for the aged were generally increasing and when the condition of the elderly has improved substantially. But at the same time, many characteristics of the aging populations have changed since the late Sixties and early Seventies, the time of the original impetus for the growth of the aging network.

Foremost among these changes has been the "aging in" of elderly populations in many neighborhoods and regions of the country. The result of "aging in" is to change very substantially the needs of the aged since there are today far greater numbers of the "old-old" and greater numbers who are frail. A senior center, for example, that had a successful program fifteen years ago may find that its program now needs to be rethought. But what should such a senior center or senior housing program do when "aging in" brings much larger numbers of "problem clients" who drain resources and make new demands the service program designed for a very different population? The answer will partly depend on ethical assumptions about access to services, advocacy, and in-take policy and limitation of programs to specific types of clients.

In the wider policy debate, aging service professionals have become familiar with the questions of "Age or need?" as the basis of entitlement. The point here is that this is not just a macro-level issue debated in the context of public policy. It arises, too, whenever human service providers must make in-take "triage" decisions about responding to clients. In short, it is impossible to avoid questions of justice and allocation whether we are addressing problems at the level of individuals, organizations, or the broadest domain of public policy.

Having looked at two cross-cutting conceptual issues—autonomy and justice—we now turn to look at some substantive ethical issues that arise in specific social or institutional contexts. It is helpful to organize this discussion around the continuum of care that can be provided to the elderly, a continuum that ranges from family caregiving in the home to the point of nursing home placement.

DILEMMAS OF FAMILY CAREGIVING

When an elderly person in need of care or services is living at home substantive ethical issues often arise. But these issues have not often been given the scrutiny they deserve, partly because they seem to be a purely private responsibility and partly because decisions are made in a less visible fashion. Yet the issues deserve attention, if only because the bulk of services for the aged today is provided not by professionals or institutions and not within the formal service system at all, but rather among families, who in fact furnish over 80 percent of the care for the frail elderly in America today (Callahan 1985; Sommers 1986).

The burden on these caregivers—mainly middle-aged women—has now become recognized as a major issue of social policy but it is an ethical matter as well. For example, a serious question concerns the limits of caregivers' responsibilities for the demented elderly. Other questions arise from the special bond between children and parents: that is, the ethics of filial responsibility. It is only recently that philosophers have given any serious analytic attention to these questions of family ethics. But any assessment of the ethics of long term care will necessarily have to take better account of the private as well as the public domain of ethical decision-making.

Questions of distributive justice arise not only in the public sphere but also in families, particularly when burdens are shared by different family members as in the case of spouses or adult children who are caregivers.

One major issue involves the nature of commitments undertaken by people who serve as caregivers. Does the caregiver entirely understand what he or she is getting into, for example, in making a commitment to keep a frail elderly relative at home rather than in an institution? What changes will be required at home rather than in an institution? What changes will be required by the caregiver as chronic disease progresses or mental impairment becomes worse? How much privacy is the caregiver prepared to give up and how far is it permissible to commit other family members to making those sacrifices? Again, what if a patient's frail spouse moves in, too? For example, when the spouse of an impaired person is about to move into the home of an adult child, what will the child's role be? What will the spouse's role be, for example, in housekeeping tasks or child care?

Another ethical dilemma that often emerges in families concerns money and inheritance. When it comes to matters of inheritance, there is often an implicit ethic of reciprocity that people take for granted. Family members may assume, "If I take care of her to the end, then she'll take care of me in the will," or some such *quid pro quo*. In cases of filial responsibility, the extent of the obligation can be a difficult matter: "He was always hard on me, deserted my mother when I was ten, and he's willed all his money to some organization. How much do I owe him?" (Mace and Rabins 1981:146).

Human service providers may have special skills in promoting communication to help deal with these vexing issues. For example, a family conference can be important in sorting out obligations and responsibilities.

In family caregiving when there are several siblings involved, there will often arise serious problems of equity or fairness in the distribution of caregiving burdens. There is no easy way to separate out current family problems or lifelong psychodynamic factors in trying to reach an "equitable" solution in these cases.

Questions of autonomy and paternalism take on one form when we are looking at communication between a doctor and a patient. But questions about paternalistic intervention become more complicated when the paternalistic decision-making involves several members of a family

Sometimes the question involves spousal responsibility, which does have a legal underpinning in our society. But filial responsibility may involve acts of supererogatory or heroic effort—above and beyond the call of duty. One problem with supererogatory efforts is that family members may undertake commitments that exceed their capacity to bear the burden or that are part of lifelong symbiotic patterns that contain an element of psychopathology. For example, the son or daughter who has never left home or, in worse cases, mixtures of guilt, frustration and aggression that can lead to elder abuse.

But, even with the best of intentions, caregivers are not always capable of carrying out the commitments they undertake, sometimes for reasons beyond their control.

The problem of good intentions leads to another ethical dilemma: the question of promise-keeping. It is not unusual for a patient, particularly in early stages of Alzheimer's disease, to tell a spouse or an adult child "Promise me you'll never put me in a nursing home." Overcome by guilt, the family member may make such a promise. Or again, perhaps a promise like this was made, in an abstract way, but much earlier, long before there was any question of Alzheimer's disease. So the question arises: can these promises be binding in conditions that surpass what people can reasonably be expected to bear?

NURSING HOME PLACEMENT

One of the most painful dilemmas comes at the point when family members must contemplate nursing home placement (Dill 1987; McCullough 1984). Nursing home placement is, for all intents and purposes, an irrevocable decision fraught with moral significance. In light of that moral significance, it is natural to raise a question about who it is who makes, or ought to make, the decision to enter a nursing home. Legal and ethical reasoning gives one clear and unequivocal answer. Our entire legal and ethical system starts with a presumption of rights and responsibilities of competent individuals, not collective social groups, such as families. Family decision-making, in short, has no ethical or legal standing.

But is this picture helpful in understanding the kinds of decisions involved in nursing home placement? Those who work with family caregivers in long-term care are apt to reply that it is not. Instead, a "decision" about long-term care is likely to emerge in a fragmentary way, over time, through a complex process of family communication that involves elements of consensus, conflict and negotiation. The decision for nursing home placement almost always embodies ambivalence, contradiction, and guilt. Lines of responsibility and authority are not easily drawn. The complex reality of family decision-making is not easily captured by the popular theories of biomedical ethics: for example, by conventional theories of informed consent.

The legal mind, with its adversary perspective, is always alert to potential conflicts of interest, and often with good reason. For example, a son or daughter-in-law who endorses a decision may, at one and the same time, be an overburdened caregiver, a presumptive heir of property, a de facto surrogate decision-maker, and finally stand in a long ambivalent psychologial relationship to the person to be placed in an institution. Each of these roles is likely to generate conflicts with others. How are such conflicts to be resolved? If the daughter-in-law, for example, is called upon to bear burdens and make extraordinary sacrifices in care of an elderly relative, does this give her special moral standing in the collective deliberation about the nursing home placement decision?

Questions of family responsibility, both spousal and filial responsibility, are also embedded in a larger context of legal entitlements and social policy. Both in turn are supported by ethical assumptions about how much caregiving is a family responsibility and how much it is a social responsibility. One can ask, how much should we, as a society, expect families to "take care of their own" before social programs—nursing home care or home care, underwritten by Medicare or Medicaid—takes care of the expenses?

NURSING HOME CARE

Among those who reach the age of 65 about one in five can expect to spend some time in a nursing home before they die, so issues of quality of life in nursing homes have enormous importance for the elderly. With the advent of deinstitutionalization of the mentally ill in the 1960s and the passage of Medicaid in 1965, there came a dramatic expansion of nursing home beds, a trend continuing into the 1970s. Before long there also followed a series of nursing home scandals in mid-'70s, greeted in turn by new laws and regulations. A widespread failure to insure rights and autonomy of institutionalized elderly was matched by attention to the issue by public interest lawyers and advocates for the elderly. For example, questions were raised about forced transfer of patients into nursing homes from one level of care to another.

By the late 1970s, enthusiasm for promoting rights of nursing home residents—for example, through the nursing home resident's "Bill of Rights"—had matured to confront more troubling questions: for example, are such rights actually enforceable? Do these rights include a so-called "right to treatment" for the mentally ill comparable to persons placed in state-run institutions? What about the use of physical or pharmacological restraints on patients who may be confused—"wanderers," for example, or those who endanger themselves? Another major issue in ethics and long-term care is the matter of nursing home placement, discussed below. Some difficult questions here involve conflicting interests of different family members and the issue of how to safeguard the rights of elderly persons who may be placed in a nursing home against their will. The questions are complicated, the answers uncertain.

CONTROVERSY OR CONSENSUS?

Reading about current controversies in ethics can easily give the impression that the problems are insoluble or, worse, merely a matter of conflicting subjective opinion. But this would be a mistaken impression. The sheer fact that there are conflicting views too quickly gives way to a conclusion of skepticism or relativism: in short, anything goes.

But in fact some ethical claims are not in dispute. For instance, there is no serious disagreement that it is morally wrong for a frail elderly person to be subjected to abuse or neglect, either at home or in an institution. Whatever "quality of life" may mean, it certainly means eliminating such abuse and neglect. The ethical mandate here is clear. The dilemma comes in when we recognize that it is sometimes hard to assess whether an elderly person's complaints are valid or not. Still worse, it is common for people to be fearful of reporting incidents of abuse or neglect because of fear of reprisals. Here we have a clear-cut case of an ethical injunction—protecting the powerless from exploitation. But how to accomplish the goal is not so clear, as the literature on the ethics of adult protective services makes clear. Nonetheless the problem may well be a practical one, not an endless dispute about principles. A solution is possible.

But a purely legalistic or regulatory approach, while sometimes necessary, is rarely sufficient to insure quality of life. There are limits to what any public oversight can be expected to accomplish. But public and private, formal and informal systems, are not necessarily mutually exclusive alternatives at all. Advocacy by private, nonprofit groups proves indispensable to avoid cooptation of professionals in the aging network. Especially valuable are steps to strengthen ties among family and friends of those who are institutionalized, both to protect against abuses and to provide a measure of individual attention that institutions can never provide.

In the end we can only expect a certain degree of guidance from the public sector, whether it is a court deciding matters of life-and-death or a regulatory agency guaranteeing quality of life. This is an important conclusion because it suggests that familiar styles government intervention have their limits in services for the aged. This observation is not a basis for wholesale deregulation but rather a recognition of the realistic limits of what regulation can be expected to accomplish. Regulatory and civil liberties solutions may not be able to do the full job for us.

We need to recognize that none of the widely touted panaceas—case management, home health care for everyone, holding families accountable for costs, Advance Directives, the patients' "Bill of Rights," etc.—really solves the thorny problems that families, professionals, and institutions must face. Law and ethics can never fully coincide on the stubborn ethical dilemmas of practice. Many of the problems are intractable, and, as the saying goes, "hard cases make bad law." Here again, we need to recognize limits to what law or regulation can achieve.

On the other hand, it would be a mistake to throw up our hands and leave matters entirely to private, ad hoc ethical judgment. We may have ethical consensus on some issues but not on others. The failure of full consensus isn't necessarily bad. It reflects our cultural ambivalence about the last stage of life. In fact, we may not need or want full ethical consensus. There are enough instances where ethical consensus does exist and where the problem is basically one of enforcement or availability of services. For example, more home health care seems desirable, even if it must still be rationed to some degree. Since families are already providing the bulk of home care services, perhaps policymakers should turn their attention away from a moralistic or punitive approach and instead look for ways to enhance family care-giving: for example, arranging for "respite" services so that exhausted caregivers can have relief from the burden from time to time. Providing enhanced home care should be an issue on which both conservatives and liberals could agree. In fact, there is already agreement at the level of rhetoric. But funding hasn't followed through to make home care services broadly available.

There's also wide consensus on the desirability of client autonomy. The problem is autonomy that is often honored in theory more than practice. At the bedside level, and especially in nursing homes, paternalism—"Doctor knows best"—is alive and well. But the practice is not limited to medical professionals: human service professionals engage in paternalistic behavior, too. Instead of denying it, perhaps we ought to move the debate to talking about when paternalistic intervention is justified and when it is not. In particular, we need to distinguish *respect* for persons from an assumption about the *autonomy* of persons. The two concepts need not be as tightly connected as commonly presumed. Above all, if we are serious about enhancing respect and dignity for elderly clients in the human services we need to examine more practical ways to make the ideal a reality, particularly with those elderly patients who have fluctuating competency or who are frail and vulnerable in other ways.

The greatest need in ethical thinking about services for the aged is a sense of realism about what is possible and what is not. A good example here is the case of institutional care-giving itself. We need to recognize that placement in a nursing home can be, not only inevitable, but, in many cases, the most desirable option. It is a tragic mistake to bombard the public with constant images of the "abandoned" elderly living in substandard nursing homes. Acceptance of that negative stereotype only encourages unnecessary guilt for those families faced with the already difficult burden of deciding to place an elderly relative in a nursing home when that time finally comes.

Instead of moralistic rhetoric about family responsibility, we need to acknowledge the real limits of what families, and medicine itself, can accomplish (Daniels 1987; Longman 1985; Litwak 1985; Schorr 1980). This sense of realism is indispensable for grappling with the genuine ethical problems of long-term care, which are difficult enough. A new recognition of limits would allow us to confront the ethical dilemmas of long term care in a more effective way. Instead of urging utopian standards for institutions or heroic standards for families, we would look at ethical decisions in light of the best available options that exist today. High quality nursing homes themselves would set a standard that lower quality institutions can be measured against. Society as a whole must decide whether to pay the price of bringing all institutions up to that level and also decide what standard of fairness is proper in allocating burdens and scarce resources.

What is clear in all these cases is how far we have come from the ethic of pure autonomy: the principle that each individual makes decisions with reference to the self alone. That individualist ethic—and its cardinal principle of informed consent—achieved wide support in the decades of the '60s and '70s. On balance, the change was a positive development. The ethic of autonomy was necessary to challenge a style of paternalism that infantilized older people. It was also necessary to deal with some very real abuses of patients rights by the health care providers.

LIVING WITHIN LIMITS

Yet, as I have argued here, the ethic of autonomy itself has serious limits, and those limits have become visible in the ethical dilemmas of services for the aged. The very real dependencies of old age are matched by the social setting of care-giving. An ethic of pure individualism is not enough, neither in services for the aged nor in wider social and public issues. Not merely must care be funded through social mechanisms, but, for chronic care, the "medical" and the "social" needs of the elderly patient are impossible to separate. This makes clear solutions, even the meaning of autonomy itself, difficult to define.

The complexity of choices in services for the aged resists any easy solution or panacea. That understanding itself is the beginning of wisdom in learning to think about human services in an aging society.

Perhaps the most important result of thinking about ethical dilemmas of services for the aged is to make us more sensitive to the "style"—and the limits—of American culture as reflected in health care politics and our social policies.

Consider some of the conventional American values—individual autonomy, progress through technology, unlimited resources for all, resolving conflicts through law, and living in one's own home and not in an institution. These are all cherished values that have profoundly influenced our thinking about health care. But every single one of these values is contradicted by the existential reality of advanced age. Fortunate, indeed, is the individual who lives to experience advanced age without confronting some of those tragic choices that have no obvious solution in conventional American values.

In an aging society, these conventional values may need reexamination and reappraisal. In the process, we can expect to see a clash and interplay of competing values in years to come. If we have the patience to apply reasoned reflection to the dilemmas, we can have hope of separating the intractable problems of the final years of life from other ethical principles that command consensus. By separating "tragic choices" from agreement about minimum decent standards of life, we might make better progress toward a society that guarantees that minimum standard to all. The resulting dialogue could open the way to a more humane service for persons of all ages. In forcing us to think more deeply about the meaning of care-giving, our elders may prompt us to move in ways that will benefit them and all of us who one day hope to reach old age ourselves.

REFERENCES

Abramson, Marcia. 1985. Caught in the middle: The professional as employee and colleague. *Generations* (Winter), pp. 35–37.

Callahan, Daniel. 1985. What do children owe elderly parents? *Hastings Center Report* (April), 15(2):32–33.

Cassel, C. K. and D. E., Meier. 1986. Selected bibliography of recent articles in ethics and geriatrics. *Journal of the American Geriatric Society* (May), 34:399–409.

Cohen, Elias. 1985. Autonomy and paternalism: Two goals in conflict. *Law, Medicine, and Health Care* (September).

Daniels, Norman. 1987. *Am I My Parent's Keeper?* New York: Cambridge University Press.

Dill, Ann E. P. et al. 1987. Coercive placement of elders: Protection or choice? *Generations* (Summer) 11:4, 48–66.

Gelfand, Donald and Jody Olson. 1984. *The Aging Network: Programs and Services*. 2d ed. New York: Springer.

Gilbert, Neil. 1981. A 'fair share' for the aged: Title XX allocation patterns, 1976–1980. *Research on Aging* (March), 4:71–86.

Kapp, M., H. E., Pies, and A. E. Doudera, eds. 1985. *Legal and Ethical Aspects of Health Care for the Elderly*, Ann Arbor, Mich.: Health Administration Press.

Litwak, Eugene. 1985. *Helping the Elderly: The Complementary Roles of Informal Networks and Formal Systems.* New York: Guilford Press.

Longman, Phillip. 1985. Justice between generations. *Atlantic Monthly* (June), 225:73–81.

Mace, N. L. and P. V. Rabins. *The 36-Hour Day*, Baltimore: Johns Hopkins University Press, 1981.

McCullough, Laurence B. 1984. Medical care for elderly patients with diminished competence: An ethical analysis. *Journal of the American Geriatrics Society*, (February), 32(2):150–153.

Moody, H. R. 1982. Ethical dilemmas in long-term care. *Journal of Gerontological Social Work* 5:97–111.

Moody, H. R. 1988. From informed consent to negotiated consent. *The Gerontologist* (Special Supplement on Autonomy and Long Term Care), 28.

Moody, H. R., ed. Ethics and aging. [Entire issue], *Generations* (Winter 1985), 10:2.

Rawls, John. 1971. *A Theory of Justice*. Cambridge: Harvard University Press.

Schorr, Alvin. 1980. *". . . Thy Father & Thy Mother": A Second Look at Filial Responsibility and Policy*. Washington, D.C.: Social Security Administration.

Sommers, Christina Hoff. 1986. Filial morality. *Journal of Philosophy* (August 8, 1986), 83:8.

Yelaja, S. A. 1982. *Ethical Issues in Social Work*, Springfield, Ill.: Thomas.

Index